A Book Of

DECISION SCIENCES

For

M.B.A. (Semester - II) & Other Management Courses
As Per Pune University's Revised Syllabus
Effective from June 2013

RANJEET H. CHITALE
B.E. (E & TC), M.B.A. (Materials, Finance, Marketing)
Associate Professor
Department of Management Sciences
University of Pune
(PUMBA)

DECISION SCIENCES
Second Edition : February 2015
© : Author

ISBN 978-93-83750-66-5

The text of this publication, or any part thereof, should not be reproduced or transmitted in any form or stored in any computer storage system or device for distribution including photocopy, recording, taping or information retrieval system or reproduced on any disc, tape, perforated media or other information storage device etc., without the written permission of Authors with whom the rights are reserved. Breach of this condition is liable for legal action.

Every effort has been made to avoid errors or omissions in this publication. In spite of this, errors may have crept in. Any mistake, error or discrepancy so noted and shall be brought to our notice shall be taken care of in the next edition. It is notified that neither the publisher nor the authors or seller shall be responsible for any damage or loss of action to any one, of any kind, in any manner, therefrom.

Published By :
NIRALI PRAKASHAN
Abhyudaya Pragati, 1312, Shivaji Nagar,
Off J.M. Road, PUNE – 411005
Tel - (020) 25512336/37/39, Fax - (020) 25511379
Email : niralipune@pragationline.com

Printed By :
Repro Knowledgecast Limited,
Thane

DISTRIBUTION CENTRES
PUNE

Nirali Prakashan
119, Budhwar Peth, Jogeshwari Mandir Lane
Pune 411002, Maharashtra
Tel : (020) 2445 2044, 66022708, Fax : (020) 2445 1538
Email : bookorder@pragationline.com

Nirali Prakashan
S. No. 28/27, Dhyari,
Near Pari Company, Pune 411041
Tel : (020) 24690204 Fax : (020) 24690316
Email : dhyari@pragationline.com
        bookorder@pragationline.com

MUMBAI
Nirali Prakashan
385, S.V.P. Road, Rasdhara Co-op. Hsg. Society Ltd.,
Girgaum, Mumbai 400004, Maharashtra
Tel : (022) 2385 6339 / 2386 9976, Fax : (022) 2386 9976
Email : niralimumbai@pragationline.com

DISTRIBUTION BRANCHES

NAGPUR
Pratibha Book Distributors
Above Maratha Mandir, Shop No. 3, First Floor,
Rani Jhanshi Square, Sitabuldi, Nagpur 440012,
Maharashtra, Tel : (0712) 254 7129

BENGALURU
Pragati Book House
House No. 1, Sanjeevappa Lane, Avenue Road Cross,
Opp. Rice Church, Bengaluru – 560002.
Tel : (080) 64513344, 64513355,
Mob : 9880582331, 9845021552
Email:bharatsavla@yahoo.com

JALGAON
Nirali Prakashan
34, V. V. Golani Market, Navi Peth, Jalgaon 425001,
Maharashtra, Tel : (0257) 222 0395
Mob : 94234 91860

KOLHAPUR
Nirali Prakashan
New Mahadvar Road,
Kedar Plaza, 1st Floor Opp. IDBI Bank
Kolhapur 416 012, Maharashtra. Mob : 9855046155

CHENNAI
Pragati Books
9/1, Montieth Road, Behind Taas Mahal, Egmore,
Chennai 600008 Tamil Nadu, Tel : (044) 6518 3535,
Mob : 94440 01782 / 98450 21552 / 98805 82331, Email : bharatsavla@yahoo.com

RETAIL OUTLETS
PUNE

Pragati Book Centre
157, Budhwar Peth, Opp. Ratan Talkies,
Pune 411002, Maharashtra
Tel : (020) 2445 8887 / 6602 2707, Fax : (020) 2445 8887
Pragati Book Centre
Amber Chamber, 28/A, Budhwar Peth,
Appa Balwant Chowk, Pune : 411002, Maharashtra,
Tel : (020) 20240335 / 66281669
Email : pbcpune@pragationline.com

Pragati Book Centre
676/B, Budhwar Peth, Opp. Jogeshwari Mandir,
Pune 411002, Maharashtra
Tel : (020) 6601 7784 / 6602 0855
PBC Book Sellers & Stationers
152, Budhwar Peth, Pune 411002, Maharashtra
Tel : (020) 2445 2254 / 6609 2463

MUMBAI
Pragati Book Corner
Indira Niwas, 111 - A, Bhavani Shankar Road, Dadar (W), Mumbai 400028, Maharashtra
Tel : (022) 2422 3526 / 6662 5254, Email : pbcmumbai@pragationline.com

www.pragationline.com

info@pragationline.com

Dedication

Dedicated To ...
   My Loving Parents

... **Ranjeet H. Chitale**

Preface

It gives me great pleasure in presenting the book titled **'Decision Sciences'** to students and readers alike.

Today's business environment is more complex and competitive, which calls for an analytical approach in the managerial decision-making process.

This book introduces to the readers, the important and commonly used Quantitative Techniques which can act as important tools while taking decisions. Written as per the recently revised syllabus for the MBA course effective from June 2013 of the University of Pune, the book exhibits a managerial perspective of solving business problems rather than a purely technical one.

The book has been divided into ten chapters for ease of understanding covering various techniques such as Linear Programming, Transportation and Assignment Models, Queuing Theory, Markov Chains and Simulation, Decision Theory and Theory of Games, the Project Management Techniques of PERT and CPM and also includes important chapters on Probability and Probability Distributions.

Each chapter includes adequate theory with illustrative examples for explaining techniques. This is followed by a large variety of completely solved problems including the problems from previous examinations for the benefit of students. The exercises at the end of each chapter would be useful for self-study and practices. This would enable the students coming from all backgrounds (sciences, commerce, arts, engineering etc.) to understand the concepts easily. However, it will be more beneficial for the students to practice more by solving the problems themselves, rather than just reading them, as it is the best way of learning a mathematical subject.

I must thank my dear students first for inspiring me to write this book. Their enthusiastic response to my earlier book on 'Statistical and Quantitative Methods' was truly rewarding. I also present my sincere thanks to all my friends and fellow colleagues at PUMBA for their suggestions, help and support.

It was indeed a pleasure to work with my publishers, Mr. Dineshbhai and Mr. Jignesh Furia of Nirali Prakashan. I would also like to extend my thanks to their team for their co-operation in the tedious editing and type-setting work and for bringing out this book in a very short period of time.

My special thanks to my parents, wife Jayanti and all my family members for their continuous encouragement and support during the entire work.

I hope that the present work would be received equally well as my earlier books by the readers and would evoke an interest and confidence among the students for the subject of Decision Sciences.

Due care has been taken while writing the book to minimise the errors - typographical or otherwise. Review, comments and suggestions, are most welcome as it would help me to improve the text in future.

Ranjeet H. Chitale
rhchitale@yahoo.com

Syllabus ...

1. **Introduction:** Decision Sciences and Role of Quantitative techniques. **(9 + 2)**
   Linear Programming: Concept, Formulation and Graphical solution.
   Assignment Models: Concept, Flood's Technique/Hungarian Method, Applications including Restricted and Multiple assignments.
   Transportation Models: Concept, Formulation, Problem types: Balanced, Unbalanced, Minimisation, Maximisation, Basic initial solution using North West Corner, Least Cost and VAM, Optimal Solution using MODI.

2. **Queuing Theory:** Concept, Single Server (M/M/I, Infinite, FIFO) and Multi Server (M/M/c, Infinite, FIFO). **(8 + 2)**
   Markov Chains and Simulation Techniques: Markov Chains: Applications related to Management Functional Areas, Implications of Steady State Probabilities, Decision Making based on the Inferences, Monte Carlo Simulation, Scope and Limitations.

3. **Decision Theory:** Concept, Decision under Risk (EMV) and Uncertainty. **(6 + 2)**
   Game Theory: Concept, 2 by 2 Zero Sum Game with Dominance, Pure and Mixed Strategy.

4. **CPM and PERT:** Concept, Drawing Network, Identifying Critical Path. **(6 + 2)**
   Network Calculations: Calculating EST, LST, EFT, LFT, Slack and Probability of Project Completion.

5. **5.1 Probability:** Concept, Addition, Conditional Probability theorem based Decision Making, (Numerical based on Functional areas of business expected). **(6 + 2)**
   5.2 Probability Distributions: Normal, Binomial, Interval estimation, Standard errors of estimation.

Contents ...

	Introduction to Decision Sciences	I.1 – I.2
1.	Linear Programming	1.1 – 1.62
2.	Transportation Models	2.1 – 2.62
3.	Assignment Models	3.1 – 3.34
4.	Queuing Theory	4.1 – 4.30
5.	Markov Chains and Simulation	5.1 – 5.52
6.	Decision Theory	6.1 – 6.32
7.	Game Theory	7.1 – 7.30
8.	CPM, PERT and Network Calculations	8.1 – 8.54
9.	Probability	9.1 – 9.36
10.	Probability Distributions	10.1 – 10.62
	Multiple Choice Questions	MCQ.1 – MCQ.14
	Appendix A	A.1 – A.2
	Appendix B	A.3 – A.3
	Appendix C	A.4 – A.5
	University Question Paper	P.1 – P.4

INTRODUCTION TO DECISION SCIENCES

Business Managers are expected to make the optimum use of the organisation's resources such as men, money, materials, machineries etc. in order to achieve the organisational goals. The typical functions of a manager involves planning, organising, staffing, directing, controlling, budgeting etc. However, integral to all these functions are the functions such as motivating and decision-making. In fact management is many times regarded as equivalent to decision-making.

In today's highly competitive and complex business world, the decisions taken by the management can have huge impact on the survival and growth of any business organisation. Again with the increased scales of business operations, decision-making becomes more difficult. One cannot use rule of thumb or intuitive approach while making the business decisions as a single wrong decision can cost a lot to the organisation. Hence today's business environment demands more of rational and objective approach towards decision-making.

Decision Sciences refer to application of scientific approach to managerial decision making. These are the set of scientific techniques intended to express the business constraints and the risks underlying a business problem into measurable terms and analysing them in a scientific manner to arrive at more rational decisions. It thus helps in reducing the decision making process to more analytical and objective one. Decision sciences are also very commonly referred to as decision modeling, quantitative techniques, management science or operations research.

These techniques originated during the second world war when in order to overcome the problem of use of limited military resources, Britain and America invited a number of scientists including physicists, statisticians, mathematicians and psychologists to apply scientific approach to many strategic and tactical problems. After the war, the industry started making use of these techniques to seek solutions to the problems caused by the increasing complexity and specialisation in the organisations.

Application of decision sciences/quantitative techniques to any business problem involves:

(i) Formulation of the Problem (consisting of defining the problem, identifying variables and developing appropriate mathematical model and acquiring the input data),

(ii) Problem Solution (identifying alternative solutions and selecting the optimum one and testing of the solution),

(iii) Interpretation (of the results and its implementation).

These techniques thus attempt to find the best or optimal solution to the problem under consideration. They involve the deterministic models (which assume that the relevant input data values are known with certainty) like the Linear Programming Models and the probabilistic models (which assume uncertainty about same input data values) such as the queuing and simulation models, game theory, decision theory etc.

The quantitative techniques thus can play a very important role as they help the managers define the problem in more structured way, analyse it systematically, identify the impact of various variables, result in optimum utilisation of the resources, identify the risk involved in the decisions and so on. They have a wide application in areas such as Marketing (deciding product mix, media planning, demand forecasting etc.), Finance (portfolio management, break even analysis, capital budgeting etc.), Production and Purchasing (production planning, supply chain networks, project planning etc.) Human Resources Management (manpower planning, scheduling of training programmes etc.).

■■■

Chapter 1...

Linear Programming

Contents ...

PART I – PROBLEM FORMULATION

1.1 Introduction

1.2 Linear Programming Problem (LPP)

1.3 Stages of LPP

1.4 Problem Formulation of LPP

   Solved Problems

   Exercise - I

PART II – GRPAHICAL METHOD OF SOLUTION

1.5 Introduction

1.6 Graphical Method of Solution

1.7 Note

   Solved Problems

   Exercise - II

PART I – PROBLEM FORMULATION

1.1 Introduction

Linear Programming is a deterministic model in decision sciences. This is an optimisation technique whereby we consider a given business problem and identify the variables concerning the same. These variables are then used to write down the objective function and the constraints for the given problem situation. Under LPP both these are expressed using the Linear Relationships only. After the formulation of the given problem we use techniques like Graphical method and Simplex method to solve it further. Problem formulation is the most critical step under LPP model.

1.2 Linear Programming Problem (LPP)

(a) **Linear Problem:** A linear relation is proportional i.e. the power of the terms (variables) in an equation is at the most raised to 1, e.g. P = ax + by + cz, where a, b, c are constants and x, y, z are variables.

The problem most commonly faced by management is to decide the manner in which the limited resources should be used to achieve the desired objectives like profit maximisation, cost minimisation, etc.

LPP is a mathematical technique for allotting the limited resources of a firm in an optimum manner and it is useful in product mix problem, media selection, transportation problems, assignment problems, portfolio selection, etc.

(b) **Decision Variables:** These are the unknowns to be determined from the solution, e.g. x, y, z in the linear equation above.

(c) **Constraints:** These represent the mathematical equations of the limitations imposed by the problem situations.

(d) **Objective Function:** This represents the mathematical equation of the major objective of the system in terms of the decision variables.

(e) **Linear Relationship:** Linear Programming deals with the problems in which the objective function as well as the constraints can be expressed as linear mathematical functions of the decision variables i.e. the functions in which each variable appears only in one term and only to the first power. Linear relationships have two properties:
  (i) Proportionality (directly proportional) e.g. 2x, – 3y etc.
  (ii) Divisibility i.e. variables can take fractional values.
    e.g. $P = ax + by + cz$ (Linear Function)
    $P = ax^2 + byz + cx$ (Quadratic Function)
    $P = ax^3 + by + c$ (Cubic Function)

(f) **Non-negativity Condition:** i.e. the decision variables must be either 0 or +ve i.e. $x, y, z \geq 0$

(g) **Feasible Solution:** A set of values of the decision variables which satisfies all the constraints and the non-negativity condition is a feasible solution. A problem can have many feasible solutions.

(h) **Optimal/Optimum Solution:** This is a feasible solution which optimises the objective function. Normally an optimal solution is unique.

1.3 Stages of LPP

Stages of LPP are:
(i) Problem identification through collection of data.
(ii) Problem formulation i.e. to formulate the mathematical problem from the given data.
(iii) Problem solving.

DECISION SCIENCES   LINEAR PROGRAMMING

1.4 Problem Formulation of LPP

Step 1: Find the key decisions to be made from the study of the problem.
Step 2: Identify the decision variables and assign symbols like x_1, x_2, x_3 or x, y, z etc.
Step 3: Mention the objective function quantitatively and express it as a linear function of the decision variables.
Step 4: Express the constraints also as linear equalities or inequalities in terms of the decision variables.
Step 5: Express the objective function, the constraints and the non-negativity condition from the steps above in an LPP format as follows:

General Form of an LPP:

Optimise (Maximise or Minimise)

$Z = C_1x_1 + C_2x_2 + \ldots + C_nx_n$ (Objective Function)

Subject to

$a_{11} x_1 + a_{12} x_2 + \ldots + a_{1n} x_n \ (\leq, =, \geq) \ b_1$
$a_{21} x_1 + a_{22} x_2 + \ldots + a_{2n} x_n \ (\leq, =, \geq) \ b_2$
$\vdots \quad\quad \vdots \quad\quad \vdots \quad\quad \vdots \quad\quad \vdots$ Constraints
$\vdots \quad\quad \vdots \quad\quad \vdots \quad\quad \vdots \quad\quad \vdots$
$a_{m1} x_1 + a_{m2} x_2 + \ldots + a_{mn} x_n \ (\leq, =, \geq) \ b_m$

and $x_1, x_2, \ldots, x_n \geq 0$ (non-negativity condition)

e.g. Maximise $Z = 5x_1 + 7x_2 + 3x_3$ (Objective function)
Subject to $2x_1 + 3x_2 + x_3 \leq 10$ (Constraint 1)
                  $x_1 + x_3 \leq 6$ (Constraint 2)
                  $x_2 \geq 2$ (Constraint 3)
where $x_1, x_2, x_3 \geq 0$ (Non-negativity condition)

Here, $x_1, x_2, \ldots, x_n$ are the decision variables;

$C_1, C_2, \ldots, C_n$ are the cost or profit co-efficients i.e. per unit contribution to the profit or cost; a_{ij} ($i = 1$ to $m, j = 1$ to n) i.e. a_{11}, a_{21} etc. are the structural co-efficients.

Example 1: Vitamins A and B are found in foods F_1 and F_2. 1 unit of food F_1 contains 3 units of vitamin A and 4 units of vitamin B. 1 unit of food F_2 contains 6 units of vitamin A and 3 units of vitamin B. 1 unit of F_1 and F_2 costs ₹ 4 and ₹ 5 respectively. The minimum daily requirement (for a person) of vitamin A and B is 80 and 100 units respectively. Assuming that anything in excess of the daily minimum requirement of vitamins A and B is not harmful, find out the optimum mixture of foods F_1 and F_2 at the minimum cost which meets the daily requirement of vitamins A and B. Formulate this as a L.P.P.

Solution: The given data can be expressed in the form of a table as:

Food	Vitamins (No. of units per unit of food)		Cost of food (₹ per unit)
	A	B	
F_1	3	4	4
F_2	6	3	5
Minimum Requirement	80	100	

1. The problem is to find the quantities of foods F_1 and F_2 so as to meet the daily minimum requirement of vitamins A and B, at minimum cost.

2. **Decision Variables:** These are the unknowns to be found out. Hence,

   Let x_1 - the quantity (number of units) of F_1 required.

   x_2 - the quantity (number of units) of F_2 required.

3. **Objective Function:** The objective is to minimise the cost of food. Now, the cost of x_1 units of food F_1 is ($x_1 \times$ per unit cost = $4x_1$). Similarly, cost of x_2 units of food F_2 is ($5x_2$). Hence, total cost is ($4x_1 + 5x_2 = C(\text{say})$). Hence, the objective function is to Minimise, $C = 4x_1 + 5x_2$

4. **Constraints:**

   (i) 1st constraint: The minimum requirement of vitamin A is 80 units. The number of units of vitamin A contained in x_1 units of food F_1 are ($x_1 \times$ number of units of A contained in 1 unit of F_1) i.e. ($3x_1$). Similarly, number of units of A contained in x_2 units of F_2 will be ($6x_2$). Thus, total intake of vitamin A will be ($3x_1 + 6x_2$) which must be at least 80 units.

   $\therefore\ 3x_1 + 6x_2 \geq 80$ ...... (1) (vitamin A constraint)

   (ii) Similarly, minimum requirement of vitamin B is 100 units.

   $\therefore\ 4x_1 + 3x_2 \geq 100$ ...... (2) (vitamin B constraint)

   (iii) Since the number of units x_1 and x_2 can not be negative, hence, $x_1, x_2 \geq 0$ (Non-negativity condition)

5. Thus, the LPP format will be,

   Minimise $C = 4x_1 + 5x_2$ (Obj. function - Cost Minimisation)

   Subject to

   $3x_1 + 6x_2 \geq 80$ (Vitamin A constraint)

   $4x_1 + 3x_2 \geq 100$ (Vitamin B constraint)

   $x_1, x_2 \geq 0$ (Non-negativity condition)

Example 2: A company makes three products X, Y, Z which go through three departments - drill, lathe and assembly. The hours of department time required by each of the products, the hours available in each of the departments and the profit contribut on of each of the products are given in the following table.

Products	Time Required per Unit (Hr.)			Profit contribution (₹ per unit)
	Drill	Lathe	Assembly	
X	3	3	8	9
Y	6	5	10	15
Z	7	4	12	20
Hrs. Available	210	240	260	

The marketing department of the company indicates that the sales potential for products X and Y is unlimited, but for Z it is not more than 30 units. Determine optimum production schedule.

Solution:
1. The objective is to maximise the total profit by selling units of X, Y and Z which are produced under the given production time constraints and sales constraint.
2. **Decision Variables:** Let
   x - Number of units of product X produced
   y - Number of units of product Y produced
   z - Number of units of product Z produced
3. **Objective Function:** Total Profit (P = 9x + 15y + 20z) must be maximised. Thus, Maximise P = 9x + 15y + 20z.
4. **Constraints:**
   (i) Drill Department Constraint: Total time required for drilling activity i.e. (3x + 5y + 7z) must be less than or equal to the time available i.e. 210 Hrs. Thus, 3x + 6y + 7z ≤ 210
   (ii) Lathe Department constraint: In similar manner, 3x + 5y + 4z ≤ 240
   (iii) Assembly Department constraint: Similarly 8x + 10y + 12z ≤ 260 OR dividing throughout by 2 we get 4x + 5y + 6z ≤ 130
   (iv) Sales constraint: For product Z the sale is not likely to exceed 30 units.
   ∴ z ≤ 30
5. ∴ The LPP format is,
   Maximise   P = 9x + 15y + 20z   (Profit maximisation)
   Subject to   3x + 6y + 7z ≤ 210   (Drill constraint)
                 3x + 5y + 4z ≤ 240   (Lathe constraint)
                 4x + 5y + 6z ≤ 130   (Assembly constraint)
                 z ≤ 30   (Sales constraint)
                 x, y, z ≥ 0   (Non-negativity condition)

Solved Problems

Problem 1: Mr. Rao, the owner of a Readymade garments shop wishes to publish advertisements in two local daily newspapers, one Marathi and one English. The expected coverage through the advertisements is 1000 people and 1500 people per advertisement respectively. Each advertisement in a Marathi newspaper costs ₹ 3000 and for an English daily it is ₹ 5,000. Mr. Rao has decided not to place more than 10 advertisements in the Marathi newspaper and wants to place at least 6 advertisements in the English daily. The total advertisement budget is ₹ 50,000/-. Formulate the problem as a LP model.

Solution: Let x_1 - Number of advertisements to be placed in Marathi newspaper

x_2 - Number of advertisements to be placed in English newspaper

1. **Objective Function:** Coverage through Marathi newspaper = 1000 x_1 and through English newspaper = 1500 x_2.

   ∴ Total coverage is C = 1000 x_1 + 1500 x_2

   ∴ Objective function is to maximise C = 1000 x_1 + 1500 x_2

2. **Constraints:**

   (i) Advertisement expenditure for Marathi newspaper = 3000 x_1

   Advertisement expenditure for English newspaper = 5000 x_2

   ∴ Total advertisement expenditure = 3000 x_1 + 5000 x_2

   Total advertisement budget = ₹ 50,000. Hence, the advertisement expenditure should not exceed the budget.

   ∴ 3000 x_1 + 5000 x_2 ≤ 50,000

   i.e. $3x_1 + 5x_2 \leq 50$

   (ii) Maximum number of advertisements in Marathi newspaper is 10

   i.e. $x_1 \leq 10$

   Similarly, minimum number of advertisements in English daily is 6

   i.e. $x_2 \geq 6$

   ∴ LP model of the problem is,

   Maximise   C = 1000 x_1 + 1500 x_2 (Coverage Maximisation)

   Subject to $3x_1 + 5x_2 \leq 50$ (Budget constraint)

                     $x_1 \leq 10$ (Marathi newspaper constraint)

                     $x_2 \geq 6$ (English daily constraint)

                     $x_1, x_2 \geq 0$ (Non-negativity condition)

Problem 2: A research lab has melts of Cu-Ni alloy to make a new alloy. The composition of the melts are as under:

Melt	Composition (Parts)	
	Cu	Ni
I	2	1
II	1	1

To make up the new alloy, at least 10 kg of Cu and 6 kg of Ni is needed. Melt I costs ₹ 25 per kg while melt II costs ₹ 30 per kg. Write the LPP for the quantities of each melt to be used to minimise the cost.

Solution: Let x_1 - Quantity of melt I (in kg) used, x_2 - Quantity of melt II (in kg) used.
1. **Objective Function:** Minimise cost $C = 25x_1 + 30x_2$
2. **Constraints:**
   Since, composition of melt I is (2 parts Cu + 1 part Ni)

   $\therefore \frac{2}{2+1} = \frac{2^{rd}}{3}$ is the proportion of Cu and $\frac{1^{rd}}{3}$ is the proportion of Ni in one unit of melt I. Similarly in melt II the proportion of Cu and Ni is $\frac{1}{1+1}$ i.e. $\frac{1}{2}$ and $\frac{1}{2}$ each.

   $\therefore$ Kg of Cu in New alloy is $\frac{2}{3}x_1 + \frac{1}{2}x_2$. Now as atleast 10 kg of Cu is needed,

   $\therefore \frac{2}{3}x_1 + \frac{1}{2}x_2 \geq 10$ i.e. (multiplying throughout by 6 i.e. LCM of 2 and 3) we get

   $4x_1 + 3x_2 \geq 60$

   (ii) Similarly for Ni,

   $\frac{1}{3}x_1 + \frac{1}{2}x_2 \geq 6$ i.e. $2x_1 + 3x_2 \geq 36$

3. $\therefore$ L.P. model of the problem is

   Minimise $C = 25x_1 + 30x_2$ (Cost minimisation)
   Subject to $4x_1 + 3x_2 \geq 60$ (Cu constraint)
                $2x_1 + 3x_2 \geq 36$ (Ni constraint)
                $x_1, x_2 \geq 0$ (Non-negativity condition)

Problem 3: A manufacturer intends to market a new fertilizer produced from a mixture of 2 ingredients A and B. The composition of the ingredients is as follows:

Ingredients	Composition			
	Bonemetal	Nitrogen	Lime	Phosphate
A	20%	30%	40%	10%
B	40%	15%	40%	5%

The management decision is such that the fertilizer
1. must be sold in bags of 20 kg. 2. must contain at least 25% Bonemetal.
3. must contain at least 15% Nitrogen. 4. must contain at least 10% Phosphate.
Cost of ingredients is ₹ 20/- per kg for A and ₹ 16/- per kg for B.
Write the LP formulation for the quantities of ingredients to be mixed to minimise the material cost.

Solution: Let x_1 - Quantity of A(in kg) in a bag of fertilizer
  x_2 - Quantity of B (in kg) in a bag of fertilizer

1. **Objective function:** Minimise costs $C = 20 x_1 + 16 x_2$
2. **Constraints:**
   (i) Each bag is of 20 kg of fertilizer produced by **mixing** A and B.
       $\therefore x_1 + x_2 = 20$ ... (1)
   (ii) A bag must have at least 25% bonemetal.

   $\therefore$ Minimum quantity of bonemetal in a bag of 20 kg = 25% of 20 kg = $\frac{25}{100}(20)$
   = 5 kg

   Now, Bonemetal contained by x_1 kg of A = 20% of $x_1 = \frac{20}{100} x_1$ and

   Bonemetal contained by x_2 kg. of B = 40% of $x_2 = \frac{40}{100} x_2$

   $\therefore$ Total bonemetal in bag $= \frac{20}{100} x_1 + \frac{40}{100} x_2$

   $\therefore \frac{20}{100} x_1 + \frac{40}{100} x_2 \geq 5$ .... (multiplying throughout by 100)
   i.e. $20 x_1 + 40 x_2 \geq 500$
   i.e. $x_1 + 2x_2 \geq 25$ ... (2)

   (iii) Each bag must have at least 15% Nitrogen.
   $\therefore \frac{30}{100} x_1 + \frac{15}{100} x_2 \geq \frac{15}{100}(20)$
   $\therefore \frac{30}{100} x_1 + \frac{15}{100} x_2 \geq 3$
   i.e. $30x_1 + 15x_2 \geq 300$ i.e. $2x_1 + x_2 \geq 20$ ... (3)

   (iv) Each bag must have at least 10% phosphate.
   $\therefore \frac{10}{100} x_1 + \frac{5}{100} x_2 \geq \frac{10}{100}(20)$ i.e. $10x_1 + 5x_2 \geq 200$
   i.e. $2x_1 + x_2 \geq 40$ ... (4)

   Now, from (3) we have $2x_1 + x_2 \geq 20$

   Hence, comparing (3) and (4) we see that constraint (3) is redundant as constraint (4) automatically indicates constraint (3).

3. Thus, the LP model is

Minimise $\quad C = 20x_1 + 16x_2 \quad$ (Cost minimisation)
Subject to $\quad x_1 + x_2 = 20 \quad$ (Bag size constraint)
$\qquad x_1 + 2x_2 \geq 25 \quad$ (Bonemetal constraint)
$\qquad 2x_1 + x_2 \geq 40 \quad$ (Phosphate and Nitrogen constraint)
$\qquad x_1, x_2 \geq 0 \quad$ (Non-negativity)

Problem 4: Consider the following problem faced by a production planner in a soft drink plant. He has two bottling machines A and B. A is designed for 250 ml bottles and B for 500 ml bottles. However each can be used in both types with some loss of efficiency. The following data is available:

Machine	Bottles per minute	
	250 ml bottles	**500 ml bottles**
A	100	40
B	60	75

The machines can be used for 8 hours per day, 5 days per week. Profit on 250 ml bottle is ₹ 1.5/- and on 500 ml bottle is ₹ 2/-. Weekly production of the softdrink can not exceed 9000 litres and the market can at the most absorb 25,000 of 250 ml bottles and there is a minimum demand of 7000 of 500 ml bottles per week. Formulate this as a LPP.

Solution: Let $\quad x_1$ - Number of 250 ml bottles produced on m/c A per week
$\qquad x_2$ - Number of 500 ml bottles produced on m/c A per week
$\qquad x_3$ - Number of 250 ml bottles produced on m/c B per week
$\qquad x_4$ - Number of 500 ml bottles produced on m/c B per week

1. **Objective Function:** Total number of 250 ml bottles = $x_1 + x_3$
   and Total number of 500 ml bottles = $x_2 + x_4$.
   $\therefore \quad$ Total profit is P = $1.5(x_1 + x_3) + 2(x_2 + x_4)$
   $\therefore \quad$ Objective function is to maximise P = $1.5x_1 + 1.5x_3 + 2x_2 + 2x_4$

2. **Constraints:**
   (i) Total time (in minutes) for which machine A can be used per week
   $= 8 \times 60 \times 5 = 2400$
   Now, machine A produces 100 bottles of 250 ml per minute
   $\therefore$ Time required to produce 1 bottle of 250 ml = $\frac{1}{100}$ minute ... **(Note this step)**
   $\therefore$ Time required to produce x_1 bottles = $\frac{1}{100} x_1$

Similarly, Time required to produce x_2 bottles of 500 ml $= \dfrac{1}{40} x_2$

∴ Total time for which the machine A is used $= \dfrac{x_1}{100} + \dfrac{x_2}{40}$

$\dfrac{x_1}{100} + \dfrac{x_2}{40} \leq 2400$

Multiplying throughout by 200 we get,
$2x_1 + 5x_2 \leq 4,80,000$

(ii) Similarly, for machine B

$\dfrac{x_3}{60} + \dfrac{x_4}{75} \leq 2400$

Multiplying throughout by 300 we get,
i.e. $5x_3 + 4x_4 \leq 7,20,000$

(iii) Total weekly production cannot exceed 9000 litres i.e. 9000×10^3 ml.
∴ $250(x_1 + x_3) + 500(x_2 + x_4) \leq 9000 \times 10^3$

(iv) Market can absorb at the most 25000 bottles of 250 ml.
∴ $x_1 + x_3 \leq 25,000$

(v) For 500 ml bottles the minimum demand is 7000 bottles
∴ $x_2 + x_4 \geq 7000$

3. ∴ The LP model for the problem is,

Maximise $P = 1.5 x_1 + 2x_2 + 1.5x_3 + 2x_4$ (Profit maximisation)
Subject to $2x_1 + 5x_2 \leq 4,80,000$ (m/c A time constraint)
$5x_3 + 4x_4 \leq 7,20,000$ (m/c B time constraint)
$250x_1 + 500x_2 + 250x_3 + 500x_4 \leq 9,000 \times 10^3$ (Production Quantity constraint)
$x_1 + x_3 \leq 25,000$ (Sales constraint for 250 ml)
$x_2 + x_4 \geq 7,000$ (Sales constraint for 500 ml)
$x_1, x_2, x_3, x_4 \geq 0$ (Non-negativity constraint)

Note: Here we have to use 4 decisions variables so that all the constraints and objective function can be expressed conveniently.

Problem 5: Formulate the following LP problem: XYZ company assembles and markets two types of calculators A and B. Some relevant facts concerning these calculators are as follows:

Type	Total component Cost per unit (₹)	Assembly Time per unit (Man-hours)	Average 'Man-minutes' of inspection and correction time per unit	Selling Price per unit (₹)
A	100	12	10	200
B	80	6	35	140

DECISION SCIENCES   LINEAR PROGRAMMING

The disparity in inspection and correction time is due to the fact that some of the components in calculator B are of cheaper and lower quality than those in A. The company employs 100 assemblers, who are paid ₹ 2 per hour actually worked and who will work to a maximum of 48 hours per week each. The inspectors, of whom there are currently four, have agreed to a plan whereby they work for an average of 40 hours per week each. However the four inspectors have certain other administrative duties which have been found to take on an average $8\frac{1}{3}$ hours per week between them. The inspectors are each paid a fixed wage of ₹ 200 per week. The only other cost is fixed overheads of ₹ 10,000 per week. Regarding marketing opportunities available, the sales manager believes that he could sell upto 300 of either type per week. Formulate the problem for the weekly production schedule that will maximise the profits.

Solution: Let x_1 - No. of units of calculator A produced per week.
x_2 - No. of units of calculator B produced per week.

1. Objective Function:

Total sales revenue per week obtained by selling the calculators = $200x_1 + 140x_2$

Total material cost per week = $100x_1 + 80x_2$

Total labour cost (assembly) per week = $(12 \times 2) x_1 + (6 \times 2) x_2$

∴ Total variable cost per week = Material cost + Labour cost

= $100x_1 + 80x_2 + 24x_1 + 12x_2 = 124x_1 + 92x_2$

Fixed wages to inspectors per week = 200×4 = ₹ 800

Fixed overheads per week = ₹ 10,000

∴ Total Fixed cost per week = 800 + 10,000 = 10,800

∴ Total cost = Variable cost + Fixed cost

= $124x_1 + 92x_2 + 10,800$

∴ Total Profit per week, P = Total sales revenue − Total cost

= $(200x_1 + 140x_2) - (124x_1 + 92x_2 + 10,800)$

= $76x_1 + 48x_2 - 10,800$

∴ Objective Function is to maximise P = $76x_1 + 48x_2 - 10,800$

2. Constraints:

(i) Assembly Time constraint:

Total weekly man hours required for the production = $12x_1 + 6x_2$

Total man-hours available for assembly

= No. of assemblers × weekly working hours for each assembler = $100 \times 48 = 4800$

∴ $12x_1 + 6x_2 \leq 4,800$

Dividing throughout by 6 we get,

$2x_1 + x_2 \leq 800$

(ii) Inspection Time Constraint:

Total man-minutes required for inspection = $10x_1 + 35x_2$

Man-Hours available for inspection

= Total man-hours for which 4 inspectors work − Time lost on administrative work

$= 4 \times 40 - 8\frac{1}{3} = 160 - \frac{25}{3} = \frac{455}{3}$ hrs.

∴ Total man-minutes available for inspection $= \frac{455}{3} \times 60 = 9{,}100$.

∴ $10x_1 + 35x_2 \leq 9{,}100$

(iii) Sales Constraint: For both types of calculators the sales can be upto 300 units. Hence, their production must not be more than 300 units i.e. $x_1 \leq 300$, $x_2 \leq 300$

3. ∴ The LP model for the problem is

Maximise $P = 76x_1 + 48x_2 - 10{,}800$ (Profit Maximisation)

Subject to $2x_1 + x_2 \leq 800$ (Assembly Time Constraint)

$10x_1 + 35x_2 \leq 9{,}100$ (Inspection Time Constraint)

$x_1 \leq 300$ (Sales Constraint for A)

$x_2 \leq 300$ (Sales Constraint for B)

$x_1, x_2 \geq 0$ (Non-negativity Condition)

Problem 6: An endowment manager is attempting to determine a best investment portfolio and is considering six alternative investments. Table below gives estimates for the price per share, the annual growth rate in price per share, the annual dividend per share and a measure of risk associated with each investment.

	Alternatives					
	1	2	3	4	5	6
Current Price per share (₹):	80	100	160	120	150	200
Projected annual growth rate:	0.08	0.87	0.1	0.12	0.09	0.15
Projected annual dividend per share (₹):	4.0	6.5	1.0	0.5	2.75	--
Projected Risk:	0.05	0.03	0.1	0.2	0.06	0.08

Risk is defined as standard deviation in return. Return on investment is defined as price per share one year hence less current price per share plus dividend per share.

The fund has ₹ 2.5 million to invest and it wishes to satisfy the following conditions:

(i) The maximum amount to be invested in alternative 6 is ₹ 2,50,000.

(ii) No more than ₹ 5,00,000 should be invested in alternatives 1 and 2 combined.

(iii) The total weighted risk should be no greater than 0.1 where

Total Weighted Risk $= \dfrac{\sum (\text{Investment in alternative j}) \times (\text{Risk of alternative j})}{\text{Total investment in all alternatives}}$

(iv) For the sake of diversity atleast 100 shares of each stock should be purchased.
(v) At least 10% of the total investment should be in alternative 1 and 2 combined.
(vi) Dividend of each year should be at least ₹ 10,000.

Formulate a Linear Programming Problem with an objective to maximise the return on investment (from both on growth and dividend together).

Solution: Let $x_1, x_2, x_3, \ldots x_6$ be the number of shares purchased, of each stocks 1, 2, ... 6 respectively.

1. **Objective Function:** The price of share 1 (having current price of 80 and growth rate 0.08) one year hence will be $(1 + 0.08) 80 = 86.4$

   ∴ Growth in price of each share = $(1 + 0.08) 80 - 80 = 0.08 \times 80 = ₹ 6.4$ and dividend per share is ₹ 4 annually.

   Hence, annual return from one share of '1' is ₹ $(6.4 + 4)$

   ∴ Annual return from x_1 number of shares = $(6.4 + 4) x_1$.

   Similarly, for each other share we can find the annual return.

   Hence, total annual return is,

   $R = (6.4 + 4)x_1 + [(0.87) 100 + 6.5]x_2 + [(0.1)160 + 1] x_3 + [(0.12) 120 + 0.5] x_4$
   $\qquad + [(0.09)150 + 2.75]x_5 + [(0.15)200 + 0]x_6$

   i.e. $R = 10.4x_1 + 93.5x_2 + 17x_3 + 14.9x_4 + 16.25x_5 + 30x_6$

   The objective function is thus, to maximise R.

2. **Constraints:**

   (i) Maximum amount to be invested in investment 6 is ₹ 2,50,000

   i.e. $200x_6 \leq 2,50,000$

   (ii) No more than ₹ 5,00,000 should be invested in alternatives 1 and 2 combined

   i.e. $80x_1 + 100x_2 \leq 5,00,000$

   (iii) Total Weighted Risk = $\dfrac{\Sigma \text{ (Investment in j) (Risk of j)}}{\text{Total investment}} \leq 0.1$

   i.e. $\dfrac{80x_1(0.05) + 100x_2(0.03) + 160x_3(0.1) + 120x_4(0.2) + 150x_5(0.06) + 200x_6(0.08)}{25,00,000}$
   $\qquad \leq 0.1$

   i.e. $\dfrac{4x_1 + 3x_2 + 16x_3 + 24x_4 + 9x_5 + 16x_6}{25,00,000} \leq 0.1$

   i.e. $4x_1 + 3x_2 + 16x_3 + 24x_4 + 9x_5 + 16x_6 \leq 2,50,000$

   (iv) At least 100 shares of each stock should be purchased

   i.e. $x_1, x_2, x_3, x_4, x_5, x_6 \geq 100$

(v) At least 10% of total investment should be in alternatives 1 and 2 combined

i.e. $80x_1 + 100x_2 \geq \dfrac{10}{100}(25,00,000)$

i.e. $80x_1 + 100x_2 \geq 2,50,000$

(vi) Dividend of each year should be at least ₹ 10,000

Now, dividend on x_1 shares of '1' = $4 \times x_1 = 4x_1$ and so on.

∴ $4x_1 + 6.5x_2 + x_3 + 0.5x_4 + 2.75x_5 \geq 10,000$.

(vii) The fund has 2.5 million i.e. $2.5 \times 10,00,000 = 25,00,000$ to invest.

∴ $80x_1 + 100x_2 + 160x_3 + 120x_4 + 150x_5 + 200x_6 = 25,00,000$

3. ∴ The LP model is,

Maximise

$R = 10.4x_1 + 93.5x_2 + 17x_3 + 14.9x_4 + 16.25x_5 + 30x_6$ (Return maximisation)

Subject to $200x_6 \leq 2,50,000$ (Investment 6 constraint)

$80x_1 + 100x_2 \leq 5,00,000$ (Max. Investment 1 and 2 constraint)

$4x_1 + 3x_2 + 16x_3 + 24x_4 + 9x_5 + 16x_6 \leq 2,50,000$

(Weighted Risk constraint)

$x_1, x_2, x_3, x_4, x_5, x_6 \geq 100$ (Diversity constraint)

$80x_1 + 100x_2 \geq 2,50,000$ (Min. Investment 1 and 2 constraint)

$4x_1 + 6.5x_2 + x_3 + 0.5x_4 + 2.75x_5 \geq 10,000$ (Dividend constraint)

$80x_1 + 100x_2 + 160x_3 + 120x_4 + 150x_5 + 200x_6 = 25,00,000$

(Fund constraint)

$x_1, x_2, x_3, x_4, x_5, x_6 \geq 0$ (Non-negativity)

Problem 7: A firm is engaged in producing two products P_1 and P_2. The relevant data are given below:

Per Unit	Product P_1	Product P_2
(i) Selling Price	₹ 200	₹ 240
(ii) Direct Materials	₹ 45	₹ 50
(iii) Direct Wages		
Dept. A	8 hrs. @ ₹ 2/hr	10 hrs. @ ₹ 2/hr
Dept. B	10 hrs @ ₹ 2.25/hr	6 hrs @ ₹ 2.25/hr
Dept. C	4 hrs @ ₹ 2.5/hr	12 hrs @ ₹ 2.5/hr
(iv) Variable Overheads	₹ 6.50	₹ 11.50

Fixed Overhead = ₹ 2,85,000 per annum

Number of employees in three departments: Dept A = 20, Dept B = 15, Dept C = 18

Number of hours/employee/week = 40 in each department

Number of weeks per annum = 50

Formulate the given problem as a Linear Programming Problem.

Solution: Let x_1 - Annual Production of product P_1 (in number of units)
x_2 - Annual Production of product P_2 (in number of units)

1. **Objective Function:**
   (i) Since the per unit selling prices for products P_1 and P_2 are ₹ 200 and ₹ 240 respectively.
   ∴ Total Sales Revenue = 200 x_1 + 240 x_2
   (ii) For product P_1,
   Total material cost = 45 x_1
   Direct wages:
   Dept. A = (No. of hours per unit) (Cost per hour) x_1 = 8 × 2 × x_1 = 16x_1
   Dept. B = 10 × 2.25 × x_1 = 22.5x_1
   Dept. C = 4 × 2.5 × x_1 = 10x_1
   Total Variable overheads = 6.5 x_1
   ∴ Total Variable Cost = 45x_1 + 16x_1 + 22.5x_1 + 10x_1 + 6.5x_1 = 100x_1
   Similarly for product P_2,
   Total variable Cost = 50x_2 + 20x_2 + 13.5x_2 + 30x_2 + 11.5x_2 = 125x_2
   ∴ Combined Total Variable Cost =100x_1 + 125x_2
   Fixed overheads = ₹ 2,85,000
   ∴ Total Annual Cost = Variable Cost + Fixed Cost = 100x_1 + 125x_2 + 2,85,000
   (iii) ∴ Total Annual Profit,
   P = Total Revenue − Total Cost = (200 x_1 + 240x_2) − (100x_1 + 125x_2 + 2,85,000)
   ∴ P = 100x_1 + 115x_2 − 2,85,000
   ∴ Objective function is profit maximisation
   i.e., Maximise P = 100 x_1 + 115x_2 − 2,85,000

2. **Constraints:**
   No. of hrs/employee/week = 40 in each department. Since, there are 20 employees in department A, the weekly man-hours available in department A = 40 × 20 and as there are 50 weeks per annum,
   ∴ Annual man-hours available with Dept A = 40 × 20 × 50 = 40,000
   Similarly, Annual man-hours with Dept B = 40 × 15 × 50 = 30,000 and
   Annual man-hours with Dept. C = 40 × 18 × 50 = 36,000
   Now, total man hours of Dept. A required for producing x_1 units of P_1 and x_2 units of P_2 are (8x_1 + 10x_2)
   ∴ 8x_1 + 10x_2 ≤ 40,000 i.e. 4x_1 + 5x_2 ≤ 20,000
   Similarly for Dept B,
   10x_1 + 6x_2 ≤ 30,000 i.e. 5x_1 + 3x_2 ≤ 15,000
   And for Dept C,
   4x_1 + 12x_2 ≤ 36,000 i.e. x_1 + 3x_2 ≤ 9,000

3. Thus, the LP model for the given problem is,
   Maximise: $P = 100x_1 + 115x_2 - 2,85,000$ (Profit Maximisation)
   Subject to $4x_1 + 5x_2 \leq 20,000$ (Dept. A constraint)
   $5x_1 + 3x_2 \leq 15,000$ (Dept. B constraint)
   $x_1 + 3x_2 \leq 9,000$ (Dept. C constraint)
   $x_1, x_2, x_3 \geq 0$ (Non-negativity condition)

Problem 8: A company has two grades of inspectors I and II who are to be assigned for a quality control inspection. It is required that at least 2000 pieces to be inspected per 8 hrs day. Grade I inspector can check pieces at the rate of 50 per hour with an accuracy of 97%. Grade II inspector can check pieces at the rate of 40 per hour with an accuracy of 95%. The wage rate of Grade I inspector is ₹ 4.50/hr. and that of grade II is ₹ 2.50 per hr. Each time an error is made by an inspector the cost to the company is one rupee. The company has available for the inspection job 10 grade I and 5 grade II inspectors. Formulate the problem to find how many grade I and grade II inspectors to be engaged to minimise the total cost.

(P.U. MBA - May 05)

Solution: Let x - number of grade I inspectors to be engaged
                  y - number of grade II inspectors to be engaged

1. **Objective Function:** The inspectors are paid wages at the rage of ₹ 4.50 per hour (for grade I) and ₹ 2.5 per hour (For grade II) for an 8 hrs day.
   ∴ Expected cost of wages
   $= 4.5 \times 8 \times x + 2.5 \times 8 \times y$
   $= 36x + 20y$

Also since the Grade I inspectors can check the pieces at the rate of 50 per hour, the number of pieces checked by x number of inspectors in 8 hours $= 50 \times 8 \times x = 400x$
Now, since the accuracy of inspection is 97%
∴ The expected error $= 100 - 97 = 3\%$ i.e. 0.03
∴ Expected number of errors by grade I inspectors
   $= 400x \times 0.03 = 12x$
Similarly for grade II inspectors, the expected number of errors $= 40 \times 8 \times y \times 0.05 = 16y$
Thus expected number of errors in an 8 hours day $= 12x + 16y$
∴ Cost of errors to the company
   $= 1 \times (12x + 16y)$ ..... as each error costs ₹ 1
   $= 12x + 16y$
∴ Total Cost $=$ Cost of wages $+$ Cost of errors
   $= (36x + 20y) + (12x + 16y)$
   $= 48x + 36y$
∴ The objective function is to minimize $C = 48x + 36y$

2. Constraints:

(i) Number of pieces checked in 8 hours
 = Pieces checked by Grade I inspectors + pieces checked by Grade II inspectors
 = 50 × 8 × x + 40 × 8 × y
 = 400x + 320y

Now, as at least 2000 pieces are to be inspected.

∴ 400 x + 320 y ≥ 2000

i.e. 5 x + 4 y ≥ 25

(ii) As 10 grade I inspectors are available with the company

∴ x ≤ 10

Similarly, y ≤ 5

3. Hence the L. P. model for the problem is:

Minimize, C = 48x + 36 y   (Cost minimization)

Subject to   5 x + 4 y ≥ 25   (Output constraint)

x ≤ 10   (Availability constraint - Grade I)

y ≤ 5   (Availability constraint - Grade II)

x, y ≤ 0   (Non - negativity condition)

Problem 9: A firm produces 3 products A, B and C. It uses 2 raw materials I and II of which 5000 and 7500 units can be used for production of A, B and C. Product A requires 3 units of raw material I and 5 units of raw material II per unit. Corresponding requirement per unit of B are 4 and 3 units of raw material I and II respectively and per unit of C, 5 units of raw material I and 5 units of raw material II. The labour time to produce 1 unit of A is twice required to produce 1 unit of B and is three times required to produce 1 unit of C. The entire labour force of the firm can produce equivalent of 3000 units of product A. The minimum demand for the 3 products is 600, 650 and 500 units respectively. Assuming profits per unit of A, B and C are ₹ 50, ₹ 60 and ₹ 80 respectively, formulate the L.P.P. to maximise profit satisfying constraints.   **(P.U. MBA - Dec. 05)**

Solution: Let x, y and z be the production quantity of the products A, B, and C respectively.

1. **Objective Function:** Since the per unit profit of A, B and C is ₹ 50, ₹ 60 and ₹ 80 respectively,

∴ Total Profit = 50x + 60y + 80z

∴ Objective Function is

Maximize, P = 50x + 60y + 80z

2. Constraints:

(i) Raw materials: Since, each unit of A, B and C requires 3, 4 and 5 units of raw material I respectively,

∴ The total units of raw material I required $= 3x + 4y + 5z$

And as a 5000 units of raw material I are available,

∴ $3x + 4y + 5z \leq 5000$

Similarly, Total number of units of raw material II required $= 5x + 3y + 5z$

And as a 7500 units are available, hence we must have

$5x + 3y + 5z \leq 7500$

(ii) Labour Time: Let a, b and c be the labour time required to produce a unit of product A, B and C respectively.

Now, as the labour time required to produce 1 unit of A is twice that for B and is thrice that for C

∴ $a = 2b$ and $a = 3c$

∴ $b = \dfrac{1}{2} a$ and $c = \dfrac{1}{3} a$

∴ Total labour time required for production

$= a \times x + b \times y + c \times z$

$= a x + \dfrac{1}{2} ay + \dfrac{1}{3} az$

Now, the labour force of the company can produce equivalent to 3000 units of product A

∴ Total labour time available $= 3000 \times a$

∴ We must have

$ax + \dfrac{1}{2} ay + \dfrac{1}{3} az \leq 3000a$

i.e. $x + \dfrac{1}{2} y + \dfrac{1}{3} z \leq 3000$

i.e. $6x + 3y + 2z \leq 18000$

(iii) Demand: The minimum demand for products A, B and C is 600, 650 and 500 units respectively. Hence, there production must be at least equal to these quantities.

∴ $x \geq 600$, $y \geq 650$ and $z \geq 500$

3. Hence, the L.P.P. formulation is

Maximize $P = 50x + 60y + 80z$ (Profit maximisation)
subject to $3x + 4y + 5z \leq 5000$ (Raw Matl. I constraint)
            $5x + 3y + 5z \leq 7500$ (Raw Matl. II constraint)
            $6x + 3y + 2z \leq 18000$ (Labour Time constraint)
            $x \geq 600$ (Demand Constraint for A)
            $y \geq 650$ (Demand Constraint for B)
            $z \geq 500$ (Demand Constraint for C)
            $x, y, z \geq 0$ (Non negativity condition)

Problem 10: A refinery makes 3 grades of petrol A, B and C from crude oils D, E and F. Crude oil F can be used in any grade but the others must satisfy the followings specifications:

Grade	Selling Price per litre (₹)	Specifications
A	₹ 48	Not less than 50% crude D Not more than 25% crude E
B	₹ 50	Not less than 25% crude D Not more than 50% crude E
C	₹ 49	No specifications

There are capacity limitations on the amounts of 3 crude elements that can be used

Crude	Capacity (kL)	Price per Litre (₹)
D	500	49.5
E	500	47.5
F	360	48.5

Formulate LPP to maximise profit.   **(P.U. MBA – May 07)**

Solution: Here, the specifications of A, B, C are expressed in terms of minimum or maximum contents of D and E. Also for calculating the profit we have to take in to account the cost of crude oils D, E, F as well as selling prices of A, B, C. Hence, it is advisable to consider the decision variables as follows: let

x_{AD} – Quantity of D (in litres) in petrol A ; x_{AE} – Quantity of E (in litres) in petrol A
x_{AF} – Quantity of F (in litres) in petrol A ; x_{BD} – Quantity of D (in litres) in petrol B
x_{BE} – Quantity of E (in litres) in petrol B ; x_{BF} – Quantity of F (in litres) in petrol B
x_{CD} – Quantity of D (in litres) in petrol C ; x_{CE} – Quantity of E (in litres) in petrol C
x_{CF} – Quantity of F (in litres) in petrol C

1. **Objective Function:**

   The total production quantity (in litres) of petrol A = $x_{AD} + x_{AE} + x_{AF}$

   Similarly, the total production quantities (in litres) of B and C are $(x_{BD} + x_{BE} + x_{BF})$ and $(x_{CD} + x_{CE} + x_{CF})$ respectively.

   Now, as the selling prices (per litre) of A, B and C are ₹ 48, 50 and 49.

   ∴ Total Revenue (by selling petrols) = $48(x_{AD} + x_{AE} + x_{AF}) + 50(x_{BD} + x_{BE} + x_{BF}) + 49(x_{CD} + x_{CE} + x_{CF})$

   Again, Total quantity (in litres) of the crude oil D used = $x_{AD} + x_{BD} + x_{CD}$

   Similarly, quantities (in litres) of the crude oils E and F used are $(x_{AE} + x_{BE} + x_{CE})$ and $(x_{AF} + x_{BF} + x_{CF})$ respectively.

   Now, as the crude oil price (per litre) for D, E and F are ₹ 49.5, ₹ 47.5 and ₹ 48.5

   ∴ Total Cost (of crude oils) = $49.5(x_{AD} + x_{BD} + x_{CD}) + 47.5(x_{AE} + x_{BE} + x_{CE}) + 48.5(x_{AF} + x_{BF} + x_{CF})$

   ∴ Total profit (P) = Total Revenue − Total Cost

   = $48(x_{AD} + x_{AE} + x_{AF}) + 50(x_{BD} + x_{BE} + x_{BF}) + 49(x_{CD} + x_{CE} + x_{CF}) - 49.5(x_{AD} + x_{BD} + x_{CD}) - 47.5(x_{AE} + x_{BE} + x_{CE}) - 48.5(x_{AF} + x_{BF} + x_{CF})$

   ∴ The objective function is to maximize

   $P = -1.5x_{AD} + 0.5x_{AE} - 0.5x_{AF} + 0.5x_{BD} + 2.5x_{BE} + 1.5x_{BF} - 0.5x_{CD} + 1.5x_{CE} + 0.5x_{CF}$

2. **Constraints:**

   (i) **Capacity:** Since the available quantity of D is 500 k ∴ i.e. 500×10^3 litres

   ∴ We must have,

   Quantity of D used $\leq 500 \times 10^3$

   i.e. $x_{AD} + x_{BD} + x_{CD} \leq 500 \times 10^3$

   Similarly, for crude oil E, $x_{AE} + x_{BE} + x_{CE} \leq 500 \times 10^3$

   and for crude oil F, $x_{AF} + x_{BF} + x_{CF} \leq 360 \times 10^3$

   (ii) **Specifications:**

   For petrol A, the quantity of crude oil D in it i.e. x_{AD} should be at least 50% (by volume)

   i.e. $x_{AD} \geq 0.50 \times$ (Quantity of petrol A)

   i.e. $x_{AD} \geq 0.5(x_{AD} + x_{AE} + x_{AF})$

   i.e. $0.5 x_{AD} - 0.5 x_{AE} - 0.5 x_{AF} \geq 0$

   i.e. $x_{AD} - x_{AE} - x_{AF} \geq 0$

   Also the quantity of crude oil E in A i.e. x_{AE} should not be more than 25%

   i.e. $x_{AE} \leq 0.25 \times$ (Quantity of petrol A)

   i.e. $x_{AE} \leq 0.25(x_{AD} + x_{AE} + x_{AF})$

   i.e. $0.75 x_{AE} - 0.25 x_{AD} - 0.25 x_{AF} \leq 0$ .... Dividing by 0.25 we get,

   i.e. $3x_{AE} - x_{AD} - x_{AF} \leq 0$

   i.e. $x_{AD} - 3x_{AE} + x_{AF} \geq 0$ .... by changing the signs

Similarly for petrol B,

$x_{BD} \geq 0.25 (x_{BD} + x_{BE} + x_{BF})$ i.e. $0.75 x_{BD} - 0.25 x_{BE} - 0.25 x_{BF} \geq 0$

i.e. $3x_{BD} - x_{BE} - x_{BF} \geq 0$ and $x_{BE} \leq 0.5 (x_{BD} + x_{BE} + x_{BF})$

i.e. $0.5x_{BE} - 0.5x_{BD} - 0.5x_{BF} \leq 0$ i.e. $x_{BE} - x_{BD} - x_{BF} \leq 0$

i.e. $x_{BD} - x_{BE} + x_{BF} \geq 0$ ..... changing sign

The petrol C has no restrictions.

3. Thus, the LPP is

Maximise

$P = -1.5 x_{AD} + 0.5 x_{AE} - 0.5x_{AF} + 0.5x_{BD} + 2.5x_{BE} + 1.5x_{BF} - 0.5 x_{CD} + 1.5x_{CE} + 0.5 x_{CF}$

(profit maximisation)

Subject to:

$x_{AD} + x_{BD} + x_{CD} \leq 500 \times 10^3$ (Capacity constraint for D)

$x_{AE} + x_{BE} + x_{CE} \leq 500 \times 10^3$ (Capacity constraint for E)

$x_{AF} + x_{BF} + x_{CF} \leq 360 \times 10^3$ (Capacity constraint for F)

$x_{AD} - x_{AE} - x_{AF} \geq 0$ (Specification of A for D)

$x_{AD} - 3x_{AE} + x_{AF} \geq 0$ (Specification of A for E)

$3x_{BD} - x_{BE} - x_{BF} \geq 0$ (Specification of B for D)

$x_{BD} - x_{BE} + x_{BF} \geq 0$ (Specification of B for E)

$x_{AD}, x_{AE}, x_{AF}, x_{BD}, x_{BE}, x_{BF}, x_{CD}, x_{CE}, x_{CF} \geq 0$ (Non - negativity condition)

Problem 11: The manager of an oil refinery must decide on an optimal mix of two possible blending processes of which the input and output per production run are given below:

Process	Input (Units)		Output (Units)	
	Crude A	Crude B	Gasoline X	Gasoline Y
I	5	3	5	8
II	4	5	4	4

Availability of crude A and B is 200 units and 150 units respectively. Market requirements show that atleast 100 units of Gasoline X and 80 units of Gasoline Y must be produced. The profit per production run from process I and process II are ₹ 300 and ₹ 400 respectively. Formulate the above LPP problem.   **(P.U. MBA - Dec. 09)**

Solution: Let x - Number of production runs of process I

y - Number of production runs of process II

1. **Objective function:** Since the profits per production run from processes I and II are ₹ 300 and ₹ 400 respectively.

∴ Total profit = 300x + 400y

∴ The objective function is,

Maximise, P = 300x + 400y

2. **Constraints:**
   (i) Crude A: Each production run of process I requires 5 units of crude A as input while that of process II requires 4 units.
   ∴ Total quantity of crude A required = 5x + 4y.
   As available quantity of A is 200 units, we must have 5x + 4y ≤ 200.
   (ii) Crude B: Similarly, requirement of crude B is 3x + 5y and as the availability is 150 units, we must have 3x + 5y ≤ 150.
   (iii) Gasoline X Sales: Each production run of process I produces 5 units of Gasoline X as its output. Similarly, each production run of process II produces 4 units of X. Hence, total production of Gasoline (through x and y number of respective production runs) is 5x + 4y.
   Now, as the market requires atleast 100 units of X be produced. Hence, we have 5x + 4y ≥ 100.
   (iv) Gasoline Y sales: Similarly, total production of Product Y is 8x + 4y and as the market requirements is atleast 80 units, we must have 8x + 4y ≥ 80 i.e. 2x + y ≥ 20.
3. Hence, the LPP formulation:

   Maximise   P = 300x + 400y   (Profit maximisation)
   Subject to   5x + 4y ≤ 200   (Crude A availability constraint)
                   3x + 5y ≤ 150   (Crude B availability constraint)
                   5x + 4y ≥ 100   (Gasoline X sales constraint)
                   2x + y ≥ 20   (Gasoline Y sales constraint)
                   x, y ≥ 0   (Non-negativity condition)

Exercise - I

1. A small manufacturing firm produces two types of gadgets A and B which are first processed in the foundry and then sent to the machine shop for finishing. The number of man-hours of labour required in each shop for the production of each unit of A and B and the number of man-hours available with the firm per week are given below:

	Foundry	Machine Shop
Gadget A	10	5
Gadget B	6	4
Firm's Capacity per week	1000	600

   Profit on sale of A is ₹ 30 per unit as compared with ₹ 20 per unit for B. Determine weekly production of A and B so that the profit is maximised. Formulate it as a L.P.P.
   (**Ans**: x_1 - No. of units of A, x_2 - No. of units of B produced per week.
   Max. P = $30x_1 + 20x_2$, subject to $10x_1 + 6x_2 \le 1000$; $5x_1 + 4x_2 \le 600$; $x_1, x_2 \ge 0$)

2. The owner of Winner Sports wishes to determine the number of advertisements to be placed in three selected monthly magazines A, B and C. His objective is to advertise in such a way that the total exposure to the principal buyers of the expensive sports goods is maximised. Percentage of readers for each magazine are known. Exposure in any particular magazine is the number of advertisements placed multiplied by the number of principal buyers. The following data may be used:

	Magazines		
	A	B	C
Readers	1 lakh	0.6 lakh	0.4 lakh
Principal Buyers	15%	15%	7%
Cost/Advt. (₹)	5,000	4,500	4,250

The budget amount at most is ₹ 1 lakh for the advertisements. The owner has already decided that magazine A will have no more than 6 advertisements and that B and C each have at least 2 advertisements. Formulate LP model for the problem.

(**Ans:** x_1, x_2, x_3 - No. of advertisements to be placed in A, B, C respectively.

Max. E = 15000 x_1 + 9000x_2 + 2800 x_3

Subject to 5000x_1 + 4500 x_2 + 4250 $x_3 \leq$ 1,00,000; $x_1 \leq$ 6; $x_2 \geq$ 2; $x_3 \geq$ 2; $x_1, x_2, x_3 \geq$ 0)

3. A pharmaceutical company has 100 kg of A, 180 kg of B and 120 kg of C available per month. They use these materials to make three basic pharma products viz. 5-10-5, 5-5-10 and 20-5-10 where the numbers in each case represent the percentage by weight of A, B, C respectively in each of the products. The cost of these raw materials are ₹ 80, ₹ 20 and ₹ 50 per kg. respectively while the inert ingredient costs ₹ 20 per kg. The selling price of the three products are ₹ 40.5, ₹ 43 and ₹ 45 per kg. respectively. There is a capacity restriction of the company for product 5-10-5 so that it can not produce more than 30 kg per month. Determine how much of each of the products the company should produce in order to maximise its monthly profit?

(**Ans:** x_1, x_2, x_3 - Quantities produced per month (in kg) of 5-10-5, 5-5-10, 20-5-10 respectively. Max. P = 16x_1 + 17x_2 + 10x_3 Subject to $x_1 \leq$ 30; 5x_1 + 5x_2 + 20x_3 $\leq$ 10,000; 10x_1 + 5x_2 + 5$x_3 \leq$ 18,000; 5x_1 + 10x_2 + 10$x_3 \leq$ 12,000; $x_1, x_2, x_3 \geq$ 0)

4. A company is making two products A and B. The cost of producing one unit of product A and B is ₹ 60 and ₹ 80 respectively. As per the agreement, the company has to supply at least 200 units of product B to its regular customers. One unit of product A requires one machine hour whereas product B has machine hours available abundantly within the company. Total machine hours available for product A are 400 hours. One unit of each product A and B requires one labour hour each and total

500 labour hours are available. The company wants to minimise the cost of production by satisfying the given requirements. Formulate the problem as a LPP.

(**Ans.:** x_1, x_2 - No. of units of A and B to be manufactured respectively

Min. C = $60x_1 + 80x_2$ Subject to $x_2 \geq 200$; $x_1 \leq 400$; $x_1 + x_2 \leq 500$; $x_1, x_2 \geq 0$)

5. A city hospital has the following minimal daily requirement of nurses.

Period	1	2	3	4	5	6
Clock time	6-10 am	10-2 pm	2-6 pm	6-10 pm	10-2 am	2-6 am
Min. no. of Nurses	2	7	15	8	20	6

The nurses report to the hospital at the beginning of each period and work for 8 hours consecutively. The hospital wants to determine the minimum number of nurses to be employed so that there will be sufficient number of them available for each period. Formulate the LP model for the problem.

(**Ans.:** $x_1, x_2, \ldots x_6$ - No. of nurses reporting during periods 1, 2, …. 6 respectively.

Min. N = $x_1 + x_2 + x_3 + x_4 + x_5 + x_6$ Subject to $x_1 + x_2 \geq 7$; $x_2 + x_3 \geq 15$; $x_3 + x_4 \geq 8$; $x_4 + x_5 \geq 20$; $x_5 + x_6 \geq 6$; $x_6 + x_1 \geq 2$; $x_1, x_2, \ldots x_6 \geq 0$)

6. A company produces two special types of soaps X and Y for which the following data is available.

Per Unit	X	Y
Selling price	₹ 18	₹ 25
Direct Material : A	2 units @ ₹ 2/unit	3 units @ ₹ 2/unit
B	1 unit @ ₹ 4/unit	2 units @ ₹ 4/unit
C	–	1 unit @ ₹ 1/unit
Direct Labour	1 man hour @ ₹ 2.5/hr	1 man hr @ ₹ 2.5/hr
Variable Overheads	₹ 1	₹ 1.5

The fixed over-heads are ₹ 1,500 per month. The quantities of materials A, B, C available for production are 500, 400 and 200 respectively per month. There are 2 workers who work for 8 hours a day for 25 days in a month. The per month market demand for X and Y is at least 200 and 150 units respectively. Formulate this as a LPP.

(**Ans.:** x, y - No. of units of X and Y produced monthly. Max. P = 6.5x + 6y − 1500 Subject to $2x + 3y \leq 500$; $x + 2y \leq 400$; $y \leq 200$; $x + y \leq 400$; $x \geq 200$; $y \geq 150$; $x, y \geq 0$)

7. A manufacturing company makes 3 products, each of which require 3 operations as a part of manufacturing process. The company can sell all of the products it can manufacture but its production capabilities are limited. Additional related data are as below:

Product	Manufacturing requirements (hours/ unit)			Cost (₹)	Selling Price (₹)
	Centre 1	Centre 2	Centre 3		
A	1	3	2	11	15
B	3	4	1	12	20
C	2	2	2	10	16
Available Hours	160	120	80		

Formulate the LPP. **(P.U. MBA - May 06)**

(**Ans.** Max $P = 4x + 8y + 6z$; s.t.: $x + 3y + 2z \leq 160$, $3x + 4y + 2z \leq 120$, $2x + y + 2z \leq 80$; $x, y, z \geq 0$)

8. A company machines and drills two castings X and Y. The time required to machine and drill one casting including machine set up time is as follows:

Casting	Machine Hours	Drilling Hours
X	4	2
Y	2	5

There are two lathe and three drilling machines. The working week is of 40 hours; there is no overtime and lost time. Variable costs for both castings are ₹ 120 per unit while total fixed costs amount to ₹ 1000 per week. The selling price of casting X is ₹ 300 per unit and that of Y is ₹ 360 per unit. There are no limitations on the number of X and Y castings that can be sold. The company wishes to maximize profits. Formulate a linear programming model for the problem.

(**Ans.:** x-casting X, y-casting Y per week; Max. $P = 180x + 240y - 1000$; s.t. $2x + y \leq 40$, $2x + 5y \leq 120$; $x, y \geq 0$)

9. A firm produces three products. These products are processed on three different machines. The time required to manufacture one unit of each of the three products and daily capacity of the three machines are given in the table below:

Machine	Time per unit (minutes)			Machine Capacity (Minutes per day)
	Product 1	Product 2	Product 3	
M_1	2	3	2	440
M_2	4	–	3	470
M_3	2	5	–	430

It is required to determine the daily number of units to be manufactured for each product. The profit per unit for product 1, 2 and 3 is ₹ 4, ₹ 3 and ₹ 6 respectively. It is assumed that all the amounts produced are consumed in the market. Formulate the LP model.

(**Ans.:** x_1 - Product 1, x_2 - Product 2, x_3 - Product 3 daily produced; Max. $P = 4x_1 + 3x_2 + 6x_3$ subject to $2x_1 + 3x_2 + 2x_3 \leq 440$, $4x_1 + 3x_3 \leq 470$, $2x_1 + 5x_2 \leq 430$; $x_1, x_2, x_3 \geq 0$)

10. A company manufactures two products A and B. The profit per unit of A and B is ₹ 60/- and ₹ 80/- respectively. The company is required to supply 200 units of product B to its regular customers. Product A requires machining on machine M_1 only and per unit of A, one hour of M_1 is required. Product B requires machine M_2 only and machine hours on M_2 has enough hours available to manufacture any number of units of product B. M_1 has 400 hours available. Product A and B both require one labour hour each and company has 500 labour hours available. To determine the number of units of A and B to be manufactured, satisfying given conditions. Formulate the LPP. **(P.U.MBA-Nov.03)**

(**Ans.:** x - A produced, y - B produced; max. P = 60x + 80y, subject to x ≥ 200, x ≤ 400, x + y ≤ 500; x, y ≥ 0)

PART II – GRPAHICAL METHOD OF SOLUTION

1.5 Introduction

After a Linear Programming Problem is expressed in the LP format, the next step is to solve it to get its solution. Before going for the solution (i.e. the set of values of the decision variables x_1, x_2 etc.), the following points must be noted:

(i) **Basic Feasible Solution:** It is a solution which satisfies the non-negativity condition as well as the constraints. Thus, a problem can have many feasible solutions.

(ii) **Optimum/Optimal Solution:** This is a basic feasible solution which optimises (maximises or minimises) the objective function. A problem normally has a unique optimal solution.

1.6 Graphical Method of Solution

This is the simplest method to solve a LP Problem involving only two decision variables. The two decision variables say x_1 and x_2 are plotted along the two coordinate axes X and Y on a graph paper. Only first quadrant of XY plane must be considered as x_1, x_2 ≥ 0.

Steps for obtaining Graphical Solution:

Step 1: Formulate the given problem in LP format.

Step 2: Plot the graph constraints:

(i) Make the constant term on the right hand side of the constraints as positive, if it is not, by changing the signs of all the terms. Change the inequality also from ≥ to ≤ or ≤ to ≥ in it.

(ii) Replace the inequality sign (≤ or ≥) in a constraint by an equality sign (=). This gives a constraint equation which represents a straight line.

(iii) Plot the constraint line: For plotting the line, identify two points on the line and join them by a straight line. The most convenient points are its points of intersection with X axis (obtained by putting x_2 = 0 in the constraint equation and solving it for x_1) and

Y axis (obtained by putting $x_1 = 0$ in the equation and solving it for x_2). Note that the lines $x_1 = a$ and $x_2 = b$ are straight lines parallel to Y and X axis at distances a and b from the origin respectively.

(iv) Repeat the procedure to draw all the constraint lines.

Step 3: Identify the Feasible Region or the Solution Space:

(i) Each constraint line divides the XY plane into two parts - one which includes the origin and the other away from the origin.

(ii) For constraints of the type ($\geq$) or ($>$), mark the region away from the origin about the constraint line. For constraints of the type ($\leq$) or ($<$) mark the region towards the origin about the constraint line. For constraint of the type ($=$) the region is the line itself, only. Use arrows ($\rightarrow$) to indicate the respective regions.

(iii) Mark the region which is common to all these regions. This is the Feasible Region, which could be an open or closed polygon.

Step 4: To find Optimum Solution:

(A) Corner Point Method:

(i) Identify all the corner points of the feasible region. To obtain their co-ordinates solve the equations of the corresponding (intersecting) constraint lines simultaneously, if necessary.

(ii) Find the value of the objective function (say Z) at all these corner points.

(iii) For a maximisation problem, the co-ordinates of the corner point where Z is maximum give the solution. Similarly, for a minimisation problem the co-ordinates of the corner point corresponding to minimum value of Z give the solution. The corresponding value of Z is its optimum value Z_{max} or Z_{min}.

(B) Iso-Profit or Iso-Cost Line Method:

Alternately we can use the Iso-Profit or Iso-Cost Line Method:

(i) Draw an objective function line (passing through the feasible region) like a constraint line by considering some positive value for Z arbitrarily. This is an iso-profit (iso-cost) line as all points on it give same value of Z.

(ii) If the problem is of maximisation (minimisation), go on shifting this line parallel to itself away (closer) from (to) the origin, until further movement takes the line completely outside the feasible region.

(iii) The co-ordinates of the point touched last by the line give the solution i.e. values of x_1 and x_2 and the value of Z for this point gives value of Z_{max} (Z_{min}.)

Example 1: Solve the following problem graphically

Maximise $Z = 3x + 4y$

Subject to $x + y \le 6$

$2x + y \le 8$

$x, y \ge 0$

Solution: The decision variables x and y are plotted along the X and Y axes.

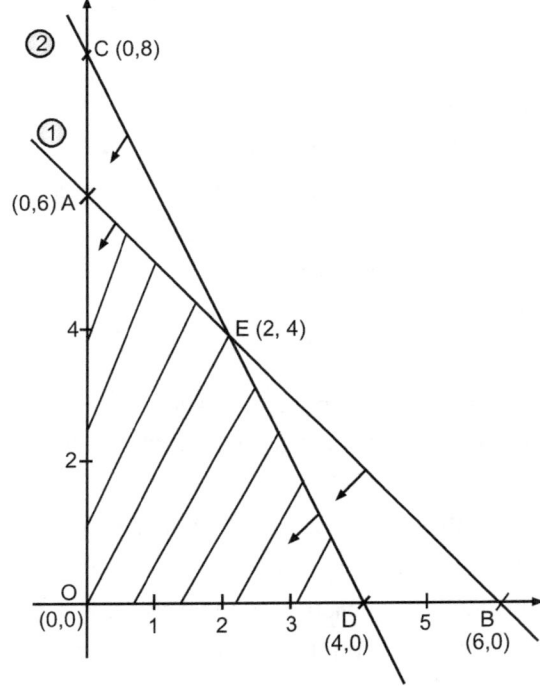

Fig. 1.1

1. **To plot the Graph Constraints:**

   (i) Consider the first constraint, $x + y \le 6$

   Replacing the inequality sign by an equality we get the first constraint equation as, $x + y = 6$ ... (1)

   This is the equation of the first constraint line. Its intersection with Y axis is obtained by putting $x = 0$ in it.

   $\therefore 0 + y = 6$ i.e. $y = 6$

   $\therefore A(x, y)$ i.e. $A(0, 6)$ is the point on Y axis

   Similarly, putting $y = 0$ in (1) we get $x = 6$

   $\therefore B(6, 0)$ is the point on X axis.

   Joining these points A and B we get the constraint line (1)

(ii) Consider the second constraint $2x + y \leq 8$. Replacing inequality by equality sign we get the constraint equation as,

$\qquad 2x + y = 8 \qquad \qquad \qquad \ldots (2)$

Put $x = 0$

$\therefore \quad y = 8$

$\therefore \quad$ C(0, 8) is point on Y axis.

Put $y = 0$

$\therefore \quad 2x = 8$

$\therefore \quad x = 4$

$\therefore \quad$ D(4, 0) is point on X axis and $\therefore$ line CD is the constraint line (2)

2. **To find the Feasible Region:**
   (i) The constraint (1) is $x + y \leq 6$ i.e. of the type $\leq$. Hence, mark the region towards the origin about line (1) by arrows as shown above.
   (ii) Constraint (2) i.e. $2x + y \leq 8$ is also of type $\leq$. Hence, mark again the region lying towards the origin about the line (2) as well.
   (iii) The region common to the above two regions is the feasible region as marked in the figure. It is a closed polygon with corner points O D E A.
   (iv) To find the co-ordinates of point E, which is a point of intersection of lines (1) and (2), solve their equations simultaneously. Thus, we have

   $\qquad x + y = 6 \qquad \qquad \qquad \ldots (1)$
   $\qquad 2x + y = 8 \qquad \qquad \qquad \ldots (2)$

   Subtracting we get, $-x + 0 = -2 \quad \therefore x = 2$.

   $\therefore \quad$ From (1), $y = 6 - x = 6 - 2 = 4$

   $\therefore \quad$ Co-ordinates of E are (2, 4)

3. **Find the values of Objective Function:**

   Finding values of $Z = 3x + 4y$ at the corner points O, D, E and A by using their co-ordinates as:

   at O (0, 0) $\quad Z_O = 3(0) + 4(0) = 0$

   D (4, 0) $\quad Z_D = 3(4) + 4(0) = 12$

   E (2, 4) $\quad Z_E = 3(2) + 4(4) = 6 + 16 = 22$

   A (0, 6) $\quad Z_A = 3(0) + 4(6) = 24$

4. **Optimum Solution:** This is a problem of maximisation. Hence, the optimum value of Z is the maximum value among the above i.e. 24. This corresponds to point A(0, 6). Thus, the co-ordinates of A i.e. $x = 0, y = 6$ is the solution for which $Z_{max.} = 24$.

Note: If this would have been a problem of minimisation i.e. Minimise $z = 3x + 4y$, the solution will correspond to point O i.e. $x = 0, y = 0$ where $Z_{min.} = 0$.

Example 2: Minimise $Z = 6x_1 + 5x_2$

Subject to
$$4x_1 + x_2 \geq 10$$
$$2x_1 + 3x_2 \geq 15$$
$$x_1 \leq 10$$
$$x_1, x_2 \geq 0$$

Solution: Plot x_1 along X axis and x_2 along Y axis.

1. **To plot Graph Constraints:**
   (i) First constraint is $4x_1 + x_2 \geq 10$
       $\therefore$ Constraint equation is $4x_1 + x_2 = 10$ ... (1)
       Put $x_1 = 0$ $\therefore x_2 = 10$ $\therefore$ A (0, 10)
       Put $x_2 = 0$, $\therefore 4x_1 = 10$ $\therefore x_1 = \dfrac{10}{4} = \dfrac{5}{2} = 2.5$ $\therefore$ B$\left(\dfrac{5}{2}, 0\right)$ or (2.5, 0)
       Join AB to get the constraint line (1)
   (ii) Second constraint is $2x_1 + 3x_2 \geq 15$
        Constraint equation is $2x_1 + 3x_2 = 15$ ... (2)
        Put $x_1 = 0$, $\therefore 3x_2 = 15$, $\therefore x_2 = 5$ $\therefore$ C (0, 5)
        Put $x_2 = 0$ $\therefore 2x_1 = 15$ $\therefore x_1 = \dfrac{15}{2} = 7.5$ $\therefore$ D$\left(\dfrac{15}{2}, 0\right)$ i.e. (7.5, 0)
   (iii) Third constraint is $x_1 \leq 10$
         $\therefore$ Constraint equation is $x_1 = 10$ ... (3)
         This is a line parallel to Y axis at a distance 10 from origin i.e. a vertical line through E(10, 0)

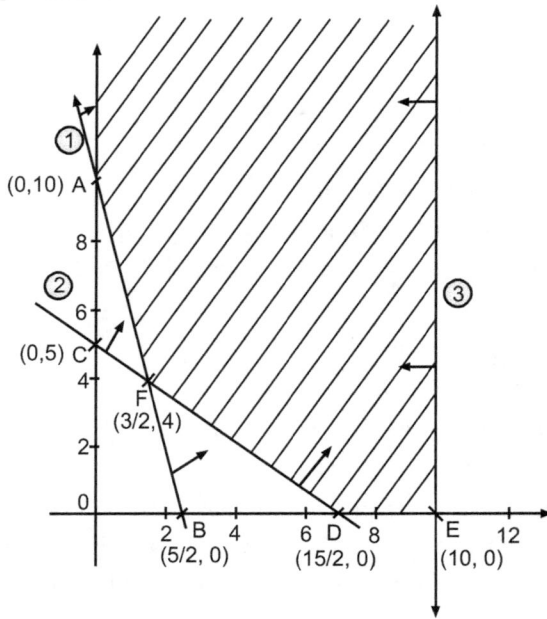

Fig. 1.2

2. To find the Feasible Region:

(i) Constraint (1) is of type $\geq$. $\therefore$ Mark the region away from origin about line (1) by arrows as shown.

(ii) Constraint (2) is also of type $\geq$. $\therefore$ Mark the region away from origin about line (2).

(iii) Constraint (3) is of type $\leq$. $\therefore$ Mark the region towards origin about line (3).

(iv) Region common to the above three regions is the feasible region. It is an open polygon with corner points AFDE and open at the top, as shown in Fig. 1.2. It extends upto infinity.

(v) To find co-ordinates of F, we solve equations of intersecting lines (1) and (2) simultaneously.

$$4x_1 + x_2 = 10 \quad \ldots (1)$$

($\times$ 3) gives $\quad 12x_1 + 3x_2 = 30$

and $\quad\quad\quad\quad 2x_1 + 3x_2 = 15 \quad \ldots (2)$

Subtracting, $\quad 10x_1 + 0 = 15$

$\therefore \quad\quad\quad\quad x_1 = \dfrac{15}{10} = \dfrac{3}{2}$

$\therefore$ From (1), $x_2 = 10 - 4x_1 = 10 - 4\left(\dfrac{3}{2}\right) = 10 - 6 = 4$

$\therefore F\left(\dfrac{3}{2}, 4\right)$

3. To find values of Objective Function: $Z = 6x_1 + 5x_2$ at corner points:

at A(0, 10), $\quad\quad Z_A = 6(0) + 5(10) = 50$

at $F\left(\dfrac{3}{2}, 4\right) \quad\quad Z_F = 6\left(\dfrac{3}{2}\right) + 5(4) = 29$

at $D\left(\dfrac{15}{2}, 0\right), \quad\quad Z_D = 6\left(\dfrac{15}{2}\right) + 0 = 45$

at E(10, 0), $\quad\quad Z_E = 6(10) + 0 = 60$

4. To find Optimum Solution:

This is a problem of minimisation. The minimum value of Z occurs at the corner point $F\left(\dfrac{3}{2}, 4\right)$.

Thus, the solution is $x_1 = \dfrac{3}{2}$, $x_2 = 4$ and $Z_{min} = 29$.

Note: If this would have been a problem of maximisation i.e. Maximise $Z = 6x_1 + 5x_2$, the solution would have been $Z_{max} = \infty$, corresponding to point (10, ∞) as the region extends upto ∞. Hence the solution would have been unbounded.

1.7 Note

For a general Linear Programming Problem having n unknowns (decision variables) $x_1, x_2, \ldots x_n$ and m constraints where m < n:

(i) **Basic Solution:** A solution obtained by setting (n–m) number of variables (from n variables $x_1, x_2, \ldots x_n$) to 0 and thus solving the m equations in m remaining variables is called a basic solution. The variables (n–m in number) that are set to zero are called as non-basic variables and the remaining m variables are called as basic variables which form the basic solution.

(ii) **Optimal Feasible Solution:** Any basic feasible solution which optimises the objective function is the optimal feasible solution.

(iii) **Degenerate Solution:** A basic solution for the system of equations is called as a degenerate solution if one or more of the basic variables become equal to zero.

Solved Problems

Problem 1: Minimise $\quad Z = 80x_1 + 120x_2$

$$\text{Subject to} \quad x_1 + x_2 \leq 9$$
$$x_1 \geq 2$$
$$x_2 \geq 3$$
$$20x_1 + 50x_2 \leq 300$$
$$x_1, x_2 \geq 0$$

Solution:

1. **To plot constraint lines:**

    (i) $x_1 + x_2 \leq 9 \quad \therefore$ Constraint equation is $x_1 + x_2 = 9$ ... (1)

    put $x_1 = 0, \quad \therefore x_2 = 9 \quad \therefore A(0, 9)$

    $x_2 = 0, \quad \therefore x_1 = 9 \quad \therefore B(9, 0)$

    (ii) $x_1 \geq 2$

    $\therefore\quad$ Constraint equation is $x_1 = 2$ ... (2)

    i.e. Line parallel to Y axis at (2, 0)

    (iii) $x_2 \geq 3$

    $\therefore\quad$ Constraint equation is, $x_2 = 3$ ... (3)

    i.e. Line parallel to X axis at (0, 3)

    (iv) $20x_1 + 50x_2 \leq 300$

    $\therefore\quad$ Constraint equation is $20x_1 + 50x_2 = 300$

    i.e. $2x_1 + 5x_2 = 30$ ... (4)

    $\therefore\quad$ Points are C(0, 6) and D(15, 0)

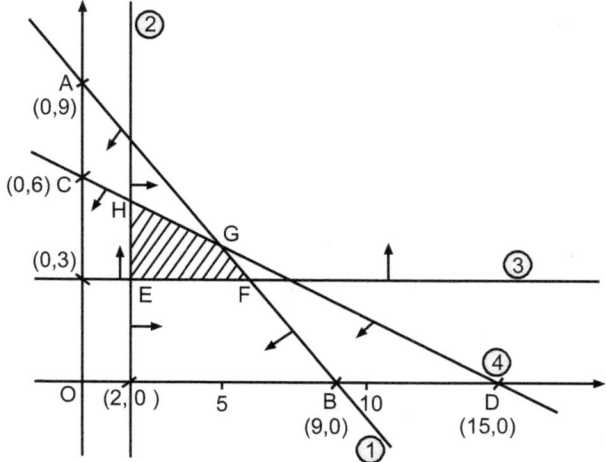

Fig. 1.3

2. To find Feasible Region:

(i) Constraint (1) is of type '≤'.   ∴ Mark region towards origin.
(ii) Constraint (2) is of type '≥'.   ∴ Mark region away from origin.
(iii) Constraint (3) is of type '≥'   ∴ Mark region away from origin.
(iv) Constraint (4) is of type '≤'   ∴ Mark region towards origin.
(v) ∴ Feasible region is the polygon EFGHE, common to all the above regions.
(vi) Since E lies on (2) and (3)
∴ $x_1 = 2$, $x_2 = 3$ ∴ E (2, 3)
F lies on (3) and (1)
∴ $x_2 = 3$
∴ From (1), $x_1 + 3 = 9$ ∴ $x_1 = 6$ ∴ F(6, 3)
G lies on (1) and (4)
∴ Solve (1) and (4) simultaneously

$$x_1 + x_2 = 9 \;\ldots\ldots (1) \;\ldots\ldots (\times 2)$$
∴ $2x_1 + 2x_2 = 18$ and
$2x_1 + 5x_2 = 30 \;\ldots\ldots (4)$
∴ Subtracting $0 - 3x_2 = -12$
∴ $x_2 = \dfrac{12}{3} = 4$
∴ From (1), $x_1 = 9 - x_2 = 9 - 4 = 5$ ∴ G(5, 4)
H lies on (2) and (4)   ∴ From (2), $x_1 = 2$

∴ From (4), $2(2) + 5x_2 = 30$
∴ $5x_2 = 30 - 4 = 26$
∴ $x_2 = \dfrac{26}{5}$
∴ $H\left(2, \dfrac{26}{5}\right)$

3. **Values of Objective Function ($Z = 80x_1 + 120x_2$) at corner points:**
   at E(2, 3) $Z_E = 80(2) + 120(3) = 160 + 360 = 520$
   at F(6, 3) $Z_F = 80(6) + 120(3) = 480 + 360 = 840$
   at G(5, 4) $Z_G = 80(5) + 120(4) = 400 + 480 = 880$
   at $H\left(2, \dfrac{26}{5}\right)$ $Z_H = 80(2) + 120\left(\dfrac{26}{5}\right) = 160 + 624 = 784$

4. Since it is a problem of minimisation
   $Z_{min.} = 520$ at E(2, 3) i.e. $x_1 = 2$, $x_2 = 3$ is the optimum solution for which $Z_{min.} = 520$.

Problem 2: (Multiple Solutions)

Maximise $Z = 3x_1 + 5x_2$
Subject to $12x_1 + 20x_2 \leq 40$
$x_1 - 4x_2 \leq 4$
$x_1, x_2 \geq 0$

Solution:

1. **Constraint Lines:**

   (i) $12x_1 + 20x_2 \leq 40$
   ∴ Constraint line is
   $12x_1 + 20x_2 = 40$
   i.e. $3x_1 + 5x_2 = 10$ ... (1)
   put $x_1 = 0$, ∴ $5x_2 = 10$
   ∴ $x_2 = 2$ ∴ A(0, 2)
   put $x_2 = 0$ ∴ $3x_1 = 10$
   ∴ $x_1 = \dfrac{10}{3} = 3.33$ ∴ $B\left(\dfrac{10}{3}, 0\right)$

   (ii) Constraint line is $x_1 - 4x_2 = 4$ ... (2)
   Put $x_1 = 0$, ∴ $-4x_2 = 4$
   ∴ $x_2 = -1$ ∴ C(0, -1)
   Put $x_2 = 0$ ∴ $x_1 = 4$ ∴ D(4, 0)

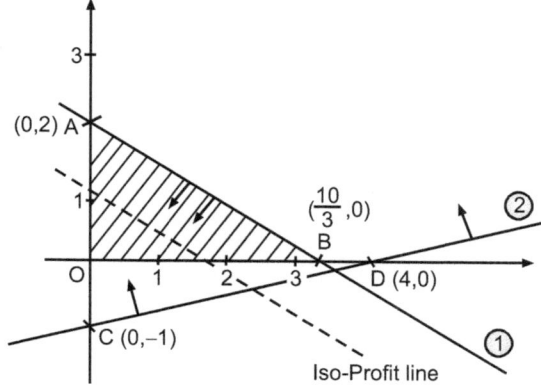

Fig. 1.4

2. **Feasible Region:**
   (i) Constraint (1) is of type '≤' ∴ Mark region towards origin.
   (ii) Constraint (2) is of type '≤' ∴ Mark region towards origin.
   (iii) Also, $x_1, x_2 \geq 0$ (Non-negativity condition).
      Hence, the region must lie in the first quadrant only
   (iv) ∴ Feasible region is the common region OBAO

3. **Values of $Z = 3x_1 + 5x_2$ at corner points:**
   at O(0, 0), $\quad Z_O = 0 + 0 = 0$
   at $B\left(\dfrac{10}{3}, 0\right)$, $\quad Z_B = 3\left(\dfrac{10}{3}\right) + 5(0) = 10$
   at A(0, 2), $\quad Z_A = 3(0) + 5(2) = 10$

4. Z max. = 10 occurs at two points A(0, 2) and B(10/3, 0)
   Hence, the problem has alternate or multiple optimum solutions. Infact, all the points lying on line segment AB give the same value of Z max. = 10. This is because line AB i.e. line (1) has equation $3x_1 + 5x_2 = 10$ i.e. $5x_2 = 10 - 3x_1$ i.e. $x_2 = -\dfrac{3}{5}x_1 + 2$ and if we plot line $3x_1 + 5x_2 = Z$ i.e. the objective function line or iso-profit line i.e. $5x_2 = -3x_1 + Z$
   i.e. $x_2 = -\dfrac{3}{5}x_1 + \dfrac{Z}{5}$

   Thus, both these lines have the same slope $\left(-\dfrac{3}{5}\right)$ OR the L.H.S. of both these equations are same i.e. $(3x_1 + 5x_2)$. Therefore they have the same slope. Hence they are parallel. Thus, for this maximisation problem, the farthest iso-profit line coincides with line AB and hence, co-ordinates of all points on AB give the optimum solution values of x_1 and x_2 and corresponding value of Z i.e. 10 gives Z max. Thus, the problem has multiple solutions.

DECISION SCIENCES — LINEAR PROGRAMMING

Problem 3: Solve using Graphical method

$$\text{Minimise} \quad Z = x_1 + 4x_2$$
$$\text{Subject to} \quad 5x_1 \geq x_2$$
$$x_1 + x_2 \leq 5$$
$$3x_1 + x_2 = 9$$
$$x_1, x_2 \geq 0$$

Solution:

1. **The Constraint Lines are:**

   (i) The constraint is $5x_1 \geq x_2$ i.e. $5x_1 - x_2 \geq 0$

   $\therefore$ Constraint line is
   $$5x_1 - x_2 = 0 \qquad \ldots (1)$$

   Put $x_1 = 0$

   $\therefore \quad -x_2 = 0 \therefore x_2 = 0 \therefore O(0, 0)$

   (if we put $x_2 = 0$ we get same point $O(0, 0)$)

   Hence to get another point on line (1) put for x_1 some value other than 0 say $x_1 = 2$ **(Note this step)**.

   $\therefore \quad 5(2) - x_2 = 0$

   $\therefore \quad x_2 = 10$

   $\therefore$ Point is A(2, 10)

   (ii) $\quad x_1 + x_2 = 5 \qquad \ldots (2)$

   $\therefore$ Points B(0, 5), C(5, 0)

   (iii) Constraint is $3x_1 + x_2 = 9$ which is of type '='.

   Hence, the constraint line is same

   i.e. $\quad 3x_1 + x_2 = 9 \qquad \ldots (3)$

   $\therefore$ Points D(0, 9), E(3, 0)

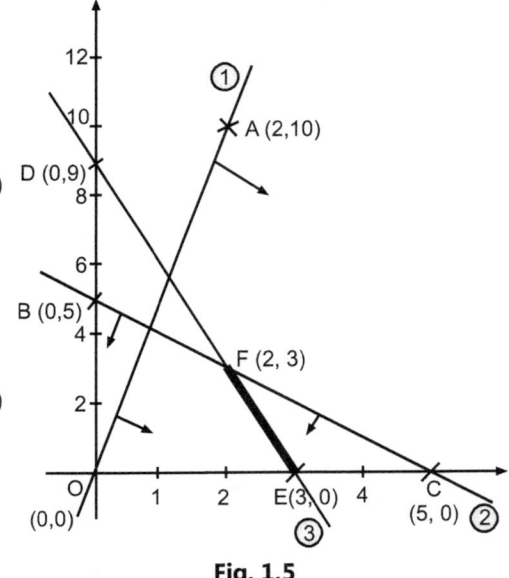

Fig. 1.5

2. **To find Feasible Region:**

   (i) The first constraint is of type '$\geq$'. But the line (1) passes through origin itself. Hence, consider any test point lying in the right portion about the line, say (1, 0) **(Note this step)**

Hence from (1) we have,

LHS = 5(1) – 0 = 5 which is > 0 which satisfies the constraint.

Similarly for test point say (0, 2) lying in the left portion about the line (1)

LHS = 5(0) – 2 = – 2 which is < 0 i.e. it violets the constraint.

Hence as the constraint is of type '≥', the region will consist of the line (1) (for =) and the part on right hand side of the line (1) (for >).

(ii) Constraint (2) is of type '≤'. Hence mark the region lying towards the origin about the line (2).

(iii) Since constraint (3) is of type '='. The region here will consist of points lying on the line (3) only.

(iv) The common region to above three regions is the feasible region. Hence the feasible region is the portion of line (3) lying in the regions common to constraints (1) and (2) i.e. it is the segment FE. Co-ordinates of F are obtained by solving (2) and (3) simultaneously as

$$x_1 + x_2 = 5 \quad \text{... from (2)}$$
$$\underline{3x_1 + x_2 = 9} \quad \text{.. from (3)}$$

Subtracting $\quad -2x_1 = -4$

∴ $\quad x_1 = \dfrac{4}{2} = 2$

∴ From (2), $\quad x_2 = 5 - x_1 = 5 - 2 = 3$

∴ F(2, 3)

3. **To find value of (Z = $x_1 + 4x_2$) at the corner points:**

   The feasible region is line segment FE

   ∴ at F(2, 3), $Z_F = 2 + 4(3) = 14$

   at E(3, 0), $Z_E = 3 + 0 = 3$

4. **Optimum Solution:**

   We have $Z_{min.} = 3$ at E(3, 0)

   Hence, the optimum solution is $x_1 = 3$, $x_2 = 0$ for which Z = 3(min.)

Problem 4: (Unbounded Solution)

Maximise $\quad Z = 4x + 5y$

Subject to $\quad x + y \geq 1$

$\quad\quad\quad\quad\quad 2x - y \geq -1$

$\quad\quad\quad\quad\quad 4x - 2y \leq 1$

$\quad\quad\quad\quad\quad x, y \geq 0$

Solution:

1. **Constraint Lines:**

   (i) $x + y = 1$ ... (1)

   $\therefore$ Points A(0, 1), B(1, 0)

   (ii) Constraint is $2x - y \geq -1$

   Changing the signs so as to make the r.h.s. +ve, we rewrite it as $-2x + y \leq 1$.
   (Note this step)

   $\therefore$ Constraint equation is $-2x + y = 1$ ... (2)

   $\therefore$ Points C(0, 1), $D\left(-\dfrac{1}{2}, 0\right)$

   (iii) $4x - 2y = 1$ ... (3)

   $\therefore$ Points $E\left(0, -\dfrac{1}{2}\right)$, $F\left(\dfrac{1}{4}, 0\right)$

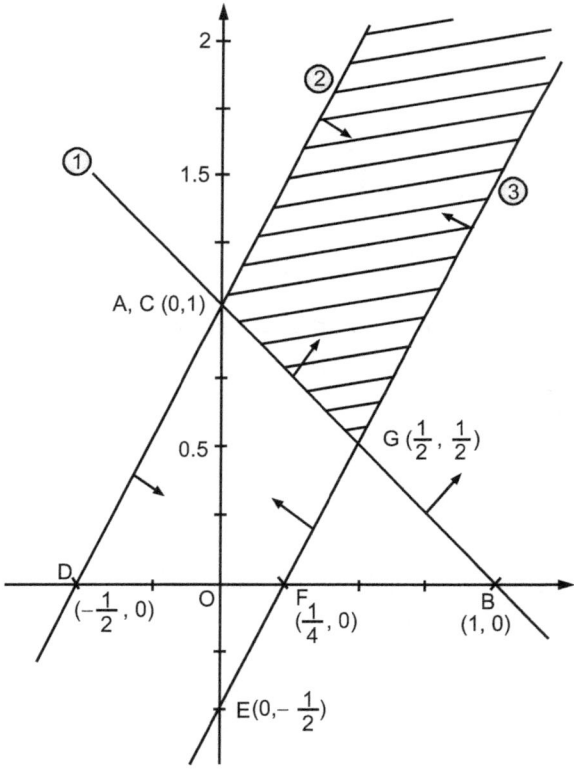

Fig. 1.6

2. Feasible region:

(i) Constraint (1) is of $\geq$ type $\quad\therefore$ Mark region away from origin.

(ii) Constraint (2) is of $\leq$ Type $\quad\therefore$ Mark region towards origin.

(iii) Constraint (3) is of $\leq$ Type $\quad\therefore$ Mark region towards origin.

$\therefore$ Feasible region is as shown in Fig. 1.6 which extends upto infinity.

G is intersection of (1) and (3)

$$x + y = 1 \quad \dots (1) \quad \dots \times 2$$

$\therefore \quad 2x + 2y = 2$ and

$$4x - 2y = 1 \qquad \dots (3)$$

adding, $6x = 3 \quad \therefore x = \dfrac{1}{2}$

$\therefore$ From (1), $y = 1 - x = 1 - \dfrac{1}{2} = \dfrac{1}{2} \quad \therefore G\left(\dfrac{1}{2}, \dfrac{1}{2}\right)$

3. Since the problem is of maximisation, the point in the region lying at infinity say (∞, ∞) will give $Z_{max.} = \infty$ which is the maximum value. Hence, the solution is unbounded.

Problem 5: (Infeasible solution)

Minimise $\qquad Z = 10x_1 + 7x_2$

Subject to $\qquad x_1 + 2x_2 \leq 4$

$\qquad\qquad\quad x_1 + x_2 \geq 5$

$\qquad\qquad\quad x_1, x_2 \geq 0$

Solution:

1. **Constraint Lines:**

   (i) $x_1 + 2x_2 = 4$ $\qquad\qquad\qquad\qquad\qquad\qquad\qquad\qquad\qquad\qquad$ ... (1)

   $\therefore$ Points A(0, 2), B(4, 0)

   (ii) $x_1 + x_2 = 5$ $\qquad\qquad\qquad\qquad\qquad\qquad\qquad\qquad\qquad\qquad\quad$ ... (2)

   $\therefore$ Points C(0, 5), D(5, 0)

2. **Feasible Region:**

   (i) (1) is of type '$\leq$' $\quad\therefore$ Region towards origin.

   (ii) (2) is of type '$\geq$' $\quad\therefore$ Region away from origin.

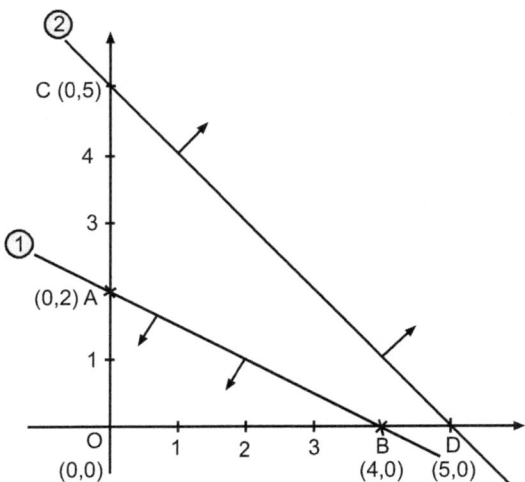

Fig. 1.7

(iii) Since there is no region common to the above two regions (in the first quadrant) hence there is no feasible region and hence the problem has infeasible solution.

Problem 6: Upon completing the construction of his house, Mr. Sharma discovers that 100 sq. feet of plywood scrap and 80 sq. feet of white pine scrap are in usable form for the construction of tables and book cases. It takes 16 sq. feet of plywood and 8 sq. feet of white pine to make a table and 12 sq. feet of plywood and 16 sq. feet of white pine are required to construct a book case. By selling the finished products to a local furniture store, Mr. Sharma can realise a profit of ₹ 125 on each table and ₹ 100 on each book case. How can he make the use of the left over scrap most profitably? Formulate the LPP and solve using graphical method.

Solution: We have,

Per Unit Requirement (sq. feet)

	Plywood	White Pine	Profit per unit (₹)
Table	16	8	125
Book case	12	16	100
Availability	100	80	–

Let x_1 - Number of tables constructed and
x_2 - Number of book cases constructed.
1. **Objective Function:** Total Profit $Z = 125 x_1 + 100 x_2$ to be maximised.
2. **Constraints:**
   (i) Plywood constraint: Plywood required is $(16x_1 + 12x_2)$ and 100 sq. feet are available
   $\therefore 16x_1 + 12x_2 \leq 100$ i.e. $4x_1 + 3x_2 \leq 25$
   (ii) White Pine constraint: White pine required is $(8x_1 + 16x_2)$ and 80 sq feet are available.
   $\therefore 8x_1 + 16x_2 \leq 80$ i.e. $x_1 + 2x_2 \leq 10$

3. ∴ **LP Model for the problem is**

Maximise $Z = 125x_1 + 100 x_2$ (Profit maximisation)
Subject to $4x_1 + 3x_2 \leq 25$ (Plywood constraint)
  $x_1 + 2x_2 \leq 10$ (White Pine constraint)
  $x_1, x_2 \geq 0$ (Non negativity condition)

4. Graphical Solution: Constraint lines are

(i) $4x_1 + 3x_2 = 25$ ... (1)
Put $x_1 = 0$ ∴ $3x_2 = 25$
∴ $x_2 = \dfrac{25}{3} = 8.33$ ∴ A(0, 8.33)

Put $x_2 = 0$
∴ $4x_1 = 25$
∴ $x_1 = \dfrac{25}{4} = 6.25$ ∴ B(6.25, 0)

(ii) $x_1 + 2x_2 = 10$ ... (2)
∴ Points are C(0, 5) and D(10, 0)

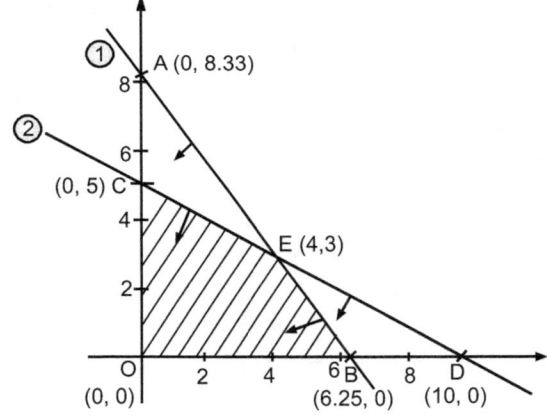

Fig. 1.8

5. Feasible Region:
Both constraints are of type '≤'. ∴ Mark regions towards origin
∴ Common region i.e. the feasible region is OBECO.
To find E, solve (1) and (2) simultaneously
$x_1 + 2x_2 = 10$ .... (2)   ..... × 4 gives
  $4x_1 + 8x_2 = 40$ and
  $4x_1 + 3x_2 = 25$ ... (1)
Subtracting $5x_2 = 15$
∴ $x_2 = 3$
From (2), $x_1 = 10 - 2x_2 = 10 - 2(3) = 4$
∴ E (4, 3)

6. **Value of (Z = 125 x_1 + 100 x_2) at corner points:**

    (i) at O(0, 0), Z_O = 0 + 0 = 0

    at B(6.25, 0) i.e. $\left(\dfrac{25}{4}, 0\right)$, Z_B = $125\left(\dfrac{25}{4}\right)$ + 100(0) = 781.25

    at E(4, 3), Z_E = 125 (4) + 100 (3) = 500 + 300 = 800

    at C(0, 5), Z_C = 0 + 100(5) = 500

7. **Optimum Solution:** We have Z max. = 800 at E(4, 3)

    Hence, Mr. Sharma can manufacture x_1 = 4 tables and x_2 = 3 bookcases to earn a maximum profit of ₹ 800.

Problem 7: Mohan-Meakins Breweries Ltd. has two bottling plants, one located at Solan and the other at Mohan-Nagar. Each plant produces three drinks, whisky, beer and fruit juices named A, B and C respectively. The number of bottles produced per day are as follows:

	Plant at	
	Solan (S)	**Mohan-nagar (M)**
Whisky A	1500	1500
Beer B	3000	1000
Fruit Juices C	2000	5000

A market survey indicates that during the month of April, there will be a demand of 20,000 bottles of whisky, 40,000 bottles of beer and 44,000 bottles of fruit juices. The operating costs per day for the plants at Solan and Mohan-nagar are 600 and 400 monetary units. For how many days each plant be run in April so as to minimise the production cost, while still meeting the market demand? Formulate the model and provide graphical solution.

Solution: Let x_1 - No. of days in a month for which plant S is run

x_2 - No. of days in a month for which plant M is run.

1. **Objective Function** is to minimise the monthly total production cost which is

    Z = 600 x_1 + 400 x_2

2. **Constraints:**

    (i) Market demand for whisky is 20,000 bottles

    ∴ 1500 x_1 + 1500x_2 ≥ 20,000   i.e. 3x_1 + 3x_2 ≥ 40

    (ii) Market demand for beer is 40,000 bottles

    ∴ 3000 x_1 + 1000 x_2 ≥ 40,000   i.e. 3x_1 + x_2 ≥ 40

    (iii) Market demand for fruit-juices is 44,000 bottles

    ∴ 2000 x_1 + 5000 x_2 ≥ 44,000   i.e. 2x_1 + 5x_2 ≥ 44

3. **Thus, the LP Model for the problem is**

   Minimise $\quad Z = 600x_1 + 400x_2 \quad$ (Cost minimisation)
   Subject to $\quad 3x_1 + 3x_2 \geq 40 \quad$ (Whisky market constraint)
   $\quad\quad\quad\quad\quad 3x_1 + x_2 \geq 40 \quad$ (Beer market constraint)
   $\quad\quad\quad\quad\quad 2x_1 + 5x_2 \geq 44 \quad$ (Fruit Juices market constraint)
   $\quad\quad\quad\quad\quad x_1, x_2 \geq 0 \quad$ (Non-negativity condition)

4. **Graphical Method:** Constraint lines are

   (i) $\quad\quad 3x_1 + 3x_2 = 40 \quad\quad\quad\quad\quad\quad\quad\quad\quad\quad\quad\quad\quad\quad\quad\quad$ ... (1)

   $\therefore$ Points are $A\left(\dfrac{40}{3}, 0\right)$ i.e. A(13.33, 0) and $B\left(0, \dfrac{40}{3}\right)$ i.e. (0, 13.33)

   (ii) $\quad 3x_1 + x_2 = 40 \quad\quad\quad\quad\quad\quad\quad\quad\quad\quad\quad\quad\quad\quad\quad\quad$ ... (2)

   $\therefore$ Points are C(0, 40), $D\left(\dfrac{40}{3}, 0\right)$ i.e. (13.33, 0)

   (iii) $\quad\quad 2x_1 + 5x_2 = 44 \quad\quad\quad\quad\quad\quad\quad\quad\quad\quad\quad\quad\quad\quad\quad\quad$ ... (3)

   $\therefore$ Points are $E\left(0, \dfrac{44}{5}\right)$ i.e. (0, 8.8), F(22, 0)

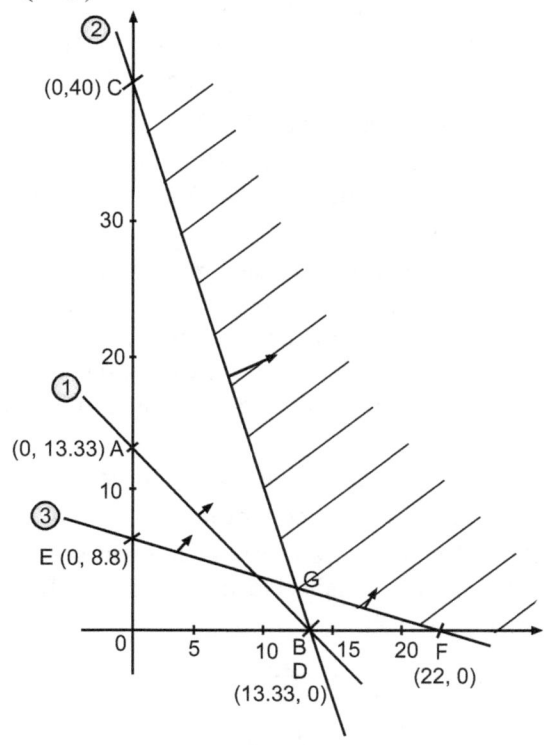

Fig. 1.9

5. Feasible Region:

Since all the constraints are of the type '≥', hence, mark the regions away from origin about these lines. Thus, the common region is the feasible region, which is the open polygon bounded by Y axis - C G F - X axis.

(Constraint (1) is infact redundent as Constraint (2) implies constraint (1) also)

Co-ordinates of G are obtained by solving equations (2) and (3) simultaneously as

$$3x_1 + x_2 = 40 \quad \ldots (2) \ldots \times 5 \text{ gives}$$
$$15x_1 + 5x_2 = 200 \text{ and}$$
$$2x_1 + 5x_2 = 44 \quad \ldots (3)$$

Subtracting $\quad 13x_1 = 156$

$$\therefore \quad x_1 = \frac{156}{13} = 12$$

$\therefore$ From (2), $x_2 = 40 - 3x_1 = 40 - 3(12) = 4$ $\therefore$ G(12, 4)

6. Value of Z = 600 x_1 + 400 x_2 at corner points

at C(0, 40), $\quad Z_C = 0 + 400 (40) = 16,000$
at G (12, 4), $\quad Z_G = 600 (12) + 400(4) = 7200 + 1600 = 8800$
at F(22, 0), $\quad Z_F = 600 (22) + 0 = 13,200$

7. Optimum solution is Z min. = 8,800 at G(12, 4).

Thus, the optimum solution is to run the Solan plant for x_1 = 12 days and Mohan-nagar plant for x_2 = 4 days in the month of April so as to keep the production cost minimum at $Z_{min.}$ = ₹ 8,800.

Problem 8: A small bank is allocating maximum of ₹ 21,00,000/- for personal and car loans. The interest rates per annum are 11% for car loans and 13% for personal loans. The loans are repaid at the end of a one-year period. The amount of personal loans can not exceed 40% of the car loans. Past experience has shown that bad debts amount to 1.2% of all personal loans. Solve the above problem to find the optimum loan allocations and bank's profit.

Solution: Let x - Amount to be allocated for personal loans.

y - Amount to be allocated for car loans.

1. **Objective Function:** The loans are repaid at the end of 1 year with 11% and 13% interest rate for car loans and personal loans respectively. The bad debts are 1.2 of all personal loans.

$\therefore$ Profit Expected is $Z = \frac{11}{100} (y) + \frac{13}{100} (x) - \left(\frac{1.2}{100}\right) x$

$= 0.11 y + (0.13 - 0.012)x = 0.11y + 0.118 x$

which is to be maximised.

2. Constraints:
(i) Total loan amount is ₹ 21,00,000 maximum

∴ $x + y \leq 21,00,000$

(ii) Amount of personal loans (x) can not exceed 40% of car loans (y)

i.e. $x \leq \frac{40}{100}(y)$ i.e. $100 x \leq 40 y$

i.e. $100 x - 40 y \leq 0$

3. Thus, the LP formulation for the problem is

Maximise $\quad Z = 0.11y + 0.118x \quad$ (Profit maximisation)

Subject to $\quad x + y \leq 21,00,000 \quad$ (Fund Availability constraint)

$\quad\quad\quad\quad 100 x - 40 y \leq 0 \quad$ (Proportion Constraint)

$\quad\quad\quad\quad x, y \geq 0 \quad$ (Non-negativity condition)

4. Graphical Solution: The Constraint lines are

(i) $\quad x + y = 21,00,000 \quad$ ... (1)

∴ Points A(0, 2100000), B(2100000, 0)

(ii) $\quad 100 x - 40y = 0 \quad$ ... (2)

i.e. $\quad 40y = 100 x$ i.e. $y = \frac{100}{40} x$ i.e. $y = 2.5 x$

i.e. a line (y = mx) passing through origin having slope (+ 2.5) OR

Points: if x = (say 0) ∴ y = 0, ∴ O(0, 0) and if y = 20,00,000 (say)

$x = \frac{20,00,000}{2.5} = 8,00,000$ ∴ C(800000, 2000000)

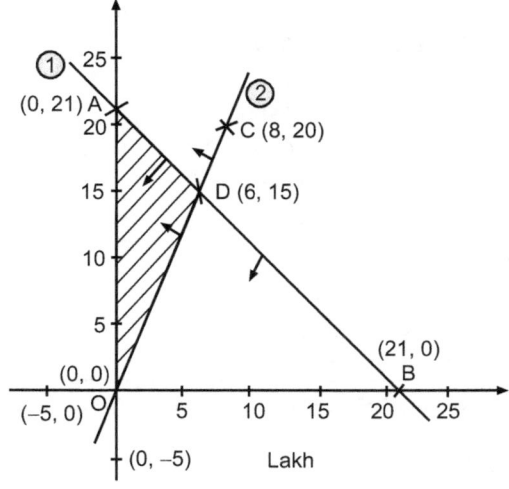

Fig. 1.10

5. To find Feasible Region:

(i) Constraint (1) is of type '≤'.
∴ Mark region lying towards origin.

(ii) Constraint (2) is also of type '≤'. But origin itself lies on line (2).
Hence, consider a test point lying on right hand side of line (2) say (5, 0)
∴ LHS = 100(5) – 0
= 500 which is > 0
Similarly consider (0, – 5) ∴ LHS = 0 – 40 (– 5) = 200 which is > 0
Hence, this part violetes constraint (2)
Now, consider points in other part say at (0, 5)
∴ LHS = 0 – 40 (5) = – 200 which is < 0.
Also at (– 5, 0), LHS = 100 (– 5) + 0 = – 500 which is < 0.
Hence, this part satisfies constraint (2). Hence mark this left hand portion about line (2).

(iii) The common region is the feasible region i.e. the region ODAO. To obtain D, solve (1) and (2) simultaneously,
From (2), $40y = 100x$
∴ $y = \dfrac{100}{40} x$

∴ From (1), $x + \dfrac{100}{40} x = 21,00,000$ i.e. $\left(1 + \dfrac{100}{40}\right) x = 21,00,000$

i.e. $\left(\dfrac{40 + 100}{40}\right) x = 21,00,000$ ∴ $x = \dfrac{40}{140} (21,00,000) = 6,00,000$

∴ From (1), $y = 21,00,000 – x = 21,00,000 – 6,00,000 = 15,00,000$

6. To find values of Z = 0.11y + 0.118x
at O(0, 0), $Z_O = 0 + 0 = 0$
at D(6, 15)   i.e. D(600000, 1500000),
$Z_D = 0.11 (15,00,000) + 0.118 (6,00,000) = 1,65,000 + 70,800 = 2,35,800$
at A(0, 21)   i.e. A(0, 21,00,000)
$Z_A = 0.11 (21,00,000) + 0 = 2,31,000$

7. Optimum Solution: Thus, we have
$Z_{max.} = 2,35,800$ at D(600000, 1500000)
Thus, the optimum loan allocations will be ₹ 6,00,000 as personal loans and ₹ 15,00,000 as car loans which gives a profit of ₹ 2,35,800 to the bank.

Problem 9: Solve graphically the following Linear Programming problem
Minimize $Z = 3X_1 + 5X_2$
Subject to $– 3X_1 + 4X_2 \leq 12$, $2X_1 – X_2 \geq – 2$
$2X_1 + 3X_2 \geq 12$, $X_1 \leq 4$, $X_2 \geq 2$ and $X_1 \geq 0$

Solution:
1. The Constraint Lines are
(i) $-3X_1 + 4X_2 = 12$ .. (1)

Put $X_1 = 0$ ∴ $4X_2 = 12$ ∴ $X_2 = 3$

∴ A(0, 3)

Put $X_2 = 0$ ∴ $-3X_1 = 12$ ∴ $X_1 = -4$

∴ B(– 4, 0)

(ii) $2X_1 - X_2 \geq -2$

Since, the rhs is – ve we change the sign through out and also change the inequality to rewrite it as $-2X_1 + X_2 \leq 2$. **(Note this step)**

∴ The constraint line is

$\qquad -2X_1 + X_2 = 2$ ... (2)

∴ Points C(0, 2) and D(– 1, 0)

(iii) $2X_1 + 3X_2 = 12$ ... (3)

∴ Points E(0, 4) and F(6, 0)

(iv) $\qquad X_1 = 4$ ... (4)

i.e. a line parallel to Y axis through G (4,0)

(v) $\qquad X_2 = 2$ ... (5)

i.e. a line parallel to X axis through H (0,2)

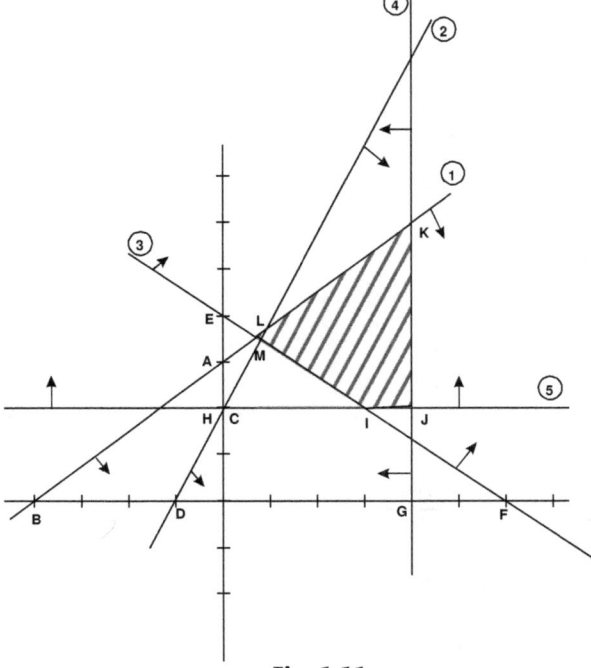

Fig. 1.11

2. **Feasible Region:** The constraints (1), (2) (modified) and (4) are of the type '≤'. ∴ Mark regions containing origin about these lines and for the constraints (3) and (5), which are of the type '≥', mark the regions away from origin.

Hence the feasible region is the polygon IJKLMI

I is intersection of lines (3) and (5)

From (5), $X_2 = 2$

∴ From (3), $2X_1 + 3(2) = 12$

∴ $2X_1 = 12 - 6 = 6$

∴ $X_1 = 3$

∴ I(3,2)

J is intersection of (4) and (5)

∴ $X_1 = 4, X_2 = 2$

∴ J(4,2)

K is intersection of (1) and (4)

From (4), $X_1 = 4$

∴ From (1), $-3(4) + 4X_2 = 12$

∴ $4X_2 = 12 + 12 = 24$

∴ $X_2 = 6$

∴ K(4, 6)

L is intersection of (1) and (2)

From (2), $-2X_1 + X_2 = 2$ .... (×4)

i.e. $\quad -8X_1 + 4X_2 = 8$

$\quad -3X_1 + 4X_2 = 12 \qquad\qquad ...(1)$

∴ Subtracting, $-5X_1 = -4$

∴ $\qquad X_1 = \dfrac{4}{5}$

∴ From (2), $\quad X_2 = 2 + 2X_1 = 2 + 2\left(\dfrac{4}{5}\right)$

$\qquad\qquad = \dfrac{10 + 8}{5}$

$\qquad\qquad = \dfrac{18}{5}$

∴ $L\left(\dfrac{4}{5}, \dfrac{18}{5}\right)$

M is intersection of (2) and (3)

$$-2X_1 + X_2 = 2 \quad \ldots (2)$$
$$2X_1 + 3X_2 = 12 \quad \ldots (3)$$

Adding, $4X_2 = 14$

$\therefore \quad X_2 = \dfrac{14}{4} = \dfrac{7}{2}$

$\therefore$ From (3), $2X_1 = 12 - 3X_2 = 12 - 3\left(\dfrac{7}{2}\right)$

$$= \dfrac{24 - 21}{2} = \dfrac{3}{2}$$

$\therefore \quad X_1 = \dfrac{3}{4}$

$\therefore \quad M\left(\dfrac{3}{4}, \dfrac{7}{2}\right)$

3. Now, value of $Z = 3X_1 + 5X_2$ at the corner points is

$Z_I = 3(3) + 5(2) = 19$

$Z_J = 3(4) + 5(2) = 22$

$Z_K = 3(4) + 5(6) = 42$

$Z_L = 3\left(\dfrac{4}{5}\right) + 5\left(\dfrac{18}{5}\right)$

$= \dfrac{12}{5} + 18$

$= \dfrac{12 + 90}{5} = \dfrac{102}{5}$

$= 20.4$

$Z_M = 3\left(\dfrac{3}{4}\right) + 5\left(\dfrac{7}{2}\right) = \dfrac{9}{4} + \dfrac{35}{2}$

$= \dfrac{9 + 70}{4} = \dfrac{79}{4}$

$= 19.75$

4. **Optimum Solution:** We have $Z_{min} = 19$ at point $I(3,2)$

$\therefore$ The optimum solution is $X_1 = 3$, $X_2 = 2$ where $Z_{min} = 19$.

Problem 10: A manufacturer of medicines is preparing a production plan of medicines A and B. There are sufficient ingredients available to make 20,000 bottles of A and 40,000 bottles of B. But there are only 45,000 bottles into which either of medicines can be put. Furthermore it takes 3 hours to prepare enough material to fill 1000 bottles of A and one hour to fill 1000 bottles of B. There are 66 hours available for this operation. The profit is ₹ 8 per bottle of A and ₹ 7 per bottle of B. Formulate and solve LPP.

Solution: Problem Formulation: Let X_1 - No. of bottles of A to be produced.

X_2 - No. of bottles of B to be produced.

1. **Objective Function:** Total profit is $P = 9X_1 + 7X_2$.

   ∴ The objective function is to Maximise $P = 8X_1 + 7X_2$.

2. **Constraints:**

   (i) Ingredient constraint: The available ingredients can be used to produce 20,000 bottles of A and 40,000 bottles of B at the most. Hence, $X_1 \leq 20,000$ and $X_2 \leq 40,000$.

   (ii) Bottles constraint: There are only 45,000 bottles available for filling up the medicines A and B.

   ∴ (Total bottles = $X_1 + X_2$) $\leq 45,000$

   (iii) Time constraint: 1000 bottles of A require 3 hours for preparing the fillup material. Hence, time required for 1 bottle of A is $\frac{3}{1000}$. Hence, X_1 bottles of A will need $\frac{3X_1}{1000}$ hours. Similarly, X_2 bottles of B will need $\left(\frac{1X_2}{1000}\right)$ hours.

   ∴ Total time required = $\frac{3X_1}{1000} + \frac{X_2}{1000}$ and since the time available is 66 hours we must have, $\frac{3X_1}{1000} + \frac{X_2}{1000} \leq 66$ i.e. $3X_1 + X_2 \leq 66,000$.

3. **Hence, the L. P. model is**

   Maximise $P = 8X_1 + 7X_2$ (Profit maximisation)
   Subject to $X_1 \leq 20,000$ (Ingredient Constraint for A)
   $X_2 \leq 40,000$ (Ingredient Constraint for B)
   $X_1 + X_2 \leq 45,000$ (Bottles constraint)
   $3X_1 + X_2 \leq 66,000$ (Time Constraint)
   $X_1, X_2 \geq 0$ (Non-negativity condition)

Graphical solution: Scale used is 1 unit: 10,000

4. **Constraint Lines:**

    (i) $X_1 = 20000$ ... (1)

    i.e. line parallel to Y axis through A (20000, 0)

    (ii) $X_2 = 40000$ ... (2)

    i.e. line parallel to X axis through B (0, 40000)

    (iii) $X_1 + X_2 = 45,000$ ... (3)

    ∴ Points: C (0,45000) and D(45000,0)

    (iv) $3X_1 + X_2 = 66000$ ... (4)

    ∴ Points: E (0,66000) and F(22000,0)

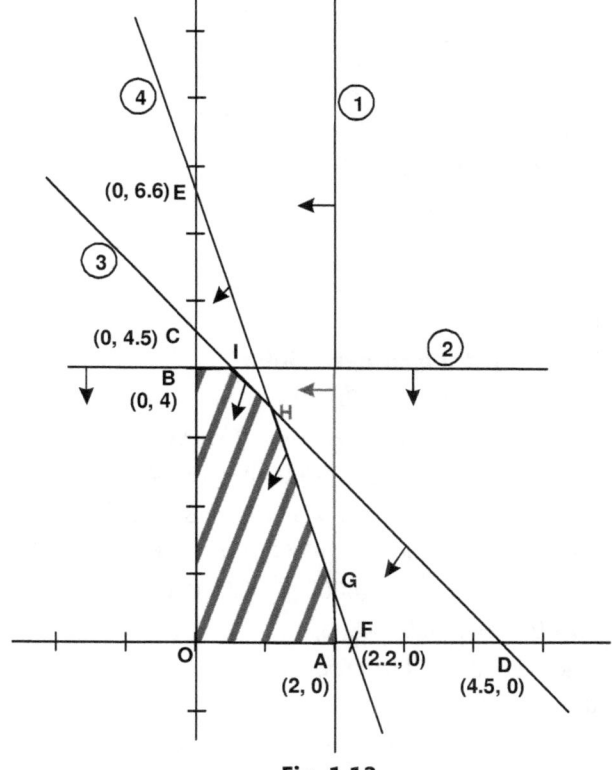

Fig. 1.12

5. **Feasible Region:** Since all the constraints are of the type '≤', hence mark the region towards origin about all the constraint lines. The common region is the feasible region OAGHIBO.

Point G is the intersection of lines (1) and (4),
From (1), $X_1 = 20000$
$\therefore$ From (4), $3(20000) + X_2 = 66000$
$\therefore X_2 = 66000 - 60000 = 6000$
$\therefore$ G (20000, 6000)
Point H is intersection of (3) and (4)
By (4) – (3) we get,
$$(3X_1 - X_1) + (X_2 - X_2) = 66000 - 45000$$
i.e. $2X_1 = 21000$
$\therefore X_1 = \dfrac{21000}{2} = 10,500$

and $\therefore$ from (3),
$$X_2 = 45000 - X_1$$
$$= 45000 - 10500 = 34500$$
$\therefore$ H (10500, 34500)
Point I is the intersection of (2) and (3),
From (2), $X_2 = 40,000$
$\therefore$ From (3), $X_1 = 45000 - X_2$
$= 45000 - 40000 = 5000$
$\therefore$ I (5000, 40000)

6. **Value of $P = 8X_1 + 7X_2$ at the corner points:**

$P_O = 8(0) + 7(0) = 0$
$P_A = 8(20000) + 7(0) = 1,60,000$
$P_G = 8(20000) + 7(6000) = 160000 + 42000 = 2,02,000$
$P_H = 8(10500) + 7(34500) = 84000 + 241500 = 3,25,500$
$P_I = 8(5000) + 7(40000) = 40000 + 280000 = 3,20,000$
$P_B = 8(0) + 7(40000) = 2,80,000$

Thus, $P_{max} = 325500$ at H(10500, 34500)
Hence, the optimum solution is to produce $X_1 = 10,500$ bottles of A and $X_2 = 34,500$ bottles of B and the expected profit is ₹ 3,25,500.

Problem 11: A company manufacturing animal feed must produce 500 kgs of mixture daily. The mixture consists of two ingredients F_1 and F_2. Ingredient F_1 costs ₹ 5 per kg and ingredient F_2 costs ₹ 8 per kg. Nutrient considerations detect that the feed contains not more than 400 kgs of F_1 and a minimum of 200 of F_2. Formulate the LPP and find the quality of each ingredient used to minimise cost. **(P.U. MBA - Dec. 10)**

Solution: Let   x - Quantity of F_1 in the mixture (in kgs)
                    y - Quantity of F_2 in the mixture (in kgs)

1. **Objective Function:** F_1 costs ₹ 5 per kg and F_2 costs ₹ 8 per kg. Hence, the cost of the mixture is (5x + 8y) which is to be minimised. Hence, the objective function is to minimise,   C = 5x + 8y

2. **Constraints:**
    (i) Mixture Quantity: As the mixture must be 500 kg, we must have,
                x + y = 500
    (ii) F_1 and F_2 requirement: The feed should not contain more than 400 kg of F_1. Hence, we must have
                x ≤ 400
    Similarly, it must have minimum 200 kgs of F_2
    ∴   y ≥ 200

3. **LPP Formulation:** Thus, the LPP formulation is
    Minimise,   C = 5x + 8y
    Subject to   x + y = 500
                     x ≤ 400
                     y ≥ 200
                     x, y ≥ 0

4. **Graphical Solution:**
    (a) The constraint lines are
    (i)   x + y = 500   ... (1)
        ∴ Points A(0, 500), B(500, 0)
    (ii)   x = 400   ...(2)
        i.e. line parallel to Y-axis through C(400, 0)
    (iii)   y = 200   ... (3)
        i.e. a line parallel to X-axis through D(0, 200).

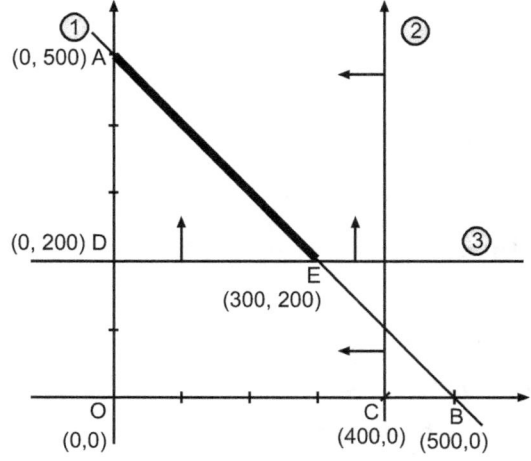

Fig. 1.13

(b) Feasible Region:

Constraint (1) is of the type '='. Hence the region will consists of the points lying on the line (1) only.

Constraint (2) is of the type '≤'. Hence mark the region about the line (2) which is lying towards the origin.

Constraint (3) is of the type '≥'. Hence mark the region about the line (3) which is lying away from the origin.

Thus, the common region is the segment AE on line (1).

As, E lies on lines (1) and (3)

∴ at E,   y = 200

∴ From (1),   x + 200 = 500   ∴ x = 300

∴ E (300, 200)

(c) Value of Objective Function C = 5x + 8y at the corner points:

at A(0, 500), C_A = 5(0) + 8(500) = 4000

at E(300, 200), C_E = 5(300) + 8(200) = 3100

(d) Optimum Solution:
We have, C_{min} = 3100 at E(300, 200). Thus, the optimum solution is to mix 300 kgs of F_1 and 200 kgs of F_2 for the mixture so that the cost is minimised to ₹ 3100.

Problem 12: Solve graphically

Minimise $z = 6x_1 + 14x_2$

Subject to $5x_1 + 4x_2 \geq 60$

                   $3x_1 + 7x_2 \leq 84$

                   $x_1 + 2x_2 \geq 18$

                   $x_1, x_2 \geq 0$ **(P.U. MBA - Dec. 11)**

Solution:

1. The Constraint Lines are:

(i) $5x_1 + 4x_2 = 60$ ... (1)

Put $x_1 = 0$, ∴ $4x_2 = 60$, ∴ $x_2 = 15$

∴ A(0, 15) is a point on the line.

Put $x_2 = 0$, ∴ $5x_1 = 60$, ∴ $x_1 = 12$

∴ B(12, 0) is a second point on the line.

(ii) $3x_1 + 7x_2 = 84$ ... (2)
   Put $x_1 = 0$, ∴ $x_2 = 12$, ∴ C(0, 12)
   Put $x_2 = 0$, ∴ $x_1 = 28$, ∴ C(28, 0)
(iii) $x_1 + 2x_2 = 18$ ... (3)
   ∴ Points are E(0, 9) and F(18, 0).

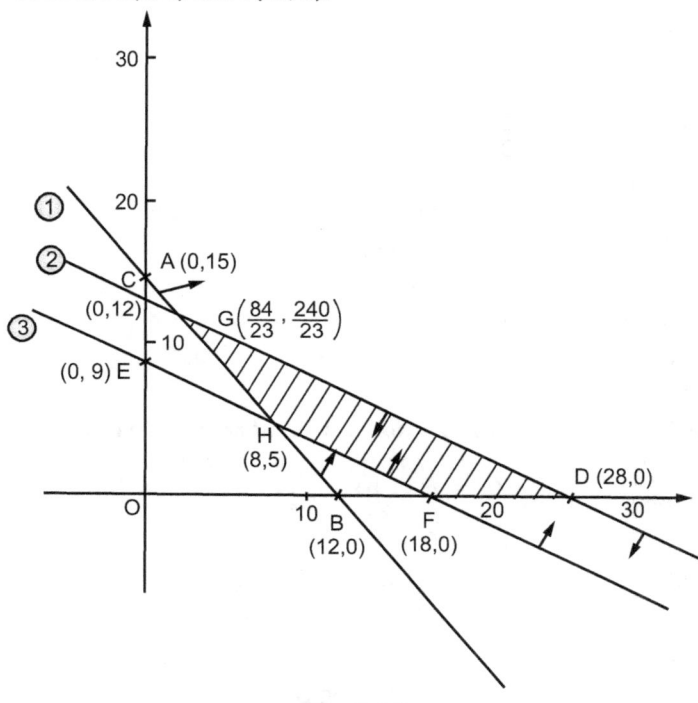

Fig. 1.14

2. **Feasible Region:**
   Constraint (1) is of the type '≥'. Hence mark the region lying away from origin.
   Constraint (2) is of the type '≤'. Hence mark the region lying towards from origin.
   Constraint (3) is of the type '≥'. Hence mark the region away from origin.
   Hence, the common region is the feasible region GHFD.
   As G lines on lines (1) and (2),

   $5x_1 + 4x_2 = 60$ ... (1) (× 3 gives)
   $15x_1 + 12x_2 = 180$

Also, $3x_1 + 7x_2 = 84$ ... (2) (× 5 gives)
   $15x_1 + 35x_2 = 420$ and we have seen above
   $15x_1 + 12x_2 = 180$

∴ Subtracting, $23x_2 = 240$ ∴ $x_2 = \dfrac{240}{23}$

∴ From (1) $5x_1 + 4\left(\dfrac{240}{23}\right) = 60$

∴ $5x_1 = 60 - \dfrac{960}{23} = \dfrac{420}{23}$

∴ $x_1 = \dfrac{84}{23}$

∴ $G\left(\dfrac{84}{23}, \dfrac{240}{23}\right)$

Again H lies on (1) and (3)

$x_1 + 2x_2 = 18$ ... (3) (× 2 gives)
$2x_1 + 4x_2 = 36$ and
$5x_1 + 4x_2 = 60$ ... (1)

∴ Subtracting, $-3x_1 = -24$ ∴ $x_1 = 8$
∴ From (3), $8 + 2x_2 = 18$ ∴ $x_2 = 5$
∴ H(8, 5)

3. **Value of Objective Function $z = 6x_1 + 14x_2$ at corner points:**

at $G\left(\dfrac{84}{23}, \dfrac{240}{23}\right)$, $Z_G = 6\left(\dfrac{84}{23}\right) + 14\left(\dfrac{240}{23}\right) = \dfrac{3864}{23} = 168$

at H (8, 5), $Z_H = 6(8) + 14(5) = 118$
at F(18, 0), $Z_F = 6(18) + 14(0) = 108$
at D(28, 0), $Z_D = 6(28) + 14(0) = 168$

4. **Optimum Solution:**

We have, $Z_{min} = 108$ at F(18, 0). Thus, the optimum solution is $x_1 = 18$, $x_2 = 0$, where $Z_{min} = 108$.

Problem 13: A manufacturer of furniture makes two products, chair and tables. The manufacturing of these two products is done on two machines A and B. A chair requires two hours on machine A and six hours on machine B. A table requires 5 hours on machine A and three hours on machine B. Profit from a chair is ₹ 20 and from table is ₹ 50. Machine A is available for 50 hours and machine B is available for 54 hours in a week. Solve the problem graphically to maximise the profits if not more than 9 tables are to be produced.

(P.U. MBA - Dec. 12)

Solution: Let, x - Number of chairs produced in a week
y - Number of tables produced in a week

1. **Objective Function:** Profit on chair is ₹ 20 per piece while that on table is ₹ 50 per piece. Hence, total profit is (20x + 50y). Thus, objective function is

   Maximise, $P = 20x + 50y$

2. Constraints:

(i) Machine A: Each chair requires 2 hours on machine A while each tables requires 5 hours on machine A. Hence, machine A is required for $(2x + 5y)$ number of hours. The availability of A is 50 hours a week. Therefore, we must have,
$$2x + 5y \leq 50$$

(ii) Machine B: Similarly we get,
$$6x + 3y \leq 54$$

(iii) Production of tables: This cannot exceed 9. Hence,
$$y \leq 9$$

3. Thus, LPP model is

Maximise $\quad\quad\quad P = 20x + 50y$
Subject to, $\quad\quad 2x + 5y \leq 50$
$\quad\quad\quad\quad\quad\quad 6x + 3y \leq 54$
$\quad\quad\quad\quad\quad\quad\quad\quad y \leq 9$
$\quad\quad\quad\quad\quad\quad x, y \geq 0$

4. Graphical Solution:

(a) Constraint lines are

$\quad\quad\quad\quad 2x + 5y = 50 \quad\quad\quad\quad\quad\quad \ldots (1)$
∴ Points A(0, 10), B(25, 0)
$\quad\quad\quad\quad 6x + 3y = 54 \quad\quad\quad\quad\quad\quad \ldots (2)$
∴ Points C(0, 18), D(9, 0)
$\quad\quad\quad\quad\quad\quad y = 9 \quad\quad\quad\quad\quad\quad\quad\quad \ldots (3)$
i.e. line parallel to x-axis at E(0, 9)

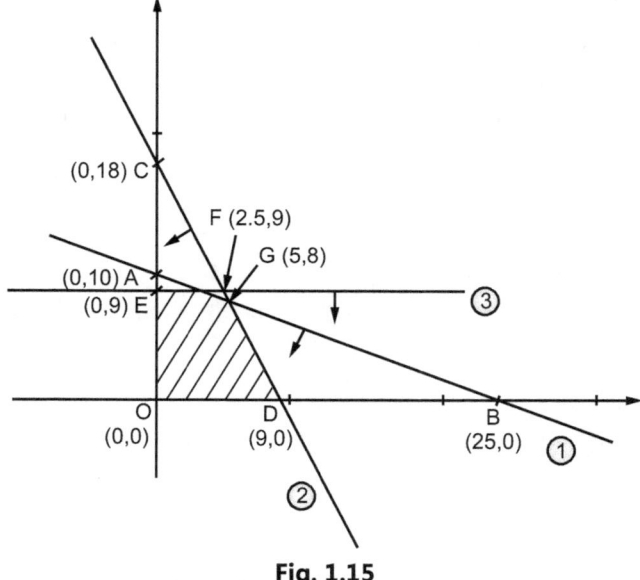

Fig. 1.15

(b) Feasible Region: All the constraints are of the type '≤'. Hence, mark the regions about them, lying towards the origin. Thus, the common region ODGFE is the feasible region.

Point lies on lines (1) and (3). Hence, solving these equations simultaneously we get F(2.5, 9)

Points G lies on lines (1) and (2). Hence, solving these equations simultaneously we get G(5,8)

(c) Value of objective function P = 20x + 50y at corner points:

at O(0, 0), P_O = 20(0) + 50(0) = 0
at D(9, 0), P_D = 20(9) + 50(0) = 180
at G(5, 8), P_G = 20(5) + 50(8) = 500
at F(2.5, 9), P_F = 20(2.5) + 50(9) = 500
at E(0, 9), P_E = 20(0) + 50(9) = 450

(d) Optimum Solution: We see that P_{max} = 500 at F and G.

Thus, the problem has multiple solutions which correspond to the coordinates of infact any point lying on the section PG of line (1).

[LHS of object function line 20x + 50y = P i.e. 2x + 5y = $\frac{P}{10}$ and that of line (1) i.e. 2x + 5y = 50 is same i.e. they have same slope. Thus, the farthest iso-profit line will coincide with line (1)].

Now, as x and y represent produced chairs and tables, they must be integers and not fractions. We see that point G(5, 8) is the only point on Section FG, having integer coordinates. Thus, the optimum solution is given at G i.e. produce 5 chairs and 8 tables which will give profit of ₹ 500.

Exercise - II

1. Describe for a Linear Programming Problem:

    (i) Basic solution (ii) Feasible solution (iii) Optimal solution (iv) Degenerate solution.

2. Use Graphical Method to solve:

    (i) Minimise   Z = 25x + 30y
        Subject to 4x + 3y ≥ 60
                    2x + 3y ≥ 36
                    x, y ≥ 0

    (**Ans.** x = 12, y = 4, Z = 420)

(ii) Maximise $Z = 10x_1 + 15x_2$
Subject to $x_1 \leq 3$
$x_2 \leq 5$
$3x_1 + 4x_2 = 29$
$x_1, x_2 \geq 0$

(**Ans.** Feasible Region is only point (3, 5) **Soln.**: $x_1 = 3, x_2 = 5, Z = 105$)

(iii) Maximise $Z = 3x_1 + 5x_2$
Subject to $3x_1 + 4x_2 \geq 12$
$2x_1 - x_2 \geq -2$
$2x_1 + 3x_2 \leq 12$
$x_1 \leq 4, x_2 \geq 2$
$x_1 x_2 \geq 0$

(**Ans.** $x_1 = 3/4, x_2 = 7/2, Z = 19.75$)

(iv) Minimise $Z = 6x + 2y$
Subject to $3x + y = 3$
$6x + 3y \geq 6$
$x, y \geq 0$

(**Ans.** Multiple solution **Soln.**: section (1, 0) to (0, 3), Z = 6)

(v) Maximise $Z = 5x_1 + 2x_2$
Subject to $x \geq -y$
$2x + y \leq 2$
$y \geq 3$
$x, y \geq 0$

(**Ans.** Infeasible solution)

3. A construction company wants to transfer the construction material from its warehouse to the project site, using two special types of trucks - A and B. Truck A can carry 1 tonne of cement and 4 tonnes of steel in one trip and truck B carries 2 tonnes of cement and three tonnes of steel at a time. The construction work needs 6 tonnes of cement and 12 tonnes of steel daily. Due to limited number of drivers, only 10 trips can be made to the site daily. The cost of one trip of A and B is ₹ 500 and ₹ 700 respectively. How many trips for each truck be planned daily, so as to minimise the transportation cost. Formulate the LPP and solve it by using Graphical method.

(**Ans.** Let x_1, x_2 : No. of trips of A and B respectively. LP model is Minimise $Z = 500 x_1 + 700 x_2$ Subject to $x_1 + 2x_2 \geq 6$; $4x_1 + 3x_2 \geq 12$; $x_1 + x_2 \leq 10$; $x_1, x_2 \geq 0$.

Soln.: $x_1 = 1.2 = 2$ trips (approx.), $x_2 = 2.4 = 2$ trips (approx.) Cost = ₹ 2,400.)

4. A furniture manufacturing company plans to make two products – chairs and tables, from its available resources which consist of 400 board feet of mahogany timber and 450 man-hours of labour. It knows that to make a chair requires 5 board feet and 10 man-hours and yields a profit of ₹ 45, while each table uses 20 board feet and 15 man-hours and has a profit of ₹ 80. The problem is to determine how many chairs and tables the company can make keeping within its resources constraints so that it maximises the profit. Formulate a linear programming model and provide its graphical solution.
   (**Ans.** Let x_1, x_2 – No. of chairs and tables produced. LP model is maximise $Z = 45x_1 + 80x_2$.
   Subject to $x_1 + 4x_2 \leq 80$; $2x_1 + 3x_2 \leq 90$; $x_1, x_2 \geq 0$
   Soln.: $x_1 = 24$ chairs, $x_2 = 14$ tables, Profit = ₹ 2,200)

5. Consider a firm that produces two products X_1 and X_2 with three fixed resources Z_1, Z_2 and Z_3. The profit contribution is ₹ 20 per unit of X_1 and ₹ 25 per unit of X_2 sold. Production of a unit of X_1 requires 10 units of Z_1 and 15 units of Z_2 while that of X_2 requires 10 units of Z_2 and 30 units of Z_3. Z_1, Z_2 and Z_3 are available in amounts of 5,000, 9,000 and 12,000 units respectively.
   (i) Find the profit maximising product mix.
   (ii) Are there any bottlenecks in the production process ?
   (**Ans.** Let x_1, x_2 – Nos. of X_1 and X_2 produced LPP – Maximise $Z = 20x_1 + 25x_2$
   Subject to $10x_1 \leq 5,000$; $15x_1 + 10x_2 \leq 9,000$; $30x_2 \leq 12,000$; $x_1, x_2 \geq 0$.
   Soln.: (i) 333 of X_1, 400 of X_2, Profit = ₹ 16,660, (ii) Since quantity of Z_2 remaining i.e. $9000 - [15(333) + 10(400)] = 5$ is very small we have 1670 units of Z_1 also unutilized).

6. A company producing three brands of Shampoos has two plants located at two places. Each plant has following production capacities per day:

Plants	Brands (Bottles per day)		
	Fresh	Blossom	Moon
I	3000	1000	2000
II	1000	1000	6000

A market survey indicates that during any particular month there will be minimum demand of 24,000 bottles of Fresh, 16,000 bottles of Blossom and 48,000 bottles of Moon. The operative costs per day of running the plants I and II are 600 monetary units and 400 monetary units respectively. The other fixed overhead costs for plants I and II are ₹ 100 and ₹ 150 per day respectively. How many days should the company run each plant during the month so that the production cost is minimised while still meeting the market demand. Use Graphical method of solution.
(**Ans.** Let x_1, x_2 - No. of days plants I and II are run in a month respectively. LPP is Minimise $Z = 600 x_1 + 400x_2 + 250$. Subject to $3x_1 + x_2 \geq 24$; $x_1 + x_2 \geq 16$; $x_1 + 3x_2 \geq 24$; $x_1, x_2 \geq 0$.
Soln.: $x_1 = 4$ days, $x_2 = 12$ days, Cost = ₹ 7,450)

7. Solve the following L.P.P. by graphical method:
   Maximise $Z = 5x_1 + 7x_2$
   Subject to $x_1 + x_2 \le 4, 3x_1 + 8x_2 \le 24, 10x_1 + 7x_2 \le 35, x_1, x_2 \ge 6$
   (**Ans.** Infeasible solution)

8. A toy company manufactures two types of dolls, a basic version – doll A and a deluxe version - doll B. Each doll of type B takes twice as long to produce as one of type A and the company would have time to make a maximum of 2000 per day. The supply of plastic is sufficient to produce 1500 dolls per day (both A and B combined). The deluxe version requires a fancy dress of which there are only 600 per day available. If the company makes a profit of ₹ 3.00 and ₹ 5.00 per doll respectively on doll A and B, then how many of each doll should be produced per day in order to maximise the total profit. Formulate and solve LPP.
   (**Ans.** Maximise $P = 3x + 5y$ s.t.: $x + y \le 1500$, $y \le 600, 2y + x \le 2000; x y \ge 0$, $P_{max} = 500$ when x i.e. A = 10 and y i.e. B = 5)

9. Solve the following LPP using graphical method
   Maximise $Z = 4X_1 + 2X_2$
   Subject to constraints: $2X_1 + 3X_2 \ge 30, X_1 + X_2 \le 14, X_1 + 2X_2 \le 18; X_1, X_2 \ge 0$
   (**Ans.** $Z_{max} = 52$ at $X_1 = 12, X_2 = 2$) **(P.U. MBA - May 06)**

10. Solve by graphical method
    Maximise $Z = 6x_1 + 14x_2$
    Subject to $5x_1 + 4x_2 \ge 60, 3x_1 + 7x_2 \ge 84, x_1 + 2x_2 \ge 18; x_1, x_2 \ge 0$
    (**Ans.** Multiple Solutions $Z_{min} = 168$) **(P.U. MBA - May 07)**

11. A firm makes two types of furniture - chairs and tables. The contribution to profit by each product as calculated by accounting department is ₹ 20 per chair and ₹ 30 per table. Both the products are to be processed on three machines M_1, M_2 and M_3. The time required in hours by each product and total time available in hours per week on each machine are as follows:

Machine	Chair	Table	Available Time (in hrs)
M_1	3	3	36
M_2	5	2	50
M_3	2	6	60

How should the manufacturer schedule the production in order to maximise the profit?
(**Ans.** 3 chairs, 9 tables, profit = 330) **(P.U. MBA - May 08)**

12. Solve the following LPP using graphical method
    (i) Maximise $Z = 5x_1 + 2x_2$. Subject to $4x_1 + 2x_2 \leq 16$, $3x_1 + x_2 \leq 9$, $3x_1 - x_2 \leq 9$; $x_1, x_2 \geq 0$.
    (**Ans.** $x_1 = 1$, $x_2 = 6$, $Z_{max} = 17$)   **(P.U. MBA - Dec. 06)**
    (ii) Maximise $Z = 5x_1 + 7x_2$. Subject to $x_1 + x_2 \leq 4$, $3x_1 + 8x_2 \leq 24$, $10x_1 + 7x_2 \leq 35$; $x_1, x_2 \geq 0$.
    (**Ans.** $x_1 = \frac{8}{5}$, $x_2 = \frac{12}{5}$, $Z_{max} = \frac{124}{5}$)   **(P.U. MBA - May 11)**

13. A firm uses lathes, milling machines and grinding machines to produce two machine parts. Table given below represents the machine times required for each part, machining times available on different machines and profits on each machine part.

Machines	Machining time required for machine part in minutes		Maximum time available (minutes)
	(I)	(II)	
Lathes	12	6	3000
Milling	4	10	2000
Grinding	2	3	900
Profit per unit (₹)	40	100	

Find the number of parts I and II to be manufactured per week to maximise the profit.

(**Ans.** Multiple solution, $P_{max.} = 20000$)   **(P.U. MBA - May 09)**

14. The Agricultural Research Institute has suggested to a farmer to spread out atleast 4800 kgs of a special phosphate fertilizer and no less than 7200 kgs of a special nitrogen fertilizer to raise the productivity of the crop in his fields. There are two sources of obtaining these mixtures. Mixture A and mixture B both are available in bags weighing 100 kg each and they cost ₹ 40 and ₹ 24 respectively. Mixture A contains phosphate and nitrogen equivalent of 20 kg and 80 kg respectively while mixture B contains these ingredients equivalent of 50 kgs each type. Determine how many bags of each type should the farmer buy in order to obtain the required at minimum cost.

(**Ans.** A - 0, B - 144, C_{min} = ₹ 3456)   **(P.U. MBA - May 13)**

■■■

Chapter 2...

Transportation Models

Contents ...
2.1 Introduction
2.2 Linear Programming Formulation of a Transportation Problem
2.3 Terminology of Transportation Problems
2.4 General Procedure for Solving a Transportation Problem
2.5 Methods for Finding the Initial Feasible Solution
2.6 Method For Finding the Optimum Solution
2.7 Special Cases in Transportation
2.8 Note
   Solved Problems
   Exercise

2.1 Introduction

It is a typical Operations Research technique intended to establish a least cost route for the transportation of goods from the sources (say a company's production plants) to the various destinations (say it's warehouses). A transportation problem is a special type of Linear Programming Problem which can be solved by the simplex method of solving these problems. However practically an alternate method called as transportation method is used to solve them.

2.2 Linear Programming Formulation of a Transportation Problem

Consider a problem of transporting goods from m sources (factories) $F_1, F_2, ... F_m$ to n destinations (warehouses) $W_1, W_2, ... W_n$. The capacities of the sources are $S_1, S_2, ... S_m$ respectively while the expected demands at the respective warehouses are $d_1, d_2 ... d_n$. C_{ij} indicates the cost of transporting one unit from the source F_i to destination W_j. Thus C_{23} is per unit transportation cost from the second factory F_2 to the third warehouse W_3. It is assumed that the total supply available at the sources will exactly satisfy the total demand required at all the destinations i.e. $S_1 + S_2 + ... + S_m = d_1 + d_2 + ... + d_n$.

Now, the above information can be written down in the form of a transportation table. It is a tabular arrangement of the data about the demands (d_j) at the destinations, the availabilities at the supply points (S_i) and the per unit transportation or shipping cost (C_{ij}) between each supply point and the destination, as shown below.

Sources	Destinations				Supply capacity
	W_1	W_2	...	W_n	
F_1	C_{11}	C_{12}	...	C_{1n}	S_1
F_2	C_{21}	C_{22}	...	C_{2n}	S_2
...	...	...	...	...	...
...	...	...	...	...	...
F_m	C_{m1}	C_{m2}	...	C_{mn}	S_m
Demand	d_1	d_2	...	d_n	N = Total Supply/Demand

The problem is to find the number of units to be transported from each of the sources to each of the destinations so that the total cost of transportation is minimised.

1. Objective Function:

Now, let X_{ij} represents the number of units to be transported from i^{th} source (i=1, 2, ... m) to the jth destination (j = 1, 2, ... n). Thus, X_{23} represents the number of units to be transported from the source F_2 to warehouse W_3. The cost of transporting these units will be ($C_{23}X_{23}$) as C_{23} is the corresponding per unit transportation cost.

∴ Total Cost
$$Z = C_{11}X_{11} + C_{12}X_{12} + ... + C_{1n}X_{1n} + C_{21}X_{21} + ... + C_{mn}X_{mn}$$
$$= \sum_{i=1}^{m} \sum_{j=1}^{n} C_{ij} X_{ij}$$

∴ The objective function is to

Minimise $$Z = \sum_{i=1}^{m} \sum_{j=1}^{n} C_{ij} X_{ij}$$

2. Constraints:

(i) Total supply from the first source to all the warehouses must be equal to S_1

i.e. $X_{11} + X_{12} + \ldots + X_{1n} = S_1$

i.e. $\sum_{j=1}^{n} X_{1j} = S_1$

Similarly, for each source. Hence in general we have,

$$\sum_{j=1}^{n} X_{ij} = S_i \text{ for each } i = 1, 2, \ldots, m$$

(ii) Similarly, for the first warehouse

$x_{11} + x_{21} + \ldots + x_{m1} = d_1$

i.e. $\sum_{i=1}^{m} X_{i1} = d_1$.

Hence in general $\sum_{i=1}^{m} X_{ij} = d_j$ for each $j = 1, 2, \ldots, n$

(iii) Similarly, the non-negativity condition is

$X_{ij} \geq 0$ for each $i = 1, 2, \ldots, m$ and $j = 1, 2, \ldots, n$

Thus, the L. P. model for the Transportation Problem is

Minimise $\quad Z = \sum_{i=1}^{m} \sum_{j=1}^{n} C_{ij} X_{ij} \quad$ ... (Cost minimisation)

Subject to $\quad \sum_{j=1}^{n} X_{ij} = S_i \text{ for } i = 1, 2, \ldots, m \quad$ ... (Supply Constraints)

$\quad \sum_{i=1}^{m} X_{ij} = d_j \text{ for } j = 1, 2, \ldots, n \quad$ ... (Demand Constraints)

$\quad x_{ij} \geq 0 \quad$ (... Non-negativity Condition)

This problem can be solved by using the simplex method of solution. But for a transportation problem we use the transportation method which is more convenient to use.

Note that the Total Supply $(S_1 + S_2 + \ldots + S_m)$ = Total Demand $(d_1 + d_2 + \ldots + d_n)$ which is called the **rim condition.**

2.3 Terminology of Transportation Problems

(i) **Balanced Transportation Problem:** Here the total capacity of the supply points or sources is equal to the total demand at the destinations.

(ii) **Unbalanced Transportation Problem:** Here the total supply is not equal to the total demand.

(iii) **Transportation Table:** It is used to represent the data about the supply at sources, demand at destinations and per unit transportation cost from each source to each destination.

Plant	Warehouse			Supply
	Delhi	Pune	Bangalore	
Mumbai	10 (300)	3 (700)	6	1000
Chennai	15 (200)	10 —	4 (1000)	1200
Kolkata	11 (300)	15 —	12 (700)	800
Demand	700	700	1000	Total = 3000

e.g. The above table has 3 rows for three sources, 3 columns corresponding to 3 warehouses along with one row and column indicating the demands and supply. Each square at the intersection of the rows and columns is called as a 'cell'. The figures in the right hand top corner for each cell indicate the per unit transportation cost between the respective source and destination, while the figures in circles indicate the number of units to be transported. E.g. 300 units to be transported from Mumbai to Delhi where unit cost of transportation is ₹ 10. We have to identify these figures to obtain the optimum solution.

(iv) **Dummy Source or Destination:** This is represented by adding an extra row or column to the transportation table with '0' per unit cost for each of its cells. It is used to balance an unbalanced problem by considering appropriate supply or demand for it.

(v) **Initial Feasible Solution:** It is a solution that satisfies the supply and demand conditions and yet it may or may not be the optimum one. There are three methods of obtaining this solution viz. North West Corner Method (NWCM), Matrix Minima or Least Cost Method (LCM) and Vogel's Approximation Method (VAM).

(vi) **Optimum Solution:** It is the feasible solution which also gives a transportation plan with minimum total cost. This can be obtained by using the Stepping Stone Method or Modified Distribution Method (MODI Method), once we get the Initial Feasible Solution.

2.4 General Procedure for Solving a Transportation Problem

Step 1: Define the objective function to be minimised with the constraints imposed on the problem.

Step 2: Set up the transportation table with m rows representing the sources and n columns representing the destinations along with their supply and demand figures as well as the unit cost figures in the cells. Add dummy row or column, if necessary, to balance the problem.

Step 3: Develop the Initial Feasible Solution to the problem using either NWCM, LCM or VAM.

Step 4: Examine the feasibility of the initial solution. The solution is feasible if it has allocations at (m+n–1) number of cells at independent positions i.e. t has (m+n–1) independent occupied cells.

Step 5: Test the solution, if found feasible, for optimality by finding out the opportunity costs for all the unoccupied or empty cells. Non-Negative (i.e. zero or positive) opportunity cost for all empty cells indicates that the solution is optimal.

Step 6: If the solution is not optimal, we improve it by using the Stepping Stone Method or the MODI method.

Step 7: Repeat steps 4, 5 and 6 until an optimal solution is obtained.

2.5 Methods for Finding the Initial Feasible Solution

(A) North - West Corner Method (NWCM):

Here we go on making maximum possible allocations to the North - West corner cells as follows:

Step 1: Select the North - West corner cell in the transportation table and allocate as many units as possible to it after checking the supply (in row) and the demand (in column) position for that cell.

Step 2: Reduce the supply and demand figures for the corresponding row and column accordingly.

Step 3: Cover the row or column where the supply or demand gets fully exhausted (i.e. becomes 0) to get a reduced transportation table.

Step 4: Go to step 1 and repeat the procedure until total supply is fully allocated to the cells so as to fulfil the total demand.

Note: Though it is easy, this method requires many further improvements to obtain the optimum solution.

Example 1: Consider the following transportation table with supply, demand and unit cost figures as shown:

	D_1	D_2	D_3	Supply
S_1	3	2	1	20
S_2	2	4	1	50
S_3	3	5	2	30
S_4	4	6	7	25
Demand	40	30	55	125

Solution: This is a balanced table with total demand = total supply = 125.

1. (i) Choose the North - West corner cell i.e. $S_1 D_1$. The row supply is 20 and column demand is 40 for this cell. Hence we can assign at most 20 units to it.

   (ii) After assigning these 20 units, the supply of S_1 becomes (20 – 20 = 0) and demand for D_1 reduces to 40 – 20 = 20.

   (iii) Thus, cover row S_1 now as its supply has been fully used, to get a reduced table.

	D_1	D_2	D_3	Supply
~~S_1~~	⑳ 3	2	1	~~20~~,0
S_2	2	4	1	50
S_3	3	5	2	30
S_4	4	6	7	25
Demand	4̶0̶,20	30	55	

2. In this table go again to the north west corner cell i.e. $S_2 D_1$ and allocate 20 units to it as it has 20 units of demand and 50 units of supply available. This reduces supply of row S_2 to 50 – 20 = 30 and demand of D_1 to 20 – 20 = 0.

	D_1	D_2	D_3	Supply
~~S_1~~	⑳ 3	2	1	~~20~~
S_2	⑳ 2	4	1	5̶0̶, 30
S_3	3	5	2	30
S_4	4	6	7	25
Demand	4̶0̶,2̶0̶,0	30	55	

Cover D_1 as its demand has been fully satisfied to get a new reduced table.

3. In this table make allocation to the northwest corner cell i.e. S_2D_2 of 30 units. This reduces both the demand of D_2 and supply of S_2 to 0. Hence, cover both S_2 and D_2.

	D_1	D_2	D_3	Supply
~~S_1~~	⑳ 3	2	1	~~20~~
~~S_2~~	⑳ 2	㉚ 4	~~1~~	~~50, 30, 0~~
S_3		3	5	㉚ 2	30
S_4		4	6	㉕ 7	25
Demand	40	30, 0	55	

4. Now, only one column D_3 with S_3D_3 and S_4D_3 remains. Make allocations directly to them of the remaining 30 and 25 units of supply. This automatically satisfies the demand for 55 units of D_3.

Thus, here we are getting a plan to transport 20 units from S_1 to D_1, 20 from S_2 to D_1, 30 from S_2 to D_2 etc. Therefore, the total cost = 20(3) + 20(2) + 30 (4) + 30(2) + 25(7) = 455. However, since the number of occupied cells (i.e. the cells to which the units have been allotted like S_1D_1, S_2D_2 etc.) is 5 which are less than (m+n–1 = 4+3–1 = 6), the solution is not feasible.

(B) Least Cost Method (LCM) or Matrix Minima Method:

Here we go on making allocations to the minimum cost cell in the table.

Step 1: (i) Select a cell with minimum unit transportation cost from the table.

(ii) If there are more than one cells with minimum unit cost i.e. there is a tie, then select that cell among them where more number of units can be allocated (after considering their row supply and column demands.) If there is a tie again, then select a cell randomly from them.

Step 2: Allocate maximum possible number of units to it. Reduce the corresponding supply and demand figures accordingly to get a reduced transportation table as in case of NWCM.

Step 3: Repeat steps 1 and 2 until entire supply is exhausted to fulfil the entire demand.

Example 2: For the same problem as in Example 1

1. (i) Choose the cell with minimum unit cost. There are two such cells S_1D_3 and S_2D_3, both having unit cost 1 i.e. there is a tie.

(ii) Hence select that cell where more units can be allocated. After considering the row supply and column demand for these cells we see that we can allocate 20 units to S_1D_3 and 50 units to S_2D_3. Hence select S_2D_3.

2. Allocate 50 units to it and then reduce its row supply and column demand by 50. Thus, the supply of S_2 gets fully exhausted and demand for D_3 becomes 5. Hence, cover S_2 to get the reduced table.

	D_1	D_2	D_3	Supply
S_1	3	2	1	20,0
~~S_2~~	~~2~~	~~4~~	~~(50) 1~~	~~50, 0~~
S_3	3	5	2	30
S_4	4	6	7	25
Demand	40	30	~~55~~, 5	

3. For the reduced table we repeat the procedure. Here the cell with minimum cost is S_1D_3. Hence we make allocation to it of 5 units after considering its row supply and remaining column demand. We then reduce the row supply and column demand by 5 and get the new reduced table by covering coulmn D_3 for which the demand becomes 0.

	D_1	D_2	D_3	Supply
S_1	3	2	(5) 1	~~20~~,15
~~S_2~~	~~2~~	~~4~~	~~(50) 1~~	~~50~~
S_3	3	5	2	30
S_4	4	6	7	25
Demand	40	30	~~55~~,~~5~~,0	

4. In the new reduced table we make allocation to the minimum cost cell i.e. S_1D_2 of 15 units and get the reduced table by reducing its row supply and column demand accordingly. We repeat the procedure once again to make allocation of 30 units to cell $S_3 D_1$.

	D_1	D_2	D_3	Supply
~~S_1~~	3	(15) 2	(5) 1	~~20,15,0~~
~~S_2~~	~~2~~	~~4~~	~~(50) 1~~	~~50~~
~~S_3~~	~~(30) 3~~	~~5~~	~~2~~	~~30,0~~
S_4	4	6	7	25
Demand	~~40~~,10	~~30~~,15	~~55~~	

5. For the remaining row S_4, we make allocations of the remaining 10 and 15 units directly to get the initial feasible solution as follows:

	D_1	D_2	D_3	Supply
S_1	3	(15) 2	(5) 1	20
S_2	2	4	(50) 1	50
S_3	(30) 3	5	2	30
S_4	(10) 4	(15) 6	7	25
Demand	40	30	55	125

Total Cost = 15(2) + 5(1) + 50(1) + 30(3) + 10(4) + 15(6) = 305

Also, since there are m + n–1 = 4 + 3–1 = 6 number of independent occupied cells, the solution is feasible.

(C) Vogel's Approximation Method (VAM):

Here we go on making allocations to the minimum cost cell of a row or column for which the penalty for not making an allocation (i.e. the opportunity cost) is high.

Step 1: Compute the penalty (ie. the difference between the two smallest unit cost figures of the cells) for each row and column.

Step 2: Identify the row or column with highest penalty and choose the cell with smallest unit cost in it.

(If there is a tie for highest penalties, select the row or column containing the minimum cost cell, among them. If there is a tie again, then select that cell where maximum allocation is possible or we can select it randomly)

Step 3: Allocate maximum possible units to the selected cell and reduce its row supply and column demand accordingly. Obtain the reduced table then as done previously.

Step 4: Recompute the penalties for the reduced table. [If a row (column) has been covered the row (column) penalties remain unchanged]. Repeat the above procedure until the entire demand and supply gets exhausted.

Example 3:

1. Considering the same problem as in Example 1 and 2 we compute the penalties for each row and column as follows: The penalty is obtained by taking the difference between two smallest unit cost figures appearing in each row and column.

	D_1	D_2	D_3	Supply	Penalty
S_1	3	2	1	20	2 – 1 = 1
S_1	2	4	1	50	2 – 1 = 1
S_3	3	5	2	30	3 – 2 = 1
S_4	4	6	7	25	6 – 4 = 2 ←
Demand	40	30	55		
Penalty	3 – 2 = 1	4 – 2 = 2 ↑	1 – 1 = 0		

2. (i) Identify the row/column with highest penalty. These are row S_4 and column D_2, both with penalty 2 i.e. there is a tie.

   (ii) From these two, select the one containing minimum cost cell: S_4 has minimum cost cell $S_4 D_1$ with cost 4 and D_2 has the minimum cost cell $S_1 D_2$ with cost 2. Hence we select D_2.

   (iii) In D_2 the cell with minimum cost i.e. $S_1 D_2$ is selected for making allocation.

3. We allocate 20 units to it (after considering its row supply and column demand) and then reduce them accordingly. We then cover S_1 as its supply gets fully exhausted to get the reduced table as follows:

	D_1	D_2	D_3	Supply	Penalty
~~S_1~~	3	②⓪ 2	1	~~20~~,0	~~1~~
S_2	2	4	1	50	1
S_3	3	5	2	30	1
S_4	4	6	7	25	2
Demand	40	~~30~~,10	55		
Penalty	1	2	0		

4. For the reduced table we recompute the penalties. As a row has been covered, the row penalties will remain unchanged while only the column penalties will change, as shown below:

	D_1	D_2	D_3	Supply	Penalty
~~S_1~~	3	②⓪ 2	1	~~20~~	~~1~~
S_2	2	4	1	50	1
S_3	3	5	2	30	1
~~S_4~~	㉕ 4	6	7	~~25~~,0	~~2~~ ←
Demand	~~40~~,15	~~30~~,10	55		
Penalty	3 - 2 = 1	5 - 4 = 1	2 - 1 = 1		

Now, the row S_4 has highest penalty. Hence we select it and make maximum allocations of 25 units to the minimum cost cell in it i.e. to $S_4 D_1$. We obtain then a new reduced transportation table as done earlier.

5. Recomputing penalties for this table, we see that all rows and columns have penalty of 1. We select row S_2 (or column D_3) containing minimum cost cell S_2D_3 with cost 1. Then we allocate 50 units to it which reduces supply of S_2 to 0.

	D_1	D_2	D_3	Supply	Penalty
~~S_1~~	3	②⓪ 2	1	~~20~~	~~1~~
~~S_2~~	~~2~~	~~4~~	㊿ 1	~~50~~,0	~~1~~ ←
S_3	3	5	2	30	1
~~S_4~~	㉕ 4	6	7	~~25~~	~~1~~
Demand	~~40~~,15	~~30~~,10	~~55~~,5		
Penalty	1	1	1		

6. We then make allocations to the remaining row S_3 directly to get the initial feasible solution as follows:

	D_1	D_2	D_3	Supply
S_1	3	⑳ 2	1	20
S_2	2	4	㊿ 1	50
S_3	⑮ 3	⑩ 5	⑤ 2	30
S_4	㉕ 4	6	7	25
Demand	40	30	55	125

Here, the total cost = 20 (2) + 50 (1) + 15 (3) + 10 (5) + 5(2) + 25(4) = 295

Also, as number of occupied cells = m+n–1 = 4+3–1 = 6, the solution is feasible.

Note: The solution obtained by VAM gives the minimum cost among all these three methods (NWCM, LCM and VAM). In fact this is the best method to get the Initial Feasible Solution which needs very few improvements further to get the optimum solution.

Example 4: Find the initial solution for the following problem using (i) NWCM (ii) LCM and (iii) VAM. The supply, demand and unit cost figures are given.

	W_1	W_2	W_3	W_4	S
P_1	190	300	500	100	70
P_2	700	300	400	600	90
P_3	400	100	400	200	180
D	50	80	70	140	340

Solution: This is a balanced table with total demand = total supply = 340.

(a) North - West Corner Method:

1.
Step 1: Select the north west corner cell i.e. P_1W_1 in the table. Its row supply is 70 and column demand is 50. Hence, we can allot maximum of 50 units to it.

Step 2: Allot 50 units to P_1W_1 and hence reduce its row supply and column demand by 50. This makes the row supply 20 while the column demand gets exhausted as 50 – 50 = 0.

Step 3: As column demand of W_1 gets exhausted fully, cover it to get the reduced table as below:

	W_1	W_2	W_3	W_4	S
P_1	㊿ 190	300	500	100	7̶0̶,20
P_2	700	300	400	600	90
P_3	400	100	400	200	180
D	5̶0̶,0	80	70	140	

2. Now repeat the procedure for this reduced table:

   Select north-west cell P_1 W_2 and allot 20 units to it. This reduces its column demand to 60 while its row supply gets fully exhausted. Hence, cover the row P_1 to get the new reduced table as follows:

	W_1	W_2	W_3	W_4	S
~~P_1~~	(50) 190	(20) 300	500	100	~~70~~,~~20~~,0
P_2	700	300	400	600	90
P_3	400	100	400	200	180
D	50	~~80~~,60	70	140	

3. Repeat the procedure similarly for making allocations of 60 units to P_2 W_2 and then of 30 units to P_2 W_3 to get the following table.

	W_1	W_2	W_3	W_4	S
~~P_1~~	(50) 190	(20) 300	500	100	70
~~P_2~~	700	(60) 300	(30) 400	600	~~90~~, ~~30~~, 0
P_3	400	100	400	200	180
D	50	~~80~~, ~~60~~, 0	~~70~~, 40	140	340

4. Since now only one row is left, make the remaining allocations to its cells directly to get the initial solution as follows:

	W_1	W_2	W_3	W_4	S
P_1	(50) 190	(20) 300	500	400	70
P_2	700	(60) 300	(30) 400	600	90
P_3	400	100	(40) 400	(140) 200	180
D	50	80	70	140	340

   Here, Total Cost = 50(190) + 20(300) + 60(300) + 30(400) + 40(400) + 140(200) = 89,500.

Note: All the operations can be carried out carefully on a single table to obtain the solution.

(b) Least Cost Method:

Here we go on making allocations to the least cost cells in the table.

1. **Step 1:** Identify the least cost cells in the table: There are two such cells P_1W_4 and P_3W_2 both with cost 100. Thus, there is a tie. Hence we select that cell where more number of allocations can be made. Considering the row supply and column demand for these cells we see that we can allot 70 units to P_1W_4 and 80 units to P_3W_2. Hence, we select P_3W_2.

DECISION SCIENCES TRANSPORTATION MODELS

Step 2: We allot 80 units to P_3W_2 and then reduce its row supply and column demand by 80. This makes the row supply (180 – 80 = 100) while the entire column demand gets exhausted. Thus, we cover column W_2 to get the reduced table as follows:

	W_1	W_2	W_3	W_4	S
P_1	190	300	500	100	70
P_2	700	300	400	600	90
P_3	400	⑧⓪100	400	200	1̶8̶0̶,100
D	50	8̶0̶, 0	70	140	

2. Repeat the procedure for the reduced table and make second allocation (of 70 units) to the least cost cell P_1W_4 in it.

	W_1	W_2	W_3	W_4	S
P̶₁	190	300	500	⑦⓪100	7̶0̶,0
P_2	700	300	400	600	90
P_3	400	⑧⓪100	400	200	1̶8̶0̶,100
D	50	8̶0̶	70	1̶4̶0̶,70	

3. In this reduced table the least cost cell is P_3W_4. Therefore make the third allocation to it.

	W_1	W_2	W_3	W_4	S
P̶₁	190	300	500	⑦⓪100	7̶0̶
P_2	700	300	400	600	90
P_3	400	⑧⓪100	400	⑦⓪200	1̶8̶0̶,1̶0̶0̶,30
D	50	8̶0̶	70	1̶4̶0̶,7̶0̶,0	

4. Now in the new reduced table make the fourth allocation to the least cost cell P_2W_3 as 70 units can be allotted to it (which is more than 30 units that can be allocated to P_3W_1 or P_3W_3).

	W_1	W_2	W_3	W_4	S
P̶₁	190	300	500	⑦⓪100	7̶0̶
P_2	700	300	⑦⓪400	600	9̶0̶,20
P_3	400	⑧⓪100	400	⑦⓪200	1̶8̶0̶,1̶0̶0̶,30
D	50	8̶0̶	7̶0̶,0	140	

2.13

Now, making further allocations directly to the cells of the remaining column W_1 we get the initial solution as follows:

	W_1	W_2	W_3	W_4	S
P_1	190	300	500	⑦ 100	70
P_2	㉒ 700	300	⑦ 400	600	90
P_3	㉚ 400	⑧ 100	400	⑦ 200	180
D	50	80	70	140	340

Here total cost = 70 (100) + 20 (700) + 70 (400) + 30 (400) + 80 (100) + 70 (200) = 83000

Note: The solution can be obtained by using one table only if the operations are carried out carefully.

(c) Vogel's Approximation Method:

Here we go on making allocations to the minimum cost cell in the row or column with highest penalty.

1. **Step 1:** We compute the penalties (i.e. the difference between two lowest per unit costs of cells) for the rows and columns as follows:

	W_1	W_2	W_3	W_4	Supply	Penalty
P_1	190	300	500	100	70	190-100=90
P_2	700	300	400	600	90	400-300=100
P_3	400	100	400	200	180	200-100=100
Demand	50	80	70	140	340	
Penalty	400-190=210	300-100=200	400-400=0	200-100=100		

↑1

Step 2: Since the maximum penalty (210) occurs for W_1, we select column W_1. Then we select the minimum unit cost cell in it i.e. P_1W_1 (with cost = 190)

Step 3: Considering the row supply (70) and column demand (50) for P_1W_1 we see that maximum 50 units can be allocated to it. Hence we allocate 50 units (1st allocation) to the cell P_1W_1 and then reduce its row supply and column demand by 50. Thus the row supply reduces to (70 – 50 = 20) and the column demand gets fully exhausted as 50 – 50 = 0. Hence, we cover the column W_1 to get a reduced table as follows:

↓1

	W_1	W_2	W_3	W_4	S
P_1	㊼ 190	300	500	100	7̸0,20
P_2		700	300	400	600	90
P_3		400	100	400	200	180
D	5̸0,0	80	70	140	

↑1

2. For the reduced table we repeat the procedure:

   (i) We recompute the penalties. As a column is covered, only the row penalties will change as follows:

   ↓2

	W_1	W_2	W_3	W_4	Supply	Penalty
P_1	㊿ 190	300	500	100	7̶0̶,20	300-100 = 200
P_2	700	300	400	600	90	400-300 =100
P_3	400	㊿ 100	400	200	1̶8̶0̶,100	200-100 =100
Demand	5̶0	8̶0̶,0	70	140		
Penalty		200	0	100		

   ↑2

   (ii) Maximum penalty (200) occurs for row P_1 as well as column W_2. Hence there is a tie. Hence, we go for the one which contains a minimum unit cost cell. However, here also there is a tie as row P_1 contains cell P_1W_4 and column W_2 contains cell P_3W_2, both of which have the same minimum cost of 100. Now, we select the cell, where maximum allocation is possible. We see that we can allocate 20 units to P_1W_4 and 80 units to P_3W_2. Hence, we select cell P_3W_2 in column W_2 for the second allocation and allocate 80 units to it. This reduces its row supply to 100 and exhausts its column demand. Thus, we cover the column W_2 to get a new reduced table as shown above.

3. We repeat the procedure once again for the new reduced table. We recompute the penalties and make allocation (3rd) of 20 units to cell P_1W_4 with (cost=100) in row P_1 with (highest penalty of 400) as follows:

   3 →

	W_1	W_2	W_3	W_4	Supply	Penalty
P_1	㊿ 190	300	500	㉇ 100	7̶0̶,2̶0̶,0	4̶0̶0̶
P_2	700	300	400	600	90	200
P_3	400	㊿ 100	400	200	1̶8̶0̶,100	200
Demand	5̶0	8̶0	70	1̶4̶0̶,120		
Penalty			0	100		

   ← 3

   This exhausts the row supply of P_1 and we get a new reduced table as above.

4. Repeat the procedure once again by recomputing the penalties. As a row is covered, only the column penalties will change.

	W₁	W₂	W₃	W₄	Supply	Penalty
P₁	㊿ 190	300	500	⑳ 100	~~70~~	—
P₂	700	300	400	600	90	200
P₃	400	⑧⓪ 100	400	⑩⓪ 200	~~180,100,0~~ ~~200~~	
Demand	5̸0	8̸0	70	1̸40,1̸20,20		
Penalty			0	400		

↑4

Select here column W₄ with highest penalty 400 and then make allocation (4th) to cell P₃W₄ (with lowest cost 200) of 100 units which exhausts the row supply of P₃.

5. As only one row is left now, we make the further allocations of the remaining units to its cells and thus get the initial solution as

	W₁	W₂	W₃	W₄	S
P₁	㊿ 190	300	500	⑳ 100	70
P₂	700	300	⑦⓪ 400	⑳ 600	90
P₃	400	⑧⓪ 100	400	⑩⓪ 200	180
D	50	80	70	140	340

Here, Total Cost = 50(190) + 20(100) + 70(400) + 20(600) + 80(100) + 100(200) = 79,500

Note:
(i) In the above tables, the numbers 1, 2 etc with the arrows near the penalty figures indicate the number of the allocation (1st, 2nd etc) that is made in that row or column while, the number with the arrows near the row and column headings indicate the number of the allocation after which, that row/column gets exhausted or covered.
(ii) All the operations can be carried out on a single table carefully to get the solution to save time as done ahead.
(iii) The NWCM, LCM and VAM may give the same solution for a problem.

2.6 Method for Finding the Optimum Solution

Once the initial solution is obtained we verify it for feasibility by finding the number of occupied cells. If the number of occupied cells (at independent positions) is equal to (number of rows + number of columns − 1 i.e. m + n − 1) then the solution is feasible, otherwise it is called as a case of degeneracy (described further in detail). Thus, if the solution is feasible we improve it further using the Stepping Stone Method or Modified Distribution Method to obtain the optimum solution. As the Modified Distribution Method is more convenient to use, only this method has been described here.

(A) Modified Distribution Method (MODI) or UV method:

Step 1: Determine the Initial Basic Feasible Solution and verify that it is feasible i.e. it has (m+n–1) independent occupied cells.

Step 2: Determine the row numbers (denoted as u_i i.e. u_1, u_2 etc) and the column numbers (denoted as v_j i.e. v_1, v_2 etc) by using the formula: $C_{ij} = u_i + v_j$ for each **occupied cell** (C_{ij} is the corresponding per unit transportation cost). Choose here one of the values of u_i or v_j as 0 arbitrarily (prefer that row or column which contains maximum number of occupied cells), and then use the formula for finding out the remaining value one by one.

Step 3: Now consider the **unoccupied cells** and find the opportunity cost (improvement index) for each of them by using the formula, Opportunity cost $\Delta_{ij} = C_{ij} - (u_i + v_j)$ for these cells.

Step 4: Check the sign of all the opportunity costs. If all of them are non-negative (i.e. zero or positive) then it implies that the solution obtained is optimum. If atleast one of the opportunity costs is negative, then it implies that the solution is not optimum and there is a scope for improvement. Then go to step 5.

Step 5: Select the unoccupied cell with highest negative opportunity cost. (If there are more than one such cells then select the cell where more units can be shifted, as described in further steps).

Step 6: For this cell, trace a closed path using most direct route through at least 3 occupied cells and then back to the unoccupied cell. Use only vertical and horizontal lines and take turns only at the occupied cells.

Step 7: Assign (+ve) and (–ve) signs alternately to each of the corner cells along the closed path, starting with a (+ve) sign for the selected unoccupied cell.

Step 8: Find the maximum number of units to be shifted to this unoccupied cell. (These are equal to the least of the number of units in the cells with (–ve) signs). Add this number of units to the cells with (+ve) sign and subtract it from the cells with (–ve) sign along the closed path.

Step 9: Go to Step 1 and repeat the procedure until an optimum solution is obtained.

Note:
(i) The initial feasible solution must have atleast one allocation in each of its rows and columns.
(ii) The allocations must be made in independent positions (i.e. the positions of cells where a closed path can not be traced as explained above) and must be (m + n – 1) in number.
(iii) The opportunity cost (Δ_{ij}) for an unoccupied cell indicates the change in the total cost if one unit is shifted to this cells. Hence a (–ve) opportunity cost indicates saving in the cost and hence we select the unoccupied cell with highest (–ve) opportunity cost.

DECISION SCIENCES — TRANSPORTATION MODELS

Example 5: Solve the following transportation problem to find its optimal solution:

	W_1	W_2	W_3	W_4	Supply
P_1	190	300	500	100	70
P_2	700	300	400	600	90
P_3	400	100	400	200	180
Demand	50	80	70	140	340

Solution:

Step 1: Using the Least Cost Method we get the initial solution of this balanced transportation problem (as done in example 4) as follows:

	W_1	W_2	W_3	W_4	S	Row No.
P_1	190	300	500	⑦ 100	70	$u_1 =$
P_2	㉒ 700	300	⑦ 400	600	90	$u_2 =$
P_3	㉚ 400	㊿ 100	400	⑦ 200	180	$u_3 = 0$
D	50	80	70	140	340	
Column No.	$v_1 =$	$v_2 =$	$v_3 =$	$v_4 =$		

It has $m + n - 1 = 3 + 4 - 1 = 6$ number of independent occupied cells. Hence, the solution is feasible. Note that total Cost = 83,000

Step 2: To find the row and column numbers (u_i and v_j):

Since the third row has maximum number of occupied cells put $u_3 = 0$. Now use the formula $C_{ij} = u_i + v_j$ for each **occupied cell** to find the other row and column numbers as follows:

For P_3W_1, $C_{31} = u_3 + v_1$ i.e. $400 = 0 + v_1$ $\therefore v_1 = 400 - 0 = 400$
For P_3W_2, $C_{32} = u_3 + v_2$ i.e. $100 = 0 + v_2$ $\therefore v_2 = 100$
For P_3W_4, $C_{34} = u_3 + v_4$ i.e. $200 = 0 + v_4$ $\therefore v_4 = 200$
Now, for P_1W_4, $100 = u_1 + v_4 = u_1 + 200$ $\therefore u_1 = 100 - 200 = -100$
For P_2W_1, $700 = u_2 + v_1 = u_2 + 400$ $\therefore u_2 = 700 - 400 = 300$ and
For P_2W_3, $400 = u_2 + v_3 = 300 + v_3$ $\therefore v_3 = 400 - 300 = 100$

Thus, we can write these values for the row and column numbers in the table as

	W_1	W_2	W_3	W_4	S	Row No.
P_1	190	300	500	⑦ 100	70	$u_1 = -100$
P_2	㉒ 700	300	⑦ 400	600	90	$u_2 = 300$
P_3	㉚ 400	㊿ 100	400	⑦ 200	180	$u_3 = 0$
D	50	80	70	140		
Column No.	$v_1 = 400$	$v_2 = 100$	$v_3 = 100$	$v_4 = 200$		

Step 3: To find the opportunity cost Δ_{ij} for each unoccupied cell:

Now, use the formula $\Delta_{ij} = C_{ij} - (u_i + v_j)$

for each **unoccupied cell** to find its opportunity cost as follows:

For P_1W_1, $\Delta = C_{11} - (u_1 + v_1) = 190 - (-100 + 400) = -110$
For P_1W_2, $\Delta = C_{12} - (u_1 + v_2) = 300 - (-100 + 100) = 300$
For P_1W_3, $\Delta = 500 - (u_1 + v_3) = 500 - (-100 + 100) = 500$
For P_2W_2, $\Delta = 300 - (u_2 + v_2) = 300 - (300 + 100) = -100$
For P_2W_4, $\Delta = 600 - (300 + 200) = 100$
For P_3W_3, $\Delta = 400 - (0 + 100) = 300$

Step 4: Since all the opportunity costs are not positive, the solution is not optimum and there is a scope for improvement.

Step 5: We now select the unoccupied cell with highest negative opportunity cost. This is the cell P_1W_1, having opportunity cost (– 110).

Step 6,7: We now trace a direct closed path for this cell using only horizontal and vertical lines and taking turn only at the occupied cells as follows (the direction of the arrows may be drawn - clockwise or anticlockwise which makes no difference):

	W₁	W₂	W₃	W₄	S
P₁	+ 190	300	500	⑦ 100	70
P₂	㉒ 700	300	⑦ 400	600	90
P₃	㉚ 400	⑧ 100	400 +	⑦ 200	180
D	50	80	70	140	

We then assign (+ve) and (–ve) signs alternately to the corner cells along the path, starting with a (+ve) sign for the unoccupied cell P_1W_1.

Step 8: Find the maximum number of units to be shifted to cell P_1W_1. The cells with (–ve) sign along the path are P_1W_4 and P_3W_1 which contain 70 and 30 units respectively. The least number between them is 30. Hence we shift 30 units to P_1W_1 along the closed path. For this, we add 30 units to the cells with (+ve) sign (i.e. P_1W_1 and P_3W_4) and subtract 30 units from the cells with negative sign (i.e. P_1W_4 and P_3W_1) to get an improved solution as follows:

	W₁	W₂	W₃	W₄	S	
P₁	㉚ 190	300	500	㊵ 100	70	$u_1 = 0$
P₂	⑳ 700	300	⑦ 400	600	90	u_2
P₃	400	⑧ 100	400	⑩ 200	180	u_3
D	50	80	70	140		
	v_1	v_2	v_3	v_4		Total Cost = 79,700

1ˢᵗ Improvement Table

Now, we repeat the procedure to find whether this solution is feasible and optimum and improve it further if necessary.

1. The table has $m + n - 1 = 6$ occupied cells. $\therefore$ It is a feasible solution.
2. Find u_i and v_j: P_1, P_2, W_1 and W_4 each contain 2 unoccupied cells. $\therefore$ Select any one of them say P_1 randomly and make $u_1 = 0$.

   Now, use the formula ($C_{ij} = u_i + v_j$) for all the occupied cells to find the values of all u_i and v_j as before.

   e.g. for P_1W_1, $190 = u_1 + v_1 = 0 + v_1$ $\therefore v_1 = 190$

   for P_1W_4, $100 = 0 + v_4$ $\therefore v_4 = 100$

   for P_2W_1, $700 = u_2 + v_1 = u_2 + 190$ $\therefore u_2 = 700 - 190 = 510$ etc.

3. Then, for all the unoccupied cells find $\Delta_{ij} = C_{ij} - (u_i + v_j)$ and write its value in the lower left hand corner of these cells as shown in the next table.

   e.g. for P_1W_2 $\Delta_{12} = 300 - (u_1 + v_2) = 300 - (0 + 0) = 300$

   for P_1W_3 $\Delta_{13} = 500 - (u_1 + v_3) = 500 - (0 - 110) = 610$

   for P_2W_2 $\Delta_{22} = 300 - (510 + 0) = -210$ etc.

Thus, we get the table as

	W_1	W_2	W_3	W_4	S	Row No.
P_1	㉚ 190 300	300 610	500	㊵ 100	70	$u_1 = 0$
P_2	⑳ 700 -210	300	⑦⓪ 400	600 -10	90	$u_2 = 510$
P_3	110 400	⑧⓪ 100 410	400	⑩⓪ 200	180	$u_3 = 100$
D	50	80	70	140		
Column No.	$v_1 = 190$	$v_2 = 0$	$v_3 = -110$	$v_4 = 100$		

4. As all the opportunity costs are not positive, the solution is not optimum and there is scope for improvement.

5. The cell with highest negative Δ_{ij} is P_2W_2. Hence, we select it and draw a closed path for it as follows (by using vertical and horizontal lines only and by taking turns only at the occupied cells) and then assign (+ve) and (–ve) signs alternately to its corner cells, starting with a (+ve) sign for P_2W_2.

	W_1	W_2	W_3	W_4	S
P_1	+ ㉚ 190	300	500	㊵ 100	70
P_2	− ⑳ 700 +	300	⑦⓪ 400	600	90
P_3	400	⑧⓪ 100 −	400	⑩⓪ 200 +	180
D	50	80	70	140	

6. Minimum number of units in the cells with (–ve) sign is 20. Hence, shift 20 units to P_2W_2 along the path. Add 20 to the cells with (+ve) sign and subtract 20 from the cells with (–ve) sign to get the following 2nd improvement table.

	W_1	W_2	W_3	W_4	S
P_1	㊿ 190	300	500	⑳ 100	70
P_2	700	⑳ 300	⑦⓪ 400	600	90
P_3	400	⑥⓪ 100	400	⑫⓪ 200	180
D	50	80	70	140	

2nd Improvement Table   **Total cost = 75,500**

This table has (m + n – 1 = 6) independent occupied cells. Hence, it is a feasible solution. We, now find u_i and v_j values and then Δ_{ij} values to see if it is optimum.
We directly write them down in the table as follows: Let $u_1 = 0$

	W_1	W_2	W_3	W_4	S	Row No.
P_1	㊿ 190	300 / 300	500 / 400	⑳ 100	70	$u_1 = 0$
P_2	210 / 700	⑳ 300	⑦⓪ 400	200 / 600	90	$u_2 = 300-0 = 300$
P_3	110 / 400	⑥⓪ 100	200 / 400	⑫⓪ 200	180	$u_3 = 200-100 = 100$
D	50	80	70	140		
Column No.	$v_1 = 190-0$ = 190	$v_2 = 100-100$ = 0	$v_3 = 400-300$ = 100	$v_4 = 100-0$ = 100		

$\Delta_{12} = 300 - (0 + 0) = 300$
$\Delta_{13} = 500 - (0 + 100) = 400$ etc.

Since all the opportunity costs (numbers in small squares) are (+ve) the solution is optimum.
Thus, we have the optimum transportation plan as follows:

Source	Destination	No. of units to be transported	Cost
P_1	W_1	50	50 × 190 = 9500
P_1	W_4	20	20 × 100 = 2000
P_2	W_2	20	20 × 300 = 6000
P_2	W_3	70	70 × 400 = 28000
P_3	W_2	60	60 × 100 = 6000
P_3	W_4	120	120 × 200 = 24000
			Total ₹ = 75,500

Note: The cost here goes on reducing from ₹ 83000 → ₹ 79,700 → ₹ 75,500 as we make the improvements.
In first improvement, cost saving = (per unit saving i.e. Δ = 110) × (No. units shifted = 30) = 3300. Similarly, in second improvement, saving = 210 × 20 = 4200.

2.7 Special Cases in Transportation

(A) Unbalanced Problem:

If the total supply from all the sources is not equal to the total demand at all the destinations, it is an unbalanced transportation problem. It is balanced by introducing a dummy row or column as follows:

  (i) If total demand is greater than total supply, add a dummy row or source with its supply equal to the difference between total demand and total supply. Consider the per unit transportation cost for all its cells as zero. The quantity supplied from this dummy source to various destinations in the optimum solution indicates the unfulfilled demand at these destinations.

  (ii) If total supply is greater than total demand, add a dummy column or destination with its demand equal to the difference between total supply and total demand. Consider the per unit cost for all its cells as zero. The quantity allotted to this dummy destination indicates the unused capacity at the respective sources.

Solve further the problem as an usual balanced transportation problem.

(B) Multiple Optimum Solution:

This is indicated by a zero opportunity cost (Δ_{ij}) for one or more unoccupied cells in the optimum transportation table. The alternate solution then can be obtained by shifting some units to this cell as we do it for the cell with a highest (–ve) opportunity cost in MODI method. This gives us a different transportation plan with same (minimum) total transportation cost.

Example 6: Four petrol dealers A, B, C, and D require 50, 40, 60 and 40 kl of petrol respectively. It is possible to supply this from three locations X, Y and Z which have 80, 100 and 50 kl respectively. The cost in ₹ for shipping each kl is shown in the table below.

	Dealers			
Location	A	B	C	D
X	7	6	6	6
Y	5	7	6	7
Z	8	5	8	6

Determine the most economical supply pattern for the company. Identify an alternate plan if any.

Solution: We have Total demand = 50 + 40 + 60 + 40 = 190 kl and

Total Supply = 80 + 100 + 50 = 230 kl. Thus, total supply > total demand. Hence, it is an unbalanced T.P. Therefore, to balance the problem we introduce a dummy dealer E with demand = 230 – 190 = 40 kl and with unit shipping cost '0' for all its cells. Now, Total Supply = Total Demand = 230 kl. and the problem is balanced.

1. To obtain the initial solution let us use the Vogel's Approximation Method for which we calculate the penalties (i.e. difference between two smallest unit costs) for each row and column as follows:

	A	B	C	D	E (Dummy)	Supply	Penalty
X	7	6	6	6	0	80	6–0=6 ← 1
Y	5	7	6	7	0	100	5–0=5
Z	8	5	8	6	0	50	5–0=5
Demand	50	40	60	40	40	230	
Penalty	7–5=2	6–5=1	6–6=0	6–6=0	0–0=0		

2. Since the maximum penalty (6) is for row X, we select row X. Then we select the cell with minimum cost in it i.e. the cell XE (with cost = 0)
3. After considering its row supply and column demand, we see that we can allocate 40 units to it (1st allocation). Hence, allocating 40 units to cell XE and then by reducing its row supply and column demand by 40 we get the reduced table as follows:

	A	B	C	D	E		Supply
X	7	6	6	6	㊵	0	8̶0̶,40
Y	5	7	6	7		0	100
Z	8	5	8	6		0	50
Demand	50	40	60	40	4̶0̶,0		

↓1 (above E column)

4. Recompute the penalties for this reduced table and repeat the procedure. As a column has been covered, only the row penalties will change.

↓2

	A	B	C	D	E		Supply	P
X	7	6	6	6	㊵	0	8̶0̶,40	0
Y	㊵ 5	7	6	7		0	1̶0̶0̶,50	1
Z	8	5	8	6		0	50	1
Demand	5̶0̶,0	40	60	40	40			
P	2	1	0	0				

↑2

Highest penalty occurs for column A. Hence select this column and make allocation to the cell with minimum unit cost in it i.e. to cell YA. We allocate 50 units here (2nd allocation) and reduce the corresponding row supply and column demand by 50 to get a new reduced table.

DECISION SCIENCES — TRANSPORTATION MODELS

5. We repeat the procedure again as follows:

    ↓3

	A	B	C	D	E	Supply	P
X	7	6	6	6	(40) 0	8̶0̶,40	0
Y	(50) 5	7	6	7	0	1̶0̶0̶,50	1
Z	8	(40) 5	8	6	0	5̶0̶,10	1	←3
Demand	5̶0̶	4̶0̶,0	60	40	4̶0̶		
P		1	0	0			

As a tie for highest penalty (1) occurs for rows Y, Z and column B, we select the one, which contains a minimum unit cost cell. Hence we select Z or B, both of which contain the same unit cost cell ZB. Then we make the 3rd allocation to it and get a new reduced table.

6. We repeat the same procedure for this table to make the 4th allocation to cell ZD in row Z of 10 units

	A	B	C	D	E	Supply	P
X	7	6	6	6	(40) 0	8̶0̶,40	0
Y	(50) 5	7	6	7	0	1̶0̶0̶,50	1
Z	8	(40) 5	8	(10) 6	0	5̶0̶,1̶0̶,0	2	←4
Demand	5̶0̶	4̶0̶	60	4̶0̶,30	4̶0̶		
P			0	0			

4→

7. Repeat the procedure once again for the new reduced table. As a row now has been covered, the column penalties will change.

	A	B	C	D	E	Supply	P
X	7	6	6	6	(40) 0	8̶0̶,40	0
Y	(50) 5	7	(50) 6	7	0	1̶0̶0̶,5̶0̶,0	1	←5
Z	8	(40) 5	8	(10) 6	0	5̶0̶	
Demand	5̶0̶	4̶0̶	6̶0̶,10	4̶0̶,30	4̶0̶		
Penalty			0	1			

5→

As tie occurs for highest penalty '1' for Y and D we go for that one which contains a minimum cost cell. Here again there is a tie as both of Y and D contain cells YC and XD with same minimum cost 6. Now we select that cell where more allocations are possible. We can allocate 30 units to XD and 50 units to YC. Hence, select cell YC to make the next allocation.

8. As the table now contains only one row X, we can make the remaining allocations directly to it to get the initial solution as follows:

	A	B	C	D	E	Supply	
X	7	6	⑩ 6	㉚ 6	㊵ 0	80	$u_1=0$
Y	㊿ 5	7	㊿ 6	7	0	100	u_2
Z	8	㊵ 5	8	⑩ 6	0	50	u_3
Demand	50	40	60	40	40	230	
Penalty	v_1	v_2	v_3	v_4	v_5		

Total cost = 10(6) + 30(6) + 40(0) + 50(5) + 50(6) + 40(5) + 10(6) = 1050

Note:
(i) The numbers 1, 2 etc with arrows near the penalty figures indicate the number of the allocation (1st, 2nd etc) that is made in that row or column while the number with arrows near the row and column headings indicates the number of the allocation after which, that row/column gets exhausted or covered.
(ii) The entire procedure can be completed using one table only if it is carried out carefully as done below.

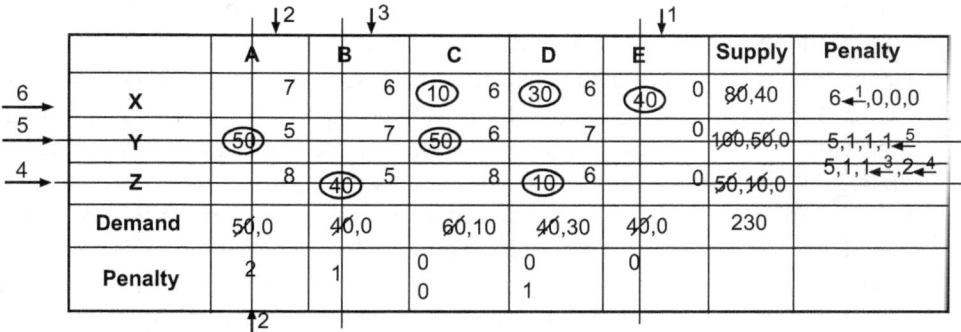

To obtain the optimum solution using MODI method:

9. Verify feasibility of the initial solution: The initial solution has 7 number of independent occupied cells which is equal to (m + n − 1 = 3 + 5 − 1 = 7). Hence, the solution is feasible.

10. To find u_i and v_j:
As row X contains maximum number of occupied cells, let $u_1=0$. Then use the formula ($C_{ij} = u_i + v_j$) for each **occupied cell** to find the remaining row and column numbers as follows.

for XC, $6=u_1+v_3=0+v_3$ ∴ $v_3=6$ for XD, $6=u_1+v_4=0+v_4$ ∴ $v_4=6$
for XE, $0=u_1+v_5=0+v_5$ ∴ $v_5=0$
Now for YC, $6=u_2+v_3=u_2+6$ ∴ $u_2=0$ for YA, $5=u_2+v_1=0+v_1$ ∴ $v_1=5$
for ZD, $6=u_3+v_4=u_3+6$ ∴ $u_3=0$ for ZB, $5=u_3+v_2=0+v_2$ ∴ $v_2=5$

Thus, we have

	A	B	C	D	E	Supply	Row No.
X	7	6	⑩ 6	㉚ 6	㊵ 0	80	$u_1 = 0$
Y	㊿ 5	7	㊿ 6	7	0	100	$u_2 = 0$
Z	8	㊵ 5	8	⑩ 6	0	50	$u_3 = 0$
Demand	50	40	60	40	40	230	
Col. No.	$v_1 = 5$	$v_2 = 5$	$v_3 = 6$	$v_4 = 6$	$v_5 = 0$		

11. Now for each **unoccupied cell**, we compute the opportunity cost (Δ_{ij}) by using the formula $\Delta_{ij} = C_{ij} - (u_i + v_j)$ as follows:

    For XA, $\Delta = 7 - (0 + 5) = 2$ XB, $\Delta = 6 - (0 + 5) = 1$ YB, $\Delta = 7 - (0 + 5) = 2$
    For YD, $\Delta = 7 - (0 + 6) = 1$ YE, $\Delta = 0 - (0 + 0) = 0$ ZA, $\Delta = 8 - (0 + 5) = 3$
    For ZC, $\Delta = 8 - (0 + 6) = 2$ ZE, $\Delta = 0 - (0 + 0) = 0$

12. As all the opportunity costs are (not negative) the solution is optimum. Thus, the optimum plan is X → C(10), X → D(30), Y → A(50), Y → C(50), Z → B(40), Z → D(10) which gives a total minimum cost of transportation = ₹ 1050.

    Note that X → Dummy E (40) has no cost as it is an allocation to a dummy dealer E. This infact indicates the unused capacity of 40kl at location X.

    Note: The same table of initial solution can be used to calculate and write u_i and v_j values. The opportunity costs can be calculated using these values and these are then written down at the bottom left corner of the unoccupied cells in the same table, in order to save time, as done ahead.

13. Multiple Solution: We see that in the optimum table above, the unoccupied cells YE and ZE have '0' opportunity cost. Hence, the problem has multiple solution.

    To obtain the alternate solution we can shift some units to these cells as we do it for cells with highest negative opportunity cost. (Since $\Delta = 0$, the saving in cost per unit shifted is 0. Hence if 'a' number of units are shifted, saving is (a × 0 = 0) i.e. the total cost remains the same, though the allocations are different).

14. (i) Thus, we draw a closed path using only vertical and horizontal lines and taking turns only at occupied cells, for the cell (say) ZE.

	A	B	C	D	E	Supply
X	7	6	⑩ 6	⁺㉚─6	㊵ 0	80
Y	㊿ 5	7	㊿ 6	7	0	100
Z	8	㊵ 5	8	⑩ 6	⁺ 0	50
Demand	50	40	60	40	40	

We also assign (+ve) and (−ve) signs alternately to the corner cells along the path, starting with a (+ve) sign for the unoccupied cell ZE.

(ii) Number of units in cells with (–ve) sign are 10 and 40. Hence, we shift 10 (i.e. least between them) to cell ZE. For this, we add 10 to cells with (+ve) sign and subtract 10 from the cells with (–ve) sign. This gives us an alternate transportation plan as follows:

	A	B	C	D	E	Supply
X	7	6	6 (10)	6 (40)	0 (30)	80
Y	5 (50)	7	6 (50)	7	0	100
Z	8	5 (40)	8	6	0 (10)	50
Demand	50	40	60	40	40	

Here also, Total Cost = 10(6) + 40(6) + 50(5) + 50(6) + 40(5) = 1050

If this plan is followed, 30 units at X and 10 units at Z will be unsued (as being supplied to dummy E).

We can get another plan with same cost = ₹ 1050, by shifting units to the other unoccupied cell YE as follows:

X → C(50), X → D(30), Y → A(50), Y → C(10), Y → Dummy E(40), Z → B(40), Z → D(10)

(C) Case of Degeneracy:

This is said to occur when the number of independent occupied cells (at any solution stage) is less than (m + n – 1). This is resolved as follows:

(i) **For degeneracy at the initial solution:** Assign an artificial quantity ε (epsilon) to one or more of the unoccupied cells, (depending upon the difference in the number of occupied cells and m+n–1) at the independent positions with lowest unit costs. ε remains until the final solution is obtained or the degeneracy is removed, whichever occurs first. (Note that ε is an infinitesimally small positive quantity, so that it does not affect the demand and supply constraints and is just used to occupy a cell temporarily so as to enable further operations).

(ii) **Degeneracy during further stages of solution:** This occurs when the reallocation or shifting of units to an unoccupied cell (in MODI method) vacates two or more occupied cells simultaneously. This is resolved by allotting ε to one or more of the recently vacated cells along the closed path, having lowest unit transportation costs. If there is a tie, assign ε arbitrarily.

Example 7: Solve the following Transportation Problem to minimise the total cost.

Origins	Destinations			Availability
	D_1	D_2	D_3	
O_1	40	70	90	300
O_2	12	80	30	400
O_3	60	90	45	200
Requirement	300	300	300	

Solution: Since Total supply = Total demand = 900, the problem is balanced.

1. Now, using Vogels Approximation Method we get its initial solution as follows:

	D_1	D_2	D_3	Availability	Penalty
O_1	(300) 40	70	90	300, 0	30 ←1
O_2	12	(100) 80	(300) 30	400, 100	18, 50 ←2
O_3	60	(200) 90	45	200	15, 45
Requirement	300, 0	300	300, 0	900	
Penalty	28	10, 10	15, 15		

 ↓1 ↓2 applied to columns; 1← applied to row O_1.

2. Thus, the initial solution has 4 independent occupied cells which is less than (m + n − 1 = 3 + 3 − 1 = 5) by 1. Thus there is a degeneracy. Hence we allocate quantity ε to an independent unoccupied cell with smallest cost i.e. to cell O_2D_1 (Here we can not draw a closed for this cell, hence it is independent, unlike cell O_3D_3). Thus, we have the initial solution with the degeneracy removed as follows.

	D_1	D_2	D_3	Availability
O_1	(300) 40	70	90	300
O_2	(ε) 12	(100) 80	(300) 30	400
O_3	60	(200) 90	45	200
Requirement	300	300	300	

This solution is thus feasible now as it has (m+n−1=5) independent occupied cells.

3. **We use MODI method now for its improvement:** Let $u_2 = 0$ and use $C_{ij} = u_i + v_j$ for **occupied cells** to find u_i and v_j. Then use $\Delta_{ij} = C_{ij} - (u_i+v_j)$ for **unoccupied cells** to get

	D_1	D_2	D_3	Availability	Row No.
O_1	(300) 40	70, −38	32	300	u_1=40−12=28
O_2	(ε) 12	(100) 80	(300) 30	400	u_2=0
O_3	38	(200) 90	5, 45	200	u_3=90−80=10
Requirement	300	300	300		
Col No.	v_1=12−0=12	v_2=80−0=80	v_3=30−0=30		

For O_1, D_2

$\Delta = 70 - (80 + 298) = -38$ etc.

As all Δ_{ij} are not positive, the solution is not optimum and we shift units to cell with highest (–ve) Δ_{ij} i.e. to cell O_1D_2. Number of units to be shifted along its closed path is 100. Thus, we get the first improvement table as follows:

	D_1	D_2	D_3	Availability
O_1	⑳⓪ 40	⑩⓪ 70	90	300
O_2	⑩⓪ 12	80	③⓪⓪ 30	400
O_3	60	⑳⓪ 90	45	200
Requirement	300	300	300	

(1st Improvement Table)

ε is very small
$\therefore \varepsilon + 100 = 100$

It is feasible as it has 5 occupied cells. (Here ε gets removed)

4. Now, for the above table we again use MODI method: Let $u_1 = 0$. Use $C_{ij} = u_i + v_j$ for occupied cells and $\Delta_{ij} = C_{ij} - (u_i + v_j)$ for unoccupied cells.

	D_1	D_2	D_3	Availability	Row No.
O_1	⑳⓪ 40 −	⑩⓪ 70	32 + / 90	300	$u_2=0$
O_2	⑩⓪ 12 +	38 / 80	③⓪⓪ 30 −	400	$u_1=12-40=-28$
O_3	0	60 ⑳⓪ −90	5 / 45 +	200	$u_3=90-70=20$
Requirement	300	300	300		
Col No.	$v_1=40-0=40$	$v_2=70-0=70$	$v_3=30-(-28)=58$		

All opportunity costs are not (+ve). Hence, solution is not optimum. Now, select O_3D_3 ($\Delta = -33$) and draw closed path as shown. We then shift 200 units along the closed path for O_3D_3, to get the second improvement table as follows:

	D_1	D_2	D_3	Availability
O_1	40	③⓪⓪ 70	90	300
O_2	③⓪⓪ 12	80	⑩⓪ 30	400
O_3	60	90	⑳⓪ 45	200
Requirement	300	300	300	

(2nd Improvement Table)

Here, number of occupied cells is 4 which is less than ($m + n - 1 = 5$). This happened as two cells O_1D_1 and O_3D_2 got vacated simultaneously during the reallocation of 200 units. Thus, there is a degeneracy. To resolve it we add ε to the **recently vacated cell with minimum cost**. Hence we add ε to O_1D_1 and proceed further by using MODI method again:

	D_1	D_2	D_3	Availability	Row No.
O_1	ⓔ ⁓ 40	ⓐ⓪⓪ 70	32 ⁓ 90	300	$u_1 = 0$
O_2	③⓪⓪ 12	38 ⁓ 80	ⓐ⓪⓪ 30	400	$u_2 = -28$
O_3	33 ⁓ 60	33 ⁓ 90	②⓪⓪ 45	200	$u_3 = -13$
Requirement	300	300	300		
Col No.	$v_1 = 40$	$v_2 = 70$	$v_3 = 58$		

As all the opportunity costs are positive, the solution is optimum. Thus the transportation plan is $O_1 \to D_2$ (300), $O_2 \to D_1$ (300), $O_2 \to D_3$ (100), $O_3 \to D_3$ (200).

ε being an artificial small quantity, it is ignored.

The total cost = 300(70) + 300(12) + 100(30) + 200(45) = 36,600

(D) Maximisation Problem:

Transportation problem method can be used for a maximisation (say profit maximisation) problem, by converting it into an equivalent minimisation problem as follows:

(i) Write down the profit table (or profit matrix) with given supply, demand and per unit profit figures.

(ii) Add a dummy source or destination to it (with '0' unit profit for its cells) if necessary.

(iii) Locate the largest per unit profit figure in the table and subtract all profit figures (including itself) from it to get an equivalent relative loss matrix.

(iv) Solve it further as a normal transportation problem to get the optimum solution table.

(v) Rewrite the optimum table by replacing the per unit cost figures by the original profit figures and then find the maximum profit for the optimum plan.

Example 8: Solve the following T.P. to maximise profit and give the criteria for optimality

Profit (₹ / Unit)

Origins	Destination				Supply
	1	2	3	4	
A	40	25	22	33	100
B	44	35	30	30	30
C	38	38	28	33	70
Demand	40	20	60	30	

Solution: This is a maximisation problem. It is an unbalanced problem also as total supply (= 200) is more than total demand (= 150).

(i) Therefore first we introduce a dummy destination '5' with its demand = 200 – 150 = 50 and with the unit profit figure for all its cells as 0 (same as in case of minimisation problem). Thus, the profit matrix/table is as follows:

	1	2	3	4	5	Supply
A	40	25	22	33	0	100
B	44	35	30	30	0	30
C	38	38	28	33	0	70
Demand	40	20	60	30	50	Total = 200

(ii) **Obtain the Relative Loss Matrix:** The highest profit figure in the above table is 44 (for B1). Thus, we get the equivalent relative loss matrix by subtracting all the profit figures (including itself) from 44 as follows:

	1	2	3	4	5	Supply
A	4	19	22	11	44	100
B	0	9	14	14	44	30
C	6	6	16	11	44	70
Demand	40	20	60	30	50	

Here, the relative importance or weightage of each cell is maintained eg. The cell B1 (with profit = 44) was the most profitable cell in profit matrix. In relative loss matrix we have the cost for B1 as 0. Hence, again it has become the least cost cell. Thus, its importance is maintained.

(iii) Now, we can solve further by using (VAM+MODI) method to get the optimum plans as follows:

A→1 (20), A→4 (30), A→5 (50), B→1 (20), B→3 (10), C→2 (20), and C→3 (50).

However, for calculating the total profit we must consider the original profit figures for these cells. Thus, we get,

Total profit = 20 (40) + 30 (33) + 0 + 20 (44) + 10 (30) + 20 (38) + 50 (28) = ₹ 5130.

Again here 50 units at A will be actually unutilised (being supplied to dummy destination '5')

(E) Prohibited Routes:

This involves problems where allocation from a source (say X) to a destination (say B) i.e. to cell XB is not permitted or is prohibited. Here we proceed as follows:

(i) For a minimisation problem we assume a very high unit cost (+M or +∞) for cell XB and solve further as usual.

(ii) For a maximisation problem we assume a very low profit (– M or – ∞) for cell XB and solve further as a normal maximisation problem.

Note: This assumption automatically makes that cell unfit for the optimum solution and thus the route gets prohibited.

Example 9: A company receives a particular component required for its production from two suppliers A and B. It has production plants at three locations X, Y and Z. Due to non-availability of proper roads, the plant Y can not receive the material from supplier A. Similarly, plant X can not receive material from supplier B. The weekly requirements of the plants and weekly availability of supply from A and B along with the respective per unit cost of transportation is given below.

	X	Y	Z	Availability
A	9	–	5	45
B	–	7	6	35
Requirement	50	25	25	

Suggest an optimum purchase plan for the company so as to minimize the total transportation cost. Identify the bottlenecks if any.

Solution: It is a problem of prohibited route, as transportation from A to Y and B to X is prohibited. Now as it is a minimisation problem, we assume the unit cost of transportation from A to Y and B to X as $(+\infty)$.

Also since total requirement ($=100$) is more than total availability ($=80$) We introduce a dummy supplier C with its supply $= 100 - 80 = 20$ and with unit cost '0' for all its cells in order to balance the problem. Now, we solve further using VAM to get the following initial solution.

		X	Y	Z	Availability	Row. No.	
	A	(30) 9	∞	(15) 5	45	4,4	
3	B	∞	(25) 7	(10) 6	35,10,0	1,∞	3
1	Dummy C	(20) 0	0	0	20,0	0	
	Requirement	50, 30	25, 0	25, 15	100		
	Penalty	9 ↑₁ ∞	7 ∞ ↑₂	5 1			

The solution is feasible as it has $m+n-1=5$ independent occupied cells. Now, we use MODI method for improvement as follows:

	X	Y	Z	Availability	Row No.
A	(30) 9	∞	(15) 5	45	$u_1 = 0$
B	∞	(25) 7	(10) 6	35	$u_2 = 1$
C	(20) 0 / 3	0 / 4	0	20	$u_3 = -9$
Requirement	50	25	25		
Col. No.	$v_1 = 9$	$v_2 = 6$	$v_3 = 5$		

Note that: for AY, $\Delta = \infty - (0+6) = \infty$

As all the opportunity costs are (+ve) the solution is optimum and hence, the optimum purchase plan will be

Supplier	Plant	No. of units Received	Cost of transportation
A	X	30	30 × 9 = 270
A	Z	15	15 × 5 = 75
B	Y	25	25 × 7 = 175
B	Z	10	10 × 6 = 60
			Total = ₹ 580

Unsatisfied demand of plant X is of 20 units (as it is received from dummy C). This is a bottleneck which must be tackled urgently by the company either by revising its production plan or by say identifying a new supplier etc.

2.8 Note

(i) It is advisable to solve a given transportation problem by using VAM and then MODI method as it gives the optimum solution in minimum number of steps.
(ii) Interchanging the rows and columns for a given T.P. does not affect the solution.

Solved Problems

Problem 1: Obtain the initial solution for the following T.P. by using i) NWCM ii) LCM iii) VAM. Use solution (ii) to obtain the optimum solution further.

	1	2	3	Supply
X	10	3	9	400
Y	12	10	5	300
Z	8	11	12	300
Requirement	200	300	500	

Find the per unit cost for (Z2) so that it is included in the optimum solution.

Solution: It is a balanced T.P. with total demand = total supply = 1000

(i) NWCM

	1	2	3	Supply
X	(200) 10	(200) 3	9	400, 200, 0
Y	12	(100) 10	(200) 5	300, 200, 0
Z	8	11	(300) 12	300
Demand	200, 0	300, 100, 0	500, 300	

Order of allocation: X1, X2, Y2, Y3, Z3   Total Cost = 8200

(ii) LCM

	1	2	3	Supply
X	10	㉚⓪ 3	⑩⓪ 9	4̶0̶0̶,100
Y	12	10	㉛⓪⓪ 5	3̶0̶0̶,0
Z	⓶⓪⓪ 8	11	⑩⓪ 12	3̶0̶0̶, 100
Demand	2̶0̶0̶, 0	3̶0̶0̶, 0	5̶0̶0̶, 200	

Order of allocation: X2, Y3, Z1, X3, Z3   Total Cost = 6100

(iii) VAM

	1	2	3	Supply	Penalty
X	10	㉚⓪ 3	⑩⓪ 9	4̶0̶0̶,100	6,1
Y	12	10	㉛⓪⓪ 5	3̶0̶0̶,0	5,7 _2
Z	⓶⓪⓪ 8	11	⑩⓪ 12	3̶0̶0̶, 100	3,4 _3
Demand	2̶0̶0̶, 0	3̶0̶0̶, 0	5̶0̶0̶, 200		
Penalty	2 2	7	4 3 ↑₁		

(column penalties: ↓3, ↓1 shown above columns 1 and 2; ←2 shown on Y row)

Order of allocation: X2, Y3, Z1, X3, Z3   Total Cost = 6100

The solution is same as that for LCM

Let us use solution in (ii) to get the optimum solution. The initial solution in (ii) is feasible as it has m+n–1=5 number of independent occupied cells.

	1	2	3	Supply	Row No.
X	10 / 5	㉚⓪ 3	⑩⓪ 9	400	$u_1 = 9$
Y	12 / 11	10 / 11	㉛⓪⓪ 5	300	$u_2 = 5$
Z	⓶⓪⓪ 8	11 / 5	⑩⓪ 12	300	$u_3 = 12$
D	200	300	500	1000	
Col No.	$v_1 = -4$	$v_2 = -6$	$v_3 = 0$		

Since all opportunity costs are (+ve), the initial solution is optimum also.

Now, if we want to include cell Z2 in the optimum solution, its opportunity cost must be 0 or negative, so that shifting units to it becomes economical.

DECISION SCIENCES TRANSPORTATION MODELS

Hence, we must have $C_{Z2} - (u_3 + v_2) \leq 0$

i.e. $C_{Z2} - (12 - 6) \leq 0$

i.e. $C_{Z2} - 6 \leq 0$

i.e. $C_{Z2} \leq 6$

Hence, the per unit cost for Z2 must be atleast 6 (or lower) so that Z2 is included in optimum solution.

Problem 2: Solve the following transportation problem.

Source	Destination				Supply
	D_1	D_2	D_3	D_4	
S_1	10	20	5	7	10
S_2	13	9	12	8	20
S_3	4	15	7	9	30
S_4	14	7	1	0	40
S_5	3	12	5	19	50
Demand	60	60	20	10	

Solution: This is a balanced problem with total supply = total demand = 150

Let us use VAM to get initial solution

	D_1	D_2	D_3	D_4	Supply	Penalty
S_1	(10) 10	20	5	7	10,0	2,5,10,4
S_2	13	(20) 9	12	8	20	1,3,4
S_3	(30) 4	15	7	9	30,0	3,3,11,3
S_4	14	(10) 7	(20) 1	(10) 0	40,30,10	1,6,2,7
S_5	(20) 3	(30) 12	5	19	50,30	2,2,9
Demand	60,30,20,0	60	20,0	10,0		
Penalty	1,7,10	2,2,2,5	4	7,1		

Arrows: $\downarrow 5$, $\downarrow 2$, $\downarrow 1$ above; $\rightarrow 4$, $\rightarrow 3$ at left.

Since number of occupied cells = 8 = (m + n−1) ∴ Feasible solution.

For Optimality Test and Improvement we use MODI method

	D_1	D_2	D_3	D_4	Supply	Row No.
S_1	10 ⑩	20 -8	5 -5	7	10	$u_1 = 10$
S_2	13	13 ⑳ 9	12	8 6	20	$u_2 = 0$
S_3	4 ㉚	15 ②	7 0	9 3	30	$u_3 = 4$
S_4	14 16	7 ⑩	1 ⑳	10 0	40	$u_4 = -2$
S_5	3 ⑳	12 ㉚	5 -1	19 14	50	$u_5 = 3$
Demand	60	60	20	10		
Col No.	$v_1 = 0$	$v_2 = 9$	$v_3 = 3$	$v_4 = +2$		

As all opportunity costs are not zero or +ve, solution is not optimum.

∴ Make reallocation to S_1D_3 of 10 units to get the 1st improvement table (S_1D_3 has maximum –ve opportunity cost of –8)

	D_1	D_2	D_3	D_4	Supply	Row No.
S_1	10 8	20 9	5 ⑩	7 3	10	$u_1 = 4$
S_2	13 13	9 ⑳	12 9	8 6	20	$u_2 = 2$
S_3	4 ㉚	15 ②	7 0	9 3	30	$u_3 = 6$
S_4	14 16	7 ⑳	1 ⑩	0 ⑩	40	$u_4 = 0$
S_5	3 ㉚	12 ⑳	5 -1	19 14	50	$u_5 = 5$
Demand	60	60	20	10		
Col No.	$v_1 = -2$	$v_2 = 7$	$v_3 = 1$	$v_4 = 0$		

(1st improvment Table)

Solution is not optimum, therefore make reallocation to S_5D_3 of 10 units.

	D_1	D_2	D_3	D_4	Supply	Row No.
S_1	10 7	20 8	5 ⑩	7 2	10	$u_1 = 0$
S_2	13 13	9 ⑳	12 ⑩	8 6	20	$u_2 = -3$
S_3	4 ㉚	15 ②	7 1	9 3	30	$u_3 = 1$
S_4	14 16	7 ㉚	1 1	0 ⑩	40	$u_4 = -5$
S_5	3 ㉚	12 ⑩	5 ⑩	19 14	50	$u_5 = 0$
Demand	60	60	20	10		
Col No.	$v_1 = 3$	$v_2 = 12$	$v_3 = 5$	$v_4 = 5$		

(2nd improvment Table)

Since all opportunity costs are +ve, the solution is optimum and optimum transportation plan is S_1D_3 (10), S_2D_2 (20), S_3D_1 (30), S_4D_2 (30), S_4D_4 (10), S_5D_1 (30), S_5D_2 (10), S_5D_3 (10) and Total min. transportation cost = $10 \times 5 + 20 \times 9 + 30 \times 4 + 30 \times 7 + 10 \times 0 + 30 \times 3 + 10 \times 12 + 10 \times 5 = ₹ 820$.

Problem 3: A company manufacturing television has four plants with a capacity of 125, 250, 175 and 100 units respectively. The company supplies TV sets to its four showrooms which have a demand of 100, 400, 90 and 60 units respectively. Due to the difference in raw material cost and the transportation cost the profits per unit (in ₹) differ which are given in the following table:

Plants	Showrooms			
	I	II	III	IV
A	90	100	120	110
B	100	105	130	117
C	111	109	110	120
D	130	125	108	113

The demand at showroom I must be supplied from plant A. By using Vogel's Approximation Method, plan the distribution programme so as to maximise the profit. Also determine the maximum total profit.

Solution: As total demand = 100 + 400 + 90 + 60 = 650 and

Total supply = 125 + 250 + 175 + 100 = 650

∴ Its a balanced transportation problem with maximisation as its objective. To get the relative loss matrix we subtract all unit profit figures from the highest figure of 130 (including itself).

Thus, the relative loss matrix is

	I	II	III	IV
A	40	30	10	20
B	30	25	0	13
C	19	21	20	10
D	0	5	12	17

Now, we use it for Vogel's Approximation method to get the initial solution. However, as the demand at showroom I must be supplied from plant A, we make this assignment first, and then use VAM as follows.

DECISION SCIENCES — TRANSPORTATION MODELS

	I	II	III	IV	Capacity	Penalty
A	⑩⓪ 40	㉕ 30	10	20	~~125~~,25	10,10
B	30	⑩⓪ 25	⑨⓪ 0	㉖⓪ 13	~~250~~,~~160~~,100	13←²,12←³
C	19	⑰⑤ 21	20	10	175	10,11
~~D~~	0	⑩⓪ 5	22	17	~~100~~,0	~~12~~
Requirement	1~~00~~,0	4~~00~~,3~~00~~	9~~0~~,0	6~~0~~,0		
Penalty		16 ↑1 4	10 10	3 3		

Arrows: ↓2, ↓3 above III and IV; ←1 at left of Requirement row.

This initial solution has 7 i.e. (m + n – 1) number of independent occupied cells. Hence, it is feasible. Now, we improve it further using modified distribution method as follows:

	I	II	III	IV	Capacity	Penalty
A	⑩⓪ 40	㉕ 30	10 [5]	20 [2]	125	$u_1=30$
B	30 [-5]	⑩⓪ 25	⑨⓪ 0	㉖⓪ 13	250	$u_2=25$
C	19 [-12]	⑰⑤ 21	20 [24]	10 [1]	175	$u_3=21$
D	0 [-15]	⑩⓪ 5	22 [42]	17 [24]	100	$u_4=5$
Requirement	100	400	90	60		
Col No.	$v_1=10$	$v_2=0$	$v_3=-25$	$v_4=-12$		

As there are some unoccupied cells with (-ve) opportunity cost, hence the solution is not optimum. However, if we draw a closed path for any of such cells (BI, CI or DI) and shift some units along it, it will change the allocation of AI (as all their closed paths will have AI as one of the corner cell). But demand at I must be fulfilled by supply from A. Hence, AI must have 100 units. Hence, we cannot improve the solution further under the given conditions. Thus, the solution is optimum. Hence, we have the distribution plan for maximum profit as follows.

From Plant	To Warehouse	No. of units	Profit
A	I	100	100 × 90 = 9000
	II	25	25 × 100 = 2500
B	II	100	100 × 105 = 10500
	III	90	90 × 130 = 11700
	IV	60	60 × 117 = 7020
C	II	175	175 × 109 = 19075
D	II	100	100 × 125 = 12500
			Total Profit = ₹ 72,295

Problem 4: A company manufacturing air coolers has two plants at Mumbai and Calcutta with a capacity of 200 units and 100 units per week respectively. The company supplies the air coolers to its four showrooms situated at Ranchi, Delhi, Lucknow and Kanpur which have maximum demand of 75, 100, 100 and 30 units respectively. Due to the differences in the raw material cost and transportation cost, the profit per unit in rupees differs which is shown in the table below:

	Ranchi	Delhi	Lucknow	Kanpur
Mumbai	90	90	100	110
Calcutta	50	70	130	85

Plan the production programme so as to maximise the profit. The company may have its production capacity at both plants partly or wholly unused.

Solution: Total capacity = 200 + 100 = 300 and Total Demand = 75 + 100 + 100 + 30 = 305

∴ A dummy plant with capacity = (305 − 300) = 5 and unit profit 0 is introduced.

	R	D	L	K	Capacity
M	90	90	100	110	200
C	50	70	130	85	100
Dummy	0	0	0	0	5
Demand	75	100	100	30	305

As it is a maximisation problem, we convert it into a relative loss matrix by subtracting each element from 130 and then solve further using VAM to get the initial solution as:

	R	D	L	K	Capacity	Penalty
M	⑦⓪ 40	⑩⓪ 40	30	㉚ 20	2̶0̶0̶, 1̶7̶0̶, 70	10,20,0
C	80	60	⑩⓪ 0	45	1̶0̶0̶, 0	4̶5̶, 1
Dummy	⑤ 130	130	130	130	5	0,0,0
Demand	75	1̶0̶0̶, 0	1̶0̶0̶, 0	3̶0̶, 0		
Penalty	40 / 90	20 / 90 ↑₃	80	25 / 110 ↑₂		

↓₃ (D), ↓₁ (L), ↓₂ (K), ←₁

Number of occupied cells (=5) < (m + n − 1) (=6)

∴ Case of Degeneracy. ∴ Introduce ε at ML and solve further using MODI method.

	R	D	L	K	Capacity	Row No.
M	+⑦ 40	⑩ 40 −	ε 30	㉚ 20	200	$u_1 = 0$
C	70 80	50 60	⑩ 0	55 45	100	$u_2 = -30$
Dummy	−⑤ 130	0 130 +	10 130	20 130	5	$u_3 = 0$
Demand	75	100	100	30		
Col No.	$v_1 = 40$	$v_2 = 40$	$v_3 = 40$	$v_4 = 20$		

This is an Optimum solution as all opportunity costs are non negative i.e. (Positive or zero). The production programme (considering original per unit profits) is

From	To	No. of Units	Profit		
Mumbai	Ranchi	70	70×90	=	6300
Mumbai	Delhi	100	100×90	=	9000
Mumbai	Kanpur	30	30×110	=	3300
Calucutta	Lucknow	100	100×130	=	13000
			Total Profit	=	31,600

(ε is ignored as it is a very small quantity. Dummy is also neglected as it has 0 profit.)

This problem has multiple solution as Δ for Dummy D is 0. We can get an alternate programme by shifting 5 units to (Dummy D) along the path shown above. This gives the following alternative plan: MR (75), MD (95), ML (ε), MK (30), CL (100), Dummy D (5).

However, Total Profit = ₹ 31,600

Problem 5: The following table shows all the necessary information on the availability of supply to each wearhouse, the requirement of each market and the unit transportation cost from each warehouse to each market.

Warehouse	Market				Supply
	P	Q	R	S	
A	6	3	5	4	22
B	5	9	2	7	15
C	5	7	8	6	8
Requirement	7	12	17	9	

The shipping clerk has worked out the following schedule from experience: 12 units from A to Q, 1 from A to R, 9 from A to S, 15 from B to R, 7 from C to P, 1 from C to R. (i) Check and see if the clerk has optimal schedule. (ii) Find the optimal schedule and minimum total transport cost (iii) The clerk is approached by a carrier to route C to Q, who offers to reduce his rate in the hope of getting some business. By how much the rate should be reduced so that the clerk will offer him the business.

Solution: The given schedule can be written as follows and we use MODI method to test its optimality.

Warehouse	P	Q	R	S	Supply	Row No.
A	6 [4]	3 ⑫	5 ① +	4 ⑨ –	22	$u_1 = 0$
B	5 [6]	9 [9]	2 ⑮	7 [6]	15	$u_2 = -3$
C	5 ⑦	7 [1]	8 ① –	6 [-1] +	8	$u_3 = 3$
Requirement	7	12	17	9	45	
Col No.	$v_1 = 2$	$v_2 = 3$	$v_3 = 5$	$v_4 = 4$		

(i) Since, the opportunity cost at cell CS is –ve, the solution is not optimum and it can be improved by making reallocation of 1 unit to this cell which gives:

Warehouse	P	Q	R	S	Supply	Row No.
A	6 [3]	3 ⑫	5 ②	4 ⑧	22	$u_1 = 0$
B	5 [5]	9 [9]	2 ⑮	7 [6]	15	$u_2 = -3$
C	5 ⑦	7 [2]	8 [1]	6 ①	8	$u_3 = 2$
Requirement	7	12	17	9		
Col No.	$v_1 = 3$	$v_2 = 3$	$v_3 = 5$	$v_4 = 4$		

Now ∵ all opportunity costs are ≥ 0, ∴ the solution is optimum

(ii) ∴ The optimum schedule is

Warehouse	Market	Units	Total cost
A	Q	12	12 × 3 = 36
A	R	2	2 × 5 = 10
A	S	8	8 × 4 = 32
B	R	15	15 × 2 = 30
C	P	7	7 × 5 = 35
C	S	1	1 × 6 = 6
			₹ 149

(iii) For having an allocation from C to Q, the route CQ must be economical i.e. the opportunity cost for the route (ie. cell CQ) must be –ve or at least 0. [Opportunity cost indicates change in cost per unit reallocated to that cell]

i.e. $C_{CQ} - (v_2 + u_3) \leq 0$

i.e. $C_{CQ} - (3 + 2) \leq 0$ ∴ $C_{CQ} \leq 5$

∴ The rate should be reduced atleast to ₹ 5 per unit so as to get the business.

(If $C_{CQ} = 5$, opp. cost = 0 and there can be an alternate schedule. If $C_{CQ} < 5$, reallocation to CQ will only give an optimum schedule).

Thus, the rate must be reduced by atleast ₹ 2 from ₹ 7 to get the business.

Problem 6: In the following T.P. the penalty costs per unit of unsatisfied demand are 15, 13 and 12 for destinations 1, 2 and 3.

Source	Destination			Supply
	1	2	3	
A	15	11	16	15
B	16	14	16	60
C	13	15	18	30
Demand	75	20	50	

Find the optimal solution. Further if the demand at destination 3 must be satisfied exactly, obtain the revised optimal solution.

Solution: (i) We have total supply = 15 + 60 + 30 = 105 and total demand = 75 + 20 + 50 = 145 ∴ we need an extra source 'D' with supply = 145 – 105 = 40. The quantities supplied from the source D to the destinations 1, 2 and 3 indicate the unsatisfied demand at these destinations (as D is a dummy source), the per unit cost (penalty) for which is given. Hence, treating this as the per unit (transportation) cost for the cells D1, D2 and D3 we write the transportation matrix as follows and then use VAM further:

		1	2	3	Supply	Penalty
1 →	A	15	11 ⓐ15	16	1̶5̶, 0	4 1 ←
	B	16 ㊺	14 ⑤	16 ⑩	60	2
3 →	C	13 ㉚	15	18	3̶0̶, 0	2̶
2 →	D	15	13	12 ㊵	4̶0̶, 0	1̶
Demand		7̶5̶, 45	2̶0̶, 5	5̶0̶, 10	145	
Penalty		2 2 3 ↑ 3	2 1 1	4 4 ↑ 2 2		

(Initial Solution)

∵ (No. of occupied cells = 6) = (m + n – 1) ∴ Feasible solution

∴ Use MODI Method for improvement.

	1	2	3	Supply	Row No.
A	15 [2]	11 (15)	16 [3]	15	$u_1 = -3$
B	16 (45)	14 (5)	16 (10)	60	$u_2 = 0$
C	13 (30)	15 [4]	18 [5]	30	$u_3 = -3$
D	15 [3]	13 [3]	12 (40)	40	$u_4 = -4$
Demand	75	20	50		
Col No.	$v_1 = 16$	$v_2 = 16$	$v_3 = 16$		

Since all $\Delta \geq 0$, ∴ Optimum Solution with the allotment as: A2(15), B1(45), B2(5), B3(10), C1(30), D3(40) and

Total Cost = $15 \times 11 + 45 \times 16 + 5 \times 14 + 30 \times 13$ + (Penalty for unsatisfied demand at '3' = 40×12)

= 1345 + 480 = ₹ 1825

(ii) Now, if the demand of 50 units at destination '3' is to be satisfied exactly, the destination '3' should not receive any units from the dummy source D as it implies unsatisfied demand as in the case above. Hence, the allotment to cell D3 must be prohibited. Hence, we consider the per unit cost for cell D3 as ∞ instead of 12 above. Thus, using VAM we get the initial solution as:

		1	2	3	Supply	Penalty
1 →	A	15	11 (15)	16	~~15~~, 0	4 ← 1
	B	16 (10)	14	16 (50)	~~60~~, 10	2, 2
2 →	~~C~~	13 (30)	15	18	~~30~~, 0	~~2~~ ← 2
	D	15 (35)	13 (5)	∞	~~40~~, 35	2, 2, ← 4
Demand		~~75~~, 45	~~20~~, ~~5~~, 0	~~50~~, 0	145	
Penalty		2, 2, 1	2, 1, 1	0, 2, ∞ ↑3		

Arrows: 4 ↓ over column 2, 3 ↓ over column 3.

(No. of occupied cells = 6) = (m + n – 1) ∴ Feasible Solution ∴ Use MODI Method for improvement.

	1	2	3	Supply	Row No.
A	15 2	11 (15)	16 3	15	$u_1 = 13$
B	16 (10) 0	14	16 (50)	60	$u_2 = 16$
C	13 (30) 4	15 5	18	30	$u_3 = 13$
D	15 (35)	13 (5) ∞	∞	40	$u_4 = 15$
Demand	75	20	50		
Col No.	$v_1 = 0$	$v_2 = -2$	$v_3 = 0$		

(Initial Solution)

∴ All $\Delta \geq 0$, ∴ Optimum solution and the optimum schedule is A2(15), B1(10), B3(50), C1(30), D1(35), D2(5) with

Total Cost = $15 \times 11 + 10 \times 16 + 50 \times 16 + 30 \times 13$ + (Penalty Cost = $35 \times 15 + 5 \times 13$)

= $1515 + 525 + 65 = 2105$

Problem 7: Given the following transportation problem:

Ware House	Market			Supply
	A	B	C	
W_1	10	12	7	180
W_2	14	11	6	100
W_3	9	5	13	160
W_4	11	7	9	120
Demand	240	200	220	

It is known that currently no units can be sent from warehouse W_1 to market A and from warehouse W_3 to market C. Determine the least cost transportation schedule. Is the optimal solution obtained by you unique? If not, what is / are the other optimal solution/s.

Solution: We have, Total Supply = 180 + 100 + 160 + 120 = 560 and Total Demand = 240 + 200 + 220 = 660. Hence, a dummy warehouse W_5 with supply capacity = 660 − 560 = 100 units is introduced. Also as the routes W_1A and W_3C are prohibited we consider the corresponding units costs as ∞ and we get the initial solution using VAM as follows:

Market ↓5 ↓3

Warehouse	A	B	C	Supply	Penalty
←4 W_1	∞	12 (60)	7 (120)	180, 60, 0	5 ←3, ∞ ←4
←2 W_2	14	11	6 (100)	100, 0	5 ←2
W_3	9 (20)	5 (140)	∞	160, 20	4, 4 ←5
W_4	11 (120)	7	9	120	2, 4
←1 W_5	0 (100)	0	0	100, 0	0
Demand	240, 140	200, 140, 0	220, 120, 0		
Penalty	9 ↑1 2 2 2	5 2 2 2	6 1 2		

No. of occupied cells = 7 = m + n − 1. ∴ Solution is feasible and we use MODI for optimality and improvement.

Warehouse	Market			Supply	Row No.
	A	B	C		
W_1	∞ ∞	− 12 (60) ←	+ 7 (120)	180	$u_1 = 16$
W_2	+ 14 −1	11 0	6 (100) → −	100	$u_2 = 15$
W_3	9 (20) ← −	5 (140) +	∞ ∞	160	$u_3 = 9$
W_4	11 (120)	7 0	9 7	120	$u_4 = 11$
W_5	0 (100)	0 4	0 9	100	$u_5 = 0$
Demand	240	200	220		
Col No.	$v_1 = 0$	$v_2 = -4$	$v_3 = -9$		

(Initial Solution)
All opportunity costs are not positive. Therefore, the solution is not optimum

∴ Shift 20 units to W_2A along the closed path to get the first improvement table as

Warehouse	Market A	Market B	Market C	Supply	Row No.
W_1	∞ / ∞	12 / 40	7 / 140	180	$u_1 = 15$
W_2	14 / 20 (+) / 0	11	6 / 80 (−)	100	$u_2 = 14$
W_3	9 / 1	5 / 160	∞ / ∞	160	$u_3 = 8$
W_4	11 / 120 (−)	7 / −1 (+)	9 / 6	120	$u_4 = 11$
W_5	0 / 100	0 / 3	0 / 8	100	$u_5 = 0$
Demand	240	200	220		
Col No.	$v_1 = 0$	$v_2 = -3$	$v_3 = -8$		

(1st Improvement Table)

No. of occupied cells = 7 ∴ Feasible Again, as all opportunity costs are not positive, the solution is not optimum. ∴ Shift 40 units to cell W_4B to get the 2nd improvement table as:

Warehouse	Market A	Market B	Market C	Supply	Row No.
W_1	∞ / ∞	12 / 1	7 / 180	180	$u_1 = 15$
W_2	14 / 60	11 / 1	6 / 40	100	$u_2 = 14$
W_3	9 / 0 (+)	5 / 160 (−)	∞ / ∞	160	$u_3 = 9$
W_4	11 / 80 (−)	7 / 40 (+)	9 / 6	120	$u_4 = 11$
W_5	0 / 100	0 / 4	0 / 8	100	$u_5 = 0$
Demand	240	200	220		
Col No.	$v_1 = 0$	$v_2 = -4$	$v_3 = -8$		

(2nd Improvement Table)

Since all the opportunity costs are ≥ 0, ∴ the solution is optimum. Hence the transportation schedule is: W_1 C(180), W_2 A(60), W_2 C(40), W_3 B(160), W_4 A(80), W_4 B(40) with the
Total Cost = $180 \times 7 + 60 \times 14 + 40 \times 6 + 160 \times 5 + 80 \times 11 + 40 \times 7$ = ₹ 4300.

Alternate Solution: Since at W_3 A, Δ = 0. Hence, the problem has an alternative solution which is obtained by shifting 80 units to W_3A along the closed path shown above. This gives us the alternate optimum table as

Warehouse	Market A	Market B	Market C	Supply
W_1	∞	12	7 (180)	180
W_2	14 (60)	11	6 (40)	100
W_3	9 (80)	5 (80)	∞	160
W_4	11	7 (120)	9	120
W_5	0 (100)	0	0	100
Demand	240	200	220	

Hence, the alternate optimal solution is:
W_1 C(180), W_2 A(60), W_2 C(40), W_3A(80), W_3 B(80), W_4 B(120) with Total Cost = ₹ 4300

Problem 8: A company has 4 factories situated at different places in the country and four sales agencies also situated at different places. The cost of production of a unit at a factory varies form factory to factory and sales prices also vary from agency to agency. The table below gives unit transportation cost from factories to sales agencies, production cost and sales price.

Unit Transportation cost ₹

Factory	Sales Agencies				Monthly capacity (units)	Cost of prod. (₹/unit)
	S_1	S_2	S_3	S_4		
F_1	7	5	6	4	10	10
F_2	3	5	4	2	15	15
F_3	4	6	4	5	20	16
F_4	12	7	6	5	15	15
Monthly Requirement (units)	8	12	18	22		
Sales Price ₹	20	22	25	18		

Find the monthly production and distribution schedule which will maximise profit.
(P.U. MBA- Dec 06)

Solution: From the given data, we can find out the profit per unit for the company for each factory-sales agency combination as:

Unit profit = unit sales price − unit production cost − unit transportation cost

Thus, for F_1 - S_1 we have, Unit profit = 20 − 10 − 7 = ₹ 3

Similarly, For F_1 - S_2 we have, Unit profit = 22 − 10 − 5 = ₹ 7 and so on.

Thus, we have the table for unit profits as:

Factory	Sales Agencies				Capacity
	S_1	S_2	S_3	S_4	
F_1	3	7	9	4	10
F_2	2	2	6	1	15
F_3	0	0	5	−3	20
F_4	−7	0	4	−2	15
Requirement	8	12	18	22	

This is a balanced problem since, Total Requirement = Total capacity = 60

Also, as it is a maximisation problem, we convert it into a relative loss matrix by subtracting each element from the highest figure of 9 to get

Factory	Sales Agencies				Capacity
	S_1	S_2	S_3	S_4	
F_1	6	2	0	5	10
F_2	7	7	3	8	15
F_3	9	9	4	12	20
F_4	16	9	5	11	15
Requirement	8	12	18	22	

Applying the Vogel's Approximation Method we get the initial solution as:

	S_1	S_2	S_3	S_4	Capacity	Penalty
F_1	6	(10) 2	0	5	10̶, 0	2
F_2	7	7	3	(15) 8	15̶, 0	4, 0
F_3	(2) 9	9	(18) 4	12	20̶, 2̶, 0	5 ←2, 0
F_4	(6) 16	(2) 9	5	(7) 11	15	4, 2
Requirement	8̶,6	12̶,2	18̶, 0	22̶, 7		
Penalty	1 2 7 ↑4	5 ↑1 2 0	3 1	3 3 ↑3 1		

Number of occupied cells = 7 = m + n −1. Hence feasible solution.

∴ Use MODI method for improvement

	S_1	S_2	S_3	S_4	Capacity	Row No.
F_1	6 -3	2 ⑩	0 -4	5 1	10	$u_1 = -7$
F_2	7 -6 (+)	7 1	3 -5	8 ⑮	15	$u_2 = -3$
F_3	9 ② (+)	9 7	4 ⑱ (−)	12 8	20	$u_3 = -7$
F_4	16 ⑥ (−)	② 	9 -6 (+)	5 11 ⑦ (+)	15	$u_4 = 0$
Requirement	8	12	18	22		
Col.No.	$v_1 = 10$	$v_2 = 9$	$v_3 = 11$	$v_4 = 11$		

(Initial Solution)

All opportunity costs are not positive. Hence the solution is not optimum. We see that there are two unoccupied cells viz. F_2S_1 and F_4S_3 which have the same highest negative opportunity cost i.e.(− 6). Hence, we consider the closed path for each of them to decide the number of units which can be shifted to them and select the one where more units can be shifted. Thus, for F_2S_1 we can shift 6 units along the closed path (shown by the solid arrows). Similarly, for the cell F_4S_3 also we can shift 6 units along the closed path (shown by dotted arrows). Thus, here also there is a tie. Hence, we select one of these cells randomly for shifting. Let us select cell F_2S_1. Thus, by shifting 6 units along the closed path for cell F_2S_1, we get the 1st Improvement Table as:

	S_1	S_2	S_3	S_4	Capacity	Row No.
F_1	6 3	2 ⑩	0 2	5 1	10	$u_1 = -4$
F_2	7 ⑥	7 1	3 1	8 ⑨	15	$u_2 = 0$
F_3	9 ②	9 1	4 ⑱	12 2	20	$u_3 = 2$
F_4	16 6	② 	9 0	5 11 ⑬	15	$u_4 = 3$
Requirement	8	12	18	22		
Col.No.	$v_1 = 7$	$v_2 = 6$	$v_3 = 2$	$v_4 = 8$		

(First Improvement Table)

Since number of occupied cells = 7 = m + n −1, ∴ it is a feasible solution.

Also, since all the opportunity costs ≥ 0. Hence the solution is optimum. Thus, considering the original profit figures, we get the optimum transportation schedule as:

Factory	Sales Agency	Units to be transported	Profit
F_1	S_2	10	$10 \times 7 = 70$
F_2	S_1	6	$6 \times 2 = 12$
F_2	S_4	9	$9 \times 1 = 9$
F_3	S_1	2	$2 \times 0 = 0$
F_3	S_3	18	$18 \times 5 = 90$
F_4	S_2	2	$2 \times 0 = 0$
F_4	S_4	13	$13 \times (-2) = -26$
		Total Profit =	₹ 155

Problem 9: Four hospitals have decided to send their patients needing linear accelerator therapy to three locations in their region. They have contract with an ambulance company which charges ₹ 2/km. Each location can handle only a certain number of outside patients per day. Find the optimal allocation of patients to locations of therapy given the following details:

Hospitals	Distance from locations (kms)			Patients
	A	B	C	
1	17	31	45	5
2	12	14	23	8
3	46	32	13	7
4	38	16	19	5
Place	5	11	5	

(P.U. MBA - Dec. 10)

Solution: This is a transportation problem where the total distance to be traveled is to be minimised (as given data refers to distance to be traveled for moving a patient for each hospital-location combination). Also, Total patients = 25 and Total places = 21. Hence, use a dummy location D with 4 places and '0' distance figures. Now using Vogel's Approximation method we get the Initial Basic Feasible Solution as:

DECISION SCIENCES — TRANSPORTATION MODELS

	A	B	C	D	Patients	Penalty
1	① 17	31	45	④ 0	5,1	17 ←¹,14,14
2	② 12	⑥ 14	23	0	8,2	12,2,2
3	① 46	32	⑤ 13	0	7,2	13,19,←² 14
4	38	⑤ 16	19	0	5,0	16,3,22 ←³
Places	5	11,6,0	5,0	4,0		
Penalty	5 5	2 17 ↑4	6	0		

↓4 ↓2 ↓1 (column arrows) ; ³→ (row arrow at row 4)

Initial Basic Feasible Solution

As it has 7 i.e. (m + n − 1 = 4 + 4 − 1) independent occupied cells, the solution is feasible. Hence use Modified Distribution (MODI) method for improvement as follows:

	A	B	C	D	Patients	Row No. (u)
1	① 17 +	31 12	45 61	→④ 0 −	5	17
2	② 12	⑥ 14 44	23 5	0	8	12
3	② 46 − -16	32	⑤ 13 -29	0 +	7	46
4	24 38	⑤ 16 38	19	3 0	5	14
Places	5	11	5	4		
Col. No. (v)	0	2	−33	−17		

As all opportunity costs, Δ are not positive or zero, solution is not optimum. Hence, we improve it by shifting 2 units cell (3D) along the closed path.

	A	B	C	D	Patients	Row No. (u)
1	③ 17 12	31 32	45	② 0	5	17
2	② 12	⑥ 14 15	23 5	0	8	12
3	29 46	13 32	⑤ 13	② 0	7	17
4	24 38	⑤ 16 9	19 3	0	5	14
Places	5	11	5	4		
Col. No. (v)	0	2	−4	−17		

1ˢᵗ Improvement Table

Solution is feasible. Also, as all Δ are positive, the solution is optimum. Thus, the optimum allocation of patients to the linear accelerator therapy locations is 1 → A(3), 1 → Dummy (2), 2 → A(2), 2 → B(6), 3 → C(5), 3 → Dummy (2), 4 → B(5).

The total (minimum) distance to be traveled is

3(17) + 2(12) + 6(14) + 5(13) + 5(16) = 304 kms.

As the ambulance company charges ₹ 2 km, the cost of transportation = 304 × 2 = ₹ 608.

Problem 10: There are three factories and four warehouses. Unit transportation cost matrix is given as below. Capacities at factories and demand at warehouses is also given. Find optimum solution.

Factory	Warehouse				Capacity (units)
	W_1	W_2	W_3	W_4	
F_1	10	30	50	10	7
F_2	70	30	40	60	9
F_3	40	8	70	20	18
Demand (units)	5	8	7	15	

(P.U. MBA - May 13)

Solution: (Total capacity = 34) ≠ (Total Demand = 35). Hence adding dummy factory and using VAM we get Basic Initial Feasible solution.

	W_1	W_2	W_3	W_4	Cap.	Penalty
F_1	⑤ 10	30	50	② 10	7̸,2̸,0̸	0,20,40
F_2	70	30	⑥ 40	③ 60	9	10,10,20
F_3	40	⑧ 8	70	⑩ 20	1̸8̸,1̸0̸,0	12,12,50
Dummy	0	0	① 0	0	1̸,0	0
Dem.	5̸,0	8̸,0	7̸,6	1̸5̸,5̸,3		
Penalty	10 30 ↑2	8 22 ↑3	40 10 10 ↑1	10 10 50 ↑5		

↓2 ↓3 (top arrows for W_2, W_3)
5→ F_1, 4→ F_3, 1→ Dummy (left arrows)
↑4 (right arrow for F_3 penalty row)

	W₁	W₂	W₃	W₄	Cap.	Row No. (u)
F₁	⑤ 10 | 32 |	30 | 60 |	50	② 10	7	10
F₂	70 | 10 |	30 | -18 |	+ ⑥ 40	③ 60 −	9	60
F₃	40 | 20 |	⑧ 8 | 70 | −	70	⑩ 20	18	20
Dummy	0 | -20 |	0 | -8 |	① − 0	0 | -20 | +	1	20
Dem.	5	8	7	15		
Col. No. (v)	0	-12	-20	0		

Initial Basic Feasible Solution

Occupied cells = 7 = (4 + 4 − 1). Hence feasible. Therefore use MODI.

Some Δ are − ve. Hence, not optimum. Consider Dummy W₁ and Dummy W₄ for shifting. '1' units can be shifted in both cases. Therefore choose randomly say cell (Dummy W₄) for shifting units along its path to get 1st Improvement Table as

	W₁	W₂	W₃	W₄	Cap.	Row No. (u)
F₁	⑤ 10 | 32 |	30 | 60 |	50	② 10	7	10
F₂	70 | 10 |	+ 30 | -18 |	⑦ 40	② 60 −	9	60
F₃	40 | 20 |	⑧ 8 | 70 | −	70	⑩ 20 +	18	20
Dummy	0 | 0 |	0 | 12 |	0 | 20 |	① 0	1	0
Dem.	5	8	7	15		
Col. No. (v)	0	-12	-20	0		

1st Improvement Table

Not optimum as all are not non-negative. Therefore improve by shifting '2' units to F₂W₂.

	W_1	W_2	W_3	W_4	Cap	Row No. (u)
F_1	⑤ 10 [32]	30 [42]	50	② 10	7	10
F_2	70 [28]	② 30	⑦ 40	60 [18]	9	42
F_3	40 [20]	⑥ 8 [52]	70	⑫ 20	18	20
Dummy	0 [0]	0 [12]	0 [2]	① 0	1	0
Dem.	5	8	7	15		
Col. No. (v)	0	−12	−2	0		

2ⁿᵈ Improvement Table

As all $\Delta \geq 0$, the solution is optimum. The optimum allocation is:

$F_1W_1(5)$, $F_1W_4(2)$, $F_2W_2(2)$, $F_2W_3(7)$, $F_3W_2(6)$, $F_3W_4(12)$, Dummy $W_4(1)$ and (minimum) Total Cost = 5(10) + 2(10) + 2(30) + 7(40) + 6(8) + 12(20) = 698.

Exercise

1. How do you express a transportation problem as a linear programming problem?
2. Explain the methods of solving Transportation Problems.
3. Write short notes on:
    (i) Vogel's Approximation Method
    (ii) Degeneracy in T. P.
    (iii) Modified Distribution Method
4. Explain:
    (i) How does a degeneracy occurs in T.P.? How can we deal with it?
    (ii) How to solve a maximisation problem using transportation method?
5. Obtain the initial solution of the following Transportation Problem using
    (i) NWCM (ii) LCM (iii) VAM

	D_1	D_2	D_3	D_4	Supply
O_1	10	20	5	7	10
O_2	13	9	12	8	20
O_3	4	15	7	9	30
O_4	14	7	1	0	40
O_5	3	12	5	19	50
Demand	60	60	20	10	

Ans. (i) NWCM: $O_1 D_1$ (10), $O_2 D_1$ (20), $O_3 D_1$ (30), $O_4 D_2$ (40), $O_5 D_2$ (20), $O_5 D_3$ (20), $O_5 D_4$ (10); Cost = 1290

(ii) LCM: $O_1 D_2$ (10), $O_2 D_2$ (20), $O_3 D_1$ (10), $O_3 D_2$ (20), $O_4 D_2$ (10), $O_4 D_3$ (20), $O_4 D_4$ (10), $O_5 D_1$ (50); Cost = 960

(iii) VAM: $O_1 D_1$ (10), $O_2 D_2$ (20), $O_3 D_1$ (30), $O_4 D_2$ (10), $O_4 D_3$ (20), $O_4 D_4$ (10), $O_5 D_1$ (20), $O_5 D_2$ (30); Cost = 910

6. Obtain an Initial basic feasible solution to the following T. P. Also find an optimal solution of it.

	Warehouses				
Factory	W_1	W_2	W_3	W_4	Capacity
F_1	19	30	50	16	7
F_2	70	30	40	60	9
F_3	40	8	70	20	18
Req.	5	8	7	14	

Ans. $F_1 W_1$ (5), $F_1 W_4$ (2), $F_2 W_2$ (2), $F_2 W_3$ (7), $F_3 W_2$ (6), $F_3 W_4$ (12); Cost = 775

7. Find the optimum solution for the following cost matrix

Unit Transportation Cost (₹)

	D_1	D_2	D_3	D_4	Availability
O_1	20	22	17	04	120
O_2	24	37	09	07	70
O_3	32	37	20	15	50
Demand	60	40	30	110	240

Ans. $O_1 D_1$ (60), $O_1 D_2$ (40), $O_1 D_4$ (20), $O_2 D_3$ (30), $O_2 D_4$ (40), $O_3 D_4$ (50); Cost = 3460

8. Find the optimum solution for

	A	B	C	D	Supply
X	1	2	1	4	30
Y	3	3	2	1	50
Z	4	2	5	9	20
Demand	20	40	30	10	

Find Alternate Solution if any.

Ans. VAM - degeneracy, XA (20), YC(50), ZA(20), ZC(10), Dummy A(ϵ), Dummy B(50); Cost = 150

Alternate: XA (20), YA(20), YC(30), ZC(30), Dummy A(ϵ), Dummy B(50)

9. A Company has four factories F_1, F_2, F_3, and F_4 manufacturing the same product. Production and raw material costs differ from factory to factory and are given in the following table in first two rows. The transportation cost from the factories to the sales depots S_1, S_2, S_3 are also given. The last two columns in the table give the sales price and the total requirement at each depot. The production capacity of each factory is given in the last row.

		F_1	F_2	F_3	F_4	Sales price per unit	Requirement
Production Cost/Unit		15	18	14	13		
Raw Material Cost/Unit		10	9	12	9		
Transportation	S_1	3	9	5	5	34	80
Cost per unit	S_2	1	7	4	5	32	120
	S_3	5	8	3	6	31	150
Production Capacity		10	150	50	100		

Determine the most profitable production and distribution schedule and the corresponding profit. The surplus production should be taken to yield zero profit.

Ans. Hint: maximisation, unit profit = Sales Price − Production Cost − Raw material Cost − Transportation Cost

$F_1 S_2$ (10), $F_2 S_2$ (90), $F_2 S_3$ (60), $F_3 S_3$ (50), $F_4 S_1$ (80), $F_4 S_2$ (20), Dummy S_3 (40); Profit = 480

10. A Company has three plants W, X and Y and three warehouses A, B, C. The supplies are transported from the plants to the warehouses which are located at varying distances from the plants. Due to this, the transportation costs from plants to warehouses vary from ₹ 8 to ₹ 24 per unit.

The company wishes to minimise the transportation costs. The costs (in ₹) from the plants to the warehouses are shown in the form of a matrix. Determine the optimum shipping schedule. Use LCM for initial solution.

Plant	Warehouse			Supply
	A	B	C	
W	12	8	18	400
X	20	10	16	350
Y	24	14	12	300
Demand	500	200	300	

Ans. Degeneracy - Twice, WA (400), XB (200), XC (150), YC (150), Dummy A (100), Dummy C (ε); Cost = 11,000.

11. A Company produces three kinds of dolls A, B and C. Their monthly production is 1000 units, 2000 units and 3000 units respectively. The dolls are sold through departmental stores X, Y and Z. 1500 units are to be supplied to each of the stores every month. However, store Z does not want any doll of type A. Profit per unit on the dolls sold to each of the stores is given below.

Dolls	Stores		
	X	Y	Z
A	15	10	–
B	16	8	9
C	12	9	11

The inventory carrying cost, for the unsold dolls is ₹ 1 per unit per month for the Company. Suggest optimum policy schedule and find the relevant profit.

Ans. Maximisation + Prohibited route. AY(1000), BX(1500), B Dummy(500), CY(500), CZ(1500), C Dummy (1000); Profit = 55000 – (1000 + 500) (1) = 53500.

12. A company has three warehouses A, B and C and four stores W, X, Y, Z. The warehouses have altogether a surplus of 150 units of a given commodity and the stores need the same as follows:

Warehouses	A	B	C	Stores	W	X	Y	Z
Units Available	50	60	40	Units Demanded	20	70	50	10

Cost in ₹ of shipping one unit of commodity from various warehouses to different stores are as follows:

Warehouses	Stores			
	W	X	Y	Z
A	50	150	70	60
B	80	70	90	10
C	15	87	79	80

Find optimum allocation and associated cost.

Ans. Degeneracy, AY (50), AZ (ε), BX (50), BZ (10), CW (20), CX (20); Cost = 9140.

13. A company has factories at A, B and C which supply warehouses at D, E, F and G. Monthly capacities are 160, 150, and 190 units respectively. Monthly warehouse requirements are 80, 90, 110 and 160 units respectively. Unit shipping costs (₹) are given as follows:

		To			
		D	E	F	G
From	A	12	18	8	7
	B	10	19	22	21
	C	3	8	10	13

What is the optimal shipping cost schedule?

Ans. Unbalanced, degeneracy; AG (160), BD(80), BE(10), B Dummy (60), CE(80), CF(120), Cost = 3850

14. Solve the following transportation problem given the unit transportation costs, demand and supply as below:

Sources	Warehouses			Supply
	A	B	C	
1	5	1	7	10
2	6	4	6	80
3	3	2	5	15
Demand	75	20	50	

(P.U. MBA - May 05, May 07)

Ans. Unbalanced 1B(10), 2A(60), 2B(10), 2C(10), 3A(15), Dummy C(40), Cost = 515.

15. Write short notes on: Uses of transportation models. **(P.U. MBA - May 05)**

16. A cement company has three factories which manufacture cement which is transported to four distribution centres. The quantity of monthly production of each factory, the demand of each distribution centre and associated transportation cost per quintal are given below:

Factory	Distribution centers				Monthly production (in quintals)
	W	X	Y	Z	
A	10	8	5	4	7000
B	7	9	15	8	8000
C	6	10	14	8	10000
Monthly demand (in quintal)	6000	6000	8000	5000	

Find the optimal solution. **(P.U. MBA - Nov 07)**

Ans. AY(7000), BX(6000), BZ(2000), CW(6000), CY(1000), CZ(3000), Cost = 179000

17. The products of 3 plants X, Y, Z are to be transported to 4 warehouses I, II, III, IV. The cost of transportation of each unit from the plant to the warehouses along with normal capacities of plants and warehouses are indicated below:

Plants	Warehouses				Availability
	I	II	III	IV	
X	25	17	25	14	300
Y	15	10	18	24	500
Z	16	20	08	13	600
Requirement	300	300	500	500	

(i) Solve the problem for minimum cost of transport.

(ii) Does there exist any alternative solution. **(P.U. MBA - May 08)**

Ans. (i) Unabalanced XIV(300), YI(200), YII(300), ZIII(500), ZIV(100), Cost = 15500, (ii) No

18. A steel company has three open hearth furnaces and five rolling mills. Transportation cost (₹ per ton) for shipping steel from furnaces to rolling mills are shown n the following table:

Furnaces	Mills					Capacity
	M_1	M_2	M_3	M_4	M_5	
F_1	4	2	3	2	6	8
F_2	5	4	5	2	1	12
F_3	6	5	4	7	3	14
Demand	4	4	6	8	8	

What is the optimal shipping cost schedule. **(P.U.MBA - May 04)**

Ans. Unbalanced, degeneracy; F_1M_2 (4), F_1M_4 (4), F_2M_4 (4), F_2M_5 (8), F_3M_1 (4), F_3M_6 (6), F_3 Dummy (4), Cost = ₹ 80. 4Tonns at F_3 will not be transported.

19. A manufacturer of jeans is interested in developing an advertising campaign that will reach 4 different age groups. Advertising campaign can be conducted through TV, Radio and magazines. The following table gives estimated cost per exposure for each group in appropriate units of money, according to medium employed. The maximum exposure levels possible in each of the media TV, radio, and magazine are 40, 30 and 20 million respectively. Also desired exposures in each age groups 12-18, 19-25, 26-35 and 36 and above are 30, 25, 15 and 10 million. The objective is to m nimise the cost of obtaining the minimum exposure level in each age group.

Media	Age Group			
	12-18	19-25	26-35	36 and above
TV	12	7	10	10
Radio	10	9	12	10
Magazine	14	12	9	12

Formulate above problem as transportation problem and find the optimal solution.

(P.U. MBA - Dec. 05)

Ans. Unbalanced + degeneracy; TV 19-25 (25), TV 36 and (10), TV Dummy (5), Radio 12-18 (30), Radio Dummy (ϵ), Magazine 26-35 (15), Magazine Dummy (5), Cost = 710 units.

20. A company has three plants and four warehouses. The supply and demand in units and the corresponding transportation costs are given. The table below has been taken from the solution procedure of a transportation problem.

Unit Transportation Cost

Plants	Warehouses				Supply
	I	II	III	IV	
A	5	10	4	5	10
B	6	8	7	2	25
C	4	2	5	7	20
Demand	25	10	15	5	55

The present distribution pattern is as follows: A to III - 10 units, B to I - 20 units, B to IV - 5 units, C to I - 5 units, C to II = 10 units, C to III - 5 units. Answer the following questions (i) Is the solution feasible? Why? (ii) Is the solution degenerate? Why? (iii) Is the solution optimum? Why? (iv) Does the problem have more than one optimum solution? If so, show all of them.

(P.U. MBA - Dec. 08)

Ans. (i) Yes, $m + n - 1 = 6$ occupied cells, (ii) No. feasible and so no independent unoccupied cell (iii) Yes, All $\Delta \geq 0$, (iv) Yes. Δ at B - III is 0. Alternative solution, A III (10), BI (15), B III (5), B IV (5), C I (10), C II (10), Cost = 235.

21. Find the initial basic feasible solution of the following transportation problem using (i) Northwest Corner method (ii) Matrix minimum method and (iii) Vogel's Approximation Method. Also find the corresponding costs.

Factory	Warehouses				Capacity (Units)
	A	B	C	D	
X	11	31	51	11	7
Y	71	31	41	61	9
Z	41	9	71	21	18
Requirement (Units)	5	8	7	15	

(P.U. MBA - May 09)

Ans. (i) NWCM - XA(5), XB(2), YB(6), YC(3), ZC(4), ZD(14), Dummy D(1), Cost = 1304, (ii) Matrix Minima (LCM) - Dummy A(1), ZB(8), XD(7), ZD(8), YC(7), YA(2), ZA(2), Cost=828, (iii) VAM - Dummy C(1), XA(5), ZB(8), ZD(10), XD(2), YC(6), YD(3), Cost = 788.

22. Solve the transportation problem for maximum profit

Per Unit Profit (₹)

Warehouse	Market			
	A	B	C	D
X	12	18	6	25
Y	8	7	10	18
Z	14	3	11	20

Availability at warehouses : X = 200, Y = 500, Z = 300 units

Demand in the markets: A = 180, B = 320, C = 100, D = 400 units

(P.U. MBA - Dec. 11)

Ans. Maximisation, XB(200), YB(120), YD(380), ZA(180), ZC(100), ZD(20), Profit = ₹ 15,300.

23. Solve the following transportation problem for minimisation

Sources	Destinations				Available Units
	D_1	D_2	D_3	D_4	
S_1	8	6	9	5	35
S_2	2	1	6	3	42
S_3	5	6	7	8	37
Demand	21	23	25	16	

(P.U. MBA - May 12)

Ans. Unbalanced, $S_1D_1(16)$, S_1 Dummy (19), $S_2D_1(19)$, $S_2D_2(23)$, $S_3D_1(2)$, $S_3D_3(25)$, S_3 Dummy (10); Cost = 326.

■■■

Chapter 3...

Assignment Models

Contents ...
3.1 Introduction
3.2 Hungarian Method of Solution / Flood's Technique
3.3 Special Cases in Assignment Problems
    Solved Problems
    Exercise

3.1 Introduction

Assignment is a typical optimisation technique practically useful in a situation where a certain number of tasks are required to be assigned to an equal number of facilities, on a one to one basis, so that the resultant effectiveness is optimised. e.g. Jobs to be assigned to machines or workers, salesmen to the sales territories, vehicles to routes etc.

Note: Assignment problem is a case of transportation problems where the number of sources is equal to the number of destinations (i.e. m = n or number of rows = number of columns) and the supply and demand figures for each of the sources and destinations is one.

Thus, a typical assignment problem is as follows:

Assignment Problem: With the available information about the payoffs (i.e. cost, efficiency, time etc.) C_{ij} for each task (i) and facility (j) combination, where i = 1, 2, 3, ... r and j = 1, 2, 3 ..... n (i.e. for n number of tasks and facilities) the problem is to determine the assignment of the n tasks to the n facilities (on a one to one basis) such that the total pay-off is optimised.

This can be formulated mathematically as,
Let x_{ij} = 1, if a task i is assigned to the jth facility and
    x_{ij} = 0, if task i is not assigned to the jth facility
Then, the objective is to Optimise (minimise or maximise) total pay off

$$Z = \sum_{i=1}^{n} \sum_{j=1}^{n} C_{ij} x_{ij}$$

subject to the constraints
(i) Each task is to be assigned to one and only one facility.
   i.e. $x_{i1} + x_{i2} + ... + x_{in} = 1$ for i = 1, 2, ... n
   i.e. $\sum_{j=1}^{n} x_{ij} = 1,$ i = 1, 2, ... n

(ii) Each facility must be assigned to one and only one task

i.e. $x_{1j} + x_{2j} + ... + x_{nj} = 1$ for $j = 1, 2, ... n$

i.e. $\sum_{i=1}^{n} x_{ij} = 1, \quad j = 1, 2, ... n$

(iii) $x_{ij} = 0$ or 1 for all i and j

This problem can be solved by using the transportation problem methods. However, it can be solved more efficiently and quickly by using an assignment problem method known as the 'Hungarian Method of Solution' or 'Flood's Technique' which is based on the concept of opportunity cost.

An Assignment Table or Matrix used in the Hungarian method consists of n rows (for say jobs 1, 2, 3, 4 etc.) and n columns (for machines A, B, C, D etc.) and its elements indicate the effectiveness (say time required for each machine to perform each of these four jobs) as:

Jobs	Machines			
	A	B	C	D
1	10	12	11	16
2	8	6	5	7
3	11	10	8	12
4	7	7	6	9

3.2 Hungarian Method of Solution / Flood's Technique

This method is useful for a balanced (i.e. n × n) assignment problem where the objective is of minimisation. It is based on the use of opportunity cost.

Step 1: In the given (n × n) assignment table or matrix, subtract the smallest element or number in each row from every element in that row.

Step 2: Subtract then, the smallest element in each column from every element of that column so as to get a reduced assignment matrix. (Steps 1 and 2 can be interchanged)

Step 3: Draw minimum number of vertical and horizontal lines necessary to cover all the zeroes in the reduced matrix, by inspection. Start with the row or column having maximum number of zeroes to draw the lines. Now,

(a) If the number of lines = number of rows/columns (i.e. n), it implies that the solution is optimum. Then go to step 4.

(b) If the number of lines is less than n, then the solution is not optimum and it needs further improvement. Then go to step 5.

Step 4: Make the assignments as follows:
(i) Check the rows successively. Mark a square ☐ around a 'single unmarked (i.e. free) zero' in a **row** (if present) and cancel all the other zeroes in its **column**.
(ii) Check the columns successively, Mark a square ☐ around a 'single unmarked zero' in a **column** (if present) and cancel all other zeroes in its **row**.
(iii) Repeat steps (i) and (ii) above until all the zeroes in the matrix are either marked with a ☐ or cancelled out.

Now, the squared zeroes represent the assignments and if there is exactly one assignment in each row and column, it indicates an optimum solution. Consider then the corresponding elements in the original matrix to find out the optimum value of the pay-off (time, cost etc.)

Step 5: If the solution is not optimum, then
(i) Select the smallest element among all the uncovered elements of the reduced matrix.
(ii) Subtract it from all the uncovered elements and add it to the elements at the intersection of the lines, keeping other elements unchanged.

Then, go to step 3 (draw lines) and repeat the procedure until the number of assignments is equal to the number of rows or columns i.e. the optimum solution is obtained.

Note: If we make assignments without drawing the lines, then we get n assignments (one in each row and column) if the solution is optimum. Otherwise we get less than n number of assignments which indicates that the solution is not optimum and it needs further improvement.

Example 1: Consider a job which requires four activities - cutting, assembly, finishing and packaging. Four workers are employed who can do all these activities. The time required by each of them (in minutes) to perform each of the activities are as follows:

Activities	Workers			
	1	2	3	4
C	14	12	15	15
A	21	18	18	22
F	14	17	12	14
P	6	5	3	6

How should these activities be assigned to the workers so that the job is completed in minimum time?

Solution:

1. Subtract the smallest element in each row from all the elements of that row. (e.g. subtract 12 from all the elements of row one, subtract 18 from all the elements of row two and so on.) Thus we get,

	1	2	3	4
C	2	0	3	3
A	3	0	0	4
F	2	5	0	2
P	3	2	0	3

2. Now, on subtracting the smallest element in each column from all the elements of that column (e.g. subtracting 2 from all the elements in column 1, subtracting 0 from all the elements in column 2 and so on), we get the reduced matrix as:

	1	2	3	4
C	0	0	3	1
A	1	0	0	2
F	0	5	0	0
P	1	2	0	1

   (The second and third columns remain unchanged as the smallest element is 0)

3. Draw minimum number of lines to cover all the zeroes:

   Column 3 contains maximum number of zeroes. Hence, draw the first line along column 3. Now, rows C and F contain two zeroes each. Therefore, draw second and third line along them. To cover the remaining single zero at A2 draw line along (row A or column 2).

   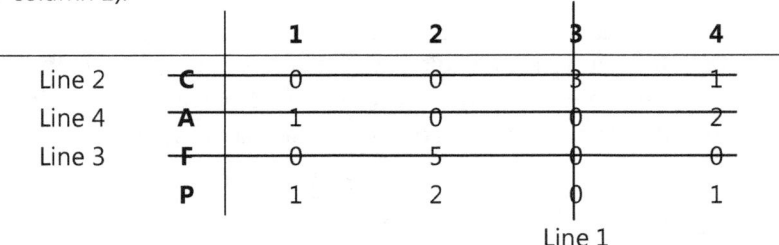

   Thus, we need minimum 4 lines (which is equal to the number of rows) to cover all the zeroes in the reduced matrix. Hence, the solution is optimum and so we make the assignments as follows:

4. Make assignments:
   (i) Choose the rows successively. First three rows have more than one unmarked zeroes (i.e. zeroes without a ☐ or cancelled out). Hence, ignore them. But in the fourth row there is a single unmarked zero in column 3 i.e. at (P3).

Hence mark it with a square ☐ and cancel all other zeroes in its column 3 as shown.

	1	2	3	4
C	0	0	3	1
A	1	0	✗	2
F	✗	5	✗	[0]
¹→P	1	2	[0]	1
				↑2

(ii) Now, proceed columnwise. First two columns have more than one unmarked zeroes. Hence neglect them. Third column has all the zeroes as marked (☐ or cancelled). Hence neglect it. But fourth column has a single unmarked zero in the third row at F4. Hence mark it with ☐ and cancel all the other zeroes in row F (F3 is already cancelled out).

(iii) Repeat steps (i) and (ii): Now we again go rowwise. As row (C) contains two unmarked zeroes, neglect it. But row A now contains only one **unmarked zero** at A2 (zero at A3 is cancelled already).

	1	2	3	4
C	[0]	✗	3	1
³→A	1	[0]	✗	2
F	✗	5	✗	[0]
¹→P	1	2	[0]	1
	↑4			↑2

Hence, mark it with ☐ and cancel other zeroes in column 2. Row F and P already have an assignment. Now, proceeding columnwise, we make last assignment at C1 in column 1 (as it is the single unmarked zero in column 1 now), so that all the zeroes in the table are either marked ☐ or cancelled out.

5. The zeroes marked with ☐ represent the assignments. As there are 4 assignments (which is equal to the number of rows or columns), with each row and column having exactly one, the solution is optimum. Hence, considering the original table we have the optimum assignment plan as:

Activity ⟶ Worker		Time Required
Cutting	1	14
Assembly	2	18
Finishing	4	14
Packaging	3	3
		Total = 49 minutes (which is minimum)

DECISION SCIENCES ASSIGNMENT MODELS

Example 2: Solve the following assignment problem for minimisation:

	1	2	3	4	5
A	8	8	8	11	12
B	4	5	6	3	4
C	12	11	10	9	8
D	18	21	18	17	15
E	10	11	10	8	12

Solution:

1. Row Subtraction: Subtracting smallest element in each row from all its elements we get the matrix as shown.

	1	2	3	4	5
A	0	0	0	3	4
B	1	2	3	0	1
C	4	3	2	1	0
D	3	6	3	2	0
E	2	3	2	0	4

2. Column Subtraction: Subtract then the smallest element in each column from all its elements. Since all the columns have zero as the smallest element, all of them remain unchanged. Thus, we have got the reduced matrix.

3. Draw minimum number of lines so as to cover all the zeroes in the reduced matrix.

   (i) Row A has maximum number of zeroes. Hence, draw first line along row A.

   (ii) Columns 4 and 5 have two zeroes each. Hence, draw vertical lines to cover them.

   (iii) Thus, all the zeroes are covered using three lines only which is less than the number of rows i.e. 5. Hence, the solution is not optimum. Hence we improve it as follows:

	1	2	3	4	5
A	0	0	0	3	4
B	1	2	3	0	1
C	4	3	2	1	0
D	3	6	3	2	0
E	2	3	2	0	4

4. First improvement:

   (i) Select the smallest element among all the uncovered elements. It is the element 1.

(ii) **Subtract** it from all the **uncovered** elements in the matrix and **add** it to the elements (3 and 4) at the **intersection** of the lines. Keep the other elements unchanged.

	1	2	3	4	5
A	0	0	0	4	5
B	0	1	2	0	1
C	3	2	1	1	0
D	2	5	2	2	0
E	1	2	1	0	4

First Improvement Matrix

5. Repeat the procedure: Now for the first improvement matrix, we can see that only 4 lines will be required to cover all its zeroes. (Row A contains maximum number of zeroes. Hence, draw first line along A. Draw second line along B as it has two zeroes. Draw the third line along column 5 as it also has two zeroes and draw the fourth line along row E or column 4 to cover the remaining zero at E4.

(We can draw lines in other manner as well so as to cover all the zeroes using minimum number of lines).

	1	2	3	4	5
A	0	0	0	4	5
B	0	1	2	0	1
C	3	2	1	1	0
D	2	5	2	2	0
E	1	2	1	0	4

Thus, as the minimum number of lines required (i.e. 4) is less than the number of rows (i.e. 5), the solution is not optimum and we improve it again as follows.

6. We subtract the smallest uncovered element (which is 1) from all the uncovered elements and add it to the elements at the intersection of the lines to get the second improvement matrix as shown.

	1	2	3	4	5
A	0	0	0	4	6
B	0	1	2	0	2
C	2	1	0	0	0
D	1	4	1	1	0
E	1	2	1	0	5

Second Improvement Matrix

This matrix needs minimum 5 lines (= No. of rows) to cover all its zeroes. Hence, it is an optimum solution.

7. **Make Assignments:**
   (i) **Choose the rows successively:** Rows A, B, C contain more than one unmarked zeroes. Hence, neglect them. Row D contains single unmarked zero at D5. Hence, mark it with a square ☐ to make the first assignment and cancel all other zeroes in column 5. Similarly, for row E make the second assignment at E4 and cancel all other zeroes in column 4.

	1	2	3	4	5
A	0	0	0	4	6
B	0	1	2	✗	2
C	2	1	0	✗	✗
¹→D	1	4	1	1	[0]
²→E	1	2	1	[0]	5

   (ii) **Proceed columnwise:** Neglect Column 1 as it has 2 unmarked zeroes. Make the third assignment at A2 (single unmarked zero) in column 2 and then cancel all other zeroes in row A. Now, in column 3 there is only one unmarked zero at C3 (zero at A3 has been just cancelled out). Hence, mark it with a square ☐ i.e. make the 4th assignment. The other zeroes in row C are already cancelled out.

   (iii) Now, again proceeding rowwise we make the last assignment at B1 to get the optimum assignment policy as follows: A → 2, B → 1, C → 3, D → 5, E → 4 and hence by using the original table we have, minimum cost = 8 + 4 + 10 + 15 + 8 = 45.

	1	2	3	4	5
A	✗	[0]	✗	4	6
⁵→B	[0]	1	2	✗	2
C	2	1	[0]	✗	✗
¹→D	1	4	1	1	[0]
²→E	1	2	1	[0]	5
		↑3	↑4		

3.3 Special Cases in Assignment Problems

(A) Unbalanced Problems:

When the number of rows is not equal to the number of columns, it is an unbalanced assignment problem. Here we add the required number of dummy rows or columns with all its elements as 0, to the matrix, so as to make it a square matrix (i.e. balanced). Use Hungarian method to solve the problem further. The assignment in the dummy row or column indicates an idle facility or task.

Example 3: The personnel manager of ABC Co. wants to assign Mr. X, Y and Z to the regional offices for which the costs are given. But the firm also has an opening in its Chennai office and would send one of them to that branch if it is more economical than a move to Delhi, Mumbai or Kolkata.

Mr. \ Office	D	M	K
X	1600	2000	2400
Y	1000	3200	2600
Z	1000	2000	4600

It will cost ₹ 2,000/- to relocate Mr. X to Chennai, ₹ 1,600/- to relocate Mr. Y there and ₹ 3,000/- to move Mr. Z. What is the optimum assignment of personnel to the offices ?

Solution:

1. From the given information we can add the fourth column corresponding to the Chennai office to the given cost matrix, which makes it a (3 × 4) matrix. Hence, it is an unbalanced problem. Thus, to balance it we add a dummy row with all its cost elements as '0' as shown.

Mr. \ Office	D	M	K	C
X	1600	2000	2400	2000
Y	1000	3200	2600	1600
Z	1000	2000	4600	3000
Dummy	0	0	0	0

2. We use Hungarian method further to solve it as a normal assignment problem as follows:

Mr. \ Office	D	M	K	C
X	1600	2000	2400	2000
Y	1000	3200	2600	1600
Z	1000	2000	4600	3000
Dummy	0	0	0	0

→

Mr. \ Office	D	M	K	C
X	0	400	800	400
Y	0	2200	1600	600
Z	0	1000	3600	2000
Dummy	0	0	0	0

Row Subtraction (Reduced matrix)

As all columns have '0' as the smallest element, column subtraction results in the same matrix. Thus, we have got the reduced matrix.

3. We need 2 lines to cover all the zeroes which is less than the number of rows (4).

Office\Mr.	D	M	K	C
X	~~0~~	400	800	400
Y	~~0~~	2200	1600	600
Z	~~0~~	1000	3600	2000
~~Dummy~~	~~0~~	~~0~~	~~0~~	~~0~~

Reduced Matrix

∴ Solution is not optimum.
∴ We subtract smallest uncovered element (400) from all the uncovered elements and add it to the element at the intersection of the lines to get the first improvement matrix as follows:

Office\Mr.	D	M	K	C
~~X~~	~~0~~	~~0~~	~~400~~	~~0~~
Y	0	1800	1200	200
Z	0	600	3200	1600
~~Dummy~~	400	~~0~~	~~0~~	~~0~~

1st Improvement Matrix

4. Now, we need 3 lines (i.e. < 4) to cover all zeroes. ∴ solution is not optimum. Thus, again using the smallest uncovered element (200), we improve it to get the second improvement matrix as shown below.

Office\Mr.	D	M	K	C
~~X~~	~~200~~	[0]	~~400~~	✗
3→ Y	✗	1600	100	[0]
1→ Z	[0]	400	3000	1400
~~Dummy~~	~~400~~	✗	[0]	✗
		↑4	↑2	

2nd Improvement Matrix

5. Here we need minimum 4 (= No. of rows) lines to cover all the zeroes. Hence, the solution is optimum and we make the assignments at the single unmarked zeroes, as shown.

Thus, the optimum assignment policy is:
X → Mumbai, Y → Chennai, Z → Delhi and Dummy → Kolkata i.e. nobody is assigned to Kolkata.

The total minimum cost of assignment = 2000 + 1600 + 1000 = ₹ 4600.

(B) Multiple Optimum Solutions:

If after making the assignments (i.e. after marking the zeroes with □) to the single unmarked zeroes in all possible rows and columns, it is found that two or more rows or columns still contain more than one unmarked zeroes, then the problem has multiple optimum solution. Then to get the alternate solutions:
  (i) Select the row or column containing maximum number of unmarked zeroes (after making assignments to the single unmarked zeroes).
  (ii) Select one of these unmarked zeroes and mark it with a square □.
  (iii) Cancel all other zeroes in its **row as well as column**.
  (iv) Proceed further in usual manner to make other assignments.
  (v) Repeat the procedure by making assignment to each of the zeroes in the row or column selected in (i) above, separately, to get the alternate solutions.
  (vi) All these alternate solutions give the same optimum value.

Example 4: Solve the following problem of assigning 4 computer programmers to 4 application programmes, where the estimated computer time in minutes required by each of them to develop the programmes is given.

		\multicolumn{4}{c}{Programmers}
		1	2	3	4
Programs	A	120	100	80	90
	B	80	90	110	70
	C	110	140	120	100
	D	90	90	80	90

Solution:

	1	2	3	4
A	120	100	80	90
B	80	90	110	70
C	110	140	120	100
D	90	90	80	90

→

	1	2	3	4
A	40	20	0	10
B	10	20	40	0
C	10	40	20	0
D	10	10	0	10

Row Subtraction

→

	1	2	3	4
A	~~30~~	~~10~~	~~0~~	~~10~~
B	~~0~~	~~10~~	~~40~~	~~0~~
C	~~0~~	~~30~~	~~20~~	~~0~~
D	~~0~~	~~0~~	~~0~~	~~10~~

Column Subtraction (Reduced Matrix)

As minimum 4 lines, which is equal to the number of rows or columns, are required to cover all the zeroes, the solution is optimum.

∴ Make assignments to single unmarked zeroes as done previously.

	1	2	3	4
A	30	10	[0]	10
B	0	10	40	0
C	0	30	20	0
D	✗	[0]	✗	10

Thus we can make assignments at A3 and D2, as shown.

But rows B and C and columns 1 and 4 still have two unmarked zeroes each (where we can not make the assignments further, using the single unmarked zeroes).

1. Thus, the problem has multiple optimum solution and we can get the alternate solutions as follows:
   (i) All B, C, 1 and 4 have same i.e. 2 unmarked zeroes.
      ∴ Select any one of them, say (B).
   (ii) Make assignment at B1 and cancel all the zeroes in its **row (B) as well as column (1)**.
   (iii) The remaining assignment is made at C4 which is the single unmarked zero now in C.

	1	2	3	4
A	30	10	[0]	10
B	[0]	10	40	⌧
C	⌧	30	20	[0]
D	⌧	[0]	⌧	10

Thus, we have the optimum assignments as:

A → 3, B → 1, C → 4, D → 2 and min. Time = 80 + 80 + 100 + 90 = 350 minutes.

2. For the second optimum solution, make assignment at B4 in row B (instead of B1). Cancel all other zeroes in row B and column 4 and make the last assignment at C1.

	1	2	3	4
A	30	10	[0]	10
B	⌧	10	40	[0]
C	[0]	30	20	⌧
D	⌧	[0]	⌧	10

Thus, the alternate assignment is

A → 3, B → 4, C → 1, D → 2 with same minimum time = 80 + 70 + 110 + 90 = 350 minutes.

(C) Maximisation Problems:

The Hungarian method for minimisation problems can be used to solve the maximisation problems as follows:

(i) Convert the given profit matrix into a relative loss matrix (or opportunity loss matrix) by subtracting all its elements from the **largest element** in it (including itself), as in case of transportation problems.
(ii) Solve further using Hungarian method to get the optimal assignments.
(iii) To find the total maximum profit, consider the original profit elements for the respective assignments.

Example 5: Solve the following problem for maximising the production output. The data refers to the production of an article for the given operators and machines.

	Machines			
	A	B	C	D
Operators 1	10	5	7	8
2	11	4	9	10
3	8	4	9	7
4	7	5	6	4
5	8	9	7	5

Solution: Given problem is of maximisation and is unbalanced also. Hence, add first a dummy column to it with all its elements as 0. Then we convert the production matrix into a relative loss matrix by subtracting each of its elements from the largest element in it i.e. 11.

	A	B	C	D	Dummy
1	10	5	7	8	0
2	11	4	9	10	0
→ 3	8	4	9	7	0
4	7	5	6	4	0
5	8	9	7	5	0

Production (Profit) Matrix

	A	B	C	D	Dummy
1	1	6	4	3	11
2	0	7	2	1	11
→ 3	3	7	2	4	11
4	4	6	5	7	11
5	3	2	4	6	11

Relative (Loss) Matrix

We use further the Hungarian Method to solve the problem.

	A	B	C	D	Dummy
1	0	5	3	2	10
2	0	7	2	1	11
→ 3	1	5	0	2	9
4	0	2	1	3	7
5	1	0	2	5	9

Row Subtraction

	A	B	C	D	Dummy
1	0	5	3	1	3
2	0	7	2	0	4
→ 3	1	5	0	1	2
4	0	2	1	2	0
5	1	0	2	4	2

Column Subtraction (Reduced Matrix)

Since 5 lines (= No. of rows/columns) are required to cover all the zeroes, the solution is optimum and hence, the assignments are:

	A	B	C	D	Dummy
1→1	[0]	5	3	1	3
2→2	✕	7	2	[0]	4
3→3	1	5	[0]	1	2
4→4	✕	2	1	2	[0]
5→5	1	[0]	2	4	2

(Using Original Production Matrix)		
Operator	M/c	Production
1	A	10
2	D	10
3	C	9
4	Dummy	0
5	B	9
		Total 38 (Maximum)

Note: We can add the dummy column after obtaining the relative loss matrix also OR after adding the dummy, we can make column subtraction first and then row subtraction to get the reduced matrix conveniently. But for both, we need one improvement further.

Again here, the operator 4 remains idle, as it is assigned to a Dummy Machine.

(D) Prohibited Assignments:

These are indicated by putting a dash (–) or cross (×) at the prohibited positions. To solve this problem:

(i) For a minimisation problem assume (+∞) cost for the prohibited position and proceed further as usual.

(ii) For a maximisation problem assume (–∞) profit for the prohibited position and proceed further as usual.

Note: This automatically makes these cells unfit for inclusion in the optimum solution.

Example 6: Consider a problem of assigning 4 clerks to four tasks. The time (Hrs.) required to complete the tasks are given. Clerk 2 can not be assigned to task A and clerk 3 can not be assigned to task B. Find the optimum assignment schedule.

		Tasks		
Clerk	A	B	C	D
1	4	7	8	6
2	–	8	7	4
3	3	–	8	3
4	6	6	4	2

Solution: It is a minimisation problem where the assignments 2 to A and 3 to B are prohibited. Hence, assume (+∞) time for 2A and 3B and solve further by using the Hungarian method as follows:

	A	B	C	D			A	B	C	D	
1	4	7	8	6		1	0	3	4	2	
2	∞	8	7	4		2	∞	4	3	0	
3	3	∞	8	3	→	3	0	∞	5	0	
4	6	6	4	2		4	4	4	2	0	(Note : ∞ – 4 = ∞)

Row Subtraction

4 lines are required. Hence, solution is optimum.

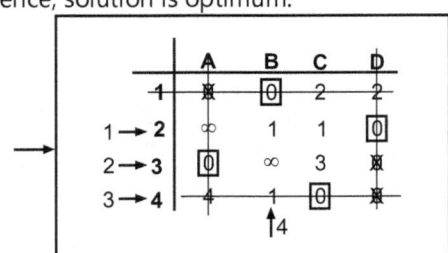

Column Subtraction
(Reduced Matrix)

Thus, we have the optimum assignment schedule as :

1 → B, 2 → D, 3 → A, 4 → C and the total optimum (minimum) time required = 7 + 4 + 3 + 4 = 18 Hr.

Note: Assuming (+ ∞) cost for 2 A and 3 B, automatically makes them unfit for the optimal solution.

Solved Problems

Problem 1: A job production unit has four jobs A, B, C, D which can be manufactured on each of the four machines. The processing cost of each job for each machine is given. How should the jobs be assigned so as to minimise the processing cost?

		Machines			
		P	Q	R	S
Jobs	A	31	25	33	25
	B	25	24	23	21
	C	19	21	23	24
	D	38	36	34	40

Solution: This is a balanced assignment problem of minimisation. Hence, we use Hungarian Method to solve it.

		Machines			
		P	Q	R	S
Jobs	A	31	25	33	25
	B	25	24	23	21
	C	19	21	23	24
	D	38	36	34	40

On subtraction along the rows we get the matrix as shown below. On subtraction along the columns, the matrix remains unchanged as each column has '0' as the smallest element. Thus we have got the reduced matrix.

		Machines			
		P	Q	R	S
Jobs	A	6	0	8	0
	B	4	3	2	0
	C	0	2	4	5
	D	4	2	0	6

Row Subtraction (Reduced matrix)

Now, we need at least four lines to cover all the zeroes in this reduced matrix, which is equal to the number of rows or columns in it. Hence, the solution is optimum. Hence, we make assignments at the single unmarked zeroes in its rows and columns as shown.

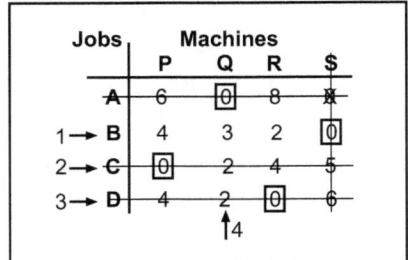

Thus, the optimum assignments for minimizing the processing cost are:
A → Q, B → S, C → P, D → R with total minimum processing cost = 25 + 21 + 19 + 34 = ₹ 99.

Problem 2: Solve the following assignment problem for minimisation. The costs are given below. Find all the alternative solutions, if any.

	X_1	X_2	X_3	X_4	X_5
A	15	29	35	20	38
B	21	27	33	17	36
C	17	25	37	15	42
D	14	31	39	21	40
E	19	30	40	19	18

Solution: It is a balanced minimisation problem. Hence, use the Hungarian Method.

	X_1	X_2	X_3	X_4	X_5			X_1	X_2	X_3	X_4	X_5
A	15	29	35	20	38		A	0	14	20	5	23
B	21	27	33	17	36		B	4	10	16	0	19
C	17	25	37	15	42	→	C	2	10	22	0	27
D	14	31	39	21	40		D	0	17	25	7	26
E	19	30	40	19	18		E	1	12	22	1	0

(Row Subtraction)

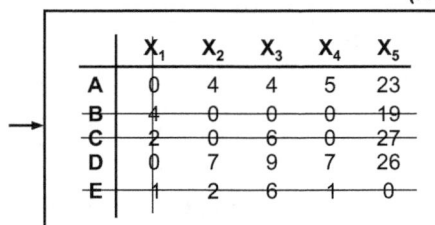

Column Subtraction (Reduced Matrix)

As 4 lines are sufficient to cover all the zeroes, which is less than 5 i.e. the number of rows, the solution is not optimum. Hence, to improve it, use the smallest unconvered element 4 to get the first improvement matrix (subtract 4 from all uncoverd elements and add it to the elements at the intersection of the lines.)

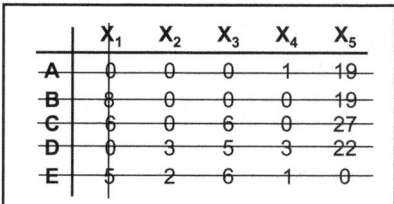

1st Improvement Matrix

As we need here 5 lines (= number of rows) to cover the zeroes, the solution is optimum and we make the assignments at the single unmarked zeroes as shown below.

	X_1	X_2	X_3	X_4	X_5
A	⊠	0	0	1	19
B	8	0	0	0	19
C	6	0	6	0	27
1→ D	[0]	3	5	3	22
2→ E	5	2	6	1	[0]

Since rows A, B, C contain more than one unmarked zeroes the problem has multiple solution. We select row B having maximum number of such zeroes and select these zeroes, one at a time, for making the assignments (and then cancel all other zeroes in its row and column). We proceed further as usual to get the following three alternate solutions.

(Solution 1 - Selecting BX_2)

	X_1	X_2	X_3	X_4	X_5
4→ A	⊠	⊠	[0]	1	19
3→ B	8	[0]	⊠	⊠	19
5→ C	6	⊠	6	[0]	27
D	[0]	3	5	3	22
E	5	2	6	1	[0]

$A \to X_3, B \to X_2, C \to X_4, D \to X_1, E \to X_5$
and Cost = 35 + 27 + 15 + 14 + 18 = 109

(Solution 2 - Selecting BX_3)

	X_1	X_2	X_3	X_4	X_5
4→ A	⊠	[0]	⊠	1	19
3→ B	8	⊠	[0]	⊠	19
5→ C	6	⊠	6	[0]	27
D	[0]	3	5	3	22
E	5	2	6	1	[0]

$A \to X_2, B \to X_3, C \to X_4, D \to X_1, E \to X_5$
Cost = 29 + 33 + 15 + 14 + 18 = 109

(Solution 3 - Selecting BX_4)

	X_1	X_2	X_3	X_4	X_5
5→ A	⊠	⊠	[0]	1	19
3→ B	8	⊠	⊠	[0]	19
4→ C	6	[0]	6	⊠	27
D	[0]	3	5	3	22
E	5	2	6	1	[0]

$A \to X_3, B \to X_4, C \to X_2, D \to X_1, E \to X_5$
and Cost = 35 + 17 + 25 + 14 + 18 = 109

Problem 3: The marketing director of a multi-unit company is faced with a problem of assigning 5 senior managers to six zones. From the past experience he knows that the efficiency percentage judged by sales, operating costs etc. depends on the manager-zone combination. The efficiency of different managers are given here. Find out which zone will be managed by a junior manager due to non-availability of senior manager.

Managers	Zones					
	I	II	III	IV	V	VI
A	73	91	87	82	78	80
B	81	85	69	76	74	85
C	75	72	83	84	78	91
D	93	96	86	91	83	82
E	90	91	79	89	69	76

Solution: This is a maximisation problem. Hence we obtain the relative loss matrix first by subtracting all its elements from the largest element 96 and then introduce a dummy row F to balance the problem. (These steps can be interchanged). Solve further as usual.

	I	II	III	IV	V	VI
A	23	5	9	14	18	16
B	15	11	27	20	22	11
C	21	24	13	12	18	5
D	3	0	10	5	13	14
E	6	5	17	7	27	20
F	0	0	0	0	0	0

(Relative Loss Matrix)

→

	I	II	III	IV	V	VI
A	18	0	4	9	13	11
B	4	0	16	9	11	0
C	16	19	8	7	13	0
D	3	0	10	5	13	14
E	1	0	12	2	22	15
F	0	0	0	0	0	0

Row Subtraction (Reduced Matrix)

3 lines (< 6) are required to cover the zeroes.

∴ Not optimum solution. Get first improvement matrix by using the smallest uncovered element 1, as follows:

	I	II	III	IV	V	VI
A	17	0	3	8	12	11
B	3	0	15	8	10	0
C	15	19	7	6	12	0
D	2	0	9	4	12	14
E	0	0	11	1	21	15
F	0	11	0	0	0	1

1st Improvement Matrix

Not optimum solution (lines 4 < 6). Improve it using '2'.

3.18

	I	II	III	IV	V	VI
A	15	0	1	6	10	11
B	1	0	13	6	8	0
C	13	19	5	4	10	0
D	0	0	7	2	10	14
E	0	2	11	1	21	17
F	0	3	0	0	0	3

2nd Improvement Matrix

Not optimum (lines 4 < 6). Improve it using '1'.

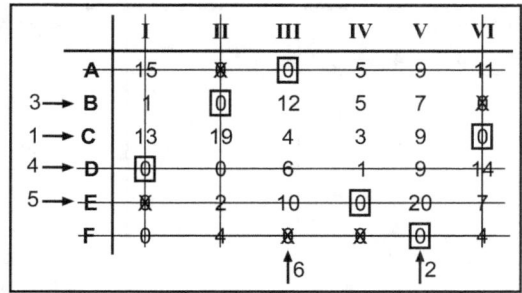

3rd Improvement matrix

Lines 6 = No. of rows are required to cover all zeroes. Hence, the solution is optimum and we have the following assignments:

A → III, B → II, C → VI, D → I, E → IV, Dummy F → V

Hence, no senior manager can be assigned to zone V. Hence, the zone V will be managed by the Junior-manager.

Problem 4: An airline Co. has drawn up a new flight schedule involving five flights. To assist in allocating five pilots to the flights it has asked them to state their preference scores by giving each flight a number out of 10. The higher the number, the greater is the preference. Certain of these flights are unsuitable to some pilots owing to some domestic reasons. These have been marked with an ×. What should be the allocation of the pilots to flights in order to meet as many preferences as possible.

		Fight Number				
		1	2	3	4	5
Pilot	A	8	2	×	5	4
	B	10	9	2	8	4
	C	5	4	9	6	×
	D	3	6	2	8	7
	E	5	6	10	4	3

Solution: This is a maximisation problem with prohibited assignments. Therefore, we assume element $(-\infty)$ for the unsuitable positions A3 and C5.

		Fight Number				
		1	2	3	4	5
	A	8	2	$-\infty$	5	4
Pilot	B	10	9	2	8	4
	C	5	4	9	6	$-\infty$
	D	3	6	2	8	7
	E	5	6	10	4	3

Let us obtain the relative loss matrix by subtracting all elements from the largest element i.e. 10 as:

		Fight Number				
		1	2	3	4	5
	A	2	8	∞	5	6
Pilot	B	0	1	8	2	6
	C	5	6	1	4	∞
	D	7	4	8	2	3
	E	5	4	0	6	7

(Relative Loss Matrix)

$\rightarrow$

		Fight Number				
		1	2	3	4	5
	A	0	6	∞	3	4
Pilot	B	0	1	8	2	6
	C	4	5	0	3	∞
	D	5	2	6	0	1
	E	5	4	0	6	7

(Row Subtraction)

Note: $10 - (-\infty) = 10 + \infty = \infty$.

$\rightarrow$

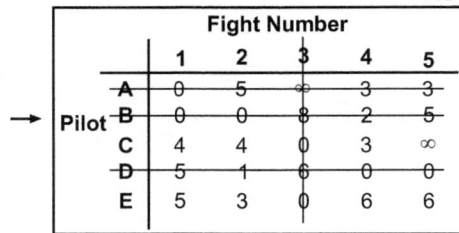

Column Subtraction (Reduced Matrix)

As (4 lines < 5) are required,
∴ Not optimum solution.
∴ Improve it by using smallest uncovered element '3'.

		1	2	3	4	5
1→	A	[0]	5	∞	3	3
2→	B	☒	[0]	11	2	5
5→	C	1	1	☒	[0]	∞
	D	5	1	9	☒	[0]
3→	E	2	☒	[0]	3	3
						↑4

1st Improvement matrix

As 5 lines = No. of rows are required, solution is optimum. ∴ The Optimum Assignment is $(A \to 1)$, $(B \to 2)$, $(C \to 4)$, $(D \to 5)$, $(E \to 3)$ [So that the total of preferences (using preference matrix) = $8 + 9 + 6 + 7 + 10 = 40$

DECISION SCIENCES

Problem 5: The purchase manager of a government department is analysing a set of bids that he has received for five projects from six bidders. The guidelines established for selecting the successful bidders require the manager to (i) minimise the total cost to complete the projects and (ii) disregard the lowest bid whenever it is more than 25 percent of and below the next lowest bid. (The assumption being that the quality of work will not be upto standards). The bids on the projects (in thousand of rupees) are shown in the table that follows:

(a) Identify which particular bidder(s) shall not be eligible for which particular contract(s) in pursuance of the requirement in (ii) above
(b) Identify the successful bidder for each of the five contracts
(c) State how much will these five contract assignments cost the department.

Bidder	A	B	C	D	E
1	7	8	8	12	7
2	9	13	10	14	5
3	3	7	6	13	11
4	17	17	7	8	8
5	8	12	7	15	16
6	10	10	10	16	8

(Contract)

Solution: As per the second guideline, if the lowest bid for a project is more than 25% of and below the next lowest bid i.e. if it is less than 75% of the next lowest bid, it will be disregarded.

Thus, for project A,   ∴ 3 < (75% of 7 i.e. 5.25) it is rejected
Similarly, for project D,   ∴ 8 < (75% of 12 i.e. 9) it is rejected
and for project E,   ∴ 5 < (75% of 7 i.e. 5.25) it is rejected.

Hence, 3A, 4D and 2E are prohibited assignments. Thus, bidder 3 is not eligible for project A, 4 is not eligible for project D and 2 for E.

Thus, the assignment matrix with the prohibited assignments (with ∞ cost) and a dummy column (so as to balance the matrix) is as follows.

	A	B	C	D	E	Dummy
1	7	8	8	12	7	0
2	9	13	10	14	∞	0
3	∞	7	6	13	11	0
4	17	17	7	∞	8	0
5	8	12	7	15	16	0
6	10	10	10	16	8	0

→

	A	B	C	D	E	Dummy
1	0	1	2	0	0	0
2	2	6	4	2	∞	0
3	∞	0	0	1	4	0
4	10	10	1	∞	1	0
5	1	5	1	3	9	0
6	3	3	4	4	1	0

Column Subtraction (Reduced Matrix)

(Row subtraction keeps the matrix unchanged)

As (3 lines) < 6, are required, the solution is not optimum. ∴ Improve it using smallest uncovered element i.e. '1'

	A	B	C	D	E	Dummy
1	0	1	2	0	0	1
2	1	5	3	1	∞	0
3	∞	0	0	1	4	1
4	9	9	0	∞	0	0
5	0	4	0	2	8	0
6	2	2	3	3	0	0

1st Improvement matrix

6 lines required. ∴ Optimum solution.
∴ The assignments are as follows:

	A	B	C	D	E	Dummy
1	✗	1	2	[0]	✗	1
2	1	5	3	1	∞	[0]
3	∞	[0]	✗	1	4	1
4	9	9	[0]	∞	✗	✗
5	[0]	4	✗	2	8	✗
6	2	2	3	3	[0]	✗

Bidder	Project	Cost
1	D	12
2	Dummy	0
3	B	7
4	C	7
5	A	8
6	E	8
	Total cost = 42 × 100 = ₹ 42,000	

Problem 6: There are 5 jobs to be performed but only 4 operators are available.
Table below gives time in hours required to complete the job. Assign operators to complete the jobs so that total time is minimum. Which job is not completed?

Operators	J_1	J_2	J_3	J_4	J_5
O_1	27	18	–	20	21
O_2	31	24	21	12	17
O_3	20	17	20	–	16
O_4	20	28	20	16	27

(P.U.MBA - May 06)

Solution: We assign a dummy operator O_5 with 0 as its elements to balance the problem. Also as assignments O_1J_3 and O_3J_4 are prohibited, we assume (+∞) time for them.

	J_1	J_2	J_3	J_4	J_5
O_1	27	18	∞	20	21
O_2	31	24	21	12	17
O_3	20	17	20	∞	16
O_4	20	28	20	16	27
O_5	0	0	0	0	0

⟶

	J_1	J_2	J_3	J_4	J_5
O_1	9	0	∞	2	3
O_2	19	12	9	0	5
O_3	4	1	4	∞	0
O_4	4	12	4	0	11
O_5	0	0	0	0	0

Row Subtraction (Reduced matrix)
(Column subtraction keeps the matrix unchanged)

	J_1	J_2	J_3	J_4	J_5
O_1	~~9~~	~~0~~	∞	~~2~~	~~3~~
O_2	19	12	9	0	5
O_3	~~4~~	~~1~~	~~4~~	∞	~~0~~
O_4	4	12	4	0	11
O_5	~~0~~	~~0~~	~~0~~	~~0~~	~~0~~

As 4 lines are sufficient to cover the zeroes which is less than the number of rows (= 5), the solution is not optimum and we improve it using the smallest uncovered element 4.

	J_1	J_2	J_3	J_4	J_5
O_1	~~9~~	~~0~~	∞	~~6~~	~~3~~
O_2	~~15~~	~~8~~	~~5~~	~~0~~	~~1~~
O_3	~~4~~	~~1~~	~~4~~	∞	~~0~~
O_4	~~0~~	~~8~~	~~0~~	~~0~~	~~7~~
O_5	~~0~~	~~0~~	~~0~~	~~4~~	~~0~~

1st Improvement Matrix

As 5 lines are now required to cover the zeroes, the solution is optimum. Also, it has multiple solutions as:

	J_1	J_2	J_3	J_4	J_5
1 → O_1	9	[0]	∞	6	3
2 → O_2	15	8	5	[0]	1
3 → O_3	4	1	4	∞	[0]
O_4	[0]	8	△	✗	7
O_5	△	✗	[0]	4	✗

Selecting $O_4 J_1$: 1st solution

Operator	Job	Time
O_1	J_2	18
O_2	J_4	12
O_3	J_5	16
O_4	J_1	20
O_5	J_3	0
		66 Hr.

or Alternate solution (selecting $O_4 J_3$): $O_1 \to J_2$, $O_2 \to J_4$, $O_3 \to J_5$, $O_4 \to J_3$, $O_5 \to J_1$, with Time = 18 + 12 + 16 + 20 + 0 = 66 Hr.

Problem 7: Finance faculty in a management school decided to hold seminars on 4 topics – leasing, portfolio management, private mutual funds and swaps and options. The seminars are to be held once a week, so that number of students unable to attend it is to be kept minimum. The past experience indicates certain number of students can not attend the seminar on a particular day of week as shown in the table below:

DECISION SCIENCES   ASSIGNMENT MODELS

	Leasing	Portfolio Management	Private Mutual Fund	Swaps & Options
Monday	50	40	60	20
Tuesday	40	30	40	30
Wednesday	60	20	30	20
Thursday	30	30	20	30
Friday	10	20	10	30

Find the optimal schedule of seminars, so that minimum number of students will miss the seminar. Find the total number of students who will be missing at least one seminar.

(P.U. MBA - Dec. 05)

Solution: The given matrix indicates the number of students remaining absent for each day-seminar combination. We have to assign the days to the seminars so that the total number of absent students is minimised. This is a typical minimisation problem, which is unbalanced one. Hence, introduce a dummy seminar D to balance the matrix and proceed as usual.

	L	P	M	S	D
M	50	40	60	20	0
T	40	30	40	30	0
W	60	20	30	20	0
TH	30	30	20	30	0
F	10	20	10	30	0

⟶

	L	P	M	S	D
M	40	20	50	0	0
T	30	10	30	10	0
W	50	0	20	0	0
TH	20	10	10	10	0
F	0	0	0	10	0

Column Subtraction (Reduced Matrix)

(Row subtraction keeps the matrix unchanged)

No. of lines (= 4) < (No. of rows = 5) ∴ Not optimum. Hence, improve it using the smallest uncovered element i.e. '10'.

	L	P	M	S	D
M	30	10	40	0	0
T	20	0	20	10	0
W	50	0	20	10	10
TH	10	0	0	10	0
F	0	0	0	20	10

3.24

5 lines required. ∴ Optimum solution. Hence, the optimum assignment is as follows:

	L	P	M	S	D
M	30	10	40	[0]	✗
T	20	✗	20	10	[0]
1→W	50	[0]	20	10	10
TH	10	✗	[0]	10	✗
F	[0]	✗	✗	20	10
	2↑		3↑	4↑	5↑

Monday → Swaps & options, Tuesday → Dummy, Wednesday → Portfolio management, Thursday → Private Mutual funds, Friday → Leasing. Thus, actually there is no seminar on Tuesday.

∴ Total number of students missing the seminars (at least one)
= 20 + 20 + 20 + 10 = 70

Problem 8: There are four manufacturing sections and five supervisors in the industry. Four of the five supervisors are to be promoted as foremen. The efficiency matrix of the supervisors is given below:

Supervisor	Manufacturing Sections			
	M_1	M_2	M_3	M_4
A	90	96	72	88
B	95	90	0	85
C	85	80	75	0
D	78	95	0	80
E	93	91	70	85

Which four supervisors should be promoted as foreman of which manufacturing sections as to the maximise the efficiency of the industry. **(P.U. MBA - Dec. 09)**

Solution: This is a maximisation problem as given are the efficiency scores. Hence, subtracting all the numbers in the given matrix from the largest number of 96 we get the relative loss matrix as below. We also add to it a dummy manufacturing sections to balance the problem and solve further using the Hungarian method.

	M_1	M_2	M_3	M_4	Dummy
A	6	0	24	8	0
B	1	6	96	11	0
C	11	16	21	96	0
D	18	1	96	16	0
E	3	5	26	11	0

Relative Loss Matrix

Column subtraction
(Row subtraction not needed)

	M_1	M_2	M_3	M_4	Dummy
A	5	0	3	0	0
B	0	6	75	3	0
C	10	16	0	88	0
D	17	1	75	8	0
E	2	5	5	3	0

Reduced Matrix

DECISION SCIENCES   ASSIGNMENT MODELS

	M₁	M₂	M₃	M₄	Dummy
A	5	0	3	0	1
B	0	6	75	3	1
C	10	16	0	88	1
D	16	0	74	7	0
E	1	4	4	2	0

Not optimum
∴ improved using '1'

1ˢᵗ Improvement Matrix

∵ 5 lines are required (= No. of rows), the solution is optimum. Hence, the assignments are made as follows:

	M₁	M₂	M₃	M₄	Dummy
A	5	✗	3	[0]	1
B	[0]	6	75	3	1
C	10	16	[0]	88	1
D	16	[0]	74	7	✗
E	1	4	4	2	[0]

Thus, the optimum assignment of the supervisors to the manufacturing sections will be: A → M₄, B → M₁, C → M₃, D → M₂, E → Dummy. As E is being assigned to the Dummy, he will not be promoted and the others i.e. A, B, C and D should be promoted. Considering also the original efficiency scores for the assignments, we get the (maximum) efficiency = 88 + 95 + 75 + 95 = 353.

Problem 9: A company has one surplus truck in each of the cities A, B, C, D and E and one deficit truck in each of the cities 1, 2, 3, 4, 5 and 6. The distance between the cities in kilometer is shown in the matrix. Find the assignment of trucks from cities in surplus to cities in deficit so that the total distance covered by vehicles is minimum. **(P.U. MBA - Dec. 12)**

	1	2	3	4	5	6
A	12	10	15	22	18	8
B	10	18	25	15	16	12
C	11	10	3	8	5	9
D	6	14	10	13	13	12
E	8	12	11	7	13	10

Solution: This is a minimisation problem. Also being unbalanced we add a dummy city F to the given distance matrix first.

	1	2	3	4	5	6
A	12	10	15	22	18	8
B	10	18	25	15	16	12
C	11	10	3	8	5	9
D	6	14	10	13	13	12
E	8	12	11	7	13	10
F	0	0	0	0	0	0

→

	1	2	3	4	5	6
A	4	2	7	14	10	0
B	0	8	15	5	6	2
C	8	7	0	5	2	6
D	0	8	4	7	7	6
E	1	5	4	0	6	3
F	0	0	0	0	0	0

Row Subtraction (Reduction Matrix)

3.26

DECISION SCIENCES — ASSIGNMENT MODELS

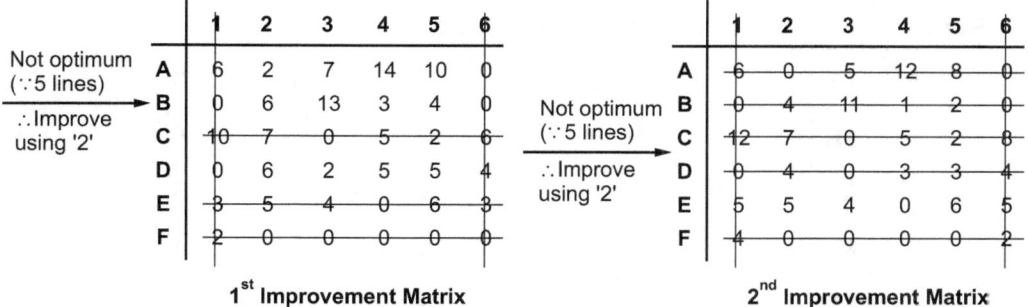

1st Improvement Matrix   **2nd Improvement Matrix**

Optimum solution as 6 (= No. of rows) lines are required.

∴ Optimum assignment is

	1	2	3	4	5	6
A	6	[0]	5	12	8	✗
B	✗	4	11	1	2	[0]
C	12	7	[0]	5	2	8
D	[0]	4	✗	3	3	4
E	5	5	4	[0]	6	5
F	4	✗	✗	✗	[0]	2

A → 2, B → 6, C → 3, D → 1, E → 4, Dummy F → 5 (i.e. city 6 does not receive a truck) and the minimum distance to be covered = 10 + 12 + 3 + 6 + 7 = 38 kilometers.

Problem 10: The following data gives the cost incurred if a job is performed on different machines. There are 4 jobs and 4 machines. Assign jobs to machines so that the total cost is minimum.

Machines	Jobs			
	A	B	C	D
M_1	3	8	5	9
M_2	4	2	1	6
M_3	3	8	5	7
M_4	4	7	10	8

(P.U. MBA - May 13)

Solution: This is a balanced and minimisation problem

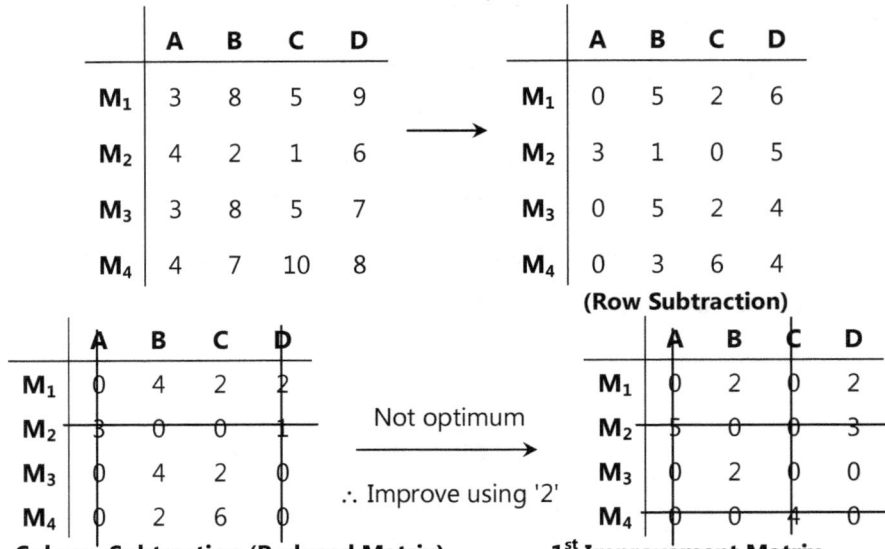

	A	B	C	D
M₁	3	8	5	9
M₂	4	2	1	6
M₃	3	8	5	7
M₄	4	7	10	8

$\longrightarrow$

	A	B	C	D
M₁	0	5	2	6
M₂	3	1	0	5
M₃	0	5	2	4
M₄	0	3	6	4

(Row Subtraction)

	A	B	C	D
M₁	0	4	2	2
M₂	3	0	0	1
M₃	0	4	2	0
M₄	0	2	6	0

Column Subtraction (Reduced Matrix)

Not optimum
$\therefore$ Improve using '2'

	A	B	C	D
M₁	0	2	0	2
M₂	5	0	0	3
M₃	0	2	0	0
M₄	0	0	4	0

1ˢᵗ Improvement Matrix

Optimum solution as 4 lines (= No. of rows) are required to cover all the zeroes. Hence, make assignments. There are no single unmarked zeroes in any row or column (there are atleast two). Hence, this is a case of multiple solutions. Thus, selecting the zeroes at M₃A, M₃C and M₃D in row three, one by one we get the solutions as:

	A	B	C	D
2→ M₁	✗	2	[0]	2
3→ M₂	5	[0]	✗	3
1→ M₃	[0]	2	✗	✗
M₄	✗	✗	4	[0]

1ˢᵗ solution
Cost = 5 + 2 + 3 + 8 = 18

	A	B	C	D
2→ M₁	[0]	2	✗	2
M₂	5	[0]	✗	3
1→ M₃	✗	2	[0]	✗
M₄	✗	✗	4	[0]

2ⁿᵈ solution
Cost = 3 + 2 + 5 + 8 = 19

	A	B	C	D
M₁	[0]	2	✗	2
M₂	5	✗	[0]	3
1→ M₃	✗	2	✗	[0]
M₄	✗	[0]	4	✗

3ʳᵈ and 4ᵗʰ solution
Cost = 3 + 1 + 7 + 7 = 18 or Cost = 5 + 2 + 7 + 4 = 18

DECISION SCIENCES   ASSIGNMENT MODELS

Exercise

1. Explain how assignment problem is a special case of transportation problem.
2. Write a note on the Hungarian Method/Flood's Technique to solve assignment problem.
3. How would you deal with assignment problems where
   (a) Some assignments are prohibited
   (b) The objective function is to be maximised.
   (c) It is not a balanced problem.
   (d) It has got multiple solutions.
4. 5 jobs are assigned to 5 people, each person will do one job only. The expected time (in hours) required for each job for each person have been estimated and are shown in the following table. Determine optimal assignments.

Job	Person				
	1	2	3	4	5
1	12	15	13	14	15
2	16	18	15	14	16
3	18	16	15	18	20
4	15	20	18	17	19
5	16	15	18	14	15

   (**Ans.** 1 → 3, 2 → 4, 3 → 2, 4 → 1, 5 → 5; Total Time = 73 Hr.)

5. In a textile sales emporium, four salesmen A, B, C and D are available for four counters W, X, Y, Z. Each salesman can handle any counter. The service time (in hour) at each counter when manned by each salesman is given here. How should the salesmen be allocated to appropriate counters so as to minimise the service time. (Each salesman must handle only one counter.)

Counter	Salesman			
	A	B	C	D
X	39	72	43	52
Y	22	32	49	65
Z	27	39	60	51
W	45	50	48	52

   (**Ans.** X → C, Y → B, Z → A, W → D, Total Time = 154 Hr.)

6. A company has a team of four salesmen and there are four districts where the company wants to start its business. The following is the profit per day in rupees for each salesman in each district. Find the assignment of salesmen to various districts which will yield maximum profit.   **(P.U. MBA - Dec. 08)**

3.29

DECISION SCIENCES   ASSIGNMENT MODELS

| | District | | | |
Salesman	D_1	D_2	D_3	D_4
A	16	10	14	11
B	14	11	15	15
C	15	15	13	12
D	13	12	14	15

(**Ans.** Maximisation; A → D_1, B → D_3, C → D_2, D → D_4; and total max. Profit = ₹61 per day)

7. A company has four machines to do 3 jobs. Each job can be assigned to one and only one machine. The cost of each job on each machine is given in the adjacent table. What are the job assignments for minimum cost? **(P.U. MBA - May 11)**

| | Machine | | | |
Job	M_1	M_2	M_3	M_4
A	17	23	27	31
B	7	12	16	18
C	9	14	18	21

(**Ans.** Unbalanced; A → M_1, B → M_2, C → M_3, Dummy → M_4 and min. cost = ₹47/-; machine M_4 is idle)

8. Solve the following assignment problem. The data given refers to the daily production (in number of units) of certain articles on the given machines. Give alternate production plans, if any.

| | Machines | | |
Articles	A	B	C
1	10	7	8
2	8	9	7
3	7	12	6
4	10	10	8

(**Ans. Plan 1:** 1 → A, 2 → Dummy, 3 → B, 4 → C; Production = 30 units; 2 is not produced. **Plan 2:** 1 → C, 2 → Dummy, 3 → B, 4 → A; Production = 30 units; 2 is not produced)

9. In a modification of a plant layout of a factory, four new machines M_1, M_2, M_3 and M_4 are to be installed in a machine shop. There are five vacant places A, B, C, D, E available. Because of limited space, machine M_2 can not be placed at C and M_3 can not be placed at A. The cost of installation of machine (i) at a place (j) in rupees hundred is shown below. Find the optimum assignment schedule.

	A	B	C	D	E
M_1	9	11	15	10	11
M_2	12	9	–	10	9
M_3	–	11	14	11	7
M_4	14	8	12	7	8

(P.U. MBA - Nov. 07)

(**Ans.** Prohibited Assignments & Unbalanced; $M_1 \rightarrow A$, $M_2 \rightarrow B$, $M_3 \rightarrow E$, $M_4 \rightarrow D$, Dummy $\rightarrow$ C; Cost = ₹ 3200; Place C is idle).

10. A Captain of a cricket team has to allot five middle batting positions to five batsmen. The average runs scored by each batsman at these positions are as given. The batsmen at the remaining batting positions are expected to score, on average, 120 runs between them. Make the assignment to the given positions so that the expected total average runs scored by the team are maximum.

Batsmen	Batting Positions				
	III	IV	V	VI	VII
A	40	40	35	25	50
B	42	30	16	25	27
C	50	48	40	60	50
D	20	19	20	18	25
E	58	60	59	55	53

(**Ans.** MaximiSation; A $\rightarrow$ VII, B $\rightarrow$ III, C $\rightarrow$ VI, D $\rightarrow$ V, E $\rightarrow$ IV; Total Score = 232 + 120 = 352)

11. A department head has three tasks to be performed with four subordinates. The subordinates differ in efficiency. The estimates of the time in hours each subordinate would take to perform is given below in the matrix. How should he allocate the tasks to each subordinate so as to minimise the total man hours?

Subordinates	Tasks		
	T1	T2	T3
A	10	27	16
B	14	28	7
C	36	21	16
D	19	31	21

(**Ans.** A $\rightarrow$ T1, B $\rightarrow$ T3, C $\rightarrow$ T2, D $\rightarrow$ Idle, Time = 38 hr.)

12. A management-consulting firm has 4 contracts. Three project leaders are available for assignment of these contracts. Because of the varying work experience of the project leaders, the profit to consulting firm will vary on the assignment as shown below:

Project Leader	Contract			
	1	2	3	4
A	13	10	9	11
B	15	17	13	20
C	6	8	11	7

Find the optimal assignment and total profit.

(**Ans.** Maximisation A $\to$ 1, B $\to$ 4, C $\to$ 3, Dummy $\to$ 2, Total Profit = 44)

13. Solve the assignment problem

Expected Sales (in ₹ Thousand) Data

Salesmen	Districts			
	D_1	D_2	D_3	D_4
S_1	20	25	22	18
S_2	25	24	19	21
S_3	18	20	22	20
S_4	25	20	17	22

(P.U. MBA - Dec. 06, May 07)

(**Ans.** Maximisation $S_1 \to D_2$, $S_2 \to D_1$, $S_3 \to D_3$, $S_4 \to D_4$, Total Sales = 94000)

14. Four engineers are available to design four projects. Engineer 2 is not competent to design project B (denoted by '–'). Given the following time estimates needed by each engineer to design a given project, find how should the engineers be assigned to projects so as to minimise the total design time of four projects.

Engineer	Project			
	A	B	C	D
1	12	10	10	8
2	14	–	15	11
3	6	10	16	4
4	8	10	9	7

(**Ans.** Prohibited: 1 $\to$ B, 2 $\to$ D, 3 $\to$ A, 4 $\to$ C and total time = 10 + 11 + 6 + 9 = 36)

DECISION SCIENCES   ASSIGNMENT MODELS

15. The owner of a company has 4 salesmen to be assigned to 5 districts. The expected sales (in Rs.'000) are given in the following table. Obtain the optimal assignment of salesmen to the districts and hence the total sales.

Salesmen	D1	D2	D3	D4	D5
A	62	78	50	73	59
B	87	92	111	101	82
C	71	84	61	71	59
D	48	64	87	77	80

(**Ans.** Maximisation, A → D4, B → D3, C → D2, D → D5, Dummy → D1, Total Sales = ₹ 3,48,000; D1 is vacant)

16. A company has to assign four workers A, B, C and D to four jobs W, X, Y, Z. The cost matrix is given below:
    (i) Find the optimum assignment schedule and total corresponding cost.
    (ii) What will be the optimum assignment if for certain reasons, worker D can not be assigned to job Y.

Worker	Job			
	W	X	Y	Z
A	1000	1200	400	900
B	600	500	300	800
C	200	300	400	500
D	600	700	300	1000

(**Ans.** (i) A → Z, B → X, C → W, D → Y, cost = ₹ 1900
(ii) DY is prohibited; A → Y, B → X, C → Z, D → W, Cost = ₹ 2,000]

17. A project work consists of four major jobs for which an equal number of contractors have submitted tenders. The tender amount quoted (in lakhs of rupees) is given in the matrix

		Job			
		a	b	c	d
	1	10	24	30	15
Contractor	2	16	22	28	12
	3	12	20	32	10
	4	9	26	34	16

Find the assignment which minimises the total cost of the Project. **(P.U. MBA May 08)**
(**Ans.** Multiple solutions; (1 → c, 2 → b, 3 → d, 4 → a), (1 → b, 2 → c, 3 → d, 4 → a), (1 → c, 2 → d, 3 → b, 4 → a); cost = ₹ 71 lacs)

3.33

18. The head of the department has five jobs A, B, C, D, E and five subordinates V, W, X, Y, Z. The number of hours each man would take to perform each job is as follows. Find the optimum allocation of jobs to the subordinates.

(P.U. MBA May 10)

	V	W	X	Y	Z
A	3	5	10	15	8
B	4	7	15	18	8
C	8	12	20	20	12
D	5	5	8	10	6
E	10	10	15	25	10

(**Ans.** A → X, B → W, C → V, D → Y, E → Z, Total time = 45 hrs)

19. The cost (₹' 000) of locating of machines to the places is estimated as follows. Find the optimal assignment schedule. **(P.U. MBA Dec. 10)**

	Places				
	A	B	C	D	E
M_1	19	21	25	20	21
M_2	27	24	–	25	24
M_3	–	24	27	24	20
M_4	22	16	20	15	16

(**Ans.** Prohibited, M_1 → A, M_2 → B, M_3 → E, M_4 → D, Dummy → C, Cost = ₹ 78,000)

Chapter 4...

Queuing Theory

Contents ...
4.1 Introduction
4.2 Elements of a Queuing System
4.3 Single Server (Channel) Queuing Model (M/M/1) : (∞/FIFO)
4.4 Multiple Servers (Channels) Queuing Model (M/M/c) : (∞/FIFO) or (M/M/k) : (∞/FIFO)
    Solved Problems
    Exercise

[Note: Readers are advised to go through the probability concepts (Chapter 9) before studying this chapter]

4.1 Introduction

The phenomena of queues or waiting lines is very common in our everyday life. Queues formed at bus stops, telephone booths, banks as well as the workers waiting at the tool crib for obtaining tools, machines waiting for repairs etc are some of its examples.

A queue is formed when either the units requiring the services (i.e. customers) wait for the service, or the service facilities (i.e. servers) stand idle and wait for the customers. Queuing Theory (or Waiting Line Theory) deals with the analysis of queues and queuing behaviour and is used for finding the solution of the problems so that the effectiveness of the service function is optimised, given that the arrival and servicing times are random.

4.2 Elements of a Queuing System

A queuing system consists of the arrival of customers, their waiting in a queue, their selection for the service by the service facility (server) according to a certain rule called service discipline, being served and their departure from the system.

A simple queue system can be represented as follows:

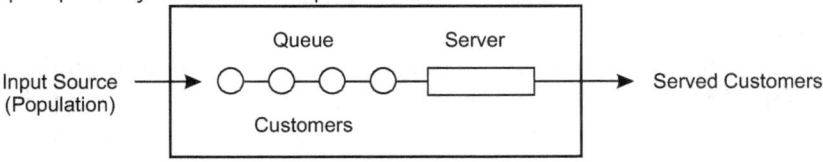

It has the following elements:

(A) **Input Process (or Arrival Pattern):** The customers (machines, workers, people etc.) arrive and join the system through an Input Process, which is characterised by:

  (i) **Size (i.e. Number of Customers Arriving):** Finite or infinite.

  (ii) **Arrival Time Distribution (i.e. Time Periods between the Arriving Customers):** Constant or random. The most commonly used random distribution is the Poisson Exponential Distribution with the mean arrival rate [i.e. the average number of arrivals per unit period (say - Hour, Minute) of time] as (lamda) λ. Hence, the mean time between successive arrivals is $\left(\frac{1}{\lambda}\right)$.

  (iii) **Customer's Behaviour:** On confronting a queue, the customers may:
   (a) Stay in the system until served (Patient customers).
   (b) Wait for certain time and leave the system if the service is not received by that time (impatient or renering customers).
   (c) Join the queue (few of them) and start demanding serivice for themselves and others (collusion of customers).
   (d) Move from one queue to other (when many servers are available) - (jockeying customers).

(B) **Queue (Waiting Line):** It refers to the customers waiting for the service and excludes those being served.

  Following characteristics are relevant here:
  (i) Waiting Time i.e. the time spent by a customer in the queue before being served.
  (ii) Service Time is the time spent by the server to render the sevice to a customer.
  (iii) Waiting Time in the system is the total time spent by the customer in the system and is equal to the waiting time plus service time.
  (iv) Queue Length i.e. the number of customers waiting in the queue (usually finite).
  (v) System length i.e. number of customers in the system i.e. those in queue plus those being served.

(C) **Service Facilities (Servers):** These are the subjects like clerks, machines etc. which render the services. These are characterised by:

  (i) **Arrangement:** The service facilities (known as servers or service channels) may be arranged in series (one after the other), in parallel or mixed. Thus, we may have Single Queue - Single Server, Single Queue - Multiple Servers (Series arrangement), Single Queue- Multiple Servers (Parallel arrangement) or Multiple Queue - Multiple Servers.

  (ii) **Service Time Distributions:** The service times (i.e. time for which the actual service is rendered) for the customers may be constant or randomly distributed. The service time in most of the situations follows a negative exponential distribution (exponent implies powers of e), which is a continuous probability distribution, with a mean service time $\left(\dfrac{1}{\mu}\right)$ where, (meu) μ is the mean or average service rate i.e. average number of customers served per unit period of time.

  (iii) **Service Discipline:** If the server is free, the arriving customers are immediately served. However, if a server is busy, the customers are selected - in order of their arrival (first come first served FCFS or first in first out FIFO) or randomly or by assigning priorities.

(D) Departure: On receiving the service completely, the customers depart from the system.

Note:

  (i) The commonly used operating characteristics of a queuing system include the queue length, system length, waiting time in queue, waiting time in system and server idle time.

  (ii) Symbolic representation of a Queuing Model (Kendall's notation): A Queuing model is usually specified completely (in terms of the important characteristics) by a symbolic notation known as Kendall's notation which is given by

   (a/b/c) : (d/e)

where

  a - The probability distribution of the number of arrivals per unit time
  b - The probability distribution of the service time
  c - Number of servers
  d - Capacity of the system
  e - Service discipline

We will consider here two queuing models viz. (M/M/1): (∞/FIFO) and (M/M/c): (∞/FIFO) where M stands for 'Markov' which implies that the 'number of arrivals in time t', and 'the number of customers served in time t' follows a Poisson process which is a continuous time Markov chain. (The description of these probability distributions / processes is beyond the scope of this book).

4.3 Single Server (Channel) Queuing Model (M/M/1) : (∞/FIFO)

(A) In this situation the customers arriving in a single queue, are served by a single server. Following are the assumptions made in this type of system:

  (i) Number of arrivals per unit time is described by Poisson Distribution (i.e. Poisson Arrivals)

  (ii) Service times are described by a Negative Exponential Distribution (i.e. exponential service times) which implies that the departures follow Poisson distribution.

  (iii) Queue discipline is First come - First served or First in First out.

  (iv) There is only one channel (or server) and only one queue.

(v) The calling population (i.e. potential customers) is infinite.
(vi) The waiting space for the customers in the queue is infinite (i.e. the capacity of the system is infinite).
(vii) Mean Arrival Rate (λ) < Mean Service Rate (μ).

(B) Formulae:

(i) Probability that the service facility is busy (i.e. Probability that there is at least one customer in the system) is given by the Traffic Intensity or Utilistion Factor, (rho) ρ as,

$$\rho = \frac{\lambda}{\mu}$$

(ii) Probability that the service facility is idle, (i.e. there is no one in the system),

$$P_o = 1 - \rho = 1 - \frac{\lambda}{\mu}$$

(iii) Probability that there are n units (customers) in the system (i.e. being served + waiting in queue),

$$P_n = P_o \left(\frac{\lambda}{\mu}\right)^n$$

(iv) Average waiting time of customers in the system (i.e. waiting time in queue + service time) is,

$$W_s = \frac{1}{\mu - \lambda}$$

(v) Average waiting time of customers (in the queue)

$$W_q = \frac{\lambda}{\mu(\mu - \lambda)}$$
$$= W_s - \frac{1}{\mu}$$

(vi) Probability that the waiting time is more than 't',

In the System $= e^{-(\mu - \lambda)t}$

In the Queue $= \frac{\lambda}{\mu} e^{-(\mu - \lambda)t}$ ..... e = 2.718

(vii) Average (expected) number of customers in the system i.e. System Length,

$$L_s = \frac{\rho}{1 - \rho} = \frac{\lambda}{\mu - \lambda} \text{ and } L_s = \lambda W_s$$

(viii) Average (expected) number of customers in the queue i.e. Queue Length,

$$L_q = \frac{\rho^2}{1 - \rho} = \frac{\lambda^2}{\mu(\mu - \lambda)}$$
$$= L_s - \frac{\lambda}{\mu} \text{ and } L_q = \lambda W_q$$

(ix) Probability that the queue size (length) is greater than or equal to k = Probability that the number of customers in system exceeds k i.e.,

$$P(n > k) = \left(\frac{\lambda}{\mu}\right)^{k+1}$$

(x) Average number of customers in a Non-empty queue (i.e. queue length, if it is formed) is,

$$L_\omega = \frac{1}{1-\rho} = \frac{\mu}{\mu-\lambda}$$

(xi) Average waiting time of a customer (in the queue), if he has to wait is

$$W_\omega = \frac{1}{\mu-\lambda}$$

(xii) Expected total cost associated with the service (per period) is equal to the sum of the expected facility cost of the server per period and the expected idle time cost of the arrivals (units) per period (= L_s × unit idle time cost per unit of arrival per period)

Note: 1. Unless Specified, Average waiting time means waiting time in the queue (and not in the system)

2. We can conveniently use Little's Formulae:

$$L_s = \lambda W_s, \; L_q = \lambda W_q, \; W_s = W_q + \frac{1}{\mu} \text{ and } L_s = L_q + \frac{\lambda}{\mu}$$

Example 1: A departmental store has a single cashier. During the rush hours, customers arrive at a rate of 20 customers per hour. The cashier takes on an average 2.5 minutes per customer for processing.

(i) What is the probability that the cashier is idle?
(ii) What is the probability that a customer shall have to wait in the queue?
(iii) What is average number of customes in the queuing system?
(iv) What is the average time spent by a customer in the system?
(v) What is the average queue length?
(vi) What is the average time a customer spends in the queue waiting for the serivce?
(vii) Find the average length of a non-empty queue and
(viii) Also find the average waiting time of an arrival who waits.

Solution: This is a case of single channel (server) model and we have,

Mean Arrival Rate (of customers), λ = 20 per hour.

As the cashier takes on average 2.5 minutes for processing each customer, hence,

Mean Service Rate i.e. average number of customers processed by the cashier per hour (i.e. in 60 minutes) is

$$\mu = \frac{60}{2.5} = 24 \text{ per hour}$$

(i) Probability that the cashier is idle

$$P_o = 1 - \frac{\lambda}{\mu} = 1 - \frac{20}{24} = 1 - \frac{5}{6} = \frac{1}{6} \text{ or } 0.17$$

(ii) Probability that a customer shall have to wait in the queue (or a queue is formed) i.e. probability that there is at least one customer in the system (who is being served) i.e. (probability that the cashier is busy) is

$$\rho = \frac{\lambda}{\mu} = \frac{20}{24} = \frac{5}{6} = 0.83$$

or $\rho = 1 - P_o = 1 - 0.17 = 0.83$

(iii) Average number of customers in the system i.e. system length is

$$L_s = \frac{\lambda}{\mu - \lambda} = \frac{20}{24 - 20} = 5 \text{ customers}$$

(iv) Average time spent by a customer in the system i.e. average waiting time in the system is

$$W_s = \frac{1}{\mu - \lambda} = \frac{1}{24 - 20} = \frac{1}{4} \text{ hour}$$

$$= \frac{1}{4}(60) = 15 \text{ minutes}$$

(v) Average Queue Length i.e. average number of customers in the queue is

$$L_q = \frac{\lambda^2}{\mu(\mu - \lambda)} = \frac{(20)(20)}{24(24 - 20)} = \frac{(20)(20)}{(24)(4)} = \frac{5(5)}{6(1)}$$

$$= 4.17 \text{ customers}$$

(vi) Average time a customer spends in the queue waiting for the service is

$$W_q = \frac{\lambda}{\mu(\mu - \lambda)} = \frac{20}{24(24 - 20)} = \frac{5}{6(4)} = \frac{5}{24} \text{ hr}$$

$$= \frac{5}{24}(60) = 12.5 \text{ minutes}$$

(vii) Average length of a non-empty queue (i.e. average number of customers in a queue, if it gets formed) is

$$L_w = \frac{\mu}{\mu - \lambda} = \frac{24}{24 - 20}$$

$$= \frac{24}{4} = 6$$

(viii) Average waiting time of an arrival who waits i.e.

$$W_\omega = \frac{1}{\mu - \lambda}$$

$$= \frac{1}{24 - 20} = \frac{1}{4} \text{ hr}$$

$$= \frac{1}{4}(60) = 15 \text{ minutes}$$

Example 2: In a company the machines that breakdown, follow a Poisson process with an average rate of four per hour. The machines are then brought to the repair section, where there is only one repairman, who provides his services on contract. The cost of non-productive machine is ₹ 50 per hour. The repairman charges ₹ 100 per hour and repairs the machines at an average rate of 6 per hour. Find:

(i) Average time for which a machine will be kept in the repair shop.
(ii) What proportion of his time is the repairman expected to be idle?
(iii) Probability that there are 3 machines in the repairshop.
(iv) Probability that there are more than 2 machines in the waiting line.
(v) Probability that a machine will be kept in the queue for at least 15 minutes before it is repaired.
(vi) Total cost incurred per hour.
(vii) If the management has decided to recruit another repairman when the utilisation of the repairman's services increases to 75%, what should be the rate of failure to justify the decision?

Solution: We have, Mean Arrival Rate of machines for repair i.e. $\lambda = 4$ per hour, Mean Service Rate i.e. $\mu = 6$ per hour.

(i) Average time for which the machine is kept in the repair shop

$$W_s = \frac{1}{\mu - \lambda} = \frac{1}{6-4} = \frac{1}{2} \text{ hour} = 30 \text{ minutes}$$

(ii) Probability that the repairman is idle (i.e. there are no machines in the repair shop i.e. system) is

$$P_o = 1 - \frac{\lambda}{\mu} = 1 - \frac{4}{6} = 1 - \frac{2}{3} = \frac{1}{3}$$

Hence, proportion of the time the repairman is idle is $\frac{1}{3} \times 100 = 33.33\%$.

(iii) Probability that there are 3 machines in the repair shop is

$$P_3 = P_o \left(\frac{\lambda}{\mu}\right)^3 = \frac{1}{3}\left(\frac{4}{6}\right)^3 = \frac{1}{3}\left(\frac{2}{3}\right)^3 = \frac{2^3}{3^4}$$

$$= \frac{8}{81} = 0.099 \cong 0.1$$

(iv) Probability that there are more than 2 machines (i.e. there are 3 or more machines) in the waiting line i.e. there are more than (2 + 1 = 3) machines in the repair shop (i.e. system) is

$$P(n > 3) = \left(\frac{\lambda}{\mu}\right)^{3+1} = \left(\frac{4}{6}\right)^4 = \left(\frac{2}{3}\right)^4 = \frac{16}{81} = 0.1975$$

(v) Probability that the machine remains unattended in the queue for at least (t = 15 minutes = ¼ Hour) before it is repaired is

$$\frac{\lambda}{\mu}e^{-(\mu-\lambda)t} = \frac{4}{6}e^{-(6-4)(\frac{1}{4})} = \frac{2}{3}e^{-\frac{1}{2}}$$

$$= \left(\frac{2}{3}\right)e^{-0.5} = \frac{2}{3}(0.6065) = 0.404$$

(vi) Total Cost per Hour
= Repairman's charges per hour + Waiting time cost for the machines lying in the repair shop.
= 100 + (Average No. of machines in the repair shop per hour) × (Non productive cost per machine per hour)
Now, Average Number of machines in the repair shop per hour is

$$L_s = \frac{\lambda}{\mu-\lambda} = \frac{4}{6-4} = 2$$

∴ Total Cost per Hour = 100 + (2) (50) = ₹ 200.

(vii) Let λ_1, be the arrival rate (breakdown rate) for which the utilisation of the repairman's services is 75% then,

Utilisation factor $\rho_1 = \frac{\lambda_1}{\mu}$ i.e. $0.75 = \frac{\lambda_1}{6}$

∴ λ_1 = 0.75 (6) = 4.5 machines per hour.

Hence, the average breakdown rate for the machines must be at least 4.5 machines per hour so as to justify the recruitment of another repairman.

4.4 Multiple Servers (Channels) Queuing Model (M/M/c): (∞/FIFO) or (M/M/k): (∞/FIFO)

(A) In this situation the customers arrive in a single queue but are served by two or more (multiple) servers which are arranged in parallel to render the service. Following are the assumptions made in this type of system:

(i) Parallel servers (say k in number) serve a single queue on a first-come first-served (i.e. First in First out) basis.

(ii) All service facilities (servers) provide the same service at the same rate (μ)

(iii) Arrivals follow Poisson Probability Distribution (with constant arrival rate λ) while the service times are exponentially distributed.

(iv) The calling population is infinite.

(v) Average arrival rate (λ) is less than the combined average service rate of all the servers (kμ)

(B) Formulae:

k - Number of servers, λ - Mean arrival rate, μ - Mean service rate at each server

(i) Probability that a server is busy i.e. utilisation factor, $\rho = \dfrac{\lambda}{k\mu}$.

(ii) Probability that there are no customers in the system i.e. the system is idle is,

$$P_o = \left[\left\{\sum_{i=0}^{k-1} \dfrac{1}{i!}\left(\dfrac{\lambda}{\mu}\right)^i\right\} + \dfrac{1}{k!}\left(\dfrac{\lambda}{\mu}\right)^k \dfrac{1}{\left(1-\dfrac{\lambda}{k\mu}\right)}\right]^{-1}$$

(iii) Probability that there are n units (customers) in the System is,

$$P_n = P_o \dfrac{(\lambda/\mu)^n}{n!} \quad \text{if } n \le k$$

$$P_n = P_o \dfrac{(\lambda/\mu)^n}{k!(k^{n-k})} \quad \text{if } n > k$$

(iv) Average waiting time of customers in the system,

$$W_s = \dfrac{\mu(\lambda/\mu)^k}{(k-1)!(k\mu-\lambda)^2} P_o + \dfrac{1}{\mu}$$

(v) Average waiting time of customers in the queue,

$$W_q = \dfrac{\mu(\lambda/\mu)^k}{(k-1)!(k\mu-\lambda)^2} P_o = W_s - \dfrac{1}{\mu}$$

(vi) Average number of customers in the system,

$$L_s = \dfrac{\lambda\mu(\lambda/\mu)^k}{(k-1)!(k\mu-\lambda)^2} P_o + \dfrac{\lambda}{\mu} \quad \text{and} \quad L_s = \lambda W_s$$

(vii) Average number of customers in the queue,

$$L_q = \dfrac{\lambda\mu(\lambda/\mu)^k}{(k-1)!(k\mu-\lambda)^2} P_o = L_s - \dfrac{\lambda}{\mu} \quad \text{and} \quad L_q = \lambda W_q$$

(viii) Average number of customer in a non-empty queue (i.e. Queue length, if it is formed) is,

$$L_w = \dfrac{\lambda}{k\mu - \lambda}$$

(ix) Average waiting time of a customer (in the queue), if he has to wait is,

$$W_w = \dfrac{1}{k\mu - \lambda}$$

Example 3: Omega Auto Service Station has 5 mechanics, each of whom can service a motorbike in 2 hours on an average. The motorbikes are registered at a single counter and then sent for servicing to different mechanics. Motorbikes arrive at the service station at an average rate of 2 per hour. Assuming the motorbike arrivals are Poisson distributed and the servicing times are distributed exponentially, determine:

(i) Probability that each mechanic is busy.
(ii) Probability that the system shall be idle.
(iii) Probability that there shall be 3 motorbikes in the station.
(iv) Probability that there shall be 8 motorbikes in the station.
(v) Expected number of motorbikes in the service station.
(vi) Expected number of motorbikes in the queue.
(vii) Average waiting time in the queue.
(viii) Average time spent by a motorbike in waiting and getting serviced.
(ix) Average number of motorbikes in a non empty queue
(x) Is it advisable to include another mechanic providing the same service at the same rate given that the mechanics are paid ₹ 5 per hour and the cost of ill-will created by waiting customer is estimated to be ₹ 12 per hour per customer.

Solution: We have, mean arrival rate, λ = 2 motorbikes/hr. As average service time is 2 hour.

∴ Mean service rate per server (mechanic), $\mu = \frac{1}{2}$ motorbikes/hr.

Number of servers (mechanics), k = 5.

(i) Probability that each mechanic is busy i.e. utilisation factor,

$$\rho = \frac{\lambda}{k\mu} = \frac{2}{5\left(\frac{1}{2}\right)} = \frac{4}{5} = 0.8$$

Hence, each mechanic is busy for 80% of his time.

(ii) Probability that the system is idle (i.e. there is no motorbike) is

$$P_o = \left[\left\{\sum_{i=0}^{k-1} \frac{1}{i!}\left(\frac{\lambda}{\mu}\right)^i\right\} + \frac{1}{k!}\left(\frac{\lambda}{\mu}\right)^k \frac{1}{1-\rho}\right]^{-1} \quad \ldots\ldots \rho = \frac{\lambda}{k\mu}$$

$$= \left[\left\{\sum_{i=0}^{5-1} \frac{1}{i!}\left(\frac{2}{0.5}\right)^i\right\} + \frac{1}{5!}\left(\frac{2}{0.5}\right)^5 \frac{1}{(1-0.8)}\right]^{-1}$$

Now, $\sum_{i=0}^{5-1} \frac{1}{i!}\left(\frac{2}{0.5}\right)^i = \sum_{i=0}^{4} \frac{1}{i!}(4)^i$

$= \frac{1}{0!}(4)^0 + \frac{1}{1!}(4)^1 + \frac{1}{2!}(4)^2 + \frac{1}{3!}(4)^3 + \frac{1}{4!}(4)^4$

$= 1 + 4 + \frac{16}{2} + \frac{64}{6} + \frac{256}{24} = \frac{103}{3} = 34.333$

and $\frac{1}{5!}\left(\frac{2}{0.5}\right)^5 \frac{1}{(1-0.8)} = \frac{1}{(120)}(4)^5 \frac{1}{(0.2)} = 42.667$

$\therefore P_o = [34.333 + 42.667]^{-1} = (77)^{-1} = \frac{1}{77} = 0.013$

(iii) Probability that there shall be ($n = 3$) motorbikes in the system: Here ($n = 3$) < ($k = 5$)

$\therefore P_n = P_o \frac{(\lambda/\mu)^n}{n!}$ $\therefore P_3 = (0.013)\frac{1}{3!}\left(\frac{2}{0.5}\right)^3$

$= \frac{0.013}{6}(4)^3 = 0.139$

(iv) Probability that there shall be ($n = 8$) motorbikes in the system: Here ($n = 8$) > ($k = 5$)

$\therefore P_n = P_o \frac{(\lambda/\mu)^n}{k!(k^{n-k})}$ $\therefore P_8 = (0.013)\frac{1}{5!}\frac{1}{5^{8-5}}\left(\frac{2}{0.5}\right)^8$

$= \frac{0.013}{(120)} \cdot \frac{1}{5^3}(4)^8 = \frac{0.013}{(120)} \cdot \frac{(65536)}{(125)} = 0.057$

(v) Expected number of motorbikes in the service station is

$\therefore L_s = \frac{\lambda\mu(\lambda/\mu)^k}{(k-1)!(k\mu-\lambda)^2}P_o + \frac{\lambda}{\mu}$

$= \frac{2\left(\frac{1}{2}\right)(4)^5}{(5-1)!\left[5\left(\frac{1}{2}\right)-2\right]^2}(0.013) + \frac{2}{0.5}$

$= \frac{4^5}{4!(0.5)^2}(0.013) + 4 = 2.22 + 4 = 6.22$

(vi) Expected number of motorbikes in the queue is

$L_q = L_s - \frac{\lambda}{\mu} = 6.22 - \left(\frac{2}{0.5}\right) = 6.22 - 4$

$= 2.22$

(vii) Average waiting time in queue is

$W_q = \frac{L_q}{\lambda} = \frac{2.22}{2} = 1.11$ hours

(viii) Average time spent by a motorbike in waiting and getting serviced i.e. average waiting time in the system is

$$W_s = \frac{L_s}{\lambda} = \frac{6.22}{2} = 3.11 \text{ hours}$$

(ix) Average number of motorbikes in a non-empty queue is

$$L_w = \frac{\lambda}{k\mu - \lambda}$$

$$= \frac{2}{5\left(\frac{1}{2}\right) - 2} = \frac{2}{\frac{1}{2}} = 4$$

(x) Now,

Total Cost (per hour) = Cost incurred on mechanics providing the Service (per hour) + Cost of ill-will (per hour)

= (No. of mechanics) (Wages per hour) + (Average number of motorbikes in system per hour) (Per hour ill-will cost per customer)

= (5) (5) + (L_s) (12) = 25 + (6.22) 12 = 25 + 74.64

= ₹ 99.64

Now, if we have an additional mechanic, then

$\lambda = 2$, $\mu = \frac{1}{2}$ and $k = 6$ for which (on using the formulae) we have, $P_o = 0.017$ and $L_s = 4.58$

∴ Total Cost (Per hour) = (6) 5 + (4.58) 12 = 30 + 54.96 = ₹ 84.96

Hence, comparing the Total Cost (per hour) for 5 and 6 mechanics we see that, it is advisable to include another mechanic, so as to reduce the total cost.

Note: Here it is convenient to use the Little's Formulae:

$L_s = \lambda W_s$, $L_q = \lambda W_q$, $W_s = W_q + \frac{1}{\mu}$ and $L_s = L_q + \frac{\lambda}{\mu}$ as shown above

Solved Problems

Problem 1: A self service store employs one cashier at its counter. Nine customers arrive on an average every 5 minutes while the cashier can serve 10 customers in 5 minutes. Assuming Poisson distribution for arrival rate and exponential distribution for service rate find:

(i) Average number of customers in the system
(ii) Average number of customers in queue or average queue length.
(iii) Average time a customer spends in the system.
(iv) Average time a customer waits before being served.

Solution: This is a case of Single Server Queuing Model (M/M/1): (∞/FIFO) where we have,

λ = Mean arrival rate
= 9 customers per unit period (of 5 minutes)
μ = Service rate
= 10 customers per unit period (of 5 minutes)

(i) Average number of customers in the system i.e. System Length

$$L_s = \frac{\lambda}{\mu - \lambda} = \frac{9}{10-9} = 9$$

(ii) Queue length, $L_q = \frac{\lambda^2}{\mu(\mu-\lambda)} = \frac{9^2}{10(10-9)} = \frac{81}{10(1)} = 8.1$

OR $L_q = L_s - \frac{\lambda}{\mu} = 9 - \frac{9}{10} = 9 - 0.9 = 8.1$

(iii) Average time a customer spends in the system is

$$W_s = \frac{1}{\mu - \lambda} = \frac{1}{10-9} = 1 \text{ unit of 5 minutes}$$

= 1 (5) = 5 minutes

OR $W_s = \frac{L_s}{\lambda} = \frac{9}{9} = 1$ unit of 5 minutes

(iv) Average time a customer waits before being served is

$$W_q = \frac{\lambda}{\mu(\mu-\lambda)} = \frac{9}{10(10-9)} = \frac{9}{10} \text{ units of 5 minutes}$$

$= \frac{9}{10}(5) = 4.5$ minutes

OR $W_q = \frac{L_q}{\lambda} = \frac{8.1}{9} = 0.9$ units of 5 minutes = 4.5 minutes

Problem 2: A milk plant distributes its products by trucks, loaded at the loading dock. It has its own fleet plus the trucks of a transporter are used. The transporter has complained that sometimes the trucks have to wait in the queue and thus he loses money. The transporter has asked the management either to go in for a second loading dock or discount prices equivalent to waiting time. The data available is:

Average Arrival Rate = 3 per hour, Average Service Rate = 4 per hour. The transporter has provided 40% of the total number of trucks. Find:
(i) The probability that a truck has to wait.
(ii) The waiting time of truck.
(iii) Expected waiting time for the transporter's trucks per day.

Solution: We have, Mean arrival rate $\lambda = 3$ trucks per hour, Mean service rate $\mu = 4$ trucks per hour.

(i) Probability that the truck has to wait i.e. the probability that the loading dock is busy is

$$\frac{\lambda}{\mu} = \frac{3}{4} = 0.75$$

(ii) Waiting time of truck (in queue)

$$W_q = \frac{\lambda}{\mu(\mu-\lambda)} = \frac{3}{4(4-3)} = \frac{3}{4} \text{ hour}$$

(iii) Expected waiting time for the transporter's trucks per day

= (Total Trucks arriving per day) (% of Transporter's Trucks) (Expected waiting time per truck)

$$= (3 \times 24)\left(\frac{40}{100}\right)\left(\frac{3}{4}\right) = 21.6 \text{ hours}$$

Problem 3: In a bank with a single server, there are two chairs for waiting customers. On an average one customer arrives every 10 minutes and each customer takes 5 minutes for getting served. Making suitable assumptions, find:

(i) Time for which the server is idle, if it works for 8 hours a day.
(ii) Average waiting time for the customers in the bank.
(iii) Probability that an arrival will get a chair to sit down.
(iv) The probability that an arrival will have to stand.
(v) Probability that there would be two customers in the queue.
(vi) How many additional chairs must be installed to accommodate the average number of waiting customers.

Solution: Let the arrival be Poisson distributed and the service time be distributed exponentially.

Here, average interarrival time = 10 minutes

∴ Average arrival rate, $\lambda = \dfrac{60}{10} = 6$ customers/hr.

Average service time = 5 minutes

∴ Average service rate, $\mu = \dfrac{60}{5} = 12$ customers/hr.

(i) Probability that the Server is idle is

$$P_o = 1 - \frac{\lambda}{\mu} = 1 - \frac{6}{12} = 1 - 0.5 = 0.5 \text{ i.e. } 50\%$$

Hence, the time for which the server is idle (out of 8 hours) per day

$$= P_o \times 8 = (0.5)\,8 = 4 \text{ hours}$$

(ii) Average waiting time for the customers in the bank is

$$W_s = \frac{1}{\mu - \lambda} = \frac{1}{12-6} = \frac{1}{6} \text{ hour} = \frac{1}{6}(60) = 10 \text{ minutes}$$

(iii) Probability that an arrival will get a chair to sit down
= Probability that there are no customers **or** one customer (being served) **or** two customers (one being served and other occupying one chair) in the system

$$= P_0 + P_1 + P_2$$

$$= P_0 + P_0\left(\frac{\lambda}{\mu}\right)^1 + P_0\left(\frac{\lambda}{\mu}\right)^2 = P_0\left[1 + \left(\frac{\lambda}{\mu}\right) + \left(\frac{\lambda}{\mu}\right)^2\right]$$

$$= \frac{1}{2}\left[1 + \frac{6}{12} + \left(\frac{6}{12}\right)^2\right] = \frac{1}{2}\left[1 + \frac{1}{2} + \frac{1}{4}\right] = \frac{1}{2}\left(\frac{7}{4}\right) = \frac{7}{8}$$

(iv) Probability that an arrival will have to stand i.e. [Probability that there are 3 or more customers in the system (1 being served + 2 in queue)]
= 1 − Probability that the arrival gets a chair to sit down

$$= 1 - \frac{7}{8} = \frac{1}{8}$$

Alternately probability that there are 3 or more customers in the system
= Probability that the number of customers in the system exceeds ($k = 2$)

$$= \left(\frac{\lambda}{\mu}\right)^{k+1} = \left(\frac{6}{12}\right)^{2+1} = \left(\frac{1}{2}\right)^3 = \frac{1}{8}$$

(v) Probability that there are two customers in the queue i.e. Probability that there are 3 customers (1 being served + 2 in queue) in the system is

$$P_3 = P_0\left(\frac{\lambda}{\mu}\right)^3 = \left(\frac{1}{2}\right)\left(\frac{6}{12}\right)^3 = \left(\frac{1}{2}\right)^4 = \frac{1}{16}$$

(vi) Average number of waiting customers i.e. queue length is

$$L_q = \frac{\lambda^2}{\mu(\mu - \lambda)} = \frac{(6)(6)}{12(12-6)} = \frac{1}{2} = 0.5$$

Since, there are two chairs available which are sufficient to accommodate the average queue length of (0.5), hence, no additional chair should be installed.

Problem 4: Arrivals at a telephone booth are considered to be Poisson, with an average time of 10 minutes between one arrival and the next. The length of a phone call is assumed to be distributed exponentially with mean of 3 minutes.
  (i) What is the probability that a person arriving at the booth will have to wait?
  (ii) The booth owner will install a second booth when convinced that an arrival would expect waiting for at least 3 minutes for the phone. By how much time should the flow of arrival increase in order to justify a second booth?

Solution: Here, mean inter arrival time of customers = 10 minutes

∴ Mean arrival rate, $\lambda = \dfrac{60}{10} = 6$ customers/hr.

Mean service time = 3 minutes

∴ Mean service rate, $\mu = \dfrac{60}{3} = 20$ customers/hr.

(i) Probability that a person arriving at the booth will have to wait i.e. Probability that the booth is busy

= utilisation factor, $\rho = \dfrac{\lambda}{\mu} = \dfrac{6}{20} = \dfrac{3}{10} = 0.3$

(ii) Let λ_1 be the arrival rate so that the waiting time is

$W_q = 3$ minutes $= \dfrac{3}{60} = \dfrac{1}{20}$ Hr.

Now ∵ $W_q = \dfrac{\lambda_1}{\mu(\mu - \lambda_1)}$

∴ $\dfrac{1}{20} = \dfrac{\lambda_1}{20(20 - \lambda_1)}$

∴ $20 - \lambda_1 = \lambda_1$ ∴ $2\lambda_1 = 20$

∴ $\lambda_1 = 10$ customers per hour

Thus, the arrival rate must increase by at least (10 – 6 = 4) arrivals per hour so as to justify the second booth.

Problem 5: A factory operates for 8 hours every day and has 240 working days in a year. It buys a large number of small machines which can be serviced by its maintenance engineer. The cost of labour and spares to be employed is estimated to be ₹ 4 per hour, fixed. The machines can alternately be serviced by the supplier at an annual contract price of ₹ 20,000 including the labour and spare-parts needed. The supplier undertakes to send a repairman as soon as a call is made but in no case more than one repairman is sent. The service times of the maintenance engineer and the supplier's repairman are both exponentially distributed with respective means of 1.7 and 1.5 days. The machine breakdown occurs randomly and follows Poisson distribution with an average of 2 in 5 days. Each hour that a machine is out of order, it costs the company ₹ 8. Which servicing alternative would you advice it to opt for?

Solution: Here, Mean Arrival (Breakdown) rate is $\lambda = \dfrac{2}{5}$ machines per day.

Now, Total cost (annual) = Annual machine idle time cost + Annual labour and spare parts cost

(i) Servicing by Maintenance Engineer:

Here, Mean service time = 1.7 days

∴ Mean Service rate, $\mu = \dfrac{1}{1.7}$ machines per day

∴ Average number of machines in the system is

$$L_s = \dfrac{\lambda}{\mu - \lambda} = \dfrac{\frac{2}{5}}{\frac{1}{1.7} - \frac{2}{5}} = \dfrac{0.4}{0.59 - 0.4} = \dfrac{0.4}{0.19} = 2.11 \text{ machines per day} \quad \textbf{(Note this step)}$$

∴ Number of machine hours lost per day = (2.11) 8 = 16.88 ... as the factory operates for 8 hours.

∴ Number of machine hours lost annually = (16.88) 240
$\qquad\qquad$ = 4051.2

∴ Annual machine idle time cost = (4051.2) (Per hour idle time cost)
$\qquad\qquad$ = (4051.2) 8 = ₹ 32409.6

Annual labour and spares cost = (Annual hours of work) (per hour labour and spares cost)
$\qquad\qquad$ = (8 × 240) (4) = 7680

∴ $\qquad\qquad$ Annual total cost = 32409.6 + 7680 = ₹ 40,089.6

(ii) Servicing by Supplier:

Here, Average service time = 1.5 days

∴ Average Service rate, $\mu = \dfrac{1}{1.5}$ machines per day

∴ $L_s = \dfrac{\lambda}{\mu - \lambda} = \dfrac{\frac{2}{5}}{\frac{1}{1.5} - \frac{2}{5}} = \dfrac{0.4}{0.67 - 0.4} = \dfrac{0.4}{0.27} = 1.48$ machines per day

∴ Annual machine idle time cost = 1.48 × 8 × 240 × 8 = 22732.8

Annual contract price for labour and spares = 20,000

∴ Annual Total Cost = 22732.8 + 20000 = ₹ 42732.8

Thus, comparing the annual total costs in both the cases, it is advisable to go for the servicing by the maintenance engineer.

Problem 6: A tax consulting firm has four stations (counters) in its office to receive people who have problems and complaints about their income, wealth and sales tax. Arrivals average 80 persons in an 8 hours service day. Each tax advisor spends an irregular amount of time servicing the arrivals which have been found to have Poisson exponential distribution. The average service time is 20 minutes. Calculate the average number of customers in the system, average number of customers waiting to be serviced, average time a customer spends in the system and the average waiting time for a customer. Calculate how many hours each week does a tax advisor spend performing his job. What is the probability that a customer has to wait before he gets the service? What is the expected number of idle tax advisors at any specific time?

Solution: This is a problem of multi server queuing model (M/M/c) : (∞/FIFO) or (M/M/k): (∞/FIFO), with

Average arrival rate $\lambda = \dfrac{80}{8} = 10$ customers per hour,

Average service rate for each advisor, $\mu = \dfrac{60}{20} = 3$ customers/hr.

and k = Number of advisors (servers) = 4

Now, Probability that there are no customers in the system is

$$P_o = \left[\left\{\sum_{i=0}^{k-1} \dfrac{1}{i!}\left(\dfrac{\lambda}{\mu}\right)^i\right\} + \dfrac{1}{k!}\left(\dfrac{\lambda}{\mu}\right)^k \dfrac{1}{\left(1-\dfrac{\lambda}{k\mu}\right)}\right]^{-1}$$

Now, $\sum_{i=0}^{k-1} \dfrac{1}{i!}\left(\dfrac{\lambda}{\mu}\right)^i = \sum_{i=0}^{3} \dfrac{1}{i!}\left(\dfrac{10}{3}\right)^i$

$$= \dfrac{1}{0!}\left(\dfrac{10}{3}\right)^0 + \dfrac{1}{1!}\left(\dfrac{10}{3}\right)^1 + \dfrac{1}{2!}\left(\dfrac{10}{3}\right)^2 + \dfrac{1}{3!}\left(\dfrac{10}{3}\right)^3$$

$$= 1 + \dfrac{10}{3} + \dfrac{1}{2}\left(\dfrac{100}{9}\right) + \dfrac{1}{6}\left(\dfrac{1000}{27}\right) = 16.06$$

and $\dfrac{1}{k!}\left(\dfrac{\lambda}{\mu}\right)^k \dfrac{1}{\left(1-\dfrac{\lambda}{k\mu}\right)} = \dfrac{1}{4!}\left(\dfrac{10}{3}\right)^4 \dfrac{1}{\left(1-\dfrac{10}{4(3)}\right)} = \dfrac{1(123.456)}{24(1-0.833)} = 30.80$

$\therefore P_o = [16.06 + 30.80]^{-1} = (46.86)^{-1} = \dfrac{1}{46.86} = 0.0213$

(i) Average number of customers in the system is

$$L_s = \dfrac{\lambda\mu(\lambda/\mu)^k}{(k-1)!(k\mu-\lambda)^2} P_o + \dfrac{\lambda}{\mu}$$

$$= \dfrac{(10)(3)\left(\dfrac{10}{3}\right)^4}{(4-1)![4(3)-10]^2}(0.0213) + \dfrac{10}{3}$$

$$= \dfrac{30(123.456)}{6(2)^2}(0.0213) + 3.333$$

$$= 3.287 + 3.333 = 6.62$$

(ii) Average number of customers waiting to be serviced is
$$L_q = L_s - \frac{\lambda}{\mu} = 6.62 - \frac{10}{3} = 6.62 - 3.333 = 3.287$$

(iii) Average time a customer spends in the system
$$W_s = \frac{L_s}{\lambda} = \frac{6.62}{10} = 0.66 \text{ hr} = 0.66(60) \cong 40 \text{ minutes}$$

(iv) Average waiting time for customer
$$W_q = \frac{L_q}{\lambda} = \frac{3.287}{10} = 0.33 \text{ hr} \cong 20 \text{ minutes}$$

(v) Now, Probability that a tax advisor is busy is given by,
$$\text{Utilisation factor, } \rho = \frac{\lambda}{k\mu} = \frac{10}{4(3)} = 0.833$$

∴ Expected time spent by an advisor in servicing a customer in a 8 hour day = 0.833 (8) = 6.66 Hr

Similarly, considering a 40 hours week, the expected number of hours spent by an Advisor in performing his job per week = (0.833) 40 = 33.3 Hours

(vi) Probability that a customer has to wait before he gets the service i.e. Probability that there are (k = 4) or more number of customers in the system is
$$P(n \geq 4) = 1 - (n < 4)$$
$$= 1 - [P_0 + P_1 + P_2 + P_3]$$
Now, $P_0 = 0.0213$ and for $(n \leq k)$ we have
$$P_n = P_0 \frac{(\lambda/\mu)^n}{n!}$$
$$\therefore P_1 = P_0 \frac{1}{1!}\left(\frac{10}{3}\right)^1 = P_0 \left(\frac{10}{3}\right) = 3.333 \, P_0$$
$$P_2 = P_0 \frac{1}{2!}\left(\frac{10}{3}\right)^2 = \frac{P_0}{2}(11.11) = 5.555 \, P_0$$
$$P_3 = P_0 \frac{1}{3!}\left(\frac{10}{3}\right)^3 = P_0 \frac{1}{6}(37.037) = 6.173 \, P_0$$
$$\therefore P(n \geq 4) = 1 - [P_0 + 3.333 \, P_0 + 5.555 \, P_0 + 6.173 \, P_0]$$
$$= 1 - 16.061 \, P_0 = 1 - (16.061)(0.0213)$$
$$= 1 - 0.342 = 0.658$$

(vii) Probability that an advisor is idle at a specific time
$$= 1 - \text{Probability that he is busy}$$
$$= 1 - \rho = 1 - 0.833 = 0.167$$

∴ Expected number of idle tax advisors at any specific time
= (Probability that an advisor is idle) (Total number of advisors)
= (0.167) 4 = 0.668

Problem 7: A bank has two tellers working on saving accounts. The first teller handles withdrawals only. The second teller handles deposits only. It has been found that the service time distributions for both deposits and withdrawals are exponential with mean service rate of 20 customers per hour. Depositors are found to arrive in Poisson fashion throughout the day with mean arrival rate 16 per hour. Withdrawers also arrive in Poisson fashion with mean arrival rate 14 per hour. What would be the effect on average waiting time for the depositors and withdrawers if each teller could handle both withdrawals and deposits? What could be the effect if this could be accomplished by increasing mean service time to 3.5 minutes?

Solution: We have,

Mean Arrival rate of depositors, λ_d = 16 per hour

Mean Arrival rate of withdrawers, λ_w = 14 per hour and mean service rate for deposits as well as withdrawals is same i.e. $\mu_d = \mu_w = 20$ per hour.

Now, considering a single server system for separate handling of deposits and withdrawals we have,

Average waiting time for depositors

$$W_{q(d)} = \frac{\lambda_d}{\mu_d(\mu_d - \lambda_d)} = \frac{16}{20(20-16)} = \frac{4}{20} = \frac{1}{5} \text{ Hr.} = \frac{1}{5}(60) = 12 \text{ minutes}$$

Similarly, Average waiting time for withdrawers

$$W_{q(w)} = \frac{\lambda_w}{\mu_w(\mu_w - \lambda_w)} = \frac{14}{20(20-14)}$$

$$= \frac{7}{10(6)} = \frac{7}{60} \text{ Hr.} = \frac{7}{60}(60) = 7 \text{ minutes}$$

Now, if each teller handles the withdrawals and the deposits as well, it becomes a case of multiple - server queuing system (M/M/k): (∞/FIFO) where mean arrival rate, $\lambda = \lambda_d + \lambda_w$ = 16 + 14 = 30 customers per hour, mean service rate of each teller, μ = 20 customers per hour and number of tellers is k = 2.

$$\therefore P_o = \left[\left\{ \sum_{i=0}^{k-1} \frac{1}{i!}\left(\frac{\lambda}{\mu}\right)^i \right\} + \frac{1}{k!}\left(\frac{\lambda}{\mu}\right)^k \frac{1}{\left(1 - \frac{\lambda}{k\mu}\right)} \right]^{-1}$$

Now, $\sum_{i=1}^{k-1} \frac{1}{i!}\left(\frac{\lambda}{\mu}\right)^i = \sum_{i=0}^{1} \frac{1}{i!}\left(\frac{30}{20}\right)^i$

$$= \frac{1}{0!}\left(\frac{3}{2}\right)^0 + \frac{1}{1!}\left(\frac{3}{2}\right)^1 = 1 + \frac{3}{2} = \frac{5}{2}$$

also, $\dfrac{1}{k!}\left(\dfrac{\lambda}{\mu}\right)^k \dfrac{1}{\left(1-\dfrac{\lambda}{k\mu}\right)} = \dfrac{1}{2!}\left(\dfrac{30}{20}\right)^2 \dfrac{1}{\left[1-\dfrac{30}{2(20)}\right]} = \dfrac{1}{2}\left(\dfrac{3}{2}\right)^2 \dfrac{1}{1-\dfrac{3}{4}}$

$= \dfrac{1}{2}\left(\dfrac{9}{4}\right)\dfrac{1}{\dfrac{1}{4}} = \dfrac{4}{2}\left(\dfrac{9}{4}\right) = \dfrac{9}{2}$

$\therefore\ P_o = \left(\dfrac{5}{2}+\dfrac{9}{2}\right)^{-1} = \left(\dfrac{14}{2}\right)^{-1} = (7)^{-1} = \dfrac{1}{7}$

∴ Average waiting time for customers (depositors + withdrawers) is

$W_q = \dfrac{\mu(\lambda/\mu)^k}{(k-1)!(k\mu-\lambda)^2} P_o = \dfrac{20\left(\dfrac{30}{20}\right)^2}{(2-1)![2(20)-30]^2}\left(\dfrac{1}{7}\right)$

$= \dfrac{20\left(\dfrac{3}{2}\right)^2}{1(10)^2}\left(\dfrac{1}{7}\right) = \dfrac{20}{100}\cdot\dfrac{9}{4}\cdot\dfrac{1}{7}$

$= \dfrac{9}{5\times 4\times 7}$ Hr $= \dfrac{9}{140}(60) = 3.86$ minutes

Thus, the average waiting time for depositors would reduce by (12 – 3.86 = 8.14) minutes and that of the withdrawers would reduce by (7 – 3.86 = 3.14) minutes.

Now, if the Mean service time is increased to 3.5 minutes we have,

Mean service rate = $\mu = \dfrac{60}{3.5} = 17.14$ customers/hr.

Proceeding in the same way, we get $P_o = 0.0638$ and hence $W_q = 0.18$ hr = 10.8 minutes.

Hence, the average waiting time for depositors would reduce by (12 – 10.8 = 1.2) minutes while that of the withdrawers will increase by (10.8 – 7 = 3.8) minutes.

Problem 8: A warehouse has only one loading dock manned by a three person crew. Trucks arrive at the loading dock at an average rate of 4 trucks per hour. The arrival rate is Poisson distributed. The loading of a truck takes 10 minutes on an average and can be assumed to be exponentially distributed. The operating cost of a truck is ₹ 20 per hour and the members of the loading crew are paid at the rate of ₹ 6 each per hour. If the second set of three person crew is employed, how the cost changes? Is it advisable to have the second set of three person crew?

Solution: We have, Mean arrival rate, $\lambda = 4$ trucks/hr

Average service time = 10 min ∴ Mean service rate, $\mu = \dfrac{60}{10} = 6$ trucks/hr.

Now, Average number of trucks waiting in the system is

$L_s = \dfrac{\lambda}{\mu-\lambda} = \dfrac{4}{6-4} = 2$

∴ Total Cost (per hour) = Loading Cost per hour + Idle time cost for trucks (per hour)
= (No. of loaders) (Loading cost per person per hour) + (Average number of trucks in system per hour) (Operating cost of a truck per hour)
= (3) 6 + (L_s) 20 = 18 + (2) 20 = ₹ 58

Now, if another set of three person crew is included, the mean service rate will be doubled hence,

μ = 2(6) = 12 trucks/hr but arrival rate is same i.e. λ = 4 trucks/hr.

∴ $L_s = \dfrac{4}{12-4} = \dfrac{1}{2}$

∴ Total cost (per hour) = (3 + 3) 6 + $\left(\dfrac{1}{2}\right)$ 20 = 36 + 10 = ₹ 46.

Thus, comparing the total costs we conclude that it is advisable to have the second set.

Problem 9: A repairman is to be hired to repair machines which breakdown at an average rate of 4 per hour. The breakdowns follow Poisson Distribution. Two repairmen A and B have been interviewed for this purpose. A charges ₹ 100 per hour and services breakdown machines at the rate of 6 per hour. B demands ₹ 125 per hour and services at an average of 8 machines per hour. If downtime of a machine costs ₹ 25 per hour, suggest which repairman should be hired.

Solution: We have, λ = Breakdown rate = 4 per hour

(i) For repairman A, μ = Repair Rate = 6 per hour

∴ Average number of machines remaining unused i.e.

$L_s = \dfrac{\lambda}{\mu - \lambda} = \dfrac{4}{6-4} = 2$ per hour

∴ Total downtime cost = (2) (25) = ₹ 50 per hour
∴ Total cost per hour = Repairman's charges + Downtime cost
= 100 + 50 = ₹ 150 per hour

(ii) For Repairman B, μ = 8

∴ $L_s = \dfrac{\lambda}{\mu - \lambda} = \dfrac{4}{8-4} = 1$ per hour

∴ Total Cost = 125 + (1) (25) = ₹ 150 per hour

Since, the total cost in case of both A and B is same, hence, any one of A and B can be hired.

Problem 10: A TV repairman finds that the time spent on his jobs has an exponential distribution with mean 30 minutes. If he repairs sets in the order the sets arrive and the arrival of the sets is approximately Poisson with an average of 10 per 8 hour day. What is the repairman's expected idle time each day? Find the average number of sets ahead of a new arrival of set.

(P.U. MBA - May 05, Dec. 05)

Solution: This is a case of the single channel (server) queuing model (M/M/1): (∞/FIFO) and we have,

Mean arrival rate of sets for repair = λ = 10 sets per (8 hr) day.
Now, ∵ mean service (repair) time for a job = 30 min
∴ for an 8 hours day,

$$\text{mean service rate} = \mu = \frac{8 \times 60}{30} = 16 \text{ sets per (8 hr) day}$$

(i) ∴ Probability that the repairman (server) is idle is

$$P_0 = 1 - \frac{\lambda}{\mu} = 1 - \frac{10}{16} = \frac{6}{16}$$

$$\therefore P_0 = \frac{3}{8}$$

∴ Repairman's expected ideal time per day

= $P_0 \times$ Number of (working) hours of a day = $\frac{3}{8} \times 8 = 3$ hrs.

(ii) Also average number of sets ahead of a new arrival of set i.e. queue length,

$$L_q = \frac{\lambda^2}{\mu(\mu - \lambda)} = \frac{10^2}{16(16 - 10)}$$

$$= \frac{100}{16(6)} = \frac{25}{4(6)} = \frac{25}{24} = 1.042 \text{ sets.}$$

Problem 11: In a railway marshalling yard, goods trains arrive at a rate of 30 trains per day. Assuming that the inter arrival time follows Poisson exponential distribution and the service time distribution is also exponential with an average of 36 minutes, calculate:
(i) The mean queue size
(ii) Average time the train spends in yard
(iii) The probability that the queue the size exceeds 10
(iv) Probability that the arriving train does not have to wait?   **(P.U. MBA - May 10)**

Solution: This is a single server model with mean arrival rate of trains, λ = 30 per day.
As the mean service time is 36 minutes.
Hence, average service rate of trains per day is

$$\mu = \frac{1}{36} \times 60 \times 24 = 40 \text{ trains per day}$$

(Note that λ and μ must be expressed in same time unit i.e. per day here)
(i) ∴ Mean queue size is

$$L_q = \frac{\lambda^2}{\mu(\mu - \lambda)}$$

$$= \frac{30 \times 30}{40(40 - 30)} = 2.25 \text{ trains}$$

(ii) Average time the mean spends in yard (i.e. system) is

$$W_s = \frac{1}{\mu - \lambda}$$

$$= \frac{1}{40 - 30} = \frac{1}{10} \text{ days}$$

$$= \frac{1}{10}(24) = 2.4 \text{ hours.}$$

(iii) Probability that the queue size exceeds 10
   i.e. Probability that the queue size is greater than or equal to 11
   i.e. Probability system length exceeds 11
   i.e. $P(n > 11) = \left(\frac{\lambda}{\mu}\right)^{11+1}$

$$= \left(\frac{30}{40}\right)^{12} = (0.75)^{12} = 0.031$$

(iv) Probability that the arriving train does not have to wait
   i.e. Probability that the yard is idle
   i.e. $P_0 = 1 - \frac{\lambda}{\mu}$

$$= 1 - \frac{30}{40} = 0.25$$

Problem 12: The tool room company's quality control department is manned by a single clerk who takes an average of 5 minutes in checking parts of each machine coming for inspection. The machines arrive once in every 8 minutes on the average. One hour of the machine is valued at ₹ 15 and a clerk's time is valued at ₹ 4 per hour. What are the average hourly queuing system costs associated with the quality control department.

(P.U. MBA - Dec. 10)

Solution: Here, mean service time for inspection = 5 minutes.

∴ Mean service rate = $\frac{60}{5}$ = 12 machines per hour

As the machines arrive with mean arrival time = 8 minutes, the mean arrival rate is

$$\lambda = \frac{60}{8} = 7.5 \text{ machines per hour}$$

Hence, the average number of machines (lying) in the quality control department is

$$L_s = \frac{\lambda}{\mu - \lambda} = \frac{7.5}{12 - 7.5}$$

$$= \frac{7.5}{4.5} = 1.67$$

Now, average hourly queuing system cost

= Hourly idle time cost of the idle machines + Hourly labour cost
= L_s × (Per hour idle time cost of a machine) + Hourly labour cost
= 1.67 × 15 + 4 = ₹ 29.04

Problem 13: A tailor specializes in ladies dresses. The no. of customers approaching the tailor appear to be Poisson with a mean of 6 customers per hour. The tailor attends the customer on first come first serve basis and customers wait if the need be. The tailor can attend the customers at an average rate of 10 customers per hour with the service time exponentially distributed. Calculate

(i) Utilisation parameter
(ii) Probability that queue - system is idle
(iii) Average time tailor is free on a 10 hour working day.
(iv) Expected number of customers in the shop
(v) Average waiting time of customer in queue before service. **(P.U. MBA - Dec. 06, 12)**

Solution: This is a case of single server (channel) queuing model with mean arrival rate of customers = λ = 6 per hour and mean service rate of the tailor = μ = 10 customers per hour

(i) Utilisation parameter
$$\rho = \frac{\lambda}{\mu} = \frac{6}{10} = \frac{3}{5}$$

(ii) Probability that the queue - system is idle i.e. there is no one in the system is
$$P_0 = 1 - \frac{\lambda}{\mu} = 1 - \rho = 1 - \frac{3}{5} = \frac{2}{5}$$

(iii) Average time the tailor is free on a 10 hour working day
= P_0 × Number of working hours of a day
= $\frac{2}{5}$ × 10 = 4 hrs.

(iv) Expected number of customers in the shop (i.e. system) is
$$L_s = \frac{\lambda}{\mu - \lambda} = \frac{6}{10 - 6} = \frac{6}{4}$$
$$= \frac{3}{2} = 1.5 \text{ customers}$$

(v) Average waiting time of customer in queue before service i.e.
$$W_q = \frac{\lambda}{\mu(\mu - \lambda)} = \frac{6}{10(10 - 6)} = \frac{3}{5(4)}$$
$$= \frac{3}{20} \text{ hr} = \frac{3}{20} \times 60 = 9 \text{ minutes}$$

Alternately, we have,

$$W_q = W_s - \frac{1}{\mu} = \frac{L_s}{\lambda} - \frac{1}{\mu} \quad \because L_s = \lambda W_s$$

$$= \frac{3/2}{6} - \frac{1}{10} \quad \because L_s = \frac{3}{2}$$

$$= \frac{1}{4} - \frac{1}{10} = \frac{3}{20} \text{ hr}$$

Problem 14: In a bank every 15 minutes one customer arrives for cashing the cheque. The staff in the only payment counter takes 10 minutes for serving a customer on an average. Find
(i) The average queue length
(ii) The management has decided to start second counter if the customers have to wait for 25 minutes or more.
(iii) Determine what should be the arrival rate if service rate remains same and waiting time of the customers is 15 minutes and more. **(P.U. MBA - May 13)**

Solution: We have Mean arrival rate of customers, $\lambda = \frac{60}{15} = 4$ per hour and

Mean service rate at the counter, $\mu = \frac{60}{10} = 6$ per hour

(i) ∴ Average Queue Length

$$L_q = \frac{\lambda^2}{\mu(\mu-\lambda)} = \frac{(4)^2}{6(6-4)} = \frac{16}{6(2)} = 1.33 \text{ customers}$$

(ii) Average waiting time in the queue is

$$W_q = \frac{\lambda}{\mu(\mu-\lambda)} = \frac{4}{6(6-4)}$$

$$= \frac{4}{6(2)} = \frac{2}{6} = \frac{1}{3} \text{ hour} = \frac{1}{3}(60) = 20 \text{ minutes}$$

Since, the second counter is opened if the waiting time for customers is 25 minutes or more, hence, with the existing arrival rate, opening of second counter is not justified.

(iii) Now, let λ_1 be the arrival rate so that the waiting time of customers is 15 minutes or more

Hence, $W_q = 15 \text{ min} = \frac{1}{4} \text{ Hr}, \lambda = \lambda_1, \mu = 6$

$$\because W_q = \frac{\lambda_1}{\mu(\mu-\lambda_1)}$$

$$\therefore \frac{1}{4} = \frac{\lambda_1}{6(6-\lambda_1)}$$

$$\therefore 6(6-\lambda_1) = 4\lambda_1 \quad \text{i.e. } 36 - 6\lambda_1 = 4\lambda_1$$

$$\therefore 10\lambda_1 = 36 \quad \therefore \lambda_1 = 3.6 \text{ customers per hour.}$$

Hence the arrival rate should be at least 3.6 customers per hour, in order to justify the second counter.

Exercise

1. What is queuing theory? What type of questions is sought after in analysing a queuing system?
2. What are the assumptions of (i) Single Server Queuing Model and (ii) Multi-Server Queuing Model.
3. Explain the characteristics of Waiting Line Problem/Queuing system.
4. In a service department manned by one server, on an average one customer arrives every 10 minutes. It has been found that each customer requires 6 minutes to be served. Find out:
   (i) Proportion of the time for which the server is idle.
   (ii) Average queue length.
   (iii) Average time spent by a customer in the system.
   (iv) Probability that there would be two customers in the queue.
   (**Ans.** 40%, 0.9 customers, 15 min., 8.64%)
5. For a certain type of machine brought at a certain repair shop, repairing time taken follows exponential distribution with a mean of 5 minutes. Machines breakdown follows Poisson Process with mean rate 3 breakdowns per hour. Find the expected idle time of a repair shop if daily shift is of 8 hours. Also find the average waiting time of the machine.
   (**Ans.** 6 hrs, 1.67 min.)
6. A child care shop dealing with children's requirements has one cashier who handles all customer payments. The cashier serves on an average 15 customers per hour. Customers come to the cashier's area in a random manner but on an average of 10 people per hour. The management received a large number of customers' complaints and decided to investigate the following questions:
   (i) What is the average length of waiting line to be expected under existing conditions?
   (ii) What is the average length of time that a customer would be expected to wait to pay for his purchase?
   (iii) If it was decided that a customer would not tolerate a wait of more than 12 minutes, what is the probability that he would have to wait at least that length of time?
   (**Ans.** 4/3 customers, 8 minutes, 0.245)
7. Patients arrive at a clinic according to Poisson distribution at the rate of 20 patients per hour. Examination time per patient is exponential with mean rate 30 per hour.
   (i) Find the traffic intensity.
   (ii) What is the probability that a new arrival does not have to wait?
   (iii) What is the average waiting time of patient before he leaves the clinic?
   (**Ans.** 0.667, 0.333, 6 minutes)

8. A repairman is to be hired to repair machines that breakdown following a Poisson Process with an average rate of four per hour. The cost of non-productive machine is ₹ 9 per hour. The company has the option of choosing either a fast repairman or a slow repairman. The fast repairman charges ₹ 6 per hour and will repair machines at an average rate of 7 per hour. The slow repairman charges ₹ 3 per hour and will repair machines at an average rate of 5 per hour. Which repairman should be hired?
   (**Ans.** Fast repairman, cost = ₹ 18 per hr; as for slow repairman, cost = ₹ 39 per hour)
9. Data have been accumulated at a banking facility regarding the waiting time for delivery of trucks to be loaded. The data shows that the average arrival rate for trucks at the loading deck is 2 per hour. The average time to load a truck using 3 loaders is 20 minutes. Find:
   (i)   The expected number of trucks in the system.
   (ii) The expected number of trucks waiting to be served.
   (iii) The expected time that a truck is in the system.
   (iv) The expected time in the waiting line.
   (v)   Probability that a truck has to wait for service.
   (vi) The probability of no units in the system.
   (vii) The management is considering hiring another loader at ₹ 5 per hour to reduce the loading time. Drivers are paid ₹ 4 per hour and truck utilisation is valued at ₹ 3 per hour. Should the additional loader be hired if an increase in the service rate to 4 truck per hour would result.
   (**Ans.** 2; 1.33; 1 hr; 0.667 hr; 0.667; 0.333; Yes ₹ 2 saving per hour with new loader as with 3 loaders, Cost = 3 (5) + (4 + 3) (2) = 29, with 4 loaders cost = 4 (5) + (4 + 3) 1 = 27)
10. In a stores, customers arrive in a Poisson stream with a mean 60 per hour. The service time is exponential with a mean of 0.005 hours. How many clerks should be available if the expected waiting time in the system should be less than 10 minutes?
    (**Ans.** No additional clerk required as $\mu \geq 66$ and for one clerk $\mu = 200$)
11. A firm has several machines and wants to install its own service facility for the repair of its machines. The average breakdown rate of the machines is 3 per day. The repair time has exponential distribution. The loss incurred due to the lost time of an inoperative machine is ₹ 40 per day. There are two repair facilities available. Facility A has an installation cost of ₹ 20,000 and the facility B costs ₹ 40,000. With facility A, the total labour cost is ₹ 5,000 per year and with facility B the total labour cost is ₹ 8,000 per year. Facility A can repair $4\frac{1}{2}$ machines per day and the facility B can repair 5 machines per day. Both facilities have a life of 4 years. Which facility should be installed?
    (**Ans.** For 4 years, Facility A: Cost = 20,000 + 4(5000) + 2 (365) (4) (40) = 1,56,800; For Facility B: Cost = 40,000 + 4(8000) + (1.5) (365) (4) (40) = 1,59,600. ∴ Facility A be installed).

12. An insurance company has 3 claim adjusters in their main office. The customers are found to arrive according to Poisson process at an average rate of 40 per 8 hours day for 6 days a week to settle claims against the company. The time spent by an adjuster with a claimant is found to have a negative exponential distribution with a mean service time of 24 minutes. Claimants are served on first-come-first served basis. Calculate:
    (i) Average number of claimants waiting to see the claim adjusters.
    (ii) Average number of claimants in the insurance office.
    (iii) Average waiting time for the claimants.
    (iv) Average time a claimant spends in the office.
    (v) The number of hours spent by an adjuster in working on the claims per week.
    (**Ans.** 0.889; 2.889; 10.66 min.; 34.66 min.; 32.02 hr.)

13. The tooth-care hospital provides free dental service to the patients on every Saturday morning. There are three dentists on duty, who are equally qualified and experienced. It takes, on average, 20 minutes for a patient to get treatment and the actual time taken is known to vary approximately exponentially around this average. The patents arrive according to Poisson distribution with an average of 6 per hour. The administrator officer of the hospital wants to investigate the following:
    (i) Expected number of patients waiting in the queue.
    (ii) The average time that a patient spends at the hospital.
    (iii) The average percentage idle time for each of the dentists.
    (iv) The fraction of time at least one dentist is idle.
    (v) Probability that a patient has to wait for the service.
    (**Ans.** 0.889, 28.9 min., 33.33%, 5/9, 4/9)

14. A milk plant distributes its products by trucks loaded at the loading dock. The data available is: Average arrival rate of trucks at the dock = 3 per hour, Average loading of the trucks = 4 per hour. Find:
    (i) The probability that a truck has to wait as the loading is busy.
    (ii) The waiting time of the truck before being loaded.
    (iii) The average queue length for all the queues.
    (**Ans.** 0.75, 45 min., 2.25 trucks)

15. At an ATM centre arrivals occur according to Poisson distribution with a rate of 5 per hour. Service time per customer is exponentially distributed with mean of 5 minutes.
    (i) Find the expected number of customers in system.
    (ii) What is the percentage of time the facility is idle. **(P.U. MBA - May 12)**
    (**Ans.** 0.7143, 58.33%)

16. Customer arrive at a service counter being manned by one individual at a rate of 25 per hour. The server takes on an average 120 seconds per customer, find (i) average waiting time of customer; (ii) average number of customers in queue. State your assumptions **(P.U. MBA - May 06)**
    (**Ans.** 10 min., 4.167)

17. Write short notes on
    (i) Characteristics of queuing system
    (ii) Multiple channel queuing system **(P.U. MBA - Dec. 05, May 11)**
    (iii) Queuing theory and its characteristics **(P.U. MBA - May 07)**
18. Customers arrive at a box office window, being manned by a single individual according to a Poisson input process with a mean rate of 30 per hour. The time required to serve a customer has an exponential distribution with a mean of 90 seconds. Find the average waiting time of a customer. Also determine the average number of customers in the system and average queue length.
    (**Ans.** 4.5 min, 3 customers, 2.25 customers) **(P.U. MBA - May 08)**
19. Arrivals at the enquiry counter of Roshanara Transport Company are Poisson distributed with an average of 6 per hour. The time that the customers spend for seeking information from the clerk stationed at the counter is known to be exponentially distributed with an average of three minutes. Using this information determine:
    (i) The probability that a customer reaching the counter shall have to wait for getting the needed information.
    (ii) The probability that a queue shall be formed.
    (iii) The expected time that a customer shall wait in the queue to obtain information.
    (**Ans.** 0.3, 0.3, 1.29 min.)
20. ABC manufacturing company operates 24 hours a day. On an average there are 648 times in a day a worker from the floor shop goes to stores to ask for tools. Assume arrival of workers to stores as Poisson exponential. One attendant at the store takes on an average 2 minutes to give the tool demanded. If we have 2 attendants in store instead of one, the service time is not reduced to half but still it is improved and on an average worker demanding the tool gets the tool in 1.2 minutes. The workers from the floor shop are paid at ₹ 15 per hour, while the attendants at the stores are paid ₹12 per hour.
    Determine whether two attendants at the stores will be a more economical system or only one attendant is more economical.
    Find average time spent by workers in waiting at the stores, total number of workers in the system on an average, utilisation factor of service in case of one attendant and two attendants.
    (**Ans.** 1 attendant: 20 min, 9, 0.9; 2 attendants: 2.61 min, 1.174, 0.54;
    Total cost per hour: 1 attendant - ₹ 147; 2 attendants - ₹ 41.61.
    Hence 2 attendants are economical]
21. Weavers in a textile mill arrive at a departmental store room to obtain spare parts needed for keeping the 100 ms running. The store is manned by one attendant. The average arrival rate of weavers per hour is 10 and the service rate is 12 per hour. Arrival rate follows Poisson distribution and service time follows exponential distribution. Determine:
    (i) Average length of waiting line
    (ii) Average time a weaver spends in the system **(P.U. MBA - Dec. 09)**
    (**Ans.** 4.16 weavers, 30 min.)

■■■

Chapter 5...
Markov Chains and Simulation

Contents ...
PART I - MARKOV CHAINS
5.1   Introduction - Definitions
5.2   Results
5.3   Uses of Markov Chains
      Solved Problems
      Exercise - I

PART II - SIMULATION
5.4   Introduction
5.5   Process of Simulation
5.6   Advantages and Disadvantages of Simulation
5.7   Simulation Model
5.8   Monte Carlo Simulation
      Solved Problems
      Exercise - II

[Note: Readers are advised to go through the probability concepts (Chapter 9) before studying this chapter]

PART I - MARKOV CHAINS

5.1 Introduction - Definitions

(a) **Markov Chains:** A sequence of events (or outcomes) in which, an event depends upon the immediate preceding event (only), but not on the other prior events is called as a Markov Chain or Markov Process. e.g. the market shares for a product during a month or year, condition of machines to be used for production each week etc.

(b) **States:** Each of these systems consist of several possible states. e.g. the various brands of the product represent the states for the market share problem, similarly 'working', 'fairly working' and 'non-working' conditions represent the states of the machines etc.

The states are assumed to be finite in number and are collectively exhaustive and mutually exclusive. A state is called as an absorbing state if there is no tendency to leave that state, otherwise it is a non-absorbing state. e.g. If a customer once uses a brand, does not change it at all, then it is an absorbing state.

Markovian Analysis is used to study the probabilities corresponding to the states at any given time period, considering the movements from one state to another.

(c) Transition Probabilities: The probabilities of the system to change from a state (i) to the state (j) is called as a transition probability and it represents the likelihood of the system to change the states, from one time period to the next. These transition probabilities are assumed to remain constant over a period of time.

e.g. Probabilities that customers change their brand of a product from say A to the others - say B and C etc.

(d) Transition Matrix (P): A matrix representing the states in one period (rows) and the states in the next period (columns), along with the transition probabilities between them is called as a transition matrix (P).

e.g. If over a time, it is found that 70% of the customers using brand A continue to use it next year while 20% shift to brand B and 10% to C. Similarly, 60% of customers using B continue to use it while 25% change it to A and 15% shift to C and for C, 75% are retained while 20% are lost to A and 5% to B then we have:

Transition Probability from A to A i.e. retention probability of A = 70% i.e. 0.7

Transition Probability from A to B = 20% i.e. 0.2 and

Transition Probability from A to C = 10% i.e. 0.1

Similarly, Transition probability from B to A = 25% i.e. 0.25

Transition Probability from B to B i.e. retention probability of B = 60% i.e. 0.6 and

Transition Probability from B to C = 15% i.e. 0.15

Similarly, we can write the transition probabilities from C to all the brands and thus, we construct the Transition Matrix as follows:

Next State (Period n = 1)

$$P = \text{Present state (Period n = 0)} \quad \begin{array}{c} \\ A \\ B \\ C \end{array} \begin{array}{ccc} A & B & C \\ \left[\begin{array}{ccc} 0.70 & 0.20 & 0.10 \\ 0.25 & 0.60 & 0.15 \\ 0.20 & 0.05 & 0.75 \end{array} \right] \end{array} \text{Retention and Gains (from)}$$

Retention and Loss (To)

(**Note:** Sum of the probabilities along each row is equal to 1.)

We can represent the states of a system and transition probabilities by two types of diagrams as:

(i) **Transition Diagram:** For the previous example, we can draw the transition diagram as:

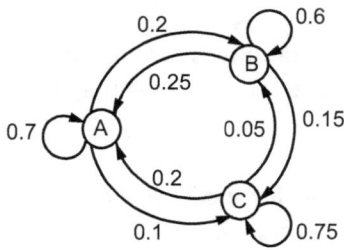

(ii) **Probability Tree Diagram:** This is drawn as follows - If a customer is buying brand A in period (n = 0) then

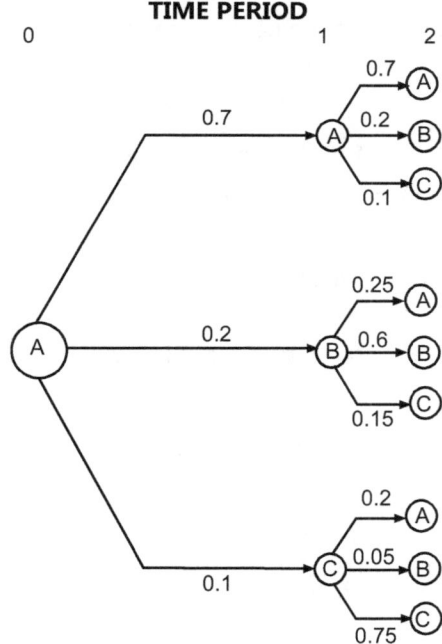

(e) **Initial Condition:** It represents the probabilities for the various states (called state probabilities), for the initial period of time.
e.g. If initially, the market share of brands A, B and C are 50%, 30% and 20% respectively, then the initial condition (for period n = 0) is given by
$$R_0 = [0.5 \quad 0.3 \quad 0.2]$$

(f) Note:
  (i) If the state probabilities at a given period of time depend only upon those of the preceding immediate period, it is a first order Markov Chain. If they depend upon the state probabilities of the last two periods, it is a second order Markov Chain and so on.
  (ii) It is assumed that the transitions between the states take place only once in one period of time. e.g. Customers shift the brand only once in a year.

5.2 Results

(A) To find the State Probabilities for the kth Period of Time:

Markov Chains can be used to predict the future. Thus, if a_1, a_2, a_3 etc. represent the probabilities for the various states (state probabilities) in the initial period (n = 0), we can represent them by a row matrix as

$$R_0 = [a_1 \quad a_2 \quad a_3 \ldots]$$

Hence, the state probabilities for the next period (n = 1) are given by the matrix product of R_0 and the transition matrix P. Thus,

$$R_1 = R_0 \times P$$

Similarly, the state probabilities for the period (n = 2) are given by

$$R_2 = R_1 \times P = R_0 \times P^2 \quad \text{where } P^2 = P \times P \text{ (matrix multiplications)}$$

P_2 is the second step transition matrix.

Thus, in general the state probabilities for the kth period are given by the row matrix (or vector)

$$R_k = R_{k-1} \times P = R_0 \times P^k$$

Note:

(i) A matrix is an ordered arrangement of elements in rows and columns.

e.g.
$$A = \begin{bmatrix} a_{11} & a_{12} & a_{13} \\ a_{21} & a_{22} & a_{23} \end{bmatrix}_{2 \times 3}$$

Row matrix
$$B = \begin{bmatrix} b_1 & b_2 & b_3 \end{bmatrix}_{1 \times 3}$$

Column Matrix
$$C = \begin{bmatrix} c_1 \\ c_2 \end{bmatrix}_{2 \times 1}$$

(ii) **Multiplication of Matrices:** For matrix multiplication, if the multiplying matrix (called pre factor) has **n columns** (say m × n matrix), then the matrix being multiplied (called post factor) must have **n number of rows** i.e. (say n × L).

And then we get the resultant matrix of size (m × L) by row column multiplication rule as follows:

$$A \times B = \begin{bmatrix} a_{11} & a_{12} & a_{13} \\ a_{21} & a_{22} & a_{23} \end{bmatrix}_{2 \times 3} \times \begin{bmatrix} b_{11} & b_{12} \\ b_{21} & b_{22} \\ b_{31} & b_{32} \end{bmatrix}_{3 \times 2}$$

$$= \begin{bmatrix} a_{11}b_{11} + a_{12}b_{21} + a_{13}b_{31} & a_{11}b_{12} + a_{12}b_{22} + a_{13}b_{32} \\ a_{21}b_{11} + a_{22}b_{21} + a_{23}b_{31} & a_{21}b_{12} + a_{22}b_{22} + a_{23}b_{32} \end{bmatrix}_{2 \times 2}$$

$$= \begin{bmatrix} 1^{st} \text{ row} \times 1^{st} \text{ column} & 1^{st} \text{ row} \times 2^{nd} \text{ column} \\ 2^{nd} \text{ row} \times 1^{st} \text{ column} & 2^{nd} \text{ row} \times 2^{nd} \text{ column} \end{bmatrix}$$

e.g.

(i) $\begin{bmatrix} 2 & 3 \\ 3 & 5 \end{bmatrix}_{2 \times 2} \begin{bmatrix} 4 & 1 & 0 \\ 1 & 2 & 3 \end{bmatrix}_{2 \times 3} = \begin{bmatrix} 2(4)+3(1) & 2(1)+3(2) & 2(0)+3(3) \\ 3(4)+5(1) & 3(1)+5(2) & 3(0)+5(3) \end{bmatrix}_{2 \times 3}$

$$= \begin{bmatrix} 11 & 8 & 9 \\ 17 & 13 & 15 \end{bmatrix}$$

(ii) $[2 \ -1 \ 3] \begin{bmatrix} 2 & 1 & 5 \\ 2 & 1 & 0 \\ 3 & 1 & 4 \end{bmatrix}$

$= [2(2) + (-1)(2) + 3(3) \quad 2(1) + (-1)(1) + (3)(1) \quad 2(5) + (-1)(0) + (3)(4)]$
$= [11 \quad 4 \quad 22]$

Example 1: Consider the case where the present market shares of three brands of soft drinks A, B and C are 60%, 30% and 10% respectively. Also, let their transition probability matrix (on the basis of the shifting pattern for a year) be

$$P = \begin{matrix} & \begin{matrix} A & B & C \end{matrix} \\ \begin{matrix} A \\ B \\ C \end{matrix} & \begin{bmatrix} 0.7 & 0.2 & 0.1 \\ 0.2 & 0.6 & 0.2 \\ 0.1 & 0.1 & 0.8 \end{bmatrix} \end{matrix}$$

Solution: Here we have, for the present year (n = 0)
$R_0 = [0.6 \quad 0.3 \quad 0.1]$ .... present 'state probabilities'
Hence, their market shares (state probabilities) after 1 year i.e. for n = 1 is

$R_1 = R_0 \times P$

$= [0.6 \quad 0.3 \quad 0.1] \begin{bmatrix} 0.7 & 0.2 & 0.1 \\ 0.2 & 0.6 & 0.2 \\ 0.1 & 0.1 & 0.8 \end{bmatrix}$

$= [(0.42 + 0.06 + 0.01) \quad (0.12 + 0.18 + 0.01) \quad (0.06 + 0.06 + 0.08)]$
$= [0.49 \quad 0.31 \quad 0.20]$

Thus, the market shares of A, B and C in the next year will be 49%, 31% and 20% respectively. Similarly, market shares after two years i.e. for the period (n = 2) are given by

$$R_2 = R_1 \times P$$

$$= [0.49 \quad 0.31 \quad 0.2] \begin{bmatrix} 0.7 & 0.2 & 0.1 \\ 0.2 & 0.6 & 0.2 \\ 0.1 & 0.1 & 0.8 \end{bmatrix}$$

$$= [0.425 \quad 0.304 \quad 0.271]$$

Thus, the market shares will be 42.5%, 30.4% and 27.1% respectively.

Also, we can use here

$$R_2 = R_0 \times P^2$$

where, P^2 i.e. second step transition matrix is

$$P^2 = P \times P = \begin{bmatrix} 0.7 & 0.2 & 0.1 \\ 0.2 & 0.6 & 0.2 \\ 0.1 & 0.1 & 0.8 \end{bmatrix} \begin{bmatrix} 0.7 & 0.2 & 0.1 \\ 0.2 & 0.6 & 0.2 \\ 0.1 & 0.1 & 0.8 \end{bmatrix}$$

$$= \begin{array}{c} \\ A \\ B \\ C \end{array} \begin{bmatrix} A & B & C \\ 0.54 & 0.27 & 0.19 \\ 0.28 & 0.42 & 0.30 \\ 0.17 & 0.16 & 0.67 \end{bmatrix}$$

Note that, the elements of the matrix P^2 represent the conditional state probabilities after 2 transitions. Thus, the element (0.27) represents the probability of a customer buying brand A initially to buy brand B after two years. Similarly, if a customer has bought brand C initially (at n = 0), the probability that he would buy brand A after 2 periods (years) is given by the element at CA i.e. 0.17.

(B) Steady State Probabilities:

If the transitions from one state to the others continue indefinitely, we reach a stage where the system becomes stable and the state probabilities tend to remain constant. This is the steady state (equilibrium) condition.

This is symbolically given by

$$R_k = R_{k-1}$$

and as we have

$$R_k = R_{k-1} \times P$$

$$\therefore \quad R_k = R_k \times P \quad \ldots \because R_{k-1} = R_k$$

Thus, if S_A, S_B, S_C etc. are the steady state probabilities then

$$[S_A \ S_B \ S_C \ldots] = [S_A \ S_B \ S_C \ldots] \times P$$

which gives us simultaneous equations in S_A, S_B, S_C etc.

Also, we always have, $S_A + S_B + S_C = 1$ which is another equation.

Solving all these equations simultaneously, we get the values of steady state probabilities S_A, S_B, S_C .... etc.

Example 2: In the previous example, if the shifting of consumers continues among the brands, then in the long run their market shares will become constant. Thus, let S_A, S_B, S_C be these steady state probabilities (market shares).

Hence,
$$[S_A\ S_B\ S_C] = [S_A\ S_B\ S_C] \times P$$
$$= [S_A\ S_B\ S_C] \times \begin{bmatrix} 0.7 & 0.2 & 0.1 \\ 0.2 & 0.6 & 0.2 \\ 0.1 & 0.1 & 0.8 \end{bmatrix}$$

$\therefore [S_A\ S_B\ S_C] = [(0.7\ S_A + 0.2\ S_B + 0.1\ S_C)\ (0.2\ S_A + 0.6\ S_B + 0.1\ S_C)\ (0.1\ S_A + 0.2\ S_B + 0.8\ S_C)]$

Thus, $S_A = 0.7\ S_A + 0.2\ S_B + 0.1\ S_C$ i.e. $0 = -0.3\ S_A + 0.2\ S_B + 0.1\ S_C$
i.e. $-3\ S_A + 2\ S_B + S_C = 0$ ..... (1) ..... (after multiplying by 10)

Also, $S_B = 0.2\ S_A + 0.6\ S_B + 0.1\ S_C$ i.e. $0.2\ S_A - 0.4\ S_B + 0.1\ S_C = 0$
i.e. $2\ S_A - 4\ S_B + S_C = 0$ ..... (2)

and $S_C = 0.1\ S_A + 0.2\ S_B + 0.8\ S_C$ i.e. $0.1\ S_A + 0.2\ S_B - 0.2\ S_C = 0$
i.e. $S_A + 2\ S_B - 2\ S_C = 0$ .... (3)

Also, the total of market shares is 100% (As the states are collectively exhaustive and mutually exclusive)

$\therefore \quad S_A + S_B + S_C = 1$ ..... (4)

We can solve equations (1) to (4) simultaneously to get S_A, S_B and S_C as follows:

By (1) − (2) we get, $-5\ S_A + 6\ S_B = 0 \quad \therefore 6\ S_B = 5\ S_A$

$\therefore \quad S_B = \dfrac{5}{6} S_A$

By (1) − (3) we get, $-4\ S_A + 3\ S_C = 0 \quad \therefore 3\ S_C = 4\ S_A$

$\therefore \quad S_C = \dfrac{4}{3} S_A$

Now, from (4) we have, $S_A + S_B + S_C = 1$

$\therefore \quad S_A + \dfrac{5}{6} S_A + \dfrac{4}{3} S_A = 1$

i.e. $\left(1 + \dfrac{5}{6} + \dfrac{4}{3}\right) S_A = 1$

i.e. $\dfrac{19}{6} S_A = 1$

$\therefore \quad S_A = \dfrac{6}{19}$

$\therefore \quad S_B = \dfrac{5}{6} S_A = \dfrac{5}{6}\left(\dfrac{6}{19}\right) = \dfrac{5}{19}$

and $S_C = \dfrac{4}{3} S_A = \dfrac{4}{3}\left(\dfrac{6}{19}\right) = \dfrac{8}{19}$

Thus, in the steady state (long run) the market share of

$$A = S_A \times 100 = \frac{6}{19} \times 100 = 31.58\%,$$

Market share of $\quad B = S_B \times 100 = \frac{5}{19} \times 100 = 26.32\%$ and

Market share of $\quad C = S_C \times 100 = \frac{8}{19} \times 100 = 42.10\%$

5.3 Uses of Markov Chains

Markov Analysis is useful for studying various business problems such as:
(i) Marketing: To study customer loyalty, switching tendencies, market share analysis etc.
(ii) Finance: Accounts Receivables, Depositors Analysis etc.
(iii) Production: Maintenance problems, Inventory management
(iv) Personnel: Manpower planning etc.

Solved Problems

Problem 1: There are three competing daily newspapers in a small city. No other daily has any effect on the current market. A survey of the last month reveals the following data.

Newspaper	Customers on Day 1	Changes during the month		Customers on Last day
		Gains	Losses	
TIME	800	250	350	700
EXPRESS	400	275	200	475
DAWN	500	150	125	525

Further analysis resulted in the gain-loss summary as follows:

Newspaper	Gains from			Losses to		
	T	E	D	T	E	D
TIME	0	150	100	0	250	100
EXPRESS	250	0	25	150	0	50
DAWN	100	50	0	100	25	0

Find the current rate of gains and losses for the newspapers (i.e. find the transition matrix)

Solution: From the data given, we see that
For TIME:
From 800 customers on day 1, the total number of customers lost during the month = 350
∴ Customers Retained = 800 – 350 = 450

∴ Retention probability (i.e. probability that a customer continues to buy the same newspaper) i.e. $p_{TT} = \dfrac{450}{800} = 0.5625$

The number of customers (out of 800) lost to EXPRESS = 250

∴ The transition probability from TIME to EXPRESS i.e. $p_{TE} = \dfrac{250}{800} = 0.3125$

Similarly, Number of customers lost to DAWN = 100

∴ Transition probability from TIME to DAWN i.e. $p_{TD} = \dfrac{100}{800} = 0.125$

(Note that $p_{TT} + p_{TE} + p_{TD} = 0.5625 + 0.3125 + 0.125 = 1$)

Now, For EXPRESS: Number of Customers on day 1 = 400

Total Number of customers lost = 200

∴ Customers retained = 400 − 200 = 200

∴ Retention probability, $p_{EE} = \dfrac{200}{400} = 0.5$

Customers lost to TIME = 150

∴ Transition probability, $p_{ET} = \dfrac{150}{400} = 0.375$

and customers lost to DAWN = 50

∴ Transition probability, $p_{ED} = \dfrac{50}{400} = 0.125$

Similarly, for DAWN: Number of customers on day 1 = 500

Retention Probability, $p_{DD} = \dfrac{500 - 125}{500} = \dfrac{375}{500} = 0.75$

Transition Probability, $p_{DT} = \dfrac{100}{500} = 0.2$ and

Transition Probability, $p_{DE} = \dfrac{25}{500} = 0.05$

Thus, writing these Retention and Transition (Loss) Probabilities along the rows we get the Transition Matrix (P) as follows:

$$P = \begin{array}{c} \\ T \\ E \\ D \end{array} \begin{array}{c} TED \\ \left[\begin{array}{ccc} 0.5625 & 0.3125 & 0.125 \\ 0.375 & 0.5 & 0.125 \\ 0.2 & 0.05 & 0.75 \end{array} \right] \end{array}$$

Problem 2: A market research organisation studied the car purchasing trends in a certain region, with a conclusion that a new car is purchased, on an average, once every 4 years. The buying pattern of the customers is as follows:

Of the current small car owners, 80% will replace the car again with a small car and 20 percent with a large car. Similarly, 60% of the large car users will replace it with a small car while 40% will replace it with another large car. Assuming the market and the preferences remaining the same:

(i) Construct the transition matrix.

(ii) If, there are currently 40,000 small cars and 20,000 large cars in the region, what will be the distribution in 8 years from now.

(iii) Find the probability that a person presently using a small car will buy a large car in the next to next purchase.

(iv) Also draw the tree diagram for the distribution in 8 years.

Solution: We are given the data where the period consists of 4 years, as the transition takes place once in a four year's period of time.

(i) Using the given data, we have the transition matrix as,

$$P = \begin{matrix} & \begin{matrix} S & L \end{matrix} \\ \begin{matrix} S \\ L \end{matrix} & \begin{bmatrix} 0.8 & 0.2 \\ 0.6 & 0.4 \end{bmatrix} \end{matrix}$$

(ii) Presently, (i.e. for period n = 0) there are, 40,000 small cars and 20,000 large cars.

Hence, present share of small cars is $\dfrac{40000}{40000 + 20000} = \dfrac{40000}{60000} = \dfrac{2}{3}$

and the present share of large cars = $\dfrac{20000}{60000} = \dfrac{1}{3}$

Thus, we have, present condition (state probabilities) for period (n = 0) as $R_0 = \begin{bmatrix} \dfrac{2}{3} & \dfrac{1}{3} \end{bmatrix}$

The distribution of the cars, is to be calculated in the 8th year from now. As each period consists of 4 years, hence, we have to find the distribution in the period $(n = \dfrac{8}{4} = 2)$.

It is given by

$R_2 = R_0 \times P^2$

where, P^2 i.e. second step transition matrix is

$$P^2 = P \times P = \begin{bmatrix} 0.8 & 0.2 \\ 0.6 & 0.4 \end{bmatrix} \begin{bmatrix} 0.8 & 0.2 \\ 0.6 & 0.4 \end{bmatrix}$$

$$= \begin{bmatrix} (0.8)(0.8)+(0.2)(0.6) & (0.8)(0.2)+(0.2)(0.4) \\ (0.6)(0.8)+(0.4)(0.6) & (0.6)(0.2)+(0.4)(0.4) \end{bmatrix}$$

... by row column multiplication rule for matrices

$$= \begin{array}{c} \\ S \\ L \end{array} \begin{array}{cc} S & L \\ \begin{bmatrix} 0.76 & 0.24 \\ 0.72 & 0.28 \end{bmatrix} \end{array}$$

$$\therefore R_2 = R_0 \times P^2 = \begin{bmatrix} \frac{2}{3} & \frac{1}{3} \end{bmatrix} \begin{bmatrix} 0.76 & 0.24 \\ 0.72 & 0.28 \end{bmatrix}$$

$= [0.747 \quad 0.253]$ ... using row column multiplication rule for matrices

Thus, the proportion of small cars after two periods (i.e. 8 years) = 0.747 i.e. 74.7% and that of the large cars = 0.253 i.e. 25.3%

Hence, if the total number of cars remains the same i.e. (40,000 + 20,000 = 60,000) then, number of small cars after 8 years = (0.747)(60,000) = 44,820 and number of large cars after 8 years = (0.253)(60,000) = 15,180

(iii) We have to find the probability that a person presently (i.e. in period n = 0) using a small car (S) will buy a large car (L) in the next-to-next purchase (i.e. in the period n = 2).

This is the conditional probability after '2' transitions. This is given by the element belonging to row (S) and column (L) in the second state transition matrix P^2.

i.e.
$$\begin{array}{c} \\ S \\ L \end{array} \begin{array}{cc} S & L \\ \begin{bmatrix} 0.76 & 0.24 \\ 0.72 & 0.28 \end{bmatrix} \end{array}$$

Hence, the required probability = 0.24

(iv) Using the transition matrix, we can construct the tree diagram for the distribution in 8 years (i.e. n = 2 periods) as follows:

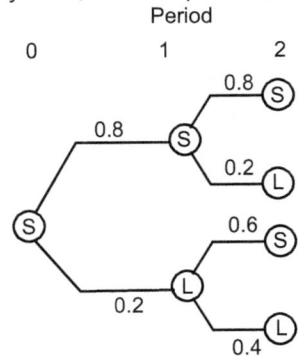

When 'Small' car is used today (n = 0)

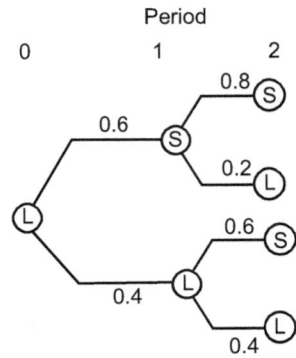

When 'Large' car is used today (n = 0)

Problem 3: A student tries to be punctual for the classes. If he is late on a day, he is 90 percent sure to be on time next day. Similarly, if he is on time, then there is a 30 per cent chance that he will be late on the next day. How often, in the long run, is he expected to be late for the class?

Solution: From the data given, we construct the transition matrix as

$$P = \begin{array}{c} \text{On Time} \\ \text{Late} \end{array} \begin{bmatrix} \text{On Time} & \text{Late} \\ 70\% & 30\% \\ 90\% & 10\% \end{bmatrix} \quad \text{i.e. } P = \begin{array}{c} O \\ L \end{array} \begin{bmatrix} O & L \\ 0.7 & 0.3 \\ 0.9 & 0.1 \end{bmatrix}$$

We have to find the long run probabilities of being 'on time' and 'late'. i.e. the steady state probabilities. Thus, let these probabilities be a (on Time) and b (Late)

Hence, we have from the steady state condition for Markov Chains,

$$[a \ b] = [a \ b] \times P$$

i.e. $[a \ b] = [a \ b] \begin{bmatrix} 0.7 & 0.3 \\ 0.9 & 0.1 \end{bmatrix} = [0.7a + 0.9b \quad 0.3a + 0.1b]$

Thus, comparing we have,

$$a = 0.7a + 0.9b$$

i.e. $0 = -0.3a + 0.9b$

i.e. $-3a + 9b = 0$

i.e. $3a - 9b = 0$ ... (1)

and, $b = 0.3a + 0.1b$

i.e. $0 = 0.3a - 0.9b$

i.e. $3a - 9b = 0$ ... (2) which is same as (1)

Also, the total of the probabilities must be 1
i.e. $a + b = 1$ .... (3)
Now, from (1), $3a = 9b$
i.e. $a = 3b$
∴ From (3) we get
        $3b + b = 1$
i.e. $4b = 1$ ∴ $b = \frac{1}{4} = 0.25$
and   ∴ $a = 3b = 3(0.25) = 0.75$

Thus, in the long run, the probability of being on time = a = 0.75 or 75% and the probability of being late = b = 0.25 i.e. 25%

Hence, the student is expected to be late for the class for 25% of times, in the long run.

Problem 4: Comment on the following transition matrix for the three brands A, B and C

$$\begin{array}{c} \\ A \\ B \\ C \end{array} \begin{array}{ccc} A & B & C \\ \left[\begin{array}{ccc} 0.8 & 0.1 & 0.1 \\ 0.1 & 0.7 & 0.2 \\ 0.0 & 0.0 & 1.0 \end{array}\right] \end{array}$$

Solution: From the row C of the transition matrix we see that the retention probability for brand C is $p_{CC} = 1$. Hence, it implies that it retains all its customers and loses nothing to the brands A and B (as $p_{CA} = p_{CB} = 0$) during one period (month, year etc.)

Also, from the column C, we conclude that, it gains 0.1 i.e. 10% of the customers of A and 0.2 i.e. 20% of the customers of B in one period.

Hence, in the long run (steady state), as it will keep on gaining the customers of A and B (without losing anything), it will grab the entire market and its market share will be 100%.

Thus, brand C represents the absorbing state.

Problem 5: Suppose that new razer blades were introduced in the market by three companies at the same time. When they were introduced, each company had equal share of the number, but during the first year some changes took place which are shown by the following transition matrix.

$$\begin{array}{c} \\ A \\ B \\ C \end{array} \begin{array}{ccc} A & B & C \\ \left[\begin{array}{ccc} 0.9 & 0.03 & 0.07 \\ 0.1 & 0.7 & 0.2 \\ 0.1 & 0.1 & 0.8 \end{array}\right] \end{array}$$

Assuming that no changes in the buying habits of the customers occur,
(i) What is the market share of the three companies at the end of the first year and second year?
(ii) What are the long-run market shares of the companies?

DECISION SCIENCES MARKOV CHAINS AND SIMULATION

Solution: We have the transition matrix as

$$P = \begin{bmatrix} 0.9 & 0.03 & 0.07 \\ 0.1 & 0.7 & 0.2 \\ 0.1 & 0.1 & 0.8 \end{bmatrix}$$

Also, as the initial market shares are equal for the three companies, we have the initial (i.e. for year n = 0) state probabilities as

$$R_0 = \begin{bmatrix} \frac{1}{3} & \frac{1}{3} & \frac{1}{3} \end{bmatrix}$$

(i) ∴ The market shares (i.e. state probabilities) at the end of year 1 i.e. (after period n = 1) will be given by

$$R_1 = R_0 \times P = \begin{bmatrix} \frac{1}{3} & \frac{1}{3} & \frac{1}{3} \end{bmatrix} \begin{bmatrix} 0.9 & 0.03 & 0.07 \\ 0.1 & 0.7 & 0.2 \\ 0.1 & 0.1 & 0.8 \end{bmatrix} = \begin{bmatrix} \frac{1.1}{3} & \frac{0.83}{3} & \frac{1.07}{3} \end{bmatrix}$$

Thus, the market shares of A, B and C at the end of one year are $\frac{1.1}{3} \times 100 = 36.67\%$, $\frac{0.83}{3} \times 100 = 27.66\%$ and $\frac{1.07}{3} \times 100 = 35.67\%$ respectively.

(ii) The market shares at the end of the second year are given by

$$R_2 = R_1 \times P = \begin{bmatrix} \frac{1.1}{3} & \frac{0.83}{3} & \frac{1.07}{3} \end{bmatrix} \begin{bmatrix} 0.9 & 0.03 & 0.07 \\ 0.1 & 0.7 & 0.2 \\ 0.1 & 0.1 & 0.8 \end{bmatrix}$$

$$= [0.3934 \quad 0.2403 \quad 0.3663]$$

Thus, the market shares are 39.34%, 24.03% and 36.63% respectively.

(We can also use $R_2 = R_0 \times P^2$, where $P^2 = P \times P$)

(iii) The long term market shares are given by the steady state probabilities for the companies A, B and C.

Let these be a, b and c respectively.

∴ From the steady state condition for Markov Chains we have

$$[a \quad b \quad c] = [a \quad b \quad c] \times P$$

$$= [a \quad b \quad c] \times \begin{bmatrix} 0.9 & 0.03 & 0.07 \\ 0.1 & 0.7 & 0.2 \\ 0.1 & 0.1 & 0.8 \end{bmatrix}$$

i.e. $[a \quad b \quad c] = [0.9a + 0.1b + 0.1c \quad 0.03a + 0.7b + 0.1c \quad 0.07a + 0.2b + 0.8c]$

∴ $a = 0.9a + 0.1b + 0.1c$

i.e. $\quad 0 = -0.1a + 0.1b + 0.1c$
i.e. $\quad -a + b + c = 0$ ... (1)

$\quad b = 0.03a + 0.7b + 0.1c$

i.e. $\quad 0 = 0.03a - 0.3b + 0.1c$

i.e. $\quad 3a - 30ab + 10c = 0$ ... (2)

and $\quad c = 0.07a + 0.2b + 0.8c$

i.e. $\quad 0 = 0.07a + 0.2b - 0.2c$

i.e. $\quad 7a + 20b - 20c = 0$ ... (3)

Also, we must have,

$\quad a + b + c = 1$ ... (4)

To find a, b and c we solve these equations simultaneously as follows:

Equation (1) × 30 gives

$\quad -30a + 30b + 30c = 0$

and $\quad 3a - 30b + 10c = 0$ ... from (2)

∴ adding, $\quad -27a + 40c = 0 \quad \therefore 40c = 27a \quad \therefore c = \dfrac{27}{40}a$

Similarly, equation (1) × 20 gives

$\quad -20a + 20b + 20c = 0$

and $\quad 7a + 20b - 20c = 0$ ... from (3)

∴ adding, $-13a + 40b = 0 \quad \therefore 40b = 13a \quad \therefore b = \dfrac{13}{40}a$

∴ From (4) we have,

$\quad a + b + c = 1 \quad$ i.e. $a + \dfrac{13}{40}a + \dfrac{27}{40}a = 1$

i.e. $\quad a\left(1 + \dfrac{13}{40} + \dfrac{27}{40}\right) = 1$

i.e. $\quad a(1 + 1) = 1$

∴ $\quad a = \dfrac{1}{2} = 0.5$ i.e. 50%

∴ $\quad b = \dfrac{13}{40}a = \dfrac{13}{40}(0.5)$

$\quad = 0.1625$ i.e. 16.25% and

$\quad c = \dfrac{27}{40}a = \dfrac{27}{40}(0.5) = 0.3375$ i.e. 33.75%

Thus, the long term market shares of A, B and C will be 50%, 16.25% and 33.75% respectively.

Problem 6: The number of units of an item that are withdrawn from the inventory on a day to day basis is a Markov Chain process in which the requirements for tomorrow depend on today's requirements. A one-day transition matrix is given below:

		Tomorrow		
		5	10	12
Today	5	0.6	0.4	0.0
	10	0.3	0.3	0.4
	12	0.1	0.3	0.6

(i) Develop a two day transition matrix.

(ii) Comment how a two-day transition matrix might be helpful to a manager who is responsible for the inventory management.

Solution:

(i) Using the given one-day transition matrix, we get the two-day transition matrix (P^2) as

$$P^2 = P \times P = \begin{bmatrix} 0.6 & 0.4 & 0.0 \\ 0.3 & 0.3 & 0.4 \\ 0.1 & 0.3 & 0.6 \end{bmatrix} \begin{bmatrix} 0.6 & 0.4 & 0.0 \\ 0.3 & 0.3 & 0.4 \\ 0.1 & 0.3 & 0.6 \end{bmatrix}$$

∴ By using row-column multiplication rule we have

$$P^2 = \begin{bmatrix} 0.6(0.6) + 0.4(0.3) + 0.0(0.1) & 0.6(0.4) + 0.4(0.3) + 0.0(0.3) & 0.6(0.0) + 0.4(0.4) + 0.0(0.6) \\ 0.3(0.6) + 0.3(0.3) + 0.4(0.1) & 0.3(0.4) + 0.3(0.3) + 0.4(0.3) & 0.3(0.0) + 0.3(0.4) + 0.4(0.6) \\ 0.1(0.6) + 0.3(0.3) + 0.6(0.1) & 0.1(0.4) + 0.3(0.3) + 0.6(0.3) & 0.1(0.0) + 0.3(0.4) + 0.6(0.6) \end{bmatrix}$$

$$= \begin{array}{c} \\ 5 \\ 10 \\ 12 \end{array} \begin{array}{ccc} 5 & 10 & 12 \end{array} \\ \begin{bmatrix} 0.48 & 0.36 & 0.16 \\ 0.31 & 0.33 & 0.36 \\ 0.21 & 0.31 & 0.48 \end{bmatrix}$$

(ii) Consider that the inventory manager places order every day. If the material so ordered reaches him after two days (i.e. lead time), then the matrix P^2 will be useful to him, for making the ordering decision.

From the two-day transition matrix P^2 we see that, if today's requirement of the item is 5, then two days later (when the ordered material will be received), the probability that 5 units will be required is 0.48, 10 units will be required is 0.36 and 12 units will be required is 0.16 and so on. Thus, these figures will guide him in deciding the quantity to be ordered today.

Problem 7: Three super markets X, Y and Z are located in a city. At the end of the last year, X had 40% of the market while its competitors Y and Z each had 30% of the market. During the last year, total revenue for the three stores was ₹ 50 lakh and the supermarket X had a net profit of 15 percent of its revenue. Both these figures are expected to remain same for the next year. The marketing manager of X has suggested a special scheme to be offered to the customers, whereby it would retain 88 percent of its customers while gaining 12% of the customers of Y and 8% of the customers of Z. As an effect of this scheme, the supermarket Y is expected to retain 85% of its customers while gaining 7% and 10% of customers from X and Z respectively. Finally, Supermarket Z would retain 82% of its customers and gain 5% and 3% of X and Y respectively. If the cost for implementing the special scheme is ₹ 50,000/-, suggest if the scheme should be implemented or not.

Solution: We are given the retention and **gain** probabilities (percentages) for the three supermarkets. Hence, writing them along the **columns** we get the transition matrix as

$$P = \begin{matrix} \\ X \\ Y \\ Z \end{matrix} \begin{matrix} X & Y & Z \\ \begin{bmatrix} 0.88 & 0.07 & 0.05 \\ 0.12 & 0.85 & 0.03 \\ 0.08 & 0.10 & 0.82 \end{bmatrix} \end{matrix}$$

The present market shares of X, Y and Z are 40%, 30% and 30% respectively. Thus, we have the present (n = 0) state probabilities as $R_0 = [0.4 \ 0.3 \ 0.3]$.

Let us find the market shares (state probabilities) for the three supermarkets, for the next year (i.e. for n = 1) as,

$$R_1 = R_0 \times P = [0.4 \ 0.3 \ 0.3] \begin{bmatrix} 0.88 & 0.07 & 0.05 \\ 0.12 & 0.85 & 0.03 \\ 0.08 & 0.10 & 0.82 \end{bmatrix}$$

$$= [0.412 \ 0.313 \ 0.275]$$

...... using row column multiplication rule.

Thus, in the next year the market share of X will be 0.412 i.e. 41.2%, if the scheme is implemented.

Now, we have for the supermarket X:

Present Profit = (Revenue for X) (net profit percentage)
= (40% of 50 lakh) × (15%)
= (0.4 × 50,00,000) (0.15) = ₹ 3,00,000

Now, if the Scheme is implemented
Profit for   X = (0.412 × 50,00,000) (0.15) − Cost of scheme
= 3,09,000 − 50,000 = ₹ 2,59,000

Hence, we see that implementing the scheme is not advisable for X.

Problem 8: A manufacturing company has a certain piece of equipment that is inspected at the end of each day and is classified as just overhauled, good, fair or inoperative. If the piece is inoperative, it is overhauled, a procedure that takes one day. Assume that the working condition of the equipment follows a Markov Chain with the transition matrix given below.

$$\begin{array}{c} \\ O \\ G \\ F \\ I \end{array} \begin{array}{cccc} O & G & F & I \\ \left[\begin{array}{cccc} 0 & 3/4 & 1/4 & 0 \\ 0 & 1/2 & 1/2 & 0 \\ 0 & 0 & 1/2 & 1/2 \\ 1 & 0 & 0 & 0 \end{array}\right] \end{array}$$

It costs ₹ 125 to overhaul a machine (including lost time) on an average and ₹ 75 as production lost if a machine is found inoperative. Using the steady state probabilities, compute the expected per day cost of maintenance.

Solution: Let the steady state probabilities for the four states of the machine: just overhauled (O), Good (G), Fair (F) and Inoperative (I) be a, b, c and d respectively.

Hence, using steady state condition for Markov Chains, we have

[a b c d] = [a b c d] × P   ... where P is the transition matrix

$$= [a \ b \ c \ d] \begin{bmatrix} 0 & 3/4 & 1/4 & 0 \\ 0 & 1/2 & 1/2 & 0 \\ 0 & 0 & 1/2 & 1/2 \\ 1 & 0 & 0 & 0 \end{bmatrix}$$

$$= \left[0+0+0+d \quad \frac{3}{4}a + \frac{1}{2}b + 0 + 0 \quad \frac{1}{4}a + \frac{1}{2}b + \frac{1}{2}c + 0 \quad 0 + 0 + \frac{1}{2}c + 0 \right]$$

... using row column multiplication rule

i.e. [a b c d] = $\left[d \quad \frac{3}{4}a + \frac{1}{2}b \quad \frac{1}{4}a + \frac{1}{2}b + \frac{1}{2}c \quad \frac{1}{2}c \right]$

Thus, comparing we get

$a = d$, $b = \frac{3}{4}a + \frac{1}{2}b$ $\therefore \frac{1}{2}b = \frac{3}{4}a$ $\therefore b = \frac{3}{2}a$

$c = \frac{1}{4}a + \frac{1}{2}b + \frac{1}{2}c$ $\therefore \frac{1}{2}c = \frac{1}{4}a + \frac{1}{2}b = \frac{1}{4}a + \frac{1}{2}\left(\frac{3}{2}\right)a = a$ $\therefore c = 2a$

and $d = \frac{1}{2}c = \frac{1}{2}(2a) = a$

Also, we must have a + b + c + d = 1

$\therefore$ $a + \dfrac{3}{2}a + 2a + a = 1$

i.e. $\dfrac{11}{2}a = 1$ $\therefore a = \dfrac{2}{11}$

$\therefore$ $b = \dfrac{3}{2}a = \dfrac{3}{2}\left(\dfrac{2}{11}\right) = \dfrac{3}{11}$, $c = 2a = 2\left(\dfrac{2}{11}\right) = \dfrac{4}{11}$, $d = a = \dfrac{2}{11}$

Thus, the machine will be overhauled for $\left(\dfrac{2}{11}\right)^{th}$ time of a day, it will be in good condition for $\left(\dfrac{3}{11}\right)^{th}$ time and will be in fair condition for $\left(\dfrac{4}{11}\right)^{th}$ time of a day. It will be inoperative for $\left(\dfrac{2}{11}\right)^{th}$ of the time in a day. **(Note this step)**

Thus, the total cost of maintenance per day (in long run)

= overhauling cost + cost due to production loss

= $\dfrac{2}{11}(125) + \dfrac{2}{11}(75) = ₹\ 36.36$

Problem 9: Market share of Brand A, B, C are 50%, 30% and 20%. Customers shift their brands. Brand switching matrix every quarter is given below:

From	To		
	A	B	C
A	50%	30%	20%
B	20%	70%	10%
C	20%	20%	60%

Find market share at the end of quarter. **(P.U. MBA - May 06)**

Solution: We have the present market shares of A, B and C as 50%, 30% and 20% respectively. Thus, for the present (initial) quarter (n = 0) we have, the state probabilities as:

$R_0 = [0.5\ \ 0.3\ \ 0.2]$

Also, since the transition matrix (or the switching matrix) is

$$P = \begin{matrix} A \\ B \\ C \end{matrix} \begin{matrix} A & B & C \end{matrix} \\ \begin{bmatrix} 0.5 & 0.3 & 0.2 \\ 0.2 & 0.7 & 0.1 \\ 0.2 & 0.2 & 0.6 \end{bmatrix}$$

Hence, the market shares at the end of the quarter i.e. after (n = 1) periods is

$R_1 = R_0 \times P$

$= [0.5 \ 0.3 \ 0.2] \begin{bmatrix} 0.5 & 0.3 & 0.2 \\ 0.2 & 0.7 & 0.1 \\ 0.2 & 0.2 & 0.6 \end{bmatrix}$

$= [0.5(0.5) + 0.3(0.2) + 0.2(0.2) \quad 0.5(0.3) + 0.3(0.7) + 0.2(0.2) \quad 0.5(0.2) + 0.3(0.1) + 0.2(0.6)]$

∴ $R_1 = [0.35 \ 0.4 \ 0.25]$

Thus, the market shares of A, B and C at the end of the quarter will be 35%, 40% and 25% respectively.

Problem 10: Market survey is made on two brands of breakfast foods A and B. Every time a customer purchases, he may buy the same brand or switch to another brand. The transition matrix is given below:

From	To	
	A	B
A	0.8	0.2
B	0.6	0.4

At present 60% of people buy brand A and 40% buy brand B. Determine market shares of brands A and B in the steady state. **(P.U. MBA - May 07)**

Solution: We have the transition matrix as:

$$P = \begin{matrix} & A & B \\ A & \begin{bmatrix} 0.8 & 0.2 \\ B & 0.6 & 0.4 \end{bmatrix} \end{matrix}$$

We have to find the steady state (long run) market shares of brand A and B i.e. we have to find steady state probabilities. Let these be a (for brand A) and b (for brand B).

Hence, we have from the steady state condition for Markov chains,

$[a \ b] = [a \ b] \times P$

i.e. $[a \ b] = [a \ b] \begin{bmatrix} 0.8 & 0.2 \\ 0.6 & 0.4 \end{bmatrix}$

i.e. $[a \ b] = [(0.8a + 0.6b) \ (0.2a + 0.4b)]$

∴ Comparing we have

$a = 0.8a + 0.6b$

∴ $0.2a - 0.6b = 0$

i.e. $a - 3b = 0$ ... (1)

and $b = 0.2a + 0.4b$

∴ $-0.2a + 0.6b = 0$
i.e. $-a + 3b = 0$
i.e. $a - 3b = 0$ which is same as (1)

Also, as the total of the state probabilities must be 1.

∴ $a + b = 1$ ... (2)

Now, from (1), $a = 3b$

∴ From (2), $3b + b = 1$

∴ $b = \dfrac{1}{4} = 0.25$

∴ $a = 3b = 3(0.25) = 0.75$

Thus, the steady state market shares of brands A and B will be 0.75, i.e. 75% and 0.25 i.e. 25% respectively.

Problem 11: It was found in the survey that that mobility of the population in a state to the village, town and city is in following percentage:

From	To		
	Village	Town	City
Village	50%	30%	20%
Town	10%	70%	20%
City	10%	40%	50%

What will be the proportion of population in village, town and city after two years given that present population is 0.7, 0.2 and 0.1 respectively. **(P.U. MBA - Dec. 10)**

Solution: Form the given information we get the transition probability matrix for the population mobility as

$$P = \begin{array}{c} \\ V \\ T \\ C \end{array} \begin{array}{c} V \quad T \quad C \\ \left[\begin{array}{ccc} 0.5 & 0.3 & 0.2 \\ 0.1 & 0.7 & 0.2 \\ 0.1 & 0.4 & 0.5 \end{array} \right] \end{array}$$

At present (i.e. for period n = 0) the population proportions in the village, town and city are 0.7, 0.2 and 0.1 respectively i.e. the present state probabilities are

$R_0 = [0.7 \quad 0.2 \quad 0.1]$

Hence, the state probabilities after two years (i.e. for n = 2) are

$R_2 = R_0 \times P^2$ ... (1)

where the second step transition matrix is

$P^2 = P \times P$

$= \begin{bmatrix} 0.5 & 0.3 & 0.2 \\ 0.1 & 0.7 & 0.2 \\ 0.1 & 0.4 & 0.5 \end{bmatrix} \begin{bmatrix} 0.5 & 0.3 & 0.2 \\ 0.1 & 0.7 & 0.2 \\ 0.1 & 0.4 & 0.5 \end{bmatrix}$

$= \begin{bmatrix} 0.30 & 0.44 & 0.26 \\ 0.14 & 0.60 & 0.26 \\ 0.14 & 0.51 & 0.35 \end{bmatrix}$ ... by row column multiplication rule for matrices

∴ From (1) we get

$R_2 = [0.7\ 0.2\ 0.1] \begin{bmatrix} 0.30 & 0.44 & 0.26 \\ 0.14 & 0.60 & 0.26 \\ 0.14 & 0.51 & 0.35 \end{bmatrix}$

$= [0.252\ 0.479\ 0.269]$

Thus, the proportion of population in village, town and city after two years will be 25.2%, 47.9% and 26.9% respectively.

Exercise - I

1. What is Markov Chain? How is it useful for managerial decisions?
2. Explain the following terms:
   (i) Transition Matrix
   (ii) Steady state conditions
3. Write a note on Markov Chain.   **(P.U. MBA - May 05, Dec. 05, May 11)**
4. There are three dairies in a town which supply the entire milk. There are 1000 customers in the town. The customers shift from one dairy to the other due to advertising, quality etc. The following table gives the flow of customers within a period of one month. The initial market shares of the three dairies are A = 25%, B = 45% and C = 30%.

Dairy	Customers (At Beginning)	Gain	Loss	Customers (At End)
A	250	62	60	262
B	450	53	50	443
C	300	50	55	295
	1000			1000

The details of the Gains and Losses are as follows:

Diary	Gain from			Loss to		
	A	B	C	A	B	C
A	0	35	27	0	25	25
B	25	0	28	35	0	25
C	25	25	0	27	28	0

Construct the Transition Matrix

(Ans.:) $\begin{bmatrix} 0.8 & 0.1 & 0.1 \\ 0.08 & 0.866 & 0.055 \\ 0.09 & 0.093 & 0.82 \end{bmatrix}$

5. In a city only two brands of a cola are sold - Royal and Nice. For a buyer buying Royal last time, there is 0.75 chance that he will buy the same next time. For a buyer of Nice, the chance that he buys Royal next time is 0.4.
   (i) Develop the transition matrix.
   (ii) Find the probability that a customer purchasing Royal today, shall buy Nice in the next-to-next purchase.
   (iii) Find the probability that three purchases from now, a customer shall buy Royal given that the present market share is Royal (60%), Nice (40%).
   (iv) Find the long run market shares of the two brands, assuming the market and customer preferences remain the same.

(Ans.: $\begin{matrix} & R & N \\ R & 0.75 & 0.25 \\ N & 0.40 & 0.60 \end{matrix}$, 0.3375, 0.61, 61.5% and 38.5%)

6. A market survey is made on three brands of breakfast foods X, Y and Z. Everytime a customer purchases new package, he may buy the same brand or switch to another. The following estimates for the shifts (in percent) are obtained

$$\begin{matrix} & & \text{Next} & \\ & X & Y & Z \\ \text{Present} \begin{matrix} X \\ Y \\ Z \end{matrix} & \begin{bmatrix} 70 & 20 & 10 \\ 30 & 50 & 20 \\ 30 & 30 & 40 \end{bmatrix} \end{matrix}$$

At this time, it is estimated that 30% of people buy brand X, 20% brand Y and 50% brand Z. What will be the distribution of the customers one and two time periods later? Also find the distribution at equilibrium.

(Ans.: 42, 31 and 27%; 46.8, 32 and 21.2%; 50, 31.25 and 18.75%)

7. A company owns three TV channels. All of them telecast one hour news program at 6.00 pm. At the end of each week, the leader is the channel with the highest estimated average fraction of the viewing audience during that time slot. Over a period of time, data have been obtained on the weekly shifts in the viewership between the channels as shown below. At present, channel A is a leader holding half of the viewing audience. The viewership fractions corresponding to channels B and C are $\frac{3}{10}$ and $\frac{2}{10}$ respectively.

$$\begin{array}{c c} & \begin{array}{ccc} A & B & C \end{array} \\ \begin{array}{c} A \\ B \\ C \end{array} & \left[\begin{array}{ccc} 0.4 & 0.35 & 0.25 \\ 0.1 & 0.7 & 0.2 \\ 0.15 & 0.25 & 0.6 \end{array} \right] \end{array}$$

If the advertisement rates for the channels are such that for a leader it is ₹ 1 lakh per week and for non leaders it is ₹ 50,000 per week, find

(i) Who will be the leader next week?

(ii) How much change will be there in the advertisement revenue for the company for the next week?

(**Ans.:** Channel B, Change = [(0.5 + 0.3 + 0.2) 100000 + (0.5 + 0.7 + 0.8) 50000] – [(0.26 + 0.435 + 0.305) 100000 + (0.54 + 0.565 + 0.695) 50000] = 200000 – 190000 = ₹ 10000 less.])

8. Explain the concept of Markov Process, giving illustration. **(P.U.MBA - Dec.06)**

9. Find the steady state probabilities for three newspapers whose transition probability matrix is given below

$$\left[\begin{array}{ccc} 0.8 & 0.125 & 0.075 \\ 0.09 & 0.9 & 0.01 \\ 0.117 & 0.017 & 0.866 \end{array} \right]$$

(P.U. MBA - Dec. 09)

(**Ans.:** 0.3307, 0.4506, 0.2187)

PART II - SIMULATION

5.4 Introduction

In the earlier chapters we dealt with mathematical models describing a given system which were solved analytically to obtain the optimal solution. However, practically there are many situations which are too complex to obtain the solution of. The simulation method is used to study these problems. It involves developing of a model of a real system and then performing experiments on it with a view of predicting the behaviour of a system over a time. It is however just a descriptive and not an optimising technique.

5.5 Process of Simulation

It involves following four phases:
(i) Defining the problem and statement of the objectives.
(ii) Development of an appropriate model so as to represent the real system. This needs a collection of appropriate data.
(iii) Experimentation (manipulation) with the model - The model so developed is then run to study the model performance. If the simulation is probabilistic (stochastic) it needs to be run many times.
(iv) Analysis and Interpretation of the results of the experiment so as to make changes in the model if necessary.

5.6 Advantages and Disadvantages of Simulation

(a) Advantages:
(i) Useful for analysing problems where conventional quantitative analytical models fail or can not be used easily.
(ii) Easier to use, flexible and less expensive.
(iii) As a model is used for analysis, risk of interference with real world systems gets avoided.
(iv) Can be used to study the interactive effect of individual components.

(b) Disadvantages:
(i) Does not give optimal solutions like other quantitative techniques and is just descriptive in nature.
(ii) Developing a model is often a complicated and time consuming process.
(iii) Not precise.
(iv) Only uncertain situations can be evaluated.

5.7 Simulation Model

Simulation is a statistical experiment where the results of a system are obtained through sampling.

The elements of a Simulation Model are:

(i) System Input: It represents the logic and the rules governing the problem.

(ii) Random Number Generation: The sampling from any probabilistic distribution is based on the use of random numbers (described ahead). These are used to simulate the given model.

(iii) Work Data Sheet: It is used to record the results of a simulation run and is used for obtaining the further results.

One of the examples of the simulation models is the Monte Carlo Simulation Model which resembles gambling establishments where the samples are selected in a purely random manner.

5.8 Monte Carlo Simulation

It is used to study probabilistic simulations where the given process has a random or chance component. Using Monte Carlo simulation, a given problem is solved by simulating the original data with random number generators.

Note: Random number are the numbers constructed by the combination of one or more digits (from 0 to 9) in such a manner that each of these 10 digits can occur with equal probability. These are generated by using dice selection, by spinning a roulette wheel or by using random number tables or can be generated by computers.

The **Monte Carlo Simulation Method** generally involves the following steps:

Step 1: Identify the input variables, collect data on them and write down the probability distributions for them. This represents the simulation model.

Step 2: Rewrite the cumulative probability distribution.

Step 3: Identify the Random Number Intervals corresponding to these cumulative probability figures. (If the probabilities are expressed in two decimal digits use random numbers from 00 to 99 and if they are in three decimal digits use random numbers from 000 to 999)

Step 4: Prepare a table for the random numbers (to be generated to simulate the model) and the expected (simulated) values of the input variables etc.

Step 5: Generate 'n' random numbers (if not given) from the random number tables. (Start with any number in the table and proceed in horizontal, vertical or diagonal direction to select n numbers consecutively). For each of the random number, identify the random number interval (found in step 3) to which it belongs. The corresponding value of the input variable is the simulated value.

Step 6: Process this simulated information and then summarise the data and interpret the results.

Note: If the problem involves more than one variables (e.g. quantity of material consumed and lead time etc.) then simulate their values separately using the above method.

Example 1: A bakery keeps stock of a popular brand of cakes. Previous experience shows the daily demand pattern for the cakes with associated probabilities as given below:

Daily Demand (Number of units):	0	10	20	30	40	50
(Corresponding) Probability:	0.01	0.20	0.15	0.50	0.12	0.02

Use the following sequence of (ten) random numbers to simulate (estimate) the demand for next 10 days. Also find the average demand per day.

Random Numbers: 25, 39, 65, 76, 12, 05, 73, 89, 19, 49.

Solution: We use Monte-Carlo simulation method to simulate the data.

1. We have the 'Daily Demand of Cakes' as the input variable for which the probability distribution is given. (The Probability Distribution represents the model to be simulated by using the random numbers)

2. **To find the Cumulative Probabilities:** We calculate the corresponding cumulative probabilities for the given values of input variable as

Daily demand	0	10	20	30	40	50
Probability	0.01	0.20	0.15	0.50	0.12	0.02
Cumulative Probability	0.01	(0.01 + 0.20) = 0.21	(0.21 + 0.15) = 0.36	(0.36 + 0.50) = 0.86	(0.86 + 0.12) = 0.98	(0.98 + 0.02) = 1.00

3. **To find Random Number Intervals:** Since the probabilities are expressed using two decimal digits, hence we consider the random numbers involving two digits i.e. 00 to 99 (which are 100 in number). Now, the total cumulative probability '1' will correspond to these 100 random numbers. Hence, considering all the cumulative probability figures, we can identify the proportionate interval of random numbers as follows:

e.g. The first cumulative probability is (0.01). This will correspond to the first (0.01 × 100 = 1) random number in 00 to 99. Thus, the corresponding interval (having only one number) is 00-00. The next cumulative probability is 0.21. This will correspond first (0.21 × 100 = 21) numbers i.e. from 00 to 20. Of these, numbers (00) belongs to the first interval. Hence, the second interval is (01 - 20). The third cumulative probability is 0.36, which will correspond to first (0.36 × 100 = 36) random numbers i.e 00 to 35. Of these, (00 to 20) belong to the first and second interval. Hence, the third interval of random numbers is (21 to 35) and so on.

Proceeding in this way we get all the random number intervals as follows:

Daily Demand (Input variable)	Probability	Cumulative Probability	Random Number Interval
0	0.01	0.01	00
10	0.20	0.21	01 - 20
20	0.15	0.36	21 - 35
30	0.50	0.86	36 - 85
40	0.12	0.98	86 - 97
50	0.02	1.00	98 - 99

Thus, (00) represents the daily demand of 0 units, (01 - 20) represents the demand of 10 units, (21 - 35) represents the demand of 20 units and so on.

4. **To Simulate (estimate) the Daily Demand for next (n = 10) days:** We use the given sequence of ten random numbers to simulate (estimate) the daily demand for next 10 days. Consider the first given random number i.e. 25. (This will correspond to the 1st day). From the above table we see that it belongs to the interval (21 - 35). Now, this interval represents the daily demand of 20 units. Hence, we estimate that for the next first day the demand will be 20.

Similarly, the 2nd random number is 39, which belongs to the interval (36 - 85). This represents the daily demand of 30 units. Hence, we estimate that the demand on the second day will be 30.

Proceeding in this way, we simulate the daily demand for the next 10 days (by using the given random numbers) as follows:

Day	R. No.	R. No. Interval	Daily Demand (simulated)	Day	R. No.	R. No. Interval	Daily Demand (simulated)
1	25	21 - 35	20	6	05	01 - 20	10
2	39	36 - 85	30	7	73	36 - 85	30
3	65	36 - 85	30	8	89	86 - 97	40
4	76	36 - 85	30	9	19	01 - 20	10
5	12	01 - 20	10	10	49	36 - 85	30

Hence, Average Demand per day $= \dfrac{20 + 30 + 30 + 30 + 10 + 10 + 30 + 40 + 10 + 30}{10}$

$= \dfrac{240}{10} = 24$ units

Example 2: For a single channel queuing model the data about the inter-arrival time of the workers at a tool-crib for collecting the tools and the service time required by the attendant at the tool-crib is as follows:

Inter arrival Time		Service Time	
Time (minutes)	Frequency	Time (minutes)	Frequency
2	10	1	4
4	6	2	12
6	2	3	10
8	2	4	8
		5	6

Simulate the queue for the next 5 arrivals and compute the following:

(a) Percentage of time the attendant is idle

(b) Average waiting time for the workers at the tool crib.

Use the random numbers:

10   21   56   74   47   for the inter arrival time and
65   59   02   71   26   for the service time

Solution:

1. We are given the frequency distributions for the input variables of inter-arrival time and service time. Hence, we first convert them into the probability distributions as

   e.g. Probability that the inter-arrival time is 2 minutes = $\dfrac{\text{Its Frequency}}{\text{Total Frequency}} = \dfrac{10}{20} = 0.5$

   and so on.

   We then calculate the cumulative probabilities and then find the random - number intervals for the given values of input variables (by considering the proportionate intervals in 00 - 99).

   This is done for both the inter-arrival time and service time as follows:

Inter Arrival Time (Min.)	Frequency	Probability	Cumulative Probability	Random No. Interval
2	10	0.50	0.50	00 - 49
4	6	0.30	0.50 + 0.30 = 0.80	50 - 79
6	2	0.10	0.80 + 0.10 = 0.90	80 - 89
8	2	0.10	0.90 + 0.10 = 1.00	90 - 99
	20			

Service Time (Min.)	Frequency	Probability	Cumulative Probability	Random No. Interval
1	4	0.10	0.10	00 - 09
2	12	0.30	0.40	10 - 39
3	10	0.25	0.65	40 - 64
4	8	0.20	0.85	65 - 84
5	6	0.15	1.00	85 - 99
	40			

2. We use now the given random numbers to simulate the interarrival times and service times for the next five arrivals.

   e.g. For the first arrival, the random number is 10 which belongs to the interval (00 - 49) corresponding to the interarrival time of 2 minutes. Hence, the simulated inter-arrival time for the first arrival is 2 minutes. We simulate the inter-arriva times for the other arrivals in the same way. Similarly, in case of the service time, the first random number is 65, which belongs to the interval (65 - 84), corresponding to the service time of 4 minutes. Hence, the simulated service time for the first arrival is 4 minutes and so on. Thus, we get the following simulation worksheet.

Arrival No.	Random Number (Inter arrival Time)	(Simulated) Inter arrival Time	Random Number (Service Time)	(Simulated) Service Time
1	10	2	65	4
2	21	2	59	3
3	56	4	02	1
4	74	4	71	4
5	47	2	26	2

3. Assuming that the shift starts at 8.00 am and considering the above Inter-arrival and Service times, we make the further calculations as follows:

Arrival No.	Inter arrival time	Service Time	Arrival Time	Service Start Time	Service End Time	Waiting Time	Idle Time
1	2	4	8.02	8.02	8.06	-	2
2	2	3	8.04	8.06	8.09	2	-
3	4	1	8.08	8.09	8.10	1	-
4	4	4	8.12	8.12	8.16	-	2
5	2	2	8.14	8.16	8.18	2	-
						5	4

(i) Now, Total Time for which the attendant is present = 8.18 − 8.00 = 18 minutes.

$\therefore$ Percentage of time the attendant is idle = $\frac{4}{18} \times 100$ = 22.22 %

(ii) Total waiting time for 5 workers = 5 minutes

$\therefore$ Average waiting time for a worker = $\frac{5}{5}$ = 1 minute

Note:

(i) The interarrival time for the 1st arrival is 2 minutes. Hence, the first worker arrives at the tool-crib at 8.02 hrs. Hence, the service facility (attendant) will be idle for 2 minutes (from 8.00 to 8.02 Hrs.) The worker is then immediately offered the service which takes 4 minutes. Hence, there is no waiting time for him and the service gets over at 8.06 Hrs.

(ii) The inter-arrival time for the second arrival (worker) is again 2 minutes. Hence, he arrives at the tool crib at (8.02 Hr + 2 min = 8.04 Hr.) As the service time for the 1st worker ends at 8.06 Hr, this second worker will have to wait for (8.06 − 8.04 = 2 minutes). The attendant will offer him the service immediately after the first worker leaves i.e. at 8.06 Hr. Hence, there is no idle time for the attendant and the service ends at (8.06 + 3 min = 8.09 Hrs.)

(iii) Similarly, for the 3rd worker, waiting time is 1 minute and the idle time for the attendant is nil. The service time for this third worker ends at 8.10 Hrs.

(iv) Now, the fourth worker arrives at (8.08 Hr + 4 min = 8.12 Hr.) However, the attendant has finished the service for the third worker at 8.10 Hr. Hence, he is idle for (8.12 − 8.10 = 2 minutes) and the worker is then immediately offered the service at 8.12 Hrs. when he arrives. Hence, the waiting time for the worker is zero.

(v) Again for the 5th arrival, waiting time is 2 minutes and the idle time for the attendant is nil.

Solved Problems

Problem 1: The management of ABC Company is considering the question of marketing a new product. The fixed cost required in the project is ₹ 4,000. Three factors are uncertain viz. the selling price, the variable cost and the annual sales volume. The product has a life of only one year. The management has the data on these three factors as under:

Selling Price (₹)	Probability	Variable Cost (₹)	Probability	Sales volume (units)	Probability
3	0.2	1	0.3	2000	0.3
4	0.5	2	0.6	3000	0.3
5	0.3	3	0.1	5000	0.4

Consider the following sequence of thirty random numbers: 81, 32, 60, 04, 46, 31, 67, 25, 24, 10, 40, 02, 39, 68, 08, 59, 66, 90, 12, 64, 79, 31, 86, 68, 82, 89, 25, 11, 98, 16.

Using the sequence (first three numbers for the first trial etc.), simulate the average profit for the above project on the basis of 10 trials.

Solution:
1. Let us find out the random number intervals for the given data.

Selling Price	Probability	Cumulative Probability	R. No. Interval	Variable Cost	Probability	Cumulative Probability	R. No. Interval
3	0.2	0.20	00 - 19	1	0.3	0.30	00 - 29
4	0.5	0.70	20 - 69	2	0.6	0.90	30 - 89
5	0.3	1.00	70 - 99	3	0.1	1.00	90 - 99

Sales Volume	Probability	Cumulative Probability	R. No. Interval
2000	0.3	0.30	00 - 29
3000	0.3	0.60	30 - 59
5000	0.4	1.00	60 - 99

2. Now, using the given random numbers we simulate the selling price, variable cost and sales volume for the next 10 trials. We identify the Random number Intervals to which the given random numbers belong and then the corresponding value (for selling price etc.) is the simulated value.

Sr. No. Trial	R. No.	Selling Price	R. No.	Variable Cost	R. No.	Sales Volume
1	81	5	32	2	60	5000
2	04	3	46	2	31	3000
3	67	4	25	1	24	2000
4	10	3	40	2	02	2000
5	39	4	68	2	08	2000
6	59	4	66	2	90	5000
7	12	3	64	2	79	5000
8	31	4	86	2	68	5000
9	82	5	89	2	25	2000
10	11	3	98	3	16	2000

Now, the profit is given as

Profit = (Selling Price – Variable Cost) Sales Volume – Fixed Cost

= (Selling Price – Variable Cost) Sales Volume – 4000

Thus, the simulated Profit is

Trial No.	Profit
1	(5 – 2) 5000 – 4000 = 11000
2	(3 – 2) 3000 – 4000 = – 1000
3	(4 – 1) 2000 – 4000 = 2000
4	(3 – 2) 2000 – 4000 = – 2000
5	(4 – 2) 2000 – 4000 = 0
6	(4 – 2) 5000 – 4000 = 6000
7	(3 – 2) 5000 – 4000 = 1000
8	(4 – 2) 5000 – 4000 = 6000
9	(5 – 2) 2000 _ 4000 = 2000
10	(3 – 3) 2000 – 4000 = – 4000
	Total = 21,000

$\therefore$ Average Profit per trial = $\dfrac{21000}{10}$ = ₹ 2100.

Problem 2: Simulate the number of machine break-downs for the next six shifts on the basis of the following data.

No. of Break-downs per shift :   0   1   2   3
Probability :   0.900 0.085 0.012 0.003

If due to operational constraints, only one machine can be repaired in a shift, find the average number of machines repaired in a shift, average number of machines lying unrepaired at the end of a shift and the proportion of time for which the repair facility is idle.

Solution: 1. Using the given information we identify the random-number intervals. As the probabilities are expressed in terms of three decimal digits, we consider the random numbers from (000 - 999) for finding out the proportionate intervals as follows:

No. of Breakdowns	Probability	Cumulative Probability	Random No. Interval
0	0.900	0.900	000 - 899
1	0.085	0.985	900 - 984
2	0.012	0.997	985 - 996
3	0.003	1.000	997 - 999

2. As the random number sequence is not given, we can select any such sequence from the random number table (given in appendix C). Thus, starting say, from the eighth row-first column element of the random number table and moving in the horizontal direction (by considering three digits at a time) we find the random number sequence as follows: 988, 371, 701, 589, 093, 959

Now, for each of these numbers, we identify the interval to which it belongs. From the interval we can simulate the corresponding number of Break downs as follows:

Shift	Random No.	R. No. Interval	No. of Breakdowns (Simulated)
1	988	985 - 996	2
2	371	000 - 899	0
3	701	000 - 899	0
4	589	000 - 899	0
5	093	000 - 899	0
6	959	900 - 984	1

Now, assuming that a machine that breaks down during a shift is attended for the repair work during the next shift we have

Shift	No. of Breakdowns	Machines to be repaired	Machines repaired	Machines unrepaired
1	2	-	-	2
2	0	2	1	1 + 0 = 1
3	0	1	1	0 + 0 = 0
4	0	0	0	0
5	0	0	0	0
6	1	0	0	0 + 1 = 1
			2	4

5.33

Hence,

(i) Average number of machines repaired in a shift $= \frac{2}{6} = \frac{1}{3}$.

(ii) Average number of machines lying unrepaired at the end of a shift $= \frac{4}{6} = \frac{2}{3}$.

(iii) Proportion of time(during a shift) for which the repair facility is idle $= \frac{6-2}{6} = \frac{4}{6} = \frac{2}{3}$.

Problem 3: A trader deals in a perishable commodity. The daily demand is a random variable. Records of past 200 days show the following distribution:

Demand of units	10	20	30	40	50
Number of days	20	40	60	60	20

The trader buys the commodity at ₹ 10 per unit and sells at ₹ 15 per unit. Calculate the profit in 10 days and the average daily profit by simulating the system. Use following random numbers: 69, 01, 08, 74, 82, 20, 72, 14, 75, 12. **(P.U. MBA - May 09)**

Solution: 1. We are given the frequency distribution for the demand. Hence, we convert it into the probability distribution first. Thus, probability that the demand is '10' $= \frac{20}{200} = 0.10$. Probability that the demand is '20' $= \frac{40}{200} = 0.20$ and so on. Using these probabilities we find the cumulative probabilities which are then used to find the Proportionate Random Number Intervals in (00 - 99) as follows:

Demand (in units)	No. of Days i.e. Frequency	Probability	Cumulative Probability	Random Number Interval
10	20	0.10	0.10	00 - 09
20	40	0.20	0.30	10 - 29
30	60	0.30	0.60	30 - 59
40	60	0.30	0.90	60 - 89
50	20	0.10	1.00	90 - 99

Now to simulate the demand for next 10 days we use the given random numbers, identify the interval to which they belong in the above table and note the corresponding demand figure (as the simulated demand) as follows:

Day	1	2	3	4	5	6	7	8	9	10
Random No.	69	01	08	74	82	20	72	14	75	12
Demand (simulated)	40	10	10	40	40	20	40	20	40	20

∴ Total demand (in 10 days) = 40 + 40 + 10 + ... = 280
and Per Unit Profit = Per Unit Selling Price – Per Unit Cost
= 15 – 10 = ₹ 5
∴ Total profit in 10 days = 280 × 5 = ₹ 1400
and ∴ Average Daily Profit = $\frac{1400}{10}$ = ₹ 140

Problem 4: An engineering firm utilises the reorder level system to replenish the stocks of its items. As per the system, a fresh order is placed when stock level of an item drops down to or becomes a pre-fixed level called reorder.

The past records of weekly demand of one such item has the following frequency distribution.

Weekly demand : 0 100 125 150 175 200 225 250
(Units)
Frequency : 1 5 12 21 2 3 4 2

When an order is placed to replenish stock, there is a delivery time lag which leads to the following frequency distribution

Lead Time (weeks) : 1 2 3 4
Frequency: 2 30 14 4

The management policy is to ensure that the proportion of stock left should be ≥ 10% of the original stock. The inventory carrying cost is ₹ 1 per unit per week, order placing cost is ₹ 100 per occurrence and loss in net revenue sale price less cost of goods is ₹ 1 per unit from shortage. Estimate average weekly cost of inventory system, with a policy of using reorder quantity of 500 units and opening balance of 1000 units. Use the technique of Monte Carlo Simulation for 20 week period.

Use the following random numbers:
For Demand: 99, 77, 82, 44, 57, 96, 82, 14, 99, 29, 55, 93, 62, 48, 13, 36, 22, 74, 53, 58
For lead time: 95, 16, 59, 46, 25, 30, 4, 77, 25, 23.

Solution: Let us simulate the weekly demand for next 20 weeks and the lead time by using the given random numbers.

As we are given the frequency distributions for the demand and the lead time, we first convert them into probability distributions to find out the corresponding Random Number Intervals as follows:

Weekly Demand:	0	100	125	150	175	200	225	250
Frequency:	1	5	12	21	2	3	4	2 (Σf= 50)
Probability:	0.02	0.1	0.24	0.42	0.04	0.06	0.08	0.04
Cumulative Probability:	0.02	0.12	0.36	0.78	0.82	0.88	0.96	1.00
Random No. interval:	00-01	02-11	12-35	36-77	78-81	82-87	88-95	96-99

The simulated demand for next 20 weeks (by identifying the interval to which the given random numbers belong) is as follows:

Week:	1	2	3	4	5	6	7	8	9	10	11	12	13	14	15	16	17	18	19	20
R. No.:	99	77	82	44	57	96	82	14	99	29	55	93	62	48	13	36	22	74	53	58
Demand:	250	150	200	150	150	250	200	125	250	125	150	225	150	150	125	150	125	150	150	150

Similarly, we find out the Random number intervals representing the given lead-times as follows:

Lead Time:	1	2	3	4	
Frequency:	2	30	14	4	($\Sigma f = 50$)
Probability:	0.04	0.60	0.28	0.08	
Cumulative probability:	0.04	0.64	0.92	1.00	
Random No. Interval:	00 - 03	04 - 63	64 - 91	92 - 99	

Using the given random numbers we simulate the lead times for the next 10 occurences as follows:

Occurence	:	1	2	3	4	5	6	7	8	9	10
Random No	:	95	16	59	46	25	30	04	77	25	23
Lead Time	:	4	2	2	2	2	2	2	3	2	2

Now, using the given information we construct the simulation worksheet as follows:

Week	Demand	Occurrence	Lead Time	Opening Balance	Consumption (Demand)	Closing Balance	10% of Opening	Order	Shortage
1	250			1000	250	750	100	-	-
2	150			750	150	600	75	-	-
3	200			600	200	400	60	-	-
4	150			400	150	250	40	-	-
5	150			250	150	100	25	-	-
6	250	1	4	100	250	0	10	500	150
7	200			0	200	0	0	-	200
8	125			0	125	0	0	-	125
9	250			0	250	0	0	-	250
10	125			0	125	0	0	-	125
11	150			(0 + 500)	150	350	50	-	-
12	225			350	225	125	35	-	-
13	150	2	2	125	150	0	12.5	500	25
14	150			0	150	0	0	-	150
15	125			0	125	0	0	-	125
16	150			(0 + 500)	150	350	50	-	-
17	125			350	125	225	35	-	-
18	150			225	150	75	22.5	-	-
19	150	3	2	75	150	0	7.5	500	75
20	150			0	150	0	0	-	150
						3225			1375

Note:

(i) Consumption during a week is the same as the demand during the week.

(ii) Opening balance for the first week = 1000 units

(iii) Closing balance = Opening balance − Consumption

(iv) The closing balance for each week is compared with the (10% of the opening balance) to decide whether the order needs to be placed or not.

If closing balance ≥ 10% of opening balance, no order is placed. e.g. for the weeks 1 to 5.

If closing balance < (10% of opening balance) an order is placed for 500 units (reorder quantity) and the unsatisfied demand represents the shortage.

e.g. for the sixth week, opening balance is 100 while the demand is 250. Hence there will be a shortage of 150 units and the closing balance will be 0. As this closing balance (0) < (10% of 100 = 10), an order for 500 units is placed. This is the first occurrence of placing an order for which the simulated lead time is 4 weeks.

(v) The order quantity is assumed to be received at the end of the week = (Week when the order is placed + Lead Time)

Thus, the first order is received at the end of (6 + 4 = 10th week)

Hence, the opening balance for the 11th week = 0 + 500 = 500

(vi) This procedure is followed for further calculations also.

Now, assuming that the inventory carrying cost is incurred on the stock remaining at the end of a week (closing stock) we have

Total Inventory carrying cost in 20 weeks

= (Total closing stock for 20 weeks) (Inventory carrying cost per unit per week)

= 3225 (1) = ₹ 3225

Number of orders placed in 20 weeks = 3

∴ Order placing cost in 20 weeks = 3 × 100 = ₹ 300

Cost of shortages = (Total shortages in 20 weeks) (Shortage loss per unit)

= (1375) (1) = ₹ 1375

∴ Total Inventory cost of the system in 20 weeks

= Inventory carrying cost + Order placing cost + Shortage cost

= 3225 + 300 + 1375 = ₹ 4,900

∴ Average Weekly Cost of Inventory System = $\dfrac{4900}{20}$ = ₹ 245

Problem 5: The manager of a book store has to decide the number of copies to be ordered of a particular tax law book. The book costs ₹ 60 and is sold for ₹ 80. Since some of the tax laws change year after year, any copies unsold while the edition is current has a scrap value of ₹ 30. From the past records, the distribution of demand for this book has been obtained as follows:

Demand in No. of copies : 15 16 17 18 19 20 21 22

Proportion : 0.05 0.08 0.20 0.45 0.10 0.07 0.03 0.02

Using the following sequence of random numbers, generate data on demand for 20 time periods (years). Calculate the average number of copies in demand and place an order for the same. Find the average profit under this number of copies to be ordered.

14, 02, 93, 99, 18, 71, 37, 30, 12, 10, 88, 13, 00, 57, 69, 32, 18, 08, 92, 73.

Solution:

1. Using the given proportions (probabilities) we compute the cumulative probabilities for the given demands. These cumulative probabilities are then used to find out the corresponding random number intervals between (00 - 99) as follows:

Copies Demanded (No.)	Probability	Cumulative Probability	Random No. Interval
15	0.05	0.05	00 - 04
16	0.08	0.13	05 - 12
17	0.20	0.33	13 - 32
18	0.45	0.78	33 - 77
19	0.10	0.88	78 - 87
20	0.07	0.95	88 - 94
21	0.03	0.98	95 - 97
22	0.02	1.00	98 - 99

2. **Simulate the demand:** Using the given 20 random numbers we simulate the demand for next 20 years (periods) as follows:

Year:	1	2	3	4	5	6	7	8	9	10	11	12	13	14	15	16	17	18	19	20
R. No.:	14	02	93	99	18	71	37	30	12	10	88	13	00	57	69	32	18	08	92	73
Demand: (x)	17	15	20	22	17	18	18	17	16	16	20	17	15	18	18	17	17	16	20	18

$\therefore$ Average Number of copies in demand $= \dfrac{\Sigma x}{20} = \dfrac{352}{20} = 17.6 \approx 18$ copies

Now, placing an order for 18 copies each year, we can calculate the corresponding profit as follows:

Year	Order Qty.	Demand Qty.	Qty. sold	Qty. Unsold	Profit on Sale	Loss on Unsold	Net Profit
1	18	17	17	1	340	30	310
2	18	15	15	3	300	90	210
3	18	20	18	-	360	-	360
4	18	22	18	-	360	-	360
5	18	17	17	1	340	30	310
6	18	18	18	-	360	-	360
7	18	18	18	-	360	-	360
8	18	17	17	1	340	30	310
9	18	16	16	2	320	60	260
10	18	16	16	2	320	60	260
11	18	20	18	-	360	-	360
12	18	17	17	1	340	30	310
13	18	15	15	3	300	90	210
14	18	18	18	-	360	-	360
15	18	18	18	-	360	-	360
16	18	17	17	1	340	30	310
17	18	17	17	1	340	30	310
18	18	16	16	2	320	60	260
19	18	20	18	-	360	-	360
20	18	18	18	-	360	-	360
							6300

Hence, the average profit per year = $\frac{6300}{20}$ = ₹ 315.

Note:
(i) Quantity sold = minimum of [the order quantity (18) available and the demanded quantity for a year]
Now, profit per copy sold = Selling price − Cost = (80 − 60) = ₹ 20
∴ Profit on sale = (Quantity sold) × 20
e.g. for first year, Quantity sold = 17 (i.e. minimum of 18 and 17)
∴ Profit on sale = 17 × 20 = 340
(ii) Unsold quantity remains only if the order quantity (18) is more than the demand for a period (year) and then Unsold Quantity = (Order Qty 18) − Demand
e.g. for first year, Unsold quantity = 18 − 17 = 1

DECISION SCIENCES MARKOV CHAINS AND SIMULATION

(iii) Scrap value of an unsold copy = ₹ 30 per copy

∴ Loss per unsold copy = Cost − Resale value = 60 − 30 = ₹ 30

∴ Loss on Unsold copies = (No. of unsold copies) (Loss per unsold copy)

= (No. of unsold copies) × 30

e.g. In first week, No. of unsold copies = 18 − 17 = 1

∴ Loss on unsold copies = 1 × 30 = ₹ 30 and so on.

(iv) Net profit = Profit on sale − Loss on unsold quantity.

e.g. for first year, Net profit = 340 − 30 = ₹ 310

Problem 6: A Company manufactures around 150 mopeds. The daily production varies from 146 to 154 depending upon the availability of raw materials and other working conditions.

Production Per day	146	147	148	149	150	151	152	153	154
Probability	0.04	0.09	0.12	0.14	0.11	0.10	0.20	0.12	0.08

The finished mopeds are transported in a specially arranged lorry accommodating only 150 mopeds. Using following random numbers: 80, 81, 76, 75, 64, 43, 18, 26, 10, 12, 65, 68, 69, 61, 57. Simulate the process to find out:

(i) What will be the average number of mopeds waiting in the factory ?

(ii) What will be the average number of empty spaces on the lorry ?

Solution:

1. Using the given probabilities, we find the cumulative probabilities which are used to find the proportionate random number intervals in (00 - 99) as follows:

Production per day	146	147	148	149	150	151	152	153	154
Probability	0.04	0.09	0.12	0.14	0.11	0.10	0.20	0.12	0.08
Cumulative Probability	0.04	0.13	0.25	0.39	0.50	0.60	0.80	0.92	1.00
Random No. Interval	00 - 03	04 - 12	13 - 24	25 - 38	39 - 49	50 - 59	60 - 79	80 - 91	92 - 99

We use the given random numbers to simulate production for next 15 days (on identifying the interval to which they belong).

5.40

Also, considering the capacity of lorry to carry 150 units, we have the simulation worksheet as follows:

Day	Random No.	Daily Production (Simulated)	Balance with Factory	Empty Spaces
1	80	153	3	-
2	81	153	3 + 3 = 6	-
3	76	152	6 + 2 = 8	-
4	75	152	8 + 2 = 10	-
5	64	152	10 + 2 =12	-
6	43	150	12 + 0 = 12	-
7	18	148	12 – 2 = 10	-
8	26	149	10 – 1 = 9	-
9	10	147	9 – 3 = 6	-
10	12	147	6 – 3 = 3	-
11	65	152	3 + 2 = 5	-
12	68	152	5 + 2 = 7	-
13	69	152	7 + 2 = 9	-
14	61	152	9 + 2 = 11	-
15	57	151	11 + 1 = 12	-
			123	-

Note:

(i) On first day excess production = 153 – 150 = 3 mopeds which will be kept in the factory as the lorry has a capacity of 150 units only. On second day excess production = 153 – 3 = 3. Hence, balance with the factory = 3 + 3 = 6 and so on.

Similarly, on 7th day shortage in production = 150 – 148 = 2 mopeds. Hence, balance that will remain with the factory (as 150 units will be transported) is 12 – 2 = 10 units and so on.

(iii) Hence, Average No. of mopeds waiting = $\frac{123}{15}$ = 8.2 and average no. of empty spaces in lorry = $\frac{0}{15} = 0$

Problem 7: At a bus terminal every bus should leave with driver. At the terminus they keep 2 drivers as reserved if any one on scheduled duty is sick and could not come. Following is the probability distribution that driver becomes sick.

Number of Sick Drivers	0	1	2	3	4	5
Probability	0.30	0.20	0.15	0.10	0.13	0.12

Simulate for 10 days and find utilisation of reserved drivers. Also find how many days and how many buses cannot run because of non-availability of drivers. Use the following random numbers: 30, 54, 34, 72, 20, 02, 76, 74, 48, 22. **(P.U. MBA - May 05, May 11)**

Solution: Using the given probabilities, we find the cumulative probabilities which are used to find the proportionate random number intervals (00 - 99) as follows:

Number of Sick Drivers	0	1	2	3	4	5
Probability	0.30	0.20	0.15	0.10	0.13	0.12
Cumulative probability	0.30	0.50	0.65	0.75	0.88	1.00
Random No. Interval	00-29	30-49	50-64	65-74	75-87	88-99

Now we use the given random numbers to simulate the number of sick drivers for next 10 days (on identifying the interval to which they belong). Also considering the availability of 2 reserved drivers, we have the simulation worksheet as follows:

Day	Random No.	Number of Sick Drivers (Simulated)	Number of Reserved Drivers Used (out of 2)	Shortage of Drivers
1	30	1	1	-
2	54	2	2	-
3	34	1	1	-
4	72	3	2	3 – 2 = 1
5	20	0	0	-
6	02	0	0	-
7	76	4	2	4 – 2 = 2
8	74	3	2	3 – 2 = 1
9	48	1	1	-
10	22	0	0	-

Note:

(i) Since 2 reserved drivers are available, on any given day at the most 2 drivers can be substituted.

(ii) Hence, on the 4th, 7th, and 8th day there is shortage of drivers as more than 2 drivers are likely to be sick. Hence, on these 3 days some buses cannot run. On 4th and 8th day 1 bus cannot run and on the 7th day 2 buses cannot run because of the shortage or non-availability of drivers.

Problem 8: The following table gives the arrival pattern at a coffee counter for 1 minute interval:

Number of Persons arriving	0	1	2	3	4	5	6	7
Frequency	5	10	15	30	20	10	5	5

Simulate the arrival using following random numbers and find average arrival. 5, 25, 16, 80, 35, 48, 67, 79, 90, 19. **(P.U. MBA - Dec. 09)**

Solution: We are given a frequency distribution for the arrivals. Hence we convert it into the probability distribution first.

e.g. Total frequency = Σf = 5 + 10 + 15 + 30 + 20 + 10 + 5 + 5 = 100.

$\therefore$ Probability that there are '0' arrivals = $\frac{5}{100}$ = 0.05 and so on.

Using these probabilities we find the cumulative probabilities which are then used to find the Proportionate Random Number Intervals in (00 - 99) as follows:

Arrivals	Frequency	Probability	Cumulative Probability	Random No. Interval
0	5	0.05	0.05	00 - 04
1	10	0.10	0.15	05 - 14
2	15	0.15	0.30	15 - 29
3	30	0.30	0.60	30 - 59
4	20	0.20	0.80	60 - 79
5	10	0.10	0.90	80 - 89
6	5	0.05	0.95	90 - 94
7	5	0.05	1.00	95 - 99
	100			

Now to simulate the next 10 arrivals, we use the given random numbers, identify their intervals above and note the corresponding arrival figures as follows:

Arrival No.	1	2	3	4	5	6	7	8	9	10	Total
Random No.	5	25	16	80	35	48	67	79	90	10	
Arrivals	1	2	2	5	3	3	4	4	6	2	32

Hence, Average arrivals per minute (over next 10 arrivals) = $\frac{32}{10}$ = 3.2

Problem 9: Modern Bakery keeps the stock of the popular brand cake. Previous experience indicates the daily demand as given below:

Daily Demand	0	10	20	30	40	50
Probability	0.02	0.19	0.16	0.45	0.13	0.05

Estimate average balance stock if the owner of the bakery decides to make 30 cakes everyday. Use following random numbers : 47, 88, 15, 91, 57, 67, 11, 54, 60, 89.

(P.U. MBA - May 10, Dec. 12)

Solution: 1. Using the given probabilities we find the cumulative probabilities which are used to find the Proportionate Random Number intervals in (00 - 99) as follows:

Daily Demand	0	10	20	30	40	50
Probability	0.02	0.19	0.16	0.45	0.13	0.05
Cumulative Probability	0.02	0.21	0.37	0.82	0.95	1.00
Random Number Interval	00-01	02-20	21-36	37-81	82-94	95-99

2. We use now the given random numbers to simulate the daily demand for next 10 days (on identifying the interval to which they belong). Also as the bakery makes 30 cakes everyday we have the simulation worksheet as follows. The daily balance quantity is the excess quantity (out of 30) over the demanded one.

Day	Random No.	Daily Demand (Simulated)	Daily Balance
1	47	30	0
2	88	40	0
3	15	10	20
4	91	40	0
5	57	30	0
6	67	30	0
7	11	10	20
8	54	30	0
9	60	30	0
10	89	40	0
			Total = 40

The average daily balance stock = $\dfrac{\text{Total balance}}{10} = \dfrac{40}{10} = 4$ cakes.

Problem 10: Haggins plumbing and heating maintains a stock of 30 gallon hot water heaters that it sells to home owners and installs for them. The owner likes the idea of having large supply on hand so as to meet all customer demand, but he also recognises that it is expensive to do so. He examines hot water heater sales over the past 50 weeks and notes the following:

Sales per week	4	5	6	7	8	9	10	
No. of weeks this number was sold	6	5	9	12	8	7	3	Total = 50

Using the random numbers given below, simulate demand for 10 weeks and answer the following questions:

(i) If stock of 8 hot water heaters is maintained, how may times will the company be stock out in 10 weeks.

(ii) What is the average number of heaters demanded per week.

(iii) Find the percentage of weeks the demand exceeds the average.

Random Nos. : 10, 24, 03, 32, 23, 59, 95, 34, 34, 51. **(P.U. MBA - Dec. 11)**

Solution: 1. We have the frequency distribution of sales. Hence, we convert it into the probability distribution first.

Probability that the demand is '4' = $\frac{6}{50}$ = 0.12 and so on.

Thus, using these probabilities we find the cumulative probabilities which are then used to find the Proportionate Random Number intervals in (00 - 99) as follows:

Sales	No. of days (i.e. frequency)	Probability	Cumulative Probability	Random No. Interval
4	6	0.12	0.12	00 - 11
5	5	0.10	0.22	12 - 21
6	9	0.18	0.40	22 - 39
7	12	0.24	0.64	40 - 63
8	8	0.16	0.80	64 - 79
9	7	0.14	0.94	80 - 93
10	3	0.06	1.00	94 - 99
	Total = 50			

2. Using the given random numbers now we simulate the demand for next 10 weeks (on identifying the interval to which they belong).

Week	Random No.	Demand (Simulated)
1	10	4
2	24	6
3	03	4
4	32	6
5	23	6
6	59	7
7	95	10
8	34	6
9	34	6
10	51	7
		Total = 62

(i) Thus, if a stock of 8 hot water heaters is maintained there will be stock out only once in 10 weeks (when the demand will be more than 8).

(ii) Total demand in 10 weeks = 62.

∴ Average weekly demand = $\frac{62}{10}$ = 6.2 units.

(iii) Out of 10 weeks, we see that the demand exceeds this average on 3 occasions. Hence, the percentage of weeks the demand exceeds the average = $\frac{3}{10} \times 100$ = 30%.

Exercise - II

1. What is Simulation model. Give suitable example.
2. Write a note on Monte Carlo Simulation.
3. Bright Bakery keeps stock of a popular brand of cake. Previous Experience indicates the daily demand as given below:

   Daily Demand :   0   10   20   30   40   50

   Probability   :   0.01 0.20 0.15 0.50 0.12 0.02

   Consider the following sequence of random numbers:

   R. No.   :   48, 78, 19, 51, 56, 77, 15, 14, 68, 09.

   Using this sequence, simulate the demand for next 10 days.

   Find daily balance stock, if the owner of the bakery decides to make 30 cakes every day.

   (**Ans.:** Demand :   30, 30, 10, 30, 30, 30, 10, 10, 30, 10

   Stock   :   –, –, 20, 20, 20, 20, 40, 60, 60, 80)

4. An electric gen-set manufacturing company manufactures gen-sets which is a variable. Following is the probability distribution for the gen-sets manufactured.

   No. of sets manufactured per day   :   23   24   25   26   27   28
   Probability   :   0.05 0.10 0.30 0.25 0.20 0.10

   According to the Company's policy, the manufactured sets are transported to the godown on the same day. The truck carrying the gen-sets is having a capacity of 25 sets. Simulate the system for next 10 days and find
   (i) Average number of sets manufactured per day.
   (ii) Number of sets transported every day.
   (iii) Average number of vacant spaces in the truck per day
   (iv) Average number of sets remaining to be transported per day.
   Use the following random numbers: 84, 06, 93, 38, 29, 59, 64, 18, 08, 45.
   (Ans.: 25.6, 25, 0, 0.6)

5. An engineering firm utilises re-order level system to replenish stock based on average demand. The demand is given as below:

   Demand per week   :   0   1   2   3   4   5   6
   Frequency   :   2   8   22 34 18 9   7

   Generate the demand for next 20 weeks using the random numbers given below and calculate average demand
   68, 46, 87, 32, 78, 72, 27, 60, 06, 40, 83, 39, 97, 11, 06, 77, 49, 31, 71, 92
   (Ans.: 3.3)

6. A small retailer has studied the weekly receipts and payments over past few weeks and has developed the following set of information:

Weekly Receipts (₹)	Frequency	Weekly Payments (₹)	Frequency
3000	4	4000	3
5000	6	6000	4
7000	8	8000	2
12000	2	10000	1

Using the following set of random numbers, simulate the weekly pattern of receipts and payments for the 12 weeks of the next quarter, assuming further that the beginning bank balance is ₹ 8000. What is the estimated balance at the end of the 12 week period? What is the highest weekly balance during the quarter? What is the average weekly balance for the quarter?

Random Numbers:

For Receipts   :   03, 91, 38, 55, 17, 46, 32, 43, 69, 72, 24, 22
For Payments   :   61, 96, 30, 32, 03, 88, 48, 28, 88, 18, 71, 99
(Ans.: Deficit ₹ 3,000; ₹ 7,000; ₹ 3,750)

7. A process involves the production of a particular component which is then installed into an end product. Past observations have indicated that the average production time for the component is 4 minutes but fluctuations about the average do occur and the following probability distribution has been derived from the past observations -

   Minutes   :   2   3   4   5   6   7
   Probability   :   0.10   0.25   0.40   0.10   0.10   0.05

   The average time taken to install a component is 30 minutes but this also fluctuates and the following probability distribution has been derived.

   Minutes   :   2   3   4   5
   Probability   :   0.30   0.45   0.15   0.10

   The current system uses one operator for installation but the company is considering employing another operator on the installation process.

   Use the following random numbers (first 10 for arrival of components and the next 10 for installations): 20, 74, 81, 22, 93, 45, 44, 16, 04, 32, 03, 62, 61, 89, 01, 27, 49, 50, 90, 98 and find: (i) Idle time for the operator.(ii) Waiting time for the components.

   (**Ans.:** 14, 4 minutes)

8. A book store wishes to carry 'Ramayana' in stock. Demand is probabilistic and replenishment of stock takes 2 days (i.e. if an order is placed on march 1, it will be delivered at the end of the day on march 3.) The probabilities of demand are given below:

   Demand (daily) :   0   1   2   3   4
   Probability   :   0.05   0.10   0.30   0.45   0.10

   Each time an order is placed, the store incurs an ordering cost of ₹ 10 per order. The store also incurs a carrying cost of ₹ 0.50 per book per day. The inventory carrying cost is calculated on the basis of stock at the end of each day.

   The manager of the book store wishes to compare two options for his inventory decision:

   (A) Order 5 books when the inventory at the beginning of the day plus order outstanding is less than 8 books.

   (B) Order 8 books when the inventory at the beginning of the day plus order outstanding is less than 8.

Currently (beginning of 1st day) the store has a stock of 8 books plus 6 books ordered two days ago and expected to arrive next day. Use Monte Carlo Simulation for 10 cycles to recommend which options the manager should choose.

The Random Numbers are: 89, 34, 78, 63, 61, 81, 39, 16, 13, 73.

(**Ans.:** B (Cost 52.50) than A (Cost 59.50))

9. A Confectioner sells confectionary items. Past data of demand per week in hundred kilograms with frequency is given below:

Demand per week :   0   5   10   15   20   25
Frequency   :   4   22   16   42   10   6

Generate the demand for the next 10 weeks. Also find out the average demand per week. Use the following random numbers: 87, 05, 35, 43, 77, 61, 09, 05, 58, 85.

(**Ans.:** 125 kg.)

10. The director of finance for a farm co - operative is concerned about the yield per acre of corn crop. The probability distribution of the yields for the current weather conditions on the basis of past years with similar weather conditions is given below:

Yield in kg per acre	120	140	160	180
Probability	0.18	0.26	0.44	0.12

Simulate the yield for next years and calculate average yield using the following random numbers: 20, 72, 34, 54, 30, 22, 48, 74, 76, 02.

(**Ans.** Average = 148 Kg)

11. In a cricket season for a one-day match a bowler bowled 50 balls. The frequency distribution of runs scored per ball is given below:

Runs / ball	0	1	2	3	4	5	6
Number of balls	15	10	10	4	8	1	2

Simulate the system for 2 overs and find average runs given in 2 overs by him. Use the following random numbers: 88, 03, 05, 29, 28, 48, 65, 19, 55, 17, 37, 82.

(P.U. MBA - Dec. 05)

(**Ans.** Average runs per ball = 14/12 = 1.167)

12. A confectionary sells items with past data of demand per week with frequency as given below:

Demand / week	0	5	10	15	20	25
Frequency	2	11	8	21	5	3

Using the following sequence of random numbers, generate the demand for the next 10 weeks. Also find the average demand per week.

Random Numbers: 35 52 90 13 23 73 34 57 35 83 **(P.U. MBA - Nov 07, Dec. 08)**

(**Ans.:** 12)

13. A company manufacturers 200 motorcycles per day which changes according to availability of raw material

Production per day	196	197	198	199	200	201	202	203	204
Probability	0.05	0.09	0.12	0.14	0.20	0.15	0.11	0.08	0.06

Using the following random numbers, simulate the procedure for 12 days and find average production of sample drawn. Random Numbers: 82, 89, 78, 24, 52, 61, 18, 45, 04, 23, 50, 77 **(P.U. MBA - May 08)**

(**Ans.:** 200)

14. At a service station a study was made over a period of 25 days to determine both the number of automobiles being brought in service and the number of automobiles serviced. The results are given below:

Number of automobiles arriving for service or completing service per day	Frequency of arrivals for service	Frequency of daily completion
0	2	3
1	4	2
2	10	12
3	5	3
4	3	4
5	1	1

Simulate arrival and service pattern for a 10 day period. Use the following random numbers

For Arrivals : 09, 54, 42, 01, 80, 06, 06, 26, 57, 79

For Service : 11, 30, 18, 11, 85, 52, 63, 18, 29, 01

(**Ans.** Simulated arrival: 1, 2, 2, 0, 3, 0, 0, 2, 2, 3; Service: 0, 2, 1, 0, 4, 2, 2, 1, 2, 0)

15. A trader deals in a perishable commodity, the daily demand and supply of which are random variables. Records of the past 500 trading days are shown below:

Supply		Demand	
Availability (kg.)	No. of days	Demand (kg.)	No. of days
10	40	10	50
20	50	20	110
30	190	30	200
40	150	40	100
50	70	50	40

The trader buys the commodity at ₹ 20 per kg and sells it at ₹ 30 per kg. Any commodity remaining at the end of a day results in a loss of ₹ 8 per kg. (after the resale). Given the following random numbers, simulate six days sales, demand and profit.

31, 18, 63, 84, 15, 79, 07, 32, 43, 75, 81, 27. Use these random numbers alternately. The first random number is for the supply and the second is for the demand.

(**Ans.** Sales Revenue: 600, 1200, 600, 300, 900, 600; Demand: 20, 40, 40, 30, 40, 20, Profit : 80, 400, 200,100, 300, – 360, Net profit = ₹ 560].

16. Find average cost of inventory from the following information using simulation technique.

Lead Time (days)   :   5   6   7   8
Probability   :   0.15   0.50   0.25   0.10
Daily Demand (Units) :   0   1   2   3   4
Probability   :   0.10   0.20   0.30   0.30   0.10

The initial balance in inventory is 20 units. Unit cost of the item is ₹ 5/- while shortage cost is ₹ 7/-. The order is placed wherever stock level is 3 or less and the cost of ordering is ₹ 10/- per order. Use following random numbers 50, 10, 87, 44 and 77 for deciding lead time and following random numbers for daily demand.

71, 21, 75, 95, 20, 19, 03, 37, 24, 39, 47, 99, 99, 09 and 72.

(**Ans.** Purchase cost = ₹ 90, Ordering cost = ₹ 10, Shortage cost = ₹ 77, Total Inventory Cost = ₹ 177, Average Inventory cost = ₹ 11.80 per day)

17. The Rainfall distribution in monsoon season is as follows:

Rain in cm.	0	1	2	3	4	5
Frequency	50	25	15	5	3	2

Simulate the rainfall for 10 days using following random numbers: 67, 63, 39, 55, 29, 78, 70, 06, 78, 76. Find average rainfall.

(**Ans.** Rainfall: 1, 1, 0, 1, 0, 2, 1, 0, 2, 2, Average = 1 cm)

18. In a management institute the first lecture starts at 9 a.m. Following is the probability distribution regarding late comers for the first lecture day.

Late by minutes	2	4	6	8	10	12
Probability	0.40	0.30	0.20	0.05	0.03	0.02

Simulate the system for 10 students and find percentage of students late by more than 6 minutes. Using the following random numbers : 99, 89, 10, 27, 50, 93, 92, 57, 50, 78. **(P.U. MBA - May 13)**

(**Ans.** 30%)

Chapter 6...
Decision Theory

Contents ...
6.1 Introduction
6.2 Elements of Decision Making Problem
6.3 Decision Models
6.4 Decision Making Under Risk
6.5 Decision Making Under Uncertainty
    Solved Problems
    Exercise

[Note: Readers are advised to go through the probability concepts (Chapter 9) before studying this chapter]

6.1 Introduction

In performing various functions like planning, organising, controlling, co-ordinating etc. a manager has to take several decisions. Decision making is a process of selecting from a set of alternative courses of action, that course, which best meets the objectives of the decision problem, as compared to the others as judged by the decision maker. In a decision making process, various alternatives are developed, based on the available data. These are then weighted logically and empirically as far as possible and feasible, before selecting the best alternative among them.

The following are the steps involved in the decision making process:
(i) Identify the problem to be solved.
(ii) Define the objective sought by the solution of the problem.
(iii) Collection of the relevant data.
(iv) Developing various alternatives for solving the problem.
(v) Evaluation of these alternatives in light of the solution objective using a suitable criterion.
(vi) Select the best alternative and implement it.

Quantitative methods are used to guide in decision making (e.g. Break even analysis to decide production level), support the decision making (e.g. forecasting techniques used in sales forecasting) or to automate programmable decisions using computers (e.g. inventory decisions).

6.2 Elements of Decision Making Problem

(i) **Decision Maker** is an individual or a group of individuals who make the decision.

(ii) **Courses of Action or Strategies:** These are the various options available to the decision maker for solving the problem. e.g. Minimum inventory to be stocked for the sale of a commodity in a given period of time. Thus, we may have,

S_1 - Strategy of stocking 15 units

S_2 - Strategy of stocking 20 units etc.

(iii) **States of Nature or Outcomes:** These are the events which indicate the occurrences which are not under the decision maker's control and which determine the level of success for a given strategy. e.g. market demand for a commodity during a given period of time. Thus, we may have,

N_1 - Market demand of 15 units

N_2 - Market demand of 20 units etc.

Each state of nature can have a probability of occurrence associated with it.

(iv) **Pay-off:** Each combination of a course of action (strategy) and a state of nature is associated with a pay-off (also called as conditional pay-off) which indicates the net gain to the decision maker for that combination. (Cost is indicated as a negative pay-off).

e.g. The pay-off associated with the strategy of stocking 20 units of a commodity when the state of nature is, say the market demand of 15 units could be ₹ 50.

(v) **Pay-off Table:** It lists a set of pay-offs for the given strategies along with all the states of nature (outcomes) that are mutually exclusive and collectively exhaustive.

Strategies	States of Nature			
	N_1	N_2	-------	N_n
	Probability of States			
	p_1	p_2	-------	p_n
S_1	x_{11}	x_{12}	-------	x_{1n}
S_2	x_{21}	x_{22}	-------	x_{2n}
⋮	⋮	⋮		⋮
S_m	x_{m1}	x_{m2}	-------	x_{mn}

Pay-off Table

The weighted pay-off associated with a given strategy-state combination, is obtained by multiplying the corresponding pay-off figure by the probability of occurrence of that state.

e.g. In the above table, weighted pay off for S_1N_1 combination = $p_1(x_{11})$

6.3 Decision Models

Decision Theory is concerned with making optimal choice from a given set of alternatives (or strategies). It identifies four models for decision making as follows:

(a) Decision making under Certainty, where the consequences of each course of action are certainly known and there is only one state of nature.

(b) Decision making under Risk, where there are several states of nature and the probabilities of occurrences for each state are known.

(c) Decision making under Uncertainty, where the probabilities of occurrences of different states of nature are not known.

(d) Decision Making under Conflict.

Decision Making under Risk and Decision Making under Uncertainty are described below.

6.4 Decision Making Under Risk

In this situation, the decision maker is aware of all the possible states of nature but does not know their occurrences with certainty. Thus, he knows or can just estimate the probabilities of their occurrences. This is based on his past experience or on the theoretical probability distributions of the states etc.

(A) Expected Monetary Value Criterion: The decision under this situation is taken on the basis of the expected pay-off or Expected Monetary Value (EMV) calculated for each strategy. EMV represents the long term gain to be expected from a strategy if the decision is repeated large number of times. Thus, for a pay-off table representing gains, we proceed as follows:

Step 1: For each strategy, calculate the Expected Monetary Value (EMV) as follows:

EMV = Σ Weighted Payoffs (along the row)

Thus, for strategy S_i

$$EMV(S_i) = \sum_{j=1}^{n} p_j (x_{ij})$$

i.e. for strategy S_1,

$$EMV(S_1) = \sum_{j=1}^{n} p_j (x_{1j}) = p_1 x_{11} + p_2 x_{12} + ... + p_n x_{1n} \text{ and so on.}$$

Step 2: Identify the maximum EMV among all these EMV values

Step 3: The strategy corresponding to the largest EMV is the optimal strategy.

Example 1: Consider the following profit table along with the given probabilities of each state:

	States		
	N_1	N_2	N_3
Strategies	Probability of States		
	0.3	0.6	0.1
S_1	20	18	–9
S_2	25	15	10
S_3	40	–10	12

Solution:
1. To find the Expected Monetary Value (EMV) for each strategy:
   For strategy S_1, we have
   EMV (S_1) = 0.3 (20) + 0.6(18) + 0.1 (–9) = 15.9
   Similarly, EMV (S_2) = 0.3(25) + 0.6(15) + 0.1 (10) = 17.5
   and   EMV (S_3) = 0.3(40) + 0.6(–10) + 0.1(12) = 7.2
2. The maximum EMV among these values is 17.5, corresponding to the strategy S_2. Hence, S_2 is the optimal strategy.

(B) Expected Value with Perfect Information: If the decision maker has a perfect information about the states before taking a decision, he can select the best strategy (giving maximum pay-off) for each of the states. This gives the Expected Value with Perfect Information. Thus, in the above case, the best strategy, if the state N_1 occurs, is S_3 as it will result in the maximum possible pay-off of 40 for that state N_1. Similarly, the best strategy for N_2 is S_1 (pay-off = 18) and that for N_3 is S_3 (pay-off = 12).

Hence, the expected value with perfect information = 0.3 (40) + 0.6(18) + 0.1 (12) = 24

(C) Value of Perfect Information (VPI): This is equal to the difference between the Expected Value with Perfect Information and the (Maximum) Expected Value without perfect information i.e. VPI = Expected value with perfect information – Max EMV.

Thus, for the above example, we have

VPI = 24 – 17.5 = 6.5

VPI helps in determining the maximum amount that should be spent for acquiring the information like the charges of consultants, expenditure on market research etc.

6.5 Decision Making Under Uncertainty

This includes those decisions where the probabilities of occurrences of the different outcomes or states of nature, can not be estimated. This happens when there is no past experience or historical data available to estimate the probabilities. e.g. when a new product is introduced in the market or when a new plant is set up. The choice of decision in this case largely depends upon the personality of the decision maker and the policy of the organisation. The different decision criteria available under the condition of uncertainty are as follows:

(A) Maximin (gain) or Minimax (loss) Criterion:

It represents pessimistic approach of the decision maker. For a Pay-off Table representing gains, we proceed as follows:

Step 1 : Write down the minimum pay-off for each strategy.

Step 2 : Identify the maximum pay-off among these minimum pay-offs i.e. we find maximin pay-off.

Step 3 : The strategy corresponding to this maximin pay-off is the optimal strategy.

Thus, here we go for the strategy or course of action which maximises the minimum possible pay-offs or gains.

For a pay-off matrix representing losses, we identify maximum pay-off for all the strategies, and then select the minimum pay-off among them i.e. minimax (to minimise the maximum possible losses). This criterion assumes the nature to be unfavourable to the decision maker.

Example 2: Consider the following Profit Table:

Strategies	States				Minimum Profit
	N_1	N_2	N_3	N_4	
S_1	30	10	10	8	8 ← **Maximin**
S_2	40	−15	5	7	− 15
S_3	50	20	−6	10	− 6

Thus, we see that,

Minimum Pay-off (profit) for Strategy S_1 = 8
Minimum Pay-off (profit) for Strategy S_2 = −15 (i.e. loss)
Minimum Pay-off (profit) for Strategy S_3 = −6 (i.e. loss)

The maximum profit among these minimas is 8, corresponding to strategy S_1. Hence, the decision is to adopt optimal strategy S_1.

(B) Maximax (gain) or Minimin (loss) Criterion:

It represents an optimistic approach of solving the problem. For a Pay-off Table representing gains, we proceed as follows:

Step 1: Write down the maximum pay-off for each strategy.

Step 2: Identify the maximum figure among these maximum pay-offs i.e. we find the maximax.

Step 3: The strategy corresponding to this maximax pay-off is the optimal strategy.

Thus, here we go for the strategy which maximises the maximum possible pay-offs or gains.

For a pay-off matrix representing losses, we identify minimum pay-off for all the strategies and then select the minimum pay-off among them i.e. minimin (to minimise the minimum possible losses). This criterion assumes the nature to be favourable to the decision maker.

Example 3: For the same previous Profit Table (Given in Example 2) we have:

Strategies	States				Maximum Profit
	N_1	N_2	N_3	N_4	
S_1	30	10	10	8	30
S_2	40	-15	5	7	40
S_3	50	20	-6	10	50 ← **Maximax**

Thus, we see that
Maximum pay-off (profit) for strategy S_1 = 30
Maximum pay-off (profit) for strategy S_2 = 40
Maximum pay-off (profit) for strategy S_3 = 50
The maximum profit among these maximas is 50, corresponding to strategy S_3.
Hence, the optimum strategy is S_3.

(C) Hurwicz Alpha Criterion:

It represents a realistic approach of the decision maker, thus avoiding the extremes of dismal pessimism (i.e. maximin) and fantastic optimism (i.e. maximax). It uses a coefficient of optimism α (alpha), $0 \le \alpha \le 1$, representing the decision maker's degree of optimism. Value of α is estimated on the basis of past experience or otherwise and $\alpha = 0$ implies pessimism (maximin) and $\alpha = 1$ implies optimism (maximax)

For a pay-off table representing gains, we proceed as follows:

Step 1: Estimate or identify value of α.
Step 2: Identify the largest payoff (M) and the smallest pay-off (m) for each strategy.
Step 3: Calculate the expected value of pay-off for each strategy as
Expected value = $\alpha M + (1 - \alpha) m$
Step 4: Identify the maximum pay-off among all these expected values.
Step 5: The strategy corresponding to this maximum pay-off, is the optimal strategy.

Example 4: Consider the previous Profit Table (Given in Example 2)

	N_1	N_2	N_3	N_4	Max. (M)	Min. (m)
S_1	30	10	10	8	30	8
S_2	40	-15	5	7	40	-15
S_3	50	20	-6	10	50	-6

Let coefficient of optimism, $\alpha = 0.7$ ∴ $1 - \alpha = 1 - 0.7 = 0.3$

∴ Expected profit for strategy $S_1 = 0.7(30) + 0.3(8) = 23.4$

Expected profit for strategy $S_2 = 0.7(40) + 0.3(-15) = 23.5$

Expected profit for strategy $S_3 = 0.7(50) + 0.3(-6) = 33.2$

∴ The strategy corresponding to the maximum expected profit of 33.2 i.e. S_3, is the optimal strategy.

(D) Laplace Criterion:

It represents a rational approach of the decision maker and is based on the principle of insufficient reason or equally likelihood of the states of nature. Thus, as the information about the probability of occurrences of the states is insufficient, we assume equal probabilities for them. For a pay-off table representing gains, we proceed as follows for making the decision:

Step 1: Find out the average expected pay-off for each strategy as,

$$\text{Average expected pay-off} = \frac{\text{Sum of all pay-offs}}{\text{Total number of States}}$$

(This is same as assuming equal probability = $\frac{1}{\text{No. of states}}$ for all the states)

Step 2: Identify the maximum figure among all these average pay-offs.

Step 3: The strategy corresponding to this maximum average pay-off, is the optimal strategy.

Example 5: For the same previous Profit Table (Given in Example 2).

	N_1	N_2	N_3	N_4	Average Expected Profit
S_1	30	10	10	8	$\frac{30 + 10 + 10 + 8}{4} = \frac{58}{4} = 14.5$
S_2	40	-15	5	7	$\frac{40 - 15 + 5 + 7}{4} = \frac{37}{4} = 9.25$
S_3	50	20	-6	10	$\frac{50 + 20 - 6 + 10}{4} = \frac{74}{4} = 18.5$ ←

Thus, the strategy corresponding to the maximum average expected profit of 18.5 i.e. S_3, is the optimal strategy.

(E) Minimax Regret Criterion:

This criterion developed by Savage uses the regret or opportunity loss (i.e. the loss for not using the best strategy) for each strategy for each state of nature.

Thus, for a pay-off table representing gains, we proceed as follows:

Step 1: Consider the first state of nature N_1.

Step 2: Identify the largest pay-off under it. (The corresponding strategy is the best strategy for this state)

Step 3: Find out the regret for each strategy now, as follows:
Regret = Largest Payoff – Payoff for the strategy

Step 4: Repeat the above steps for each state of nature to get the regret table

Step 5: Identify the maximum regret for each strategy.

Step 6: Find out the minimum regret figure among all these maximum regrets (minimax).

Step 7: The strategy corresponding to this minimax regret is the optimal strategy.

Note: For a loss matrix we proceed in the same way but select the strategy corresponding to maximin.

Example 6: Consider the previous Profit Table (Given in Example 2).

Strategies	States			
	N_1	N_2	N_3	N_4
S_1	30	10	10	8
S_2	40	–15	5	7
S_3	50	20	–6	10

Solution:

1. To find out the regrets corresponding to state N_1:
   Here, the best strategy is S_3, which represents the largest profit of 50.
   Hence, the regret for strategy S_1, is
   Regret = Largest Profit – Pay-off for S_1 = 50 – 30 = 20
   Similarly, for strategy S_2, regret = 50 – 40 = 10
   and for strategy S_3, regret = 50 – 50 = 0
   [The opportunity loss (i.e. regret) for S_1, represents the loss incurred for not using the best strategy S_3 if strategy S_1 is adopted instead and so on]

2. Similarly, for state N_2, largest profit = 20
   ∴ regret for S_1 = 20 – 10 = 10, regret for S_2 = 20 – (–15) = 35.
   and regret for S_3 = 20 – 20 = 0

3. Again for N_3, largest profit = 10
   ∴ regret for S_1 = 10 – 10 = 0, regret for S_2 = 10 – 5 = 5 and
   regret for S_3 = 10 – (– 6) = 16
   And finally for N_4, we get the regrets as S_1 (2), S_2 (3), S_3 (0)

4. Thus, using these regrets we get the Regret Table as

	N_1	N_2	N_3	N_4	Maximum Regret	
S_1	20	10	0	2	20	
S_2	10	35	5	3	35	
S_3	0	0	16	0	16	← Minimax

The minimum regret among all the maximum regrets (of the strategies) is 16. Hence, the corresponding strategy S_3 is the optimal strategy.

Note: For a Cost or Loss Table, it is convenient to obtain the equivalent Profit Table and then use any of the above criteria to solve it further as usual. To obtain the Profit Table, simply change the signs for all the pay-offs in the cost matrix (as cost is indicated by a negative profit)

Solved Problems

Problem 1: A major consumer goods manufacturer, wishes to decide which of the two new products to bring out in the market and what level of advertising to use. The profit tables for these products are as follows (profits are in units of ₹ 10,000):

Demand	OZONE			LIFE		
	A_1	A_2	A_3	A_1	A_2	A_3
S_1 High	140	160	200	200	210	230
S_2 Average	100	130	160	160	170	190
S_3 Low	80	120	140	120	130	140

where A_1 - low expenditure advertising programme
 A_2 - medium expenditure advertising programme
 A_3 - high expenditure advertising programme

The prior probability distributions of demand are:

S_i	OZONE $P(S_i)$	LIFE $P(S_i)$
S_1	0.4	0.2
S_2	0.5	0.2
S_3	0.1	0.6

(i) Which product and advertising level would you recommend?
(ii) What is the expected value of perfect information for each product?

Solution: Here S_1, S_2, S_3 represent the states of nature and A_1, A_2, A_3 represent the strategies (advertisement levels). Hence, we rewrite the table as follows and use the (EMV) criterion (as the probabilities of states are given) to find out the required result.

For the product - OZONE.

Strategies	States			EMV
	S_1 (0.4)	S_2 (0.5)	S_3 (0.1)	
A_1	140	100	80	[0.4 (140) + 0.5 (100) + 0.1 (80)] = 114
A_2	160	130	120	[0.4 (160) + 0.5 (130) + 0.1 (120)] = 141
A_3	200	160	140	[0.4 (200) + 0.5 (160) + 0.1 (140)] = 174 ← **Max.**

Hence, the maximum expected pay-off for OZONE is ₹ (174) × 10,000 = ₹ 17,40,000 and the Expected Monetary Value with perfect information is

$$\text{EMVPI} = 0.4 (200) + 0.5 (160) + 0.1 (140) = 174 \text{ (units of 10,000)}$$
$$= ₹ 17,40,000$$

Thus, Value of Perfect Information (VPI) is

$$\text{VPI} = \text{EMVPI} - \text{Max. EMV} = 174 - 174 = 0$$

Now, for product LIFE we have

Strategies	States			EMV
	S_1 (0.2)	S_2 (0.2)	S_3 (0.6)	
A_1	200	160	120	[0.2 (200) + 0.2 (160) + 0.6 (120)] = 144
A_2	210	170	130	[0.2 (210) + 0.2 (170) + 0.6 (130)] = 154
A_3	230	190	140	[0.2 (230) + 0.2 (190) + 0.6 (140)] = 168 ← **Max.**

Thus, Maximum (EMV) = 168 × (10,000) = ₹ 16,80,000

$$\text{EMVPI} = 0.2 (230) + 0.2 (190) + 0.6 (140) = 168 \text{ (units of 10,000)}$$
$$= 16,80,000$$

Thus, VPI = EMVPI – Max. EMV = 16,80,000 – 16,80,000 = 0.

Now, we see that between the two products OZONE and LIFE, maximum EMV corresponds to OZONE which is of 17,40,000 (as compared to 16,80,000 for LIFE). Hence, product OZONE should be selected.

Now, for OZONE, this maximum EMV corresponds to the strategy A_3 i.e. the strategy of high expenditure on advertisement programme. Hence, this strategy is selected. Thus, the manufacturer should bring out the product OZONE to the market with high expenditure on advertisement.

Problem 2: Suresh finds the probability of demand distribution of luxury car 'S' as follows:

Probability of Demand : 0.2 0.4 0.1 0.3
Demand for car each day : 1 2 3 4

The Selling Price of car is ₹ 10,00,000 and it costs to Suresh ₹ 6,00,000. Suresh has always followed a rule for initial purchase - purchase 3 cars.

Find the expected daily profit under the decision rule of buying three each morning. If fees for perfect information is ₹ 1,00,000, calculate the expected monetary value of the venture with perfect information (EMVPI). **(P.U. MBA - Dec. 13)**

Solution:

Let N_1 - State that the demand is 1, N_2 - State that the demand is 2,
      N_3 - State that the demand is 3, N_4 - State that the demand is 4
and S_1 - Strategy of buying 1 car, S_2 - Strategy of buying 2 cars.
      S_3 - Strategy of buying 3 cars, S_4 - Strategy of buying 4 cars.

Now, we can find the conditional profit per day (pay-off) to Suresh for each strategy-state combination as

$$\text{Pay-off (profit)} = \text{(cars sold)(profit per car)} - \text{(cars unsold)(cost)}$$
$$= \text{(cars sold)}(10{,}00{,}000 - 6{,}00{,}000) - \text{(cars unsold)}(6{,}00{,}000)$$
$$= 4{,}00{,}000 \text{ (cars sold)} - 6{,}00{,}000 \text{ (cars unsold)}$$

Thus, for S_1N_1,   Profit = $1(4) - 0 = ₹\,4$ lakh
for S_1N_2,   Profit = $1(4) - 0 = ₹\,4$ lakh etc.
Similarly, for S_2N_1, Profit = $(1)4 - (2-1)(6) = 4 - 6 = -2$ lakh
        for S_2N_2, Profit = $2(4) - 0 = 8$ lakh. etc.
        for S_3N_1, Profit = $1(4) - (3-1)6 = 4 - 12 = -8$ lakh
        for S_3N_2, Profit = $2(4) - (3-2)6 = 8 - 6 = 2$ lakh and so on.

Thus, we get the pay-off table as follows:

	N_1 (0.2)	N_2 (0.4)	N_3 (0.1)	N_4 (0.3)	Expected Profit (EMV)
S_1	4	4	4	4	4
S_2	−2	8	8	8	6 ← **Max**
S_3	−8	2	12	12	4
S_4	−14	−4	6	16	1

Thus, the expected daily profit under the decision rule of buying three cars in the morning i.e. $S_3 = 0.2(-8) + 0.4(2) + 0.1(12) + 0.3(12) = ₹\,4$ lakh

As we see that the maximum (EMV) of ₹ 6 lakh, corresponds to strategy S_2, hence, infact, S_2 is the optimal decision policy.

Now, the Expected Montary Value with perfect information
(EMVPI) = $0.2(4) + 0.4(8) + 0.1(12) + 0.3(16) = ₹\,10$ lakh

Note: Value of Perfect Information = EMVPI − Maximum EMV
                                         = $10 - 6 = ₹\,4$ lakh

Thus, Suresh should pay maximum fee for perfect information upto ₹ 4 lakh. As the fees (₹ 1 lakh) are less than this, he should opt for it.

Problem 3: A certain output is manufactured at ₹ 8 and sold at ₹ 14 per unit. The product is such that if it is produced but not sold during a day time it becomes worthless. The daily sales records in the past are as follows.

Demand per day: 30   40   50   60   70
No. of days each sales
level was recorded: 24   24   36   24   12

(i) Calculate the average expected sales of a day.
(ii) Find the expected pay-offs and the optimum policy.
(iii) Also find the value of perfect information.

Solution:

We have, x = demand per day and
f = No. of days, with that demand

(i) ∴   Average expected daily sales $= \frac{\Sigma fx}{\Sigma f}$

$$= \frac{24(30) + 24(40) + 36(50) + 24(60) + 12(70)}{24 + 24 + 36 + 24 + 12}$$

$$= \frac{5760}{120} = 48 \text{ units}$$

(ii) Let S_1 - Strategy of producing 30 units per day
S_2 - Strategy of producing 40 units per day and so on.

Similarly, let the states of nature be

N_1 - Daily demand is of 30 units.
N_2 - Daily demand is of 40 units and so on.

Hence, we have the probabilities of occurrences of these states as

p_1 = Probability of occurrence of state N_1 = $\frac{\text{No. of days with demand '30'}}{\text{Total No. of days}} = \frac{24}{120} = 0.2$

$p_2 = \frac{24}{120} = 0.2$, $p_3 = \frac{36}{120} = 0.3$, $p_4 = \frac{24}{120} = 0.2$ and $p_5 = \frac{12}{120} = 0.1$

Now, Pay-off = (Quantity sold) (Profit per unit) – (Quantity unsold) (Cost per unit)
= (Quantity sold) (14 – 8) – (Quantity unsold) 8
= 6 (Quantity sold) – 8 (Quantity unsold)

e.g. if quantity produced is 30 and demand is 40, all the produced quantity will be sold and there will be no unsold quantity.

∴   Pay-off = 6 (30) – 8 (0) = 180

Similarly, if produced quantity is 40 units and demand is 30 units, only 30 units will be sold and 10 units will be the unsold quantity.

∴   Pay-off = 6(30) – 8(10) = 180 – 80 = 100

Thus, proceeding in this way we get the pay-off matrix as follows:

Strategies	States of Nature					EMV
	N_1	N_2	N_3	N_4	N_5	
	Probability					
	0.2	0.2	0.3	0.2	0.1	
S_1	180	180	180	180	180	180
S_2	100	240	240	240	240	212
S_3	20	160	300	300	300	216 ← Max
S_4	– 60	80	220	360	360	178
S_5	– 140	0	140	280	420	112

Hence, the strategy S_3 i.e. of producing 50 units daily is the optimal strategy.

(iii) Now, the value with perfect information =

= 180 (0.2) + 240 (0.2) + 300 (0.3) + 360 (0.2) + 420 (0.1) = ₹ 288

Hence, value of perfect information = 288 – Max. EMV = 288 – 216 = ₹ 72

Problem 4: Using various criteria for decision making, find the optimal strategy for the marketing manager of an automobile company. The conditional pay-offs in crores of rupees for the two models of a car for the various likely sales figures are as follows:

Model	Sales (Units)		
	1 lakh	2 lakh	3 lakh
X	30	10	10
Y	55	20	3

Solution: We have,

S_1 - Strategy of selling model X, S_2 - Strategy of selling model Y.

N_1 - State that the likely sales are 1 lakh units

N_2 - State that the likely sales are 2 lakh units.

N_3 - State that the likely sales are 3 lakh units.

Also, we do not know the probabilities for each state. Hence, it is a case of decision making under uncertainty.

Thus, we have the pay-off (profit) table as

	N_1	N_2	N_3	Minimum Profit	Maximum Profit	Average Profit
S_1(X)	30	10	10	10 ← Maximin	30	16.67
S_2(Y)	55	20	3	3	55 ← Maximax	26 ← Max.

(i) Using Maximin Criterion (pessimism) - Comparing the minimum profits for both the strategies, we see that maximum between these two i.e. maximin is 10. Hence, optimal strategy as per this criterion is S_1 i.e. to sell model X and the expected profit will be ₹ 10 crores.

(ii) Using Maximax Criterion (optimism) - Comparing the maximum profit for both the strategies we see that the maximum between them i.e. maximax is 55 corresponding to S_2. Hence the optimal strategy would be S_2 i.e. to sell model Y with expected profit = ₹ 55 crores.

(iii) Laplace Criterion (rationalism) - For using this criterion, we find out the average expected profit for both the strategies S_1 and S_2 (i.e. we assume the probabilities of all the states as equal) as average profit for $S_1 = \frac{30 + 10 + 10}{3} = \frac{50}{3} = ₹ 16.67$ crores, average profit for $S_2 = \frac{55 + 20 + 3}{3} = \frac{78}{3} = ₹ 26$ crores.

The maximum among these two is ₹ 26 crores corresponding to S_2. Hence S_2 i.e. to sell model Y is the best strategy, under this criterion. The corresponding expected profit is ₹ 26 crore.

(iv) We can not use Hurwitz Criterion as we do not know the coefficient of optimism α for the marketing manager.

(v) Regret Criterion - Here, we find out the regrets for each strategy corresponding to each state by using
Regret = Maximum pay off for the State – Pay-off for the strategy.
Thus, for state N_1, maximum pay off = 55
∴ Regret of S_1 = 55 – 30 = 25 and Regret of S_2 = 55 – 55 = 0
Similarly, for N_2,
Regret of S_1 = 20 – 10 = 10 and Regret of S_2 = 20 – 20 = 0 and so on.
Thus, we get the Regret Table as

	N_1	N_2	N_3	Minimum Regret
S_1	25	10	0	25
S_2	0	0	7	7 ← Min.

The minimum between the maximum regrets is 7 corresponding to S_2. Hence S_2 i.e. to sell model Y is the optimal strategy.

Problem 5: A bakery owner has to buy 100 units of cakes A and B from the producer at the beginning of a week. The cake A costs him ₹ 5 which he sells at ₹ 9 per unit. Similarly, cake B costs him ₹ 4 per unit which he sells for ₹ 7. The expected demands per week for these cakes could be 80, 90, 100 or 110 units. Any quantity of cakes remaining at the end of a week is collected back by the producer for ₹ 2 per unit. Identify which of the cakes A or B should the bakery owner buy using - (i) Maximin Criterion (ii) Maximax Criterion (iii) Hurwicz Criterion when the bakery owner is 80% optimum about the likely demand (iv) Laplace Criterion and (v) Minimax Regret Criterion.

Solution: We have the Strategies as S_1 - To buy cakes A and S_2 - To buy cakes B and the states of Nature are

N_1 - demand for 80 units, N_2 - demand for 90 units.
N_3 - demand for 100 units, N_4 - demand for 110 units.
We calculate the pay-off (profit) as follows:
Profit = (Quantity sold) (Profit per unit) - (Quantity unsold) (Loss per unit)
Here, profit per unit of cake A sold = Selling Price – Cost = 9 – 5 = ₹ 4 and
loss per unit of cake A unsold = Cost – Resale Price = 5 – 2 = ₹ 3.
Similarly, profit per unit of cake B sold = 7 – 4 = ₹ 3 and
loss per unit of cake B unsold = 4 – 2 = ₹ 2.
Hence, for cake A, (i.e. strategy S_1) as the quantity purchased is 100 units,
∴ Profit if the demand is 80 = (80) 4 – (100 – 80) 3 = 320 – 60 = ₹ 260
Profit if the demand is 90 = (90) 4 – (100 – 90) 3 = 360 – 30 = ₹ 330
Profit if the demand is 100 = (100) 4 – 0 = 400
Profit if the demand is 110 = (100) 4 – 0 = ₹ 400, as only 100 units are available.

Proceeding similarly we can find the profits for strategy S_2 (of buying cake B) and thus write the pay off table as

Strategies	N_1	N_2	N_3	N_4	Minimum Profit	Maximum Profit	Expected Profit	Average Profit
S_1	260	330	400	400	260 (Maximin)	400 (Maximax)	372 (Max)	347.5 (Max)
S_2	200	250	300	300	200	300	280	262.5

(i) Using Maximin Criterion - The maximum among the minimum pay-offs for strategies S_1 and S_2 is ₹ 260 corresponding to strategy S_1. Hence, this is the optimal strategy and he should buy cakes A.

(ii) Using Maximax Criterion - The maximum among the maximum pay-offs for the strategies S_1 and S_2 is ₹ 400 corresponding to S_1. Hence he should select this strategy S_1 of buying cakes A.

(iii) Hurwitz Criterion - Considering, coefficient of optimism, α = 80% i.e. $\frac{80}{100}$ = 0.8

we calculate the expected profit for each of the strategies as

for S_1, expected profit = α (max) + $(1 - \alpha)$ (min)
$= (0.8)(400) + (1 - 0.8) 260 = 320 + 52 = ₹ 372$

and for S_2, expected profit = $(0.8) 300 + (0.2) 200 = 240 + 40 = ₹ 280$

The maximum between these two values is ₹ 372. Hence, he should go for S_1 i.e. buy cakes A.

(iv) **Laplace Criterion** - Here we find the average expected profit for each strategy as

for S_1, average profit $= \dfrac{260 + 330 + 400 + 400}{4} = \dfrac{1390}{4} = ₹ 347.5$

and for S_2, average profit $= \dfrac{200 + 250 + 300 + 300}{4} = \dfrac{1050}{4} = ₹ 262.5$

Hence, he should select strategy corresponding to the maximum between these two average profits i.e. strategy S_1 and hence should buy cakes A.

(v) **Minimax Regret Criterion** - We find out the regrets for each strategy, corresponding to each state as

Regret = Maximum profit for the state − Profit for the strategy

∴ for state N_1,

Regret of $S_1 = 260 − 260 = 0$ and regret of $S_2 = 260 − 200 = 60$

Find out the other regrets similarly to get the regret table as:

	N_1	N_2	N_3	N_4	Minimum Regret
S_1	0	0	0	0	0 (Minimax)
S_2	60	80	100	100	100

The minimum regret among the maximum regrets for the strategies S_1 and S_2 is 0 corresponding to S_1. Hence, the optimal strategy is S_1 i.e. to buy cakes A.

Problem 6: A food product company is contemplating the introduction of a revolutionary new product with new packaging to replace the existing product at much higher price (S_1) or a moderate change in the composition of the existing product with a new packaging at a small increase in price (S_2) or a small change in the composition of the existing except the word 'New' with a negligible increase in the price (S_3). The three possible states of nature of the events are (i) high increase in sales (A_1) (ii) no change in sales (A_2) and (iii) decrease in sales (A_3). The marketing department of the company worked out the pay-offs in terms of the yearly net profits for each of the strategies for these events (expected sales). This is represented in the following table:

Pay-offs (in ₹)

State of Nature	Strategies		
	S_1	S_2	S_3
A_1	7,00,000	3,00,000	1,50,000
A_2	5,00,000	4,50,000	0
A_3	3,00,000	3,00,000	3,00,000

Which strategy should the executive concerned choose on the basis of (i) Maximin Criterion (ii) Maximax Criterion (iii) Minimax regret criterion and (iv) Laplace Criterion

Solution: Rewriting the Pay-off Table with the strategies as the row-headings and the states as the column headings we have

	A₁	A₂	A₃	Minimum Pay-off	Maximum Pay-off	Average Pay-off
S₁	700000	500000	300000	300000 (Maximin)	700000 (Maximax)	500000 (Max)
S₂	300000	450000	300000	300000 (Maximin)	450000	350000
S₃	150000	0	300000	0	300000	150000

(i) Using Maximin Criterion - We see that the maximum among the minimum pay-offs for all the strategies i.e. maximin is ₹ 3,00,000 which corresponds to two strategies S_1 and S_2. Hence, any one of them can be selected.

(ii) Using Maximax Criterion - The maximum among the maximum payoffs for all the strategies i.e. maximax is ₹ 7,00,000, corresponding to strategy S_1. Hence, S_1 is the optimal strategy.

(iii) Using Laplace Criterion - Here we calculate the average expected payoff for all the strategies, assuming equal probability of occurrence for all the states.

Thus, for S_1, Average Payoff $= \dfrac{700000 + 500000 + 300000}{3} = \dfrac{1500000}{3}$

$= ₹ 5,00,000$ etc.

The maximum among such average payoffs for all the strategies is ₹ 5,00,000. Hence, the corresponding strategy S_1 should be selected.

(iv) Using Minimax Regret Criterion - Here we construct the regret matrix first, by finding out the regrets for each strategy corresponding to each state as

Regret = Maximum Payoff for the State – Pay off for the Strategy

Thus, for State A_1,

Regret of S_1 = 7,00,000 – 7,00,000 = 0, Regret of S_2 = 7,00,000 – 3,00,000 = 4,00,000 etc.

Thus, the Regret Table is

	A₁	A₂	A₃	Maximum Regret
S₁	0	0	0	0 (Minimax)
S₂	400000	50000	0	400000
S₃	550000	500000	0	550000

As, the minimum regret among the maximum regrets of all the strategies is 0, the corresponding strategy S_1 should be selected.

Problem 7: Hindustan sales corporation is a dealer firm in white goods. It finds that the weekly holding cost per unit of an Air cooler is ₹ 30 per week. Non-availability of an air cooler results in losing a customer. The cost for losing a customer is estimated to be ₹ 80. The dealer, expects that the weekly demand for an air cooler will range from 0 to 3 units per week.

(a) Construct a Pay-off matrix.

(b) Determine the optimal quantity to be stocked per week and the corresponding weekly cost using: (i) Maximin Criterion (ii) Maximax Criterion (iii) Laplace Criterion (iv) Regret Criterion (v) Hurwicz Criterion if the dealer is optimistic about the demand for 60% of times (vi) If the probability distribution of the demand is as follows:

0	1	2	3
0.1	0.3	0.4	0.2

Solution: We have the four possible outcomes for the weekly demands for the coolers i.e. states of nature as

N_0 - Demand for 0 units, N_1 - Demand for 1 unit

N_2 - Demand for 2 units, N_3 - Demand for 3 units.

Hence, the possible strategies could be

S_0 - To stock 0 units, S_1 - To stock 1 unit

S_2 - To stock 2 units, S_3 - To stock 3 units.

Assuming that the weekly holding cost is incurred on the air coolers (units) lying unsold at the end of a week, we can find the pay-offs (cost) associated with each strategy as:

Cost = (Number of customers lost) (Cost of losing a customer)

+ (Number of units unsold at the end of week) (Weekly per unit holding cost)

Thus, if stocked quantity is 1 (i.e. S_1) and Demand is 0 (i.e. N_0) then

Cost $(S_1 N_0) = 0 (80) + (1 - 0) 30 = 30$.

Similarly, if the demand is 1, i.e. N_1 there are no lost customers as well as no quantity remains unsold.

∴ Cost $(S_1 N_1) = 0 (80) + 0(30) = 0$

Similarly, Cost $(S_1 N_2) = (2 - 1) 80 + 0(30) = 80$ and so on.

Thus, we can calculate the **costs (payoffs)** for each strategy-state combination to get the Pay-off (cost) Table as

Strategy	States			
	N_0	N_1	N_2	N_3
S_0	0	80	160	240
S_1	30	0	80	160
S_2	60	30	0	80
S_3	90	60	30	0

Now, before using any of the criteria, it is convenient to convert it into an equivalent profit matrix. Thus, considering each cost as a negative profit we can write the equivalent profit table as below and then proceed further as usual. **(Note this step)**

Strategy	N_0	N_1	N_2	N_3	Minimum Profit	Maximum Profit	Average Profit	Expected Profit (Hurwicz)
S_0	0	– 80	– 160	– 240	– 240	0 (Maximax)	– 160	– 96
S_1	– 30	0	– 80	– 160	– 160	0 (Maximax)	– 90	– 64
S_2	– 60	– 30	0	– 80	– 80 (Maximin)	0 (Maximax)	– 56.67 (Max).	– 32 (Max.)
S_3	– 90	– 60	– 30	0	– 90	0 (Maximax)	– 60	– 36

(i) Using Maximin Criterion - The maximum figure among the minimum profits for all the strategies is (– 80) corresponding to S_2. Hence, the optimal strategy is to stock 2 air coolers. This strategy would give profit of (– 80) i.e. cost of ₹ 80.

(ii) Using Maximax Criterion - The maximum figure among the maximum profits is 0, which corresponds to all the strategies. Hence, any of the four strategies S_0, S_1, S_2 or S_3 can be adopted which will cost 0 i.e. nothing to the dealer.

(iii) Laplace Criterion - Here we calculate the average profit for each strategy. The maximum among these is (–56.67) corresponding to S_2. Thus, the optimal strategy is S_2. i.e. to stock 2 coolers so that the (minimum) weekly cost is ₹ 56.67.

(iv) Hurwicz Criterion - We have α = coefficient of optimism = 60% = 60/100 = 0.6

∴ using, expected profit = $\alpha M + (1 - \alpha)m$, we find the expected profits for all strategies. The maximum among these is (– 32). Hence, strategy S_2 of stocking 2 coolers is optimal which will minimise the cost to ₹ 32.

(v) Using Regret Criterion - For this, we calculate the regrets for all strategies for all the states by using, Regret = Maximum Pay-off for a state – Pay-off for the strategy.

Thus, for state N_0
Regret of $S_0 = 0 – 0 = 0$,   Regret of $S_1 = 0 – (–30) = 30$
Regret of $S_2 = 0 – (– 60) = 60$,   Regret of $S_3 = 0 – (– 90) = 90$ and so on.

This gives the regret table which is same as the original cost table as

Strategy	N_1	N_2	N_3	N_4	Maximum Regret
S_0	0	80	160	240	240
S_1	30	0	80	160	160
S_2	60	30	0	80	80 ← Minimax
S_3	90	60	30	0	90

Thus, the minimum regret among the maximum regrets for all the strategies is 80 corresponding S_2. Thus, S_2 is the optimal strategy.

(vi) As the probability distribution for the demands is given, it is a case of decision making under risk and hence we find the Expected Monetary Value (EMV) for all the strategies first. We use the equivalent profit table along with the probabilities of states as

Strategy	N_0 0.1	N_1 0.3	N_2 0.4	N_3 0.2	EMV
S_0	0	– 80	– 160	– 240	– 136
S_1	– 30	0	– 80	– 160	– 67
S_2	– 60	– 30	0	– 80	– 31 ← Max.
S_3	– 90	– 60	– 30	0	– 39

Here, EMV for S_0 = 0.1 (0) + 0.3 (– 80) + 0.4 (– 160) + 0.2 (– 240) = – 136 and so on.
The maximum EMV corresponds to strategy S_2. Hence, it is the optimal strategy.

Problem 8: The past experience shows that the number of copies of tax laws in demand vary between 25 and 30 copies. Some taxes change every year as such if the copies are not sold during the year its value is reduced. Some agency purchases such unsold copies for ₹ 30. The vendor purchases the copies at ₹ 80 each and sells them at ₹ 100 each.

Prepare pay-off table for his purchasing copies between 25 and 30 and state different decisions that will be taken under:

(i) Maximax
(ii) Maximin
(iii) Laplace criterion
(iv) Regret criterion
(v) EMV criterion, if probability of demand is known as:

Demand	25	26	27	28	29	30
Probability	0.05	0.10	0.35	0.30	0.15	0.05

Solution: Let N_1 - State of nature that the demand is of 25 copies.
N_2 - State of nature that the demand is of 26 copies etc.
and S_1 - Strategy of purchasing 25 copies.
S_2 - Strategy of purchasing 26 copies etc.

Now, Profit per copy sold = 100 – 80 = ₹ 20 and
Loss per copy unsold = 80 – 30 = ₹ 50

Hence, we can find the conditional profit per year (pay-off) for each strategy-state combination as:

Pay-off (Profit) = (Copies Sold) (Profit per copy) – (Copies unsold) (Loss per copy)
= (Copies sold) (20) – (Copies unsold) (50)

Thus, for S_1N_1, Profit = 25(20) − (0)(50) = 500
for S_1N_2, Profit = 25(20) − (0)(50) = 500 etc.

Similarly,

For S_2N_1, Profit = 25(20) − (26 − 25)(50) = 500 − 50 = 450
For S_2N_2, Profit = 26(20) − (0)(50) = 520 etc.
For S_3N_1, Profit = 25(20) − (27−25)(50) = 500 − 100 = 400
For S_3N_2, Profit = 26(20) − (27−26)(50) = 520 − 50 = 470
For S_3N_3, Profit = 27(20) − (0)(50) = 540 etc.

Thus, we get the Pay-off table as:

Probability Strategy	States						Maximum Profit	Minimum Profit	Average Profit	EMV
	(0.05) N_1	(0.1) N_2	(0.35) N_3	(0.3) N_4	(0.15) N_5	(0.05) N_6				
S_1	500	500	500	500	500	500	500	500 (Maxi min)	500	500
S_2	450	520	520	520	520	520	520	450	$\frac{3050}{6}$ = 508.33 (max)	516.5
S_3	400	470	540	540	540	540	540	400	$\frac{3030}{6}$ = 505	526 (max)
S_4	350	420	490	560	560	560	560	350	$\frac{2940}{6}$ = 490	511
S_5	300	370	440	510	580	580	580	300	$\frac{2780}{6}$ = 463.33	475
S_6	250	320	390	460	530	600	600 (maxi max)	250	$\frac{2550}{6}$ = 425	428.5

Thus, we have:

(i) Using maximax criterion: Maximax Profit = 600 for strategy S_6. Hence, the vendor should purchase 30 copies.

(ii) Using maximin criterion: Maximin = 500 for S_1. Hence, the vendor should purchase 25 copies.

(iii) **Laplace criterion:** The average expected profit = 508.33 for S_2. Hence, the vendor should purchase 26 copies

(iv) **EMV criterion:** Considering the given probabilities of demand, we have,

EMV for S_1 = (0.01) 500 + (0.1) 500 + (0.35) 500 + (0.3) 500 + (0.15) 500 + (0.05) 500 = 500

EMV for S_2 = (0.05) 450 + (0.1) 520 + (0.35) 520 + (0.3) 520 + (0.15) 520 + (0.05) 520 = 516.5 etc.

Thus, maximum EMV = 526 for S_3. Hence, the vendor should purchase 27 copies.

(v) **Regret criterion:** We have for any state:

Regret for a strategy = (Max. pay off for state) − (Pay off for strategy)

Thus, for state N_1:

Regret of S_1 = 500 − 500 = 0, Regret of S_2 = 500 − 450 = 50, Regret of S_3 = 500 − 400 = 100 etc.

For state N_2:

Regret of S_1 = 520 − 500 = 20, Regret of S_2 = 520 − 520 = 0, Regret of S_3 = 520 − 470 = 50 etc.

Hence, we get the regret matrix as:

	N_1	N_2	N_3	N_4	N_5	N_6	Maximum Regret
S_1	0	20	40	60	80	100	100
S_2	50	0	20	40	60	80	80 (minimax)
S_3	100	50	0	20	40	60	100
S_4	150	100	50	0	20	40	150
S_5	200	150	100	50	0	20	200
S_6	250	200	150	100	50	0	250

Thus, the minimum regret among the maximum regrets for all strategies is 80, for strategy S_2. Hence the vendor should purchase 26 copies.

Problem 9: Find the regret table from the following pay-off table:

Events	Actions			
	A_1	A_2	A_3	A_4
E_1	80	430	−20	30
E_2	330	30	230	330
E_3	−120	130	30	330
E_4	80	30	130	30

Also find expected regret for each action if

$P(E_1) = 0.15$, $P(E_2) = 0.45$, $P(E_3) = 0.25$, $P(E_4) = 0.15$ **(P.U. MBA - May 05)**

Solution: Rewriting the given pay-off table with the actions (strategies) along the rows and the events (i.e. the states of nature) as the columns we get

Actions	Events			
	E_1	E_2	E_3	E_4
A_1	80	330	–120	80
A_2	430	30	130	30
A_3	–20	230	30	130
A_4	30	330	330	30

Now, we calculate the regrets corresponding to each action as:

Regret for an action = Maximum pay-off for the event – Pay-off for the action

Consider the column E_1:

∵ Maximum pay-off for E_1 is 430

∴ Regret for A_1 = 430 – 80 = 350

For A_2 = 430 – 430 = 0

For A_3 = 430 – (–20) = 450

For A_4 = 430 – (30) = 400

Similarly, for column E_2: Maximum pay-off = 330

∴ Regret for A_1 = 330 – 330 = 0

For A_2 = 330 – 30 = 300

For A_3 = 330 – 230 = 100

For A_4 = 330 – 330 = 0

Proceeding similarly we get the regret table as:

Actions	Events			
	E_1	E_2	E_3	E_4
A_1	350	0	450	50
A_2	0	300	200	100
A_3	450	100	300	0
A_4	400	0	0	100

Now, if $P(E_1) = 0.15$, $P(E_2) = 0.45$, $P(E_3) = 0.25$, $P(E_4) = 0.15$

∴ Expected regrets for each of the actions are:

Expected regret for A_1 = 350(0.15) + 0(0.45) + 450(0.25) + 50(0.15) = 172.5

Expected regret for A_2 = 0(0.15) + 300(0.45) + 200(0.25) + 100(0.15) = 200

Expected regret for A_3 = 450(0.15) + 100(0.45) + 300(0.25) + 0(0.15) = 187.5

Expected regret for A_4 = 400(0.15) + 0(0.45) + 0(0.25) + 100(0.15) = 75

Problem 10: A small industry finds from past data that the cost of making an item is ₹ 25/-. The selling price of an item is ₹ 30/-. If it is not sold within a week, it could be disposed off at ₹ 20/- at the end of a week. Data for sales is given below. Find optimum number of items per week the industry should purchase find EVPI.

Weekly Sales	4	5	6	7
No. of Weeks	10	20	40	30

(P.U. MBA - Dec. 08)

Solution: Let N_1 - state that the demand is 4 units
N_2 - state that the demand is 5 units etc. and
S_1 - Strategy of purchasing 4 units
S_2 - Strategy of purchasing 5 units etc.

Now, per unit profit on Sale = Selling price − Cost = 30 − 25 = 5 and per unit loss due to unsold quantity = Cost − Resale value = 25 − 20 = 5. Hence, the conditional profit per week (i.e. pay-off) for each strategy state combination can be found as:

Profit (Pay-off) = (Quantity sold) (Per Unit Profit) − (Quantity Unsold) (Per Unit Loss)
= (Quantity sold) (5) − (Quantity Unsold) (5)

∴ For combination,
S_1N_1, Profit = 4(5) − 0(5) = 20
For S_1N_2, Profit = 4(5) − 0(5) = 20 etc.
For S_2N_1, Profit = 4(5) − 1(5) = 15
For S_2N_2, Profit = 5(5) − 0(5) = 25
For S_2N_3, Profit = 5(5) − 0(5) = 25 etc.
For S_3N_1, Profit = 4(5) − 2(5) = 10 etc.

Thus, we get the pay-off table as given below.

Also, as the frequency distribution of weekly sales (with total no. of weeks = 10 + 20 + 40 + 30 = 100) is given, we convert it into probability distribution. Thus, probability that the weekly sales is 4 (i.e. probability of state N_1).

$= \dfrac{10}{100} = 0.10$

Similarly, Probability of N_2 (i.e. sale of 5 units) $= \dfrac{20}{100} = 0.20$

Probability of N_3 = 0.40 and
Probability of N_4 = 0.30

As these probabilities of states of nature are known, we find Expected Monetary Value (EMV) for each strategy as follows:

Strategies	States				EMV
	N_0 0.1	N_1 0.3	N_2 0.4	N_3 0.2	
S_1	20	20	20	20	20(0.1) + 20(0.2) + 20(0.4) + 20(0.3) = 20
S_2	15	25	25	25	15(0.1) + 25(0.2) + 25(0.4) + 25(0.3) = 24
S_3	10	20	30	30	26 ← Max.
S_4	5	15	25	35	24

Thus, the industry should adopt strategy S_3 (having maximum EMV) and should purchase 6 items per week.

Also, the Expected (monetary) Value with Perfect Information is
$$\text{EVPI} = 20(0.1) + 25(0.2) + 30(0.4) + 35(0.3) = ₹\ 29.5$$

[Hence, the Value of Perfect Information is
$$\text{VPI} = \text{EVPI} - \text{Max. EMV}$$
$$= 29.5 - 26 = 3.5]$$

Problem 11: A farmer wants to decide which of the three crops he should plant. The farmer has categorised the amount of rainfall as high, medium and low. Estimated profit is given below:

Rainfall	Estimated Profit (in ₹)		
	Crop A	Crop B	Crop C
High	8000	3500	5000
Medium	4500	4500	4900
Low	2000	5000	4000

Farmer wishes to plant one crop. Decide the best crop using:
(i) Hurwicz criteria (take degree 0.6).
(ii) Laplace criteria
(iii) Minimax regret criteria **(P.U. MBA - Dec. 10)**

Solution: Rewriting the pay-off table with the actions/strategies (of crop to be planted) as the row-headings and the events/states of nature (of the level of rainfall) as column-headings we have,

Strategies (Crops)	States (Rainfall)			Pay-off = α(max) + (1−α)(min)	Average Payoff
	High	Medium	Low		
A	8000	4500	2000	0.5 (8000) + 0.4 (2000) = 5600 ← Max.	$\dfrac{14500}{3}$ = 4833.33 ← Max.
B	3500	4500	5000	0.6 (5000) + 0.4 (3500) = 4400	$\dfrac{13000}{3}$ = 4333.33
C	5000	4900	4000	4600	4633.33

(i) **Hurwicz Criteria:** Finding the Expected Payoff = α (Maximum) + $(1 - \alpha)$ (Minimum) [... where degree of optimism, $\alpha = 0.6$ (given)] we see that, the expected pay-off is maximum (i.e. 5600) in case of crop A. Thus, the best crop is crop A.

(ii) **Laplace Criteria:** Finding the average pay-off for each crop, we see that it is maximum (i.e. 4833.33) for crop A. Hence, the best crop is crop A.

(iii) **Minimax Regret Criteria:** We calculate for all states regret for a strategy = (Max. pay-off for state) – (Pay-off for strategy).

∴ For State - High.

Regret for strategy A = 8000 – 8000 = 0
Regret for strategy B = 8000 – 3500 = 4500
Regret for strategy C = 8000 – 5000 = 3000 etc.

Thus, the Regret Matrix is

	H	M	L	Maximum Regret
A	0	400	3000	3000 ← Min.
B	4500	400	0	4500
C	3000	0	1000	3000 ← Min.

Thus, the minimum among the maximum regrets for all the crops (strategies) is 3000 for crops A and C. Hence, the farmer should plant crops A or C.

[**Note:** The actions which are under the control of the decision maker are the strategies, which are written as row headings of pay-off matrix. Similarly, the events that are outside the scope of decision maker and which are decided by the external factors are the states of nature that are written as column headings of pay-off matrix].

Problem 12: Given the following pay-off matrix use (i) maximax, (ii) maximin and (iii) Hurwicz criteria and find which action to be taken (given: $\alpha = 0.7$).

States of Nature	Actions			
	A_1	A_2	A_3	A_4
S_1	10	5	8	6
S_2	3	9	15	2
S_3	–3	4	6	10

(P.U. MBA - May 13)

Solution: Rewriting the actions (i.e. strategies) as row headings and states of nature as column headings we have

	States			Maximum Profit	Minimum Profit	Expected Profit (Hurwicz = α (max) + (1 – α) (min)
	S_1	S_2	S_3			
A_1	10	3	–3	10	–3	0.7(10) + 0.3(–3) = 6.1
A_2	5	9	4	9	4	0.7(9) + 0.3(4) = 7.5
A_3	8	15	6	15 ← Max.	6 ← Max.	12.3 ← Max.
A_4	6	2	10	10	2	7.6

(i) **Maximax:** The maximum among the maximum profits for all actions (strategies) is 15 for A_3. Hence, use A_3.

(ii) **Maximin:** The maximum among the minimum profits for all action is 6 for A_3. Hence use A_3.

(iii) **Hurwicz:** The maximum of the expected profits (by Hurwicz criteria) is 12.3 for action A_3. Hence use A_3.

Exercise

1. What is decision making? What is the difference between 'decision making under risk' and 'decision making under uncertainty'?
2. Describe the 5 criteria of decision making under uncertainty.
3. Omega manufacturing company Ltd. is proposing to introduce two models of a Radio set X and Y which vary in complexity, but the company has sufficient capacity to manufacture only one model. An analysis of the probable acceptance of the two models has been carried out and the resulting profits (in ₹ Ten thousands) are

Model Acceptance	Probability	Model X	Model Y
Excellent	0.3	120	100
Moderate	0.5	80	70
Poor	0.2	– 30	– 20

(i) Which model should the company introduce?
(ii) How much is the worth to know the model acceptance level before making the decision?

(**Ans.:** Model X, Worth = 7,20,000 – 7,00,000 = 20,000)

4. A trader of boats has estimated the following distribution of demand for a particular kind of a boat

| No. Demanded: | 0 | 1 | 2 | 3 | 4 |
| Probability: | 0.05 | 0.2 | 0.35 | 0.25 | 0.15 |

Each boat costs him ₹ 7,000 and he sells them for ₹ 10,000 each. Boats that are left unsold at the end of the season must be disposed of for ₹ 6,000 each. How many boats should be stocked so as to maximise his expected profit? Also solve the problem by ignoring the given probabilities.

(**Ans.:** 3 boats at Max. EMV = 5,400; Maximin (0); Maximax (4); Laplace (3); Regret (3))

5. The probability distribution of monthly sales of an item is as follows:

   Monthly sales (units): 0   1   2   3   4   5   6
   Probabilities: 0.01 0.06 0.25 0.30 0.22 0.10 0.06

   The cost of carrying inventory (unsold during the month) is ₹ 30 per unit per month and cost of unit shortage is ₹ 70. Determine the optimum stock to minimise the expected cost.

   (**Ans.:** 4 units per month)

6. A businessman has 3 alternative actions, that he can take. Each of these follow 4 possible events. The conditional pay-offs for each action event combination are as under:

Actions	Events			
	A	B	C	D
I	4	0	-5	3
II	-2	6	9	1
III	7	3	2	4

   Find optimal decision under: (i) Maximin Criterion (ii) Regret Criterion (iii) Laplace Criterion.

   (**Ans.:** III, III, III)

7. A film distributor is faced with the problem of selecting one of the two films for distribution. The profit depends upon the market acceptability of the films, which is uncertain. But it has been broadly classified into four categories as - Excellent, Good, Fair and Poor. The profits expected from the release of these films at different levels of market acceptability are as follows:

Market Acceptability	Profit (in ₹ per day)	
	Film A	Film B
Excellent	60,000	78,000
Good	28,000	30,000
Fair	18,000	8,000
Poor	8,000	– 12,000

Using various Criteria, suggest the film to be distributed. Let $\alpha = 0.7$.

(Ans.: Maximin (A), Maximax (B), Hurwicz (B), Laplace (A), Regret (A))

8. Two companies, Hindustan Electro-Carbon Ltd. and Poly Chemicals Ltd., expect to announce plans for next year's operations on the same day. One of the vital issue that the shareholders of each company as well as the general public have an interest in, is the position that each of the companies will take regarding the problem of pollution. If one company, for example declares its intent to take action towards stopping pollution, its public image will be greatly improved. But on the other hand, such action could increase its costs and put it in a bad position with respect to its competitor, if the competitor chooses not to take the same course of action. Each company can take any of the following three actions:

(i) Adoption of a policy towards ending pollution.

(ii) Complete avoidance of the issue or

(iii) Intention to continue as in the past. The pay-offs for the actions are:

Hindustan Electro-Carbon Ltd.	Poly Chemicals Ltd.		
	Action (i)	Action (ii)	Action (iii)
Action (i)	3	– 2	4
Action (ii)	– 1	4	2
Action (iii)	2	2	6

Determine the optimal course of action for Hindustan Electro-Carbon Ltd.

(Ans.: Maximin (iii), Maximax (iii), Laplace (iii), Regret (iii))

9. The conditional pay-offs in crores of rupees for the three models of a car for the various likely sales figures are as follows:

Model	Sales (Units)		
	1 lakh	2 lakh	3 lakh
X	30	10	10
Y	55	20	3
Z	15	35	65

Find strategy using: (i) Maximax (ii) Maximin (iii) Laplace.

(**Ans.:** Z, Z, Z)   (**P.U. MBA - May 11**)

10. Under a sales promotion programme, it is proposed to allow sale of newspapers on the buses during off - peak hours. The vendor can purchase the newspaper at a concessional rate of 75 paise per copy against the selling price of 1 ₹. Unsold copies are, however a dead loss. The vendor has estimated the following probability distribution of the number of copies demanded.

Number of Copies demanded	15	16	17	18	19	20
Probability	0.04	0.19	0.33	0.26	0.11	0.07

How many copies should he order so that his expected profit will be maximum?

(**Ans.:** 17 copies, profit = ₹ 3.98)

11. Write a note on Decision Theory.   (**P.U. MBA - Dec. 05**)

12. Pay-offs of three acts X, Y, Z and the states of Nature of L, M, N are given below:

States of Nature	Acts		
	X	Y	Z
L	– 20	– 50	200
M	200	–100	50
N	400	600	300

The probabilities of the States of Nature are 0.3, 0.4 and 0.3 respectively. Calculate VPI for the above data.   (**P.U. MBA - Dec. 2012**)

(**Ans.:** VPI = 320 – 194 = 126)

13. A newspaper vendor has to decide how many copies of a particular magazine he should buy for the coming month. Each magazine costs him ₹ 5 which he sells for ₹ 10. At the end of the month the unsold magazines are thrown away. The demand distribution of the magazines is as follows:

   No. of copies demanded: 10   11   12
   Probability: 1/3   1/3   1/3

   Construct a pay off table. According to maximin criterion how many copies should be stocked? Which number of copies will maximize the expected pay-off?

   (**Ans.:** maximin = ₹ 50 for '10' copies, expected pay-off = ₹ 51.67 for '11' copies)

14. The Probability distribution of demand for cakes is given below:

No. of Cakes demanded (in arbitrary units)	0	1	2	3	4	5
Probability	0.05	0.10	0.25	0.30	0.20	0.10

    If the cost per cake is ₹ 3 per unit and selling price is ₹ 4 per unit, how many cakes should the baker make to maximise his profit. Assume that if cake is not sold at the end of the day its value is zero.

    (**Ans.:** 2 cakes)

15. In the toy manufacturing company, suppose the product acceptance probability are not known, but the following data is known:

Product	Anticipated 1st year Profit (₹'000)		
	Acceptance		
	Full	Partial	Minimal
Good	8	70	50
Fair	50	45	40
Poor	–25	–10	0

    Determine the optimal decision under each of the following criteria:

    (i) Maximax

    (ii) Maximin

    (iii) Minimax Regret   (**P.U. MBA - Nov 07**)

    (**Ans.:** (i) Good, (ii) Fair, (iii) Fair)

16. Following table gives Profit Matrix for different events and actions. Calculate EVPI.

Events (States of Nature)	Probability	Actions		
		A_1	A_2	A_3
E_1	0.20	40	52	45
E_2	0.35	70	28	40
E_3	0.35	30	70	– 50
E_4	0.10	30	– 50	– 70

(P.U. MBA - May 09)

(**Ans.:** 62.4)

17. Given the following pay-off matrix, prepare a Regret Matrix

States of Nature	Actions				
	A_1	A_2	A_3	A_4	A_5
S_1	5	6	– 2	3	8
S_2	4	2	6	3	5
S_3	– 4	3	2	– 1	7
S_4	10	5	2	3	4

(P.U. MBA - May 12)

(**Ans.:** A_1 : 3, 2, 11, 0; A_2 : 2, 4, 4, 5; A_3 : 10, 0, 5, 8; A_4 : 5, 3, 8, 7; A_5 : 0, 1, 0, 6]

18. Define: (i) Minimax regret criterion (ii) EMV, (iii) EVPI.

(P.U. MBA - Dec. 09)

■■■

Chapter 7...
Game Theory

Contents ...
7.1 Introduction
7.2 Terminology
7.3 Pure Strategy Games
7.4 Mixed Strategy Games
7.5 Principle of Dominance
7.6 Limitations of Game Theory
 Solved Problems
 Exercise

7.1 Introduction

A business firm may come across a situation where there are two (or more) opposing parties with conflicting interests and where, the action of one depends upon the actions of the opponents. These are the competitive situations, e.g. two companies fighting to increase their market shares. The Game Theory helps in determining the best course of action (or strategy) for a firm, in view of the expected counter moves (or strategies) from the competitors.

Thus, **Game Theory** may be defined as *an Operations Research Technique that deals with making decisions when two or more intelligent and rational opponents are involved under conditions of conflict and competition.*

7.2 Terminology

(a) **Player:** Each participant is called a Player.

(b) **Play:** A play occurs when each player selects one of his strategies.

(c) **Strategy:** The strategies are the finite number of possible courses of action, which are available to a player, e.g. in order to increase the market share, a player either reduces his price or will maintain the price.

There are two types of strategies:

(i) **Pure Strategy:** It is a decision of the players (in advance of all the plays) to always select a particular strategy.

(ii) **Mixed Strategy:** It is a decision of the players (in advance of all the plays) to choose more than one strategy with fixed probabilities. It is advantageous because it keeps the opponent guessing.

(d) **Pay-off:** The outcome of playing a game is known as a pay-off. It represents the 'net gain' for the firms for each combination of strategies adopted by them.

E.g. if both firms, say A and B, reduce their prices to increase the market share, it may result in gain of ₹ 'K' for the maximising player A (i.e. loss of ₹ K for the minimising player B). This is the pay-off (+ve for A and – ve for B).

(e) **Pay-off Matrix:** It is a table showing the pay-offs for the different strategies of the game.

e.g.

	Strategies → ↓	**Player B (Minimising)**		
		B_1	B_2	B_3
Player A	A_1	a_{11}	a_{12}	a_{13}
(Maximising)	A_2	a_{21}	a_{22}	a_{23}

where a_{11} is the pay-off corresponding to A using strategy A_1 and B using strategy B_1, and so on.

(f) **Optimum Strategy:** *The strategy which puts the player in the most preferred position, irrespective of the strategy of his competitors,* is called as an optimal strategy.

(g) **Value of the Game:** *It is the expected pay-off of the play when all the players follow their optimal strategies.* The game is called fair if the value of the game is zero and unfair if it is non-zero.

(h) **Types of Games:** A game represents the competitive situation which has more than one player.

(i) When there are two competing players, it is known as a 'Two-Person Game', and if there are more than two (say n) competing players, it is a 'Multiple Person Game or n-Person Game'.

(ii) If the sum of the gains of all the winners is equal to the sum of the losses by all the losers, then it is a 'Zero-Sum game'. Thus, the algebric sum of the gains and losses of all the players is zero. On the other hand, if the sum is not zero (i.e. the sum of all gains is not equal to the sum of all losses) then it is called as a 'Non-zero sum game'.

(iii) Thus, a game with two players, where the gain of one player is the loss to the other is known as a 'Two-Person Zero-sum game (or a rectangular game)'.

A two person - game having two strategies for each player is called a Two-person 2×2 game. Similarly, the game with two strategies for one player and more than 2 (say n) strategies for the other is a 'Two-Person 2 × n game' and so on.

7.3 Pure Strategy Games

In pure strategy games, the players stay with one strategy throughout the game. These are solved as follows:

Step 1: Write down the pay-off matrix with the maximising player's strategies along the rows and the minimising player's strategies along the columns.

Step 2: Write down the minimum element in each row (row minima) on its right. Identify the largest element among these elements and mark it with an arrow. This principle of identifying the maximum element among the row minimas is called as 'Maximin' (maximum of minimums). This indicates a conservative approach for the maximising player.

Step 3: Write down the maximum element in each column at its bottom (column maxima) and mark the smallest element among them with an arrow. This principle of identifying the minimum element among the column maximas is called as 'Minimax' (minimum of maximums). This also indicates a conservative approach for the minimising player.

Step 4: If these two arrowed elements (i.e. maximin and minimax) are same, then the element lying at the intersection of the corresponding row and column is called as a 'Saddle Point'.

Step 5: The strategies corresponding to the saddle point (represented by the corresponding row and column headings) are the optimal strategies for the two players, while the saddle point is the value of the game.

Step 6: If there are more than one saddle points, then there are more than one solution, one for each saddle point.

Step 7: If the arrowed elements (maximin and minimax) are not same, then there is no saddle point and the value of the game lies between these two values. This is a case of mixed strategy games.

Example 1: Let there be two firms: A (with two strategies) and B (with three strategies). Their strategies and corresponding pay-offs are as given below:

$$\text{Firm A} \begin{array}{c} \\ A_1 \\ A_2 \end{array} \begin{bmatrix} \begin{array}{ccc} B_1 & B_2 & B_3 \end{array} \\ \begin{array}{ccc} 2 & 8 & 4 \\ 7 & 10 & 6 \end{array} \end{bmatrix}$$

Firm B

Solution:

(i) In the given table, firm A is a maximising player and firm B is a minimising player

(ii) To find maximin for rows: For row A_1, write down the minimum element (row minima) i.e. 2 on the right hand side. Similarly, for row A_2, the row minima is 6. Now, the maximum among these two row minimas is 6. Hence, mark this maximin element 6 with an arrow.

Note: Firm A is a maximising player and the row elements represent the gains for A on adopting the corresponding strategies. Thus, if A adopts strategy A_1, then it will have a gain of 2 (if B adopts B_1), 8 (if B adopts B_2) or 4 (if B adopts B_3). Thus, the minimum expected gain for A on adopting strategy A_1 is 2, irrespective of the strategy adopted by B. Similarly, minimum expected gain on adopting A_2 is 6. These are the row minimas. Now, A would go for the maximum of the gain figures among these two row minimas i.e. maximin '6'. Hence, he will prefer strategy corresponding to the maximin '6' i.e. pure strategy A_2.

$$A \begin{array}{c} \\ A_1 \\ A_2 \end{array} \begin{array}{ccc} B_1 & B_2 & B_3 \\ \begin{bmatrix} 2 & 8 & 4 \\ 7 & 10 & 6 \end{bmatrix} \end{array} \begin{array}{l} \text{Row minima} \\ 2 \\ 6 \leftarrow \text{maximin} \end{array}$$

Column maxima 7 10 6
                    ↑
               minimax

(iii) To find minimax for Columns: For Column B_1, write down the maximum element i.e. 7 at the bottom. Similarly, the column maximas (10 for B_2) and (6 for B_3) are written for the other columns. The minimum element among these elements is 6. Hence, mark this minimax element 6 with an arrow as shown.

Note: B is a minimising player. Hence, the pay-offs represent the losses for it. The maximum loss on adopting strategy B_1 is 7, irrespective of the strategy adopted by A. Similarly, the maximum loss on adopting strategies B_2 and B_3 are 10 and 6 respectively. These are the column maximas. Now, as B wants to minimise the losses, he would go for the minimum loss figure among these column maximas i.e. minimax, 6. Hence, he will prefer strategy corresponding to the minimax, 6 i.e. pure strategy B_3.

(iv) As the maximin is same as the minimax i.e. 6, hence, the element 6 at the intersection of row A_2 and column B_3 i.e. at cell A_2B_3 is the saddle point.

(v) The strategies represented by the row and the column corresponding to the saddle point are the optimal strategies. Thus, for firm A, strategy A_2 is the optimal strategy and for firm B, strategy B_3 is optimal. It is represented as A (0,1) i.e. probability of A using A_1 is 0 and that of using A_2 is 1 i.e. 100%. Similarly, for B we have B (0, 0, 1). Thus, the optimal strategies are pure or fixed. The optimal value of the game is given by the saddle point i.e. 6. Hence, A will gain maximum 6 units per play and B will lose minimum 6 units per play i.e. B makes payment to A in this game. Also as the value of the game is non-zero, the game is unfair.

Example 2: Solve the following game to determine the optimal strategies for X and Y. Also find the value of the game. The pay-off is for Player X.

$$X \begin{bmatrix} 4 & 4 & -5 & 6 \\ -3 & -4 & -5 & -2 \\ 6 & 7 & -8 & -9 \\ 7 & 9 & -9 & 5 \end{bmatrix}$$

Solution: Write down the row minima and then mark the maximin. Similarly, write down the column maxima and then mark the minimax. This gives:

		Y				
		I	II	III	IV	Row minima
X	I	4	4	−5	6	−5 ← maximin
	II	−3	−4	−5	−2	−5 ← maximin
	III	6	7	−8	−9	−9
	IV	7	9	−9	5	−9
Column maxima		7	9	−5	6	

↑ minimax

Thus, we have maximin = −5 (occuring for two rows) and minimax = −5. As, maximin = minimax, the game has a saddle point, in fact two saddle points at cells (I-III) and (II-III). Thus, it is a pure strategy game and the players will stick to one strategy throughout. However, player X has an alternative strategy resulting in the same value of the game.

Thus, the optimal strategy for player X is I i.e. (1, 0, 0, 0) or II i.e. (0, 1, 0, 0) and the optimal strategy for Y is III i.e. (0, 0, 1, 0). The value of the game in both the cases is equal to the saddle point (−5). Thus, the maximum gain for X is (−5) i.e. it has a loss of 5 per play and the minimum loss for Y is (−5) i.e. it has a gain of 5 per play. Thus, in this game X makes payment to Y.

7.4 Mixed Strategy Games

When, for a given game, we do not get a saddle point (i.e. maximin ≠ minimax), it is a case of mixed strategy game. Here, the players mix the different strategies with certain probabilities or proportions (to be found out) so as to optimise the expected pay-off.

We use the Algebraic Method to find the solution of a 2 × 2 game with mixed strategy (i.e. without saddle point) as follows:

Consider the pay-off matrix

		B	
		$B_1(q)$	$B_2(1-q)$
A	$A_1(p)$	a_{11}	a_{12}
	$A_2(1-p)$	a_{21}	a_{22}

Step 1: Let
$$p = \text{Probability that A uses strategy } A_1$$
$$\therefore 1-p = \text{Probability that A uses strategy } A_2$$
$$q = \text{Probability that B uses strategy } B_1$$
$$\therefore 1-q = \text{Probability that B uses strategy } B_2$$

Step 2: For Player A, p and (1 – p) should be such that he should have same pay-offs, irrespective of B using B_1 or B_2. Thus,

Expected pay-off to A when B uses B_1 = Expected pay-off to A when B uses B_2

i.e. $a_{11}p + a_{21}(1-p) = a_{12}p + a_{22}(1-p)$

$\therefore$ Solving we get, $p = \dfrac{a_{22} - a_{21}}{a_{11} + a_{22} - a_{21} - a_{12}}$

and then we can find (1 – p). Hence, optimal strategy for A is (p, 1 – p).

Similarly, for B we must have

Expected pay-off to B when A uses A_1 = Expected pay-off to B when A uses A_2

i.e. $a_{11}q + a_{12}(1-q) = a_{21}q + a_{22}(1-q)$

$\therefore$ Solving we get, $q = \dfrac{a_{22} - a_{12}}{a_{11} + a_{22} - a_{21} - a_{12}}$

and then we can find (1 – q). Hence, optimal strategy for B is (q, 1 – q).

Step 3: Now, the value of the game (for A) i.e.

v = (Expected pay-off to A when B uses B_1) (Probability that B uses B_1) + (Expected pay-off to A when B uses B_2) (Probability that B uses B_2)

= [a_{11} p + a_{21} (1 – p)] q + [a_{12} p + a_{22} (1 – p)] (1 – q)

Putting values of p and q and solving we get,

$$v = \dfrac{a_{11}a_{22} - a_{21}a_{12}}{a_{11} + a_{22} - a_{21} - a_{12}}$$

The value of the game for B will be (– v).

Note: We can remember the above formulae easily as follows:

Find the denominator by considering the diagonal elements of the pay-off matrix as

$$D = a_{11} + a_{22} - a_{21} - a_{12}$$

Now, probability of using first row A_1, is
$$p = \frac{\text{Second row difference starting with } a_{22}}{D} = \frac{a_{22} - a_{21}}{D}$$

Similarly, probability of using first column B_1, is
$$q = \frac{\text{Second column difference starting with } a_{22}}{D} = \frac{a_{22} - a_{12}}{D}$$

and Value of the game for A is
$$v = \frac{\text{Difference of cross products of diagonal elements}}{D}$$
$$= \frac{a_{11}a_{22} - a_{21}a_{12}}{D}$$

Example 3: Solve the following game:

		Player B	
		B_1	B_2
Player A	A_1	3	5
	A_2	4	1

Solution:
1. Check if there is a saddle point:
   The row minimas are 3 and 1. Hence, maximin is 3.
   The column maximas are 4 and 5. Hence, minimax is 4.
   As, maximin ≠ minimax, hence there is no saddle point and it is a mixed strategy game.

2. Let p = Probability that A uses A_1,
   ∴ 1 − p = Probability of A using A_2
   q = Probability of B using B_1
   ∴ 1 − q = Probability of B using B_2

		Player B	
		B_1 (q)	B_2 (1 − q)
Player A	A_1 (p)	3	5
	A_2 (1 − p)	4	1

3. To find p and q:
   Use the diagonal elements to get
   $D = 3 + 1 - 4 - 5 = -5$
   $$\therefore p = \frac{\text{Second row difference starting with } (a_{22} = 1)}{D}$$
   $$= \frac{1-4}{-5} = \frac{-3}{-5} = \frac{3}{5}$$

   and $$q = \frac{\text{Second column difference starting with } (a_{22} = 1)}{D}$$
   $$= \frac{1-5}{-5} = \frac{-4}{-5} = \frac{4}{5}$$

   $\therefore 1 - p = 1 - \frac{3}{5} = \frac{2}{5}$ and $1 - q = 1 - \frac{4}{5} = \frac{1}{5}$

The maximum gain for A will be given by the value of the game,

$$v = \frac{\text{Difference of cross products of diagonal elements}}{D}$$

$$= \frac{3(1) - 4(5)}{-5} = \frac{-17}{-5} = \frac{17}{5}$$

Hence, the optimal strategy for player A is (p, 1 − p) i.e. $\left(\frac{3}{5}, \frac{2}{5}\right)$ or (0.6, 0.4) or (60%, 40%) and the optimal strategy for player B is (q, 1 − q) i.e. $\left(\frac{4}{5}, \frac{1}{5}\right)$ or (0.8, 0.2) or (80%, 20%).

Thus, A should mix the strategies so as to use the strategy A_1 for $\frac{3}{5}^{th}$ (or 60%) of the times and strategy A_2 for $\frac{2}{5}^{th}$ (or 40%) of the times. This would result in an average gain of maximum $\left(\frac{17}{5}\right)$ units per play to A. Similarly, the mixed strategy of B of using B_1 for $\frac{4}{5}^{th}$ (or 80%) of the times and B_2 for $\frac{1}{5}^{th}$ (or 20%) of the times, would result in the minimum loss of $\left(\frac{17}{5}\right)$ units per play to him. Thus, B will make payment to A in this game.

7.5 Principle of Dominance

The Principle of Dominance states that, if a strategy of a player dominates over another strategy in all conditions (i.e. for all counter strategies by the other player), then the later strategy (being dominated) can be ignored. A strategy dominates over the other strategy, only if, it is preferable over the other, under all conditions.

This principle can be applied to any (m×n) size problem. In case of a pure strategy problem, it directly gives the solution and for a mixed strategy problem, it can help reduce the problem to (2×2) size which can be solved further using the algebric method. [For problems reducing to size (2×n) or (m×2), Graphical method is used while for problems of size (3×3) or more, it can be solved by Linear Programming Technique. [Both these methods are beyond the scope of this book].

Thus, to solve a given (m×n) problem we proceed as follows:

Step 1: Check if there is a saddle point. If a saddle point is there, the optimal solution is directly obtained.

Step 2: If the problem does not have a saddle point, then reduce it to (2 × 2) size by using the following rules of dominance:
(i) If all the elements in a row (say i^{th} row) are **less than or equal to (≤)** the corresponding elements of **any other row** (say j^{th} row), then neglect the ith row.

(ii) If all the elements in a column (say r^{th} column) are **greater than or equal to** ($\geq$) the corresponding elements of **any other column** (say s^{th} column), then neglect the rth column.

(iii) A pure strategy may be dominated if it is inferior to the combination of two other strategies in a certain fixed proportion (k : 1− k).

Step 3: On getting the reduced pay-off matrix of size (2×2) (after using the above rules successively), we solve it further using the Algebric Method to get the optimal solution.

Example 4: Solve the following game

$$A \begin{array}{c} \\ A_1 \\ A_2 \\ A_3 \end{array} \begin{array}{c} B \\ \begin{array}{ccc} B_1 & B_2 & B_3 \end{array} \\ \begin{bmatrix} 1 & 2 & 7 \\ 6 & 7 & 2 \\ 6 & 6 & 1 \end{bmatrix} \end{array}$$

Solution:

1. Find maximin and minimax as follows:

		B			Row minima	
		B_1	B_2	B_3		
A	A_1	1	2	7	1	
	A_2	6	7	2	2	← Maximin
	A_3	6	6	1	1	
Column maxima		6 ↑ Minimax	7	7		

Since, Maximin ≠ Minimax, hence there is no saddle point.

2. To reduce the pay-off matrix using Principle of Dominance:

(i) We see that all the elements of row A_3 are ≤ the corresponding elements of row A_2. Hence, the gain to the maximising player A for using strategy A_3 is always less than or equal to the gain on using strategy A_2 (irrespective of the strategy used by B). Hence, strategy A_3 is dominated by strategy A_2. Hence, we neglect it to get the reduced pay-off matrix as

$$\begin{array}{c} \\ A_1 \\ A_2 \end{array} \begin{array}{c} \begin{array}{ccc} B_1 & B_2 & B_3 \end{array} \\ \begin{bmatrix} 1 & 2 & 7 \\ 6 & 7 & 2 \end{bmatrix} \end{array}$$

(ii) In this matrix, the elements of column B_2 are greater than corresponding elements of column B_1. Thus, for the minimising player B, the loss on adopting strategy B_2 is always greater than the loss on adopting strategy B_1 (irrespective of the strategy used by A). Hence, strategy B_2 is dominated by strategy B_1. Hence, we neglect B_2 to get the reduced pay-off matrix as shown.

$$\begin{array}{c} & B_1 \quad B_3 \\ A_1 & \begin{bmatrix} 1 & 7 \\ 6 & 2 \end{bmatrix} \\ A_2 & \end{array}$$

We cannot use here the dominance rule again to reduce it further. This (2×2) matrix, thus, has no saddle point and hence, we use algebric method to solve it as follows:

3. **Algebric Method:**

$$D = 1 + 2 - 6 - 7 = -10$$

$$\therefore p = \frac{2-6}{-10} = \frac{-4}{-10} = \frac{2}{5} \qquad \therefore 1 - p = 1 - \frac{2}{5} = \frac{3}{5}$$

and $\qquad q = \dfrac{2-7}{-10} = \dfrac{-5}{-10} = \dfrac{1}{2} \qquad \therefore 1 - q = 1 - \dfrac{1}{2} = \dfrac{1}{2}$

Also, value of the game, $\quad v = \dfrac{1(2) - 6(7)}{-10} = \dfrac{-40}{-10} = 4$

Thus, the optimal strategy for A is $\left(\dfrac{2}{5}, \dfrac{3}{5}, 0\right)$ (i.e. he should use A_1 - 40% of times, A_2 - 60% of times and should not use A_3) and for B it is $\left(\dfrac{1}{2}, 0, \dfrac{1}{2}\right)$ (i.e. he should use B_1 - 50% of times, B_2 - should not be used and B_3 - 50% of times). The value of the game is 4 for A. Thus, A cannot get more than ₹ 4 and B cannot reduce his loss below ₹ 4, in this game.

7.6 Limitations of Game Theory

(i) The assumption of Game Theory that the players have the knowledge about their own and other's pay-offs is unrealistic and only guess is possible here.
(ii) As the number of players increase, the analysis of gaming strategies becomes complex and difficult and in practice there are many firms in an oligopoly situation. Hence, the theory is not very useful.
(iii) The assumptions of maximin and minimax imply that the players are conservative or risk-averse and have complete knowledge of the strategies. This is not possible practically.
(iv) In oligopoly situations, the players will allow each other to share the secrets of business in order to work in collusion instead of working under uncertainty. Thus, the mixed strategies are also not very useful.

Solved Problems

Problem 1: Solve the following game: (a) Directly, (b) By using Dominance Rule:

$$\text{Player X} \begin{array}{c} \\ \text{I} \\ \text{II} \\ \text{III} \\ \text{IV} \end{array} \begin{array}{c} \text{Player Y} \\ \begin{array}{ccccc} 1 & 2 & 3 & 4 & 5 \end{array} \\ \begin{bmatrix} 1 & 3 & 2 & 7 & 4 \\ 3 & 4 & 1 & 5 & 6 \\ 6 & 5 & 7 & 6 & 5 \\ 2 & 0 & 6 & 3 & 1 \end{bmatrix} \end{array}$$

Solution:

(a) Let us find the row minimas and hence maximin and column maximas and hence minimax as follows:

		Y					Row Minima	
		1	2	3	4	5		
	I	1	3	2	7	4	1	
X	II	3	4	1	5	6	1	
	III	6	5	7	6	5	5	← Maximin
	IV	2	0	6	3	1	0	
Column Maxima		6	5	7	7	6		
			↑				Saddle Point = 5	
			Minimax					

Thus, as maximin = minimax, a saddle point exists. Hence, it is a pure strategy game and the optimal strategy for X is III i.e. (0, 0, 1, 0) and optimal strategy for Y is 2 i.e. (0, 1, 0, 0, 0). The value of the game = saddle point = 5

(b) We can solve the problem alternately by using the dominance rule as follows:

(i) As (all elements in row IV) are < (corresponding elements in row III), hence neglect row IV to get reduced pay-off matrix as

			Y			
		1	2	3	4	5
	I	1	3	2	7	4
X	II	3	4	1	5	6
	III	6	5	7	6	5

(ii) In the reduced matrix,
(all elements in column 4) ≥ (corresponding elements in column 1) and
(all elements in column 5) ≥ (corresponding elements in column 2)

Hence, neglect columns 4 and 5 to get the reduced matrix as

	1	2	3
I	1	3	2
II	3	4	1
III	6	5	7

(iii) Repeating the procedure we see that
(all elements in row I as well as II) < (corresponding elements in row III).
Hence, neglect rows I and II to get

	1	2	3
III	6	5	7

(iv) Here, (elements in columns 1 and 3) > (corresponding element in column 2)
Hence, neglect columns 1 and 3. Thus, we have

	2
III	5

(v) Hence, the optimal strategy for X is III and for Y it is 2, with the value of the game = 5

Note: If not specified exclusively, it is advisable to solve pure strategy problem by direct method (by finding out the saddle point directly). If there is no saddle point, then we reduce the problem using dominance rule.

Problem 2: Solve the following (2×2) game

$$\begin{bmatrix} 6 & -3 \\ -3 & 0 \end{bmatrix}$$

Solution: We have (P.U. MBA - May 12, May 13)

	B_1	B_2	Row Minima
A_1	6	-3	-3 ← Maximin
A_2	-3	0	-3 ← Maximin
Column Maxima	6	0 ↑ Minimax	

As, maximin ≠ minimax, the problem has no saddle point and hence, it is a mixed strategy game.

Now, we use algebric method to solve it further as follows:
We have,

$$D = 6 + 0 - (-3) - (-3) = 6 + 3 + 3 = 12$$

Probability of using row A_1 is, $p = \dfrac{\text{Second row difference starting with } (a_{22}=0)}{D}$

$= \dfrac{0-(-3)}{12} = \dfrac{3}{12} = \dfrac{1}{4}$ or 25%

$\therefore 1-p = 1-\dfrac{1}{4} = \dfrac{3}{4}$ or 75%

Probability of using column B_1 is

$q = \dfrac{\text{Second column difference starting with } (a_{22}=0)}{D}$

$= \dfrac{0-(-3)}{12} = \dfrac{3}{12} = \dfrac{1}{4}$ or 25%

and $\therefore 1-q = 1-\dfrac{1}{4} = \dfrac{3}{4}$ i.e. 75%

The value of the game for A is

$v = \dfrac{\text{Difference of cross products of diagonal elements}}{D}$

$= \dfrac{6(0)-(-3)(-3)}{12} = \dfrac{0-9}{12} = \dfrac{-3}{4}$

Thus, optimal strategy for A is $(p, 1-p)$ i.e. $\left(\dfrac{1}{4}, \dfrac{3}{4}\right)$ i.e. to use A_1 for 25% of times and A_2 for 75% of times. Similarly, the optimal strategy for B is $\left(\dfrac{1}{4}, \dfrac{3}{4}\right)$ i.e. to use B_1 for 25% of times and B_2 for 75% of times. The maximum gain for A is $\left(\dfrac{-3}{4}\right)$ i.e. he will lose at least $\dfrac{3}{4}$ units per play to B.

Problem 3: Solve the following game by using the principle of dominance

		Player B					
		I	II	III	IV	V	VI
	1	4	2	0	2	1	1
Player A	2	4	3	1	3	2	2
	3	4	3	7	−5	1	2
	4	4	3	4	−1	2	2
	5	4	3	3	−2	2	2

(P.U. MBA - Dec. 13)

Solution: The pay off matrix has no saddle point. Hence, its a mixed strategy game and we reduce the matrix using dominance rule as follows:

(i) Row 1 is dominated by Row 2 as (all elements in row 1) ≤ (corresponding elements in row 2)

Also, row 5 is dominated by row 4. Hence, neglect rows 1 and 5 to get the reduced matrix

	I	II	III	IV	V	VI
2	4	3	1	3	2	2
3	4	3	7	−5	1	2
4	4	3	4	−1	2	2

(ii) Here:

(all elements in column I and II) ≥ (corresponding elements in column IV).

Hence, columns I and II are dominated by column IV.

∴ Neglect them.

Also, column VI is dominated by column V

∴ Neglect it also to get the reduced matrix as shown.

	III	IV	V
2	1	3	2
3	7	−5	1
4	4	−1	2

(iii) Now, no single row or column dominates another row or column i.e. no pure strategy of A or B is inferior to any other pure strategy. However, by inspection (decided by trial and error) we see that on combining columns III and IV in the proportion $\left(\frac{1}{2} : 1 - \frac{1}{2}\right)$ (i.e. $k : 1 - k$ for $k = \frac{1}{2}$) or $\frac{1}{2} : \frac{1}{2}$, we get $\frac{1}{2}(1) + \frac{1}{2}(3) = 2$, $\frac{1}{2}(7) + \frac{1}{2}(-5) = 1$, $\frac{1}{2}(4) + \frac{1}{2}(-1) = \frac{3}{2}$ i.e. $\left(2, 1, \frac{3}{2}\right)$

Now, since all the elements in column V i.e. (2, 1, 2) are ≥ these corresponding elements, hence, pure strategy V is dominated by the above combination of strategies III and IV. Hence, neglect V to get

	III	IV
2	1	3
3	7	−5
4	4	−1

(iv) Here also we see that on combining rows 2 and 3 in $\left(\frac{1}{2} : \frac{1}{2}\right)$ we get (4, −1) which is same as elements of row 4. Hence, neglect row 4 to get a reduced (2 × 2) matrix.

	III	IV
2	1	3
3	7	−5

which has no saddle point. Hence, we use Algebraic method further to solve this mixed strategy game as follows:

$$D = 1 + (-5) - 7 - 3 = -14$$

∴ Probability of using '2' is, $p = \dfrac{-5-7}{-14} = \dfrac{12}{14} = \dfrac{6}{7}$ ∴ $1 - p = 1 - \dfrac{6}{7} = \dfrac{1}{7}$

and Probability of using 'III' is, $q = \dfrac{-5-3}{-14} = \dfrac{8}{14} = \dfrac{4}{7}$ ∴ $1 - q = 1 - \dfrac{4}{7} = \dfrac{3}{7}$

∴ Optimal strategy for A is $\left(0, \dfrac{6}{7}, \dfrac{1}{7}, 0, 0\right)$ and for B it is $\left(0, 0, \dfrac{4}{7}, \dfrac{3}{7}, 0, 0\right)$ and value of the game to player A is

$$v = \dfrac{1(-5) - (7)(3)}{-14} = \dfrac{-26}{-14} = \dfrac{13}{7}$$

Problem 4: Two competing firms want to open their new branch at one of the three cities A, B and C, whose distance profile is given. If both the companies open their branches in the same city, they will split the business evenly. However, if they open the branches in different cities, the Company that is closer to a given city will get all that city's business. If all the three cities have the same amount of business, where should the firms open their branches? Will it be a fair game?

Distance Profile
From A to B 35 km
From A to C 24 km
From B to C 28 km

Solution: Let us construct the pay-off matrix with Company 1 as a maximising firm and Company 2 as a minimising firm. Their strategies could be to open the branch at A, B or C. If they open branch in the same city, the business is split equally hence, there is no gain for them over the other. Hence, the diagonal elements are zero.

		Firm 2		
		A	B	C
	A	0	1	−1
Firm 1	B	−1	0	−1
	C	1	1	0

If Firm 1 opens a branch in A and Firm 2 opens it in B, they will get the same business from these cities. However, city C being closer to A, its business will go to Firm 1. As the businesses of all the cities are equal, hence it will imply a gain to Firm 1 of 1 city's business. Now, if Firm opens 2 a branch in C it will gain the business of city B as it is closer to city B as compared to Firm 1 with its Branch in A. Hence, this will amount to a loss of 1 city's business to Firm 1. Thus, proceeding similarly, we get the pay-off matrix as shown above.

Let us check it for a saddle point. As, maximin = minimax, hence there exists a saddle point and thus its a pure strategy game. The saddle point occurs at cell C-C. Hence, optimal strategy for both the firms is to open branches in city C. And as the value of the game = saddle point = 0, hence, its a fair game.

		Firm 2			
		A	B	C	Row minima
	A	0	1	−1	−1
Firm 1	B	−1	0	−1	−1
	C	1	1	0	0 ← maximin
	Column maxima	1	1	0	Saddle point = 0
			Minimax ↑		

Problem 5: Two companies X and Y, competing for the same product are sharing a market. Each of them attempts to raise its market share. An advertising campaign by X can increase its market share by six percent provided that Y does nothing. Company Y contemplates invoking a price cut if it is worthwhile. The price cut shall cause a five percent gain to the company Y only if X takes no action. If X goes for advertising campaign here, the gain to Y will be just two percent. No action on the part of both the companies shall leave the market share of them undisturbed at 40 : 60. Construct a pay-off matrix and suggest the best strategy for each of the companies.

Solution: Considering X as a maximising player and Y as a minimising player, we can use the given information to construct the pay-off matrix as follows:

		Y		
		No Action	Price Cut	Row Minima
X	Advertise	6	−2	−2 ← Maximin
	No Action	0	−5	−5
	Column Maxima	6	−2	Saddle Point
			↑	= −2
			Minimax	

As maximin = minimax, a saddle point exists. Hence, the best strategy for X is to Advertise and for Y the best strategy is to Cut the price. This would result in a loss of 2% market share for X and a gain of 2% for Y, which is the optimum outcome for both.

Problem 6: A Company Management and the Labour Union are negotiating a new 3 year settlement. Each player has 4 strategies; they are:
I. Hard and aggressive bargaining
II. Reasoning and logical approach
III. Legalistic strategy
IV. Conciliatory approach

The costs to the Company (in the form of average wage rise in ₹) are given for every pair of strategy choices.

		Union Strategies			
		I	II	III	IV
Company Strategies	I	20	25	40	−5
	II	15	14	2	4
	III	12	8	10	11
	IV	35	10	5	0

Which strategy will the two sides adopt? Also determine the value of the game.

Solution: Given figures indicate the costs to the Company. Hence, the Company is a minimising player while the Union is a maximising player. Hence, we rewrite the table to represent the Union Strategies along the rows and the Company Strategies along the column as shown. **(Note this step)**

		Company			
		I	II	III	IV
Union	I	20	15	12	35
	II	25	14	8	10
	III	40	2	10	5
	IV	−5	4	11	0

Let us check the matrix for a saddle point:

		Company				Row Minima
		I	II	III	IV	
Union	I	20	15	12	35	12 ← Maximin
	II	25	14	8	10	8
	III	40	2	10	5	2
	IV	−5	4	11	0	−5
Column Maxima		40	15 Minimax ↑	12	35	Saddle Point=12

DECISION SCIENCES   GAME THEORY

Since, Maximin = Minimax, the saddle point exists and hence it is a pure strategy game. Thus, the optimal strategy for Union is (1,0,0,0) i.e. the strategy of Hard and aggressive bargaining. The optimal strategy for the Company is (0,0,1,0) i.e. the Legalistic strategy. The value of the game is given by the saddle point as 12. Hence, the optimal strategies will result in a maximum gain of ₹ 12 as wage rise to the Union. Similarly, the minimum loss to the Company will be of ₹ 12. Hence, the Company will pay ₹ 12 as an average rise in wages to the Union in this game.

Problem 7: In a small town, there are only two stores that handle sundry goods - Kohinoor and Akash. The total number of customers are equally divided between the two, because the price and quality are equal. Both the stores have a reputation in the community for the equally good services they render. Assume that a gain of customer by Kohinoor is a loss to Akash and vice-versa. Both stores plan to run a pre-Diwali Sale during the first week of October. Sales are advertised through local press, radio and cable TV with the aid of an advertising firm. Kohinoor has estimated its percentage market share gain as a pay-off matrix given below:

Determine Optimum Strategies and the worth of them for both Kohinoor and Akash.

		Akash		
		Local press	Radio	Cable TV
	Local Press	30	40	– 80
Kohinoor	Radio	0	15	– 20
	Cable TV	90	20	50

Solution:
1. Let us check the matrix for a saddle point first:

		Akash			Row Minima
		LP	RD	CT	
	LP	30	40	– 80	– 80
Kohinoor	RD	0	15	– 20	– 20
	CT	90	20	50	20 ← Maximin
Column Maxima		90	40 ↑ Minimax	50	

As, Maximin ≠ Minimax, the game has no saddle point and hence, it is a mixed, strategy game.

2. As it is a (3×3) game we use the Principle of Dominance to reduce it as follows:
   (i) As (all elements in row 2 i.e. RD) < (corresponding elements in row 3 i.e. CT), hence neglect row 2 to get a reduced matrix as shown.

	LP	RD	CT
LP	30	40	-80
CT	90	20	50

   (ii) Here, (all elements in column 1 i.e. LP) > (corresponding elements in column 3 i.e. CT),
   ∴ Neglect column 1 to get the reduced (2×2) pay off matrix as shown.

		Akash	
		RD	CT
Kohinoor	LP	40	-80
	CT	20	50

3. This clearly, has no saddle point and we use algebraic method to solve this (2×2) pay-off matrix for mixed strategy as follows:

   We have, $D = 40 + 50 - (20) - (-80) = 150$

   ∴ Probability of Kohinoor using strategy 1 i.e. LP is

   $$p = \frac{50-20}{150} = \frac{30}{150} = \frac{1}{5} \quad \text{i.e.} \quad \frac{1}{5} \times 100 = 20\%$$

   ∴ Probability of Kohinoor using strategy 2 i.e. CT is

   $$1 - p = 1 - \frac{1}{5} = \frac{4}{5} \quad \text{i.e. 80\%}$$

   Similarly, probability of Akash using strategy 1 i.e. RD is

   $$q = \frac{50-(-80)}{150} = \frac{130}{150} = \frac{13}{15} \quad \text{i.e.} \quad \frac{13}{15} \times 100 = 86.67\%$$

   and probability of Akash using strategy 2 i.e. CT is

   $$1 - q = 1 - \frac{13}{15} = \frac{2}{15} \quad \text{i.e. 13.33\%}$$

   Also, value of the game for Kohinoor is

   $$v = \frac{40(50)-(20)(-80)}{150} = \frac{2000+1600}{150} = \frac{3600}{150} = \frac{72}{3} = 24$$

   Hence, optimal strategy for Kohinoor is (20%, 0, 80%) and the optimal strategy for Akash is (0%, 86.67%, 13.33%). This would result in a maximum gain of 24% market share to Kohinoor and a minimum loss of 24% market share for Akash. Thus, Akash will lose 24% market share to Kohinoor.

Problem 8: Shruti Ltd. and Purnima Ltd. are two competitors in the market. Shruti has devised 4 strategies S_1, S_2, S_3 and S_4 and Purnima 3 strategies P_1, P_2, P_3. The pay-offs corresponding to all 12 combinations of strategies are given below. Considering the information stated which strategy is better for Shruti? Which is better for Purnima? What is the value of the game? Is the game fair?

Pay-offs

Shruti's Strategies	Purnima's Strategies		
	P_1	P_2	P_3
S_1	30000	– 21000	1000
S_2	18000	14000	12000
S_3	– 6000	28000	4000
S_4	18000	6000	2000

(P.U. MBA – Dec 06)

Solution: Let us check the given matrix for a saddle point:

Shruti	Purnima			Row Minima
	P_1	P_2	P_3	
S_1	30000	–21000	1000	–21000
S_2	18000	14000	12000	12000 ← maximin
S_3	– 6000	28000	4000	– 6000
S_4	18000	6000	2000	2000
Column Maxima	30000	28000	12000 ↑minimax	

Since maximin = 12000 = minimax, the saddle point exists and hence it is a pure strategy game. The optimal strategy for Shruti is (0, 1, 0, 0) i.e. the strategy S_2. The optimal strategy for Purnima is (0, 0, 1) i.e. the strategy P_3.

The value of the game is given by the saddle point i.e. 12000. Thus, the optimal strategies will result in a maximum gain of 12000 for Shruti and the minimum loss for Purnima will also be 12000. Thus, Purnima will pay 12000 to Shruti. Since, the value of the game i.e. 12000 ≠ 0, hence, it is not a fair game.

Problem 9: Solve the following game

Pay-offs

		Player B			
		B_1	B_2	B_3	B_4
Player A	A_1	3	2	4	0
	A_2	3	4	2	4
	A_3	4	2	4	0
	A_4	0	4	0	8

(P.U. MBA - Dec. 05, Dec. 11)

Solution: We have

		B				Row Minima
		B_1	B_2	B_3	B_4	
	A_1	3	2	4	0	0
A	A_2	3	4	2	4	2 ← Maximin
	A_3	4	2	4	0	0
	A_4	0	4	0	8	0
Column Maxima		4 ↑	4 ↑	4 ↑	8	
			Minimax			

1. As maximin ≠ minimax, the problem has no saddle point and hence it is a mixed strategy game.
2. As it is a (4 × 4) game, we use the principle of dominance to reduce it as follows:
   (i) As (all elements in row A_1) ≤ (Corresponding elements in row A_3), hence neglect row A_1 so as to get the reduced matrix as

			B		
		B_1	B_2	B_3	B_4
	A_2	3	4	2	4
A	A_3	4	2	4	0
	A_4	0	4	0	8

   (ii) Here (all elements of column B_1) ≥ (Corresponding elements of column B_3)
   ∴ Neglect Column B_1 to get reduced matrix

			B	
		B_2	B_3	B_4
	A_2	4	2	4
A	A_3	2	4	0
	A_4	4	0	8

   (iii) Now no single row or column dominates another row or column i.e. no pure strategy of A of B is inferior to any other pure strategy. However, by inspection (trial and error) we see that on combining columns B_3 and B_4 in the proportion $(\frac{1}{2} : 1 - \frac{1}{2})$ (i.e. k : 1 − k for k = $\frac{1}{2}$) i.e. $\frac{1}{2} : \frac{1}{2}$,
   We get $\frac{1}{2}(2) + \frac{1}{2}(4) = 3$, $\frac{1}{2}(4) + \frac{1}{2}(0) = 2$, $\frac{1}{2}(0) + \frac{1}{2}(8) = 4$ i.e. (3, 2, 4.)

Now, since all elements of column B_2 viz. (4, 2, 4) are ≥ these corresponding elements (3, 2, 4) hence, pure strategy B_2 is dominated by the above mentioned combination ($\frac{1}{2}:\frac{1}{2}$) of strategies B_3 and B_4. Hence neglect B_2 to get

		B	
		B_3	B_4
	A_2	2	4
A	A_3	4	0
	A_4	0	8

(iv) Here we see that on combining rows A_3 and A_4 in ratio ($\frac{1}{2}:\frac{1}{2}$) we get (2, 4) which is same as the elements of row A_2. Hence, neglect row A_2 to get the reduced (2 × 2) matrix.

		B	
		B_3	B_4
A	A_3	4	0
	A_4	0	8

which has no saddle point.

3. We use further the Algebraic method to solve this mixed strategy game as follows:

$D = 4 + 8 - 0 - 0 = 12$

∴ Probability of using A_3 is $p = \frac{8-0}{12} = \frac{2}{3}$

∴ Probability of using A_4 is $1 - p = 1 - \frac{2}{3} = \frac{1}{3}$

Also, Probability of using B_3 is $q = \frac{8-0}{12} = \frac{2}{3}$

∴ Probability of using B_4 is $1 - q = 1 - \frac{2}{3} = \frac{1}{3}$

∴ Optimal strategy for A is (0, 0, $\frac{2}{3}$, $\frac{1}{3}$) and for B it is (0, 0, $\frac{2}{3}$, $\frac{1}{3}$) and the value of the game to player A is $v = \frac{(4)(8) - (0)(0)}{12} = \frac{32}{12} = \frac{8}{3}$

Problem 10: Find the value of the game and the optimal actions for the players

Player A	Player B	
	B_1	B_2
A_1	11	7
A_2	9	10

(P.U. MBA - May 09, May 11)

Solution: We have,

	B_1	B_2	Row Minimia
A_1	11	7	7
A_2	9	10	9 ← Maximin
Column maxima	11	10 ↑ Minimax	

As, maximin ≠ minimax, the problem has no saddle point and it is a mixed strategy game.

∴ Use algebraic method:

$$D = 11 + 10 - 9 - 7 = 5$$

∴ Probability of player A using action A_1 is

$$p = \frac{10-9}{5} = \frac{1}{5} \quad \text{i.e. 20\%}$$

∴ Probability of using action A_2 is

$$1 - p = 1 - \frac{1}{5} = \frac{4}{5} \quad \text{i.e. 80\%}$$

Also, probability of player B using action B_1 is

$$q = \frac{10-7}{5} = \frac{3}{5} \quad \text{i.e. 60\%}$$

∴ Probability of using action B_2 is

$$1 - q = 1 - \frac{3}{5} = \frac{2}{5} \quad \text{i.e. 40\%}$$

Also, value of the game for A is

$$v = \frac{11(10) - 9(7)}{5} = \frac{47}{5} = 9.4$$

Thus, optimal actions of A is $\left(\frac{1}{5}, \frac{4}{5}\right)$ and for B is $\left(\frac{3}{5}, \frac{2}{5}\right)$ and the maximum gain for A is 9.4.

Problem 11: Solve the game

$$\begin{array}{c} & \begin{array}{cc} B_1 & B_2 \end{array} \\ \begin{array}{c} A_1 \\ A_2 \\ A_3 \end{array} & \left[\begin{array}{cc} 28 & 0 \\ 2 & 12 \\ 4 & 7 \end{array}\right] \end{array}$$

(P.U. MBA - Dec. 12)

Solution: We have

	B₁	B₂	Row Minimia
A₁	28	0	0
A₂	2	12	2
A₃	4	7	4 ← Maximin
Column maxima	28	12 ↑ Minimax	

As, maximin ≠ minimax, the problem has no saddle point and hence it is a mixed strategy game. Also, as it is a (3 × 2) game we use principle of dominance.

We observe here that (by trial and error) on combining rows A_1 and A_2 in the proportion $\left(k : 1-k \text{ for } k = \frac{1}{4}\right)$ i.e. $\left(\frac{1}{4} : 1 - \frac{1}{4}\right)$ i.e. $\left(\frac{1}{4} : \frac{3}{4}\right)$ we get $\frac{1}{4}(28) + \frac{3}{4}(2) = 8.5, \frac{1}{4}(0) + \frac{3}{4}(12) = 9$.
Now, as all elements of A_3 i.e. (4 and 7) ≤ these corresponding elements (i.e. 8.5 and 9), A_3 is dominated by the combination of A_1 and A_3. Thus neglecting A_3 we get the reduced matrix

	B₁	B₂
A₁	28	0
A₂	2	12

which has no saddle point.
∴ Using algebraic method:
$$D = 28 + 12 - 2 - 0 = 38$$
∴ Probability of using A_1 is $p = \frac{12-2}{38} = \frac{10}{38} = \frac{5}{19}$

∴ Probability of using A_2 is $1 - p = 1 - \frac{5}{9} = \frac{14}{19}$

Also, probability of using B_1 is $q = \frac{12-0}{38} = \frac{6}{19}$

and probability of using B_2 is $1 - q = 1 - \frac{6}{19} = \frac{13}{19}$

Also value of game for A is
$$v = \frac{28(12) - 2(0)}{38} = \frac{168}{19}$$

Thus, optimal strategy for A is $\left(\frac{5}{19}, \frac{14}{19}, 0\right)$ and for B is $\left(\frac{6}{19}, \frac{13}{19}\right)$ and the value of the game for A is $\frac{168}{19}$.

Exercise

1. What is game theory? Discuss its importance to business decisions.

2. Explain the following:

   (i) Saddle point

   (ii) Pure strategy

   (iii) Mixed strategy

   (iv) Maximin and Minimax principle of game theory

3. Discuss briefly the steps involved in solving a two-person zero-sum game.

4. Find the saddle point and determine the optimal strategies for the games.

   (i) $\begin{bmatrix} 4 & 0 & 2 \\ 6 & -1 & 4 \\ 8 & -5 & -3 \end{bmatrix}$

   (**Ans.:** 0; A_1 and B_2; fair game)

   (ii) $\begin{bmatrix} 9 & 3 & 1 & 8 & 0 \\ 6 & 4 & 4 & 6 & 7 \\ 2 & 4 & 3 & 3 & 8 \\ 3 & 2 & 2 & 5 & 1 \end{bmatrix}$

   (**Ans.:** 4; A_2, B_2 or A_2, B_3)

   (iii) $\begin{bmatrix} -4 & -12 & 10 \\ 0 & -2 & 6 \\ 7 & -3 & 9 \\ 11 & -5 & -4 \end{bmatrix}$

   (**Ans.:** -2; A_2, B_2)

5. Solve the following games for optimal strategy

   (i)
   $$A \begin{array}{c} \\ A_1 \\ A_2 \end{array} \begin{array}{c} B \\ \begin{array}{cc} B_1 & B_2 \end{array} \\ \begin{bmatrix} 8 & -7 \\ -6 & 4 \end{bmatrix} \end{array}$$

   (**Ans.:** Mixed; $A\left(\dfrac{2}{5}, \dfrac{3}{5}\right)$; $B\left(\dfrac{11}{25}, \dfrac{14}{25}\right)$; value $= -\dfrac{2}{5}$)

(ii) $\quad A \begin{array}{c} \\ A_1 \\ A_2 \end{array} \begin{array}{c} B \\ \begin{array}{cc} B_1 & B_2 \end{array} \\ \begin{bmatrix} 3 & -4 \\ -3 & 4 \end{bmatrix} \end{array}$

(**Ans.:** Mixed; $A\left(\dfrac{1}{2}, \dfrac{1}{2}\right)$; $B\left(\dfrac{4}{7}, \dfrac{3}{7}\right)$; value = 0)

6. Reduce by method of dominance and solve:

(i) $\begin{bmatrix} 7 & 6 & 8 & 9 \\ -4 & -3 & 9 & 10 \\ 3 & 0 & 4 & 2 \\ 10 & 5 & -2 & 0 \end{bmatrix}$

(**Ans.:** A_1, B_2; value = 6)

(ii) $\begin{array}{c} A_1 \\ A_2 \\ A_3 \end{array} \begin{array}{c} \begin{array}{cc} B_1 & B_2 \end{array} \\ \begin{bmatrix} 28 & 0 \\ 2 & 12 \\ 4 & 7 \end{bmatrix} \end{array}$

(**Ans.:** $A\left(\dfrac{5}{19}, \dfrac{14}{19}, 0\right)$, $B\left(\dfrac{6}{19}, \dfrac{13}{19}\right)$; value = $\dfrac{168}{19}$

Hint: $k : 1 - k = \dfrac{1}{4} : \dfrac{3}{4}$)

7. Two players A and B, without showing each other, put on a table a coin each, heads or tails up. If the coins show the same side (both heads or both tails) the player A takes both the coins, otherwise B gets them. Compile the pay-off matrix and solve.

(**Ans.:** $\begin{bmatrix} 1 & -1 \\ -1 & 1 \end{bmatrix}$; $A\left(\dfrac{1}{2}, \dfrac{1}{2}\right)$, $B\left(\dfrac{1}{2}, \dfrac{1}{2}\right)$; value = 0)

8. Two leading firms A and B are planning to make fund allocation for advertising their product. The matrix given below shows the percentage of market share of firm A and B for their various advertising strategies.

		Firm B		
		Low	Medium	Heavy
	Low	60	50	40
Firm A	Medium	70	60	50
	Heavy	80	60	75

Find the optimum strategies for the two firms and the corresponding expected outcome.

(**Ans.:** A-Heavy, B-Medium; outcome = 60 for A)

9. The management and the union of a company are discussing the wage agreement. The table gives the pay-offs in the form of rise in the wages for the workers. If both follow a same approach in negotiations, there is no change in the wages. If the union is casual, it will have to lose ₹ 40 if the management is assertive and will lose ₹ 100 if the management is aggressive. If the management is casual, the union will gain ₹ 30 or ₹ 60 on being assertive or aggressive, respectively. Assertive union and aggressive management makes a loss of ₹ 50 while an aggressive approach by the union and an assertive approach by the management can result in wage loss of ₹ 10 only.

   (i) Construct a pay off matrix

   (ii) Suggest optimal strategies for the union and the management and the value of the game

   (**Ans.:** Union $\left(0, \frac{1}{6}, \frac{5}{6}\right)$, mgmt $\left(0, \frac{5}{6}, \frac{1}{6}\right)$; union will lose ₹ 8.33)

10. Two breakfast food manufacturing firms A and B are competing for an increased market share. To improve its market share, both the firms decide to launch the following strategies.

    A_1, B_1 - Give coupons;

    A_2, B_2 - Decrease price,

    A_3, B_3 - Maintain present strategy;

    A_4, B_4 - Increase advertising.

    The pay-off matrix shown in the following table describes the increase in the market share for firm A and decrease in the market share for firm B.

Firm A	Firm B			
	B_1	B_2	B_3	B_4
A_1	35	65	25	5
A_2	30	20	15	0
A_3	40	50	0	10
A_4	55	60	10	15

    Determine the optimal strategies for each firm and the value of the game.

    (P.U. MBA - Dec. 09)

    (**Ans.:** A $\left(\frac{1}{5}, 0, 0, \frac{4}{5}\right)$, B $\left(0, 0, \frac{2}{5}, \frac{3}{5}\right)$ and value = 13 for A)

DECISION SCIENCES   GAME THEORY

11. Solve the following game, given the pay-off matrix as below:

	Player B	
Player A	B_1	B_2
A_1	1	7
A_2	6	2

(**Ans.**: A: $\left(\dfrac{2}{5},\dfrac{3}{5}\right)$, B: $\left(\dfrac{1}{2},\dfrac{1}{2}\right)$, value = 4 for A)

12. Solve the following two person game and find the value of the game.

	Player B	
Player A	B_1	B_2
A_1	−2	−4
A_2	3	5

(**Ans.**: A_2 & B_1, value = 3)

13. The following is the pay-off matrix of a game being played by A and B. Determine the optimal strategies for the players and value of the game.

	Player B		
Player A	B_1	B_2	B_3
A_1	12	−8	−2
A_2	6	7	3
A_3	−10	−6	2

(**Ans.**: A_2, B_3; value = 3)

14. Solve the game with pay-off matrix as below:

	Player B		
Player A	B_1	B_2	B_3
A_1	1	7	2
A_2	6	2	7
A_3	5	1	6

(**P.U. MBA - May 05**)

(**Ans.**: A $\left(\dfrac{2}{5},\dfrac{3}{5},0\right)$, B $\left(\dfrac{1}{2},\dfrac{1}{2},0\right)$, value = 4)

15. Write a note on Game Theory. **(P.U. MBA - May 06)**

16. Determine the optimal strategies of both the players and value of the game.

$$A \begin{array}{c} a \\ b \\ c \\ d \end{array} \begin{pmatrix} \text{I} & \text{II} & \text{III} & \text{IV} \\ 2 & -2 & 4 & 1 \\ 6 & 1 & 12 & 3 \\ -3 & 2 & 0 & 6 \\ 2 & -3 & 7 & 1 \end{pmatrix}$$

(with column labels B: I, II, III, IV)

(P.U. MBA - Nov 07)

(**Ans.:** A: $(0, \frac{1}{2}, \frac{1}{2}, 0)$, B: $(\frac{1}{10}, \frac{9}{10}, 0, 0)$, Value = 1.5 for A)

17. Find the value of the following game. Also determine the optimal strategies of both the players

$$\text{Player A} \begin{array}{c} A_1 \\ A_2 \end{array} \begin{pmatrix} B_1 & B_2 \\ -5 & 2 \\ -7 & -4 \end{pmatrix}$$

(P.U. MBA - May 08)

(**Ans.:** Value = -5, A_1, B_1)

18. Find the optimal strategies for A and B in the following game. Also obtain the value of the game.

$$\text{A's strategy} \begin{array}{c} a_1 \\ a_2 \\ a_3 \end{array} \begin{pmatrix} b_1 & b_2 & b_3 \\ 9 & 8 & -7 \\ 3 & -6 & 4 \\ 6 & 7 & -7 \end{pmatrix}$$

(P.U. MBA - May 07)

(**Ans.:** A(40%, 60%, 0), B(0, 44%, 56%), $-\frac{2}{5}$)

19. Explain the term pure strategy regarding a 2 × 2 game. **(P.U. MBA - May 09)**

20. Solve the following game

$$\begin{array}{c} \\ \text{Player A} \end{array} \begin{array}{c} \\ a_1 \\ a_2 \\ a_3 \\ a_4 \end{array} \begin{bmatrix} b_1 & b_2 & b_3 & b_4 & b_5 \\ 3 & 5 & 4 & 9 & 6 \\ 5 & 6 & 3 & 7 & 8 \\ 8 & 7 & 9 & 8 & 7 \\ 4 & 4 & 8 & 5 & 3 \end{bmatrix}$$

(P.U. MBA - May 10)

(**Ans.:** A(0,0,1,0), B(0,1,0,0,0), Value = Saddle point = 7]

■■■

Chapter 8...
CPM, PERT and Network Calculations

Contents ...
8.1 Introduction
8.2 Steps in PERT/CPM Techniques
8.3 PERT/CPM – Network Construction
8.4 Network Components and Precedence Relationships
8.5 Rules for Network Construction
8.6 Drawing a Network Diagram
8.7 Network Analysis
8.8 Critical Path
8.9 Determination of Slacks/Floats
8.10 Programme Evaluation and Review Technique (PERT)
     Solved Problems
     Exercise

[Note: Readers are advised to go through the concepts of Normal Probability Distribution (Chapter 10) before studying this chapter]

8.1 Introduction

Any commercial project, small or large, consists of a number of interrelated activities which are required to be completed in the given time, should be carried out in the required sequence and should make optimum consumption of the resources such as time, money, material etc. The project could be construction of a mall, erection and commissioning of a power plant, developing a new product, launching of a product in the market, setting up a new office etc. The techniques of PERT and CPM are used for project planning, scheduling and controlling so that the above stated objectives are achieved effectively.

Programme Evaluation and Review Technique (PERT) was developed as a result of US Navy's Polaris Missile Project in 1950's while Critical Path Method (CPM) was developed for planning and construction of chemical plants by DuPont company along with Remington Rand Corporation. Both these techniques though developed independently, had some common features such as: constructing a network diagram involving the various project activities, determining the scheduling of the activities and analysing the network for deciding the critical path for the completion of the project. However there are also some differences such as:

(i) PERT is probabilistic in nature and makes use of three completion time estimates of the activities. CPM on the other hand is deterministic in nature and makes use of a single fixed time estimate for each activity.

(ii) Thus PERT is used for projects involving non-repetitive activities (where time durations are uncertain) such as research and development projects, launching of a product in a new market etc. CPM is used for projects consisting of repetitive activities (where time durations are fairly certain and known) such as construction of a building.

(iii) In PERT, there is more emphasis on the completion of a task or event. It prepares the networks from the events and is thus an event oriented technique. CPM uses the activities to develop the network and is thus an activity oriented technique.

(iv) PERT makes use only of time calculations in the analysis while CPM establishes time-cost trade-offs for a project.

8.2 Steps in PERT/CPM Techniques

Application of PERT/CPM technique for any project involves the following basic steps:

1. **Project Planning:** This involves identification of various activities to be performed, stating their interrelationships, determining the resources required such as time, money etc.

2. **Construction** of Project Network Diagram using standard conventions so as to depict the activities and the events involved in the project.

3. **Network Analysis:** This involves scheduling the activities and deciding the critical path of activities for the project. This also contains identification of the slacks or floats and probability calculations related with project completion etc.

4. **Project Control:** It involves aspects such as resource analysis and allocation and readjustment of the project flow.

8.3 PERT/CPM – Network Construction

Depending upon the nature of the project, it is required to be broken down into its basic well-defined activities. These must be independent in nature and they can be ordered so that they can be performed in a technological sequence. The technological sequence specifies the inter dependence of these activities which is usually stated in the form of precedence relationships which form the basis of the network diagram.

8.4 Network Components and Precedence Relationships

A network is a diagrammatic representation (in the form of arrows and circles) of the activities comprising the project. It consists of the following components:

(a) Events:

The events or nodes in a network diagram represent milestones in a project and they occur at a particular point of time. They only indicate specific accomplishments along the progress of the project and do not consume any resources nor require any time for themselves. Examples of events are 'Fabrication of Subassembly Completed', 'Start of Brochure Printing Work' etc. In a network, the events are represented by circles called as 'nodes' and they are numbered in a sequential order. They signify the beginning and completion of the activities, which are indicated by arrows.

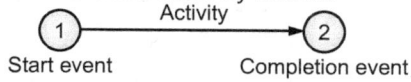

Fig. 8.1

When more than one activity start from an event, it is called a 'burst event' and when more than one activity terminate in an event, it is called a 'merge event'. An event, where more than one activity start as well as terminate, is called a 'merge and burst event'.

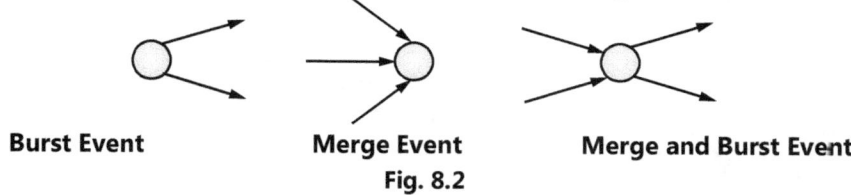

Burst Event **Merge Event** **Merge and Burst Event**

Fig. 8.2

Note that for any event, no activity can start from it unless all the activities terminating into it are completed.

(b) Activities:

These are the basic project operations or tasks to be performed such as 'Fabrication of a Subassembly', 'Printing of Information Brochure' etc. In a network diagram, these are represented by arrows which are also called as arcs. The head of the arrow indicates the direction of the progress of the project. The activities (except the dummy activities) unlike the events, consume time and other resources. They are a recognisable part of the project and represent passage of time. Every activity starts at an event, called tail or initial event (say i) and it ends at an event called head or terminal event (say j) and is represented as activity (i - j). The description of the activity is usually written above arrow and its duration is written below it or next to it in a parenethesis. e.g. The activity (1-2) of printing which takes 4 days is represented as:

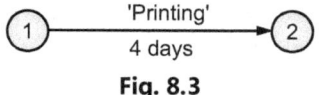

Fig. 8.3

Note that the length of the arrow is just a matter of convenience and it does not signify the time duration of the activity.

The activity which must be completed before an activity under consideration is called a 'Predecessor' activity. The activity which starts immediately after the completion of an activity under consideration is called a 'Successor' activity. The activities which can be carried out concurrently are called 'Concurrent' activities. Sometimes we use 'Dummy activities' in the network diagram, which do not consume any time or other resources and they are represented by broken or dashed arrows.

(c) Relationships:

Graphical Representation	Activity Relationship
Fig. 8.4	Activity A (i.e. 1-2) is a predecessor or preceding activity and B (i.e. 2-3) is a successor or succeeding activity. Activity B can not start until activity A is completed.
Fig. 8.5	A is a preceding activity while B and C are succeeding activities. B and C are also concurrent activities. '2' is a 'burst node'. Activities B and C cannot start until activity A is completed.
Fig. 8.6	A and B are the preceding activities and thus activity C can not start until both A and B are completed. A and B may not finish simultaneously.
Fig. 8.7	Both A and B must be finished before the start of C as well as D. A and B are preceding activities while C and D are succeeding.
Fig. 8.8	A and B must be completed, before C starts. However, only B is required to be completed for D to start. E is a dummy activity. Thus, A and B are preceding activities to C while only B is the preceding activity to D. Alternately, C is the succeeding activity to A and B, while D also is a succeeding activity to B.

(d) Dummy Activities:

A dummy activity is added to the network to clarify the activity pattern as follows:
(i) When two or more activities have a common starting (or tail) event and terminal (or head) events.

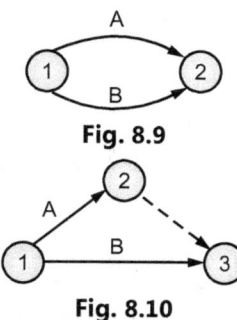

Fig. 8.9

Fig. 8.10

Thus here both activities A and B have the same tail and head events (so that both will be represented as '1-2'). Hence we introduce a dummy activity as shown so that activities A (i.e. '1-2') and B (i.e. '1-3') can have different representation in terms of the event numbers. Note that the dummy activity (called 'identify dummy') does not consume any time and is used to ensure that the concerned activities can be identified by unique end events.

(ii) When two or more activities have some (but not all) of their immediate predecessor activities in common. If an activity C depends on A and B; activity D depends on B. Thus, only B is a common predecessor activity to C and D. Here we use dummy activity (called 'logic dummy') as follows:

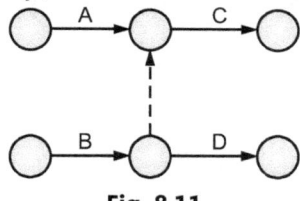

Fig. 8.11

The dummy activities are not usually listed with the real activities and are only shown in the network.

8.5 Rules for Network Construction

1. A network should have only one initial node (event) and only one terminal node (event). All other nodes should be tied to the network on both the sides.
2. Each activity in the network should be represented by one and only one arrow. Each arrow connects the tail node (which indicates the 'activity start' event) to the head node (indicating the 'activity end' event) and its direction gives the general progression in time. No two or more activities can have the same tail and head nodes (If it is so, dummy activities are used to differentiate them).
3. An activity can not start until all its preceding activities are completed. The network should clearly depict the predecessor – successor relationship between the activities and should indicate logical progression of the activities in the forward (i.e. left to right) direction.

4. The arrows should be straight and should not be crossed, unless it is unavoidable.
5. Each event (node) in a network is identified by a unique number. The initial event (node) is numbered '1' and the other events are assigned numbers in their progressive logical order. In general, the head events (say 'j') should always be numbered higher than the tail events (say 'i') i.e. for an activity 'i-j', i<j. This can be ensured by following the Fulkerson's Rule as follows:
    (i) Number the initial node as '1'.
    (ii) Delete the outgoing arrows starting from this numbered node.
    (iii) Number the nodes which now do not have any incoming arrows and number them consecutively as 2, 3...,
    (iv) Repeat the steps (ii and iii) until the terminal node is numbered.

Example 1: Consider the following network diagram having the activities A, B, C ... etc. and the events or nodes a, b, c ,... etc. as shown. Use Fulkerson's Rule to number the events.

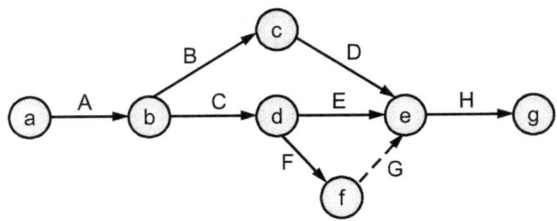

Fig. 8.12

Solution:
(i) The network starts with the node 'a' having no incoming arrows. Thus, it is the initial node. Hence we number it as node '1'.
(ii) Delete the outgoing arrows from this node, which is arrow for activity A.
(iii) This makes the node 'b', without any incoming arrows. Hence, we assign it the next (consecutive) number i.e. '2'.
(iv) Now, we repeat the steps (ii) and (iii) above for this node '2'. Hence delete arrows B and C, which results in making nodes 'c' and 'd' without any incoming arrows. Hence we assign them the next consecutive numbers '3' and '4' respectively (we prefer to assign the numbers in the top-down direction i.e. the node located on upper side is assigned the number first).
(v) Repeat the Procedure: Delete all the outgoing arrows from the nodes c (i.e. 3) and d (i.e. 4). Hence, deleting arrows D, E and F results in the node f without any incoming arrows. (Node e still has one incoming arrow representing dummy activity G). Hence we assign next number i.e. '5' to this node f.

(vi) **Repeat the Procedure:** Delete outgoing arrow G from node f (i.e. 5). Arrows D and E are already deleted in previous step (They are kept deleted for this step also, as their head node 'e' is not yet numbered). Thus, node 'e' now does not have any incoming arrows. Hence, now it is assigned the next number '6'. Proceeding similarly, the terminal node 'g' is assigned the last number '7'.

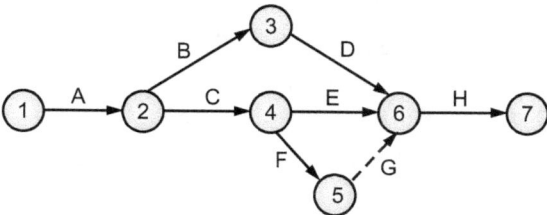

Fig. 8.13

Note:

1. Now, the activities can also be represented as (i, j) or 'i-j'. E.g. A: (1,2) or '1-2'; B: (2,3) or '2-3'; C: (2, 4) or '2-4'. Note that for all activities (i, j) we have, i < j i.e. the head node is numbered higher than the tail node.
2. If the time durations for completion of the activities are known, we write them in a bracket along with the activity name.

Note: The following errors must be avoided while drawing a network:

(a) Looping: Looping as shown in the following diagram represents an error in the logic and hence should not be present in the network diagram. Here, activity E cannot start until D is over, D cannot start until C and F are over, while F can not start until E is over. Thus, activity E can never start as it depends on itself.

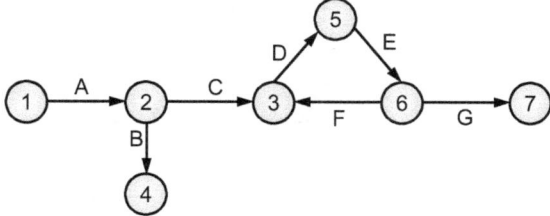

Fig. 8.14

(b) Dangling: Any disconnect of an activity before the completion of all the activities in a network diagram is called Dangling. Here the activity B is not the last activity and hence must be tied to the network. Such error must be avoided.

8.6 Drawing a Network Diagram

Once the activities which comprise the project are defined and their precedence relationships are identified, the project network diagram can be drawn. It is started with the first activity and then the subsequent activities can be drawn step by step, by considering their relationships and by following the network construction rules. However it may need more iterations and can consume more time for a bigger and complex network. This can be minimised by following the steps as shown in the examples below:

Example 2: Draw a network for a project of erecting a storage steel shed for an industrial unit. The activities involved in the project are as follows:

Activity	Description	Immediate Predecessor Activity
A	Erect a site workshop	–
B	Fence the site	–
C	Bend reinforcement (i.e. steel bars for foundation)	A
D	Dig foundation	B
E	Fabricate steel work	A
F	Install concrete making plant	B
G	Place the reinforcement	C, D
H	Concrete the foundation	G, F
I	Paint steel work	E
J	Erect steel structure	H, I
K	Give finishing touch.	J

Solution: Rewrite the precedence relationships by placing the predecessor activities as column 1 and given sequenced activities in sequence in column 2 as follows:

Predecessor Activities	Given Activities
–	A
–	B
A	C
B	D
A	E
B	F
C, D	G
G, F	H
E	I
H, I	J
J	K

We can now consider the precedence relationships using the columns above, one by one, to draw the network directly as follows:

Fig. 8.15	(i) Activities A and B do not have a predecessor. Hence, they start from the initial node.
Fig. 8.16	(ii) Now, we see that A is a preceding activity to C and E (i.e. C and E succeed or follow A). Hence, the head node of arrow A is the tail node of arrows C and E. So we draw them accordingly. Similarly we draw D and F, having B as their predecessor.
Fig. 8.17	(iii) Now C and D precede G. Hence, their head node is the tail node of G. So we draw it accordingly. (The positions of C and E are interchanged here so that the arrows do not intersect further). Also, E precedes I and F precedes H. Hence we also draw H and I accordingly.
Fig. 8.18	(iv) Now, I precedes J; G precedes H and H also precedes J. Hence, we draw them accordingly.

(v) J precedes K. Now, K is not a predecessor to any activity as it does not appear in column 1. Thus, K is the last activity of the network and hence it will terminate in the terminal node of the network. Thus, we draw K accordingly and can draw the networks neatly as:

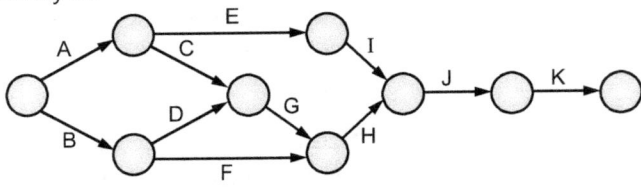

Fig. 8.19

Note:
1. We can use Fulkerson's Rule for the above network diagram to assign numbers to the nodes or events as follows:

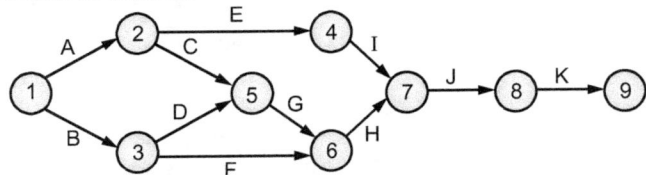

Fig. 8.20

The activities can now be also represented as: A i.e. '1-2', B i.e. '1-3', C i.e. '2-5' etc.

Example 3: A project has fourteen activities A through M. The relationships obtained among these activities are given here: Construct the network and number them.

(i) A is the first operation.
(ii) B and C can be performed in parallel and are immediate successors to A.
(iii) D, E and F follow B.
(iv) G follows E.
(v) H follows D, but it can not start until E is complete.
(vi) I and J succeed G.
(vii) F and J precede K.
(viii) H and I precede L.
(ix) M succeeds L and K.
(x) The last operation N succeeds M and C.

Solution:

Step 1: Considering the given data we can write the precedence relationships column wise. First we write 'Column 2' starting with activity A upto N in regular sequence one by one.

Then considering the given data we write the predecessors for each of these activities to their left in 'Column 1' as follows:

Column 1 (Predecessors)	Column 2 (Activities)
–	A
A	B
A	C
B	D
B	E
B	F
E	G
D, E	H
G	I
G	J
F, J	K
H, I	L
L, K	M
M, C	N

We can now consider the precedence relationships (using the columns above) one by one to draw the network directly as follows:

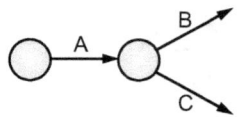

Fig. 8.21

(i) Activity A does not have a predecessor. Hence, it starts from the initial node.

(ii) Now, as A precedes B and C, the head node of A is the tail node of B and C.

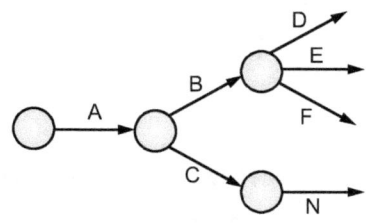

Fig. 8.22

(iii) Further we see that B precedes D, E and F while C precedes N. Hence, we draw them accordingly.

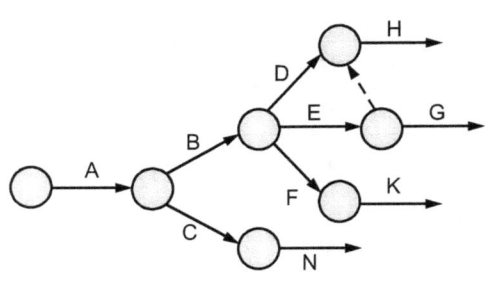

Fig. 8.23

(iv) Now D precedes H and E precedes G and H. Thus, H has two predecessors D and E of which E is common with D. Hence, we have to use a (logic) dummy as shown. Also, as F precedes K, we draw K accordingly. N is not a predecessor. Hence, it will terminate into the terminal node, which we will show in the end.

(v) H precedes L; G precedes I and J; and K precedes M. Hence, we draw them accordingly:

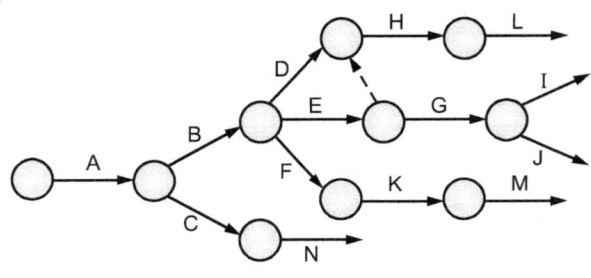

Fig. 8.24

(vi) Now, L precedes M; I precedes L; J precedes K and M precedes N. Hence, we draw the network accordingly as below:

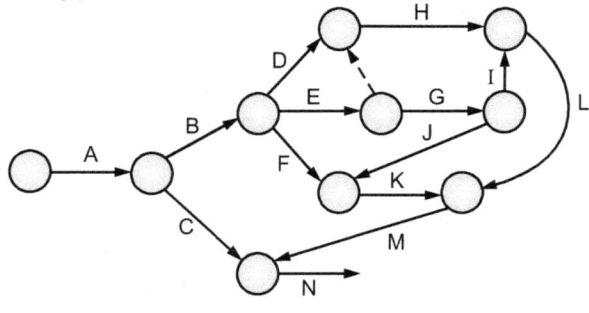

Fig. 8.25

(vii) Now, as N terminates into the terminal node we can neatly re-draw the network as below. Fulkerson's Rule can be further applied to number the nodes as shown.

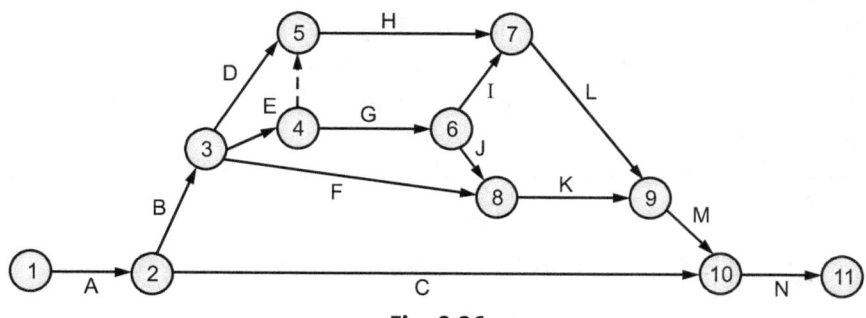

Fig. 8.26

Alternately we can proceed more systematically as follows:

We can use the above relationships (in step 1) to identify the activity chains as follows:

Column 1 (Predecessor)		Column 2 (Activity)
–		A
A^1	$\xrightarrow{1}$	B
A^2	$\xrightarrow{2}$	C
B^1	$\xrightarrow{1}$	D
B^3	$\xrightarrow{3}$	E
B^4	$\xrightarrow{4}$	F
E^3	$\xrightarrow{3}$	G
D^1, E^5	$\xrightarrow{1,5}$	H
G^3	$\xrightarrow{3}$	I
G^6	$\xrightarrow{6}$	J
F^4, J^6	$\xrightarrow{4,6}$	K
H^1, I^3	$\xrightarrow{1,3}$	L
L^1, K^4	$\xrightarrow{1,4}$	M
M^1, C^2	$\xrightarrow{1,2}$	N

1. **Chain 1:** Start with 1st activity in 'column 1' i.e. activity A. Connect it to B against it by arrow. Write '1' as superscript to A and also above the arrow. The arrow is connected to B in column 2. Now look out for first appearance of B in column 1. Connect it to D against it. Write again '1' as superscript to B and also above the arrow. Proceeding similarly we reach to the last activity N. Thus, the first chain is: A B D H L M N.

(The chain activities are given by those with superscript 1 in 'Column 1' viz. A, B, D, H, L, M. (The last activity M is connected to N by arrow. Hence, N is the last activity in the chain. Thus, the chain is : A B D H L M N).

2. **Chain 2:** Start with first non-connected activity (i.e. one without a superscript number) under column 1 i.e. activity A which is against activity C. Join it to C using an arrow. Write 2 as superscript to A and above the arrow. Now locate first non-connected (i.e. without superscript number) activity C under column 1. This already has an arrow against it. Hence, just write '2' as a superscript to C and write '2' also above the arrow. Thus, looking at superscript '2' in column 1 and the last connecting arrow, we get the second chain as: A C N.

3. **Proceeding similarly we get the other chains of activities as:**

    Chain 3: B E G I L; Chain 4: B F K M; Chain 5: E H and Chain 6: G J K.

    We already have, Chain 1: A B D H L M N and Chain 2: A C N.

4. Obviously, only activity A has no preceding activity. Hence it starts from the initial node. Also, Chain 1 is the longest and ends with activity N which is the last given activity. There is no activity that succeeds N. Hence, it is the only activity that terminates into the terminal node. Thus, we can draw the first chain as:

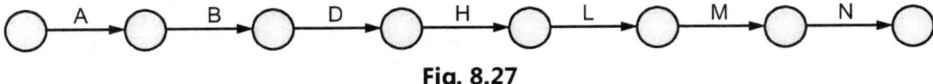

Fig. 8.27

Adding Chains 2, 3, 5 and 6 (by trial and error), we get the network as:

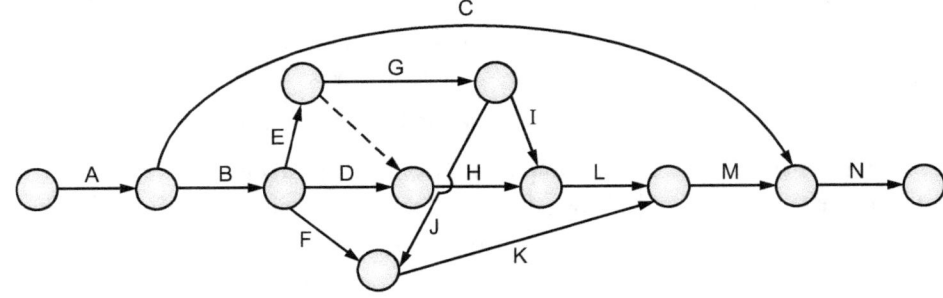

Fig. 8.28

Here we have to use a crossed over arrow J. Again, as the Chain 5 is E H, we use a dummy activity as shown. We can redraw the above network to avoid the crossover of activity J as:

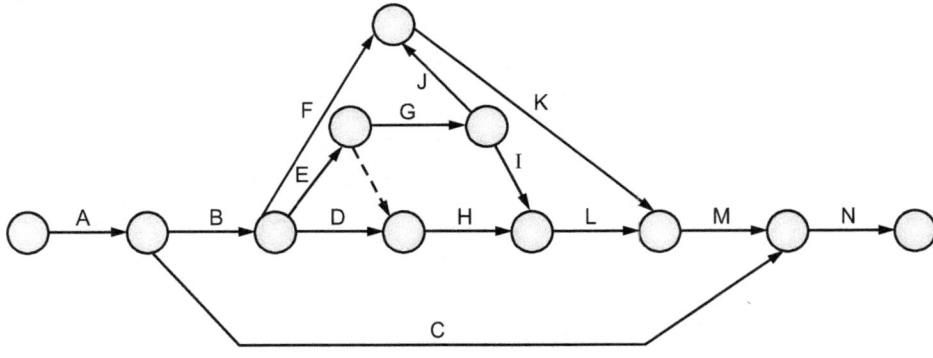

Fig. 8.29

Note:
1. Both the networks (drawn directly or by using activity chains as above) are the same. We can use direct method for networks involving relatively smaller number of activities, while the activity chains method can be used when the network is bigger and has complex relationships.
2. Only immediate predecessor activities should be used while drawing networks. Sometimes predecessors to predecessors are also given. Hence, they become

redundant. E.g. If A, B precede C and A, B, C precede D. Here A, B precede C and as C precedes D, hence A, B automatically precede D. But they are actually immediate predecessors of C and C is immediate predecessor of D. Hence, their precedence relationship with D is redundant. Hence, consider only C as immediate predecessor of D. This reduces number of dummies in the diagram, otherwise the results are the same.

8.7 Network Analysis

After the network diagram is drawn and on getting the estimates of time durations for all the activities, we can analyse the network in order to schedule the performance of the activities; estimate the duration for the completion of the project; identify the critical activities and find out the flexibility in scheduling the activities etc. Here we will consider the analysis in the context of 'time' only, though analysis for other resources like cost is also possible. Note that for the Critical Path Method (CPM) the duration for each activity is uniquely determined while in case of PERT, we use three time estimates to determine the duration (which is described later). Now, consider the following network diagram, along with the time durations of the activities which are written in a bracket next to them.

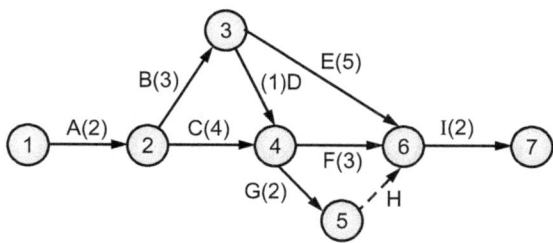

Fig. 8.30

Thus, activity '1-2' i.e. A takes (2) days, '2-3' i.e. B takes (3) days for completion etc.

The time analysis of a network requires the determination of the 'Earliest and Latest times for Starting and Finishing' the activities. For this purpose let us use the following notations:

- **(i, j)** : Activity (i, j) where i is the tail node/event number and j is the head node/event number.
- **E_i** : Earliest occurrence time of event i.
- **L_i** : Latest occurrence time of event i.
- **t_{ij}** : Time duration estimate of activity (i, j).
- **ES_{ij}** : Earliest Starting time for activity (i, j).
- **EF_{ij}** : Earliest Finishing time for activity (i, j).
- **LS_{ij}** : Latest Starting time for activity (i, j).
- **LF_{ij}** : Latest Finishing time for activity (i, j).

All these are calculated such that they do not delay the project completion time.

(A) Foreword Pass Calculations (Determining EST and EFT):

Here we begin with the fixed occurrence time of the initial event '1'. Then we proceed in forward direction to calculate the Earliest Starting and Finishing Time of all the activities one by one. This also yields the earliest expected occurrence time for each event in the network.

1. We assume the Earliest Occurrence Time for the initial node or event as zero. Thus, $E_1 = 0$.
2. For any activity (i, j):
   (i) Earliest Starting Time (ES_{ij}) is the Earliest Occurrence Time (E_i) of its tail event i, i.e. $ES_{ij} = E_i$
   (ii) Earliest Finishing Time (EF_{ij}) is then obtained by adding its duration (t_{ij}) to its Earliest Starting Time (ES_{ij})
   i.e. $EF_{ij} = ES_{ij} + t_{ij}$
   Thus, $EF_{ij} = E_i + t_{ij}$ ... $\because ES_{ij} = E_i$
3. For the head event j of the activities, the Earliest Occurrence Time (E_j) is given by the maximum among the Earliest Finishing Times (EF_{ij}) of all the activities ending into it.
   i.e. E_j = Maximum of EF_{ij}
   Thus, E_j = Max of $[E_i + t_{ij}]$

Note:
(i) Relations in steps above are used first for calculating the Earliest Occurrence Times (E) of the successive events/nodes, starting from the initial node 1 to the terminal node (say) N.
(ii) These values can then be written in the lower left part of the nodes/circles representing the events in the network diagram.
(iii) The EST and EFT values for all the activities can be readily calculated from the values of (E) obtained above and using the above relations appropriately.

(B) Backward Pass Calculations (Determining LST and LFT):

Here we begin with the occurrence time of the terminal event (say N). We then proceed in the backward direction to calculate the Latest Finishing and Starting Time of all the activities one by one. This also yields the Latest Expected Occurrence Time for each event in the network.

1. We assume the Latest occurrence time for the terminal event/node (L_N) as equal to its Earliest Occurrence Time (E_N) as found at the end of the Forward Pass calculations done before. Thus, $L_N = E_N$
2. For any activity (i, j):
   (i) Latest Finishing Time (LF_{ij}) is the Latest occurrence time (L_j) of its head event j.
   i.e. $LF_{ij} = L_j$

(ii) Latest Starting Time (LS_{ij}) is obtained by subtracting its duration (t_{ij}) from its Latest Finishing Time (LF_{ij}).

i.e. $LS_{ij} = LF_{ij} - t_{ij}$

Also, $LS_{ij} = L_j - t_{ij}$ ... ∵ $LF_{ij} = L_j$

3. For the tail event i of the activities, the Latest Occurrence Time (L_i) is given by the minimum among the Latest Starting Times (LS_{ij}) of all activities starting from it.

i.e. L_i = Minimum of LS_{ij}

Thus, L_i = Minimum of $[L_j - t_{ij}]$

Note:

(i) The relations in the steps above are used first for calculating the Latest occurrence times (L) of the preceding events/nodes (i.e. in reverse order) starting from the terminal node (say) N to the initial node 1.

(ii) These values can then be written in the lower right part of the nodes/circles representing the events in the network diagram.

(iii) The LST and LFT values for all the activities can be readily calculated from the values of (L) obtained above and using the above relations appropriately.

Example 4: Reconsider the earlier network (with activity durations in days).

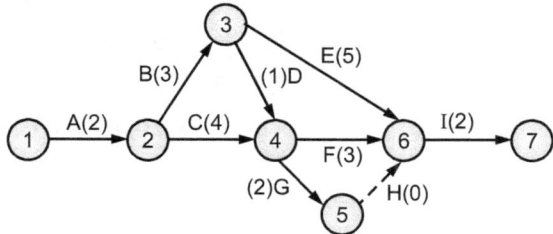

Fig. 8.31

Solution: Let us determine the Earliest and Latest times for the activities (as well as the events).

1. **Forward Pass Calculations:**

We have, for any event j:

$E_j = E_i + t_{ij}$ ... if only one activity ends into it

= Max of $[E_i + t_{ij}]$ ... if more than one activity ends into it

Also, we assume $E_1 = 0$.

(Now refer to the network diagram).

∴ $E_2 = E_1 + t_{12} = 0 + 2 = 2$ ... as only A (1, 2) ends into node 2 and $t_{12} = 2$

∴ $E_3 = E_2 + t_{23} = 2 + 3 = 5$ ... as only B (2, 3) ends into node 3 and $t_{23} = 3$

∴ E_4 = Max of $[E_3 + t_{34}, E_2 + t_{24}]$ ... as D (3, 4) and C (2, 4) end into node 4
    = Max of $[5 + 1, 2 + 4]$ ... ∵ $t_{34} = 1$, $t_{24} = 4$
    = Max of $[6, 6] = 6$

∴ $E_5 = E_4 + t_{45} = 6 + 2 = 8$

∴ E_6 = Max of $[E_3 + t_{36}, E_4 + t_{46}, E_5 + t_{56}]$ ... as E, F, G end into node 6
    = Max of $[5 + 5, 6 + 3, 8 + 0]$ ... ∵ $t_{36} = 5$, $t_{46} = 3$ and $t_{56} = 0$, H being dummy
    = Max of $[10, 9, 8] = 10$

∴ $E_7 = E_6 + t_{67} = 10 + 2 = 12$

2. **Backward Pass Calculations:**

We have for any tail event i:

$L_i = L_j - t_{ij}$ ... if only one activity starts from it
    = Min of $[L_j - t_{ij}]$ ... if more than one activities start from it

Also, we assume, for the terminal node/event (say N),

$L_N = E_N$ (Where E_N is obtained in the Forward Pass Calculations).

Thus, here, for the last node 7:

$L_7 = E_7 = 12$ ... as $E_7 = 12$

∴ $L_6 = L_7 - t_{67} = 12 - 2 = 10$ ... as only I (6, 7) starts from node 7 and $t_{67} = 2$.

∴ $L_5 = L_6 - t_{56} = 10 - 0 = 10$ ... as only H (5, 6) starts from node 6 and $t_{56} = 0$

∴ L_4 = Min of $[L_6 - t_{46}, L_5 - t_{45}]$ ... as F (4, 6) and G (4, 5) start from node 4
    = Min of $[10 - 3, 10 - 2]$ ... ∵ $t_{46} = 3$ and $t_{45} = 2$
    = Min of $[7, 8] = 7$

∴ L_3 = Min of $[L_6 - t_{36}, L_4 - t_{34}]$ ... as D and E start from node 3
    = Min of $[10 - 5, 7 - 1]$ ... ∵ $t_{36} = 5$ and $t_{34} = 1$
    = Min of $[5, 6] = 5$

∴ L_2 = Min of $[L_3 - t_{23}, L_4 - t_{24}]$
    = Min of $[5 - 3, 7 - 4]$
    = Min of $[2, 3] = 2$

∴ $L_1 = L_2 - t_{12} = 2 - 2 = 0$.

3. **The Earliest Starting and Finishing Times (EST and EFT)** as well as the Latest Starting and Finishing Times (LST and LFT) can now be easily calculated for all the activities (from the values of E and L for all events and by considering the relations in Forward and Backward Pass Calculations described earlier) as follows:

(1)	(2)	(3) →	(4)	(5) ←	(6)
Activity (i–j)	Duration t_{ij}	EST $ES_{ij} = E_i$	EFT $EF_{ij} = ES_{ij} + t_{ij}$	LST $LS_{ij} = LF_{ij} - t_{ij}$	LFT $LF_{ij} = L_j$
A: 1 – 2	2	= E_1 i.e. 0	= 0 + 2 = 2	= 2 – 2 = 0	= L_2 i.e. 2
B: 2 – 3	3	= E_2 i.e. 2	= 2 + 3 = 5	= 5 – 3 = 2	= L_3 i.e. 5
C: 2 – 4	4	= E_2 i.e. 2	= 2 + 4 = 6	= 7 – 4 = 3	= L_4 i.e. 7
D: 3 – 4	1	= E_3 i.e. 5	= 5 + 1 = 6	= 7 – 1 = 6	= L_4 i.e. 7
E: 3 – 6	5	= E_3 i.e. 5	= 5 + 5 = 10	= 10 – 5 = 5	= L_6 i.e. 10
F: 4 – 6	3	6	9	7	10
G: 4 – 5	2	6	8	8	10
H: 5 – 6	0	8	8	10	10
I: 6 – 7	2	10	12	10	12

Note:

1. Here first we can write the EST (i.e. Column 3) values for each activity as $ES_{ij} = E_i$ where i is the tail node of the activity (i – j). Then we add the duration (t_{ij}) to these values to get EFT i.e. (column 4) values as shown.
2. Similarly, we write LFT (i.e. column 6) values first as $LF_{ij} = L_j$ where j is the head node of the activity (i – j). Then we subtract (t_{ij}) from these values to get LST (i.e. column 5) values as shown.

8.8 Critical Path

Critical Activities: Certain activities in a project network are called 'Critical Activities' because any delay in their execution causes delay in the completion of the entire project.

Critical Path: Critical path is a sequence of the critical activities which starts from the initial event/node and goes upto the last event/node through the network. It is the longest duration path and it determines the minimum time that will be required to complete the project. It is shown by a thick line or by double lines on a network diagram. The length of the critical path is obtained by taking the sum of the durations of all the (critical) activities lying along it.

Identifying a Critical Path:

1. For a simple network, we can write down all possible paths (i.e. the sequences starting from the initial to the terminal node). Then we find the durations of all these paths by summing up the durations of all activities along them. The path having the longest duration, is the critical path.

2. However, for a bigger and complex network, this procedure becomes more tedious and time consuming. Here we make use of the Earliest and Latest Time Calculations as done earlier. We identify those nodes for which the Earliest Occurrence Time (E) = Latest Occurrence Time (L). These are the critical events/nodes. The activities connecting these critical nodes are the critical activities. Their sequence gives the critical path.

[Alternately, we can directly find out the critical activities from the time calculations. We identify the activities for which Earliest Finishing Times (EFT) = Latest Finishing Times (LFT). These are the critical activities which constitute the critical path. In fact, for the critical activities we also have Earliest Starting Times (EST) = Latest Starting Times (LST)].

Note:
1. Every network has a critical path and it may have less number of activities than the non-critical path (though it has the longest duration).
2. A critical path can involve a dummy activity also.
3. Critical path helps in identifying critical activities of the project which call for better managerial control on them in the form of monitoring, resource allocation etc.
4. As for critical activities, EFT = LFT. Hence, there is no scope (called float) for delaying them. If a critical activity is delayed by a day, the entire project also gets delayed by a day (unless the further critical activity times are shortened accordingly). Mere allocation of additional resources to the project, does not ensure the reduction. Thus to shorten the project duration, some of its critical activities must be shortened.
5. Any variation in actual execution time of the activities (critical or non-critical) can affect the critical path determination and related calculations. Hence, these calculations must be reworked if any change has occurred.

Example 5: Consider the network in the earlier example on which forward and backward pass calculations were done. It is shown below, where for all events/nodes, the previously computed Earliest Occurrence Times (E) are written in lower left part of the node/circle. The Latest Occurrence Times (L) are written in the lower right part.

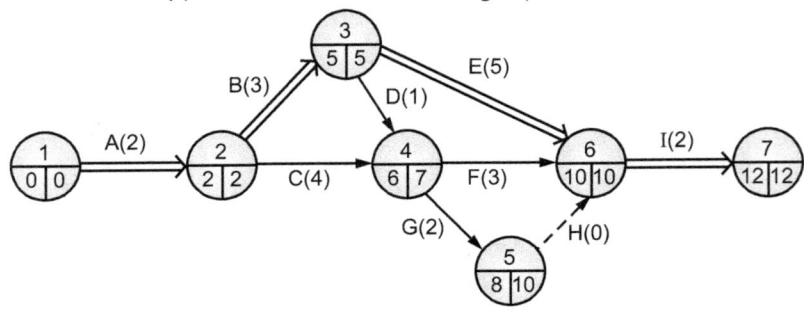

Fig. 8.32

Solution: We can determine here, the critical path as:
1. We write down all the paths (starting from initial node 1 to the terminal node 7) as:

Path	Path Duration	
	(=Summation of Activity Durations)	
A-B-E-I	2 + 3 + 5 + 2	= 12 days.
A-B-D-F-I	2 + 3 + 1 + 3 + 2	= 11 days.
A-B-D-G-H-I	2 + 3 + 1 + 2 + 0 + 2	= 10 days.
A-C-F-I	2 + 4 + 3 + 2	= 11 days.
A-C-G-H-I	2 + 4 + 2 + 0 + 2	= 10 days.

Thus, the path with longest duration of 12 days is (A-B-E-I). Hence, it is the critical path and A, B, E and I are the critical activities. This also implies that the minimum duration that will be required for completing the project is 12 days. Here, we do not make use of the event occurrence times.

2. Alternately, we see that the Earliest occurrence times (E) are equal to the Latest occurrence times (L) for the events (1, 2, 3, 6 and 10). These are thus the critical events and hence the path connecting them (i.e. A-B-E-I) is the critical path. The duration of the critical path gives the minimum completion time for the project as before.

8.9 Determination of Slacks/Floats

1. Event Slack:

The float of an event, which is called as 'slack' is the difference between its latest and earliest occurrence times. Thus, Slack of event (i) = $L_i - E_i$

It shows the time duration by which the occurrence of the event can be delayed without delaying the completion of the entire project. Now, for critical event (i), we have, $E_i = L_i$. Hence, for a critical event, slack = 0.

2. Activity Float:

The float/slack of an activity is the available time by which its duration can be delayed. There are three main types of floats which can be found out.

(A) Total Float/Slack:

It is the time duration by which the completion of an activity could be delayed beyond its earliest expected finishing time without delaying the **overall completion of the entire project**. Thus, for an activity (i, j), its total float (TF_{ij}) is given by the difference between its Latest Finishing Time (LF_{ij}) and the Earliest Finishing Time (EF_{ij}). Thus,

$$TF_{ij} = LF_{ij} - EF_{ij} \qquad \ldots (1)$$
$$= (LS_{ij} + t_{ij}) - (ES_{ij} + t_{ij}) \qquad \ldots \because LF_{ij} = LS_{ij} + t_{ij} \text{ and } EF_{ij} = ES_{ij} + t_{ij}$$
(Relations in forward and backward pass calculations).
$$\therefore TF_{ij} = LS_{ij} - ES_{ij} \qquad \ldots (2)$$

Again from (1), we can write:

$$TF_{ij} = LF_{ij} - (ES_{ij} + t_{ij}) \quad \ldots \because EF_{ij} = ES_{ij} + t_{ij}$$
$$\therefore TF_{ij} = L_j - E_i - t_{ij} \quad \ldots (3) \quad \ldots \because LF_{ij} = L_j \text{ and } ES_{ij} = E_i$$

Note:
(i) The last relation is quite useful in calculating the total float once the earliest and latest event times are known through the forward and backward pass calculations.
(ii) Now, for a critical activity, EFT = LFT and EST = LST. Hence, from the above relations, we can easily see that for the critical activities, total float is zero.
(iii) Negative value of float implies that the resources are inadequate and so the activity may not be finished in time. This calls for providing extra resources or for 'crashing' (i.e. shortening or compressing) the critical path. Zero value of float signifies that the resources are just sufficient for completing the activity and it can not be delayed (i.e. the activity is critical). Positive value of float implies that the resources are excess for the activity so that they can be reallocated or the activity can be delayed accordingly.
(iv) Total float is the most important float, which is concerned with the completion of the entire project.
(v) It signifies the difference between the 'total time available' for an activity and the time 'required' for its execution.

(B) Free Float/Slack:

It is the time duration by which the completion of an activity can be delayed beyond its earliest expected finishing time without delaying the **earliest expected starting time of its any immediate succeeding activities**. Thus, for an activity (i, j), its free float (FF_{ij}) is given by the difference between the minimum of the earliest starting times of all its succeeding activities starting from its head node (j) and its earliest finishing time (EF_{ij}). Thus,

FF_{ij} = Min of [ES of all succeeding activities having tail node j] – EF_{ij}

... as the succeeding activities start from the node (j), it is their tail node.

$$= E_j - (E_i + t_{ij}) \quad \ldots \text{using Forward Pass Relations.}$$
$$\therefore FF_{ij} = E_j - E_i - t_{ij}$$

Note:
(i) We have seen previously that, Total Float:

$$TF_{ij} = L_j - E_i - t_{ij}$$
$$\therefore L_j = TF_{ij} + E_i + t_{ij}$$

Now, for any event (j), its earliest occurrence time is always less than or equal to the latest occurrence time i.e. $E_j \leq L_j$ i.e. $E_j \leq TF_{ij} + E_i + t_{ij}$

$$\therefore E_j - E_i - t_{ij} \leq TF_{ij}$$
i.e. $\quad FF_{ij} \leq TF_{ij} \quad \ldots \because FF_{ij} = E_j - E_i - t_{ij}$

Thus, free float of any activity can have value from zero upto that of total float, but it can never be greater than the total float.

(ii) Again, we have,
$$TF_{ij} = L_j - E_i - t_{ij}$$
$$= (L_j - E_j) + (E_j - E_i - t_{ij})$$
i.e. Total Float = Head Event Slack + Free Float ... ∵ Slack of event (j) = $L_j - E_j$
i.e. Free Float = Total Float – Head Slack

(iii) Free float is concerned with the timely commencement of the succeeding activities. Thus it does not affect the float of succeeding activities but can affect those of the previous.

(iv) Free float results when all the preceding as well as succeeding activities start at their earliest (tail) event occurrence times.

(v) It is helpful in rescheduling the project activities with minimum disruption of the earlier plans.

(C) Independent Float/Slack:

It is the time duration by which the **start of an activity** can be delayed without delaying the earliest expected **starting time of its any immediate succeeding** activities, assuming that the preceding activities have **finished at their latest finish time**. Thus, for an activity (i, j), its Independent Float (IF_{ij}) can be found as follows:

First we find the difference between the minimum of the earliest starting times of all its succeeding activities starting from its head node (j) and the maximum of the latest finishing times of all its preceding activities ending into its tail node (i). This gives the minimum time available for performing the activity (i-j). Then from this minimum available time, we deduct the activity time t_{ij} to get the Independent Float (IF_{ij}). Thus,

$$IF_{ij} = \text{Minimum available time} - t_{ij}$$
$$= \{\text{Min of [ES of all succeeding activities having tail node j]} -$$
$$\text{Max of [LF of all preceding activities having head node i]}\} - t_{ij}$$

... as for succeeding activities, j is the tail node and for the preceding activities,

i is the head node.

$$= (E_j - L_i) - t_{ij} \quad \text{... using Forward and Backward pass relations}$$

Thus, $IF_{ij} = E_j - L_i - t_{ij}$

Note:

(i) We have seen previously that, Free Float:
$$FF_{ij} = E_j - E_i - t_{ij}$$
∴ $$E_i = E_j - t_{ij} - FF_{ij}$$

Now, for any event (i), $E_i \leq L_i$

∴ $\quad E_j - t_{ij} - FF_{ij} \leq L_i$

∴ $\quad E_j - L_i - t_{ij} \leq FF_{ij}$

i.e. $\quad IF_{ij} \leq FF_{ij}$

Thus, Independent float of an activity can have value at the most equal to free float but it can never be greater than it.

(ii) We can obtain a negative value for Independent float. However in that case we consider it as zero.

(iii) Again we have, $\quad IF_{ij} = E_j - L_i - t_{ij}$
$$= (E_j - E_i - t_{ij}) + E_i - L_i$$
$$= FF_{ij} - (L_i - E_i)$$

i.e. Independent float = Free Float − Tail Slack   ... ∵ For (Tail) event i, slack = $L_i - E_i$

(iv) The independent float provides a measure of variation in starting time of an activity without affecting the preceding and succeeding ones.

3. We can summarise the above relations as follows:

(i) Slack of event (i) = $L_i - E_i$

(ii) For Activity (i, j):

Total Float, $\quad TF_{ij} = LF_{ij} - EF_{ij}$
$$= LS_{ij} - ES_{ij}$$
$$= L_j - E_i - t_{ij}$$
$$= \text{Maximum available time − Activity duration}$$

Free Float, $\quad FF_{ij} = E_j - E_i - t_{ij}$

Also, Free Float = Total Float − Head Slack

Independent Float, $IF_{ij} = E_j - L_i - t_{ij}$
$$= \text{Minimum available time − Activity duration}$$

Also, Independent Float = Free Float − Tail Slack

Again, Independent Float ≤ Free Float ≤ Total Float

(iii) For critical events, Slack = 0

For critical activities, Total Float = 0

(iv) Slacks or floats represent the available spare times. 'Slacks' are used with reference to events only whereas 'floats' are used for activities.

(v) Understanding of various floats helps the project manager in identifying the underutilised resources, flexibility in scheduling and resource management.

(vi) Once the float of an activity is changed, the float of all other activities are disturbed and are required to be recalculated.

Example 6: Let us continue with the earlier example again. Its network diagram and the table representing the Earliest and Latest times of the events and activities (which were calculated using Forward pass and Backward pass procedures as described earlier) are reproduced here for ready reference:

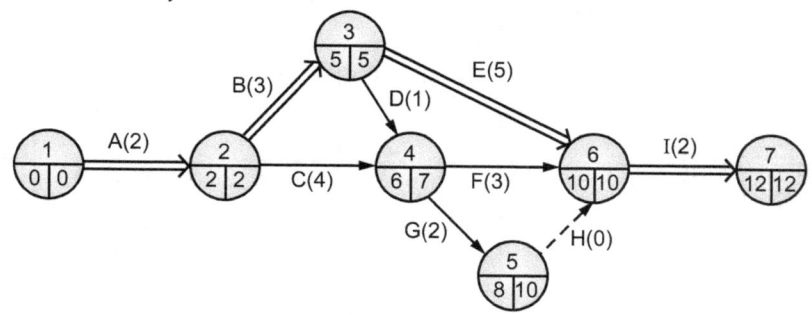

Fig. 8.32 (a)

Activity Start /Finish Times Calculations:

(1)	(2)	(3)	(4)	(5)	(6)
Activity (i–j)	Duration t_{ij}	EST $ES_{ij} = E_i$	EFT $EF_{ij} = ES_{ij} + t_{ij}$	LST $LS_{ij} = LF_{ij} - t_{ij}$	LFT $LF_{ij} = L_j$
A: 1 – 2	2	0	2	0	2
B: 2 – 3	3	2	5	2	5
C: 2 – 4	4	2	6	3	7
D: 3 – 4	1	5	6	6	7
E: 3 – 6	5	5	10	5	10
F: 4 – 6	3	6	9	7	10
G: 4 – 5	2	6	8	8	10
H: 5 – 6	0	8	8	10	10
I: 6 – 7	2	10	12	10	12

We proceed now to calculate the floats.

Activity Float Calculations

(1) Activity (i–j)	(2) Duration t_{ij}	(7) Total Float $TF_{ij} = LS_{ij} - ES_{ij}$ (i.e. LST–EST)	(8) Head Slack $S_j = L_j - E_j$	(9) Free Float = Total Float – Head Slack	(10) Tail Slack $S_i = L_i - E_i$	(11) Independent float = Free Float – Tail Slack
A: 1 – 2	2	0 – 0 = 0	$S_2 = L_2 - E_2$ = 2 – 2 = 0	0 – 0 = 0	$S_1 = L_1 - E_1$ = 0 – 0 = 0	0 – 0 = 0
B: 2 – 3	3	2 – 2 = 0	$S_3 = L_3 - E_3$ = 5 – 5 = 0	0 – 0 = 0	$S_2 = L_2 - E_2$ = 2 – 2 = 0	0 – 0 = 0
C: 2 – 4	4	3 – 2 = 1	7 – 6 = 1	1 – 1 = 0	2 – 2 = 0	0 – 0 = 0
D: 3 – 4	1	6 – 5 = 1	7 – 6 = 1	1 – 1 = 0	5 – 5 = 0	0 – 0 = 0
E: 3 – 6	5	5 – 5 = 0	10 – 10 = 0	0 – 0 = 0	5 – 5 = 0	0 – 0 = 0
F: 4 – 6	3	7 – 6 = 1	10 – 10 = 0	1 – 0 = 1	7 – 6 = 1	1 – 1 = 0
G: 4 – 5	2	2	2	0	1	–1 i.e. 0*
H: 5 – 6	0	2	0	2	2	0
I: 6–7	2	0	0	0	0	0

* IF being negative is considered as zero.

Note:
1. Here to find the Total float for each activity (i–j), we subtract its EST (i.e. ES_{ij}) value in column 3 from the LST (i.e. LS_{ij}) value in column 5.
   [Alternately, we can also use, TF = LFT (i.e. LF_{ij}) – EFT (i.e. EF_{ij})]
2. Then we write the column 8 of Head slacks (for head events j) as:
   $S_j = L_j - E_j$ where the L and E values can be read from the lower parts of the nodes/circles in the network diagram. We then subtract these values from the total floats calculated above in column 7 to get Free Floats.
3. Then we write the column 10 of Tail Slacks (for Tail Events i) as: $S_i = L_i - E_i$. We then subtract these values from the Free Floats in column 9 to get Independent Floats.
4. For all activities, TF ≥ FF ≥ IF. Only for critical activities A, B, E, I (shown by double line in the network), TF = 0. In fact for them all floats are zero. For non-critical activities, TF ≠ 0. However, they may have Free Floats or Independent Floats as zero.
5. The columns for Head and Tail Slacks may not be included in the table. However, using them as above makes the calculations easy.

6. Alternately, the Floats can be directly found as:

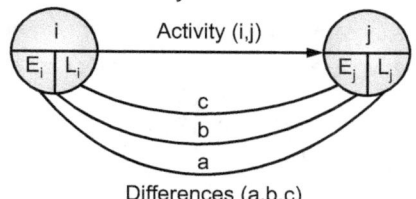

Differences (a,b,c)

Fig. 8.33

$$TF_{ij} = (L_j - E_i) - t_{ij}$$
$$= a - t_{ij} \quad \ldots \text{(See Fig. 8.33)}$$

∴ For, A (1 – 2): $TF_{12} = (2 - 0) - 2 = 0$
   C (2 – 4): $TF_{24} = (7 - 2) - 4 = 1$
   G (4 – 5): $TF_{45} = (10 - 6) - 2 = 2$ etc.

$$FF_{ij} = (E_j - E_i) - t_{ij}$$
$$= b - t_{ij} \quad \ldots \text{(See Fig. 8.33)}$$

∴ For, A (1 – 2): $FF_{12} = (2 - 0) - 2 = 0$
   C (2 – 4): $FF_{24} = (6 - 2) - 4 = 0$
   G (4 – 5): $FF_{45} = (8 - 6) - 2 = 0$ etc.

$$IF_{ij} = (E_j - L_i) - t_{ij}$$
$$= c - t_{ij} \quad \ldots \text{(See Fig. 8.33)}$$

∴ For, A (1 – 2): $IF_{12} = (2 - 0) - 2 = 0$
   C (2 – 4): $IF_{24} = (6 - 2) - 4 = 0$
   G (4 – 5): $IF_{45} = (8 - 7) - 2 = -1$ (i.e. 0 being negative) etc.

Example 7: The following table gives the activities in a construction project and other relevant information.

Activity	:	1 – 2	1 – 3	2 – 3	2 – 4	3 – 4	4 – 5
Duration (Days)	:	20	25	10	12	6	10

(i) Draw the network for the project.
(ii) Find the critical path.
(iii) Determine the expected project completion time.
(iv) Prepare an activity schedule (showing ES, EF, LS, LF and float for each activity).

Solution:

(i) Here the activities are already given in terms of their tail and head nodes. Hence, we can easily draw the network diagram for the project as:

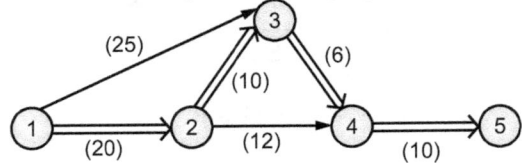

Fig. 8.34

(ii) Identifying the critical path: Here there are three paths connecting the initial node to the terminal node for which we can find the durations (by adding the activity durations along them) as follows:

Paths	Durations
1–3–4–5	25 + 6 + 10 = 41
1–2–3–4–5	20 + 10 + 6 + 10 = 46
1–2–4–5	20 + 12 + 10 = 32

Thus, the critical path is (1–2–3–4–5) as it has the longest duration i.e. 46 days. Here as the network is small we need not use the network time calculations for finding the critical path.

(iii) The expected project completion time is given by the length of the critical path. Thus, the project can be expected to complete in 46 days.

(iv) For preparing the activity schedule for the project we proceed with the forward and backward pass calculations as follows (Refer to the network diagram).

1. Forward Pass Calculations:

We assume $E_1 = 0$

$\therefore \quad E_2 = E_1 + t_{12} \quad \ldots \because E_j = E_i + t_{ij}$ and as only one activity (1-2) ends into node 2
$= 0 + 20 = 20$

Now, $\quad E_3 = \text{Max}[E_1 + t_{13}, E_2 + t_{23}]$
$\ldots \because$ more than one activity i.e. 2 activities (1-3) and (2-3) end into node 3
$= \text{Max}[0+25, 20+10]$
$= \text{Max}[25, 30]$

$\therefore \quad E_3 = 30$

Similarly now,
$E_4 = \text{Max}[E_2+t_{24}, E_3+t_{34}]$
$= \text{Max}[20+12, 30+6]$
$= \text{Max}[32, 36]$

$\therefore \quad E_4 = 36$

and $\quad E_5 = E_4 + t_{45}$
$= 36 + 10 = 46$

2. Backward Pass Calculations:

We assume, $L_5 = E_5$

$\therefore \quad L_5 = 46$ ... $\because E_5 = 46$ as found above

Now, $\quad L_4 = L_5 - t_{45}$

... $\because L_i = L_j - t_{ij}$ and as only one activity (4–5) starts from node 4

$\quad = 46 - 10 = 36$

Similarly now,

$\quad L_3 = L_4 - t_{34} = 36 - 6 = 30$ and,

Now, $\quad L_2 = $ Min of $[L_4 - t_{24}, L_3 - t_{23}]$

... $\because$ more than one activities i.e. 2 activities (2–4) and (2–3) start from node 2

$\quad = $ Min $[36 - 12, 30 - 10] = $ Min $[24, 20]$

$\therefore \quad L_2 = 20$

Similarly now,

$\quad L_1 = $ Min $[L_3 - t_{13}, L_2 - t_{12}]$

$\quad = $ Min $[30-25, 20-20]$

$\quad = $ Min $[5, 0]$

$\therefore \quad L_1 = 0$

[We can now enter these E and L values for all the nodes in the lower part of the circles for ready reference during calculations ahead. By practice, we can directly calculate and write them on the diagram].

Thus, we can redraw the network diagram as:

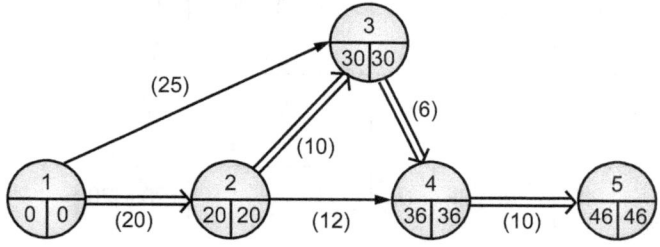

Fig. 8.35

[We can see that all the nodes are critical as for all of them E = L. The critical path can be drawn along the activities connecting all of them successively as shown].

(By practice we can directly calculate and write E and L values in the nodes).

3. We can now prepare the activity schedule as:

Activity Time Schedule:

(1)	(2)	EARLIEST		LATEST	
		Start (3) →	Finish (4)	Start (5) ←	Finish (6)
Activity	Duration	EST $ES_{ij} = E_i$	EFT (EF_{ij}) = $ES_{ij} + t_{ij}$	LST (LS_{ij}) = $LF_{ij} - t_{ij}$	LFT $LF_{ij} = L_j$
1 – 2	20	$E_1 = 0$	0 + 20 = 20	20 – 20 = 0	$L_2 = 20$
1 – 3	25	$E_1 = 0$	0 + 25 = 25	30 – 25 = 5	$L_3 = 30$
2 – 3	10	$E_2 = 20$	20 + 10 = 30	30 – 10 = 20	$L_3 = 30$
2 – 4	12	$E_2 = 20$	20 + 12 = 32	36 – 12 = 24	$L_4 = 36$
3 – 4	6	30	36	30	36
4 – 5	10	36	46	36	46

Activity Floats (Table Continued):

(1)	(7)	(8)	(9)	(10)	(11)
Activity	Total Float $TF_{ij} = LS_{ij} - ES_{ij}$	Head Slack $S_j = L_j - E_j$	Free Float = Total float – Head Slack.	Tail Slack $S_i = L_i - E_i$	Independent Float = Free Float – Tail Slack.
1 – 2	0 – 0 = 0	$L_2 - E_2$ = 20 – 20 = 0	0 – 0 = 0	$L_1 - E_1$ = 0 – 0 = 0	0 – 0 = 0
1 – 3	5 – 0 = 5	$L_3 - E_3$ = 30 – 30 = 0	5 – 0 = 5	$L_1 - E_1$ = 0 – 0 = 0	5 – 0 = 5
2 – 3	20 – 20 = 0	30 – 30 = 0	0 – 0 = 0	20 – 20 = 0	0 – 0 = 0
2 – 4	24 – 20 = 4	36 – 36 = 0	4 – 0 = 4	20 – 20 = 0	4 – 0 = 4
3 – 4	0	0	0	0	0
4 – 5	0	0	0	0	0

Note: The total floats for all critical activities are zero.

8.10 Programme Evaluation and Review Technique (PERT)

[Readers are advised to go through the concepts of Normal Probability Distribution (Chapter 10) before studying this Section].

In the Critical Path Method (CPM) technique, which we have studied so far, the project activity durations (tij) we assumed to be known with certainly or fixed i.e. deterministic. However, in practice they may not be so and may be uncertain i.e. probabilistic. The PERT takes into account this uncertain nature of project activities, and here we work out the expected time durations for all the activities which are based on three estimates which are:

(i) **Optimistic Time (a):** It is the activity time estimate if everything assumed goes as per the plans. It represents the practically shortest possible time.

(ii) **Most Likely Time (m):** It is the time which an activity will take most frequently if executed a number of times i.e. it is the 'modal' value of activity time.

(iii) **Pessimistic Time (b):** It is the activity time estimate under very unfavourable conditions. It represents the conceivably longest possible activity time.

The three estimates a, m and b are typically assumed to follow beta (β) probability distribution where a and b form its end points while m represents its mode.

Hence, the (single) expected (mean) time duration of an activity (say i) is given by (the following weighted average formula):

$$t_{ei} = \frac{a + 4m + b}{6}$$

Also, the standard deviation of activity time duration is given by:

$$\sigma_i = \frac{b - a}{6}$$

so that its Variance is:

$$\sigma_i^2 = \left(\frac{b-a}{6}\right)^2 \qquad \ldots \because \text{Variance} = (\text{Std. Deviation})^2$$

[Detailed description of beta distribution is beyond the scope of this book. Again t_{ei} represents the arithmetic mean (i.e. average) of activity times while the standard deviation measures the overall variation in them from this average].

Now, we draw the network diagram (as done earlier in CPM) and use these calculated expected activity durations to identify the critical path as done before. The activities lying along the critical path will be the critical activities and the project length (duration) will be given by the sum of the critical activity durations. Being sum of the activity durations (having no fixed values), the project duration (say T) will also not have a fixed value. This however will follow the Normal Probability Distribution. [This is based on the assumption of Central Limit Theorem which states that the 'sum of several independent activity durations will tend to be normally distributed with a mean (value) equal to the sum of their individual activity times and variance equal to sum of their individual activity variances].

Thus, if the critical activities are say 1, 2, ... k, then the project duration (T) will be following a Normal Probability Distribution with mean.

Mean: $T_e = \sum_{i=1}^{k} t_{ei} = t_{ei} + t_{e2} + t_{e3} + \ldots + t_{ek}$, and

Variance: $\sigma_T^2 = \sigma_1^2 + \sigma_2^2 + \sigma_3^2 + \ldots + \sigma_k^2$

(i.e. with Standard Deviation, $\sigma_T = \sqrt{\sigma_1^2 + \sigma_2^2 + \sigma_3^2 + \ldots + \sigma_k^2}$)

This can help us workout the probability of completing the project in the scheduled time duration (say T_s). This is given by:

$P(T < T_s) = P(z < z_s)$ where $z = \dfrac{T - T_e}{\sigma_T}$ is the Standard Normal Variate so that $z_s = \dfrac{T_s - T_e}{\sigma_T}$.

This can be found out by referring to the table of area under the Standard Normal Curve (Appendix A). [Refer to the chapter on 'Probability Distributions' for the details].

Note:
(i) We can also use the above expression to find the project duration corresponding to given probability.
(ii) If there are more than one critical path, then we use the one with the largest variance value σ_T^2.
(iii) Similar procedure can be used for probability calculations related to occurrence of any intermediate events in the network. Here we consider the largest path leading from the initial event to the concerned intermediate event. This is just as considering the critical path for the calculations of project duration which is indicated by the completion of the terminal i.e. last node in the network.
(iv) PERT is a suitable technique for projects where time estimates of activities are uncertain, like research and development. However it suffers from limitations such as its emphasis only on time and not on cost; the dynamic activity durations affect several aspects such as the critical path; assumptions of independence of project activities is unrealistic; it needs frequent revision for better control of activities which is a very costly affair.

Example 8: A project is represented by the following network diagram and has the following time estimates (in weeks) for its activities.

Activity	A	B	C	D	E	F	G	H
Most Optimistic Time (a)	2	10	8	10	7	9	3	5
Most Likely Time (m)	4	12	9	15	7.5	9	3.5	5
Most Pessimistic Time (b)	12	26	10	20	11	9	7	5

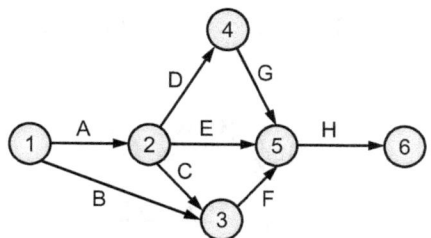

Fig. 8.36

(i) Find the critical path and expected project length.
(ii) Find the probability that the project is completed two weeks before the expected time.
(iii) If a 30 weeks deadline is imposed, what is the probability that the project will be finished within the limit?
(iv) If failing to meet the above deadline costs Rs. 1000 per week as a penalty to the project management company, what is the probability that a penalty, but not exceeding ₹ 3000 will be paid.
(v) What should be the due date to have 0.90 probability of project completion?
(vi) If the project manager wants to be 99% sure that the project is completed on the scheduled date, how many weeks before that date should he start the project?

Solution: The network diagram along with node numbers is already given. We hence, first proceed to find the expected activity durations and their variances using the following formulae:

Expected Time $t_{ei} = \dfrac{a + 4m + b}{6}$ and Variance $\sigma_i^2 = \left(\dfrac{b-a}{6}\right)^2$

Activity	Time Estimates: a	m	b	Expected Time: $t_{ei} = \dfrac{a+4m+b}{6}$	Variance: $\sigma_i^2 = \left(\dfrac{b-a}{6}\right)^2$
A	2	4	12	$\dfrac{2+4(4)+12}{6} = 5$	$\left(\dfrac{12-2}{6}\right)^2 = \left(\dfrac{5}{3}\right)^2 = \dfrac{25}{9}$
B	10	12	26	$\dfrac{10+4(12)+26}{6} = 14$	$\left(\dfrac{26-10}{6}\right)^2 = \left(\dfrac{8}{3}\right)^2 = \dfrac{64}{9}$
C	8	9	10	$\dfrac{8+4(9)+10}{6} = 9$	$\left(\dfrac{10-8}{6}\right)^2 = \left(\dfrac{1}{3}\right)^2 = \dfrac{1}{9}$
D	10	15	20	15	25/9
E	7	7.5	11	8	4/9
F	9	9	9	9	0
G	3	3.5	7	4	4/9
H	5	5	5	5	0

Now, we redraw given the PERT network along with the expected time durations for the activities found above as:

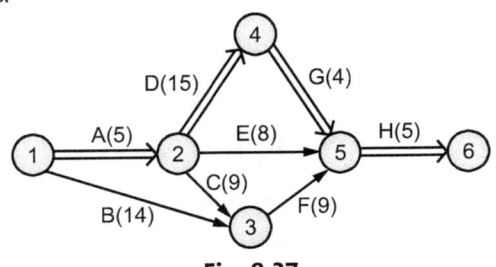

Fig. 8.37

(i) Finding the Critical Path:
The paths along the network have the following durations.

Path	Path Duration
1–2–4–5–6	5 + 15 + 4 + 5 = 29
1–2–5–6	5 + 8 + 5 = 18
1–2–3–5–6	5 + 9 + 9 + 5 = 28
1–3–5–6	14 + 9 + 5 = 28

Thus, the critical path is (1–2–4–5–6) and the critical activities are A, D, G and H. The expected time for the completion of the project (i.e. the mean project duration or length) is:

$T_e = t_{eA} + t_{eD} + t_{eG} + t_{eH} = 5 + 15 + 4 + 5 = 29$ weeks.

Also, the project duration variance is given by

$$\sigma_T^2 = \sigma_A^2 + \sigma_D^2 + \sigma_G^2 + \sigma_H^2 = \frac{25}{9} + \frac{25}{9} + \frac{4}{9} + 0 = \frac{54}{9} = 6$$

∴ Project Standard Deviation is $\sigma_T = \sqrt{\text{Variance}} = \sqrt{6} = 2.45$ weeks.

Now, the Project Duration (T) follows normal distribution with mean, $T_e = 29$ weeks and standard deviation, $\sigma_T = 2.45$

∴ The standard normal variate is $z = \dfrac{T - T_e}{\sigma_T} = \dfrac{T - 29}{2.45}$

(ii) We have to find the probability that the project is completed 2 weeks before the expected time (of 29 weeks) i.e. in scheduled duration of $T_s = 29 - 2 = 27$ weeks.

i.e. $P(T \leq 27) = P(z \leq z_s)$ where, $z = \dfrac{T - 29}{2.45}$ and $z_s = \dfrac{27 - 29}{2.45} = -0.82$

$= P(z \leq -0.82)$
$= P(z \leq 0.82)$ ... by symmetry of standard normal curve.
$= 0.5 - P(0 \leq z \leq 0.82)$
$= 0.5 - 0.2930$ ... reading value from area under standard normal curve (Appendix A).
$= 0.207$

Fig. 8.38

(iii) Similarly, here $T_s = 30$ weeks.

∴ P (Completing Project in 30 weeks)

$$= P(T \leq 30)$$
$$= P(z \leq 0.41) \quad \quad \ldots \because z_s = \frac{30-29}{2.45} = 0.41$$
$$= P(-\infty < z \leq 0.41)$$
$$= 0.5 + P(0 \leq z < 0.41)$$
$$= 0.5 + 0.1591 \quad \quad \ldots \text{using Table (Appendix A)}.$$
$$= 0.6591$$

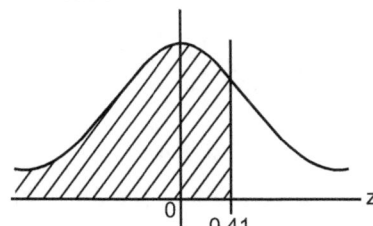

Fig. 8.39

(iv) We have to find the probability that the company pays a fine but it is not more than ₹ 3,000. It will pay a fine of ₹ 1,000 per week delay in excess of 30 weeks. Thus, at most it should exceed by $\frac{3,000}{1,000} = 3$ days. Also, it must take minimum 30 weeks (as only then it has to pay the fine).

∴ Required Probability = $P(30 < T \leq 33)$

$$= P(z_1 < z \leq z_2) \text{ where, } z_1 = \frac{30-29}{2.45} = 0.41 \text{ and } z_2 = \frac{33-29}{2.45} = 1.63$$
$$= P(0.41 < z \leq 1.63)$$
$$= P(0 < z \leq 1.63) - P(0 < z < 0.41)$$
$$= 0.4484 - 0.1591 \quad \quad \ldots \text{using Table}$$
$$= 0.2893$$

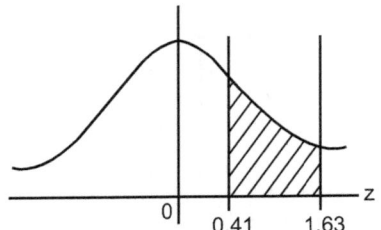

Fig. 8.40

(v) Here we have to first work out scheduled duration (T_s), so that the probability of project completion within duration is 0.90

i.e. $\quad P(T < T_s) = 0.9$

i.e. $\quad P(z < z_s) = 0.9$

i.e. $\quad 0.5 + P(0 < z < z_s) = 0.9$

i.e. $\quad P(0 < z < z_s) = 0.4$

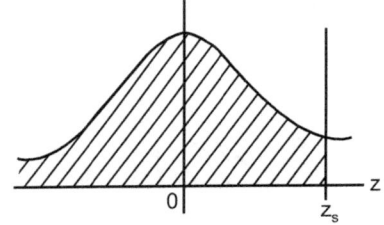

Fig. 8.41

Now reading the value of z from the table of 'Area Under Standard Normal Curve' in reverse order, we see that for probability value of 0.90, z =1.28

∴ $\quad z_s = 1.28$

i.e. $\quad \dfrac{T_s - 29}{2.45} = 1.28$

∴ $\quad T_s = 32.13$ weeks.

Thus, the due date should be 32.13 weeks from start (so that chances of project completion by the due date are 0.90.)

(vi) The project manager wants to be 99% sure that the project is completed on the scheduled date.

∴ We have to first find Ts such that,

$\quad P(T < T_s) = 0.99$

i.e. $\quad P(z < z_s) = 0.99$

∴ $0.5 + P(0 < z < z_s) = 0.99$

∴ P (0 < z < z_s) = 0.49

∴ z_s = 2.33 ... using Table.

i.e. $\dfrac{T_s - 29}{2.45}$ = 2.33

∴ T_s = 34.7 weeks which is the required duration. Hence, he should start 34.7 weeks before the due date.

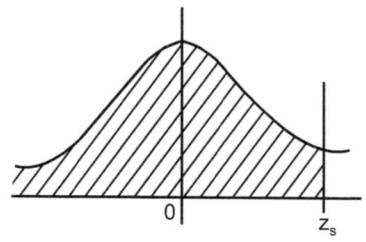

Fig. 8.42

Solved Problems

Problem 1: The following information is gathered for a project:

Activity	Preceding Activity	Duration (Weeks)
A	–	1
B	A	3
C	A	4
D	A	3
E	D	2
F	B, C, E	4
G	D	9
H	D	5
I	H	2
J	F, G, I	2

(a) Draw the network diagram.

(b) Determine critical path and project duration.

(c) What is effect on the project duration if:
  (i) D is changed to 6 weeks.
  (ii) F is changed to 8 weeks.

(P.U. MBA - May 11)

Solution:

(a) Considering the given precedence relationships we develop the network diagram directly. For convenience we write the preceding activities in the first column, followed by the given activities and then its duration.

Preceding Activity	Activity	Duration (Weeks)
–	A	1
A	B	3
A	C	4
A	D	3
D	E	2
B, C, E	F	4
D	G	9
D	H	5
H	I	2
F, G, I	J	2

A has no predecessor while, it precedes B, C and D.

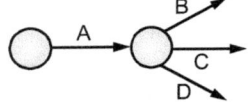

Fig. 8.43

B and C precede F hence we use a dummy (D1). D precedes E, G and H. Hence,

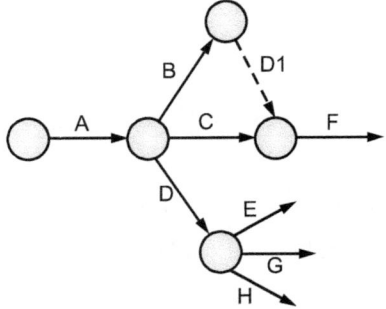

Fig. 8.44

Now, E precedes F, while F and G precede J, and H precedes I.

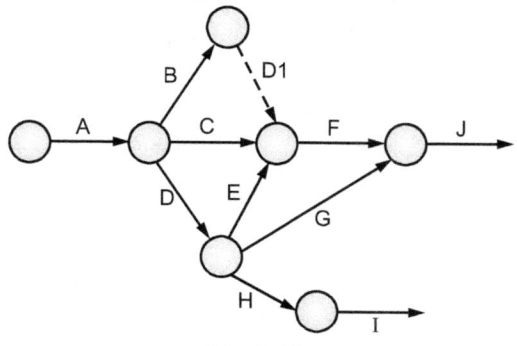

Fig. 8.45

Finally as I precedes J and J is not a predecessor of any activity, it is the last activity terminating into the terminal node. Thus, we draw the final network diagram (including the activity durations) as follows. The nodes are also numbered then in logical sequence from left to right (or by using Fulkerson's Rule), ensuring that tail node number (i) < head node number (j).

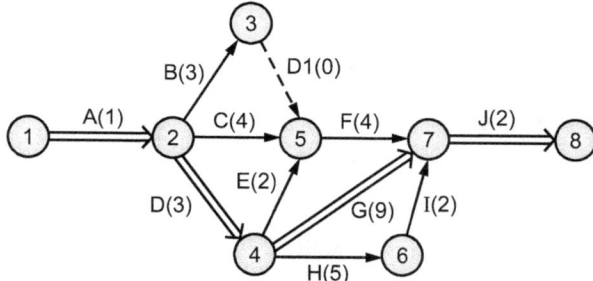

Fig. 8.46

(b) Critical Path: Identifying all the paths through the network (from node 1 to 8) and finding their durations, we get:

Sr. No.	Path	Activities	Duration
I	1-2-3-5-7-8	A B D1 F J	1 + 3 + 0 + 4 + 2 = 10
II	1-2-5-7-8	A C F J	1 + 4 + 4 + 2 = 11
III	1-2-4-5-7-8	A D E F J	1 + 3 + 2 + 4 + 2 = 12
IV	1-2-4-7-8	A D G J	1 + 3 + 9 + 2 = 15
V	1-2-4-6-7-8	A D H I J	1 + 3 + 5 + 2 + 2 = 13

Thus, path IV (i.e. 1-2-4-7-8 or A-D-G-J) is having maximum duration of 15 weeks. Thus it is the critical path and hence the project duration is 15 weeks.

(c) (i) If D (i.e. activity 2-4) is changed to 6 weeks (i.e. increases by 6 – 3 = 3 weeks), the durations of paths III, IV and V will increase by 3 weeks to become 12 + 3 = 15, 15 + 3 = 18 and 13 + 3 = 16 weeks respectively. But here again among all the paths the path A D G J remains longest i.e. critical with duration 18 weeks. Thus, the project duration will increase to 18 weeks but the critical path is unchanged.

(ii) If F (i.e. activity 5-7) increases to 8 weeks (i.e. increases by 8 – 4 = 4 weeks), the durations of paths I, II and III will increase by 4 weeks to become 10 + 4 = 14, 11 + 4 = 15 and 12 + 4 = 16 weeks. Thus, now the path III (i.e. 1–2–4–5–7–8 or A D E F J) will be the longest i.e. critical. Thus, the project duration will increase to 18 weeks and the critical path will also be changed.

Problem 2: A project has been defined to contain the following list of activities along with their required time of completion.

Activity:	A	B	C	D	E	F	G	H	I
Time in Days:	1	4	3	7	6	2	7	9	4
Immediate Predecessor:	–	A	A	A	B	C	E, F	D	G, H

(a) Draw the network diagram.
(b) Show early start time and early finish time.
(c) Identify critical path.
(d) What would happen if duration of activity F is taken as four days instead of two?

(P.U. MBA - Dec. 10)

Solution:

(a) Considering the given precedence relationships, we can draw the network diagram for the project as follows:

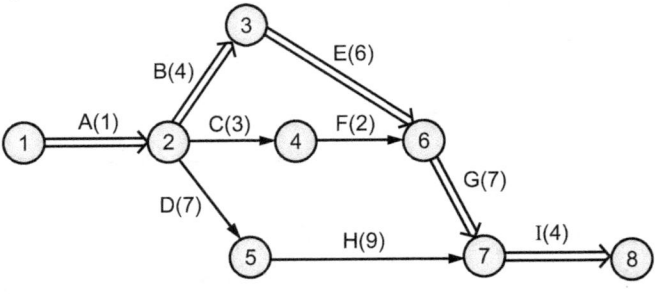

Fig. 8.47

(b) In order to find the Early Start Time (EST) and Early Finish Time (EFT) we first use the Forward Pass calculations for finding the Earliest Occurrence Times (E) of the events/nodes as follows:

Let $E_1 = 0$

$\therefore E_2 = E_1 + t_{12} = 0 + 1 = 1$ ... $\because E_j = E_i + t_{ij}$

$\therefore E_3 = E_2 + t_{23} = 1 + 4 = 5$

$E_4 = E_2 + t_{24} = 1 + 3 = 4$

$E_5 = E_2 + t_{25} = 1 + 7 = 8$

$\therefore E_6$ = Max of $[E_3 + t_{36}, E_4 + t_{46}]$ ... $\because$ 2 activities merge into node 6.

= Max of $[5 + 6, 4 + 2]$ = Max of $[11, 6]$ = 11

E_7 = Max of $E_6 + t_{67}, E_5 + t_{57}]$

= Max of $[11 + 7, 8 + 9]$ = Max of $[18, 17]$ = 18

$E_8 = E_7 + t_{78} = 18 + 4 = 22$

Now, we find the Early Start Times (EST) and Early Finish Times (EFT) for all the activities as follows:

Activity (i–j)	Duration t_{ij}	EST $ES_{ij} = E_i$	EFT $EF_{ij} = ES_{ij} + t_{ij}$
A: 1 – 2	1	$E_1 = 0$	$0 + 1 = 1$
B: 2 – 3	4	$E_2 = 1$	$1 + 4 = 5$
C: 2 – 4	3	$E_2 = 1$	4
D: 2 – 5	7	1	8
E: 3 – 6	6	5	11
F: 4 – 6	2	4	6
G: 6 – 7	7	11	18
H: 5 – 7	9	8	17
I: 7 – 8	4	18	22

(c) Critical Path: We find all the paths through the network and their durations as:

Sr. No.	Path	Activities	Duration
I	1-2-3-6-7-8	A B E G I	$1 + 4 + 6 + 7 + 4 = 22$
II	1-2-4-6-7-8	A C F G I	$1 + 3 + 2 + 7 + 4 = 17$
III	1-2-5-7-8	A D H I	$1 + 7 + 9 + 4 = 21$

The path with the longest duration i.e. path I (1-2-3-6-7-8 or A-B-E-G-I) is the critical path which gives the duration of the project as 22 days.

(d) If the duration of the activity F (i.e. 4–6) is taken as four days instead of two, the duration of path II will increase by two days to 17 + 2 = 19 days. Thus, the critical path remains unchanged and the project duration as well.

(**Note:** This will not even change the ESTs of the activities as E_6 = Max $[E_3 + t_{36}, E_4 + t_{46}]$ = Max $[5 + 6, 4 + 4]$ = Max $[11, 8]$ = 11. i.e. remains unchanged and so E_7 and E_8 as well.)

Problem 3: The activities of a project and estimated time in days for each activity are given below:

Activity	1-2	1-3	1-4	2-3	2-6	3-5	4-5	4-6	5-6
Duration (in Days)	8	10	8	10	16	17	18	14	9

(a) Draw a PERT network for this project.
(b) Find the critical path.
(c) What is the minimum time of completion for the project.
(d) Prepare activity schedule showing the ES, EF, LS, LF and total and free floats for the non-critical activities.
(e) Will the critical path change if the activity (3–5) takes:
   (i) 20 days instead of 17.
   (ii) 14 days instead of 17.

Solution:

(a) Using the given information (about the tail (i) and head (j) nodes of activities), we can roughly draw the PERT network directly as follows:

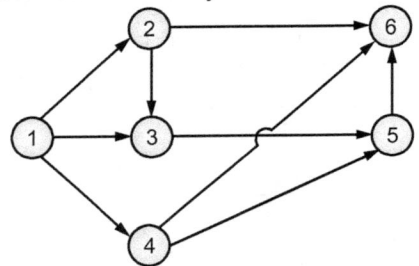

Fig. 8.48

This can be neatly redrawn (along with activity names say A, B, C and durations) as:

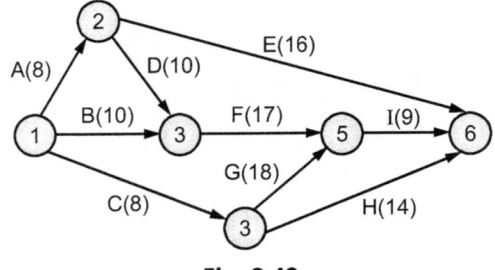

Fig. 8.49

(b) To find the critical path, we consider all paths [starting from initial node (1) to terminal node (6)] of the network and their durations (given by adding the activity durations along them) as:

Sr. No.	Path	Activities	Duration
I	1-2-6	A-E	8 + 16 = 24
II	1-2-3-5-6	A-D-F-I	8 + 10+ 17+ 9 = 44
III	1-3-5-6	B-F-I	10 + 17+ 9 = 36
IV	1-4-5-6	C-G-I	8 + 18+ 9 = 35
V	1-4-6	C-H	8 + 14 = 22

Thus, the critical path is II (1–2–3–5–6 or A–D–F–I) being of the longest duration of 44 days. The critical activities are thus A (1-2), D (2-3), F (3-5) and I (5-6).

(c) The minimum time required for the completion of the project is given by the length of the critical path i.e. 44 days.

(d) To Prepare the Activity Schedule:

First, we find the Earliest Occurrence Time (E_i) and Latest Occurrence Time (L_i) for all the event nodes as:

Using Forward Pass calculations to find E_i:

Assume, $E_1 = 0$

∴ $E_2 = E_1 + t_{12}$ ... ∵ $E_j = E_i + t_{ij}$ where t_{ij} is the activity (i-j) duration.

$= 0 + 8 = 8$

$E_3 = \text{Max}[E_1 + t_{13}, E_2 + t_{23}]$ ... ∵ 2 activities merge in node 3

$= \text{Max}[0 + 10, 8 + 10] = 18$

$E_4 = E_1 + t_{14} = 0 + 8 = 8$

$E_5 = E_3 + t_{35} = 18 + 17 = 35$

$E_6 = \text{Max}[E_2 + t_{26}, E_5 + t_{56}, E_4 + t_{46}]$

$= \text{Max}[8 + 16, 35 + 9, 8 + 14] = 44$

Now, using Backward Pass calculations (to find L_i):

For the terminal node,

$L_6 = E_6 = 44$ ... ∵ $E_6 = 44$

∴ $L_5 = L_6 - t_{56}$ ... ∵ $L_i = L_j - t_{ij}$

$= 44 - 9 = 35$

∴ $L_4 = \text{Min}[L_5 - t_{45}, L_6 - t_{46}]$ ... ∵ 2 activities burst from node 4

$= \text{Min}[35 - 18, 44 - 14] = 17$

Now, $L_3 = L_5 - t_{35} = 35 - 17 = 18$
∴ $L_2 = \text{Min } [L_6 - t_{26}, L_3 - t_{23}]$
     $= \text{Min } [44 - 16, 18 - 10] = 8$
and ∴ $L_1 = \text{Min } [L_2 - t_{12}, L_3 - t_{13}, L_4 - t_{14}]$
     $= \text{Min } [8 - 8, 18 - 10, 17 - 8] = 0$

Thus, we can redraw the network with these values (for our convenience in calculations) as:

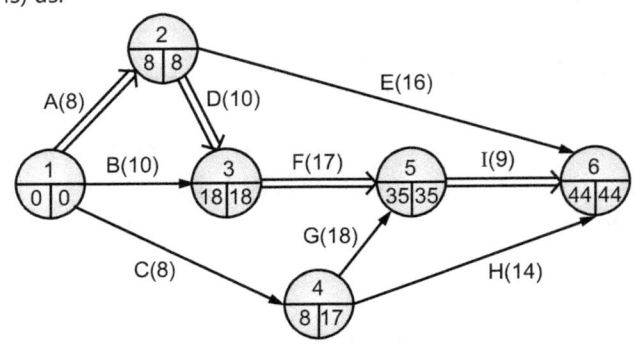

Fig. 8.50

We can now write (by referring to the above diagram) the activity schedule as:

Activity (i-j)	Duration t_{ij}	EST $ES_{ij} = E_i$	EFT $EF_{ij} = ES_{ij} + t_{ij}$	LST $LS_{ij} = LF_{ij} - t_{ij}$	LFT $LF_{ij} = L_j$	Total Float $TF_{ij} = \text{LST} - \text{EST}$	Head Slack $S_j = L_j - E_j$	Free Float = Total Float − Head Slack = $TF_{ij} - S_j$
A(1-2)	8	$E_1 = 0$	$0 + 8 = 8$	$8 - 8 = 0$	$L_2 = 8$	$0 - 0 = 0$	$L_2 - E_2 = 8 - 8 = 0$	$0 - 0 = 0$
B(1-3)	10	$E_1 = 0$	$0 + 10 = 10$	$18 - 10 = 8$	$L_3 = 18$	$8 - 0 = 8$	$L_3 - E_3 = 18 - 18 = 0$	$8 - 0 = 8$
C(1-4)	8	$E_1 = 0$	8	$17 - 8 = 9$	$L_4 = 17$	$9 - 0 = 9$	$L_4 - E_4 = 17 - 8 = 9$	$9 - 9 = 9$
D(2-3)	10	8	18	8	18	0	0	0
E(2-6)	16	8	24	28	44	20	0	20
F(3-5)	17	18	35	18	35	0	0	0
G(4-5)	18	8	26	17	35	9	0	9
H(4-6)	14	8	22	30	44	22	0	22
I(5-6)	9	35	44	35	44	0	0	0

Note:
1. For all critical events 1, 2, 3, 5 and 6 : E = L.
2. For all critical activities A, D, F, I : TF = 0 and FF = 0.
3. For non-critical activities B, C, E, G, H : TF ≠ 0. Thus they may be delayed beyond EFT by this time (=TF) without affecting the project duration.
4. We can find the free floats directly as:
$$FF_{ij} = E_j - E_i - t_{ij}$$
∴ $FF_{12} = E_2 - E_1 - t_{12} = 8 - 0 - 8 = 0$
$FF_{13} = E_3 - E_1 - t_{13} = 18 - 0 - 10 = 8$
5. For all activities, FF ≤ TF

(e) Changing duration of activity F (3-5):
  (i) F is a critical activity. Hence if it takes 20 days instead of 17 (i.e. 3 days more) the project duration will also increase by 3 days to become 47. The critical path will remain unchanged (i.e. A-D-F-I). The next critical path B-F-I (having second longest duration of 36 days) will also have an increased duration of 36 + 3 = 39 days. Other paths will remain unchanged. (However the floats of other activities will change)
  (ii) If F (3-5) takes 14 days instead of 17 (i.e. 3 days less), the duration of path A-D-F-I will be 44 - 3 = 41 days and that of B-F-I will be 36 - 3 = 33 days. Thus, A-D-F-I being still the longest, it will remain to be critical. However, the next critical path now will be CGI (having second longest duration of 35 days.)

Problem 4: Following are the activities of a project:

Activity	Immediate Predecessor Activity	Activity Times in Weeks		
		Most Optimistic	Most Likely	Most Pessimistic
A	None	4	7	13
B	A	6	9	11
C	A	5	7	9
D	B	3	5	7
E	C	7	8	10
F	D	2	3	5
G	E	6	7	8
H	F & G	2	3	4

(a) Calculate the expected time of each activity.
(b) Draw the network and indicate the expected time on each activity.
(c) Compute the earliest completion time of the project.
(d) Identify the critical path in the diagram. **(P.U. MBA - Dec. 12)**

Solution: The data pertains to PERT network as it involves the three activity time estimates.

(a) We rewrite the given information in the following order to calculate the expected time for each activity as:

Predecessor Activity	Activity	Activity Times: a	m	b	Expected Time: $t_{ei} = \dfrac{a+4m+b}{6}$
–	A	4	7	13	$\dfrac{4 + 4(7) + 13}{6} = 45/6$
A	B	6	9	11	$\dfrac{6 + 4(9) + 11}{6} = 53/6$
A	C	5	7	9	42/6
B	D	3	5	7	30/6
C	E	7	8	10	49/6
D	F	2	3	5	19/6
E	G	6	7	8	42/6
F & G	H	2	3	4	18/6

(b) Now, using the given precedence relationships among the activities we can draw the network as follows:

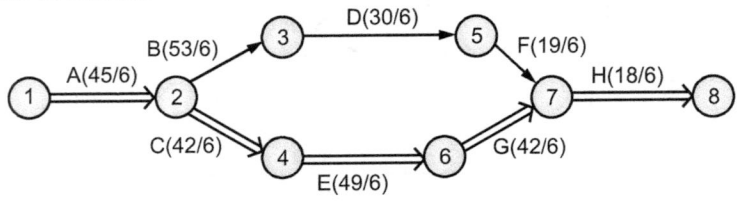

Fig. 8.51

We also write the expected activity times (t_{ei}) and number the nodes logically from left to right [ensuring that tail node number (i) < head node number (j)] as shown.

(c) We have to compute the earliest completion time of the project. This is given by the length of the critical path.

Note: This is same as the earliest occurrence time of the terminal event 8 i.e. E_8. This can be found out using forward pass calculations.

This is also the same as the latest occurrence time of event 8 i.e. L_8. This is because the terminal node is always a critical node of the network (for which we have $E = L$). This corresponds to the value of the longest path duration i.e. the duration of the critical path].

Now, the network has two paths viz. 1-2-3-5-7-8 (i.e. A-B-D-F-H) with duration $\left(\frac{45}{6} + \frac{53}{6} + \frac{30}{6} + \frac{19}{6} + \frac{18}{6} = \frac{165}{6} = 27.5 \text{ weeks}\right)$ and 1-2-4-6-7-8 i.e. A-C-E-G-H with duration $\left(\frac{45}{6} + \frac{42}{6} + \frac{49}{6} + \frac{42}{6} + \frac{18}{6} = \frac{196}{6} = 32.67 \text{ weeks}\right)$. Thus, the critical path is A-C-E-G-H and the duration of the project is 32.67 weeks. The earliest completion time of the project is thus (same as this i.e.) 32.67 weeks.

Problem 5: A publisher has just signed a contract for publishing a book. What is the earliest time by which the book can be ready for distribution? The tasks given in the table are involved, with the time estimates given in weeks.

Task	Precedence	Most Likely	Optimistic	Pessimistic
(A) Appraisal of book by reviewers	–	8	4	10
(B) Initial pricing of the book	–	2	2	2
(C) Assessment of marketability	A, B	2	1	3
(D) Revisions by author	A	6	4	12
(E) Editing of final draft	C, D	4	3	5
(F) Typesetting of text	E	3	3	3
(G) Plates for artwork	E	4	3	5
(H) Designing & printing of jacket	C, D	6	4	9
(I) Printing & binding of book	F, G	8	6	16
(J) Inspection & final assembly	I, H	1	1	1

(i) For this PERT network, find the expected task durations and the variance of task durations.

(ii) Draw a network and find the critical path. What is the expected length of the critical path and what is its variance?

(iii) What is the probability that the length of the critical path does not exceed 32 weeks? 36 weeks?

(iv) What is the probability that the task E is completed one week before the expected time?

(v) If this task is to be completed by December 31 of the given year and the publisher wants to be 95% sure of meeting this deadline, when should he start the project?

Solution:

(i) For the given PERT network, the expected (i.e. mean) activity time durations (t_{ei}) and variances (σ_i^2) will be as follows:

Precedence	Activity	Optimistic (a)	Most likely (m)	Pessimistic (b)	Expected Time $t_{ei} = \dfrac{a+4m+b}{6}$	Variance $\sigma_i^2 = \left(\dfrac{b-a}{6}\right)^2$
–	A	4	8	10	$\dfrac{4+4(8)+10}{6} = 46/6$	$\left(\dfrac{10-4}{6}\right)^2 = \left(\dfrac{6}{6}\right)^2$
–	B	2	2	2	$\dfrac{2+4(2)+2}{6} = 12/6$	$\left(\dfrac{2-2}{6}\right)^2 = 0$
A, B	C	1	2	3	12/6	$(2/6)^2$
A	D	4	6	12	40/6	$(8/6)^2$
C, D	E	3	4	5	24/6	$(2/6)^2$
E	F	3	3	3	18/6	0
E	G	3	4	5	24/6	$(2/6)^2$
C, D	H	6	6	9	39/6	$(3/6)^2$
F, G	I	4	8	16	52/6	$(12/6)^2$
I, H	J	1	1	1	6/6	0

(ii) Drawing Network: Using the given precedence relationships among the tasks/activities, we can draw a rough PERT network as:

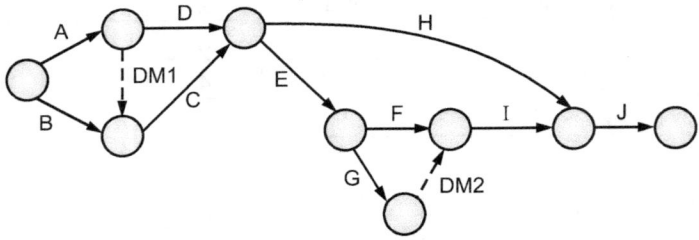

Fig. 8.52

This can be neatly redrawn with activity durations and node numbers which are assigned from left to right ensuring ($i < j$) or using Fulkerson's Rule as:

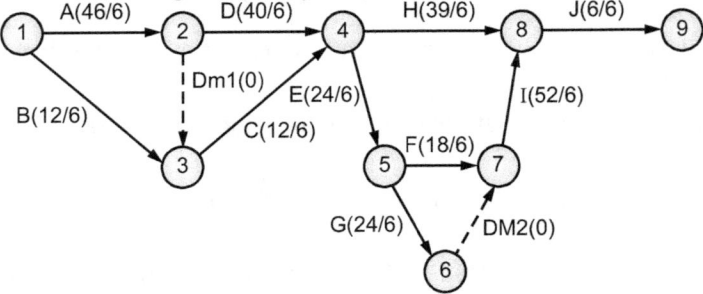

Fig. 8.53

To find the critical path we consider all paths of the network with their durations as:

Path		Duration
I	: 1-2-4-8-9	$\dfrac{46+40+39+6}{6} = \dfrac{131}{6}$
II	: 1-2-4-5-7-8-9	$\dfrac{46+40+24+18+52+6}{6} = \dfrac{186}{6}$
III	: 1-2-4-5-6-7-8-9	192/6
IV	: 1-2-3-4-8-9	103/6
V	: 1-2-3-4-5-7-8-9	158/6
VI	: 1-2-3-4-5-6-7-8-9	164/6
VII	: 1-3-4-8-9	69/6
VIII	: 1-3-4-5-7-8-9	124/6
IX	: 1-3-4-5-6-7-8-9	130/6

Thus, the critical path is III (1-2-4-5-6-7-8-9 i.e. A-D-E-G-I-J) having duration 192/6 = 32 weeks. (The dummy activity is not mentioned). Now, the expected length of the critical path (i.e. project duration) is given by:

$$T_e = \Sigma\, t_{ei} \text{ (along critical path)}$$

$$= 32 \text{ weeks and the variance is given by:}$$

$$\sigma_T^2 = \Sigma\, \sigma_i^2 \text{ (along critical path)}$$

$$= \sigma_A^2 + \sigma_D^2 + \sigma_E^2 + \sigma_G^2 + \sigma_I^2 + \sigma_J^2$$

$$= \left(\dfrac{6}{6}\right)^2 + \left(\dfrac{8}{6}\right)^2 + \left(\dfrac{2}{6}\right)^2 + \left(\dfrac{2}{6}\right)^2 + \left(\dfrac{12}{6}\right)^2 + 0 = \dfrac{252}{36} = 7$$

(iii) Now as the critical path length i.e. (project duration T follows Normal Distribution with (mean) expected duration = 32 weeks and variance 7 (i.e. standard deviation $\sigma_T = \sqrt{7} = 2.65$), the standard normal variate is:

$$z = \dfrac{T - T_e}{\sigma_T} = \dfrac{T - 32}{2.65}$$

$\therefore$ P (Critical path does not exceed T_s = 32 weeks)

$= P(T \leq 32)$

$= P(z \leq 0)$ ... $\because z_s = \dfrac{T - 32}{2.65} = \dfrac{32 - 32}{2.65} = 0$

$= 0.5$ ... area lying to the left of z = 0

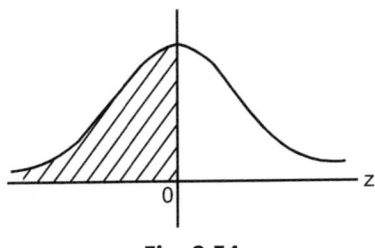

Fig. 8.54

Similarly, $P(T \le 36) = P(z \le 1.51)$ $\therefore z_s = \dfrac{36 - 32}{2.65} = 1.51$

$= 0.5 + P(0 < z \le 1.51)$

$= 0.5 + 0.4345$ ... using table of area

$= 0.9345$ under standard normal curve (Appendix A)

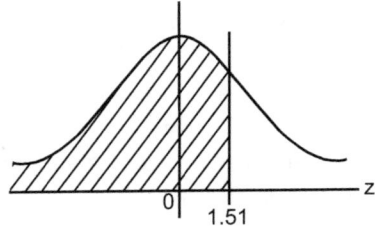

Fig. 8.55

(iv) The task E i.e. editing of the final draft is to be completed i.e. the event 5 must occur. Thus, we now identify the longest path from node 1 to node 5 (just like we considered the critical path for the completion of entire project) as:

1-2-4-5 (i.e. A-D-E) with its length $\left(= \dfrac{46}{6} + \dfrac{40}{6} + \dfrac{24}{6} = \dfrac{110}{6} = 18.33 \text{ weeks} \right)$

Thus, the expected completion time for the task E is: $T_e = T_{eA} + T_{eD} + T_{eE} = 18.33$ weeks.

Similarly, its variance is:

$\sigma_T^2 = \sigma_A^2 + \sigma_D^2 + \sigma_E^2 = \left(\dfrac{6}{6}\right)^2 + \left(\dfrac{8}{6}\right)^2 + \left(\dfrac{2}{6}\right)^2 = \dfrac{104}{36} = 2.89$

The duration T here is assumed to follow normal distribution with mean = 18.33 weeks and variance = 2.89 i.e. (std. dev. = $\sqrt{2.89}$ = 1.7), so that the

$z = \dfrac{T - T_e}{\sigma_T} = \dfrac{T - 18.33}{1.7}$.

∴ P (Task E is completed one week before the expected time)

= P (T ≤ T_s) where T_s = 18.33 − 1 = 17.33

= P (z ≤ z_s) where $z_s = \dfrac{17.33 - 18.33}{1.7} = -0.59$

= P (z ≤ − 0.59)

= P (z ≥ 0.59) ... by symmetry

= 0.5 − P (0 < z ≤ 0.59)

= 0.5 − 0.2224 ... from table

= 0.2776

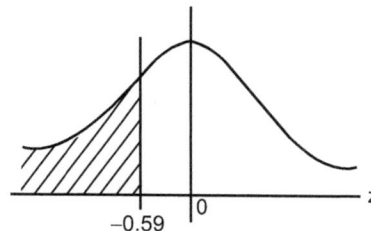

Fig. 8.56

(v) The publisher wants to be 95% sure that the task E is finished by 31st December. Thus we have to find the scheduled duration (Ts) upto this event, such that P(T≤Ts) = 0.95.

i.e. P (z ≤ z_s) = 0.95 where $z_s = \dfrac{T_s - 18.33}{1.7}$

i.e. 0.5 + P (0 < z ≤ z_s) = 0.95 i.e., P (0 < z ≤ z_s) = 0.45

Now, reading value of z from the table of 'Area under standard normal curve' corresponding to probability value of 0.45 is z_s = 1.645 (i.e. average of 1.64 and 1.65)

i.e. $\dfrac{T_s - 18.33}{1.7} = 1.645$

∴ T_s = 1.7 (1.645) + 18.33 = 21.13 ≅ 21 weeks.

Thus, the project should start 21 weeks prior to 31st December i.e. on 6th August of the year.

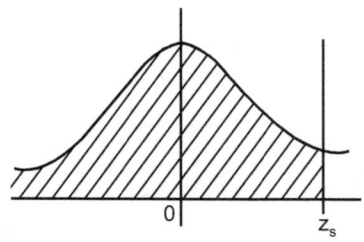

Fig. 8.57

Exercise

1. Describe the characteristics of CPM and PERT model.
2. Describe briefly the basic steps to be followed in developing a PERT/CPM programme.
3. Explain the usefulness of PERT and CPM techniques in decision making. State their limitations.
4. Explain the following in terms of PERT/CPM.
   (i) Earliest Time
   (ii) Latest Time
   (iii) Total Activity Slack
   (iv) Event Slack
   (v) Critical Path.
5. Distinguish between PERT and CPM.
6. An assembly is to be made from two parts X and Y. Both parts must be turned on a lathe and Y must be polished whereas X need not be polished. The sequence of activities together with their predecessors is given below:

Activity	Description	Predecessor Activity
A	Open work order	–
B	Get material for X	A
C	Get material for Y	A
D	Turn X on lathe	B
E	Turn Y on lathe	B, C
F	Polish Y	E
G	Assemble X and Y	D, F
H	Pack	G

   Draw a network diagram for the project.

   (**Ans.** A(1-2), B(2-3), C(2-4), Dummy (3-4), D(3-6), E(4-5), F(5-6), G(6-7), H(7-8))

7. Draw a network diagram from the following activities:

Activity:	A	B	C	D	E	F	G	H	I	J	K
Immediate Predecessor:	–	A	A	A	B	C	C	C, D	E, F	G, H	I, J
Duration (Days):	3	2	3	2	5	2	4	3	2	2	1

   Also, determine critical path and minimum time required to complete the project.

   (**Ans.** A(1-2), B(2-4), C(2-3), D(2-5), Dummy(3-5), E(4-6), F(3-6), G(3-7), H(5-7), I(6-8), J(7-8), K(8-9); CP: ACGJK & ABEIK; Project duration = 13 days)

8. The activities of a project and estimated time in days for each activity are given below:

Activity:	1-2	2-3	2-4	2-5	3-7	4-5	4-7	5-6	6-7
Duration (in Days)	3	4	4	5	4	2	2	3	2

   (a) Draw the network diagram.
   (b) Calculate project duration and determine critical path.
   (c) Find latest start and finish times for the activities. Also find their total floats.
   (d) If the duration of activity (2-5) is taken as follows, what will be its effect on project duration? (i) 7 days, (ii) 3 days. **(P.U. MBA - Dec. 11)**
   (**Ans.** (b) CP: 1-2-4-5-6-7, Project duration: 14 days), (c) 1-2 (0, 3, 0), 2-3 (6, 10, 3), 2-4 (3, 7, 0), 2-5 (4, 9, 1), 3-7 (10, 14, 3), 4-5 (7, 9, 0), 4-7 (12, 14, 5), 5-6 (9, 12, 0), 6-7 (12, 14, 0), (d) (i) 15 days, New CP: 1-2-5-6-7
   (ii) 14 days, CP: Unchanged.

9. Given the following information:

Activity:	1-2	1-3	1-4	2-6	3-5	4-5	4-7	5-6	5-7	6-8	7-8
Optimistic Time:	6	1	1	1	1	1	2	4	4	2	2
Pessimistic Time:	8	9	7	3	9	9	8	4	10	14	8
Most Likely Time:	7	2	4	2	2	5	2	4	4	5	2

   (a) Construct the project network.
   (b) Find the expected duration and variance of each activity.
   (c) Find the critical path and the expected project completion time.
   (d) What is the probability of completing the project on or before 25 weeks?
   (e) If the probability of completing the project is 0.84, find the expected project completion time.
   (**Ans.** (b) 1-2 (7, 0.11), 1-3 (3, 1.78), 1-4 (4, 1), 2-6 (2, 0.11), 3-5 (3, 1.78), 4-5 (5, 1.78), 4-7 (3, 1), 5-6 (4, 0), 5-7 (5, 1), 6-8 (6, 4), 7-8 (3, 1), (c) 1-2-3-5-6-8; Time = 20 weeks, (d) 0.9803, (e) 22.4 weeks from start)

10. A nationalised bank wishes to plan and schedule the development and installation of a new computerised cheque processing system. The change over in cheque-processing procedures requires employment of additional personnel to operate the new system, development of new system (computer software) and modification of existing cheque sorting equipment. The activities required to complete the project along with three time estimates and the precedence relationship among the activities have been determined by bank management and are given in the following table:

Activity	Description	Predecessor	Time Estimates (in Days)		
			Optimistic	Most Likely	Pessimistic
A	Position Recruiting	–	5	8	17
B	System Development	–	3	12	15
C	System Training	A	4	7	10
D	Equipment Training	A	5	8	23
E	Manual System Test	B, C	1	1	1
F	Preliminary System Changeover	B, C	1	4	13
G	Computer-Personnel Interface	D, E	3	6	9
H	Equipment Modification	D, E	1	2.5	7
I	Equipment Testing	H	1	1	1
J	System Debugging & Installation	F, G	2	2	2
K	Equipment Changeover	G, I	5	8	11

(a) Draw a network diagram for this project and find critical path and its length.

(b) Calculate total, free and independent floats for non-critical activities.

(c) What is the probability that the project is completed in not more than (i) 40 days, (ii) 35 days?

(d) What should be due date to have 0.90 probability of completion?

(**Ans.** (a) 1-2 (Time = 9, Variance = 2), 1-3 (11, 2), 2-3 (7, 1), 2-4 (10, 3), 3-4 (1, 0), 3-8 (5, 2), 4-6 (6, 1), 4-5 (3, 1), 5-7 (1, 0), Dummy 6-7 (0, 0), Dummy 6-8 (0, 0), 7-9 (8, 1), 8-9 (2, 0); CP: 1-2-4-6-7-9 i.e. ADG (DM1)K. Length = 33 days., (b) B (7, 5, 5), C (2, 0, 0), E (2, 2, 0), F (10, 4, 2), H (2, 0, 0), I (2, 2, 0), J (6, 6, 0), (c) (i) 0.9959, (ii) 0.7734, (d) 36.39 weeks from start)

■■■

Chapter 9...
Probability

Contents ...
9.1 Definitions
9.2 Theorems of Probability
9.3 Mathematical Preliminaries
    List of Formulae
    Solved Problems
    Exercise

9.1 Definitions

(i) **Trial and Event:** In the theory of probability an experiment is called as 'Trial' and its outcome is called as an 'Event or Case'. (e.g. throw of Coin-experiment/trial and Head or Tail-outcome/event). The events are generally denoted by A, B, C, etc. The experiments where the results may be altogether different even though they are performed under identical conditions are called as 'Random Experiments'.

(ii) **Equally Likely:** The outcomes of a trial are said to be equally likely if anyone of them cannot be expected to occur in preference to another (e.g. Getting a Head or a Tail, if an unbiased coin is thrown.)

(iii) **Mutually Exclusive:** The events are said to be mutually exclusive if the happening of an event excludes the happening of all other events i.e. the events cannot happen simultaneously in a single trial. (e.g. Getting 1 at uppermost face excludes the occurrence of 2, 3, 4 etc. automatically in a throw of a die.) These events can be connected by the words "either...or". Thus A, B, C are mutually exclusive if either A or B or C can occur.

(iv) **Exhaustive:** All possible outcomes of a trial form exhaustive sets of cases or events e.g. Events of Head and Tail, Appearance of 1, 2, 3, 4, 5 and 6 in a throw of a die etc. Similarly if two coins are tossed, the events (H,H), (H,T), (T,H) and (T,T) are exhaustive events.

(v) **Sample Space:** A set of all possible outcomes of a trial which are exhaustive is called a sample space and each outcome is called a sample point (e.g. In case of tossing a coin once, the sample space = S = { H, T }).

(vi) **Independent and Dependent Events**: The events are said to be independent if the happening or not happening of an event does not depend on the occurrence or non-occurrence of other events. If the happening of an event is affected by the occurrence of others, the events are called as dependent events. (e.g. If two cards are drawn successively from a well shuffled pack without replacement, then getting say a king at a second draw will depend upon the result of the first draw. Thus these are dependent events. However, if the first card is replaced, then getting a king in second draw is independent of the first draw.) Note that independent events are quite different from mutually exclusive events.

(vii) **Simple and Compound Events:** When two or more events occur in connection with each other, the simultaneous occurrence is called as a compound event e.g. when a die is thrown, getting '3 or 4' is a compound event. In case of simple events we consider the probability of the happening or not happening of a single event only. e.g. getting 3 for a die.

(viii) **Probability:** If a trial results in n exhaustive cases which are mutually exclusive and equally likely and out of which m are favourable to the happening of event A, then the probability p of the happening of event A is given by,

$$p = P(A) = \frac{m}{n}$$

e.g. Probability of getting a king when a card is drawn from a well-shuffled pack. Here A = Event of getting a king. ∴ m = No. of favourable outcomes = 4 and n = Total No. of possible outcomes = 52

$$\therefore P(A) = \frac{m}{n} = \frac{4}{52} = \frac{1}{13}$$

If $\bar{A}$ denotes the non-happening of A, then its probability

$$q = P(\bar{A}) = \frac{n-m}{n} = 1 - \frac{m}{n} = 1 - P(A)$$

Thus, probability of not getting a king is $P(\bar{A}) = 1 - P(A) = 1 - \frac{1}{13} = \frac{12}{13}$

Thus, $P(A) + P(\bar{A}) = p + q = 1$

And if an event A is certain to occur then $P(A) = 1$ and $\therefore P(\bar{A}) = 0$

Note: $P(A) = \frac{m}{n}$ is expressed sometimes by saying that the odds in favour of A are m : (n − m) or the odds against A are (n − m) : m.

9.2 Theorems of Probability

Note:
(i) $A \cup B$ is the event **either A or B or both** and is also denoted as (A+B) and is read as 'A union B'.
(ii) $A \cap B$ is the event **both A and B** and is also denoted as AB and is real as 'A intersection B'.
(iii) A or $\overline{A}$ is the event 'Not A'.
(iv) (A − B) is the event 'A but not B'.
(v) For mutually exclusive events we have $A \cap B = \phi$ i.e. null set.

1. Addition Theorem:
If A and B are any two events then
$$P(A \cup B) = P(A+B) = P(A) + P(B) - P(A \cap B)$$
e.g. P(King or Heart Card) = P(King) + P(Heart) − P(King and Heart)
$$= \frac{4}{52} + \frac{13}{52} - \frac{1}{52} = \frac{16}{52} = \frac{4}{13}$$

If A and B are mutually exclusive then $P(A \cup B) = P(A) + P(B)$. .... $\because A \cap B \neq \phi$

e.g. P (King or Queen) = P (King)+P (Queen) = $\frac{4}{52} + \frac{4}{52} = \frac{8}{52} = \frac{2}{13}$ as here $P(A \cap B) = 0$.

Similarly, for three events A, B and C we have,
$$P(A \cup B \cup C) = P(A) + P(B) + P(C) - P(A \cap B) - P(B \cap C) - P(C \cap A) + P(A \cap B \cap C)$$
Now, if $A_1, A_2, A_3 ... A_n$ are mutually exclusive events then,
$$P(A_1 \cup A_2 \cup A_3 ... \cup A_n) = P(A_1) + P(A_2) + ... + P(A_n)$$

Thus, in general "or" implies addition of probabilities for mutually exclusive events.

Example 1: A bag contains 30 balls numbered from 1 to 30. One ball is drawn at random. Find the probability that the number of the ball drawn will be (i) a multiple of 5 or 7 (ii) a multiple of 4 or 6 and (iii) even number or a multiple of 5.

Solution: Total number of possible outcomes is n = 30
(i) Let A - Event that the ball drawn has a number which is a multiple of 5.
Let B- Event that the ball drawn has a number which is a multiple of 7.
∴ No. of favourable outcomes to event A which are {5, 10, 15, 20, 25, 30} is m = 6
∴ Probability that the number is a multiple of 5 = $P(A) = \frac{m}{n} = \frac{6}{30}$

Similarly, Probability that the number is a multiple of 7, which are {7, 14, 21, 28} is $P(B) = \frac{4}{30}$

∴ Probability that the number is a 'multiple of 5 or 7' which are mutually exclusive events (since no number is common to them) is,

$$P(A \text{ or } B) \text{ i.e. } P(A \cup B) = P(A) + P(B) = \frac{6}{30} + \frac{4}{30} = \frac{10}{30} = \frac{1}{3}$$

∵ "or" = ⇒ Addition for mutually exclusive events.

(ii) Probability that the number is a multiple of 4 i.e. {4, 8, 12, 16, 20, 24, 28} is say $P(C) = \frac{7}{30}$.

Probability that the number is a multiple of 6 i.e. {6, 12, 18, 24, 30} is say $P(D) = \frac{5}{30}$.

Now, these are not mutually exclusive events as the numbers 12 and 24 are common to both these events.

∴ Probability that the number is a multiple of 4 as well as 6 is $P(C \cap D) = \frac{2}{30}$ and hence,

∴ $P(C \text{ or } D)$ i.e. $P(C \cup D) = P(C) + P(D) - P(C \cap D)$

... as C and D are not mutually exclusive

$$= \frac{7}{30} + \frac{5}{30} - \frac{2}{30} = \frac{10}{30} = \frac{1}{3}$$

(iii) Similarly, the probability that the number is even or a multiple of 5

$$= P(\text{even}) + P(\text{multiple of 5}) - P(\text{even and multiple of 5})$$

$$= \frac{15}{30} + \frac{6}{30} - \frac{3}{30} = \frac{18}{30} = \frac{3}{5}$$

2. Theorem on Compound Probability:

For dependent events A and B, the probability of their simultaneous occurrence is

$P(A \text{ and } B) = P(A \cap B) = P(A) \times P(B/A) = P(B) \times P(A/B)$

where, $P(B/A)$ called as the conditional probability, implies the probability of occurrence of event B given that the event A has already occurred.

E.g. If one card is drawn from a pack and then the second is drawn without replacing the first, the probability of the second draw is dependent on the first draw.

Now, if A and B are independent events, then

$P(B/A) = P(B)$ or $P(A/B) = P(A)$ so that

$P(A \text{ and } B) = P(A \cap B) = P(A) \times P(B)$ ... Multiplication Theorem

Similarly, for three events A, B, and C

$P(A \cap B \cap C) = P(A) \cdot P(B/A) \cdot P(C/A \cap B)$

and if A, B and C are independent then

$P(A \cap B \cap C) = P(A) \cdot P(B) \cdot P(C)$

Thus, in general for independent events 'and' implies multiplication of the probabilities.

Note:

(i) For independent events $A_1, A_2, \ldots A_n$ we have

P{Happening of at least one of the events $A_1, A_2, \ldots A_n$}

$= 1 - $ P{Happening of none of the events $A_1, A_2, \ldots A_n$}

(iii) Also from the above formulae we have,

$P(B/A) = \dfrac{P(A \cap B)}{P(A)}$ and $P(A/B) = \dfrac{P(A \cap B)}{P(B)}$

Example 2: Find the probability of drawing a queen and a king in that order from a pack of cards in two consecutive draws when the cards drawn are (i) not being replaced (ii) being replaced.

Solution: Let A - event that the first card drawn is a queen

$$\therefore \quad P(A) = \frac{4}{52}$$

(i) Now, if the card is not replaced, there will be 51 cards in the pack and hence, the second event B of drawing a king from this pack is **dependent** on the first.

Hence, probability of drawing a king from the remaining pack of 51 cards is

$$\therefore \quad P(B/A) = \frac{4}{51}$$

Hence, Probability of drawing a queen followed by a king is

$$\therefore P(A \text{ and } B) \text{ i.e., } P(A \cap B) = P(A) \times P(B/A) = \frac{4}{52} \times \frac{4}{51}$$

(ii) If the card is replaced back, the event B of drawing of a king is **independent** of the first event, as there would be 52 cards again.

Hence, $\quad P(B) = \frac{4}{52}$

$\therefore$ P(A and B) i.e.,

$$P(A \cap B) = P(A) \times P(B) = \frac{4}{52} \times \frac{4}{52}$$

$\because$ "and" $\Rightarrow$ multiplication for independent events

---

3. **Bayes' Theorem:**

If $A_1, A_2, \ldots A_k \ldots A_n$ are mutually exclusive and collectively exhaustive events and B is any other event that occurs in conjunction with events $A_1, A_2, \ldots A_n$.

Then, $P(A_k/B) = \dfrac{P(A_k) \times P(B/A_k)}{\sum\limits_{k=1}^{n} P(A_k) \times P(B/A_k)}$

Hence, for three such events A_1, A_2, A_3.

$$P(A_1/B) = \frac{P(A_1) P(B/A_1)}{\sum\limits_{k=1}^{3} P(A_k) P(B/A_k)} = \frac{P(A_1) P(B/A_1)}{P(A_1) P(B/A_1) + P(A_2) P(B/A_2) + P(A_3) P(B/A_3)}$$

Example 3: A factory has two machines A and B, A producing 300 units and B producing 700 units, forming the total output. 5% of the items produced on A are defective and only 1% produced by B are defective. If a defective item is drawn at random, what is the probability that it is produced by machine A? Also, find the probability that an item drawn randomly from the output is defective.

Solution: Let A_1 - The event that the item is produced on machine A.
A_2 - The event that the item is produced on machine B.
and D - The item is defective.

(i) We have to find the probability that the item is produced on machine A given that it is defective i.e. $P(A_1/D)$, Here A_1 and A_2 are mutually exclusively (as only one of them can happen at a time) and collectively exhaustive (as these are the only possible events which form the total output). Also, event D can happen in conjunction with both A_1 and A_2.

∴ By Bayes' Theorem

$$P(A_1/D) = \frac{P(A_1) \times P(D/A_1)}{\sum_{k=1}^{2} P(A_k) \times P(D/A_k)} = \frac{P(A_1) P(D/A_1)}{P(A_1) P(D/A_1) + P(A_2) P(D/A_2)}$$

Now, Total output = 300 + 700 = 1000

∴ $P(A_1) = \frac{300}{1000} = 0.3$ and $P(A_2) = \frac{700}{1000} = 0.7$

Also, since A produces 5% defective items

∴ $P(D/A_1) = \frac{5}{100} = 0.05$

Similarly, $P(D/A_2) = 0.01$

∴ $P(A_1/D) = \frac{(0.3)(0.05)}{(0.3)(0.05)+(0.7)(0.01)} = \frac{0.015}{0.015+0.007} = \frac{0.015}{0.022}$

= 0.682

Similarly, $P(A_2/D) = \frac{0.007}{0.022} = 0.318$

(ii) Now, the probability that the item drawn randomly from the total output is defective is

P(D) = P[(item is produced on A and is defective) or (item is produced on B and is defective)]

= $P(A_1 \cap D) + P(A_2 \cap D)$

... ∵ $(A_1 \cap D)$ and $(A_2 \cap D)$ are mutually exclusive

= $P(A_1) P(D/A_1) + P(A_2) P(D/A_2)$

... ∵ Events D & A_1, A_2 are dependent

(Note that this is the denominator term in Bayes' Theroem)

∴ P(D) = (0.3) (0.05) + (0.7) (0.01)

= 0.015 + 0.007 = 0.022

Note: Bayes' Theorem is based on the proposition that the probabilities should be revised when new information is available. This is required in order to make better use of the available information and thereby reduce the element of risk involved in making decisions under uncertainty. On the basis of this theorem the probabilities of various outcomes are revised upwards or downwards depending upon the evidence obtained. Thus, if the probability of exporting successfully to a country is 1/10 and if after some initial survey there is an indication of an untapped market in that country, the probability of exporting successfully will be revised upwards. However, sometimes such additional information may be misleading also. The probabilities before revision are called 'Prior Probabilities' and those after revision are called 'Posterior Probabilities'.

9.3 Mathematical Preliminaries

(a) **Factorial Notation**: If n is a positive integer then n factorial (denoted as n! or n) is
$$n! = n \times (n-1) \times (n-2) \times ... 3 \times 2 \times 1$$
e.g. $\quad 7! = 7 \times 6 \times 5 \times 4 \times 3 \times 2 \times 1$

Note that,
(i) $n! = n \times (n-1)!$
(ii) $0! = 1$

(b) **Permutations**: Each **arrangement** of r objects at a time drawn out of n different objects is called a 'Permutation'. The possible total number of such permutations is given by

$$^nP_r = \frac{n!}{(n-r)!} \qquad \therefore \; ^nP_n = n!$$

e.g. We can arrange the 5 letters in the word 'LOTUS' in $^5P_5 = 5! = 120$ number of ways.

(c) **Combination**: The **selection** of r objects at a time from n different objects is called a 'Combination'. The total number of possible combinations i.e. the number of ways in which r items can be selected from a total of n items is

$$^nC_r = \frac{n!}{r!\,(n-r)!}$$

Note that,
(i) $^nC_r = \,^nC_{n-r} \qquad \therefore \; ^{10}C_4 = \,^{10}C_6$
(ii) $^nC_1 = n$
(iii) $^nC_n = \,^nC_0 = 1$

e.g. The total number of ways in which 4 cards can be drawn from a total of 10 cards is

$$^{10}C_4 = \frac{10!}{4!(10-4)!} = \frac{10!}{4!\,(6!)}$$
$$= \frac{10 \times 9 \times 8 \times 7 \times (6!)}{4 \times 3 \times 2 \times 1 \times (6!)} = \frac{10 \times 9 \times 8 \times 7}{1 \times 2 \times 3 \times 4} = 210$$

List of Formulae

1. $p = P(A) = \dfrac{\text{No. of favourable cases}}{\text{Total number of cases}} = \dfrac{m}{n}$

   $q = P(\text{not } A) = P(\bar{A}) = 1 - P(A) = 1 - p$

2. Theorems:

   (a) Addition Theorem:

   $P(A \text{ or } B) = P(A \cup B) = P(A) + P(B) - P(A \cap B)$

   $\qquad\qquad\qquad\qquad\quad = P(A) + P(B) \qquad$ ... for Mutually Exclusive Events

   $P(A \cup B \cup C) = P(A) + P(B) + P(C) - P(A \cap B) - P(B \cap C) - P(A \cap C) + P(A \cap B \cap C)$

   $\qquad\qquad\qquad\quad = P(A) + P(B) + P(C) \qquad$ ... for Mutually Exclusive Events

   In general, 'or' $\Rightarrow$ Addition of probabilities for mutually exclusive events.

   (b) Compound Probability Theorem:

   $P(A \text{ and } B) = P(A \cap B) = P(A) P(B/A) = P(B) P(A/B)$

   $\therefore P(B/A) = \dfrac{P(A \cap B)}{P(A)}$, $P(A/B) = \dfrac{P(A \cap B)}{P(B)}$

   For Independent Events:

   $P(A \cap B) = P(A) \cdot P(B)$

   In general, 'and' $\Rightarrow$ Multiplication of probabilities for independent events.

3. P{Happening of at least one of $A_1, A_2, \ldots A_n$}

   $= 1 - P$ {Happening of none of $A_1, A_2, \ldots A_n$}

4. Bayes' Theorem:

   $P(A_1/B) = \dfrac{P(A_1) P(B/A_1)}{\sum_{k=1}^{n} P(A_k) P(B/A_k)} = \dfrac{P(A_1) P(B/A_1)}{P(A_1) P(B/A_1) + P(A_2) P(B/A_2) + \ldots + P(A_n) P(B/A_n)}$

5. $n! = n \times (n-1) \times (n-2) \times \ldots 3 \times 2 \times 1$

   $0! = 1,\ n! = n(n-1)!$

6. $^nC_r = \dfrac{n!}{n!(n-r)!}$

   e.g. $^{10}C_4 = \dfrac{10!}{4!6!} = \dfrac{10 \times 9 \times 8 \times 7}{1 \times 2 \times 3 \times 4}$

   $^nC_r = {}^nC_{n-r},\ {}^nC_1 = n,\ {}^nC_n = {}^nC_0 = 1$

Solved Problems

Problem 1: A card is drawn at random from a well shuffled pack. Find the probability that: (i) it is not a spade (ii) it is a face card.

Solution: Total number of possible outcomes, n = 52

(i) Let A - Event that a non-spade card is selected.

Now, there are (53 – 13) = 39 non-spade cards

∴ Favourable outcomes for A are m = 39

∴ $P(A) = \dfrac{m}{n} = \dfrac{39}{52} = \dfrac{3}{4}$

(ii) Let B - Event that the card is a face (King, Queen or Jack) card

∴ Favourable outcomes, m = 3 × 4 = 12

∴ $P(B) = \dfrac{m}{n} = \dfrac{12}{52} = \dfrac{3}{13}$

Problem 2: A pair of dice is thrown. Find the probability of getting the sum (i) more than nine (ii) multiple of 3 (iii) divisible by 3 or 4.

Solution: The sample space i.e. (all possible outcomes) consists of

$$S = \{(1, 1), (1, 2), \ldots (1, 6), (2, 1), (2, 2) \ldots (2, 6), (3, 1) \ldots (6, 6)\}$$

i.e. n = Total possible outcomes = 6^2 = 36

(i) A - Event that the sum is more than 9

The favourable outcomes where the sum is more than 9

i.e. The sum is 10 OR 11 OR 12 are {(4, 6), (5, 5), (6, 4), (5, 6), (6, 5), (6, 6)} i.e.

m = No. of favourable outcomes = 6

∴ $P(A) = \dfrac{m}{n} = \dfrac{6}{36} = \dfrac{1}{6}$

(ii) B - Event that the sum is a multiple of 3

The outcomes where the sum is a multiple of 3 are

{(1, 2), (1, 5), (2, 1), (2, 4), (3, 3), (3, 6), (4, 2), (4, 5), (5, 1), (5, 4), (6, 3), (6, 6)}

i.e. m = 12

∴ $P(B) = \dfrac{m}{n} = \dfrac{12}{36} = \dfrac{1}{3}$

(iii) C - Event that the sum is a multiple of 4

∴ Favourable outcomes are {(1, 3), (2, 2), (2, 6), (3, 1), (3, 5), (4, 4), (5, 3), (6, 2), (6, 6)}

i.e. m = 9

∴ $P(C) = \dfrac{9}{36} = \dfrac{1}{4}$

Of these outcomes, {(6, 6)} is common to events B and C

∴ P(sum is a multiple of 3 **and** 4)

$= P(B \cap C) = \dfrac{1}{36}$

∴ Probability that the sum is divisible by 3 or 4 i.e. it is a multiple of 3 or 4 is

$P(B \cup C) = P(B) + P(C) - P(B \cap C)$

$= \dfrac{1}{3} + \dfrac{1}{4} - \dfrac{1}{36} = \dfrac{4+3}{12} - \dfrac{1}{36} = \dfrac{7}{12} - \dfrac{1}{36} = \dfrac{21-1}{36} = \dfrac{20}{36} = \dfrac{5}{9}$

Problem 3: What is the probability that a leap year selected at random will have 53 Mondays?

Solution: A leap year has 366 days. Now, 52 weeks cover (52 × 7) = 364 days.

Thus, there are 52 full weeks containing 52 Mondays. Now, the remaining (366 – 364 = 2) days could be Sun-Mon., Mon.-Tue, Tue-Wed, ... etc. i.e.7 possible combinations. Out of these, only 2 combinations will have a Monday in them. Hence, the probability that there will be a 53rd Monday $= \dfrac{2}{7}$

i.e. The probability that the leap year will have 53 Mondays $= \dfrac{2}{7}$

Problem 4: The daily production (in number of units) for a week in a factory is 56, 59, 62, 57, 53, 60, 66 units. If it is checked at random on a day, what is the probability that it will be less than the average?

Solution: Number of days considered, n = 7

Let, x - The daily production

∴ Average production $= \dfrac{\Sigma x}{7} = \dfrac{56 + 59 + 62 + 57 + 53 + 60 + 66}{7} = \dfrac{413}{7} = 59$

Let A - Event that the production is less than the average on a day i.e. {56, 57, 53}

∴ m = 3

∴ $P(A) = \dfrac{3}{7}$

Problem 5: Two friends A and B apply for two vacancies at the same post. The probabilities of their selection are 1/4 and 1/5 respectively. What is the chance that (i) One of them will be selected, (ii) Both will be selected, (iii) None will be selected, (iv) At least one will be selected.

Solution: Let A - Event that A is Selected, B - Event that B is selected

∴ P(A) = 1/4 and P(B) = 1/5

∴ P(A not selected) = $P(\bar{A}) = 1 - P(A) = 1 - \frac{1}{4} = \frac{3}{4}$ and $P(\bar{B}) = 1 - P(B) = 1 - \frac{1}{5} = \frac{4}{5}$

(i) Now, if only one is selected i.e. (A is selected **and** B is not) **or** (B is selected **and** A is not) then Required probability

= P(A∩B̄) + P(B∩Ā) ... mutually exclusive events
= $P(A) \cdot P(\bar{B}) + P(B) \cdot P(\bar{A})$ ... independent events
= $\left(\frac{1}{4}\right)\left(\frac{4}{5}\right) + \left(\frac{1}{5}\right)\left(\frac{3}{4}\right) = \frac{4}{20} + \frac{3}{20} = \frac{7}{20}$

(ii) If both are selected, then

Required probability

= P(A∩B)

= P(A) · P(B) ... independent events

= $\left(\frac{1}{4}\right)\left(\frac{1}{5}\right) = \frac{1}{20}$

(iii) P(None of them is selected) = 1 – P(at least one is selected)

= 1 – P (one is selected **or** both are selected)

= $1 - \left[\frac{7}{20} + \frac{1}{20}\right] = 1 - \frac{8}{20} = \frac{12}{20} = \frac{3}{5}$

Alternately, P(none is selected) i.e. $P(\bar{A} \cap \bar{B}) = P(\bar{A}) \cdot P(\bar{B}) = \left(\frac{3}{4}\right)\left(\frac{4}{5}\right) = \frac{3}{5}$

(iv) P(At least one will be selected)

= P (one is selected **or** both are selected)

= P (one selected) + P(both are selected)

= $\frac{7}{20} + \frac{1}{20} = \frac{8}{20} = \frac{2}{5}$

Problem 6: Probability that a man will be alive 25 years hence is 0.3 and the probability that his wife will be alive 25 years hence is 0.4. Find the probability that 25 years hence (i) both will be alive, (ii) only the man will be alive, (iii) only the woman will be alive, (iv) at least one of them will be alive.

Solution: Let A – The man will be alive 25 years hence, B – His wife will be alive 25 years hence,

∴ We have P(A) = 0.3 and P(B) = 0.4

∴ P(man will not be alive) = $P(\bar{A}) = 1 - P(A) = 1 - 0.3 = 0.7$

Similarly, $P(\bar{B}) = 1 - 0.4 = 0.6$

(i) Probability that, both man and his wife will be alive, is

∴ P(A∩B) = P(A) × P(B)   ... as events are independent
= (0.3) (0.4) = 0.12

(ii) Probability that only the man will be alive i.e. the man will be alive and his wife not,

i.e. P(A∩B̄) = P(A) · P(B̄) = (0.3) (0.6) = 0.18

(iii) Similarly, Probability that only the woman will be alive is

P(Ā∩B) = P(Ā) · P(B) = (0.7) (0.4) = 0.28

(iv) Probability that at least one of them is alive i.e. Probability that either man or woman is alive

i.e. P(A∪B) = P(A) + P(B) − P(A∩B) = (0.3) + (0.4) − (0.12) = 0.58

Alternately, Probability that at least one of them is alive

= 1 − Probability that none of them is alive.

= 1 − (Ā∩B̄) = 1 − P(Ā) · P(B̄) = 1 − (0.7) (0.6) = 1 − 0.42 = 0.58

Problem 7: 12% of the items produced on a machine are defective. The quality inspector makes incorrect classification of the items 10% of the time during its testing further. If 600 items are supplied, how many of them are expected to be defectives?

Solution: Let D - Item produced is defective and I - Classification is incorrect.

∴ P(D) = 0.12

∴ $P(\bar{D}) = 1 - 0.12 = 0.88$ and

P(I) = 0.1   ∴ $P(\bar{I}) = 1 - 0.1 = 0.9$

∴ P (Item is classified as good for supply)

= P [(It is non-defective **and** correctly classified) **or** (it is defective **and** incorrectly classified)]

= P(D̄∩Ī) + P(D∩I)   ... Mutually Exclusive Events

= P(D̄) P(Ī) + P(D) P(I)   ... Independent events

= (0.88) (0.9) + (0.12) (0.1) = 0.792 + 0.012 = 0.804

Out of these, probability of defective items = P(D∩I) = P(D) P(I) = (0.12) (0.1) = 0.012

This implies that if 1 items is produced, (0.804) of it will be supplied and 0.012 of it will be defectives.

∴ Probability that the item supplied is defective = $\frac{0.012}{0.804} = 0.015$

Thus, if one item is supplied (0.015) of it is defective

∴ If 600 items are supplied, No. of defective items = (0.015) (600) = 9.

Similarly, percentage defective items supplied = (0.015) (100) = 1.5%.

Problem 8: A can hit a target 1 out of 4 times. B can hit the target 2 out of 3 times and C can hit the target 3 out of 4 times. Find the probability that, (i) The target is hit, (ii) At least two hit the target.

Solution: We have, $P(A) = \frac{1}{4}$, $P(B) = \frac{2}{3}$, $P(C) = \frac{3}{4}$

∴ P(A not hitting the target) i.e. $P(\bar{A}) = 1 - P(A) = 1 - \frac{1}{4} = \frac{3}{4}$

Similarly, $P(\bar{B}) = 1 - \frac{2}{3} = \frac{1}{3}$, $P(\bar{C}) = 1 - \frac{3}{4} = \frac{1}{4}$

(i) ∴ Probability that the target is hit i.e. Probability that at least one hits the target

= 1 − P(No one hits the target)

= 1 − Probability that (A does not hit and B does not hit and C does not hit)

= 1 − P($\bar{A} \cap \bar{B} \cap \bar{C}$)

= $1 - P(\bar{A}) \cdot P(\bar{B}) \cdot P(\bar{C})$ ...independent events

= $1 - \left(\frac{3}{4}\right)\left(\frac{1}{3}\right)\left(\frac{1}{4}\right) = 1 - \frac{1}{16} = \frac{15}{16} = 0.94$

(ii) If at least two hit the target i.e. either two or all hit the target i.e. events

($\bar{A} \cap B \cap C$) **or** ($A \cap \bar{B} \cap C$) **or** ($A \cap B \cap \bar{C}$) **or** ($A \cap B \cap C$) take place.

∴ Required Probability

= P($\bar{A} \cap B \cap C$) + P($A \cap \bar{B} \cap C$) + P($A \cap B \cap \bar{C}$) + P($A \cap B \cap C$) ... mutually exclusively events

= $\left(\frac{3}{4}\right)\left(\frac{2}{3}\right)\left(\frac{3}{4}\right) + \left(\frac{1}{4}\right)\left(\frac{1}{3}\right)\left(\frac{3}{4}\right) + \left(\frac{1}{4}\right)\left(\frac{2}{3}\right)\left(\frac{1}{4}\right) + \left(\frac{1}{4}\right)\left(\frac{2}{3}\right)\left(\frac{3}{4}\right)$ ... independent events

= $\frac{3}{8} + \frac{1}{16} + \frac{1}{24} + \frac{1}{8} = \frac{29}{48} = 0.604$

Problem 9: In a certain examination three papers were administered and following were the results: 30%, 20%, and 25% of the candidates failed in papers 1, 2, and 3 respectively. 10% failed in both papers 1 and 2, 8% failed in papers 2 and 3 and 6% failed in papers 1 and 3. 2% failed in all papers. If a candidate is selected at random find:

(i) The probability that he has failed in either of the three papers.

(ii) Probability that the candidate has passed in all 3 papers.

Solution: Let A - Event that candidate fails in paper 1. B - Event that candidate fails in paper 2. C - Event that candidate fails in paper 3.

∴ We have, P(A) = 0.30, P(B) = 0.20, P(C) = 0.25 and

P(A∩B) = 0.1, P(B∩C) = 0.08, P(A∩C) = 0.06 and P(A∩B∩C) = 0.02.

(i) Probability that the candidate has failed in either of the three papers

= P(A∪B∪C)

= P(A) + P(B) + P(C) − P(A∩B) − P(B∩C) − P(A∩C) + P(A∩B∩C)

= 0.30 + 0.20 + 0.25 − 0.1 − 0.08 − 0.06 + 0.02

= 0.53

(ii) Probability that the candidate passes in all papers = 1 − Probability that he fails in either of the three papers

i.e. $P(\bar{A} \cap \bar{B} \cap \bar{C})$ = 1 − P(A∪B∪C) = 1 − 0.53 = 0.47

Problem 10: Four cards are drawn at random from a pack of 52 cards. Find the probability that:

(i) They are a king, a queen, a jack, and an ace.

(ii) Two are kings and two are jacks

(iii) All are clubs

(iv) All are red or all are blacks.

Solution: Four cards can be drawn from a well shuffled pack in n = $^{52}C_4$ number of ways.

(i) One king can be drawn from 4 kings in $^4C_1$ number of ways. Similarly a queen, a jack and an ace each can be drawn in $^4C_1$ number of ways. Since all must be drawn **simultaneously**, the total number of favourable cases will be $^4C_1 \times {}^4C_1 \times {}^4C_1 \times {}^4C_1$.

∴ Required Probability = $\dfrac{{}^4C_1 \times {}^4C_1 \times {}^4C_1 \times {}^4C_1}{{}^{52}C_4} = \dfrac{4 \times 4 \times 4 \times 4}{{}^{52}C_4} = \dfrac{256}{{}^{52}C_4}$

(ii) Here number of favourable cases will be $^4C_2 \times {}^4C_2$

∴ Required Probability = $\dfrac{{}^4C_2 \times {}^4C_2}{{}^{52}C_4} = \dfrac{\frac{4 \times 3}{1 \times 2} \times \frac{4 \times 3}{1 \times 2}}{{}^{52}C_4} = \dfrac{36}{{}^{52}C_4}$

(iii) Here number of favourable cases = $^{13}C_4$

∴ Required Probability = $\dfrac{^{13}C_4}{^{52}C_4}$

(iv) 4 red cards (Hearts and Diamonds) can be drawn in $^{26}C_4$ ways. Similarly, black cards can be drawn in $^{26}C_4$ ways. Also, there are no common cards. We have to find probability of drawing all red or all black cards, which are mutually exclusive events.

∴ Favourable cases = $^{26}C_4 + {}^{26}C_4$

∴ Required probability = $\dfrac{^{26}C_4 + {}^{26}C_4}{^{52}C_4} = \dfrac{2 \times {}^{26}C_4}{^{52}C_4} = \dfrac{2 \times \dfrac{26 \times 25 \times 24 \times 23}{1 \times 2 \times 3 \times 4}}{^{52}C_4}$

$= \dfrac{2 \times 26 \times 25 \times 23}{^{52}C_4} = \dfrac{52 \times 25 \times 23}{\dfrac{52 \times 51 \times 50 \times 49}{1 \times 2 \times 3 \times 4}}$

$= \dfrac{52 \times 25 \times 23 \times 2 \times 3 \times 4}{52 \times 51 \times 50 \times 49} = 0.11$

Problem 11: An urn contains 8 white and 3 red balls. If two balls are drawn at random, what is the chance that, (i) both are white, (ii) both are red, (iii) one is of each colour, (iv) both are red or both are white.

Solution: There are in all 8+3 = 11 balls in the urn. Out of these 2 balls can be drawn in $n = {}^{11}C_2 = \dfrac{11 \times 10}{1 \times 2}$ number of ways. ∴ Exhaustive number of cases = n = 55.

(i) Two balls from 8 white balls can be drawn in $^8C_2 = \dfrac{8 \times 7}{1 \times 2} = 28$ number of ways.

∴ No. of favourable outcomes = 28.

∴ Required probability = $\dfrac{28}{55}$

(ii) Two red balls can be drawn from 3 balls in $^3C_2 = \dfrac{8 \times 7}{1 \times 2} = 3$ number of ways.

∴ Required probability = $\dfrac{3}{55}$

(iii) One white ball can be drawn from 8 balls in $^8C_1 = 8$ number of ways. Also one red ball is drawn from 3 balls in $^3C_1 = 3$ number of ways. As, this must happen **simultaneously**, total number of favourable cases = 8× 3 = 24

..... as the events are independent.

∴ Required probability = $\dfrac{24}{55}$

(iv) Since the events are mutually exclusive, the number of favourable cases where both are red or both are white = $^8C_2 + {}^3C_2$ = 28 + 3 = 31.

∴ Required probability = $\dfrac{31}{55}$

OR   P (Red or White) = P (Red) + P (White)

$$= \dfrac{{}^8C_2}{55} + \dfrac{{}^3C_2}{55} = \dfrac{28}{55} + \dfrac{3}{55} = \dfrac{31}{55}$$

Problem 12: If 3 out of 20 tubes in a lot are defective and if 4 of them are randomly chosen for inspection, then what is the probability that only one of the defective tubes will be selected.

Solution: 4 tubes can be selected from a lot of 20 tubes in

$$n = {}^{20}C_4 = \dfrac{20!}{4!(20-4)!} = \dfrac{20!}{4!(16!)} = \dfrac{20 \times 19 \times 18 \times 17}{1 \times 2 \times 3 \times 4} \text{ ways.}$$

The sample of 4 tubes should have only one defective tube. Hence, there should be 1 defective tube (out of 3) and 3 non defective tubes (out of remaining 17) simultaneously. Now one tube can be selected from 3 defective tubes in $^3C_1$ = 3 ways and 3 tubes can be selected from 17 non-defective tubes in $^{17}C_3 = \dfrac{17 \times 16 \times 15}{1 \times 2 \times 3}$ ways.

No. of ways in which one defective **and** 3 non defective tubes are selected = $^3C_1 \times {}^{17}C_3$

∴ Required probability = $\dfrac{{}^3C_1 \times {}^{17}C_3}{{}^{20}C_4} = \dfrac{3 \times \dfrac{17 \times 16 \times 15}{1 \times 2 \times 3}}{\dfrac{20 \times 19 \times 18 \times 17}{1 \times 2 \times 3 \times 4}}$

$$= \dfrac{3 \times 17 \times 16 \times 15}{2 \times 3} \times \dfrac{2 \times 3 \times 4}{20 \times 19 \times 18 \times 17} = \dfrac{8}{19} = 0.421$$

Problem 13: A committee of four has to be formed from among 3 economists, 4 engineers, 2 statisticians and 1 doctor.

(i) What is the probability that each of four professions is represented in the committee?

(ii) What is the probability that the committee consists of the doctor and at least one economist?

Solution: There are 3 + 4 + 2 + 1 = 10 members in all.

∴ A committee of 4 can be formed in total of n = $^{10}C_4 = \dfrac{10 \times 9 \times 8 \times 7}{1 \times 2 \times 3 \times 4}$ number of ways.

(i) One economist can be included from 3 in $^3C_1 = 3$ number of ways. Similarly 1 engineer, 1 statistician and 1 doctor can be included in $^4C_1, ^2C_1$ and $^1C_1$ number of ways respectively. This must happen **simultaneously** and as these are **independent events**, the total number of favourable cases = $^3C_1 \times ^4C_1 \times ^2C_1 \times ^1C_1 = 3 \times 4 \times 2 \times 1 = 24$.

∴ Required probability = $\dfrac{24}{210} = \dfrac{4}{35}$

(ii) The committee must have one doctor and at least one economist. Hence, the composition could be: [1 doctor **and** 1 economist **and** 2 others (from 4 + 2 = 6)] **or** [1 doctor **and** 2 economists **and** 1 other] **or** [1 doctor **and** 3 economists]

These are mutually exclusive cases.

∴ Required probability = $\dfrac{^1C_1 \times ^3C_1 \times ^6C_2}{^{10}C_4} + \dfrac{^1C_1 \times ^3C_2 \times ^6C_1}{^{10}C_4} + \dfrac{^1C_1 \times ^3C_3}{^{10}C_4}$

$= \dfrac{1}{^{10}C_4}\left[1 \times 3 \times \dfrac{6 \times 5}{1 \times 2} + 1 \times \dfrac{3 \times 2}{1 \times 2} \times 6 + 1 \times 1\right]$

$= \dfrac{(45 + 18 + 1)}{210} = \dfrac{64}{210} = 0.305$

Problem 14: There are 4 hotels in a certain town. If 3 men check into hotels in a day, what is the chance that each checks into a different hotel.

Solution: Since each man can check into any one of the four hotels i.e. in $^4C_1 = 4$ number of ways and as there are 3 men, Total number of exhaustive cases = $4 \times 4 \times 4 = 64$.

Now, they must check into different hotels. Thus, first man can check into any of the four hotels in $^4C_1 = 4$ ways, the second can check into any one of the remaining 3 hotels in $^3C_1 = 3$ ways and the third man can check into any one of the remaining 2 hotels in $^2C_1 = 2$ number of ways. This must happen simultaneously. Hence, total number of favourable cases = $4 \times 3 \times 2 = 24$.

∴ Required probability = $\dfrac{24}{64} = 0.375$

Problem 15: A box contains 25 articles including 5 defectives. Two articles are drawn one after the other at random. What is the probability that they are both defective when, (i) The first is replaced before drawing the second, (ii) The first is not replaced.

Solution: A - Event of drawing a defective article in first draw.

B - Event of drawing a defective article in second draw.

(i) Here, the events are independent as the article is replaced. Thus, for second draw also there will be 25 articles in the box.

Now, $P(A) = \dfrac{5}{25} = \dfrac{1}{5}$

Also, $P(B) = \dfrac{5}{25} = \dfrac{1}{5}$

∴ $P(A \cap B) = P(A) \cdot P(B) = \dfrac{1}{5} \cdot \dfrac{1}{5} = \dfrac{1}{25}$

(ii) If the first article is not replaced then for the second draw there will be 24 articles including 4 defectives as one defective article is already drawn. Thus, the events are dependent.

∴ $P(A) = \dfrac{5}{25} = \dfrac{1}{5}$

and probability of drawing defective article when the first event A has taken place is

$P(B/A) = \dfrac{4}{24} = \dfrac{1}{6}$

∴ $P(A \cap B) = P(A) \cdot P(B/A) = \dfrac{1}{5} \cdot \dfrac{1}{6} = \dfrac{1}{30}$

Problem 16: A box contains six white and eight red balls. The second box contains nine white and ten red balls. One ball is drawn at random from the first box and put in the second box without noticing it's colour. A ball is drawn at random from the second box. What is the probability that it is red?

Solution: First box contains 6(W) + 8(R) = 14 balls.

∴ Probability of drawing a white ball from the first box is, $P(W) = \dfrac{6}{14}$

and probability of drawing a red ball is, $P(R) = \dfrac{8}{14}$

Now, two dependent cases can take place:

(i) The ball drawn from first box and kept in second box is white.

∴ Second box has (9+1)(W) + 10(R) = 20 balls.

∴ Probability of drawing a red ball now = $P(R/W) = \dfrac{10}{20}$

(ii) If the first ball is red, then second box will have 9(W) + (10 + 1)(R) = 20 balls again

and probability of drawing a red ball now = $P(R/R) = \dfrac{11}{20}$.

Thus we have,

Probability of drawing a red ball from second box

= P(Transferring white ball and drawing red ball) or P(Transferring red ball and drawing red ball)

= P(W) . P(R/W) + P(R) . P(R/R)

$$= \left(\frac{6}{14}\right)\left(\frac{10}{20}\right)+\left(\frac{8}{14}\right)\left(\frac{11}{20}\right)=\frac{60+88}{(14)(20)}=\frac{148}{280}=\frac{37}{70}=0.523$$

Problem 17: A card is drawn from a pack of cards. What is the chance of drawing a red queen given that the card drawn was a face card?

Solution: We have, n = 52.

Let A - Event of drawing a red queen (Heart or Diamond)

B - Event of drawing a face card (King, Queen or Jack)

$$\therefore P(A) = \frac{2}{52}$$

and $$P(B) = \frac{3 \times 4}{52} = \frac{12}{52}$$

We have to find the probability that the card is a red queen given that it is a face card i.e. P(A/B)

Now, $$P(A \cap B) = P(B) . P(A/B)$$

$$\therefore P(A/B) = \frac{P(A \cap B)}{P(B)}$$

Now, m i.e. number of favourable cases for (A∩B) = 2,

$$\therefore P(A \cap B) = \frac{2}{52}$$

$$\therefore P(A/B) = \frac{\frac{2}{52}}{\frac{12}{52}} = \frac{2}{12} = \frac{1}{6}$$

Problem 18: The probability that a person stopping at a petrol pump will get his tyre checked 0.12, the probability that he will get his oil checked is 0.29 and the probability that he will get both checked is 0.07.

(i) What is the probability that the person will have neither his tyres nor oil checked?

(ii) Find the probability that a person who has his oil checked will also have tyres checked.

(iii) Find the probability that a person checks tyres but not oil.   **(P.U. MBA- Dec.05)**

Solution: Let A - Event that the person will have his tyres checked.

B - Event that the person will have his oil checked.

∴ We have, $P(A) = 0.12$, $P(B) = 0.29$ and $P(A \cap B) = 0.07$

(i) P(Person will have neither checked)

$$= 1 - P(\text{person will have either tyre or oil checked})$$
$$= 1 - P(A \cup B) = 1 - [P(A) + P(B) - P(A \cap B)]$$
$$= 1 - (0.12 + 0.29 - 0.07) = 1 - (0.34) = 0.66$$

(ii) Probability that the person will have his tyres checked who already has his oil checked i.e.

$$P(A/B) = \frac{(A \cap B)}{P(B)} = \frac{0.07}{0.29} = 0.24$$

(iii) We have to find the probability that person checks tyres but not oil i.e. $P(A \cap \bar{B})$

Now ∵ we have, $P(A) = P(A \cap B) + P(A \cap \bar{B})$ **(Note this step)**

∴ $P(A \cap \bar{B}) = P(A) - P(A \cap B)$

$$= 0.12 - 0.07 = 0.05$$

Problem 19: It is known that 15% of the males and 10% of the females in a town having equal number of them, are unemployed. A person is selected at random from the town. What is the probability that

(i) He is employed.

(ii) He is male known that he is employed.

Solution: Let M - Person selected is a male   F - Person selected is a female

E - Person selected is employed

∴ $\bar{E}$ = Person selected is unemployed

Since, the population of males and females is same

∴ $P(M) = 0.5$ and $P(F) = 0.5$.

Also, $P(\bar{E}/M) = 15\% = 0.15$, $P(\bar{E}/F) = 10\% = 0.1$

∴ P(Person is employed given that he is male)

$$= P(E/M) = 1 - P(\bar{E}/M) = 1 - 0.15 = 0.85$$ **(Note this step)**

Similarly, $P(E/F) = 1 - 0.1 = 0.9$

(i) Now, P(The person is Employed) i.e.

$P(E)$ = P(Person is a male and he is employed) + P(Person is a female and is employed)

$= P(M \cap E) + P(F \cap E)$

$= P(M) P(E/M) + P(F) P(E/F)$

$= (0.5)(0.85) + (0.5)(0.9)$

$= 0.425 + 0.45 = 0.875$

(ii) We have to find the probability that the person is a male given that he is employed i.e. P(M/E)

$$\therefore P(M/E) = \frac{P(M \cap E)}{P(E)} = \frac{P(M) P(E/M)}{P(E)}$$

$$= \frac{(0.5)(0.85)}{0.875} = 0.486$$

Alternately, by Bayes' Theorem,

We have, $$P(M/E) = \frac{P(M) P(E/M)}{P(M) P(E/M) + P(F) P(E/F)}$$

$$= \frac{(0.5)(0.85)}{(0.5)(0.85) + (0.5)(0.9)}$$

$$= \frac{0.425}{0.425 + 0.45} = \frac{0.425}{0.875} = 0.486$$

Problem 20: The probability that a car one year old will pass the pollution test is 0.992 and not pass the pollution test is 0.008. An insurance company intends to sell the car owners of one year old cars a policy of ₹ 10,000/- for a premium of ₹ 100/-. Find the insurance company's expected gain.

Solution: We have,

p = Probability that the car will pass the pollution test
= 0.992

and q = Probability that the car will not pass the pollution test
= 0.008

Now, if the Insurance Company offers the scheme, the revenue received per car = premium = ₹ 100/-

However, it will have to make payments to the claimants whose probability is 0.008.

Hence, the amount which the company has to pay to settle the claims (i.e. the amount to be paid if the car fails the test)

= (Probability of failure) (Amount of policy)

= (0.008)10,000 = ₹80/-

Thus, the company has to spend ₹80/- per car

∴ Net expected gain per car = 100 – 80 = ₹ 20/-

Problem 21: At the college entrance examination, each candidate is admitted or rejected according to whether he has passed or failed at the test. Of the candidates who are really capable 75% pass the test and of the incapable 25% pass the test. Given that 40% of the candidates are really capable, find the proportion of capable college students.

Solution: Let there be x number of total candidates

∴ Number of capable candidates = 40% of x = $\dfrac{40}{100} \times x = \dfrac{4x}{10}$

∴ Number of incapable candidates = $x - \dfrac{4x}{10} = \dfrac{6x}{10}$

75% of capable candidates pass the examination

∴ Number of capable students = $\dfrac{75}{100}\left(\dfrac{4x}{10}\right) = \dfrac{3}{4}\left(\dfrac{4x}{10}\right) = \dfrac{3x}{10}$

Similarly, Number of incapable students = $\dfrac{25}{100}\left(\dfrac{6x}{10}\right) = \dfrac{1}{4}\left(\dfrac{6x}{10}\right) = \dfrac{3x}{20}$

∴ Total Number of students = $\dfrac{3x}{10} + \dfrac{3x}{20} = \dfrac{6x + 3x}{20} = \dfrac{9x}{20}$

∴ Proportion of capable students = $\dfrac{\text{Number of capable students}}{\text{Total number of students}}$

$= \dfrac{\dfrac{3x}{10}}{\dfrac{9x}{20}} = \dfrac{3x}{10} \times \dfrac{20}{9x} = \dfrac{2}{3}$

Problem 22: A movie house is filled with 700 people of which 60% are females. 70% are seated in no smoking area including 300 females. A person is selected at random. Find the probability that:

(i) Person is a male,
(ii) Person is a male or non-smoker,
(iii) Person is a smoker, if person is known to be male.

Solution: Total Number of People = n = 700

Number of females = $\dfrac{60}{100}(700) = 420$

∴ Number of males = 700 − 420 = 280

Number of Non-smoking people = $\dfrac{70}{100}(700) = 490$

Of these 300 are females.

∴ Number of Non-smoking males = 490 – 300 = 190

∴ Number of smoking males = 280 – 190 = 90 and

Number of smoking females = 420 – 300 = 120

∴ Total number of smoking people = 90 + 120 = 210

(i) ∴ Probability that the person selected is a male = $\dfrac{280}{700} = \dfrac{4}{10} = 0.4$

(ii) Probability (male or non-smoker)

= P(male) + P(non-smoker) – P(male and non-smoker)

= $\dfrac{280}{700} + \dfrac{490}{700} - \dfrac{190}{700} = \dfrac{580}{700} = \dfrac{29}{35} = 0.828$

(iii) Let A - Event that the person is smoker

B - Event that the person is male,

$P(A) = \dfrac{210}{700}$ and $P(B) = \dfrac{280}{700}$ and P(smoking males) = $P(A \cap B) = \dfrac{90}{700}$.

We have to find the probability that the person is a smoker if he is known to be male i.e. P(A/B)

Now, $P(A/B) = \dfrac{P(A \cap B)}{P(B)}$

$= \dfrac{\frac{90}{700}}{\frac{280}{700}} = \dfrac{90}{280} = 0.321$

Problem 23: In 1989 there were three candidates for the position of principal Mr. Chatterji, Mr. Ayangar and Dr. Singh, whose chances of getting the appointment are in the proportion 4 : 2 : 3 respectively. The probability that Mr. Chatterji if selected, would introduce co-education in the college is 0.3. The probabilities of Mr. Ayangar and Dr. Singh doing the same are respectively 0.5 and 0.8. What is the probability that there is co-education in the college in 1990?

Solution : Let A_1 - Event that Mr. Chatterji is appointed

A_2 - Event that Mr. Ayangar is appointed

A_3 - Event that Dr. Singh is appointed and

E - Event that Co-education is introduced.

Now, Co-education will be introduced if events
(A_1 and E) **or** (A_2 and E) **or** (A_3 and E) take place

∴ $P(E) = P(A_1 \cap E) + P(A_2 \cap E) + P(A_3 \cap E)$
$= P(A_1) \cdot P(E/A_1) + P(A_2) \cdot P(E/A_2) + P(A_3) \cdot P(E/A_3)$

...as events A_1 and E etc., are dependent.

As the proportions of the selection chances are given as 4 : 2 : 3.

∴ $P(A_1) = \dfrac{4}{4+2+3} = \dfrac{4}{9}$, $P(A_2) = \dfrac{2}{9}$ and $P(A_3) = \dfrac{3}{9}$

Also, probabilities of each person, introducing co-education are given

∴ $P(E/A_1) = 0.3$, $P(E/A_2) = 0.5$, $P(E/A_3) = 0.8$,

∴ $P(E) = \dfrac{4}{9}(0.3) + \dfrac{2}{9}(0.5) + \dfrac{3}{9}(0.8)$

$= 0.1333 + 0.1111 + 0.2667 = 0.5111$

∴ Required Probability is 0.51

Problem 24: The probability that there is at least one error in an account statement prepared by A is 0.2, for B and C they are 0.25 and 0.4 respectively. A, B and C prepared 10, 16 and 20 statements respectively. Find the expected number of correct statements in all.

Solution: We have,

P(A) = Probability that there is at least one error in an account statement prepared by A.
= Probability that the account statement prepared by A is incorrect.
= 0.2

Similarly, P(B) = 0.25 and P(C) = 0.4

∴ If A prepares 10 statements,

No. of incorrect statements = 10 × P(A) = 10 × 0.2 = 2

Similarly, No. of incorrect statements of B = 16 × P(B) = 16 × 0.25 = 4

and No. of incorrect statements of C = 20 × P(C) = 20 × 0.4 = 8

∴ Total Number of incorrect statements = 2 + 4 + 8 = 14

∴ Expected Number of Correct Statements = (10 + 16 + 20) − 14 = 46 − 14 = 32

Problem 25: A candidate is selected for interview for three posts. For the first post there are three candidates, for the second there are 4, and for the third there are 2. What is the probability that a candidate is selected for at least one post.

Solution: Let A - Event that the candidate is selected for the first post.
B - Event that the candidate is selected for the second post.
C - Event that the candidate is selected for the third post.

∴ We have,

$$P(A) = \frac{1}{3}, P(B) = \frac{1}{4} \text{ and } P(C) = \frac{1}{2}$$

∴ $P(\bar{A}) = 1 - P(A) = 1 - \frac{1}{3} = \frac{2}{3}$, $P(\bar{B}) = 1 - \frac{1}{4} = \frac{3}{4}$ and $P(\bar{C}) = 1 - \frac{1}{2} = \frac{1}{2}$

P (candidate is selected at least for one post)
= 1 − P (candidate is not selected for any of the posts)
= 1 − P($\bar{A} \cap \bar{B} \cap \bar{C}$)
= 1 − P($\bar{A}$) P($\bar{B}$) P($\bar{C}$)   ∵ $\bar{A}, \bar{B}, \bar{C}$ are independent events
= $1 - \frac{2}{3} \cdot \frac{3}{4} \cdot \frac{1}{2} = 1 - \frac{1}{4}$
= $\frac{3}{4}$

Problem 26: There are two identical boxes containing respectively 4 white and 3 red balls, and 3 white and 7 red balls. A box is chosen at random and a ball is drawn from it. If the ball is white, what is the probability that it is from the first box.

Solution: Let A - Event that the first box is chosen.
                     B - Event that the second box is chosen.
                     W - A ball selected is white.

∴ Since, a box is chosen randomly from the two boxes,

∴ $P(A) = \frac{1}{2}$ and $P(B) = \frac{1}{2}$

Now, we have to find the probability that the ball is drawn from the first box given that it is a white ball i.e. P(A/W)

∴ By Bayes' Theorem

$$P(A/W) = \frac{P(A)\,P(W/A)}{P(A)\,P(W/A) + P(B)\,P(W/B)}$$

Now, since the first box has 4 white and 3 red balls,

∴ $P(W/B) = \frac{4}{4+3} = \frac{4}{7}$ and

as the second box has 3 white and 7 red balls,

∴ $P(W/B) = \frac{3}{3+7} = \frac{3}{10}$

$$\therefore \quad P(A/W) = \frac{\left(\dfrac{1}{2}\right)\left(\dfrac{4}{7}\right)}{\left(\dfrac{1}{2}\right)\left(\dfrac{4}{7}\right)+\left(\dfrac{1}{2}\right)\left(\dfrac{3}{10}\right)} = \frac{\dfrac{4}{7}}{\dfrac{4}{7}+\dfrac{3}{10}}$$

$$= \frac{\dfrac{4}{7}}{\dfrac{61}{70}} = \frac{4}{7} \cdot \frac{70}{61} = \frac{40}{61}$$

$$= 0.656$$

Problem 27: There are 50 applications for a job in a factory. Some of them are MBA's and some are not. Some of them have at least 2 years experience and some have not with the following exact breakdown.

	MBA	Non-MBA
At least 2 years experience	11	6
Less than 2 years experience	19	14

If the order in which the applicants are interviewed by the factory manager is random. M is the event that first applicant interviewed is a MBA and E is the event that first applicant interviewed has at least 2 years experience. Find (i) P(M) (ii) P(E') (iii) P(M/E) (iv) P(M'∩E') (v) P(E'/M').

Solution: We have,

M - Event that the first applicant is MBA

$\therefore$ M' - Event that the first applicant is Non-MBA

Similarly,

E - Event that the first applicant has at least 2 years work experience.

$\therefore$ E' - Event that the first applicant has less than 2 years experience.

Now, total number of applicants = n = 50

(i) No. of MBA applicants = m = 11+19 = 30

$$\therefore \quad P(M) = \frac{m}{n} = \frac{30}{50} = \frac{3}{5}$$

(ii) Now, Number of applicants with less than 2 years experience = 19 + 14 = 33

$$\therefore \quad P(E') = \frac{33}{50}$$

(iii) We have, $\quad P(M\cap E) = P(E)\, P(M/E)$ ... (1)

Now, No. of applicants who are both MBA and experienced = 11

$$\therefore \quad P(M\cap E) = \frac{11}{50}$$

Also, no. of experienced candidates = 11 + 6 = 17

∴ $P(E) = \dfrac{17}{50}$

∴ From (1), $\dfrac{11}{50} = \dfrac{17}{50} P(M/E)$

∴ $P(M/E) = \dfrac{11}{17}$

Alternately, we have, No. of Experienced Candidates = 11 + 6 = 17 and
No. of MBA Candidates among the Experienced = 11

$P(M/E)$ = P(Candidate is MBA given that he is experienced) = $\dfrac{11}{17}$

(iv) We have,

Number of candidates who are Non-MBA's (i.e. M') and not having experience (i.e. E') = 14

∴ $P(M' \cap E') = \dfrac{14}{50}$

(v) Number of Non-MBA Candidates = 6+14 = 20

Number of inexperienced candidates among these Non-MBA's = 14

∴ $P(E'/M')$ = P(Candidate is inexperienced given that he is Non-MBA)

$= \dfrac{14}{20} = \dfrac{7}{10}$

Alternately, $P(M' \cap E') = P(M') P(E'/M')$

∴ $P(E'/M') = \dfrac{P(M' \cap E')}{P(M')} = \dfrac{\frac{14}{50}}{1 - P(M)} = \dfrac{\frac{14}{50}}{1 - \frac{3}{5}} = \dfrac{\frac{14}{50}}{\frac{2}{5}}$

$= \dfrac{14}{50} \cdot \dfrac{5}{2} = \dfrac{7}{10}$

Problem 28: From a computer tally based on employee records, the personnel manager of a large manufacturing firm finds that 15% of the firm's employees are supervisors and 25% of the firm's employees are college graduates. He also discovers that 5% of the firms employees are both supervisors and college graduates. Suppose that an employee is selected at random from the firm's personnel record find the

(i) Probability of selecting a person who is both a college graduate and a supervisor.

(ii) Probability of selecting a person who is neither a supervisor nor a college graduate.

Solution: Let S - Event than an employee is a Supervisor
C - Event that an employee is a college graduate.
∵ 15% of the employees are supervisors
∴   P(S) = 0.15
Similarly,   P(C) = 0.25
Also, P (an employee is a supervisor and a college graduate)
= P(S∩C) = 0.05
(i) P (A person selected is both a college graduate and a supervisor)
= P(C∩S) = P(S∩C) = 0.05
(ii) P (A person selected is neither a supervisor nor a college graduate)
= 1 – P (The person is a supervisor or a college graduate)
= 1 – P(S∪C)
= 1 – [P(S) + P(C) – P(S∩C)]
= 1 – [0.15 + 0.25 – 0.05] = 1 – 0.35
= 0.65

Problem 29: An insurance company insured 1500 scooter drivers, 3500 car drivers and 5000 truck drivers. The probability of an accident is 0.05, 0.02 and 0.10 respectively in case of scooter, car and truck drivers. One of the insured person meets an accident. What is the probability that he is a car driver? **(P.U.MBA - May 05)**

Solution: Let S - Event that an insured driver is a scooter driver
C - Event that an insured driver is a car driver
T - Event that an insured driver is a Truck driver
and   A - Event that an insured driver meets with an accident.

We have to find the probability that the person met with an accident is a car driver i.e. probability that the person is a car driver given that he has met with an accident i.e. P(C/A)
Here, total number of drivers = 1500 + 3500 + 5000 = 10000

∴ Probability that a driver is a scooter driver i.e. P(S) = $\dfrac{1500}{10000}$ = 0.15

Similarly, P(C) = $\dfrac{3500}{10000}$ = 0.35 and P(T) = $\dfrac{5000}{10000}$ = 0.50

Also, probability of an accident in case of a scooter driver = 0.05 (given)
i.e. P (a driver meets an accident given that he is a scooter driver)
i.e.   P(A/S) = 0.05
Similarly,   P(A/C) = 0.02
and   P(A/T) = 0.10
Now, we have to find the probability P(C/A)

∴ By using Bayes' Theorem we have,

$$P(C/A) = \frac{P(C)\ P(A/C)}{P(S)\ P(A/S) + P(C)\ P(A/C) + P(T)\ P(A/T)}$$

$$= \frac{(0.35)(0.02)}{(0.15)(0.05) + (0.35)(0.02) + (0.50)(0.10)}$$

$$= \frac{0.007}{0.0075 + 0.007 + 0.05} = \frac{0.007}{0.0645} = 0.109$$

Note: Similarly, we can find P(the person is a scooter driver given that he has met with an accident)

i.e.
$$P(S/A) = \frac{P(S)\ P(A/S)}{P(S)\ P(A/S) + P(C)\ P(A/C) + P(T)\ P(A/T)} = \frac{0.0075}{0.0645} = 0.116$$

and
$$P(T/A) = \frac{P(T)\ P(A/T)}{P(S)\ P(A/S) + P(C)\ P(A/C) + P(T)\ P(A/T)} = \frac{0.05}{0.0645} = 0.775$$

Problem 30: An investment firm purchases 3 stocks for one week trading purposes. It assesses the probability that the stocks will increase in value in the week is 0.8, 0.7 and 0.6 respectively. What is the chance that (i) All three stocks will increase, (ii) Atleast two stocks will increase, (iii) Only one will increase. **(P.U.MBA - May 09)**

Solution: Let
A - Event that the value of 1st stock will increase
B - Even that the value of 2nd stock will increase
C - Event that the value of 3rd stock will increase

∴ We have, P(A) = 0.8, P(B) = 0.7 and P(C) = 0.6
∴ P(1st stock will not increase)

i.e. $P(\overline{A}) = 1 - P(A) = 1 - 0.8 = 0.2$

Similarly, $P(\overline{B}) = 1 - 0.7 = 0.3$

and $P(\overline{C}) = 1 - 0.6 = 0.4$

(i) ∴ P (All three stocks will increase)
= P(1st will increase and 2nd will increase and 3rd will increase)
= P(A∩B∩C)
= P(A) · P(B) · (C) ... being independent events
= 0.8 (0.7) (0.6) = 0.336

(ii) P (At least two stocks will increase)
= P(two stocks will increase or three stocks will increase)
= P(two stocks will increase) + P(three stocks will increase)
... these being mutually exclusive events
= P[(A∩B∩$\overline{C}$) or (A∩$\overline{B}$∩C) or ($\overline{A}$∩B∩C)] + P(A∩B∩C)

$= P(A \cap B \cap \bar{C}) + P(A \cap \bar{B} \cap C) + P(\bar{A} \cap B \cap C) + P(A \cap B \cap C)$

... again the events being mutually exclusive

$= P(A) \cdot P(B) \cdot P(\bar{C}) + P(A) P(\bar{B}) P(C) + P(\bar{A}) P(B) P(C) + 0.336$

... being independent events

and $\because P(A \cap B \cap C) = 0.336$ from earlier

$= 0.8(0.7)(0.4) + 0.8(0.3)(0.6) + 0.2(0.7)(0.6) + 0.336$

$= 0.224 + 0.144 + 0.084 + 0.336 = 0.788$

(iii) Again P(only one will increase)

$= P[(A \cap \bar{B} \cap \bar{C}) \cup (\bar{A} \cap B \cap \bar{C}) \cup (\bar{A} \cap \bar{B} \cap C)]$

$= P(A \cap \bar{B} \cap \bar{C}) + P(\bar{A} \cap B \cap \bar{C}) + P(\bar{A} \cap \bar{B} \cap C)]$

$= P(A) \cdot P(\bar{B}) \cdot P(\bar{C}) + P(\bar{A}) \cdot P(B) \cdot P(\bar{C}) + P(\bar{A}) P(\bar{B}) \cdot P(C)$

$= 0.8(0.3)(0.4) + 0.2(0.7)(0.4) + 0.2(0.3)(0.6)$

$= 0.096 + 0.056 + 0.036 = 0.188$

Problem 31: Probability that a man will be alive 5 years hence is 0.35 and probability that his wife will be alive 5 years hence is 0.42. Find the probability that 5 years hence (i) only wife is alive, (ii) Exactly one of them is alive, (iii) none of them is alive. **(P.U. MBA - May 10)**

Solution: Let A - Event that the man is alive 5 years hence

B - Event that his wife is alive 5 years hence

Hence, we have

$P(A) = 0.35$ and $P(B) = 0.42$

∴ P(The man is not alive 5 years hence)

i.e. $P(\bar{A}) = 1 - P(A)$

$= 1 - 0.35 = 0.65$

Similarly, $P(\bar{B}) = 1 - P(B)$

$= 1 - 0.42 = 0.58$

(i) Probability that only wife is alive

i.e. P(Wife is alive and the mean is not alive)

$= P(B \cap \bar{A})$

$= P(B) \cdot P(\bar{A})$ ... B and $\bar{A}$ being independent events

$= 0.42 (0.65) = 0.273$

(ii) P(exactly one of them is alive)

i.e. P[(Man is alive and wife is not) or (Man is not alive and wife is alive)]

$$= P[(A \cap \bar{B}) \cup (\bar{A} \cap B)]$$

$$= P(A \cap \bar{B}) + P(\bar{A} \cap B) \quad \ldots (A \cap \bar{B}) \text{ and } (\bar{A} \cap B) \text{ being mutually exclusive events}$$
as only one of them is possible at a time

$$= P(A) \cdot P(\bar{B}) + P(\bar{A}) \cdot P(B) \quad \ldots \text{being independent events}$$

$$= (0.35)(0.58) + (0.65)(0.42)$$

$$= 0.203 + 0.273 = 0.476$$

(iii) P(None of them is alive)

i.e. P(man is not alive and wife is not alive)

$$= P(\bar{A} \cap \bar{B})$$

$$= P(\bar{A}) \cdot P(\bar{B}) \quad \ldots \text{independent events}$$

$$= (0.65)(0.58) = 0.377$$

Problem 32: The contents of three urns 1, 2, 3 are as follows:
1 White, 2 Black, 3 Red Balls; 2 White, 1 Black, 1 Red Balls; 4 White, 5 Black, 3 Red Balls. One urn is selected at random and two balls drawn. They happen to be White and Red. What is the probability that they came from urn 2. **(P.U. MBA - Dec. 10)**

Solution: Let A - Event that the first urn is selected

B - Event that the second urn is selected

C - Event that the third urn is selected

D - Event that a combination of 1 White and 1 Red ball is selected

We have to find the probability that urn 2 is selected when the 2 balls selected happen to be White and Red i.e. P(B/D).

This is given by Bayes' Theorem as

$$P(B/D) = \frac{P(B)\,P(D/B)}{P(A)\,P(D/A) + P(B)\,P(D/B) + P(C)\,P(D/C)} \quad \ldots (1)$$

Now obviously, the chance of selecting the urns will be same

i.e. $P(A) = P(B) = P(C) = \frac{1}{3}$

Now, consider urn 1 which has (1W + 2B + 3R = Total 6 balls).

The total number of ways in which 2 balls can be selected is $n = {}^6C_2$.

Number of ways in which the combination 1 White (out of 1) **and** 1 Red (out of 3) is selected (i.e. event D) is,

$$m = {}^1C_1 \times {}^3C_1$$

DECISION SCIENCES   PROBABILITY

$$\therefore \quad P(D/A) = \frac{m}{n} = \frac{{}^1C_1 \times {}^3C_1}{{}^6C_2}$$

$$= \frac{1 \times 3}{\frac{6 \times 5}{1 \times 2}} = \frac{3}{15} = 0.20$$

Similarly, $\quad P(D/B) = \frac{{}^2C_1 \times {}^1C_1}{{}^4C_2}$

$$= \frac{2 \times 1}{\frac{4 \times 3}{1 \times 2}} = \frac{1}{3} = 0.333$$

and $\quad P(D/C) = \frac{{}^4C_1 \times {}^3C_1}{{}^{12}C_2}$

$$= \frac{4 \times 3}{\frac{12 \times 11}{1 \times 2}} = \frac{12}{66} = 0.182$$

$\therefore$ From (1) we get required probability i.e.

$$P(B/D) = \frac{\frac{1}{3}(0.333)}{\frac{1}{3}(0.20) + \frac{1}{3}(0.333) + \frac{1}{3}(0.182)}$$

$$= \frac{0.333}{0.715} = 0.466$$

Problem 33: There are three stocks items, each of which can be substituted for the other. Each has stockout probability of 0.03 and is independent of others. The materials manager wants to know the probability that (i) All items in the stock, (ii) No item in the stock.

(P.U. MBA - May 12)

Solution: Let
- A - Event that the first item is not in the stack
- B - Event that the second item is not in the stock
- C - Event that the third item is not in the stock

$\therefore$ We have,

$$P(A) = P(B) = P(C) = 0.03 \quad (\text{given})$$

Hence, Probability that the first items is in the stock is

$$P(\bar{A}) = 1 - P(A)$$
$$= 1 - 0.03 = 0.97$$

Similarly, $P(\bar{B}) = P(\bar{C}) = 0.97$

(i) ∴ P (all items are in the stock)

$$= P(\bar{A} \cap \bar{B} \cap \bar{C})$$
$$= P(\bar{A}) \cdot P(\bar{B}) \cdot P(\bar{C}) \qquad \text{... being independent events}$$
$$= 0.97 \, (0.97) \, (0.97) = 0.913$$

(ii) P (No items in the stock)

$$= P(A \cap B \cap C)$$
$$= P(A) \cdot P(B) \cdot P(C) \qquad \text{... being independent events}$$
$$= 0.03 \, (0.03) \, (0.03)$$
$$= 0.000027$$

Problem 34: It has been found that 80% of all the tourists who visit India visit Delhi, 70% of them visit Mumbai and 60% of them visit both. What is the probability that a tourist will visit at least one city? Also find the probability that he will visit neither city?

(P.U.MBA - Dec. 11)

Solution: Let D - Event that a tourist visits Delhi and
M - Event that a tourist visits Mumbai

Now ∵ 80% of the tourists visiting India visit Delhi

∴ Probability that a (randomly selected) tourist will visit Delhi

i.e. $\qquad P(D) = \dfrac{80}{100} = 0.8$

Similarly, $\qquad P(M) = \dfrac{70}{100} = 0.7$

Also, ∵ 60% of tourists visit both Delhi and Mumbai

∴ P(D and M) i.e. $P(D \cap M) = \dfrac{60}{100} = 0.6$

(i) Now, Probability that a tourist will visit at least one city

= Probability that he will visit Delhi **or** Mumbai **or** Both
= $P(D \cup M)$
= $P(D) + P(M) - P(D \cap M) \qquad$ ... by Addition Theorem of Probabilities
= $0.8 + 0.7 - 0.6$
= $0.9 \qquad\qquad\qquad\qquad\qquad\qquad\qquad\qquad$ ... (1)

(ii) Probability that he will visit neither city

= 1 - probability that he will visit at least one of the cities
= $1 - 0.9 \qquad\qquad\qquad\qquad\qquad\qquad\qquad$ ... using (1)
= 0.1

Exercise

1. Explain the concept of probability. Give two examples.
2. Define the following terms:
   (i) Event, (ii) Equally likely events, (iii) Mutually exclusive events, (iv) Exhaustive events. (v) Dependent and Independent events.
3. State various Theorems of Probability.
4. Write a note on: Conditional Probability and Bayes' Theorem.
5. Three coins are tossed simultaneously. What is the probability that
   (i) They will show all heads.
   (ii) They will show odd number of tails.
   (iii) There will be at least one tail.
   (**Ans.:** 1/8, 1/2, 7/8)
6. A committee of 5 is to be formed from a group of 8 boys and 7 girls. Find the probability that the committee consists of 3 boys and 2 girls.
   (**Ans.:** 0.392)
7. Following data gives the service time required for first 50 customers in a bank. Find the probability that:
   (i) New customer will require 4.5 to 6.5 minutes.
   (ii) The customer will require more than 10.5 minutes.
   (iii) Customer will require less than 6.5 minutes.

Service Time (Class intervals) in min.	0.0-2.5	2.5-4.5	4.5-6.5	6.5-8.5	8.5-10.5	10.5-12.5	12.5-14.5
No. of customers	3	7	15	10	6	7	2

   (**Ans.:** 0.3, 0.18, 0.5)
8. In a certain college there are 320 students. 160 of them play cricket, 80 play football and 35 play both the games. If one is selected at random what is the chance that he plays either cricket or football?
   (**Ans.:** 0.64)
9. The probability that the two newly released films X and Y will succeed at the box-office are 0.6 and 0.7 respectively. What is the probability that, (i) only X will succeed, (ii) only Y will succeed, (iii) none of them will succeed, (iv) at least one will succeed, (v) only one will succeed, (vi) both will succeed.
   (**Ans.:** 0.15, 0.3, 0.1, 0.9, 0.45, 0.45)

10. What is the chance that a non-leap year should have fifty-three Sundays.
    (**Ans.:** 1/7)
11. In a certain hospital 60% of the patients are suffering from Typhoid, 50% are suffering from Cholera and 30% are suffering from both the diseases. If a patient is selected at random, what is the chance that he will be (i) Suffering from Typhoid or Cholera (ii) Suffering from neither of the diseases.
    (**Ans.:** 0.8, 0.2)
12. A textile mill produces cloth in three different shades - blue, black, and brown. Production of these shades is 30%, 50% and 20% respectively of the total production. It is found from experience that 2%, 3%, and 4% of blue, black and brown shades respectively are defective. On general inspection of the entire production a specimen is selected at random. Find the probability that: (i) It is defective. (ii) If it is defective, it is of black shade.
    (**Ans.:** 0.029, 0.517)
13. Suppose that one of three men a politician, a businessman and an educationist will be appointed as the Vice Chancellor of a University. The respective probabilities of their appointments are 0.50, 0.30 and 0.20. The probabilities that research activities will be promoted by these people if they are appointed are 0.30, 0.70 and 0.80 respectively. What is the probability that research will be promoted by the new Vice Chancellor?
    (**Ans.:** 0.52)
14. In the dairy the milk is filled in sachets of 500 gms by machines A, B and C respectively, 25%, 35% and 40% of the total output. It is also found that 5, 4 and 2 percent of the sachets respectively by machine A, B and C have either over filling or under filling of milk. A government inspector made a random check and found that the sachet was under filled and booked a case against the dairy. What are the probabilities that it was filled by machine A, B, C?
    (**Ans.:** 0.362, 0.406, 0.232)
15. In a certain locality there were 320 patients. 10 were suffering from typhoid, 12 were suffering from malaria and 2 were suffering from both. If one is selected at random, what is the probability that he is suffering either from typhoid or malaria.

    (P.U. MBA - May 05)

    (**Ans.:** 0.0625)
16. It is known that 18% of males and 12% of females in a town having equal number of them are unemployed. A person is selected at random, what is the probability that he is employed? **(P.U. MBA - Nov. 07, Dec. 11)**
    (**Ans.:** 0.85)

17. In a certain hospital 60% of the patients are suffering from tyophoid, 50% are suffering from cholera and 30% are suffering from both the diseases. If a patient is selected at random what is the chance that (i) he will be suffering from typhoid or cholera. (ii) He is suffering from only cholera.
    (**Ans.:** (i) 0.8 (ii) 0.2) **(P.U. MBA - Nov. 07)**

18. Two unbiased dice are thrown. Find the probability that the total of the numbers on the dice is 8.
    (**Ans.:** 0.1389)

19. Three machines A, B and C with capacities proportional to 4 : 2 : 3 are producing identical items. The percentage that the machine produce defectives are 4%, 3% and 5% respectively. At the end of a day from the total production one item is selected at random and is found defective. What is the chance that it came from machine B?
    (**Ans.:** 0.163)

20. A product is manufactured by a company for which it has three machines M_1, M_2 and M_3. M_1 produces 50%, M_2 produces 30% and M_3 produces 20% of the total product. Past experience shows that M_1 produces 4% defectives, M_2 produces 5% defectives and M_3 produces 6% defectives. At the end of a day from the total production, 1 unit of production is selected at random and is found to be defective. What is the chance that machine M_1 has produced it?
    (**Ans.:** 0.426)

21. There are 3 men aged 60, 65 and 70 years. The probability that they live 5 more years is 0.8 for a 60 year old, 0.6 for a 65 year old and 0.3 for a 70 year old person. Find the probability that at least two of the 3 persons will live 5 years more.
    (**Ans.:** 0.612) **(P.U.MBA - May 07)**

22. Define the following terms with illustrations:
    (i) Independent events
    (ii) Mutually exclusive events
    (iii) Occurrence of atleast one of two events
    (iv) Exhaustive Events. **(P.U MBA - Dec. 09)**

23. Probability of x, y, z becoming managers are $\frac{4}{9}, \frac{2}{9}$ and $\frac{1}{3}$ respectively. Probability that bonus scheme will be introduced if x, y, z, become managers are $\frac{3}{10}, \frac{1}{2}$ and $\frac{4}{5}$ respectively. What is probability that bonus scheme will be introduced? What is the probability that manage was x if bonus scheme is introduced.
    (**Ans.:** $\frac{23}{45}, \frac{6}{23}$) **(P.U. MBA - Dec. 08)**

24. An urn contains 4 White and 5 Black balls. A second urn contains 5 white and 4 Black balls. One ball is transferred from the first to second urn then a ball is drawn from the second urn. What is the probability that it is White? **(P.U. MBA - Dec. 09)**
    (**Ans.:** 0.544)

■■■

Chapter 10...
Probability Distributions

Contents ...
10.1 Definitions
10.2 Binomial Distribution
10.3 Poisson Distribution
10.4 Normal Distribution
10.5 Characteristics of Normal Distribution
10.6 Standard Normal Distribution
10.7 Sampling Distributions
10.8 Statistical Estimation
   List of Formulae
   Solved Problems
   Exercise

10.1 Definitions

(i) **Random Variable:** A variable whose value is determined by the outcome of a random experiment is called as a random variable or chance variable.

(ii) **Continuous Random Variable:** If the random variable takes on all values in a certain interval, then it is a Continuous Random Variable. e.g. Weight or height of students can have all values - integral as well as fractional.

(iii) **Discrete Random Variable:** If the random variable takes on only particular numerical values (say, integer values 0, 1, 2, ... etc) or separate attributes, it is called as a discrete random variable.

E.g. Number of defective items in a lot (like 1, 2, etc.), suits of playing cards (like club, heart) etc.

Now, if X is a variable assuming values $x_1, x_2, \ldots x_n$ and if $X = x_1, X = x_2, \ldots, X = x_n$ are mutually exclusive such that

$P(X = x_1) + P(X = x_2) + \ldots + P(X = x_n) = 1$.

i.e. $\sum_{i=1}^{n} P(X = x_i) = 1$ or sum of the probabilities for all values of X is 1 then X is a Discrete Random Variable.

(iv) Mathematical Expectation or Expected Value E(X): If X is a discrete random variable assuming values $x_1, x_2, ... x_n$ with their probabilities of occurrences as $P(x_1)$, $P(x_2)$, ..., $P(x_n)$, then the mathematical expectation or expected value of X is defined as:

$$E(X) = x_1 P(x_1) + x_2 P(x_2) + ... + x_n P(x_n)$$
$$= \sum_{i=1}^{n} x_i P(x_i)$$

It is the value, on average, that X takes i.e. it is the arithmetic mean of X i.e. $\bar{X}$ Also, Variance (σ^2) of X is given by variance = $\sigma^2 = E(X^2) - [E(X)]^2$.

Note: For any data there is a tendency to concentrate about a particular value, called as central tendency and that particular value is called as the measure of central tendency or average. Arithmetic mean (or simply mean or average) is the most commonly used measure of central tendency and for a variable x having N observations, it is given by

$$\bar{x} = \frac{\Sigma x}{N}$$
$$= \frac{\Sigma fx}{N} \text{ where } N = \Sigma f$$

[When the data is in the form of frequency distribution (i.e. a listing of values of x and their frequency i.e. number of occurrences - in the data)].

Mean is thus a single figure which is a representative value (figure) of the entire data. However, it does not indicate the variation (or dispersion or scatteredness or spread) in the data values. Standard deviation (σ) is a powerful measure of this dispersion and it gives the overall extent to which the values in the data vary from the average (i.e. arithmetic mean). It is given by

$$\sigma = \sqrt{\frac{1}{N}\Sigma(x-\bar{x})^2}$$
$$= \sqrt{\frac{1}{N}\Sigma f(x-\bar{x})^2} \quad \text{... for frequency distribution}$$

Variance is the square of standard deviation and is also sometimes used to describe the dispersion. Thus, variance = σ^2.

Example - Consider a retail chain having the average daily sales at its 40 stores in a city as ₹ 30,000 with a standard deviation of ₹ 5,000. Thus, it implies that the sales recorded at its any store are typically ₹ 30,000 (this being the arithmetic mean or average). Obviously, some stores will have sales above and some will have sales below it. The typical variation about the average of ₹ 30,000 is here ₹ 5,000 (this being the standard deviation).

(v) Probability Distributions: The probability distribution for a discrete random variable is a mutually exclusive listing of all the possible outcomes (for that variable) and the corresponding probabilities of occurrences of these outcomes. E.g. Consider an experiment involving simultaneous throw of three coins and let the variable be X = number of heads displayed on the coins. Thus, X can have values 0, 1, 2 or 3 i.e. X is a discrete random variable.

Now, $P(X = 0) = P(TTT) = \frac{1}{2} \cdot \frac{1}{2} \cdot \frac{1}{2} = \frac{1}{8}$,

$P(X = 1) = P(HTT) + P(THT) + P(TTH)$

$= \frac{1}{2} \cdot \frac{1}{2} \cdot \frac{1}{2} + \frac{1}{2} \cdot \frac{1}{2} \cdot \frac{1}{2} + \frac{1}{2} \cdot \frac{1}{2} \cdot \frac{1}{2} = \frac{3}{8}$

Similarly, $P(X = 2) = \frac{3}{8}$ and $P(X = 3) = \frac{1}{8}$

Thus, we have the Probability Distribution as

X = x :	0	1	2	3
P(X = x):	$\frac{1}{8}$	$\frac{3}{8}$	$\frac{3}{8}$	$\frac{1}{8}$

and P (X) which is a function of variable X is called as its Probability Function.

If the variable X is discrete, the probability function P (X) is called as Probability Mass Function. E.g. In the above experiment we can express the probability of X i.e. P (x) in terms of x as

$$P(x) = {}^3C_x \cdot \left(\frac{1}{2}\right)^3, \quad x = 0, 1, 2, 3$$

i.e. The probability mass function is $P(x) = \frac{1}{8} {}^3C_x$ x = 1, 2, 3.

Similarly, if X is a continuous variable, P(X) is called as the Probability Density Function.

Note: The frequency distribution of X is the listing of the values of X and their corresponding number of occurrences in a given data i.e. their frequencies. This is very commonly used form of any data. E.g. Marks obtained by students and their corresponding frequencies. However, in certain situations, it is possible to deduce mathematically what the frequency distribution could be. These distributions, which are based on the previous experience or theoretical considerations are known as the 'Theoretical Distributions or Probability Distributions'. Thus, the values of the variable may be distributed according to some definite probability law, which can be expressed mathematically, and it gives the corresponding theoretical probability distribution. These distributions provide us a data to assess the results of actual observations and help in arriving at rational and dependable decisions. There are three most popular and widely used theoretical distributions viz. Binomial Distribution, Poisson Distribution (both are discrete probability distributions) and Normal Distribution (which is a continuous probability distribution).

10.2 Binomial Distribution

Consider an experiment with only two possible outcomes (called as Bernoulli's Trial), namely a success with (constant) probability p and a failure with (constant) probability q.

Hence $\quad p + q = 1$

E.g. If a fair coin is tossed, we either get a success (say head) with probability $p = \frac{1}{2}$ or a failure (i.e. tail) with probability $q = \frac{1}{2}$.

Now, consider 'n' such independent trials. Also, let r = Number of successes in n trials.

(Hence r can take values 0, 1, 2, ..., n since we can get no success, one success, ..., all successes etc.).

Then, the probability of getting r successes in n trials is given by

$$P(r) = {}^nC_r p^r q^{n-r}, \quad r = 0,1,2,\ldots n$$

This is the Binomial Probability Distribution denoted as B (n, p, r) where n and p are called as the parameters of the distribution (which must be known).

[Note: P(r) here, corresponds to the terms of Binomial Expansion given by

$$(q+p)^n = q^n + {}^nC_1 q^{n-1} p^1 + {}^nC_2 q^{n-2} p^2 + \ldots + {}^nC_r q^{n-r} p^r + \ldots + p^n \text{ , hence the name}]$$

Note:

(i) We have, $P(0) + P(1) + \ldots + P(n) = 1$ i.e. $\sum_{r=0}^{n} P(r) = 1$

(ii) p and q must not be too small and n must be finite and fixed.

(iii) Probability that there will be success at most r times i.e. Probability that there will be 1 or 2 or 3 ...or r successes in n trials is

$$P(0) + P(1) + \ldots + P(r) = {}^nC_0 p^0 q^n + {}^nC_1 p^1 q^{n-1} + \ldots + {}^nC_r p^r q^{n-r}$$

Similarly, Probability of getting at least r successes in n trials is

$$P(r) + P(r+1) + \ldots + P(n) = {}^nC_r p^r q^{n-r} + {}^nC_{r+1} p^{r+1} q^{n-r-1} + \ldots + {}^nC_n p^n q^0$$

(iv) For a Binomial Distribution, Expected Value of the distribution i.e. mean of the distribution is $E(r) = \text{mean } (\bar{r}) = np$ and its variance, $\sigma^2 = npq$ so that standard deviation, $\sigma = \sqrt{npq}$

(v) If the set of n trials is repeated N times, then the expected (theoretical) frequency of getting r successes is given by $f(r) = N \times P(r) = N \times {}^nC_r p^r q^{n-r}, \quad r = 0, 1, 2, \ldots n$.

Example 1: 10 unbiased coins are tossed simultaneously, find the probability that there will be (i) Exactly 5 heads (ii) At least 8 heads (iii) Not more than 3 heads (iv) At least one head. (v) If this exercise is carried out 50 times, how many times we can get exactly 5 heads?

Solution: Here, let p = Probability of getting a head (success) in one trial = $\frac{1}{2}$.

Similarly, q = probability of getting a tail (failure) in one trial = $1-p = 1-\frac{1}{2} = \frac{1}{2}$.

Also, the experiment is performed using 10 coins i.e. it is carried out n = 10 number of times. Thus, there are 10 independent trials. Hence, the probability of getting r successes (heads) in 10 trials is given by the Binomial Probability Function as

$$P(r) = {}^{10}C_r p^r q^{10-r} = {}^{10}C_r \left(\frac{1}{2}\right)^r \cdot \left(\frac{1}{2}\right)^{10-r} = {}^{10}C_r \left(\frac{1}{2}\right)^{10} = \frac{1}{1024} {}^{10}C_r$$

(i) ∴ Probability of getting 5 heads i.e. r = 5 is

$$P(5) = \frac{1}{1024} {}^{10}C_5 = \frac{1}{1024} \times \frac{10 \times 9 \times 8 \times 7 \times 6}{1 \times 2 \times 3 \times 4 \times 5} = 0.246$$

(ii) Probability of getting atleast 8 heads i.e.

P(r ≥ 8) = P(r = 8 or 9 or 10) = P(8) + P(9) + P(10)

... being mutually exclusive events

$$= \frac{1}{1024}\left({}^{10}C_8 + {}^{10}C_9 + {}^{10}C_{10}\right) = \frac{1}{1024}\left({}^{10}C_2 + {}^{10}C_1 + 1\right) \quad \ldots (\because {}^nC_r = {}^nC_{n-r})$$

$$= \frac{1}{1024}\left(\frac{10 \times 9}{1 \times 2} + 10 + 1\right) = \frac{1}{1024}(56) = 0.055$$

(iii) P(Not more than 3 heads) i.e. P(r ≤ 3) = P(r = 0 or 1 or 2 or 3)

= P(0) + P(1) + P(2) + P(3)

$$= \frac{1}{1024}\left({}^{10}C_0 + {}^{10}C_1 + {}^{10}C_2 + {}^{10}C_3\right) = \frac{1}{1024}\left(1 + 10 + \frac{10 \times 9}{1 \times 2} + \frac{10 \times 9 \times 8}{1 \times 2 \times 3}\right)$$

$$= \frac{1}{1024}(1+10+45+120) = \frac{176}{1024} = 0.172$$

(iv) P (At least one head)

i.e. P(r ≥ 1) = 1 − P(r < 1) = 1 − P(no head) = 1 − P(0)

$$= 1 - \frac{1}{1024}({}^{10}C_0) = 1 - \frac{1}{1024} = \frac{1023}{1024} = 0.9$$

(v) If the exercise of throwing n = 10 coins is repeated N = 50 times, then the number of times (i.e. frequency) we expect to get 5 heads = f(5) = N × P(5) = 50 (0.246) = 12.3 ≈ 12.

Example 2: The mean and variance of a Binomial Distribution are 3 and 2 respectively. Find the probability that the variate takes values (i) Exactly 2 (ii) at most 2.

Solution: For a Binomial Distribution, mean = np and variance = npq

∴ np = 3 and npq = 2

∴ Dividing, $\dfrac{npq}{np} = \dfrac{2}{3}$ i.e. $q = \dfrac{2}{3}$ ∴ $p = 1 - q = 1 - \dfrac{2}{3} = \dfrac{1}{3}$

Now, mean, np = 3 ∴ $n = \dfrac{3}{p} = \dfrac{3}{1/3} = 9$

Thus, $p = \dfrac{1}{3}$, $q = \dfrac{2}{3}$ and n = 9

∴ Probability that the variate takes value r is

$$P(r) = {}^nC_r p^r q^{n-r} = {}^9C_r \left(\dfrac{1}{3}\right)^r \left(\dfrac{2}{3}\right)^{9-r}$$

(i) ∴ $P(2) = {}^9C_2 \left(\dfrac{1}{3}\right)^2 \left(\dfrac{2}{3}\right)^{9-2} = \dfrac{9 \times 8}{1 \times 2} \left(\dfrac{1}{9}\right)\left(\dfrac{2}{3}\right)^7$

$= 4\left(\dfrac{2}{3}\right)^7 = 4(0.667)^7 = 4(0.0587) = 0.235$

(ii) $P(r \le 2) = P(0) + P(1) + P(2)$

$= {}^9C_0 \left(\dfrac{1}{3}\right)^0 \left(\dfrac{2}{3}\right)^9 + {}^9C_1 \left(\dfrac{1}{3}\right)^1 \left(\dfrac{2}{3}\right)^8 + {}^9C_2 \left(\dfrac{1}{3}\right)^2 \left(\dfrac{2}{3}\right)^7$

$= 1.1\left(\dfrac{2}{3}\right)^9 + 9\left(\dfrac{1}{3}\right)\left(\dfrac{2}{3}\right)^8 + \dfrac{9 \times 8}{1 \times 2}\left(\dfrac{1}{9}\right)\left(\dfrac{2}{3}\right)^7$

$= \left(\dfrac{2}{3}\right)^7 \left[\left(\dfrac{2}{3}\right)^2 + 3\left(\dfrac{2}{3}\right) + 4\right] = (0.667)^7 \left(\dfrac{4}{9} + 2 + 4\right)$

$= 0.0587 \left(\dfrac{58}{9}\right) = 0.378$

10.3 Poisson Distribution

This is another type of discrete probability distribution which is a limiting case of the Binomial Distribution under the following conditions:

(i) The number of trials i.e. n is very large.
(ii) The constant probability of success for each trial i.e. p is very small (near '0') or very large (near '1').
(iii) np = mean m (say) is finite and positive

Here, the probability function becomes

$$P(r) = \frac{e^{-m} m^r}{r!}, \qquad r = 0, 1, 2, \ldots$$

where, P(r) is the probability of getting r successes (i.e. occurrences of the event), e is the base of natural logarithm = 2.7183 (approx.) and mean m = np which is the parameter of the distribution.

Note:

(i) $\sum_{r=0}^{\infty} P(r) = 1$

(ii) For Poisson Distribution:
 $E(r)$ = mean $(\bar{r})$ = m, also variance = σ^2 = m

(iii) This distribution is useful in the study of rare events like finding the number of telephone calls received in a given time, number of customers arriving at a service counter in a given time, number of accidents or defects in manufacturing, number of printing mistakes in a page etc.

(iv) If there are N sets of n trials each, then the expected frequency of occurence of r successes is $f(r) = N \times P(r)$.

Example 3: If 5% of electric bulbs manufactured by a company are defective, use Poisson Distribution to find the probability that in a box of 100 bulbs: (i) None is defective (ii) 3 bulbs are defective (iii) More than 3 bulbs are defective. (Given e^{-5} = 0.007).

Solution: We have, p = probability that a bulb is defective = 5% = $\frac{5}{100}$ = 0.05 (which is very small) and n = number of bulbs in a box = 100 (which is relatively large). Hence, it is a case of Poisson Distribution and $\therefore$ m = np = 100 (0.05) = 5

$\therefore$ Probability of getting r defective bulbs in a box of (n = 100) bulbs is

$$P(r) = \frac{e^{-m} m^r}{r!} = \frac{e^{-5} \cdot 5^r}{r!} = \frac{(0.007) 5^r}{r!} \qquad \because e^{-5} = 0.007$$

(i) $\therefore$ Probability that no bulb is defective is

$$P(r = 0) = \frac{(0.007) 5^0}{0!} = \frac{(0.007)(1)}{1} = 0.007$$

(ii) Probability that 3 bulbs are defective i.e.

$$P(r = 3) = \frac{(0.007) 5^3}{3!} = \frac{(0.007)(125)}{3 \times 2 \times 1} = 0.146$$

(iii) P(r > 3) = 1 − P(r ≤ 3)
= 1 − [P(0) + P(1) + P(2) + P(3)]
$$= 1 - \left[\frac{(0.007)5^0}{0!} + \frac{(0.007)5^1}{1!} + \frac{(0.007)5^2}{2!} + \frac{(0.007)5^3}{3!}\right]$$
$$= 1 - (0.007)\left[\frac{1}{1} + \frac{5}{1} + \frac{25}{2\times 1} + \frac{125}{3\times 2\times 1}\right] = 1 - (0.007)(6+12.5+20.83)$$
= 1 − (0.007) (39.33)
= 1 − 0.275 = 0.725

Note: If (N = 10) such boxes are delivered, then the number of boxes containing more than 3 defective bulbs will be f(r > 3) = N × P(r > 3) = 10 (0.725) = 7.25 i.e. 7 (rounded off).

Example 4: For a Poisson Distribution Mean = 7 and variance = 6. Comment.

Solution: For a Poisson Distribution, the mean and variance both must be same. Hence, the given statement is wrong.

10.4 Normal Distribution

It is one of the most important continuous probability distributions, which is also called as Gaussian Distribution. Here, the probability function for a continuous random variable x, called as Probability Density Function is given by

$$P(x) = \frac{1}{\sigma\sqrt{2\pi}} \cdot e^{-\frac{1}{2}\left(\frac{x-m}{\sigma}\right)^2} \quad \text{...for } -\infty < x < \infty$$

where, m is the mean and σ is the standard deviation of the distribution, which are its parameters.

Thus, it is denoted as x~ N (m,σ). i.e. read as x follows normal distribution with mean m and s.d. σ. It is a limiting case of Binomial Distribution where n is very large but p and q are not very small.

10.5 Characteristics of Normal Distribution

(i) The normal Curve [graph of P(x) versus x] is a bell shaped curve symmetric about the line x = m (mean) and extending on both the sides up to ∞. The exact shape depends on the values of m and σ.

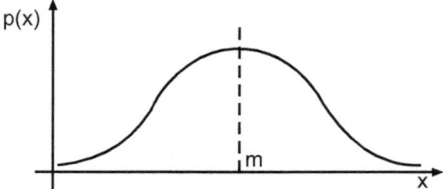

(ii) Probability that x lies between x_1 and x_2 i.e. $P(x_1 \leq x \leq x_2)$ = Area under the normal curve between lines $x = x_1$ and $x = x_2$.

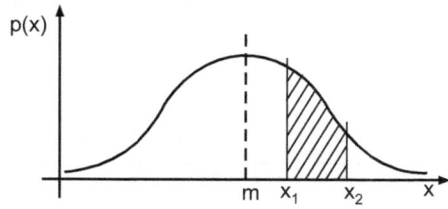

(iii) $P(-\infty < x < \infty) = 1$ = area under the entire curve.

(iv) $P(-\infty < x \leq m) = \dfrac{1}{2} = P(m \leq x < \infty)$ i.e. $P(x \leq m) = P(x \geq m) = \dfrac{1}{2}$

(v) $P(m - \sigma \leq x \leq m + \sigma) = 0.6826$ i.e. the range $(m \pm \sigma)$ of x covers 68.26% of the observations. Similarly $P(m - 2\sigma \leq x \leq m + 2\sigma) = 0.9544$ and $P(m - 3\sigma \leq x \leq m + 3\sigma) = 0.9973$. Hence, practically, the range $(m \pm 3\sigma)$ covers all the observations.

(vi) For the normal distribution, mean = median = mode = m.

(vii) Practically we come across many situations which follow the normal distribution.

10.6 Standard Normal Distribution

For all practical purposes we use the substitution, $z = \dfrac{x - m}{\sigma}$, where z is called as the Standard Normal Variate. This reduces the probability density function to the form:

$$P(z) = \dfrac{1}{\sqrt{2\pi}} e^{-\dfrac{z^2}{2}}, \quad -\infty < z < \infty \text{ as for } z, \text{ mean} = 0 \text{ and } \sigma = 1.$$

Hence, the Standard Normal Curve
[P(z) versus z] is symmetric about the line $z = 0$ (mean)

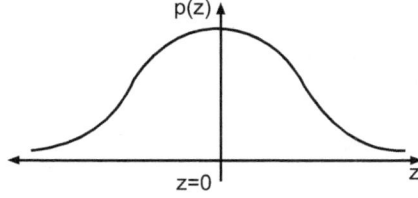

Note: Now we have,

(i) $P(x_1 \leq x \leq x_2) = P(z_1 \leq z \leq z_2)$

where, we find $z_1 = \dfrac{x_1 - m}{\sigma}$ and $z_2 = \dfrac{x_2 - m}{\sigma}$

And $P(z_1 \leq z \leq z_2)$ = Area under the standard normal curve between ($z = z_1$) and ($z = z_2$)

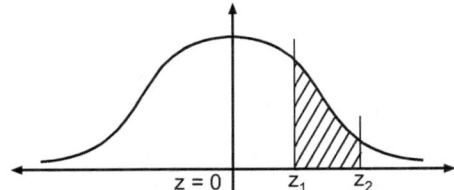

(ii) $P(-\infty < z < \infty) = 1$

$P(-\infty < z \leq 0) = P(0 \leq z < \infty) = \dfrac{1}{2}$

$P(m \leq x \leq x_1) = P(0 \leq z \leq z_1)$

$P(-z_1 \leq z \leq 0) = P(0 \leq z \leq z_1)$ as the curve is symmetric about $z = 0$.

$P(m - \sigma \leq x \leq m + \sigma) = P(-1 \leq z \leq 1) = 0.6826$ etc.

(iii) To find the area under the standard normal curve from $z = 0$ to $z = z_1$ i.e. $P(0 \leq z \leq z_1)$, we use the values from the Standard Table for area under Standard Normal Curve. **(See Appendix A)**

(iv) The number of cases where ($x_1 \leq x \leq x_2$) from the total number of N cases is given by $f(x_1 \leq x \leq x_2) = N \times P(x_1 \leq x \leq x_2) = N \times P(z_1 \leq z \leq z_2)$ etc.

Example 5: Using the 'Area Under the Normal Curve Table' **(Appendix A)** we have:

(i) $P(0 \leq z \leq 1.25)$ = Area under curve from ($z = 0$) to ($z = 1.25$) = 0.3944

(ii) $P(-1.25 \leq z \leq 0) = P(0 \leq z \leq 1.25)$
                = 0.3944   ... by symmetry

(iii) $P(0.6 \leq z \leq 1.25)$
= Area under curve from ($z = 0.6$) to ($z = 1.25$)
= (Area under curve from $z = 0$ to $z = 1.25$)
  − (Area under curve from $z = 0$ to $z = 0.6$)
= $P(0 \leq z \leq 1.25) - P(0 \leq z \leq 0.6)$
= $0.3944 - 0.2257 = 0.1687$

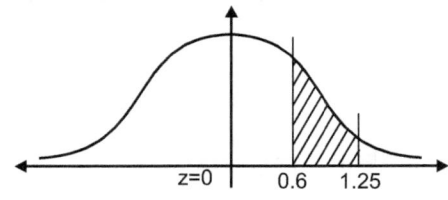

(iv) P(z ≥ 2.5) = P(2.5 ≤ z < ∞)
= P(0 ≤ z < ∞) − P(0 ≤ z ≤ 2.5)
= 0.5 − 0.4938 = 0.0062   ... ∵ P(0 ≤ z ≤ ∞) = 0.5

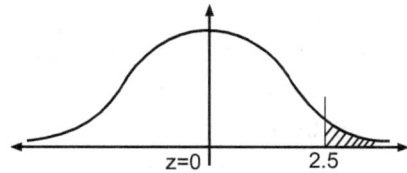

(v) P(z ≤ 2.5) = P(−∞ ≤ z ≤ 2.5)
= P(−∞ ≤ z ≤ 0) + P(0 ≤ z ≤ 2.5)
= 0.5 + 0.4938 = 0.9938

(vi) P(z ≥ −2.5) = P(−2.5 ≤ z < ∞) = P(−2.5 ≤ z ≤ 0) + P(0 ≤ z < ∞)
= P(0 ≤ z ≤ 2.5) + 0.5   ... by symmetry
= 0.4938 + 0.5 = 0.9938

(vii) P(z ≤ − 2.5) = P(z ≥ 2.5)   ... by Symmetry
= 0.0062

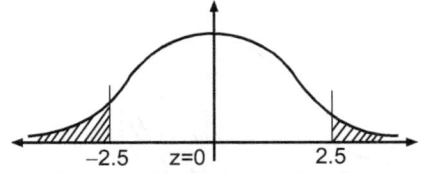

(viii)   P(−2.5 ≤ z ≤ 1.25) = P(−2.5 ≤ z ≤ 0) + P (0 ≤ z ≤ 1.25)
= P (0 ≤ z ≤ 2.5) + P (0 ≤ z ≤ 1.25)   ... by symmetry
= 0.4938 + 0.3944
= 0.8882

Example 6: The weekly wages of 1000 workers are normally distributed around a mean of ₹ 70 and Standard Deviation of ₹ 5. Estimate the number of workers whose weekly wages will be:

(i) Between ₹ 70 and 72 (ii) Between ₹ 69 and 72 (iii) More than ₹ 75 (iv) Less than ₹ 63, (v) Also, estimate the lowest weekly wages of the 100 highest paid workers.

Solution: Let x denote the weekly wages in ₹ Thus, x is a normal variable with mean m = 70 and σ = 5.

∴   Standard normal variate corresponding to x is

$$z = \frac{x - m}{\sigma} = \frac{x - 70}{5}$$

(i) Let us find P (wages between ₹ 70 and 72) i.e. P(70 ≤ x ≤ 72)

Now, when $x_1 = 70$, $z_1 = \dfrac{70-70}{5} = 0$ and $x_2 = 72$, $z_2 = \dfrac{72-70}{5} = 0.4$

∴ P(70 ≤ x ≤ 72) = P(0 ≤ z ≤ 0.4) = 0.1554   **... from the table (See Appendix A)**

∴ Probability that the workers will have weekly wages between ₹ 70 and 72 is 0.1554
Hence, the number of such workers among the 1000 workers will be

        f(70 ≤ x ≤ 72) = 1000 × P(70 ≤ x ≤ 72)

                            = 1000 × 0.1554 = 155.4 ≃ 155

(ii) For, $x = 69$, $z = \dfrac{69-70}{5} = -0.2$

∴   P(69 ≤ x ≤ 72) = P(– 0.2 ≤ z ≤ 0.4)
                          = P(–0.2 ≤ z ≤ 0) + P(0 ≤ z ≤ 0.4)
                          = P(0 ≤ z ≤ 0.2) + P(0 ≤ z ≤ 0.4)   ... by symmetry
                          = 0.0793 + 0.1554 = 0.2347   **Using Table (Appendix A)**

∴ Number of workers with wages between ₹ 69 and 72 = 1000 × (0.2347) = 234.7

≃ 235

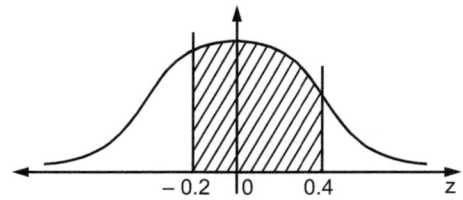

(iii) We want to find P(x ≥ 75)

When $x = 75$, $z = \dfrac{75-70}{5} = 1$

∴   P(x ≥ 75) = P(z ≥ 1) = P(1 ≤ z ≤ ∞)
                   = P(0 ≤ x ≤ ∞) – P(0 ≤ x ≤ 1)
                   = 0.5 – 0.3413 = 0.1587

∴ Number of workers with wages more than ₹ 75 = 1000 × (0.1587) = 158.7 ≃ 159

(iv) We want to find P(x ≤ 63)

When, $x = 63$, $z = \dfrac{63-70}{5} = \dfrac{-7}{5} = -1.4$

∴   P(x ≤ 63) = P(z ≤ –1.4) = P(z ≥ 1.4)   ... by symmetry
                 = P(0 ≤ z ≤∞) – P(0 ≤ z ≤ 1.4) = 0.5 – 0.4192 = 0.0808

∴ Number of workers with wages less than ₹ 63 = 1000 × (0.0808) = 80.8 ≃ 81

(v) The proportion of 100 highest paid workers in total of 1000 workers is $\frac{100}{1000} = 0.1$

Hence, if x_1 are the lowest weekly wages of the 100 highest paid workers, then we have to find, x_1 such that
$P(x \geq x_1) = 0.1$

Now, when $x = x_1$, $z_1 = \frac{x_1 - 70}{5}$

Thus, we have to find z_1 such that $P(z \geq z_1) = 0.1$
i.e. $P(z_1 \leq z \leq \infty) = 0.1$

Thus, the area lying on the right side of the ordinate (line) $z = z_1$ is 0.1.

Also we know that the area lying to the right side of the line $z = 0$ is 0.5 (which is more than 0.1). Hence the line $z = z_1$ will lie in the right half of the normal curve as shown.

Thus $P(z_1 \leq z \leq \infty) = 0.1$
i.e. $P(0 \leq z < \infty) - P(0 \leq z \leq z_1) = 0.1$
i.e. $0.5 - P(0 \leq z \leq z_1) = 0.1$
∴ $P(0 \leq z \leq z_1) = 0.5 - 0.1 = 0.4$

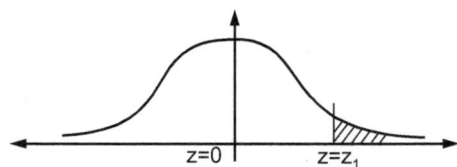

∴ Reading the value of z_1 corresponding to the probability (i.e. the area under the normal curve) 0.4 from the table in the reverse order we see that, $z_1 \simeq 1.28$

∴ $z_1 = \frac{x_1 - 70}{5} = 1.28$

∴ $x_1 - 70 = (1.28)\,5 = 6.4$

∴ $x_1 = 70 + 6.4 = 76.4$

∴ The required lowest wages are ₹ 76.40

10.7 Sampling Distributions

(A) Introduction

Sampling Technique is used very commonly for estimating the values of a certain characteristic say the arithmetic mean of the entire population. The value of a characteristic (say mean) of a sample of say n number of objects i.e. sampling units (out of the population of N objects) is called as a statistic (say $\bar{x}$) whereas the corresponding value for the entire population is called as a parameter (say meu–μ). Sampling analysis is used for estimating the parameter from a given statistic.

(B) Sampling Distributions

If we take all possible number of samples (= say m) of equal size (n) from the entire population, we can find the statistic for each sample (say the value of mean, standard deviation, etc.). Thus we will have a set of statistics, corresponding to m samples taken. Then we can write down the frequency distribution for these 'm' statistics and can also find the relative frequencies for each value of the statistics. Thus, from the relative frequency values we can write down the probability distribution for these values of statistics. For example, consider the number of workers (x) in (N = 5) small scale units be x: 2, 4, 6, 8, 10 which forms the population.

$\therefore \quad \mu$ = mean number of workers in a unit

$$= \frac{\Sigma x}{N}$$

$$= \frac{2 + 4 + 6 + 8 + 10}{5}$$

$$= \frac{30}{5} = 6$$

Now, consider all possible samples of size say (n = 2) drawn from the above population so that we will have m = 10 such samples which will have their means ($\bar{x}$) as follows:

Sample No.	Mean
1 : (2, 4)	$\bar{x}_1 = 3$
2 : (2, 6)	$\bar{x}_2 = 4$
3 : (2, 8)	$\bar{x}_3 = 5$
4 : (2, 10)	$\bar{x}_4 = 6$
5 : (4, 6)	$\bar{x}_5 = 5$
6 : (4, 8)	$\bar{x}_6 = 6$
7 : (4, 10)	$\bar{x}_7 = 7$
8 : (6, 8)	$\bar{x}_8 = 7$
9 : (6, 10)	$\bar{x}_9 = 8$
10 : (8, 10)	$\bar{x}_{10} = 9$

Thus, for the above values of statistics ($\bar{x}$) we have,

Sample mean ($\bar{x}$)	Frequency (f) i.e. No. of occurrences	Relative frequency	Probability (p)
3	1	1/10	0.1
4	1	1/10	0.1
5	2	2/10	0.2
6	2	2/10	0.2
7	2	2/10	0.2
8	1	1/10	0.1
9	1	1/10	0.1
	Σf = 10		Σp = 1

This probability distribution of the sample means is called as the sampling distribution of the mean and we have, the mean of the sampling distribution

$$\mu_{\bar{x}} \text{ or } \bar{\bar{x}} = \frac{\Sigma f \bar{x}}{m} = \frac{3(1) + 4(1) + 5(2) + 6(2) + 7(2) + 8(1) + 9(1)}{10} = \frac{60}{10}$$

∴ $\mu_{\bar{x}}$ or $\bar{\bar{x}}$ = 6 = μ i.e. same as the population mean

Note:
1. We can have a sampling distribution of any statistical measure like mean, median, standard deviation, proportion etc.
2. Each item in a sampling distribution is a particular statistic of a sample.
3. If the number of samples (m) is large, the sampling distribution tends quiet closer to the normal distribution.
4. Mean of sampling distribution is same as the mean of the population.

Thus, the mean of the sampling distribution of standard deviations is same as the standard deviation of the population.

The commonly used sampling distributions are: Sampling distribution of mean, Sampling distribution of proportion, Student's 't' distribution, 'F' distribution and Chi-square distribution.

(C) Sampling Distribution of Mean

1. Definition: It is the probability distribution of all possible sample means of a given size, selected from a population. The example considered earlier is a case of sampling distribution of means. Here we have, mean of the sampling distribution is equal to the mean of the population. This is true only when all possible samples of the given size are taken from the sample. If only some of such samples are taken the mean of the sampling distribution of the means $\left(\text{i.e. } \mu_{\bar{x}} \text{ or } \bar{\bar{x}}\right)$ may not be same as the population mean (i.e. μ), but will be closer to it.

2. **Central Limit Theorem:** It states that: "Irrespective of the shape of the distribution of the population, the distribution of the sample means approaches the normal probability distribution as the sample size increases". This is the most important theorem in statistical inference and it assures that the sampling distribution of the means approaches normal distribution as the sample size increases (i.e. practically when the sample size n ≥ 30). It enables us to draw inferences about the population parameters without knowing the shape and frequency distribution of the population.

3. **Standard Error of the Mean** $\left(\sigma_{\bar{x}}\right)$: It is the measure of the dispersion of the distribution of sample means (similar to the standard deviation in a frequency distribution) which is given by

$$\left(\sigma_{\bar{x}}\right) = \sqrt{\frac{\Sigma\left(\bar{x} - \mu_{\bar{x}}\right)^2}{M}}$$

where, $\bar{x}$ = Sample means
$\mu_{\bar{x}}$ = Mean of sample means
M = Total number of sample means under consideration

Thus, for the earlier example

$\bar{x}$	3	4	5	5	6	6	7	7	8	9
$\mu_{\bar{x}}$	6	6	6	6	6	6	6	6	6	6
$\left(\bar{x} - \mu_{\bar{x}}\right)^2$	9	4	1	1	0	0	1	1	4	9

∴ $\Sigma\left(\bar{x} - \mu_{\bar{x}}\right)^2 = 30$

∴ $\sigma_{\bar{x}} = \sqrt{\frac{30}{7}} = \sqrt{4.2857} = 2.07$

Also, we have, for a finite population, a standard formula

$$\sigma_{\bar{x}} = \frac{\sigma}{\sqrt{n}} \sqrt{\frac{N-n}{N-1}}$$

where, σ = Standard deviation of the population
$\sigma_{\bar{x}}$ = Standard error of the mean
N = Size of the population
n = Sample size

Note: If the sample size n is smaller than 5% of the population size N i.e. when the population size is large, the 'finite correction factor' $\sqrt{\frac{N-n}{N-1}} \simeq 1$ (approximately).

∴ For large (or infinite) populations,

$$\sigma_{\bar{x}} = \frac{\sigma}{\sqrt{n}}$$

Thus, as the sample size increases, $\sigma_{\bar{x}}$ decreases. Also, with increased sample size, the sampling distribution approaches normal distribution (by Central Limit Theorem). Now, due to the property of normal distribution, there is 68.26% chance of the population mean $(\mu = \mu_{\bar{x}})$ being within the range of $(\pm \sigma_{\bar{x}})$ of the sample mean $\bar{x}$. Hence, if $\sigma_{\bar{x}}$ is smaller, the population mean will be closer to the sample mean.

(D) Sampling Distribution of Proportion (or Percentage)

If we are interested in estimating the proportion of the units in a population possessing a given characteristic, based on the proportion of units possessing that characteristic from a given sample, the sampling distribution of the proportions would be useful. Thus, the sampling distribution of proportions can be defined as the probability distribution of the proportions of all possible random samples of a fixed size n selected from the given population. This is similiar to the sampling distribution of the means, but is useful in the analysis of qualitative data. e.g. Based on the proportion of the defective parts from a sample of the parts produced on an assembly line, we can estimate their proportion in the entire production.

Consider, (N = 5) parts produced on a machine and if we have the following results.

Sr. No. of Part	Status
1.	Defective
2.	Not defective
3.	Not defective
4.	Defective
5.	Not defective

Thus, proportion of defectives produced in the population (denoted as pi-π) is

$$\pi = \frac{\text{No. of defectives}}{N} = \frac{2}{5} = 0.4 \text{ or } 40\%$$

Now, if we take all possible samples of size (n = 4) from this population of size (N = 5) then we have the following (m = 5) such samples:

Samples	Proportion of Defectives (p)
Parts: 1, 2, 3, 4	2/4 = 0.5
Parts: 1, 2, 3, 5	1/4 = 0.25
Parts: 1, 2, 4, 5	2/4 = 0.5
Parts: 1, 3, 4, 5	2/4 = 0.5
Parts: 2, 3, 4, 5	1/4 = 0.25
	Σp = 2

∴ Average of sample proportions is
$$\mu_p = \frac{\Sigma p}{m} = \frac{2}{5} = 0.4$$
Thus, $\mu_p = \pi$ = population proportion

Standard Error of Proportions (σ_p): For a finite population

$$\sigma_p = \sqrt{\frac{\pi(1-\pi)}{n}} \sqrt{\frac{N-n}{N-1}}$$

where, σ_p = Standard error of proportion
π = Proportion of (success) in population
N = Size of Population and
n = Sample size

and for a large population compared to the sample size, we have, $\sqrt{\frac{N-n}{N-1}} \simeq 1$ and

∴ $$\sigma_p = \sqrt{\frac{\pi(1-\pi)}{n}}$$

The central limit theorem also applies to the sampling distribution of proportions and hence for large sample size, the distribution behaves like a normal probability distribution.

(E) Standard Error

The standard deviation of the sampling distribution of a statistic is known as its standard error (S.E.) e.g. standard error of mean $\sigma_{\bar{x}}$ or standard error of proportions σ_p.

Utility of Standard Error:
1. Standard error helps us in determining whether the difference between the observed and expected values of a characteristic or frequencies is due to chance (where the difference is called as not significant) or not (where it is treated as significant).
   Thus, the standard error is an important measure is 'Significance Test' or in examining the research hypothesis.
2. The standard error also gives us an idea bout the reliability and precision of a sample. Smaller the value of S.E., greater is the uniformity of the sampling distribution and hence greater is the reliability of the sample.
3. It also enables us to specify the limits within which the population parameter is expected to lie with a given degree of confidence (which is described ahead).

10.8 Statistical Estimation

One of the aims of statistical inferencing is to estimate the value of a parameter (say man μ) of the population, based on the calculated value of the corresponding sample statistic (say mean of a sample, $\bar{x}$). Here, we can make two types of estimates:

(A) Point Estimate: Here, we use a single sample value to estimate the desired population parameter e.g. the sample mean $\bar{x}$ is considered as a point estimate of the population mean μ. Thus, we write $\mu = \bar{x}$. Similarly, the standard deviation of a sample (s) will be the point estimate of the population standard deviation (σ). Thus, here the estimated parameter (μ or σ) is a specific single value. Hence, in order to get the best estimate, the statistic $(\bar{x}$ or $s)$ must be drawn from a truly representative sample and should be unbiased, consistent, efficient and sufficient.

(B) Interval Estimation: In case of point estimate, it may not give the correct value of the parameter and there is some level of uncertainty. If there is a difference between the statistic (say $\bar{x}$) and the parameter (μ), we do not come to know the possible error and again a point estimate does not specify as to how confident we can be that the estimate is close to the parameter. Hence, we use an interval estimate where the estimated value of the population parameter is expressed in terms of a range of values.

In this method, we find the point estimate $(\text{say } \bar{x})$ first and then construct an interval on both sides of it, within which we can be reasonably confident that the true parameter (μ) will lie.

Obviously, greater the interval, more likely it is that the parameter will lie in this range. This degree of likelihood is known as the confidence level and the corresponding range around the sample statistics (say $\bar{x}$) is known as the confidence interval at a given confidence level, assuming the sample to be large.

(a) Interval Estimate of Population Mean (Population Variance Known)

By central limit theorem, for a large sample, sampling distribution of means approaches a normal distribution and we have mean of sampling distribution = mean of the population.

i.e. $\bar{\bar{x}} = \mu$

and $\sigma_{\bar{x}}$ = standard deviation of the distribution, called as standard error of means.

Hence, transforming the sampling distribution into the standard normal distribution we have,

$$z = \frac{\bar{x} - \mu}{\sigma_{\bar{x}}}$$

$\therefore \quad \bar{x} - \mu = z\, \sigma_{\bar{x}}$

$\therefore \quad \mu = \bar{x} - z\, \sigma_{\bar{x}}$

Now, as μ can fall within a range of values equidistant from $\bar{x}$,

∴ $\mu = \bar{x} \pm z \sigma_{\bar{x}}$

and hence, $\left(x_1 = \bar{x} - z\sigma_{\bar{x}}\right) \leq \mu \leq \left(x_2 = \bar{x} + z\sigma_{\bar{x}}\right)$ is the range of μ.

Now, if say, $z = 3$

∴ $\bar{x} - 3\sigma_{\bar{x}} \leq \mu \leq \bar{x} + 3\sigma_{\bar{x}}$ is the range of μ.

Now, we know that for a normal curve, total area under the curve = 1 and the interval $\left(\bar{x} \pm 3\sigma_{\bar{x}}\right)$ will cover 99.73% area under the curve. [Similarly $\left(\bar{x} \pm 2\sigma_{\bar{x}}\right)$ will cover 95.44% of the area under the curve]. Thus, there is 99.73% likelihood (confidence) that the parameter μ will lie in this range and $\left(\bar{x} \pm 3\sigma_{\bar{x}}\right)$ will represent the confidence interval at 99.73% level of confidence.

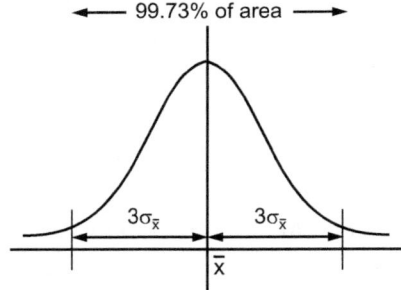

Similarly, for confidence level of 95% we get $z = 1.96$ as $\left(\bar{x} \pm 1.96 \sigma_{\bar{x}}\right)$ covers 95% of the area under the normal curve.

Hence, $\left(\bar{x} \pm 1.96 \sigma_{\bar{x}}\right)$ represents the confidence interval at 95% level of confidence and here we will be confident 95% of the times that the population parameter (μ) will lie in the range $\left(x_1 = \bar{x} - 1.96\sigma_{\bar{x}} \text{ to } x_2 = \bar{x} + 1.96\sigma_{\bar{x}}\right)$ about the sample mean $\bar{x}$. Obviously, the chance that it will lie outside this interval will be 5% (2.5% on either sides). This is known as the level of significance (α). Thus, at 95% confidence level (or 5% significance level i.e. α = 0.05), the critical value of z is 1.96.

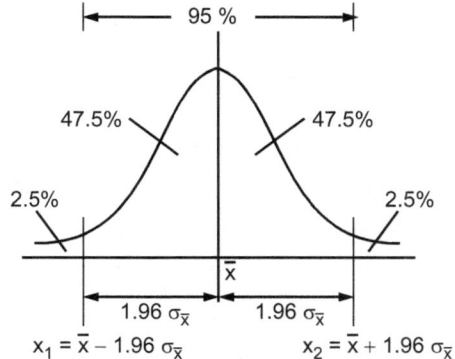

Similarly, at 99% level of confidence (i.e. at 1% level of significance) the critical value of z is 2.575.

And at 90% level of confidence (i.e. at 10% level of significance) the critical value of z is 1.645.

Note:

(i) We have, the standard error of means,

$$\sigma_{\bar{x}} = \frac{\sigma}{\sqrt{n}}$$

where σ is the standard deviation of the population (and therefore its variance = σ^2) and n = sample size

Now, if the population standard deviation σ (or variance σ^2) is not known, then for a large sample size (i.e. n ≥ 30) it is approximated by the standard deviation (s) of the sample so that we have,

$$s_{\bar{x}} = \frac{s}{\sqrt{n}}$$

and hence, the confidence interval is

$$\bar{x} \pm z\, s_{\bar{x}}$$

∴ at 95% level of confidence we have the interval as

$$\bar{x} \pm 1.96\, s_{\bar{x}}$$

(ii) $\bar{x} \pm z\, \sigma_{\bar{x}}$ (or $\bar{x} \pm z\, s_{\bar{x}}$) gives the interval estimation of the population mean (μ) and $\sigma_{\bar{x}}$ (or $s_{\bar{x}}$) represents the standard error of estimation (of population mean) at the given confidence level (or level of significance, α).

Example 7: A company wants to estimate the average age of its workers. A random sample of 64 workers showed that the average age was 27 years with a standard deviation of 4 years.

(i) Estimate a 95% confidence interval estimate of the average age of all its workers.

(ii) How will these limits change if the confidence level is increased from 95% to 99%.

Solution: Since the sample size (n = 64) is large (as n > 30), we approximate the population standard deviation σ (which is unknown), by the sample standard deviation, s.

(i) Thus, we have, sample mean, $\bar{x}$ = 27 years

Sample s.d., s = 4 years and at 95% confidence level, the critical value of z is 1.96.

$\therefore$ Confidence interval is

$\bar{x} \pm z\, s_{\bar{x}}$ where $s_{\bar{x}} = \dfrac{s}{\sqrt{n}} = \dfrac{4}{\sqrt{64}} = \dfrac{4}{8} = 0.5$

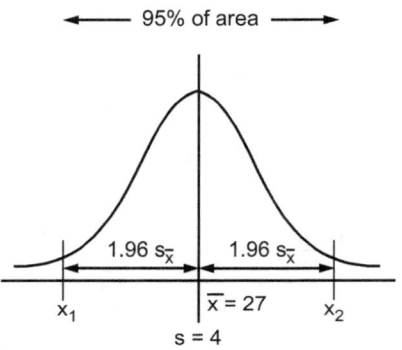

i.e. $27 \pm 1.96\,(0.5)$ i.e. 27 ± 0.98

i.e. $x_1 = 27 - 0.98 = 26.02$

and $x_2 = 27 + 0.98 = 27.98$

and hence, the estimated population mean (i.e. average age of all workers) is μ such that $26.02 \le \mu \le 27.98$ at 95% level of confidence (or at significance level, $\alpha = 0.05$).

Thus, we can say with 95% confidence that the average age of workers will lie between 26.02 and 27.98 years.

(ii) Here for 99% level of confidence, the critical value of z is z = 2.575.

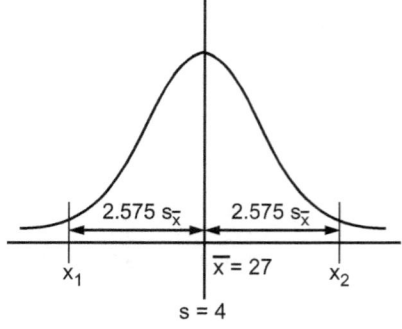

$\therefore$ The confidence interval is

$\bar{x} \pm z\, s_{\bar{x}}$ i.e. $27 \pm 2.575\,(0.5)$

i.e. 27 ± 1.29

i.e. $x_1 = 27 - 1.29 = 25.71$ years and $x_2 = 27 + 1.29 = 28.29$ years so that $25.71 \le \mu \le 28.29$ at 99% level of confidence.

(b) Interval Estimate of Population Proportion

As the sampling distribution of proportions also follows the central limit theorem, hence, for 95% level of confidence (i.e. at 5% level of significance), the confidence interval will be ($p \pm 1.96\ \sigma_p$).

where, p = sample proportion of the desired attribute (say proportion of defectives in a sample)

and σ_p = standard error of proportion which is given by

$$\sigma_p = \sqrt{\frac{\pi(1-\pi)}{n}}$$

where, n = Sample size

and π = Population proportion

Thus, it is 95% likely that the population proportion will lie within this range.

Similarly, the confidence interval at 99% and 90% level of confidence is ($p \pm 2.575\ \sigma_p$) and ($p \pm 1.645\ \sigma_p$) respectively.

Note:

1. For large samples, where $np \geq 5$ and $nq \geq 5$, where p = probability of success (i.e. probability of presence of the desired attribute, say defectiveness in an item) and $q = 1 - p$ = probability of failure, then the binomial distribution (which is referred for the analysis of the attributes) is approximated to a normal distribution.

2. If the population proportion (π) is not known, then it can be approximated by the sample proportion (p) so that

$$\sigma_p = \sqrt{\frac{p(1-p)}{n}}$$

3. $p \pm z\ \sigma_p$ gives the interval estimation of the population proportion (π) and σ_p represent the standard error of estimation (of population proportion) at a given confidence level (or level of significance, α).

Example 8: A large company is worried about the smoking habits among its workers. A random survey of 300 workers across all its plants showed that 120 of these workers were smokers. Construct 90% and 95% confidence interval of true proportion.

Solution: The sample size is $n = 300$ and the sample proportion of the smokers is

$$p = \frac{120}{300} = 0.4$$

Also, as the population proportion (π) is not known, we estimate the standard error of proportion as

$$\sigma_p = \sqrt{\frac{p(1-p)}{n}}$$

$$= \sqrt{\frac{0.4(1-0.4)}{300}} = \sqrt{\frac{0.4(0.6)}{300}}$$

$$= \sqrt{\frac{0.24}{300}} = \sqrt{0.0008}$$

$\therefore \quad \sigma_p = 0.028$

Hence,
(i) At 90% level of confidence, (i.e. at 10% level of significance i.e. $\alpha = 0.10$)

$p_1 = p - 1.645 \, \sigma_p$ .... as critical value of $z = 1.645$
$= 0.4 - 1.645 (0.028) = 0.4 - 0.046$
$= 0.354$ i.e. 35.4%

and $\quad p_2 = p + 1.645 \, \sigma_p$
$= 0.4 + 0.046 = 0.446$ i.e. 44.6%

$\therefore$ The interval estimate of population proportion (i.e. the proportion of smokers in the entire company) i.e. π is

$p_1 \leq \pi \leq p_2$ i.e. $0.354 \leq \pi \leq 0.446$

So that we can be 90% confident that the proportion of workers in the entire company with smoking habits will be in the interval (or range) of (0.354 to 0.446) i.e. (35.4% to 44.6%).

(ii) Similarly, at 95% level of confidence,

$p_1 = p - 1.96 \, \sigma_p$ .... as critical value of $z = 1.96$
$= 0.4 - 1.96 (0.028) = 0.4 - 0.055$
$= 0.345$

and $\quad p_2 = p + 1.96 \, \sigma_p$
$= 0.4 + 0.055 = 0.455$

So that the confidence interval is $(0.345 \leq \mu \leq 0.455)$

List of Formulae

1. Binomial Distribution:

(i) Parameters are n and p and P(r successes in n trials) i.e.

$$P(r) = {}^nC_r p^r q^{n-r} \quad , r = 0, 1, 2, \ldots n$$

where p = probability of getting success in one trial and $q = 1 - p$

(ii) mean or E(r) i.e. $\bar{r} = np$ and Variance $= \sigma^2 = npq$

(iii) Number of sets in which r successes are achieved in n trials, from total number of N sets is $f(r) = N \, P(r)$.

2. **Poisson Distribution:** $n \to \infty$ and $p \to 0$ or 1

   (i) Parameter is $m = np$ and $P(r) = \dfrac{e^{-m} m^r}{r!}$, $r = 0, 1, 2, ...$

   Find e^{-m} directly or use its value from the table of e^{-m} (appendix B)

   (ii) mean = variance = $m = np$

   (iii) $f(r) = N\, P(r)$

3. **Normal Distribution:**

   (i) Parameters are mean m and standard deviation σ

   Standard Normal Variate is $z = \dfrac{x - m}{\sigma}$

   $\therefore P(x_1 \le x \le x_2) = P(z_1 \le z \le z_2)$ = Area under Standard Normal Curve from the ordinate (line) $z = z_1$ to $z = z_2$

   Use Standard table to read the value of $P(0 \le z \le z_1)$ for z_1 etc. **(Appendix A)**

   (ii) $f(x_1 \le x \le x_2) = N\, P(x_1 \le x \le x_2) = N\, P(z_1 \le z \le z_2)$

   (iii) $P(-\infty < z < \infty) = 1$, $P(-\infty < z \le 0) = P(0 \le z < \infty) = 0.5$

   Standard Normal Curve is symmetric about $z = 0$.

4. **Interval Estimates:**

   (i) Of population mean (μ) : $\bar{x} \pm z\, \sigma_{\bar{x}}$

   i.e. $(\bar{x} - z\, \sigma_{\bar{x}} \le \mu \le \bar{x} + z\, \sigma_{\bar{x}})$

   where $\bar{x}$ = Sample mean

   $\sigma_{\bar{x}}$ = Standard error of mean (estimation)

   $= \dfrac{\sigma}{\sqrt{n}} \sqrt{\dfrac{N - n}{N - 1}}$ ... for finite population

   $= \dfrac{\sigma}{\sqrt{n}}$ ... for large population

   where σ = Population Standard Deviation

   If σ is not known then,

   Interval estimate: $\bar{x} \pm z\, s_{\bar{x}}$

   where, $s_{\bar{x}} = \dfrac{s}{\sqrt{n}}$ ... s = sample standard deviation

DECISION SCIENCES   PROBABILITY DISTRIBUTIONS

(ii) of population proportion (π): $p \pm z\, \sigma_p$

i.e. $p - z\, \sigma_p \leq \pi \leq p + z\, \sigma_p$

where, p = Sample proportion

σ_p = Standard error of proportion (estimation)

$= \sqrt{\dfrac{p(1-p)}{n}}$

(iii) Critical values of z:

For 90% confidence level (i.e. 10% level of significance or $\alpha = 0.10$). $z = 1.645$.

For 95% confidence level (i.e. $\alpha = 0.05$): $z = 1.96$.

For 99% confidence level (i.e. $\alpha = 0.01$): $z = 2.575$.

Solved Problems

Problem 1: If the dividend amounts expected on a share of face value ₹ 100 of a Company XYZ along with their likely probabilities are as follows:

Dividend (₹):	00	10	20	30	40
Probability:	0.2	0.25	0.30	0.15	0.10

Should Mr. Sharma purchase the shares if he expects a minimum rate of return of 15%.

Solution: We have to find the expected gain i.e. mean of the return on investment, given its probability distribution.

Thus,

x:	00	10	20	30	40
P(x):	0.20	0.25	0.30	0.15	0.10
xP(x):	00	2.5	6.0	4.5	4.0

$\therefore$ Expected Gain, $E(x) = \Sigma\, x\, P(x) = 17$

Since expected gain is ₹ 17/- on the share of face value 100. $\therefore$ Expected gain is 17% which is more than 15%. Hence, Mr. Sharma should purchase the shares.

Problem 2: An experiment succeeds twice as many times as it fails. Find the chance that in 5 trials there will be at least one success.

Solution: We have, p = Probability of success, q = Probability of failure

$\therefore p + q = 1$ Now, $p = 2q$ ... (given)

$\therefore 2q + q = 1$ $\therefore q = \dfrac{1}{3}$ $\therefore p = 2\left(\dfrac{1}{3}\right) = \dfrac{2}{3}$

Also, $n = 5$ $\therefore$ By Law of Binomial Distribution, $P(r) = {}^nC_r\, p^r\, q^{n-r} = {}^5C_r \left(\dfrac{2}{3}\right)^r \left(\dfrac{1}{3}\right)^{5-r}$

∴ Required Probability = $P(r \geq 1) = 1 - P(r < 1) = 1 - P(0)$

$$= 1 - {}^5C_0 \left(\frac{2}{3}\right)^0 \left(\frac{1}{3}\right)^{5-0} = 1 - 1(1)\frac{1}{3^5}$$

$$= 1 - \frac{1}{3^5}$$

Problem 3: Assume that half of the population is vegetarian so that the chance of an individual being a vegetarian is $\frac{1}{2}$. Assuming that 100 investigators each take a sample of 10 individuals to see whether they are vegetarians, how many investigators would you expect to report that three people or less were vegetarians.

Solution: We have, p = probability that an individual is vegetarian = $\frac{1}{2}$

∴ $q = 1 - p = 1 - \frac{1}{2} = \frac{1}{2}$

Also, n = 10 ∴ By Binomial Probability Law the probability that there are r number of vegetarians in a sample of n = 10 is

$$P(r) = {}^nC_r p^r q^{n-r} = {}^{10}C_r \left(\frac{1}{2}\right)^r \left(\frac{1}{2}\right)^{10-r} = {}^{10}C_r \left(\frac{1}{2}\right)^{10}$$

$$= \frac{1}{1024} {}^{10}C_r$$

∴ P(there are three or less vegetarians) = $P(r \leq 3)$
= P(0) + P(1) + P(2) + P(3)

$$= \frac{1}{1024}{}^{10}C_0 + \frac{1}{1024}{}^{10}C_1 + \frac{1}{1024}{}^{10}C_2 + \frac{1}{1024}{}^{10}C_3$$

$$= \frac{1}{1024}\left(1 + 10 + \frac{10 \times 9}{1 \times 2} + \frac{10 \times 9 \times 8}{1 \times 2 \times 3}\right) = \frac{1}{1024}(1 + 10 + 45 + 120)$$

$$= \frac{1}{1024}(176) = 0.172$$

Now in all (N = 100) investigators took the survey of (n=10) individuals each. Hence, the required expected number of investigators = N $P(r \leq 3)$ = 100(0.172) = 17.2 ≈ 17.

Problem 4: The incidence of a certain disease is such that on average, 20% of workers suffer from it. If 10 workers are selected at random, find the probability that
   (i) Exactly 2 workers suffer from the disease
   (ii) Not more than 2 workers suffer from the disease
   (iii) Atleast 9 workers suffer from the disease

Solution: Probability that a worker suffers from the disease = 20% = $\frac{20}{100} = \frac{1}{5}$

∴ $q = 1 - p = 1 - \frac{1}{5} = \frac{4}{5}$ Also, n = Number of workers selected = 10

∴ By Binomial Probability Law, the probability that r workers out of these (n = 10) workers suffer from the disease is

$$P(r) = {}^nC_r p^r q^{n-r} = {}^{10}C_r \left(\frac{1}{5}\right)^r \left(\frac{4}{5}\right)^{10-r} = {}^{10}C_r \frac{4^{10-r}}{5^{10}}$$

(i) ∴ Probability that exactly (r = 2) workers suffer from the disease i.e.

$$P(r = 2) = {}^{10}C_2 \frac{4^{10-2}}{5^{10}} = \frac{10 \times 9}{1 \times 2} = \frac{4^8}{5^{10}} = 0.302$$

(ii) Required Probability = $P(r \leq 2) = P(r = 0) + P(r = 1) + P(r = 2)$

$$= {}^{10}C_0 \frac{4^{10}}{5^{10}} + {}^{10}C_1 \frac{4^9}{5^{10}} + {}^{10}C_2 \frac{4^8}{5^{10}}$$

$$= \frac{1}{5^{10}} \left(1 \times 4^{10} + 10 \times 4^9 + \frac{10 \times 9}{1 \times 2} \cdot 4^8\right) = \frac{4^8}{5^{10}} [4^2 + 10(4) + 45]$$

$$= \frac{4^8}{5^{10}} (101) = 0.678$$

(iii) Required Probability = $P(r \geq 9) = P(r = 9) + P(r = 10)$

$$= {}^{10}C_9 \frac{4^{10-9}}{5^{10}} + {}^{10}C_{10} \frac{4^{10-10}}{5^{10}} = {}^{10}C_1 \frac{4^1}{5^{10}} + 1 \cdot \frac{4^0}{5^{10}} \quad \ldots \because {}^nC_r = {}^nC_{n-r}$$

$$= \frac{1}{5^{10}} (10 \times 4 + 1 \times 1) = \frac{41}{5^{10}} = (4.2) \times 10^{-6}$$

Problem 5: Comment on the following: For a Binomial Distribution, mean = 7 and variance = 11.

Solution: For a Binomial Distribution, we have mean = np and variance = npq

∴ np = 7 and npq = 11

∴ Dividing we get, $\frac{npq}{np} = q = \frac{11}{7} = 1.6$

i.e. Probability of failure = 1.6

Since the probability must always lie between (0 and 1), hence the given statement is wrong.

Problem 6: If on an average 8 ships out of 10, arrive safely at a port. Find the mean and standard deviation of the number of ships arriving safely out of a total of 1200 ships.

Solution: We have, p = probability of a safe arrival = $\frac{8}{10}$ = 0.8.

$$\therefore q = 1 - p = 1 - 0.8 = 0.2$$

Also, n = Total number of ships = 1200

∴ Mean no. of ships arriving safely = np
$$= 1200 (0.8) = 960$$

and Standard Deviation,
$$\sigma = \sqrt{\text{Variance}}$$
$$= \sqrt{npq} = \sqrt{(1200)(0.8)(0.2)} = \sqrt{192}$$
$$= 13.86$$

Problem 7: Five fair coins were tossed 100 times. From the following outcomes find the expected frequencies.

No. heads up:	0	1	2	3	4	5
Observed Frequency:	2	10	24	35	18	8

Solution: We have p = probability of head = $\frac{1}{2}$, ∴ $q = 1 - p = \frac{1}{2}$ and n = 5

Thus, by Binomial Probability Law,

$$P(r) = {}^nC_r p^r q^{n-r} = {}^5C_r \left(\frac{1}{2}\right)^r \left(\frac{1}{2}\right)^{5-r} = {}^5C_r \left(\frac{1}{2}\right)^5 = \frac{1}{32} {}^5C_r$$

∴ And if N = 100, we have corresponding expected frequencies as

$$f(r) = N \times P(r) = 100 \left(\frac{1}{32} {}^5C_r\right) = (3.125) \, {}^5C_r$$

∴ $f(0) = (3.125) \, {}^5C_0 = (3.125)(1) = 3.125$

$f(1) = (3.125) \, {}^5C_1 = (3.125)(5) = 15.625$

$f(2) = (3.125) \, {}^5C_2 = (3.125) \left(\frac{5 \times 4}{1 \times 2}\right) = 31.25$

$f(3) = (3.125) \, {}^5C_3 = (3.125) \, {}^5C_2 = 31.25$ ... ∵ ${}^nC_r = {}^nC_{n-r}$

$f(4) = (3.125) \, {}^5C_4 = (3.125) \, {}^5C_1 = 15.625$ and

$f(5) = (3.125) \, {}^5C_5 = (3.125) \, {}^5C_0 = 3.125$

Problem 8: In a certain factory, it was found that the variance of the number of absentees is 4 workers per shift. Find the probability that on a given shift (i) Exactly two workers will be absent (ii) At least two workers will be absent (iii) Not more than two workers will be absent. Use Poisson distribution.

Solution: We have, for the factory, variance of absentees per shift = 4

For a Poisson distribution, mean of the absentees per shift (m) = variance

∴ m = 4

∴ By Poisson Probability Law

P(r number of absentees in a shift) = $\dfrac{e^{-m}m^r}{r!} = \dfrac{e^{-4}4^r}{r!} = \dfrac{(0.0183)4^r}{r!}$

... using table **(Appendix B)** or otherwise

(i) ∴ P(two workers are absent) i.e. P (r = 2) = $\dfrac{0.0183(4)^2}{2!} = \dfrac{0.0183(16)}{2 \times 1} = 0.1464$

(ii) P (at least 2 absentees) i.e. P (r ≥ 2)

$= 1 - $ P (less than two absentees) $= 1 - $ P(r < 2)

$= 1 - $ P (0 or 1 absentee) $= 1 - $ P(r = 0 or r = 1)

$= 1 - [P(0) + P(1)] = 1 - \left[0.0183\dfrac{(4)^0}{0!} + 0.0183\dfrac{(4)^1}{1!} \right]$

$= 1 - 0.0183\left[\dfrac{1}{1} + \dfrac{4}{1}\right] = 1 - 0.0183(5) = 1 - 0.0915 = 0.9085$

(iii) Similarly, P(not more than two absentees) i.e. P (r ≤ 2)

$= $ P(r = 0 or 1 or 2) $=$ P (0) + P (1) + P (2)

$= 0.0183\left[\dfrac{(4)^0}{0!} + \dfrac{(4)^1}{1!} + \dfrac{(4)^2}{2!}\right]$

$= 0.0183\left(\dfrac{1}{1} + \dfrac{4}{1} + \dfrac{16}{2 \times 1}\right) = 0.0183 (1 + 4 + 8)$

$= 0.2379$

Problem 9: In a certain factory turning out razor blades, there is a small chance $\dfrac{1}{500}$ for any blade to be defective. The blades are supplied in a packet of 10. Use Poisson distribution to calculate approximately, the number of packets containing (i) No defective and (ii) Two defective blades, in a consignment of 10,000 packets.

Solution: We have, p = Probability that a razor blade is defective = $\frac{1}{500}$ = 0.002.

Also, n = Number of blades in a packet = 10
∴ Average Number of defective blades in a packet = m = np = 10(0.002) = 0.02
∴ By Poisson Probability Law, the probability that a packet will contain r defective blades is

$$P(r) = \frac{e^{-m}m^r}{r!} = \frac{e^{-0.02}(0.02)^r}{r!} = \frac{(0.9802)(0.02)^r}{r!}$$

(i) ∴ Probability that a packet contains no defective blade i.e.

$$P(r=0) = \frac{(0.9802)(0.02)^0}{0!} = \frac{(0.9802)(1)}{1} = 0.9802$$

∴ Number of such packets in a consignment of (N=10,000) packets
= N.P(0) = 10,000(0.9802) = 9802

Similarly, $P(r=2) = \frac{(0.9802)(0.02)^2}{2!} = \frac{(0.9802)(0.0004)}{2 \times 1} = 1.96 \times 10^{-4}$

∴ Number of packets containing two defective blades in the consignment of (N = 10,000) packets = 10,000 (1.96 × 10⁻⁴) = 1.96 ≈ 2 packets.

Problem 10: In a sample of 1000 scores, the mean of a certain test is 14 and the standard deviation is 2.5. Assuming the distribution to be Normal, find:
(i) How many students have scored between 12 and 15?
(ii) How many scored above 18?
(iii) How many scored below 8?
(iv) How many scored 16?

Solution: Let x - marks scored by the students in the given test,

We have, mean of marks, m = $\bar{x}$ = 14 and standard deviation (s.d.) as σ = 2.5.
Also, N = Total Number of students = 1000

Let, z = $\frac{x-m}{\sigma} = \frac{x-14}{2.5}$ be the Standard Normal Variate

(i) Let us find, Probability (student scores between 12 and 15) i.e. P(12 ≤ x ≤ 15)

Now when, x = 12, z = $\frac{12-14}{2.5}$ = –0.8 and when x = 15, z = $\frac{15-14}{2.5}$ = 0.4

∴ P(12 ≤ x ≤ 15) = P(−0.8 ≤ z ≤ 0.4)
= P(−0.8 ≤ z ≤ 0) + P(0 ≤ z ≤ 0.4)
= P(0 ≤ z ≤ 0.8) + P(0 ≤ z ≤ 0.4)   ... by symmetry
= 0.2881 + 0.1554
              ... from table of area under Normal Curve (Appendix A)
= 0.4435

∴ Number of students who have scored between 12 and 15
= N× P(12 ≤ x ≤ 15) = 1000(0.4435) = 443.5 = 444 (approx.)

(ii) For x = 18, $z = \dfrac{18-14}{2.5} = 1.6$

∴ P(student scores above 18) i.e.

$$P(x \geq 18) = P(z \geq 1.6) = P(1.6 \leq z < \infty)$$
$$= P(0 \leq z < \infty) - P(0 \leq z \leq 1.6)$$
$$= 0.5 - 0.4452$$
$$= 0.0548$$

... from table of area under normal curve (Appendix A)

∴ Number of students scoring above 18 = 1000 (0.0548) = 54.8 ≃ 55

(iii) If x = 8, $z = \dfrac{8-14}{2.5} = -2.4$

∴ $P(x \leq 8) = P(z \leq -2.4) = P(z \geq 2.4)$ ... by symmetry
$$= P(2.4 \leq z < \infty) = P(0 \leq z < \infty) - P(0 \leq z \leq 2.4)$$
$$= 0.5 - P(0 \leq z \leq 2.4) = 0.5 - 0.4918 = 0.0082$$

∴ Number of students scoring marks below 8 = 1000 (0.0082) = 8.2 ≃ 8

(iv) Assuming that the fractional marks are rounded of to the nearest integer, we have, students scoring (x = 16) marks = students scoring marks in the range (x = 15.5 to x = 16.5).

Thus, P(x = 16) = P(15.5 ≤ x ≤ 16.5)

When, x = 15.5, $z = \dfrac{15.5-14}{2.5} = 0.6$ and when x = 16.5, $z = \dfrac{16.5-14}{2.5} = 1$

∴ $P(x = 16) = P(0.6 \leq z \leq 1) = P(0 \leq z \leq 1) - P(0 \leq z \leq 0.6)$
$$= 0.3413 - 0.2257 = 0.1156$$

∴ Number of students scoring 16 marks = 1000 (0.1156) = 115.6 ≃ 116

Problem 11: Assume the mean height of soldiers to be 68.22 inches with a variance of 10.8 inches. How many soldiers in a regiment of 1000 would you expect to be i) over 6 feet tall and ii) below 5.5 feet. iii) What is the percentage of soldiers having height between 5.5 feet and 6 feet. Assume the heights to be normally distributed.

Solution: Let x- height of a soldier. Also we have mean height = m = 68.22 inches, and variance σ^2 = 10.8 inches

∴ Standard deviation, $\sigma = \sqrt{10.8} = 3.286$.

Also, let $z = \dfrac{x-m}{\sigma} = \dfrac{x-68.22}{3.286}$ be the standard normal variate and N = Total number of soldiers in the regiment = 1000.

(i) If x = 6 feet = 6×12 = 72 inches

$$\therefore z = \frac{72 - 68.22}{3.286} = 1.15$$

∴ Probability (height is above 6 feet) i.e. P(x ≥ 72 inches)

$$= P(z \geq 1.15)$$
$$= P(1.15 \leq z < \infty) = P(0 \leq z < \infty) - P(0 \leq z \leq 1.15)$$
$$= 0.5 - P(0 \leq z \leq 1.15)$$
$$= 0.5 - 0.3749$$

... by using table of area under normal curve (Appendix A)

$$= 0.1251$$

∴ Number of soldiers over 6 feet tall = N × P(x ≥ 72) = 1000 (0.1251) = 125.1 ≃ 125

(ii) For x = 5.5 feet = 5.5 × 12 = 66 inches, $z = \frac{66 - 68.22}{3.286} = -0.6756$

∴ Probability (height is below 5.5 feet) i.e.

P(x ≤ 66) = P(z ≤ −0.6756) = P(z ≥ 0.6756)   ... by symmetry
$$= P(0.6756 \leq z < \infty) = P(0 \leq z < \infty) - P(0 \leq z \leq 0.6756)$$
$$= 0.5 - 0.2502 \quad \text{... from table, taking average of 0.2486 and 0.2517}$$
$$= 0.2498$$

∴ Number of soldiers with height below 5.5 feet = 1000 (0.2498) = 249.8 ≃ 250

(iii) P(height between 5.5 feet and 6 feet) i.e.

P(66 ≤ x ≤ 72) = P(−0.6756 ≤ z ≤ 1.15)
$$= P(-0.6756 \leq z \leq 0) + P(0 \leq z \leq 1.15)$$
$$= P(0 \leq z \leq 0.6756) + P(0 \leq z \leq 1.15) \quad \text{... by symmetry}$$
$$= 0.2502 + 0.3749 = 0.6251$$

∴ Percentage or proportion of soldiers having height between 5.5 and 6 feet = 62.51% and

∴ Number of soldiers with height between (5.5 feet and 6 feet) = 1000 (0.6251) = 625.1 ≃ 625

Note: Total probability P (−∞ < z < ∞) = 1
i.e. P(z ≤ 66) + P(66 ≤ z ≤ 72) + P(z ≥ 72) = 1
i.e. 0.2498 + 0.6251 + 0.1251 = 1
Also, Total number of soldiers = 250 + 625 + 125 = 1000

Problem 12: The mean inside diameter of a sample of 500 washers produced by a machine is 5.02 mm and the standard deviation is 0.05 mm. The purpose for which these washers are intended allows a maximum tolerance in diameter from 4.96 to 5.08 mm, otherwise, the washers are considered defective. Determine the percentage of defective washers produced by the machine assuming the diameters are normally distributed.

Solution: Let x - diameter of washer, m = 5.02 mm, σ = 0.05 mm and $z = \dfrac{x-m}{\sigma} = \dfrac{x-5.02}{0.05}$

Since the tolerances are given, the washers with diameters in the range (4.96 ≤ x ≤ 5.08) would be allowed.

Now, when x = 4.96, $z = \dfrac{4.96-5.02}{0.05} = -1.2$ and x = 5.08, $z = \dfrac{5.08-5.02}{0.05} = 1.2$

∴ P(diameter is in the acceptable range) i.e.

P(4.96 ≤ x ≤ 5.08) = P(−1.2 ≤ z ≤ 1.2) = P(−1.2 ≤ z ≤ 0) + P(0 ≤ z ≤ 1.2)
= P(0 ≤ z ≤ 1.2) + P(0 ≤ z ≤ 1.2)   ... by symmetry
= 2 P(0 ≤ z ≤ 1.2) = 2(0.3849) = 0.7698

∴ Percentage of non-defective washers = 100 (0.7698) = 76.98% ≈ 77%

∴ Percentage of defective washers = 100 − 77 = 23%

Problem 13: A set of examination marks is approximately normally distributed with a mean of 75 and standard deviation of 5. If the top 5% of the students get grade A and the bottom 25% get grade F, what mark is the lowest A and what mark is the highest F?

(P.U. MBA - May 10)

Solution: Let x − marks obtained by students in the examination
We have, mean marks, m = 75 and standard deviation, σ = 5

Let $z = \dfrac{x-m}{\sigma} = \dfrac{x-75}{5}$ be the Standard Normal Variate.

Let x = x' be the lowest marks obtained by the students getting grade A

$$\therefore z' = \dfrac{x'-75}{5}$$

Now, top 5% of the students get grade A i.e. they get marks more than x'.

Hence, P (marks more than x') = 5% i.e. $\dfrac{5}{100} = 0.05$

i.e. P(x ≥ x') = 0.05

∴ P(x ≥ x') = P(z ≥ z') = P(z' ≤ z < ∞) = 0.05

∴ Area to the right of ordinate (line) z = z' is 0.05 which is less than area (0.5) lying to the right of z = 0 [i.e. between (0≤ z <∞)] Hence, z' lies in right portion of normal curve.

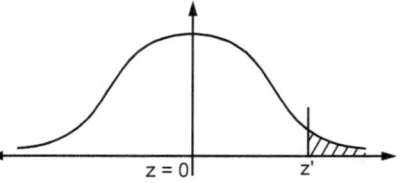

Now, $P(z \geq z') = 0.05$

∴ $P(0 \leq z < \infty) - P(0 \leq z \leq z') = 0.05$

∴ $0.5 - P(0 \leq z \leq z') = 0.05$

∴ $P(0 \leq z \leq z') = 0.5 - 0.05 = 0.45$

Reading the table of the area under standard normal curve (appendix A) in reverse order, the value of z corresponding to area of (0.45) is (average of 1.64 and 1.65 i.e.) 1.645

∴ $z' = 1.645$ i.e. $\dfrac{x' - 75}{5} = 1.645$ ... (1)

∴ $x' = 5(1.645) + 75 = 83.225 \simeq 83$

(ii) Let $x = x''$ be the highest marks obtained by students getting grade F

∴ $z'' = \dfrac{x'' - 75}{5}$

Now, since bottom 25% of the students get F

∴ P(marks less than x") = 25% = 0.25

i.e. $P(x \leq x'') = P(z \leq z'') = 0.25$

∴ Area to the left of ordinate $z = z''$ is 0.25 which is less than the total area (0.5) to the left of $z = 0$.

Hence, z" lies in the left portion of the normal curve.

Now, $P(z \leq z'') = 0.25$

∴ $P(z \geq -z'') = 0.25$ ... by symmetry

∴ $P(-z'' \leq z < \infty) = 0.25$

i.e. $P(0 \leq z < \infty) - P(0 \leq z \leq -z'') = 0.25$

i.e. $0.5 - P(0 \leq z \leq -z'') = 0.25$

∴ $P(0 \leq z \leq -z'') = 0.5 - 0.25 = 0.25$

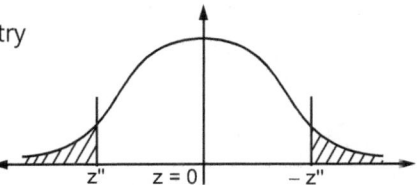

∴ From table, $-z'' = 0.675$ (average of 0.67 and 0.68)

∴ $z'' = -0.675$ i.e. $\dfrac{x'' - 75}{5} = -0.675$

∴ $x'' = 5(-0.675) + 75 = 71.625 \simeq 72$

Problem 14: In an intelligence test administered to 1000 students, the average score was 42 and standard deviation 24. Find (a) The number of students lying between 30 and 54 marks (b) The value of score exceeded by top 100 students.

Solution: Let x – Score of students, m = 42, σ = 24

$$z = \dfrac{x - m}{\sigma} = \dfrac{x - 42}{24}$$

(a) If $x = 30$, $z = \dfrac{30 - 42}{24} = -0.5$ and $x = 54$, $z = \dfrac{54 - 42}{24} = 0.5$

∴ P(30 ≤ x ≤ 54) = P(– 0.5 ≤ z < 0.5)
               = 2P(0 ≤ z ≤ 0.5)   ... by symmetry
               = 2(0.1915) = 0.383   ... using table
∴ Number of students lying between 30 and 54 = 1000(0.383) = 383

(b) Let the score be x' ∴ $z' = \dfrac{x' - 42}{24}$

∴ Number of students with score exceeding x' = 100

∴ P(Student scores more than x') = $\dfrac{100}{\text{Total No.}} = \dfrac{100}{1000} = 0.1$

i.e. P(x ≥ x') = P(z ≥ z') = 0.1. Thus z' will be in the right half of curve
∴ 0.5 – P(0 ≤ z ≤ z') = 0.1
∴ P(0 ≤ z ≤ z') = 0.5 – 0.1 = 0.4

∴ z' = 1.28   i.e. $\dfrac{x' - 42}{24} = 1.28$ ... using table in reverse order

∴ x' = 24 (1.28) + 42 = 72.72 ≈ 73

Problem 15: In a distribution exactly normal, 7% of the items are under 35 and 89% are under 63. What is the mean and standard deviation of the distribution?

Solution: Let x be the variate whose mean is m and s.d. σ

∴ Standard Normal Variate is $z = \dfrac{x - m}{\sigma}$

If x = 35, $z = \dfrac{35 - m}{\sigma} = z_1$ (say) and x = 63, $z = \dfrac{63 - m}{\sigma}$ (say)

Since, 7% of the items have value under 35

∴ P(x ≤ 35) = 7% = $\dfrac{7}{100}$ = 0.07

∴ P(z ≤ z_1) = 0.07

Hence, area to the left of ordinate (line) z = z_1 is 0.07 which is less than the area (0.5) to the left of line z = 0 under the standard normal curve.
Hence, z = z_1 will lie in the left portion.

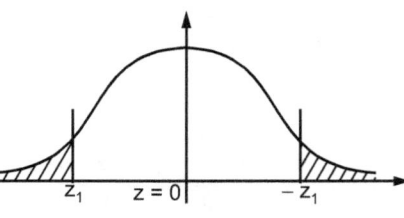

Now,   ∵ P(z ≤ z_1) = 0.07
∴   P(z ≥ – z_1) = 0.07   ... by symmetry
∴   P(–z_1 ≤ z < ∞) = 0.07
i.e. P(0 ≤ z < ∞) – P(0 ≤ z ≤ – z_1) = 0.07
∴   0.5 – P(0 ≤ z ≤ –z_1) = 0.07
∴ P(0 ≤ z ≤ –z_1) = 0.5 – 0.07 = 0.43

∴ Using the table for area under the normal curve in the reverse order we see that value corresponding to 0.43 is 1.48 (approx.)

∴ $-z_1 = 1.48$

∴ $z_1 = -1.48$ i.e. $\dfrac{35-m}{\sigma} = -1.48$ ... (1)

Also, since 89% items are under value of 63

∴ $P(x \le 63) = 89\% = 0.89$

i.e. $P(z \le z_2) = 0.89$

∴ Area to the left of ordinate $z = z_2$ is 0.89 which is greater than total area to the left of $z = 0$ which is 0.5. Hence, $z = z_2$ will lie in the right hand portion.

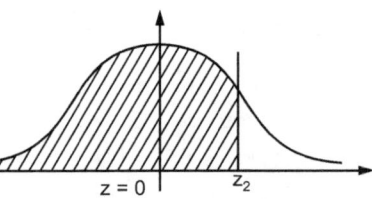

Now, $P(z \le z_2) = 0.89$

i.e. $P(-\infty < z \le z_2) = 0.89$

i.e. $P(-\infty < z \le 0) + P(0 \le z \le z_2) = 0.89$

i.e. $0.5 + P(0 \le z \le z_2) = 0.89$

∴ $P(0 \le z \le z_2) = 0.89 - 0.5 = 0.39$

∴ Reading the table in reverse order,

$z_2 = 1.23$ i.e. $\dfrac{63-m}{\sigma} = 1.23$ ... (2)

Also, $\dfrac{35-m}{\sigma} = -1.48$ ... (1)

∴ Dividing, $\dfrac{\frac{63-m}{\sigma}}{\frac{35-m}{\sigma}} = \dfrac{1.23}{-1.48}$

i.e. $\dfrac{63-m}{35-m} = -\dfrac{1.23}{1.48} = -\dfrac{123}{148}$

∴ $148(63 - m) = -123(35 - m)$

i.e. $9324 - 148m = -4305 + 123m$

∴ $123m + 148m = 9324 + 4305$

i.e. $271m = 13629$

∴ $m = \dfrac{13629}{271} = 50.3 =$ mean

∴ From (2), $\dfrac{63 - 50.3}{\sigma} = 1.23$

∴ $\sigma = \dfrac{12.7}{1.23} = 10.33 =$ S.D.

Problem 16: Of a large group of men, 5 percent are under 60 inches in height and 40 percent are between 60 and 65 inches. Assuming a normal distribution, find the mean height and standard deviation. **(P.U. MBA - Dec. 10)**

Solution: Let x – height of the men. Let mean be m and s.d. σ

Also, let $z = \dfrac{x - m}{\sigma}$

(i) When $x = 60$, $z = \dfrac{60 - m}{\sigma} = z_1$ (say)

Since 5% of men have height under $x = 60$ inches

$\therefore P(x \leq 60) = P(z \leq z_1) = 5\% = 0.05$.

Thus, area to the left of ordinate i.e. line $z = z_1$ is 0.05 which is less than total area to the left of line $z = 0$ which is 0.5

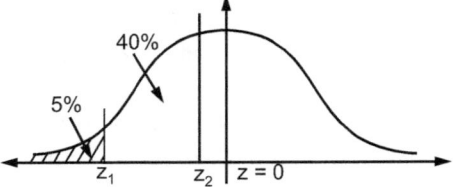

$\therefore z_1$ lies in left hand portion

$\because \qquad\qquad P(z \leq z_1) = 0.05$

$\therefore \qquad\qquad P(z \geq -z_1) = 0.05 \qquad\qquad$ ... by symmetry

$\therefore \qquad\qquad P(-z_1 \leq z < \infty) = 0.05$

i.e. $P(0 \leq z < \infty) - P(0 \leq z \leq -z_1) = 0.05$

i.e. $\qquad\qquad 0.5 - P(0 \leq z \leq -z_1) = 0.05$

$\therefore \qquad\qquad P(0 \leq z \leq -z_1) = 0.5 - 0.05 = 0.45$

$\therefore$ Reading the table of area under normal curve in reverse manner we have,

$\qquad\qquad -z_1 = 1.645 \qquad\qquad$ (taking average of 1.64 and 1.65)

$\therefore \qquad\qquad z_1 = -1.645$

$\therefore \qquad\qquad \dfrac{60 - m}{\sigma} = -1.645 \qquad\qquad$ ... (1)

Now, when $x = 65$, $z = \dfrac{65 - m}{\sigma} = z_2$ (say)

Since 40% of the men have height between 60 and 65 inches.

$\therefore \qquad\qquad P(60 \leq x \leq 65) = P(z_1 \leq z \leq z_2) = 40\%$ i.e. 0.4

Now, $\qquad\qquad P(z \leq z_2) = P(z \leq z_1) + P(z_1 \leq z \leq z_2)$

$\qquad\qquad\qquad\qquad = 0.05 + 0.4 = 0.45 \qquad\qquad$ (which is again less than 0.5)

(Note this step)

$\therefore z_2$ also lies in the left portion

$\therefore \qquad\qquad P(z \geq -z_2) = 0.45 \qquad\qquad$ ... by symmetry

$\therefore \qquad\qquad 0.5 - P(0 \leq z \leq -z_2) = 0.45$

$\therefore \qquad\qquad P(0 \leq z \leq -z_2) = 0.5 - 0.45 = 0.05$

∴ From table, $-z_2 = 0.13$ ∴ $z_2 = -0.13$

i.e. $\dfrac{65 - m}{\sigma} = -0.13$ ... (2)

Also, $\dfrac{60 - m}{\sigma} = -1.645$ ... from (1)

Dividing we get, $\dfrac{65 - m}{60 - m} = \dfrac{0.13}{1.645} = \dfrac{13}{164.5}$

∴ $164.5(65 - m) = 13(60 - m)$ i.e. $10692.5 - 164.5m = 780 - 13m$

∴ $164.5m - 13m = 10692.5 - 780 = 9912.5$ i.e. $151.5 m = 9912.5$

∴ $m = \dfrac{9912.5}{151.5} = 65.43$

∴ From (2), $\dfrac{65 - 65.43}{\sigma} = -0.13$

∴ $\sigma = \dfrac{-(0.43)}{-(0.13)} = 3.3$

Problem 17: The income distribution of workers in a certain factory was found to be normal with mean of ₹ 500 and S.D of ₹ 50. There were 228 workers getting above ₹ 600. How many workers were there in all?

Solution: Let there be N number of workers in the factory and x – income of a worker, $m = 500, \sigma = 50$

$$\therefore z = \dfrac{x - m}{\sigma} = \dfrac{x - 500}{50}$$

Now, P(a worker has income more than 600) $= \dfrac{228}{N}$

i.e. $P(x \geq 600) = \dfrac{228}{N}$ ... (1)

Now, using normal distribution, for $x = 600$, $z = \dfrac{600 - 500}{50} = 2$

∴ $P(x \geq 600) = P(z \geq 2)$

$= 0.5 - P(0 \leq z \leq 2) = 0.5 - 0.4772$

$= 0.0228$

∴ From (1) we have,

$0.0228 = \dfrac{228}{N}$

∴ $N = \dfrac{228}{0.0228} = 10{,}000$

Problem 18: There are 600 business students in a management institute and the probability for any student to need a copy of a particular text book from the library on any day is 0.05. How many copies of the book should be kept in the library so that the probability may be greater than 0.9 that none of the students needing a copy from the library has to come back disappointed. Use normal approximation to the Binomial probability law.

Solution: Let n = number of students = 600 and p = probability for any student to need a copy from library = 0.05

∴ q = 1 − p = 1 − 0.05 = 0.95

∴ For Binomial Distribution, mean no. of students who need the book is, m = np = 600 (0.05) = 30 and its standard deviation, $\sigma = \sqrt{npq} = \sqrt{600\,(0.05)\,(0.95)} = 5.34$.

Now, let x − Number of copies required in the library

∴ Mean number of copies required = mean number of students who need the book = m = 30 and σ = 5.34.

$$\therefore z = \frac{x-m}{\sigma} = \frac{x-30}{5.34}$$

Let x = x' be the minimum number of copies required in the library so that the probability of a student getting a copy is more than 0.9

i.e. the Probability (No. of copies required by students is less than x') ≥ 0.9

i.e. P(x ≤ x') ≥ 0.9

i.e. P(z ≤ z') ≥ 0.9

∴ Area to the left of z = z' is more than or equal to 0.9 (which is more than area 0.5 to the left of z = 0)

∴ z' must lie in the right hand portion.

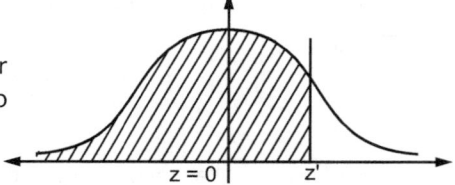

Now,   P(z ≤ z') ≥ 0.9

∴   P(−∞ < z ≤ z') ≥ 0.9

∴   0.5 + P(0 ≤ z ≤ z') ≥ 0.9

∴   P(0 ≤ z ≤ z') ≥ 0.9 − 0.5

i.e.   P(0 ≤ z ≤ z') ≥ 0.4

∴   z' ≥ 1.28   ... from table

i.e. $\dfrac{x'-30}{5.34} \geq 1.28$

i.e.   x' − 30 ≥ 5.34 (1.28)

i.e.   x' ≥ 5.34 (1.28) + 30

∴   x' ≥ 36.84

∴ Minimum number of books to be kept = 37

Problem 19: You are incharge of a soft drink distribution agency. The following reports are available for the daily supply (in no. of bottles) for two cities (with same size) in your area.

City	Mean	S.D
A	2000	350
B	1750	100

The estimated requirement is 2500 bottles daily and the absolute minimum requirement is of 1000 bottles for both the cities. Comment on the reported figures and determine which area needs more urgent attention for supply.

Solution: Let us assume the daily supply of the soft drink to be normally distributed for both the cities A and B. We know that the range (Mean ± 3σ) covers 99.73% of the distribution for a Normal distribution.

Hence,

City A	City B
Mean ± 3 σ	Mean ± 3 σ
= 2000 ± 3 (350)	= 1750 ± 3(100)
i.e. 2000 – 1050 to 2000 + 1050	i.e. 1750 – 300 to 1750 + 300
i.e. 950 to 3050	i.e. 1450 to 2050

Thus, the daily supply for B, ranges from 1450 bottles to 2050 which is fairly larger than the minimum requirement of 1000 bottles. However, the daily supply for A varies from 950 bottles to 3050 bottles which is critical as the minimum daily requirement is of 1000 bottles. Thus, there is a chance of short supply for city A. Hence, city A needs more urgent attention for supply.

Problem 20: A random sample of 100 soap cakes was taken from a large consignment. Upon weighing them the average weight of a cake was found to be 110 gm with a variance of 100. Calculate the interval estimate for the mean weight of the soap cakes for the entire consignment using (i) 90%, (ii) 95% and (iii) 99% confidence level.

Solution: We have,

n = Sample size of the soaps = 100

$\bar{x}$ = Sample mean of weights = 110 gm

Variance of sample weights = 100

∴ Sample standard deviation of soap weights

i.e. $s = \sqrt{\text{Variance}}$

i.e. $s = \sqrt{100} = 10$ gm

Now, the interval estimate for the mean weight of the soap cakes for the entire consignment i.e. the population mean weight (μ) is given by

$$\mu = \bar{x} \pm z\sigma_{\bar{x}}$$

where, $\sigma_{\bar{x}}$ = Standard error of mean (estimation)

Now, $\sigma_{\bar{x}} \simeq S_{\bar{x}} = \dfrac{s}{\sqrt{n}}$

$= \dfrac{10}{\sqrt{100}} = \dfrac{10}{10} = 1$

∴ Interval estimate to μ : $110 \pm z(1)$

(i) Now at 90% confidence level, critical value of $z = 1.645$.
∴ Interval $= 110 \pm 1.645 (1)$ i.e. $110 - 1.645$ to $110 + 1.645$
$= 108.36$ to 111.65
i.e. $108.36 \leq \mu \leq 111.65$ gm

(ii) The critical value of z at 95% confidence level is 1.96.
∴ Interval estimate of (μ) $= 110 \pm 1.96 (1)$
i.e. $= 110 - 1.96$ to $110 + 1.96$
$= 108.04$ to 111.96
i.e. $108.04 \leq \mu \leq 111.96$ gm

(iii) The critical value of z at 99% confidence level is 2.575
∴ Interval estimate of (μ) $= 110 \pm 2.575 (1)$
$= 110 - 2.575$ to $110 + 2.575$
$= 107.43$ to 112.58
i.e. $107.43 \leq \mu \leq 112.58$ gm

Problem 21: In a random survey of 70 employees recently joining a BPO firm, 50 were college going students. Estimate the percentage of college students among all the newly joined employees at confidence level of (i) 0.95, (ii) 0.99.

Solution: Here, n = sample size = 70
and No. of college students in the sample = 50
∴ p = Sample proportion of students
$= \dfrac{50}{70} = 0.714$

∴ Interval estimate for the proportion of students in all the newly joined employees i.e. population proportion (π) is $p \pm z\,\sigma_p$.

where, σ_p = Standard error of proportion (estimation)

$$= \sqrt{\frac{p(1-p)}{n}}$$

$$= \sqrt{\frac{0.714(1-0.714)}{70}} = \sqrt{\frac{0.204}{70}}$$

$$= \sqrt{0.0029} = 0.054$$

∴ Interval estimate of (π) : $0.714 \pm z(0.054)$

(i) At confidence level of 0.95 i.e. 95%, critical value of z = 1.96.

∴ Interval : $0.714 \pm 1.96(0.054)$ i.e. 0.714 ± 0.106

i.e. 0.714 − 0.106 to 0.714 + 0.106

i.e. 0.608 + 0.82 i.e. 60.8% to 82%

∴ at 95% confidence level, the estimated percentage of college students is 60.8% to 82%.

[i.e. we are 95% confident that the percentage will belong to this range]

(ii) Similarly, at confidence level of 0.99 i.e. 99%, the critical value of z = 2.575.

∴ Interval estimate of (π): $0.714 \pm 2.575(0.054)$

i.e. 0.714 ± 0.14

i.e. 0.714 − 0.14 to 0.714 + 0.14

i.e. 0.574 to 0.854 i.e. 57.4% to 85.4%

∴ At 99% confidence level, the estimated percentage of college students is 57.4% to 85.4%.

Problem 22: A sample of 900 articles was found to have a mean weight of 3.47 kg. Can it be reasonably regarded as a simple sample from a large population with mean 3.23 kg and standard deviation of 2.31 kg?

Solution: We have,

Sample size, $\quad n = 900$

Sample mean, $\quad \bar{x} = 3.47$ kg

Also, population standard deviation, $\sigma = 2.31$ kg.

∴ Standard error mean, $\sigma_{\bar{x}} = \dfrac{\sigma}{\sqrt{n}}$

$$= \frac{2.31}{\sqrt{900}} = \frac{2.31}{30} = 0.077$$

Now, consider 99 confidence level of estimating the interval for population mean (μ). (This is the wider range). Also, the critical value of z is 2.575.

∴ Interval estimate for population mean (μ) is

$\bar{x} \pm z\sigma_{\bar{x}}$ i.e. $3.47 \pm 2.575 (0.077)$

i.e. 3.47 ± 0.20 i.e. $3.47 - 0.20$ to $3.47 + 0.20$

i.e. 3.27 to 3.67.

Thus, we will be 99% confident (i.e. almost sure) that the population mean will i.e. between 3.27 to 3.67 kg. However, the population mean is 3.23 kg which is outside the range. Thus, the estimate based on the given sample is not very accurate. Thus, our sample cannot be considered as a simple sample from the population.

Problem 23: If the probability that one of the telephone lines is engaged at an instant is 0.2. A company has 10 telephone lines. Find the probability that:

(i) 5 out of these are engaged and

(ii) All the 10 lines are engaged.

Solution: This is a problem of Binomial Distribution.

Let p = probability that line is engaged = 0.2

∴ q = probability that the line is not engaged = $1 - p = 1 - 0.2 = 0.8$

Now, n = 10 lines, p = 0.2 and q = 0.8

∴ By Binomial Distribution Law, we have, probability that r lines out of 10 are engaged is $P(r) = {}^nC_r p^r q^{n-r} = {}^{10}C_r (0.2)^r (0.8)^{10-r}$

(i) Probability that 5 out of 10 lines are engaged i.e.

$P(r = 5) = {}^{10}C_5 (0.2)^5 (0.8)^{10-5} = \frac{10 \times 9 \times 8 \times 7 \times 6}{1 \times 2 \times 3 \times 4 \times 5} (0.00032)(0.3277)$

$= (9 \times 4 \times 7)(0.00032)(0.3277) = 0.0264$

(ii) Probability that all the 10 lines are engaged is

$P(r=10) = {}^{10}C_{10} (0.2)^{10} (0.8)^{10-10} = 1 \left(\frac{1}{5}\right)^{10} (0.8)^0 = \frac{1}{5^{10}}$

Problem 24: In a business it is assumed that average daily sales in ₹ follows normal distribution. It is given that the probability that the average daily sales is less than ₹ 1240 is 0.0287 and the probability that it exceeds ₹ 2700 is 0.4599. Find the mean daily sales and standard deviation of the daily sales.

Solution: Let x – daily sales in ₹, m – mean of sales, and σ - standard deviation

Also, $z = \frac{x - m}{\sigma}$

For, x = 1240, $z = \frac{1240 - m}{\sigma}$ = say (z_1) ... (1)

and for x = 2700, $z = \frac{2700 - m}{\sigma}$ = say (z_2) ... (2)

Now, we have P(x ≤ 1240) = P(z ≤ z_1) = 0.0287

∴ Area to the left of line (z = z_1) is 0.0287

Since, it is less than 0.5 (which is the total area to the left of z = 0) z_1, will lie in the left portion as shown

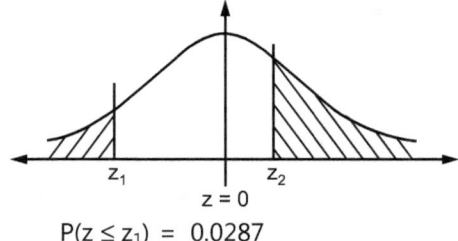

∵		P(z ≤ z_1) = 0.0287	
∴		P (z ≥ – z_1) = 0.0287 ... by symmetry	
i.e.	P(0 ≤ z ≤ ∞) – P(0 ≤ z ≤ –z_1) = 0.0287		
∴	0.5 – P(0 ≤ z ≤ –z_1) = 0.0287		
	P (0 ≤ z ≤ –z_1) = 0.5 – 0.0287 = 0.4713		
∴	From table,	– z_1 = 1.9	
∴		z_1 = – 1.9	
∴	From (1),	$\dfrac{1240 - m}{\sigma}$ = – 1.9	... (3)

Also, P(x ≥ 2700) = P(z ≥ z_2) = 0.4599

∴ Area to the right of line (z ≥ z_2) is 0.4599

Since, it is also less than 0.5 (which is the total area to the right of z = 0), z_2 will lie in right portion as shown

∵	P(z ≥ z_2) = P(z_2 ≤ z < ∞) = 0.4599		
∴	0.5 – P(0 ≤ z ≤ z_2) = 0.4599		
∴	P(0 ≤ z ≤ z_2) = 0.5 – 0.4599 = 0.0401		
∴	from table,	z_2 = 0.1 (approx.)	
∴	from (2),	$\dfrac{2700 - m}{\sigma}$ = 0.1	... (4)
Also,		$\dfrac{1240 - m}{\sigma}$ = – 1.9	... (from (3))
∴	Dividing,	$\dfrac{2700 - m}{1240 - m} = -\dfrac{0.1}{1.9} = -\dfrac{1}{19}$	
∴		19(2700 – m) = – 1 (1240 – m)	
∴		51300 – 19m = –1240 + m	

∴ m + 19m = 51300 + 1240 = 52540

∴ $m = \dfrac{52540}{20} = 2627$

∴ from (4), $\dfrac{2700 - 2627}{\sigma} = 0.1$

∴ $\dfrac{73}{\sigma} = 0.1$

∴ $\sigma = \dfrac{73}{0.1} = 730$

∴ Mean = ₹ 2627 and Std. deviation = ₹ 730

Problem 25: In a certain examination 10% of the students who appeared for the paper in Statistical Methods got less than 30 marks and 97% of the students got less than 62 marks. Assuming the distribution to be normal, find the mean and standard deviation of the distribution given that 40% of the area of the normal curve is between the ordinates corresponding to t = 0 and t = 1.3 and 7% of the area is between t = 1.3 and t = 1.9 where $t = \dfrac{x - \bar{x}}{\sigma}$.

Solution: Let x – marks scored by students in the examination and $t = \dfrac{x - \bar{x}}{\sigma}$ which is the Standard Normal Variate. We are given that the area between ordinates (lines) corresponding to t = 0 and t = 1.3 is 40%

i.e. P(0 ≤ t ≤ 1.3) = 40% = 0.4
Also, P(1.3 ≤ t ≤ 1.9) = 7% = 0.07   ... (1)

Now, for x = 30, $t = \dfrac{30 - \bar{x}}{\sigma} = t_1$ (say) and for x = 62, $t = \dfrac{62 - \bar{x}}{\sigma} = t_2$ (say)

Since 10% of the students got less than 30 marks

P(x ≤ 30) = 0.1

i.e. $P(t \le t_1)$ = 0.1

∴ t_1 lies in the left portion,

∴ $P(t \ge -t_1)$ = 0.1   ... by symmetry

∴ $0.5 - P(0 \le t \le -t_1)$ = 0.1

∴ $P(0 \le t \le -t_1)$ = 0.5 – 0.1 = 0.4

∴ Comparing with (1), we have, $-t_1 = 1.3$

∴ $t_1 = -1.3$

∴ $\dfrac{30 - \bar{x}}{\sigma} = -1.3$ ... (2)

Similarly, 97% students got less than 62 marks.

∴ $P(x \leq 62) = 97\% = 0.97$

∴ $P(t \leq t_2) = 0.97$

∴ 97% of the area lies to the left of t_2 (which is more than 50% of the area that lies to the left of $t = 0$) hence t_2 must lie in the right portion.

∴ $P(-\infty < t \leq t_2) = 0.97$

i.e. $P(-\infty < t \leq 0) + P(0 \leq t \leq t_2) = 0.97$

i.e. $0.5 + P(0 \leq t \leq t_2) = 0.97$

∴ $P(0 \leq t \leq t_2) = 0.97 - 0.5 = 0.47$

Now, from (1),

$P(0 \leq t \leq 1.3) + P(1.3 \leq t \leq 1.9) = 0.4 + 0.07 = 0.47$

i.e. $P(0 \leq t \leq 1.9) = 0.47$

∴ We must have, $t_2 = 1.9$ i.e. $\dfrac{62 - \bar{x}}{\sigma} = 1.9$ ... (3)

and ∴ $\dfrac{30 - \bar{x}}{\sigma} = -1.3$ ... (from (2))

∴ Dividing, $\dfrac{62 - \bar{x}}{30 - \bar{x}} = -\dfrac{1.9}{1.3} = -\dfrac{19}{13}$

∴ $13(62 - \bar{x}) = -19(30 - \bar{x})$

i.e. $806 - 13\bar{x} = -570 + 19\bar{x}$

∴ $19\bar{x} + 13\bar{x} = 806 + 570 = 1376$

∴ $\bar{x} = \dfrac{1376}{32} = 43$ i.e. mean

∴ from (3), $\dfrac{62 - 43}{\sigma} = 1.9$

∴ $\sigma = \dfrac{19}{1.9} = 10$ i.e. Standard deviation.

Problem 26: A particular breed of hens lay eggs four days in a week, one egg on a day. If the poultry has 10 hens, find the probability that on a particular day poultry gets 4 eggs.

Solution: Within 7 days (i.e. a week) a hen lays eggs on 4 days. Hence, the probability that a hen lays an egg in a day is $\dfrac{4}{7}$ i.e. $p = \dfrac{4}{7}$

∴ Probability that a hen does not lay an egg in a day $= q = 1 - p = 1 - \dfrac{4}{7} = \dfrac{3}{7}$

Thus, p and q are not very small. We have to find the probability for 10 hens i.e. n = 10 which is not very large.

∴ It is a problem of Binomial Distribution.

Now, we have to find the probability that on a particular day the poultry gets 4 eggs i.e. the probability that on a particular day (r = 4) out of the (n = 10) hens lay eggs, as each lays only one egg on a day.

∴ The required probability = $P(r=4) = {}^nC_r p^r q^{n-r} = {}^{10}C_4 \left(\dfrac{4}{7}\right)^4 \left(\dfrac{3}{7}\right)^{10-4}$

$= \dfrac{10 \times 9 \times 8 \times 7}{1 \times 2 \times 3 \times 4} \left(\dfrac{4}{7}\right)^4 \left(\dfrac{3}{7}\right)^6$

$= (210)(0.5714)^4 (0.4286)^6 = (210)(0.1066)(6.12 \times 10^{-3})$

$= 137 \times 10^{-3} = 0.137$

Problem 27: Wages of workers in a factory are normally distributed with average wage ₹ 4000, with standard deviation of ₹ 400. Find the highest wage of lowest paid 10% workers, percentage of workers whose wages are between ₹ 3500 and ₹ 4200. Also find the lowest wages of highest paid 15% of workers.

Solution: Let x – wages of workers, mean m = ₹ 4000, s.d. σ = ₹ 400.

Also let $z = \dfrac{x - m}{\sigma} = \dfrac{x - 4000}{400}$

(i) Let x' be the highest wage of lowest paid 10% workers so that $z' = \dfrac{x' - 4000}{400}$

Also, we must have, P(x ≤ x') = 10% i.e. 0.1

∴ P(z ≤ z') = 0.1
∴ z' lies in the left portion
∴ P(z ≥ – z') = 0.1 ...by symmetry
∴ 0.5 – P(0 ≤ z ≤ – z') = 0.1
∴ P(0 ≤ z ≤ – z') = 0.5 – 0.1 = 0.4
∴ from table, – z' = 1.28 ∴ z' = – 1.28

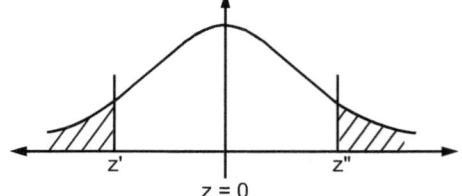

i.e. $\dfrac{x' - 4000}{400} = -1.28$ ∴ x' = 400(– 1.28) + 4000 = ₹ 3488

(ii) If x = 3500, $z = \dfrac{3500 - 4000}{400} = -1.25$ and x = 4200

∴ $z = \dfrac{4200 - 4000}{400} = 0.5$

∴ P(3500 ≤ x ≤ 4200) = P(– 1.25 ≤ z ≤ 0.5) = P(– 1.25 ≤ z ≤ 0) + P(0 ≤ z ≤ 0.5)
= P(0 ≤ z ≤ 1.25) + P(0 ≤ z ≤ 0.5)   ... by symmetry
= 0.3499 + 0.1915 = 0.5414

∴ Percentage of workers with wages between ₹ 3500 and ₹ 4200 = 54.14%

(iii) Let x" be the lowest wages of highest paid 15% of the workers.

$z" = \dfrac{x" - 4000}{400}$ and $P(x \geq x") = P(z \geq z") = 15\% = 0.15$

∴ Area to the right of line z = z" is 0.15 and
∴ z" lies in the right portion.
∴ $0.5 - P(0 \leq z \leq z") = 0.15$
∴ $P(0 \leq z \leq z") = 0.5 - 0.15 = 0.35$
∴ From table, z" = 1.04 ∴ $z" = \dfrac{x" - 4000}{400} = 1.04$
∴ x" = 400(1.04) + 4000 = ₹ 4416

Problem 28: Two teams A and B play a series of independent games until one of them wins four games. The probability that team A wins a game is 0.60. Find the probability that the series will end in at most six games.

Solution: We have, p = Probability of team A winning a game = 0.6
∴ q = Probability of team A losing a game
= Probability of team B winning a game = 1 − p = 1 − 0.6 = 0.4

Now, the series gets over when one of A or B wins four games. Also, the series must get over in at most six games. Hence, in a series there could be (n = 4) OR (n = 5) OR (n = 6) games.

Hence, P(at most six games) = P(4 games) + P(5 games) + P(6 games) ... (1)

Now, if the series gets over in (n = 4) games, hence, either team A must win all (r = 4) games or it must win (r = 0) games (so that team B wins all four games) as per our requirement.

Thus, P(four games) = P(r = 4) + P(r = 0)
Here, n = 4, p = 0.6, q = 0.4

Now, By Binomial Probability Distribution = $P(r) = {}^nC_r p^r q^{n-r}$

∴ P(4 games) = ${}^4C_4 (0.6)^4 (0.4)^0 + {}^4C_0 (0.6)^0 (0.4)^4 = 1(0.6)^4(1) + 1(1)(0.4)^4$

= $(0.6)^4 + (0.4)^4$ ... (2)

Now, if the series gets over in (n=5) games, A must win (r = 4) games or win (r = 1) game out of them so that B wins the remaining games (as winning 4 games ends the series)

∴ P(5 games) = ${}^5C_4 (0.6)^4 (0.4)^1 + {}^5C_1 (0.6)^1 (0.4)^4$

= ${}^5C_1 (0.6)^4 (0.4)^1 + {}^5C_1 (0.6)^1 (0.4)^4$ ... ∵ ${}^nC_r = {}^nC_{n-r}$

= $5(0.6)^4 (0.4) + 5(0.6)(0.4)^4 = 5\left[(0.6)^4(0.4) + (0.6)(0.4)^4\right]$ ... (3)

Similarly, if there are (n = 6) games, A must win (r = 4) games or win (r = 2) games out of them so that B wins the remaining 4.

$\therefore$ P(6 games) = $^6C_4(0.6)^4(0.4)^2 + {}^6C_2(0.6)^2(0.4)^4 = {}^6C_2(0.6)^4(0.4)^2 + {}^6C_2(0.6)^2(0.4)^4$

$= {}^6C_2\left[(0.6)^4(0.4)^2 + (0.6)^2(0.4)^4\right] = \dfrac{6 \times 5}{1 \times 2}\left[(0.6)^4(0.4)^2 + (0.6)^2(0.4)^4\right]$

$= 15\left[(0.6)^4(0.4)^2 + (0.6)^2(0.4)^4\right]$ ..... (4)

$\therefore$ Substituting in (1) from (2), (3) and (4) we get the probability that the series will end in at most 6 games as,

P(at most 6 games)

$= \left[(0.6)^4 + (0.4)^4\right] + 5\left[(0.6)^4(0.4) + (0.6)(0.4)^4\right] + 15\left[(0.6)^4(0.4)^2 + (0.6)^2(0.4)^4\right]$

$= \left[(0.6)^4 + (0.4)^4\right] + \left[2(0.6)^4 + 3(0.4)^4\right] + 15\left[(0.6)^4(0.16) + (0.36)(0.4)^4\right]$

$= \left[(0.6)^4 + (0.4)^4\right] + \left[2(0.6)^4 + 3(0.4)^4\right] + \left[2.4(0.6)^4 + 5.4(0.4)^4\right]$

$= (1 + 2 + 2.4)(0.6)^4 + (1 + 3 + 5.4)(0.4)^4$

$= (5.4)(0.1296) + (9.4)(0.0256) = 0.6998 + 0.2406 = 0.9404$

Problem 29: The local authorities in a certain city installed 20,000 sodium lamps in the main streets of the city. The life of the lamp is assumed to follow normal distribution with mean life of 1350 burning hours with a standard deviation of 300 burning hours.
  (i) Find the number of lamps expected to fail in first 900 hours.
  (ii) Find the period of burning hours before which 10% of lamps would have failed.
  (iii) Find the period of burning hours after which only 12% of the lamps would have survived?

Solution: Let x – Number of burning hours of a lamp, m = 1350hr., σ = 300hr.

$\therefore z = \dfrac{x - m}{\sigma} = \dfrac{x - 1350}{300}$ Also, N = Total number of lamps = 20,000

(i) If x = 900, $z = \dfrac{900 - 1350}{300} = -1.5$

$\therefore$ P(lamp fails in first 900hrs)

i.e. P(x $\leq$ 900) = P(z $\leq$ –1.5) = P(z $\geq$ 1.5)   ... by symmetry

$= 0.5 - P(0 \leq z \leq 1.5) = 0.5 - 0.4332 = 0.0668$ **... using table (Appendix A)**

$\therefore$ Number of lamps expected to fail in first 900 hr.

$= N \times P(x \leq 900)$

$= 20000\,(0.0668) = 1336$

(ii) Let x' be the required period

$$\therefore z' = \frac{x' - 1350}{300}$$

10% of lamps fail before the burning period of x' hours

i.e. P(x ≤ x') = 10% = 0.1

i.e. P(z ≤ z') = 0.1 ∴ z' lies in the left portion

∴ P(z ≥ –z') = 0.1 ... by symmetry

∴ 0.5 – P(0 ≤ z ≤ –z') = 0.1

∴ P(0 ≤ z ≤ –z') = 0.5 – 0.1 = 0.4

∴ from table, –z' = 1.28 ∴ z' = –1.28

i.e. $\frac{x' - 1350}{300} = -1.28$ ∴ x' = 300(–1.28) + 1350 = 966 hrs.

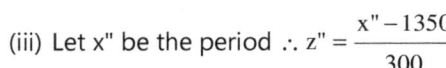

(iii) Let x" be the period ∴ $z" = \frac{x" - 1350}{300}$

Now, 12% of lamps survive after x" hrs

∴ P(x ≥ x") = P(z ≥ z") = 12% i.e. 0.12

∴ z" lies in the right portion

∴ 0.5 – P(0 ≤ z ≤ z") = 0.12

∴ P(0 ≤ z ≤ z") = 0.5 – 0.12 = 0.38

∴ from table, z" = 1.175 (average of 1.7 and 1.8) i.e. $\frac{x" - 1350}{300} = 1.175$

∴ x" = 300(1.175) + 1350 = 1702.5 hr.

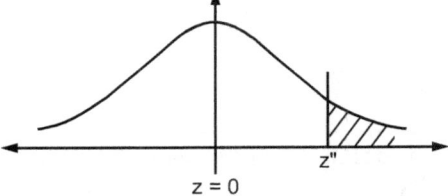

Problem 30: Given below are the weekly wages (in ₹) of six workers in a factory - 1620, 1900, 1780, 1850, 1790, 1680. If two of these workers are selected at random to serve as representatives, what is the probability that at least one will have a wage lower than the average.

Solution: Let x - wages of workers and we have N = total number of workers = 6

∴ Average wage i.e. $\bar{x} = \frac{\Sigma x}{N}$

$$= \frac{1620 + 1900 + 1780 + 1850 + 1790 + 1680}{6}$$

$$= \frac{10620}{6} = 1770$$

∴ No. of workers having wage less than the average i.e. {1620, 1680} = 2

∴ p = Probability that a worker has a wage less than the average = $\frac{2}{6} = \frac{1}{3}$

∴ $q = 1 - p = 1 - \frac{1}{3} = \frac{2}{3}$

Now, n = 2 workers have been selected at random.

∴ Using Binomial Probability Distribution,

P (at least r = 1 worker out of n = 2 has wage less than average)

= P (r ≥ 1) = 1 − P(r < 1)

= 1 − P(r = 0)

= $1 - {}^2C_0 \left(\frac{1}{3}\right)^0 \left(\frac{2}{3}\right)^{2-0}$ ∵ $P(r) = {}^nC_r \, p^r q^{n-r}$

= $1 - 1(1)\left(\frac{2}{3}\right)^2 = 1 - \frac{4}{9}$

= $\frac{9-4}{9} = \frac{5}{9}$

Problem 31: The average daily sale of 500 branch offices was ₹ 150 thousand and the standard deviation ₹ 15 thousand. Assuming the distribution to be normal, indicate how many branches have sales between ₹ 120 thousand and ₹ 145 thousand.

[Given: Z   0.33   2.0
         Area   0.1293   0.4772]

Solution: We have for the given Normal Distribution

Let, x - daily sale of a branch

Average daily sale m = ₹ 150 thousand and Std. deviation, σ = ₹ 15 thousand

∴ Std. Normal Variate is $z = \frac{x - m}{\sigma} = \frac{x - 150}{15}$

Now, if x_1 = 120 thousand

∴ $z_1 = \frac{120 - 150}{15} = -2$

and x_2 = 145 thousand

∴ $z_2 = \frac{145 - 150}{15} = \frac{-5}{15}$

= − 0.33

∴ Probability that a branch has sales between $x_1 = 120$ and $x_2 = 145$ is

$P(120 \leq x \leq 145)$
$= P(z_1 \leq z \leq z_2) = P(-2 \leq z \leq -0.33)$
$= P(0.33 \leq z \leq 2)$ .... by symmetry of std. normal curve
$= P(0 \leq z \leq 2) - P(0 \leq z \leq 0.33)$
$= 0.4772 - 0.1293$ ....using given data for area under normal curve
$= 0.3479$

∴ Number of branches out of $N = 500$ having sales between ₹ 120 and ₹ 145 thousand
$= N \times P(120 \leq x \leq 145)$
$= 500 \times 0.3479 = 173.95 \approx 174$ branches

Problem 32: Suppose that the probability that a light in a class room will be burnt out is 1/3. The class room has in all 5 lights and it is unusable if the number of lights burning is less than two. What is the probability that the class room is unusable on a random occasion?

Solution: We have, p = Probability that a light is burnt out = 1/3

∴ $q = 1 - p = 1 - \dfrac{1}{3} = \dfrac{2}{3}$

The number of lights in the classroom = 5

Now, the class room is unusable if the number of lights burning is less than 2 i.e. if the number of lights burning is 0 or 1 i.e. if the number of lights burnt out (out of 5) is (5 − 0 = 5) or (5 − 1 = 4)

Now, by Binominal Probability Law $P(r) = {}^nC_r \, p^r \, q^{n-r}$

∴ Required probability
$= P(r = 4 \text{ or } r = 5)$
$= P(r = 4) + P(r = 5)$
$= {}^5C_4 \, p^4 \, q^{5-4} + {}^5C_5 \, p^5 \, q^{5-5}$
$= {}^5C_1 \, p^4 \, q^1 + 1 \, p^5 \, q^0$ .... ∵ ${}^nC_r = {}^nC_{n-r}$ and ${}^nC_n = 1$
$= 5 \left(\dfrac{1}{3}\right)^4 \left(\dfrac{2}{3}\right) + 1 \left(\dfrac{1}{3}\right)^5 (1)$ .... ∵ $p = \dfrac{1}{3}, q = \dfrac{2}{3}$
$= \left(\dfrac{1}{3}\right)^4 \left[5\left(\dfrac{2}{3}\right) + \dfrac{1}{3}\right] = \dfrac{1}{3^4}\left(\dfrac{11}{3}\right)$
$= \dfrac{11}{81(3)}$
$= 0.0452$

Problem 33: It is observed that 80% of TV viewers watch Aap ki Adalat program. What is the probability that at least 80% of viewers in a random sample of 5 watch this program?

(P.U. MBA - May 05)

Solution: Since 80% of TV viewers watch Aap Ki Adalat,

∴ p = Probability that a TV viewer watches Aap Ki Adalat

$$= \frac{80}{100} = 0.8$$

∴ q = 1 − 0.8 = 0.2

Now,

P(at least 80% of viewers in a random sample of n = 5 watch this program)
= P(at least 4 viewers watch the program) ∵ 80% of 5 = 0.8(5) = 4
= P (r = 4 or r = 5 watch the program)
= P (r = 4) + P (r = 5)

Now, by Binomial Probability Law, $P(r) = {}^nC_r\, p^r\, q^{n-r}$

∴ Required probability
= P (r = 4) + P (r = 5)
= ${}^5C_4\, p^4\, q^{5-4} + {}^5C_5\, p^5\, q^{5-5}$
= ${}^5C_1\, p^4 q^1 + 1\, p^5 q^0$
= $5(0.8)^4(0.2) + 1(0.8)^5(1)$
= $(0.8)^4[5(0.2) + 0.8]$
= 0.4096 (1.8) = 0.737

Problem 34: The mean of binomial distribution is 4 and variance is $\frac{4}{3}$. Find the probability of getting (i) no success (ii) at least 5 successes. **(P.U. MBA - May 08)**

Solution: We have for the given binomial distribution

mean = np = 4 ..... (1)   .... ∵ for a binomial distribution, mean = np

and variance = npq = $\frac{4}{3}$ ... (2) ... ∵ for a binomial distribution, variance = npq

∴ dividing (2) by (1) we get, $\frac{npq}{np} = \frac{4/3}{4}$

i.e. $q = \frac{1}{3}$

∴ $p = 1 - q = 1 - \frac{1}{3} = \frac{2}{3}$

and from (1), $n = \frac{4}{p} = \frac{4}{2/3}$

∴ $n = 4 \times \frac{3}{2} = 6$

Thus, for the given binomial distribution, n = 6, $p = \frac{2}{3}$, $q = \frac{1}{3}$

Now for a binomial distribution,

P(getting r number of success in n number of trials) i.e.

$P(r) = {}^nC_r \, p^r \, q^{n-r}$ .... binomial probability law

$\therefore \quad P(r) = {}^6C_r \left(\dfrac{2}{3}\right)^r \left(\dfrac{1}{3}\right)^{n-r}$ .... (3)

(i) $\therefore$ P(no success) i.e.

$$P(r = 0) = {}^6C_0 \left(\dfrac{2}{3}\right)^0 \left(\dfrac{1}{3}\right)^{6-0}$$

$$= 1.1 \cdot \left(\dfrac{1}{3}\right)^6 = \dfrac{1}{3^6}$$

(ii) P (Getting at least 5 successes) i.e.

$P(r \geq 5) = P(r = 5 \text{ or } r = 6)$

$= P(r = 5) + P(r = 6)$ ..... being mutually exclusive events

$= {}^6C_5 \left(\dfrac{2}{3}\right)^5 \left(\dfrac{1}{3}\right)^{6-5} + {}^6C_6 \left(\dfrac{2}{3}\right)^6 \left(\dfrac{1}{3}\right)^{6-6}$

$= {}^6C_1 \left(\dfrac{2}{3}\right)^5 \left(\dfrac{1}{3}\right) + {}^6C_0 \left(\dfrac{2}{3}\right)^6 \left(\dfrac{1}{3}\right)^0$ .... $\because {}^nC_r = {}^nC_{n-r}$

$= 6\left(\dfrac{2}{3}\right)^5 \left(\dfrac{1}{3}\right) + 1\left(\dfrac{2}{3}\right)^6 \cdot 1 = \left(\dfrac{2}{3}\right)^5 \left(2 + \dfrac{2}{3}\right) = \left(\dfrac{2}{3}\right)^5 \left(\dfrac{8}{3}\right)$

$= \dfrac{2^5}{3^5} \cdot \dfrac{2^3}{3} = \dfrac{2^8}{3^6}$

Problem 35: The mean life of a battery follows normal distribution with average life time 50 hours and 5% of the values are greater than 60 (i) Find the standard deviation of this distribution, (ii) Also find the lowest life time of highest 15% batteries. **(P.U. MBA - Dec. 09)**

Solution: Let x - life of the battery which follows normal distribution. Its mean s m = 50 hours and let σ be its standard deviation.

Also, Let $\quad z = \dfrac{x - m}{\sigma} = \dfrac{x - 50}{\sigma}$

(i) Now, when x = 60, $z = \dfrac{60 - 50}{\sigma} = \dfrac{10}{\sigma} = z_1$ (say)

Since, 5% of the values are greater than 60.

$\therefore \quad P(x > 60) = P(z > z_1) = \dfrac{5}{100} = 0.05$

$\therefore$ Area to the right of line (z = z_1) is 0.05 (which is less than the total area to the right of z = 0 i.e. 0.5). Hence, z_1 lies in the right half under standard normal curve.

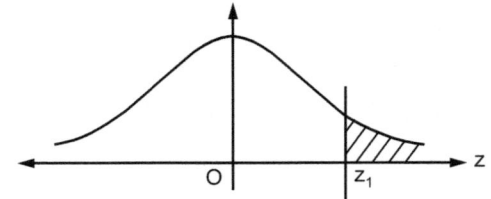

Now, $\quad P(z > z_1) = 0.05$
i.e. $\quad P(z_1 < z < \infty) = 0.05$
i.e. $\quad P(0 < z < \infty) - P(0 < z < z_1) = 0.05$
i.e. $\quad 0.5 - P(0 < z < z_1) = 0.5$
$\therefore \quad P(0 < z < z_1) = 0.45$

Now, pending value of z in reverse order from table of area under standard normal curve (Appendix A) we have,

$$z_1 = 1.645 \qquad \text{(average of 1.64 and 1.65)}$$

$\therefore \quad z_1 = \dfrac{10}{\sigma} = 1.645$

$\therefore \quad \sigma = \dfrac{10}{1.645} = 6.08$

(ii) Now, let x' be the lowest life time of highest 15% batteries.

$\therefore \quad P(x > x') = \dfrac{15}{100} = 0.15$

i.e. $\quad P(z > z') = 0.15 \quad$ where $\quad z' = \dfrac{x' - m}{\sigma} = \dfrac{x' - 50}{6.08}$

$\therefore$ z' lies in the right half.

Now, $\quad P(z > z') = 0.15$
i.e. $\quad P(z' < z < \infty) = 0.15$
i.e. $P(0 < z < \infty) - P(0 < z < z') = 0.15$
i.e. $\quad 0.5 - P(0 < z < z') = 0.15$
$\therefore \quad P(0 < z < z') = 0.35$
$\therefore \quad z' = 1.04 \quad$ **... from table (Appendix A)**
$\therefore \quad \dfrac{x' - 50}{6.08} = 1.04$
$\therefore \quad x' = 1.04\,(6.08) + 50$
$\quad = 56.32 \text{ hours}$

Problem 36: Life of Car batteries is normally distributed with an average life 5 years and standard deviation 2 month. What should the guarantee period be if the company wishes to replace not more than 15% of the batteries. Given area under normal curve for z = 1.03 is 0.3485, z = 1.04 is 0.3506 and z = 1.05 is 0.3531. **(P.U. MBA - Dec. 11)**

Solution: Let x - Life of car batteries (in months)

We have, mean of x = m = 5 years = 60 months and s.d. σ = 2 months

Also, let $z = \dfrac{x - m}{\sigma} = \dfrac{x - 60}{2}$

The distribution of x is given to be normal.

Now, let the guarantee period be x' so that $z' = \dfrac{x' - 60}{2}$ ... (1)

Now, the company does not want to replace more than 15% of the batteries. Hence, the chance (probability) that the car battery will fail before this period (x') should not exceed 15% i.e. $\dfrac{15}{100} = 0.15$

∴ P(x ≤ x') ≤ 0.15 i.e. P(z ≤ z') ≤ 0.15

Hence, area to the left of line z = z' is less than area (0.5) to the left of z = 0

∴ z = z' must lie in the left hand portion of the normal curve

Now, P(z ≤ z') ≤ 0.15

∴ P(z ≥ – z') ≤ 0.15 ... by symmetry

∴ 0.5 – P(0 ≤ z ≤ –z') ≤ 0.15

∴ 0.5 – 0.15 ≤ P(0 ≤ z ≤ –z')

∴ P(0 ≤ z ≤ –z') ≥ 0.35

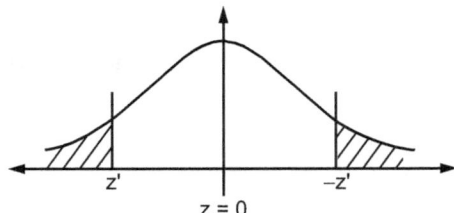

∴ Using the given values, we have the value of z corresponding to area of (0.35) as 1.04 (approx.)

∴ – z' ≥ 1.04 ∴ z' ≤ – 1.04   (signs change ⇒ inequality change)

∴ From (1), $\dfrac{x' - 60}{2} \leq -1.04$

∴ x' – 60 ≤ – 2.08

∴ x' ≤ 60 –2.08 i.e. x' ≤ 57.92 months

∴ Guarantee period should be 57 months.

Exercise

1. What is a random variable? State its types. Give Examples.
2. What do you mean by the Expected Value and Variance of a random variable?
3. Write short notes on:
   (i) Probability Distribution
   (ii) Binomial Distribution
   (iii) Poisson Distribution
   (iv) Normal Probability Distribution
4. (a) Comment: The mean of a Binomial Distribution is 15 and its standard deviation is 5.
   (b) Find the Binomial distribution whose mean is 6 and variance 4.

   $\left(\text{Ans.: (a) wrong (b) } (q + p)^n = \left(\frac{2}{3} + \frac{1}{3}\right)^{18}\right)$

5. Out of 320 families with 5 children each, what percentage would be expected to have (i) 2 boys and 3 girls (ii) at least one boy? Assume equal probability for boys and girls.

   (**Ans.:** 31.25%, 97%)

6. The incidence of an occupational disease in an industry is such that the workmen have a 20% chance of suffering from it. What is the probability that out of six workmen, 4 or more will contract the diseases.

   (**Ans.:** 0.017)

7. On an average a box containing 10 articles is likely to have 2 defectives. If we consider a consignment of 100 boxes, how many of them are expected to have at the most 3 defectives.

   (**Ans.:** 88)

8. Find the probability that the value of an item drawn of random from a normal distribution with mean 20 and standard deviation 10 will be (i) between −5 and 10 (ii) less than 10 (iii) between 15 and 25 (iv) more than 25.

   (**Ans.:** 0.1525, 0.1587, 0.3830, 0.3085)

9. A sample of 500 dry battery cells tested to find the length of life produced the results - $\bar{x} = 12$ hours, $\sigma = 3$ hours. Assuming the data to be normally distributed, what percentage of the battery cells are expected to have life: (i) More than 15 hours (ii) less than 6 hours (iii) between 10 and 14 hours. State their number in the sample also.

   (**Ans.:** 15.87%, 79, 2.28%, 11, 49.74%, 249)

10. The income of a group of 10,000 persons was found to be normally distributed with mean of ₹ 750 and S.D of ₹ 50. Show that, of this group 95% had income exceeding ₹ 668 and only 5% had income exceeding ₹ 832. What was the lowest income among the richest 100?

    (**Ans.:** ₹ 866.5)

11. 1000 light bulbs with a mean life of 120 days are installed in a new factory, their length of life normally distributed with S.D.20 days (i) How many bulbs will expire in less than 90 days (ii) It is decided to replace all the bulbs together, what intervals should be allowed between replacements if not more than 10% should expire before replacements?

    (**Ans.:** 67, 94 days)

12. In a normal distribution, 31% of the items are under 45 and 8% are over 64. Find the mean and standard deviation of the distribution.

    (**Ans.:** 50, 10)

13. The lives of brand X coils are normally distributed with a mean of 700 hours and s.d of 20 hours. Its manufacturer guarantees to replace free of charge, if it burns before the expiry of a certain time period. How long should the guarantee be given so that no more than 5% of the coils have to be replaced?

    (**Ans.:** 667 hours)

14. In order to introduce same incentive for higher balance in savings accounts, a random sample of 64 savings accounts at a bank's branch was studied to estimate the average monthly balance in savings bank accounts. The mean and standard deviation were found to be ₹ 8,500 and ₹ 2,000 respectively. Estimate the intervals in which the mean monthly balance in the accounts is expected to lie. Use (i) 90%, (ii) 95% and (iii) 99% confidence levels.

    (**Ans.:** (i) 8088.75 to 8911.25, (ii) 8010 to 8990, (iii) 7856 to 9144)

15. One of the properties of a good quality paper is its bursting strength. Suppose a sample of 16 specimen yields mean bursting strength of 25 units and it is known from the history of such tests that s.d. among specimens is 5 units. Assuming normality of tests results, what are the (i) 95% and (ii) 98% confidence limits for the mean bursting strength from this sample.

    (**Ans.:** (i) 22.55 to 27.45, (ii) z = 2.327; 22.09 to 27.91)

16. The last month's sales at an electronics shop showed that out of 30 TV sets sold, 20 were LCD TVs. Estimate the proportion of buyers preferring to buy LCD TVs in the given locality at (i) 80% (ii) 90% (iii) 95% and (iv) 99% level of confidence.

    (**Ans.:** (i) z = 1.28; 0.56 to 0.78 i.e. 56% to 78%, (ii) 0.53 to 0.81, (iii) 0.50 to 0.84, (iv) 0.45 to 0.89).

17. The life time of a certain type of battery have a mean of 300 hours and s.d. of 35 hours. Assuming that the distribution of the life is normal, find: (i) the probability of batteries having life time between 225 and 355 hours (ii) the life in hours above which we will find the best 20% of the batteries.

z	0.84	1.57	2.14
Area from z = 0 to	0.30	0.4418	0.4884

    (**Ans.:** 0.93, 329.4 hours)

18. In an aptitude test administered to 1000 children the score is supposed to follow normal distribution with average score 42 and s.d. 24. (i) find the number of children exceeding the score 60 and (ii) what is the score of the children so that 10% of the children exceed this score.
    (**Ans.:** 227, 73)

19. A grinding machine is set so that its production of shafts has an average diameter of 10.10 cm and a standard deviation of 0.20 cm. The product specifications call for the shaft diameters between 10.05 cm and 10.20 cm. What proportion of output meets the specifications presuming normal distribution?
    (**Ans.:** 29.02%)

20. The diameter of ball bearings are normally distributed with mean 0.6140 inches and S.D. 0.0025 inches. Calculate the percentage of ball bearings with diameter: (i) between 0.610 and 0.618 inches (ii) greater than 0.617 inches (iii) less than 0.608 inches.
    (**Ans.:** 89.04, 11.51, 0.82)

21. Six coins are tossed simultaneously. What is the probability of getting: (i) Exactly 2 heads (ii) More than 2 heads on upper face.
    (**Ans.:** 0.2344, 0.6563)

22. The mean quantity of rice filled in a sachet by a sachet filling machine is 500 gms with the standard deviation of 3 gms. The contractor will lose if there is over filling and will have to pay penalty if the rice is less than 495 gms in any sachet. Determine the percentage of times the rice is more than 503 gms in a sachet and also the percentage of times rice is in a sachet will be less than 494 gms.
    (**Ans.:** 0.1507, 0.0277)

23. The life of battery cells supplied by company A was tested and it was found that the average life is 50 hours with a standard deviation 3 hours. If the company has supplied 1000 battery cells (i) How many of these will have life more than 55 hours, (ii) How many of these will have life less than 44 hours. Given area under normal curve for (i) Z = 1.67 is 0.4525 and (ii) Z = 2 is 0.4722
    (**Ans.:** 0.0475, 0.0228) (**P.U. MBA - Dec. 05**)

24. The mean yield of one acre plot is 662 Kg, with a s.d. of 32 Kg. Assuming normal distribution how many one acre plots in a batch of 1000 plots would you expect to have (i) over 700 kgs. (ii) below 650 kgs (iii) what is the lowest yield of the best 100 plots. **(P.U. MBA - May 03)**

   (**Ans.:** (i) 117, (ii) 354, (iii) 702.96 kg)

25. A large departmental store has 4500 accounts receivables. The amounts of these accounts is normally distributed with a mean amount ₹ 150 and a standard deviation of ₹ 25. (i) How many accounts are expected to be between ₹ 115 and ₹ 165? (ii) How many accounts are expected to be of an amount less than ₹ 100 (iii) What is the amount of bills so that 10% of the accounts receivable exceed this amount.

   (**Ans.:** 2902, 103, ₹ 182)

26. From the past experience a stock broker finds that 70% of the telephone calls he receives during the business hours are orders and remaining are for other business. What is the probability that out of first 8 telephone calls during a day exactly 5 calls are order calls.

   (**Ans.:** 0.2541)

27. For a binomial distribution the mean is 6 and the standard deviation is $\sqrt{2}$. Find n, p and q.

   (**Ans.:** 9, 2/3, 1/3)

28. A sample of 100 dry battery cells tested to find the length of life, produced the following result: $\bar{x}$ = 12 hrs, σ = 3 hours. Assuming that the data are normally distributed, what percentage of battery cells are expected to have life
   (i)   More than 15 hours
   (ii) Less than 6 hours
   (iii) Between 10 and 14 hours

   (**Ans.:** (i) 15.87%, (ii) 2.28%, (iii) 49.72%)

29. Of a large group of men 30% are under 165 cms and 60% are between 165 cms and 185 cms in height. Find the mean and standard deviation of the group of men assuming heights are normally distributed.
   Given: Z :   0.525   1.28
   Area under SNV from   Z = 0 :   0.2000   0.4000   **(P.U. MBA - Dec. 06)**

   (**Ans.:** m = 170.82, σ = 11.078)

30. 44% of candidates get marks 55 or less and 6% of candidates get marks 80 or more. Assume that the distribution in normal, find average marks and standard deviation of marks.

    Given:

z	0.15	1.55
Area from z = 0 to	0.06	0.44

    (**Ans.:** 58, 20) **(P.U. MBA - Dec. 08)**

31. The incidence of a certain disease is such that on the average 20% of workers suffer from it. If 10 workers are selected at random, find the probability that more than 2 workers suffer from the disease. **(P.U. MBA - Dec. 08)**
    (**Ans.:** 0.322)

32. An experiment succeeds twice as many times as it fails. Find the chance that in six trials there will be atleast one success. **(P.U. MBA - May 13)**
    (**Ans.:** $1 - \frac{1}{3^6} = 0.998$)

Multiple Choice Questions

Chapter 1: Linear Programming

1. The first step in solving operations research problem is
   - (a) model building
   - (b) obtain alternate solutions
   - (b) interpreting the variables
   - (d) formulation of the problem

2. The distinguishing feature of an LP model is
   - (a) relationship among all the variables is linear
   - (b) it has single objective function and constraints
   - (c) value of the decision variables is non-negative
   - (d) all of the above

3. The constraints of a maximisation problem are normally of
   - (a) less than or equal type
   - (b) greater than or equal type
   - (c) less than type
   - (d) greater than type

4. Resources in a LP problem are indicated by
   - (a) objective function
   - (b) decision variables
   - (c) constraint equations
   - (d) slack variables

5. In graphical solution of solving LP problem, to convert inequalities into equations we
   - (a) use slack variables
   - (b) use surplus variables
   - (c) draw lines
   - (d) simply assume them as equations

6. For constraints of the type '≤' we mark the feasible region as
   - (a) the region not containing region
   - (b) the region containing the origin
   - (c) the region on the line
   - (d) the region in the first quadrant

7. An iso-profit line represents
   - (a) an infinite number of solutions all of which yield the same profit
   - (b) an infinite number of solutions all of which yield the maximum profit
   - (c) an infinite number of optimal solutions
   - (d) a boundary of the feasible region

8. In a graphical solution of minimisation problem, we move the iso-cost line
   - (a) towards right
   - (b) towards left
   - (c) towards the origin
   - (d) away from the origin

9. In a graphical method of LP problem, the optimal solution happens to be
   (a) one of the constraint line
   (b) origin
   (c) one of the corner point
   (d) one of the central point
10. If an iso-profit line yielding the optimal solutions coincides with a constraint line, then
   (a) the solution is unbounded
   (b) the solution is infeasible
   (c) the coinciding constraint is redundant
   (d) none of the above.

ANSWERS

| 1. (d) | 2. (a) | 3. (b) | 4. (c) | 5. (d) | 6. (b) | 7. (a) | 8. (c) | 9. (c) | 10. (d) |

■■■

Chapter 2: Transportation Models

1. The dummy source or destination in a transportation problem is added to
   (a) satisfy the rim conditions
   (b) present solution from becoming degenerate
   (c) ensure that the total cost does not exceed a limit
   (d) none of the above
2. The solution of a transportation problem with m-rows (supplies) and n-columns (destinations) is feasible if the number of occupied cells are
   (a) m + n
   (b) m × n
   (c) m + n − 1
   (d) m + n + 1
3. While improving a solution of transportation problem, we reallocate units to the unoccupied cell having its opportunity cost as
   (a) equal to zero
   (b) most negative number
   (c) most positive number
   (d) any value
4. Multiple optimal solutions for a transportation problem are indicated in the optimum table by
   (a) occupied cells with positive opportunity costs
   (b) unoccupied cells with zero opportunity costs
   (c) occupied cells with zero opportunity costs
   (d) unoccupied cells with positive opportunity costs

5. To solve a transportation problem for minimisation, the relative loss matrix is obtained by
   (a) subtracting all elements from the largest element of the matrix
   (b) subtracting smallest element from all elements of the matrix
   (c) treating maximum elements at ∞
   (d) adding a dummy row or column

6. Allocations to the dummy row cells in the optimum solution of a transportation problem indicate
   (a) unutilised resources at the respective origins
   (b) shortage of resources of the respective origins
   (c) unutilised demand at the respective destinations
   (d) unfulfilled demand at the respective destinations

7. MODI stands for
   (a) modern distributions
   (b) markov distribution method
   (c) modified distribution method
   (d) model index method

8. The opportunity cost/penalty of a row in VAM is obtained by
   (a) deducting smallest element in the row from all other elements of the row
   (b) deducting the smallest elements in the row from the next highest elements of the row
   (c) deducting smallest element from the highest element of the row
   (d) adding smallest element in the row to the next highest element of the row

9. Transportation problem is basically a
   (a) iconic model
   (b) transshipment model
   (c) maximisation model
   (d) minimisation model

10. The prohibited cell in transportation problem is considered by considering its cost
    (a) ∞
    (b) −∞
    (c) 0
    (d) negative

ANSWERS

| 1. (a) | 2. (c) | 3. (b) | 4. (b) | 5. (a) | 6. (d) | 7. (c) | 8. (b) | 9. (d) | 10. (a) |

Chapter 3: Assignment Models

1. Assignment problem is solved by
   (a) Simplex method
   (b) Graphical method
   (c) Vector method
   (d) Hungarian method

2. In Hungarian method of solving assignment problems, the row opportunity cost matrix is obtained by
   (a) subtracting all elements of the row from the largest element in the row
   (b) subtracting smallest element in the row from all the elements of the row
   (c) subtracting all elements of the row from the largest element in the matrix
   (d) dividing each element by smallest uncovered element

3. The property of the optimum assignment matrix is
   (a) it will have zero as elements of one diagonal
   (b) it will have zero as elements of at least one row or column
   (c) it will have atleast one zero in each row and column
   (d) it will not have zero as its element

4. To balance an assignment matrix we have to
   (a) add a dummy row or column depending on given situation
   (b) add a dummy row
   (c) add a dummy column
   (d) remove a row or column depending upon the given situation

5. An optimum assignment requires that the minimum number of lines which can be drawn through the squares with zero opportunity cost to be equal to the number of
   (a) rows or columns
   (b) rows and columns
   (c) rows + columns − 1
   (d) rows + columns + 1

6. The assignment problem
   (a) requires that only one activity be assigned to each resource
   (b) is a special case of transportation problems
   (c) can be used for maximisation objective
   (d) all of the above

7. To convert the assignment problem into a maximisation problem
   (a) deduct smallest element in the matrix from all other elements
   (b) deduct all elements of the matrix form the largest element in it
   (c) deduct smallest element of each row from other elements in it
   (d) deduct all elements of each row from the largest element in it

8. If the assignment matrix is not optional (after drawing the lines) then to improve it
    (a) add smallest uncovered element to the elements on the lines
    (b) subtract smallest uncovered element from the inter section elements of the lines
    (c) subtract smallest uncovered element from all uncovered elements
    (d) subtract smallest element from the elements on the lines
9. Flood's technique of solving an assignment matrix uses the concept of
    (a) maximum cost					(b) minimum cost
    (c) opportunity cost				(d) negative cost
10. Prohibited assignment in an assignment problem is addressed by
    (a) considering its cost as negative	(b) considering its cost as ∞
    (c) considering its cost as zero		(d) none of the above

ANSWERS

| 1. (d) | 2. (b) | 3. (c) | 4. (a) | 5. (a) | 6. (d) | 7. (a) | 8. (c) | 9. (c) | 10. (b) |

■■■

Chapter 4: Queuing Theory

1. The characteristics of a queuing model is independent of
    (a) number of servers				(b) limit of queue length
    (c) service pattern					(d) queue discipline
2. In (M/M/1) : (∞/FCFS) model, the system length L_s is given by
    (a) $\dfrac{\rho}{1-\rho}$			(b) $\dfrac{\lambda^2}{\mu-\lambda}$
    (c) $\dfrac{1}{\mu-\lambda}$		(d) $\dfrac{P^2}{1-P}$
3. In the queue model notation (a/b/c) : (d/e), what does c represent
    (a) arrival pattern					(b) service pattern
    (c) number of services				(d) capacity of the system
4. With respect to a simple queue model which of the following is not true
    (a) $L_q = \lambda W_q$				(b) $L_s = L_q + P$
    (c) $W_s = W_q + P$					(d) $L_s = \lambda W_s$
5. For a (M/M/c) : (∞/FCFS) Queue model, the steady state exists if
    (a) $\lambda = k\mu$				(b) $\lambda > k\mu$
    (c) $\mu = k\lambda$				(d) $\lambda < k\mu$

6. For a (M/M/c) : (∞/FCFS) Queue model, the waiting time in the queue is given by

   (a) $\dfrac{\mu\left(\dfrac{\lambda}{\mu}\right)^c}{(c-1)!\,(c\mu-\lambda)^2} P_0 + \dfrac{1}{\mu}$

   (b) $\dfrac{\mu\left(\dfrac{\lambda}{\mu}\right)^c}{(c-1)!\,(c\mu-\lambda)^2} P_0$

   (c) $\dfrac{\lambda}{c\mu-\lambda}$

   (d) none of the above

7. For a simple queue, traffic intensity is given by
   (a) mean arrival rate/mean service rate
   (b) number present in the queue/number served
   (c) $\lambda \times \mu$
   (d) $\dfrac{\mu}{\lambda}$

8. Which of the following cost estimates and performance measures are not used for economic analysis of a queuing system
   (a) cost per server per unit of time
   (b) cost per unit of time for a customer waiting in the system
   (c) average number of customers in the system
   (d) average waiting time of customers in the system

9. Customer behaviour in which he moves from one queue to another in multiple channel situation is
   (a) backing
   (b) reneging
   (c) jockeying
   (d) alternating

10. A calling population in a queue system is considered to be infinite when
    (a) all customers arrive at once
    (b) arrivals are independent of each other
    (c) arrivals are depending upon each other
    (d) all of the above

11. Which of the following is not an assumption of the single server queuing method
    (a) service times are Poisson distributed
    (b) queue discipline is not first came first serve
    (c) mean arrival rate < mean service rate
    (d) arrivals follow Poisson distribution

ANSWERS

1. (d)	2. (a)	3. (c)	4. (c)	5. (d)	6. (b)	7. (a)	8. (d)	9. (c)	10. (b)
11. (a)									

Chapter 5: Markov Chains and Simulation

1. In a matrix of transition probability, the probability values should add upto 1 in each
   (a) row
   (b) column
   (c) diagonal
   (d) all of the above

2. While calculating the state probabilities for a Markov process, it is assumed that
   (a) there is a single absorbing state
   (b) transition probabilities remain unchanged
   (c) there is a single non-absorbing state
   (d) none of the above

3. Which of the following is not an assumption of Markov Analysis
   (a) the number of possible states are limited
   (b) the transition probabilities are not changed over time
   (c) there are limited number of future periods
   (d) future state can be predicted from preceding state

4. If R_0 represent state probabilities of present period then the state probabilities at the end of second period are given by
   (a) $R_2 = R_1 \times P^2$
   (b) $R_2 = R_0 \times P^2$
   (c) $R_2 = P \times R_1$
   (d) none of the above

5. In the transition probability matrix, the diagonal elements represents the probability of
   (a) gain
   (b) loss
   (c) transition
   (d) retention

6. Simulation, not being an analytical method, its results must be viewed as
   (a) unrealistic
   (b) exact
   (c) approximation
   (d) simplified

7. In Monte Carlo Simulation Random numbers are used to
   (a) calculate the probabilities
   (b) calculate cumulative probabilities
   (c) simulate the values of the variable
   (d) summarise the output

8. While using random numbers in Monte Carlo Simulation it is
   (a) not necessary to assign the exact range of random numbers
   (b) necessary to find out the cumulative probability distribution
   (c) necessary to use particular random numbers
   (d) none of the above

9. The purpose of simulation technique is to
   (a) create a real world situation
   (b) avoid cost of experimenting on real situation
   (c) approximately understand the behaviour of real life situation
   (d) all of the above
10. In Monte Carlo Simulation, the solutions obtained using different set of random number will be
    (a) different
    (b) exactly same
    (c) non-real
    (d) none of the above

ANSWERS

1. (a)	2. (b)	3. (c)	4. (b)	5. (d)	6. (c)	7. (c)	8. (b)	9. (d)	10. (a)

Chapter 6: Decision Theory

1. Which of the following criteria is not used for decision making under uncertainty
   (a) maximin
   (b) maximax
   (c) minimax
   (d) minimise expected loss
2. The decision maker's knowledge and experience may influence the decision-making process while using the criterion of
   (a) maximax
   (b) minimax regret
   (c) realism
   (d) maximin
3. The difference between the maximum expected monetary value (i.e. profit) under conditions of risk and the expected profit with perfect information is called
   (a) expected value of perfect information
   (b) expected marginal loss
   (c) expected opportunity loss
   (d) none of the above
4. When the probabilities of states of nature can be worked out, it becomes a case of decision-making under
   (a) certainty
   (b) risk
   (c) uncertainty
   (d) none of the above
5. The value of coefficient of optimism (α) is required while using the criteria of
   (a) Laplace
   (b) Savage
   (c) Hurwicz
   (d) Maximax

6. Decisions that are meant to solve repetitive and well structured problems are known as
   (a) structured decisions
   (b) programmed decisions
   (c) non-programmed decisions
   (d) linear programming decisions
7. Maximin criterion represents
   (a) optimistic approach
   (b) pessimistic approach
   (c) realistic approach
   (d) retrieval approach
8. Expected monetary value is given by the summation of weighted pay-offs along
   (a) the strategies
   (b) states of nature
   (c) all elements of pay-off matrix
   (d) none of the above
9. States of nature are the factors
   (a) within the scope of decision maker
   (b) decided by the top management
   (c) outside the scope of decision maker
   (d) none of the above
10. Regret for each strategy is calculated by
    (a) subtracting its pay-off from the maximum pay-off
    (b) subtracting all pay-offs along its row from the maximum pay-off
    (c) subtracting the minimum pay-off for each state of nature from its pay-off
    (d) subtracting its pay-off from maximum pay-off for each state of nature

ANSWERS

| 1. (d) | 2. (c) | 3. (a) | 4. (b) | 5. (c) | 6. (b) | 7. (b) | 8. (a) | 9. (c) | 10. (d) |

■■■

Chapter 7: Game Theory

1. If the loss of a player is a gain of the other player in two player game, then the game is known as
   (a) fair game
   (b) unfair game
   (c) non-zero sum game
   (d) zero sum game
2. Which of the following is not true
   (a) game without a saddle point is probabilistic
   (b) game with saddle point will have pure strategies
   (c) game with saddle point requires use of dominance rule
   (d) game without saddle point uses mixed strategies
3. The size of the pay-off matrix of a game can be reduced by using the principle of
   (a) game inversion
   (b) dominance
   (c) rotation reduction
   (d) game transpose

4. A row is dominated by another row if
   (a) least of the row ≥ highest of another row
   (b) least of the row ≤ highest of another row
   (c) every element of the row ≥ corresponding element of another row
   (d) every element of the row ≤ corresponding element of another row
5. Saddle point in a game exists if
   (a) row maximin = column minimax
   (b) row minimax = column maximin
   (c) row maximax = column minimin
   (d) row minimin = column maximax
6. For the following game, the player A should:

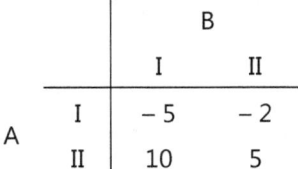

   (a) first strategy
   (b) second strategy
   (c) mixed strategy
   (d) no strategy
7. If the value of a game is zero it is called
   (a) zero sum game
   (b) non-zero sum game
   (c) fair game
   (d) unfair game
8. The negative values in a pay-off matrix of a game with row player A and column player B represents
   (a) payments from A to B
   (b) payments from B to A
   (c) loss of both the players
   (d) gain of both the players
9. Value of the following game is

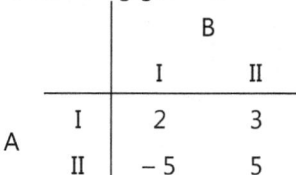

   (a) 3
   (b) – 5
   (c) 5
   (d) 2
10. Games involving more than two players are called
    (a) conflicting games
    (b) negotiable games
    (c) N-person games
    (d) none of the above

ANSWERS

| 1. (d) | 2. (c) | 3. (b) | 4. (d) | 5. (a) | 6. (b) | 7. (c) | 8. (a) | 9. (d) | 10. (c) |

Chapter 8: CPM, PERT and Network Calculations

1. Network models have advantage in terms of project
   (a) planning
   (b) planning and scheduling
   (c) planning, scheduling and controlling
   (d) scheduling
2. The technique of PERT is more useful for the projects that are
   (a) repetitive in nature
   (b) non-repetitive in nature
   (c) deterministic in nature
   (d) none of the above
3. If one activity ends and two activities start from an event then it will be a
   (a) terminal event
   (b) merge and burst event
   (c) initial event
   (d) burst event
4. For an activity (i-j) in a network
   (a) $EF_{ij} = ES_{ij} - t_{ij}$
   (b) $EF_{ij} = ES_{ij} + t_{ij}$
   (c) $EF_{ij} = \text{Max}[ES_{ij} + t_{ij}]$
   (d) None of the above
5. For a non-critical event (j), which of the following is not true
   (a) $L_j = LF_{ij}$
   (b) $L_j = LS_{ij} + t_{ij}$
   (c) $E_j < L_j$
   (d) $L_j = E_j$
6. The critical path of a network has
   (a) shortest duration
   (b) odd number of nodes
   (c) longest duration
   (d) none of the above
7. Along a critical path, which of the following is not true
   (a) $ES_{ij} = LS_{ij}$
   (b) $EF_{ij} = LF_{ij}$
   (c) $E_i < L_j$
   (d) $E_i \neq L_i$
8. For an activity which of the following is not true
   (a) $TF_{ij} = E_j - L_i - t_{ij}$
   (b) $TF_{ij} = LF_{ij} - EF_{ij}$
   (c) $TF_{ij} = LS_{ij} - ES_{ij}$
   (d) $TF_{ij} = L_j - E_i - t_{ij}$
9. For an activity
   (a) Independent Float ≤ Total Float ≤ Free Float
   (b) Independent Float ≤ Free Float ≤ Total Float
   (c) Free Float ≤ Independent Float ≤ Total Float
   (d) Free Float ≥ Independent Float ≥ Total Float

10. Which of the following is not a difference between PERT & CPM
    (a) PERT is probabilistic and CPM is deterministic
    (b) PERT is based on time considerations and CPM is based on time and cost considerations
    (c) PERT is event oriented and CPM is activity oriented technique
    (d) PERT makes use of critical path while CPM does not use a critical path

11. In PERT calculations, the expected time of an activity (having optimistic, most likely and pessimistic time estimates a, m, b respectively) is found out by
    (a) $\dfrac{a+4m+b}{6}$
    (b) $\dfrac{a+6m+b}{4}$
    (c) $\dfrac{b-a}{6}$
    (d) $\left(\dfrac{b-a}{6}\right)^2$

12. The project duration of a PERT network the following is not true
    (a) its standard deviation is equal to sum of the standard deviations of critical activities
    (b) it follows normal probability distribution
    (c) its expected time is the sum of the expected times of the critical activities
    (d) its expected time is given by the length of critical path

ANSWERS

1. (c)	2. (b)	3. (d)	4. (b)	5. (c)	6. (c)	7. (d)	8. (a)	9. (b)	10. (d)
11. (a)	12. (a)								

■■■

Chapter 9: Probability

1. Mutually exclusive events are the events where
    (a) each event is independent of the others
    (b) if one event takes place the others are ruled out
    (c) can happen mutually
    (d) none of the above

2. The sample space consists of
    (a) all possible simple events
    (b) all the exhaustive events
    (c) events such that at least one of them must happen at a time
    (d) all of the above

3. For mutually exclusive events, A, B and C
   (a) P(A∪B) = P(A) + P(B) − P(A∩B)
   (b) P(A∪B) = P(A) + P(B) + P(C)
   (c) P(A∪B) = P(A) + P(B)
   (d) P(A/B) = P(A) + P(B)

4. For dependent events A and B
   (a) P(A∩B) = P(A) · P(B/A)
   (b) P(A∩B) = P(A) · P(B)
   (c) P(A∩B) = P(A) + P(B)
   (d) P(A∪B) = P(A) + P(B)

5. P(A/B) indicates
   (a) the probability of event 'A' not 'B'
   (b) conditional probability of event A given that the event has taken place
   (c) a reciprocal of P(B/A)
   (d) simultaneous occurrence of event A and B.

ANSWERS

| 1. (b) | 2. (d) | 3. (c) | 4. (a) | 5. (b) |

■■■

Chapter 10: Probability Distributions

1. Probability distribution is
   (a) same as frequency distribution
   (b) random distribution of probability
   (c) listing of values of a variable and their probability of occurrence
   (d) none of the above

2. For a binomial probability distribution x ~ B(n, p, r)
   (a) $P(r) = {}^nC_r \, p^r \, q^{n-r}$
   (b) mean = n p r
   (c) variance = $\sqrt{n \, p \, r}$
   (d) none of the above

3. Which of the following is not a characteristic of a normal curve
   (a) it is a bell shaped curve
   (b) area under the curve is one
   (c) mean = media = mode
   (d) it lies in the first quadrant

4. $P(x_1 < x < x_2)$ where x follows a normal probability distribution is obtained by
   (a) $P(x_2) - P(x_1)$
   (b) Finding the area under the normal curve between lines $x = x_1$ and $x = x_2$
   (c) substituting values of x_1 and x_2 in the probability density function $P(x)$
   (d) none of the above
5. The range (± 3σ) about the mean for a normal probability distribution covers
   (a) 68.26% of the observations
   (b) 95.44% of the observations
   (c) 99.73% of the observations
   (d) none of the above

ANSWERS

| 1. (c) | 2. (a) | 3. (d) | 4. (b) | 5. (c) |

Appendix A

TABLE OF AREAS UNDER NORMAL CURVE

Normal Probability Curve is given by the Equation:

$$P(x) = \frac{1}{\sigma\sqrt{2\pi}} e^{-\frac{1}{2}\left(\frac{x-m}{\sigma}\right)^2}, -\infty < x < \infty$$

and Standard Normal Probability curve is given by:

$$P(z) = \frac{1}{\sqrt{2\pi}} e^{-\frac{z^2}{2}}, -\infty < z < \infty \quad \text{where, } z = \frac{x-m}{\sigma}$$

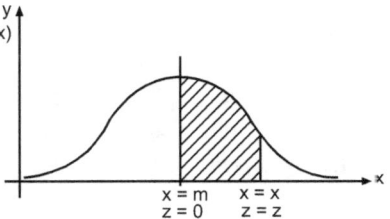

The following table gives the shaded area in the diagram viz. $P(0 \leq z \leq Z)$ for different values of Z. e.g. For finding $P(0 \leq z \leq 1.25)$, see first for (1.2) vertically and then for (5) horizontally.

∴ $P(0 \leq z \leq 1.25) = 0.3944$.

AREAS UNDER STANDARD NORMAL PROBABILITY CURVE

↓z→	0	1	2	3	4	5	6	7	8	9
.0	.0000	.0040	.0080	.0120	.0169	.0199	.0239	.0279	.0319	.0359
.1	.0398	.0438	.0478	.0517	.0557	.0596	.0636	.0675	.0714	.0753
.2	.0793	.0832	.0871	.0910	.0948	.0987	.1026	.1064	.1103	.1141
.3	.1179	.1217	.1255	.1293	.1331	.1368	.1406	.1443	.1480	.1517
.4	.1554	.1591	.1628	.1664	.1700	.1736	.1772	.1808	.1844	.1879
.5	.1915	.1950	.1985	.2019	.2054	.2088	.2123	.2157	.2190	.2224
.6	.2257	.2291	.2324	.2357	.2389	.2422	.2454	.2486	.2517	.2549
.7	.2580	.2611	.2642	.2673	.2703	.2734	.2764	.2794	.2823	.2852
.8	.2881	.2910	.2930	.2967	.2995	.3023	.3051	.3078	.3106	.3133
.9	.3159	.3186	.3212	.3238	.3264	.3289	.3315	.3340	.3365	.3389

↓Z→	0	1	2	3	4	5	6	7	8	9
1.0	.3413	.3438	.3461	.3485	.3506	.3531	.3554	.3577	.3599	.3621
1.1	.3643	.3665	.3686	.3708	.3729	.3749	.3770	.3790	.3810	.3830
1.2	.3849	.3869	.3888	.3907	.3925	.3944	.3962	.3980	.3997	.4015
1.3	.4032	.4049	.4066	.4082	.4099	.4115	.4131	.4147	.4162	.4177
1.4	.4192	.4207	.4222	.4236	.4251	.4265	.4279	.4292	.4306	.4319
1.5	.4332	.4345	.4357	.4370	.4382	.4394	.4406	.4418	.4429	.4441
1.6	.4452	.4463	.4474	.4484	.4495	.4505	.4515	.4525	.4535	.4545
1.7	.4554	.4564	.4573	.4582	.4591	.4599	.4608	.4616	.4625	.4633
1.8	.4641	.4649	.4656	.4664	.4671	.4678	.4686	.4693	.4699	.4706
1.9	.4713	.4719	.4726	.4732	.4738	.4744	.4750	.4756	.4761	.4767
2.0	.4772	.4778	.4783	.4788	.4793	.4798	.4803	.4808	.4812	.4817
2.1	.4821	.4826	.4830	.4834	.4838	.4842	.4846	.4850	.4854	.4857
2.2	.4861	.4864	.4868	.4871	.4875	.4878	.4881	.4884	.4887	.4890
2.3	.4893	.4896	.4898	.4901	.4904	.4906	.4909	.4911	.4913	.4916
2.4	.4918	.4920	.4922	.4925	.4927	.4929	.4931	.4932	.4934	.4936
2.5	.4938	.4940	.4941	.4943	.4945	.4946	.4948	.4949	.4951	.4952
2.6	.4953	.4955	.4956	.4957	.4959	.4960	.4961	.4962	.4963	.4964
2.7	.4965	.4966	.4967	.4968	.4969	.4970	.4971	.4972	.4973	.4974
2.8	.4974	.4975	.4976	.4977	.4977	.4978	.4979	.4979	.4980	.4981
2.9	.4981	.4982	.4982	.4983	.4984	.4984	.4985	.4985	.4986	.4986
3.0	.4987	.4987	.4987	.4988	.4988	.4989	.4989	.4989	.4990	.4990
3.1	.4990	.4991	.4991	.4991	.4992	.4992	.4992	.4992	.4993	.4993
3.2	.4993	.4993	.4994	.4994	.4994	.4994	.4994	.4995	.4995	.4995
3.3	.4995	.4995	.4995	.4996	.4996	.4996	.4996	.4996	.4996	.4997
3.4	.4997	.4997	.4997	.4997	.4997	.4997	.4997	.4997	.4997	.4998
3.5	.4998	.4998	.4998	.4998	.4998	.4998	.4998	.4998	.4998	4.998
3.6	.4998	.4998	.4999	.4999	.4999	.4999	.4999	.4999	.4999	.4999
3.7	.4999	.4999	.4999	.4999	.4999	.4999	.4999	.4999	.4999	.4999
3.8	.4999	.4999	.4999	.4999	.4999	.4999	.4999	.4999	.4999	.4999
3.9	.5000	.5000	.5000	.5000	.5000	.5000	.5000	.5000	.5000	.5000

Note: Sometimes the table starts with a figure of (0.5000) for Z = 0.00. It actually gives $P(-\infty < z \leq Z)$.

Hence, subtract 0.5 from all the figures in that table so as to get the figures in the above table and then use them for further calculations.

■■■

Appendix B

TABLE FOR VALUES OF e^{-m}
($0 < m < 1$)

m	0	1	2	3	4	5	6	7	8	9
0.0	1.0000	.9900	.9802	.9704	.9608	.9512	.9418	.9324	.9231	.9139
0.1	.9048	.8958	.8869	.8781	.8694	.8607	.8521	.8437	.8353	.8270
0.2	.8187	.8106	.8025	.7945	.7866	.7788	.7711	.7634	.7558	.7483
0.3	.7408	.7334	.7261	.7189	.7118	.7047	.6977	.6907	.6839	.6771
0.4	.6703	.6636	.6570	.6505	.6440	.6376	.6313	.6250	.6188	.6126
0.5	.6065	.6005	.5945	.5886	.5827	.5770	.5712	.5655	.5599	.5543
0.6	.5488	.5434	.5379	.5326	.5273	.5220	.5169	.5117	.5066	.5016
0.7	.4966	.4916	.4868	.4819	.4771	.4724	.4677	.4630	.4584	.4538
0.8	.4493	.4449	.4404	.4360	.4317	.4274	.4232	.4190	.4148	.4107
0.9	.4066	.4025	.3985	.3946	.3906	.3867	.3829	.3791	.3753	.3716

($m = 1, 2, 3, ... 10$)

m	1	2	3	4	5	6	7	8	9	10
e^{-m}	.36788	.13534	.04979	.01832	.00638	.002479	.00091	.000335	.000153	.000045

Note: To obtain values of e^{-m} for other values of m, use the laws of exponents.

e.g. $e^{-2.35} = (e^{-2.00})(e^{-0.35}) = (.13534)(.7047) = .095374$.

Appendix C

TABLE OF RANDOM NUMBERS

```
39 65 76 45 45   19 90 69 64 61   20 26 36 31 62   58 24 97 14 97   95 06 70 99 00
73 71 23 70 90   65 97 60 12 11   31 56 34 19 19   47 83 75 51 53   30 62 38 20 44
72 20 47 33 84   61 67 47 97 19   98 40 07 17 66   23 05 09 51 80   59 78 11 52 69
75 17 25 69 17   17 95 21 78 48   24 33 45 77 48   69 81 84 09 29   93 22 70 45 80
37 48 79 88 74   63 52 06 34 30   01 31 60 10 27   35 07 79 71 53   28 99 52 01 41

02 89 08 16 94   85 53 83 29 95   56 27 09 24 43   21 78 55 09 82   72 61 88 73 61
87 18 15 70 07   37 40 79 12 38   48 13 93 15 96   41 92 45 71 51   09 18 25 58 94
98 83 71 70 15   89 09 39 59 24   00 06 41 41 20   14 36 59 25 47   54 45 17 24 89
10 08 58 07 04   76 62 60 48 68   58 76 17 14 86   59 53 11 52 21   66 04 18 72 87
17 90 56 37 31   71 82 13 50 41   27 55 10 24 92   28 04 67 53 44   95 23 00 84 47

93 05 31 03 07   34 18 04 52 35   74 13 39 55 22   68 95 23 92 35   36 63 70 35 31
21 80 11 47 99   11 20 99 45 18   76 51 94 84 86   13 79 93 37 55   98 16 04 41 67
95 18 94 36 97   23 37 83 28 71   79 57 95 13 91   09 61 87 25 21   56 20 11 32 44
97 08 31 55 73   10 65 81 92 59   77 31 61 95 46   20 44 90 32 64   23 99 76 75 63
69 26 88 86 13   59 71 74 17 32   48 38 75 93 29   73 37 32 04 05   60 82 29 20 25

41 27 10 25 03   87 63 93 95 17   81 83 83 04 49   77 45 85 50 51   79 88 01 97 30
91 94 50 63 62   08 61 74 51 68   92 79 43 83 79   29 18 94 51 23   14 85 11 47 23
80 06 54 18 47   08 52 85 08 40   48 40 35 94 22   72 65 71 08 86   50 03 42 99 36
76 72 77 63 99   89 85 84 46 06   64 71 06 21 66   89 37 20 70 01   61 65 70 22 12
59 40 24 13 75   42 29 82 23 19   07 94 76 10 08   81 30 15 89 14   81 83 17 16 33

63 62 06 34 41   79 53 36 02 95   94 61 09 43 62   20 21 14 68 86   84 95 48 46 45
78 47 23 53 90   79 93 96 38 63   34 85 52 05 09   85 43 01 72 73   14 93 87 81 40
87 68 62 15 43   97 48 72 66 48   53 16 71 13 81   59 97 50 99 92   24 62 20 42 30
47 60 92 10 77   26 97 05 73 51   88 46 38 00 58   72 63 49 29 31   75 70 16 08 24
56 88 87 59 41   06 87 37 78 48   65 88 69 58 39   88 02 84 27 82   85 81 56 39 38
```

```
22 17 68 65 84   86 02 22 57 51   68 69 80 95 44   11 29 01 95 80   49 34 35 86 47
19 36 27 59 46   39 77 32 77 09   79 57 92 36 59   89 74 39 82 15   05 50 94 34 74
16 77 23 02 77   28 06 24 25 93   22 45 44 84 11   87 80 61 65 31   09 71 91 74 25
78 43 66 07 61   97 66 63 99 61   80 45 67 93 82   59 73 19 85 23   53 33 65 97 21
03 28 28 26 08   69 30 16 09 05   53 58 47 70 93   66 56 45 65 79   45 56 20 19 47

04 31 17 21 56   33 63 99 19 87   26 72 39 27 67   53 77 57 68 93   60 61 97 22 61
61 06 98 03 91   87 14 77 43 96   43 00 65 98 50   45 60 33 01 07   98 90 46 50 47
23 58 35 26 00   99 53 93 61 28   52 70 05 48 34   56 65 05 61 86   90 92 10 79 80
15 39 25 70 99   93 86 52 77 65   15 35 59 05 28   22 87 26 07 47   86 96 98 29 06
58 71 96 30 24   18 46 23 34 27   85 13 99 24 44   49 18 09 79 49   74 16 32 23 02

93 22 53 64 39   07 10 63 76 35   37 03 04 79 88   08 33 33 85 51   55 34 57 72 69
78 76 58 54 74   92 38 70 96 92   52 06 79 79 45   82 63 18 27 44   69 66 92 19 09
61 81 31 96 82   00 57 25 60 56   46 72 60 18 77   55 66 12 62 11   09 99 55 64 57
42 88 07 10 05   24 98 65 08 21   47 21 61 88 32   27 80 30 21 60   10 92 35 36 12
77 94 30 05 33   28 10 99 00 27   12 73 73 99 12   39 99 57 94 82   96 88 87 17 91
```

DECISION SCIENCES   UNIVERSITY QUESTION PAPER

Winter 2014

Time : 2.5 Hours   **Max. Marks : 50**

Instructions to the candidates:
1. All questions are compulsory.
2. Each question has an internal option.
3. Each question carries 10 marks.
4. Figures to the right indicates full marks for that question/sub-question.
5. Your answer should be specific and to the point.
6. Graph papers will not be provided, draw neat diagrams on answer sheet only.
7. Use of non-scientific calculator is permitted.

SECTION - I

Q.1 (a) (i) Maximize $Z = 50 X_1 + 30 X_2$ [5]
Subject to
$$2X_1 + X_2 \geq 18$$
$$X_1 + X_2 \geq 12$$
$$3X_1 + 2X_2 \leq 34$$
$$X_1, X_2 \geq 0$$
Solve LP by graphical method.

(ii) Solve the following assignment [5]

	X1	X2	X3	X4	X5
A	15	29	35	20	38
B	21	27	33	17	36
C	17	25	37	15	42
D	14	31	39	21	40
E	19	30	40	19	18

OR

(b) Find the optimum solution.

Warehouse	Cost per unit (₹) at Places				Supply (Units)
	A1	A2	A3	A4	
M1	16	12	18	10	70
M2	4	2	12	6	84
M3	10	12	14	16	74
Demand (Units)	42	46	50	32	

P.1

Q.2 (a) A maintenance service facility has Poisson arrival rates, negative exponential service times and operates on first time served queue discipline. Break down occurs on an average of three per day with a range of zero to eight. The maintenance crew can service, on an average, six machines per day, with a range from zero to seven find the [10]
   (i) Utilization factor of the service facility
   (ii) Mean waiting time in the system
   (iii) Mean number machine in the system
   (iv) Mean waiting time of machine in the queue

OR

(b) A bakery keeps stock of popular brand of cakes. Previous experience shows that the daily demand pattern for the item with associated probabilities are as given below: [10]

Daily demand	0	10	20	30	40	50
Probability	0.01	0.20	0.15	0.50	0.12	0.02

Use the following sequence random numbers to stimulate the demand for next 10 days.

25, 39, 65, 76, 12, 65, 73, 89, 19, 49

Q.3 (a) (i) Explain the various quantitative methods that are useful for decision making under uncertainty. [5]
   (ii) From the following payoff matrix calculate:
   (A) Maximin
   (B) Maximax
   (C) Equal probability (Laplace)
   (D) Minimax regret [5]

State of nature	Strategy		
	S1	S2	S3
N1	4000	20000	20000
N2	−100	5000	15000
N3	6000	400	−2000
N4	18000	0	1000

OR

(b) (i) Explain (Any Two) [5]
   (A) Saddle point
   (B) Principle of dominance
   (C) Mixed strategy game

(ii) Solve the following game [5]

Player A	Player B		
	B1	B2	B3
A1	1	7	2
A2	6	2	7
A3	6	1	6

Q.4 (a) (i) Discuss various steps in application of CRM and PERT. [5]

(ii) Draw network diagram [5]

Activity	1-2	2-3	2-4	2-5	3-7	4-5	4-7	5-6	6-7
Duration in weeks	10	11	11	12	11	9	9	10	9

(b) Given the following information: [10]

Activity	Optimistic time (Weeks)	Pessimistic time (Weeks)	Most likely time (Weeks)
1-2	6	8	7
1-3	1	9	2
1-4	1	7	4
2-6	1	3	2
3-5	1	9	2
4-5	1	9	5
4-7	2	8	2
5-6	4	4	4
5-7	4	10	4
6-8	2	14	5
7-8	2	8	2

(i) Construct the project network diagram

(ii) Find the expected duration

(iii) Calculate Earliest Start Time (EST) and Latest Finish Time (LFT)

Q.5 (a) (i) Explain the concept of probability. Give two applications of probability in any businesses. [5]
 (ii) A product is manufactured by a company for which it has three machines M1, M2 and M3. Machine M1 produces 50%, M2 produces 30%, M3 produces 20% of the total output. Past experience shows that M1 produces 4% defectives, M2 produces 5% defectives and M3 produces 6% defectives. At the end of the day from total production one unit of production is selected at random and is found to be defective. What is the chance that Machine M1 has produced it? [5]

OR

(b) (i) Write a short note on Binomial or Normal Distribution. [5]
 (ii) In a sample of 1000 scores, the mean of a certain test is 14 and the standard deviation is 2.5, assuming the distribution to be normal, find:
  (A) How many students have scored between 12 and 15
  (B) How many scored above 18

www.ingramcontent.com/pod-product-compliance
Lightning Source LLC
Chambersburg PA
CBHW060503300426
44112CB00017B/2534